TCHAIKOVSKY

A Self-Portrait

Tchaikovsky

A Self-Portrait

ALEXANDRA ORLOVA

Translated by R. M. Davison
with a Foreword by
David Brown

Oxford   New York
OXFORD UNIVERSITY PRESS
1990

Oxford University Press, Walton Street, Oxford OX2 6DP

Oxford New York Toronto
Delhi Bombay Calcutta Madras Karachi
Petaling Jaya Singapore Hong Kong Tokyo
Nairobi Dar es Salaam Cape Town
Melbourne Auckland

and associated companies in
Berlin Ibadan

Oxford is a trade mark of Oxford University Press

Published in the United States
by Oxford University Press, New York

British Library Cataloguing in Publication Data
Data available

Library of Congress Cataloging in Publication Data
Data available

Set by Eta Services (Typesetters) Ltd., Beccles, Suffolk
Printed in Great Britain by Courier International Ltd., Tiptree, Essex

FOREWORD

I first encountered the name of Alexandra Orlova over twenty years ago while working on my biographical and critical study of Mikhail Glinka. At a time when most Soviet archives were closed (as many still are) to scholars from the West, I found invaluable her distinguished editorial work upon source material fundamental to any study of this 'father' of Russian music, and I assumed from the quantity and authority of her publications that she was one of the favoured élite within the circles of Soviet musical scholarship.

My first contact with her came after the publication of my book. I had done my best, I thought, by this remarkable seminal composer, but in the eyes of Soviet orthodoxy I had failed miserably, the leading Russian music periodical, *Sovyetskaya Muzyka*, greeting my effort with the most blistering condemnation I have ever received in print. Mrs Orlova's response was not what I might have expected. She had read the review, been intrigued, and finding no copy of my book in Leningrad, wrote asking whether I would send her one. This I did, adding upon the opening leaf a little inscription which I later discovered the customs authorities had torn out. But the book was let through; evidently the bomb was felt to be safe as long as the fuse had been removed.

For several years Mrs Orlova and I corresponded decorously, aware of the scrutiny of the censor. Then, in 1979, came a letter saying she was leaving Leningrad, and I should not write until she gave me her new address. I waited some months, then received a letter postmarked Rome. It emerged that she had been planning to leave the Soviet Union, but had not dared tell me for fear of compromising her exit visa. Now, however, she could reveal that she had for long been no part of the Soviet establishment. As a young scholar she had indeed worked within various archives such as the Tchaikovsky Museum at Klin, with free access to all materials. But in 1949, a year after the notorious Zhdanov denunciation of the work of such as Prokofiev and Shostakovich had inaugurated one of the most extreme periods of cultural reaction in the history of the Soviet Union, Mrs Orlova was a casualty of an antisemitic campaign and was expelled from the Research Institute of Theatre and Music; subsequently she had been compelled to continue her work and bring up her two sons by 'private enterprise', as it was ironically termed in the Soviet Union. Now she was to join one of these sons in the United States.

For the last ten years she has been living in Jersey City, and the invaluable day-by-day biographies she had assembled on Glinka and Musorgsky before her emigration have already been published in English editions. And now, in this present volume, comes her portrait of Tchaikovsky himself as projected from his own words. In my study of the composer I have also drawn upon such documents (letters, diaries, and so on), but in attempting the more conventional biographical approach of building my own image of the man as I perceive him, I am aware that such insights as I offer are liable to be offset by misperceptions. The supreme value of Mrs Orlova's present 'autobiographical' volume is that it confronts the reader in the most direct way with the subject himself, and includes much that has not before appeared in English. True, she has had to choose what documents to include, and the process of selection is in itself an act of interpretation. But there are two particular reasons why her selection deserves special attention. First, it is made by one who has a deeper knowledge of such materials than any Western scholar not merely because she has lived with them so long, but because her approach is conditioned by the knowledge and insights she acquired during the many years when she had free access to much that has been deliberately excluded from the printed editions which are all that I and other Western scholars have been able to see. Second, a Russian is bound to see a compatriot in a different light from a foreigner; her selection of materials will therefore be rather different, afford different emphases, and the image that builds from these is bound to differ from that which a racial outsider might project.

The single, most intriguing passage in what follows is the account of the court of honour set up by a group of Tchaikovsky's former schoolfellows to forestall a public scandal from a homosexual relationship in which the composer was accused of engaging; they decreed he should take his own life to ensure the honour of their old school was not soiled. Since Mrs Orlova smuggled this story to the West ten years ago, corroboration has come from a second, quite separate source. It is, of course, unlikely that evidence proving conclusively the truth (or otherwise) of this extraordinary incident will ever come to light; nevertheless, it is no stranger than some other incidents in the composer's life story, and it simply cannot be dismissed out of hand, as some have tried to do.

But the prime interest of this book lies in the vivid cumulative portrait it builds of the composer. For the reader who wants to come as close to Tchaikovsky *himself* as is possible a century after his death, who wants to know how he reacted to people, to things, to circumstances, what he thought about life, his art, politics, religion, and everything around him that engaged or compelled his interest—above all, for the reader who wants to know what he was *really* like as a man—the following pages provide the answer.

Braishfield, Hampshire   DAVID BROWN
November, 1989

PREFACE TO THE ENGLISH EDITION

No one can describe a man's life better than he himself. His inner state of mind, his real life, are known only to himself.

(Rousseau *Confessions*)

The idea of a book about Tchaikovsky in the form of an autobiographical narrative goes back very many years to the time when I was working as a young musicologist in the Tchaikovsky Museum at Klin. Over a period of two years (1938–9) I assisted in compiling a chronicle of the composer's life and work[1] and in addition I compiled a subject index for his unpublished letters to his brothers. This work gave me the opportunity to carry out a detailed study of Tchaikovsky's correspondence and to go so far into the depths of his personality that there arose the complete illusion of actually being in communication with the composer, an illusion which was reinforced by the circumstances of working in the house at Klin.

Every day before I began work I used to go upstairs and spend some time wandering on my own through the composer's rooms. I particularly liked to linger by his desk. To this very day the blotting-paper bears traces of his letters, as well as hasty notes of an address, a number, even sometimes a scrap of music. Standing by this desk where Tchaikovsky wrote to his correspondents, where he wrote them the selfsame letters which I was now reading, I had the feeling that I might at any moment hear his voice or even see him. It seemed that he had just gone out for a second and would soon come in and catch me indulging my indiscreet curiosity.

I wanted to ask his forgiveness for concerning myself so much with his private affairs, which was in itself an insult to his memory. His own words in a letter to Mme von Meck were burnt into my mind in letters of fire: 'The idea that an interest in my music will stimulate interest in me personally is very burdensome... The notion that some day people will try to probe into the private world of my thoughts and feelings, into everything that I have so carefully hidden throughout my life... is very sad and unpleasant.'[2]

And yet here I was deliberately going against Tchaikovsky's will, trying to penetrate the intimate world of his emotions. Moreover, it afforded me

[1] V. Yakovlev (ed.), *Dni i gody P. I. Chaykovskovo. Letopis zhizni i tvorchestva* (Moscow–Leningrad, 1940). (*Tchaikovsky's Days and Years. A Chronicle of his Life and Works.*)

[2] Letter of 10 Aug. 1880. *Polnoye sobraniye sochineniy* (Moscow, 1965), ix. 233–4 (*Collected Works*).

enormous pleasure and I became increasingly convinced that a knowledge of the composer's personality would aid the understanding of his works.

I was consoled by the knowledge that Tchaikovsky himself would have understood that an ever-growing interest in his private thoughts and feelings, in all the details of his biography, was, of course, inevitable. Indeed in the same letter he acknowledged that 'there is even an element of tragedy in the conflict between the aspiration to fame and revulsion from its consequences'.[3]

In other words he *knew* that it was inevitable. He had also always known that his tastes, opinions, likes and dislikes, and his private comments were bound to attract the attention of biographers. In his diary for 1886 he wrote: 'Probably when I am dead people will find it not without interest to know what my musical preferences and prejudices were, all the more so since I have rarely mentioned them in conversation.'[4] *Not without interest* . . . thus does he express himself in his *diary*, the most private of all documents. Then Tchaikovsky goes on to record his views on Beethoven, Mozart, Glinka, and Dargomyzhsky.

And I continued to study his letters. The more I got into them, the more acutely was I aware of how important it was to make Tchaikovsky's 'Confessions' available to a wider public. It now became possible to understand much that had previously been unclear, sometimes inexplicable, or which could only be guessed at.

Whence came the unfulfilled longings of Romeo and Juliet, and of Tatyana? Why should a composer who was, in his own words, 'illustrating' a simple children's tale about the nutcracker create in his imagination the infernal images of the mouse kingdom, or the heart-rending *pas de deux* in the second act? What was the source of that note of suffering in Princess Aurora's theme and of the grim tread of death in the theme of Carabosse in *The Sleeping Beauty*? In *The Queen of Spades* the story itself evokes such images but their appearance in the bright world of Perrault's lyrical tale would seem to be inexplicable . . . Then finally, what tortures, what spiritual torments led Tchaikovsky to the eerie sonorities of the first movement of the Sixth Symphony and the funereal tones of the Finale? For these are after all the works of an artist who had known success and recognition in two continents, who was in his lifetime covered with glory, with affection, with adulation. So why the sadness, the pain, the torment?

The theories of Tchaikovsky's biographers and of the students of his work may appear arguable, unprovable, even far-fetched. It can scarcely be accidental that both from the performing and from the musicological aspect it is possible to take completely opposing views of a number of works,

---

[3] Letter of 10 Aug. 1880. *Polnoye sobraniye sochineniy* (Moscow, 1965), ix. 233–4 (*Collected Works*).

[4] P. I. Tchaikovsky, *Dnevniki* (Moscow–Petrograd, 1923), 212. (*Tchaikovsky's Diaries*) [*Diaries*].

including the Fifth Symphony and the Finale in particular (from exultation in the forces of light on the one hand, to the triumph of cruel fate on the other!). Yet the composer himself answers all these questions for us ... He answers them in what he has to say in his letters.

However, Tchaikovsky left an enormous number of letters, to be counted in thousands. The general reader cannot be overwhelmed with this mass of documents in the hope that he may find a few pearls. After all, just like anybody else's, Tchaikovsky's letters are full of everyday trivia, business affairs, purely practical issues, and frequent repetition of the same information directed to different people. Should it not be possible to make a distillation, to extract the quintessential elements of what Tchaikovsky had to say?

It was in fact when I was working at the Klin museum that I conceived the idea of making such a compilation—of Tchaikovsky's views on music (in the first instance!). There were masses of all sorts of interesting material which I tried to organize but if it was to attract the general reader something was lacking. What was it?

Whilst I was pondering over the material and trying to think of something more attractive for the reader, Kunin published his series.[5] I realized what I would have to avoid. I would have to present what Tchaikovsky had to say about himself, as well as his views on various musical problems; and his views on music would have to be seen not in isolation but in the context of his life. In short, I would have to show the man as a whole. But how was this to be done? I wanted to compile a book in which Tchaikovsky's voice would come through loud and clear, but *naturally*, not in a string of aphorisms.

It took many years of experience acquired in work on documentary monographs on Glinka, Musorgsky, and Rimsky-Korsakov before I realized how my idea could be brought to fruition.

In the early 1970s I decided to compile Tchaikovsky's 'autobiography' on the basis of his letters, diaries, and articles.

I was, however, confronted with numerous difficulties. Foremost amongst these was the fact that I could not now make use of the unpublished materials in the Klin archive: there is in effect no access to them and in recent years some items have apparently been destroyed. It was, for example, possible to use Tchaikovsky's letters only in their published form i.e. with omissions.

Difficulties also arose with the censorship. It is common knowledge that in the Soviet Union there are two topics concerning Tchaikovsky which may not be mentioned and on which no light may be cast: his

[5] A series of four books: *P. I. Chaykovsky o kompizitorskom masterstve* (*Tchaikovsky on the Art of Composing*); *P. I. Chaykovsky o programmnoy muzyke* (*Tchaikovsky on Programme Music*); *P. I. Chaykovsky o narodnom i natsionalnom elemente v muzyke* (*Tchaikovsky on the Folk and National Element in Music*); *P. I. Chaykovsky ob opere* (*Tchaikovsky on Opera*) (Moscow–Leningrad, 1952).

homosexuality and the truth about his death, two topics which are, incidentally, closely related. As in tsarist Russia, the former is regarded as a
vice and is punishable in law. As to Tchaikovsky's suicide, it is simply
denied, although everybody knows about it, particularly in Leningrad,
where it is a living oral tradition passed on from grandparents to grandchildren. No Soviet author would dare to touch these two themes.

For this reason, in the book which I published in 1976[6] there is not a
word about the cause of the composer's death and his marriage is treated in
such a way that the true state of affairs can only be understood by those who
are already fully in the picture about Tchaikovsky's life. The Soviet edition
contained evasions, and was also incomplete in that many of Tchaikovsky's
negative observations about a number of other musicians had to be
abridged (on the principle that one great man 'has no right' to dislike
another great man). All reflections on religious and political themes were
excluded too.

The English edition offers the opportunity to show Tchaikovsky as he
really was, warts and all. He does not suffer in any way from such a treatment; rather do we have before us a fuller picture of a man of remarkable
charm, of spiritual sensitivity, a man with a many-sided intellect and broad
interests. The richness of his character, his modesty, his kindness, his love
of children, his love of nature can evoke nothing but our warmest sympathy. What Tchaikovsky suffered because of his homosexuality certainly
does not evoke either contempt or censure, but rather deep compassion and
pity. There were, after all, many people in his position, even at that time,
who were not at all burdened by the fact that they had similar proclivities;
but for a man of Tchaikovsky's psychological sensitivity it was a terrible,
irretrievable disaster beyond his capacity to bear.

The sense of isolation, which he felt as a misfortune and something
shameful, the attempts to conquer his own nature, to be like everybody
else, his tragic marriage and the subsequent crisis—all this must be condemned by any unprejudiced observer who has not been infected by the
'morality' of Soviet social amorality. And how much then becomes clear in
Tchaikovsky's music!

There are deep psychological and physiological roots for Tchaikovsky's
intensely personal, tragic view of the world, for his spiritual disharmony.
Without a knowledge of this aspect of the composer's life it is impossible to
trace the sources of that tremulous anguish in search of unattainable happiness which characterizes his musical treatment of love. No other composer
gives such sublime expression to this feeling. This applies not only to
Romeo and Juliet, a work which, according to his brother and biographer
Modest, Tchaikovsky was able to write solely because in his youth he had
suffered the torments of an unrequited love for his school-fellow Vladimir

⁶ A. Orlova, *P. I. Tchaikovsky o muzyke, o zhizni, o sebye* [*Tchaikovsky on Music, on Life, on Himself*] (Leningrad, 1976).

Gerard;[7] it applies to all of Tchaikovsky's work, which reveals itself to us in all its fullness only if we are aware of the composer's mental sufferings.

He said himself: '...have I known *non-Platonic love?* *Yes* and *no.* If we put the question a different way and ask whether I have known complete happiness in love then the answer is *No, no, and no again!* In any case the question is answered in my music. [... As to] whether I understand the full force, the immeasurable power of this feeling [...] I would answer *Yes, yes, and yes again* and I would say yet again that my repeated efforts to express in music the torments and, at the same time, the bliss of love have themselves been efforts lovingly made.'[8]

The work of every artist is always in some way or other an inseparable part of his biography. Tchaikovsky, who had an astonishingly acute insight into his own character, maintained that he was to be seen in his works as God created him and as he had been influenced by the particular time and place in which he lived and worked.

When speaking of the close link between Tchaikovsky's music and his inner world it is fitting to recall the words of Tolstoy, that great seer into the human heart whom he idolized: 'Art is a microscope which the artist trains upon the mysteries of his soul and which shows these shared mysteries to other people.'[9]

If Tchaikovsky is seen in the dual capacity of composer and psychologist, the most important 'subject of study' in his works is, in fact, the inner life of man. This feature permeates all his works and is apparent also in the style, the tone of his letters, which show a rare gift of self-analysis and an ability to reach into the innermost recesses of the human heart. In this tale told, in truth, by Tchaikovsky himself in the present work, he stands before the reader just as he was in real life. He is here in all his aspects—in the sensitivity of his unfading emotions and thoughts, just as in his subjective and sometimes unfair judgements, and in the impulses of his nervous nature. It is precisely in this truthful and uncontrived re-creation of Tchaikovsky's personality that we see the advantages of this type of 'autobiography' over reminiscences written by others.

In memoirs there is always an admixture of piety, a degree of polishing-up, and very often there are inaccuracies and lapses of memory. But when Tchaikovsky talks about himself, in most cases, moreover, not retrospectively but under the direct and immediate impression of events, there is no question of an incomplete, half-finished picture, to say nothing of an inaccurate one. We have, in fact, the utmost in truthfulness and accuracy.

[7] Modest Tchaikovsky recounts this in his unpublished reminiscences which are in the archives of the Tchaikovsky Museum at Klin. Access to them is not now granted; I read Modest's reminiscences and diaries when I was working at the Museum in 1938–9.

[8] *Polnoye sobraniye sochineniy* (Moscow, 1962), vii. 105 (*Collected Works*).

[9] L. N. Tolstoy, *Polnoye sobraniye sochineniy* (Moscow, 1953), liii. 94 (*Collected Works*). Diaries for 1896.

Tchaikovsky was not only a composer of genius: he was a talented writer as well. His 'epistolary prose' (Pushkin's expression) is quite outstanding. What he writes is notable above all for its thoughtfulness but also for its sharp, distinctive style. Reading Tchaikovsky is a source of aesthetic pleasure and not just of information.

He was willing to write about himself and to chat to people whom he held in affection. The most mercilessly frank letters are addressed to his favourite brothers, the twins Anatoly and Modest. He tells them about all the most private aspects of his life and bares to them the most intimate secrets of his heart. His letters to Taneyev, his pupil and friend, are full of serious reflections on music; his letters to Balakirev, Rimsky-Korsakov, and Glazunov in St Petersburg, many of his letters to his publisher and friend Jurgenson, to his cousin Anna Merkling, and to his nephew Vladimir ('Bob') Davydov are valuable for the light which they throw on his creative work. A special place is occupied by his letters to the poet K.R. (the Grand Duke Konstantin) which are in the nature of literary essays.

Tchaikovsky was usually reticent and reserved but when he was dealing with people whom he liked he opened up very easily. We need only mention Pogozhev, the assistant to the Director of the Imperial Theatres, who was an admirer of the composer and to whom Tchaikovsky wrote remarkably significant letters not only about his musical work but about life in general.

Even so, were it not for Tchaikovsky's correspondence with Nadezhda von Meck we would be without a great deal of material, much of it crucial, about his inner life and his creative personality; without this correspondence it would have been impossible to carry out a deep and thorough analysis of the emotional side of his character. With no one else did Tchaikovsky share his recollections of the past; no one else did he allow to approach so close to his creative workshop, to no one else did he talk about the process of composition as he did to his 'best friend' (as Tchaikovsky himself called Mme von Meck). This remarkable woman had been able to understand the composer's character and see the value of his work when his talent was only just beginning to flower. To her he expressed his religious doubts and his innermost thoughts, avoiding, of course, only one topic: the misfortune of his homosexuality.

With the passage of the years his correspondence with Mme von Meck lost its former intensity but even then Tchaikovsky retained his habit of telling his friend more than anyone else about all that was happening to him, initiating her into all his affairs, his ideas, and his feelings. Perhaps a friendship of this nature was made possible not only by Mme von Meck's generous character, but also because Tchaikovsky never met her and their only form of contact was by correspondence. However that may be, his letters to Mme von Meck are fundamental to Tchaikovsky's biography from the end of the 1870s to 1890, when the break occurred (for more detail see pp. 373–5).

And so, Tchaikovsky the man and Tchaikovsky the artist are to be seen to the full in his letters. His articles and diaries also contribute much, both on purely musical matters and on his attitudes in general.

Tchaikovsky's observations always have a quality of passionate, frank confession, of self-revelation, of self-analysis. The tender sensitivity of his character from early childhood marked him out from others of his own age. The family called him 'a hothouse plant': he never changed...

It is possible that an as yet latent sense of being different played an important role in the years of his childhood and boyhood. We know nothing of his youthful experiences except for Modest Tchaikovsky's story of his tragic affection for Gerard. The first admissions which he makes himself date from the Moscow period, when his brothers—the only people with whom Tchaikovsky was completely frank—were older and could understand him. It was, moreover, a bitter blow to discover that one of his brothers (Modest) was 'the same' as he was himself. Many of the composer's letters to his brothers are also marked by a fear of being exposed. As he admitted himself, this sword of Damocles was to hang over him all his life.

Tchaikovsky was early aware of his artistic mission in life, of his creative powers. His thoughts when he was no more than considering becoming a professional musician are evidence of this. But by 1877 he will proudly say that he can feel an enormous creative power within himself and that he is sure he will bring honour to his country.

He is very ready to talk about the secrets of his creative workshop, to reveal the processes of composing. He tries to explain the ideas, images, and feelings in his works which it is difficult to put into words; in this respect his attempt to give a verbal interpretation of the Fourth Symphony is of particular interest, though, of course, it is far from complete and is even inaccurate, as Tchaikovsky himself admits.

Tchaikovsky's remarks on matters of aesthetics are of enormous interest, not merely because they reveal his views and explain much about his own work: they are of general interest as representing the opinions about various aspects of the arts, about music in the first instance, of a man who was himself a skilled practitioner in the field. There is much in his assessments which is too subjective and perhaps arguable; some things will strike the modern reader as being outmoded or naïve. No doubt many will find a great deal to disagree with, but Tchaikovsky will certainly have his supporters too.

For instance, I always want to argue with him about his underestimation of Glinka's intellect which is unfair, though in general typical of its time. I want to show him, to prove to him that his opinion really is superficial, that it is ill-founded and short-sighted. Nor, of course, can I agree with his rejection of Musorgsky's music, any more than I can accept Musorgsky's harsh criticism of Tchaikovsky: this was a clash between two aesthetic parties which provoked mutual misunderstanding and rejection. Each reader will doubtless find something to argue with Tchaikovsky about, but if we are to understand his artistic views we must see them in all their variety, complexity, and contradiction.

Tchaikovsky's work has very strong links with world literature. Amongst Russian writers his main source of inspiration was Pushkin, on whose works he based his three operas: *Eugene Onegin*, *Mazepa*, and *The Queen of Spades*.[10] Gogol's *Christmas Eve* provided the subject for one of the brightest of his operas: *Cherevichki* (*Vakula the Smith* in its first version).

Tchaikovsky drew equally on the resources of foreign literature. His musical imagination was stimulated by Dante (*Francesca da Rimini*), by Schiller (*The Maid of Orleans*), and especially by Shakespeare and Byron. Over a period of many years Tchaikovsky turned to Shakespeare's works to create such masterpieces as *The Tempest*, *Romeo and Juliet*, and *Hamlet*. He also wrote music for the play *Hamlet* and throughout his life he more than once formed the intention of writing an opera on *Romeo and Juliet*: he maintained, not without some justification, that there was no subject to which his personality was better suited than to this one. The duet for Romeo and Juliet found amongst Tchaikovsky's papers after his death and published posthumously is one of the finest interpretations of Shakespeare's tragedy. One of the peaks of his symphonic achievement was the programme symphony *Manfred*, after Byron, in which Tchaikovsky gave an entirely individual, subjective, and personal presentation of Byron's great poem.

Tchaikovsky had always been particularly attracted by English literature. His favourite authors were Thackeray and Dickens. He learnt English when he was no longer a young man so as to read Dickens in the original. The works of Dickens are not directly represented in Tchaikovsky's music, but he had a passionate liking for this writer whose goodness, whose lyricism and gentle humour were so indescribably dear to one whose own love for mankind permeates all his works.

Similarly there is no direct connection between Tchaikovsky's works and those of his other favourite author—Tolstoy. But what Tchaikovsky had to say about him is as revealing about what lay behind his own works as it is of the development of his attitude to Tolstoy. Tolstoy's psychological insight, his love and compassion for mankind, about which Tchaikovsky writes with such moving enthusiasm—are these 'Tolstoyan elements' not also characteristic of the composer who saw as deeply into the human heart as

[10] *Mazepa* is not so well known in the West, yet it is one of the peaks of Tchaikovsky's operatic writing. This work is an organic fusion of Tchaikovsky's characteristic delicate lyricism with Musorgsky's principles of the historical music drama. One need only compare the scenes between Mariya and Mazepa or the stunning finale (Mariya's lullaby to the corpse of Andrey) with the scenes of Kochubey's interrogation and execution. The drunken Cossack episode, in particular, in the execution scene could have come from the pages of *Khovanshchina* or *Boris Godunov*, both of them works of which Tchaikovsky disapproved!

did the writer? It was precisely such features which Tchaikovsky found attractive in Dostoyevsky, but he rejected other aspects which he regarded as morbid and pathological.[11]

Tchaikovsky was one of the first to appreciate Chekhov's gifts. Their mutual attraction and that note of delicate lyricism characteristic of both men drew them together in their personal relations as much as in their works.

Tchaikovsky's remarks scattered over many years make it possible to trace the tortuous path of his religious quest. The naïve belief of the child gives way to complete lack of belief in youth and early manhood. Thus we read in one of his letters to Modest that although Tchaikovsky is glad to know that his brother has religious faith, he does not share his convictions and is ready to argue with him about everything.[12] However, the catastrophe of his marriage and the appearance in his life of his benefactress and friend Nadezhda von Meck caused Tchaikovsky to reflect on a Providence which was concerning itself with him. He still speaks at this time of his doubts and hesitations, of his rejections of the dogmas of Christianity, yet equally he acknowledges the aesthetic attraction of the externals of Orthodox worship; this is also apparent in his work in that he wrote music for the Church. A few years later Nikolay Rubinstein died and his death was a heavy blow to Tchaikovsky: now he admitted that he was saved from utter despair by the beginnings of a faith in the inscrutable will of God.

By 1887 Tchaikovsky had evolved a definite religious outlook; he had worked out his own creed, which he even intended to set down, but he never managed to do so. We can, however, hazard some guesses, in particular on the basis of the parallels between the Lord of Sabaoth and Beethoven, between Christ and Mozart; we may take account also of his thoughts on the Roman Catholic requiem, of his rejection of God the avenger and his admiration for the kindness and humanity of Christ.

The fear of death pursued Tchaikovsky all his life and betrays the insecurity of his religious convictions, his lack of belief in a life after death (which he admitted himself). He denied the possibility of personal immortality and objected to the dogma of retribution, but in the last years of his life Tchaikovsky was attracted to the mercy of Christ. He was also given to moods of pantheism which were part of his passionate love for nature and the amazing vigour of his response to its beauties. His descriptions of nature, of how he becomes part of it, breathe a lyrical charm reminiscent of poems in prose.

The present work also reflects Tchaikovsky's interest in philosophy: his criticism of Schopenhauer's teaching and of Tolstoy's philosophical views,

[11] Another comparison and parallel inevitably suggests itself at this point: Tolstoy/Tchaikovsky and Dostoyevsky/Musorgsky. But that is another story.
[12] Precise references are not given here but in the main body of the text.

the attention which he paid to the works of Vladimir Solovyov and of
Chicherin, and finally, in the last years of his life, his study of Spinoza.
Tchaikovsky himself admitted that he had no inclination to become deeply
involved in philosophy and that his interest was fairly superficial. Yet there
is evidence here of the breadth of Tchaikovsky's erudition, as well as of that
quest which finds particularly vivid representation in his later works.

Tchaikovsky's approach to politics was a moral one. His political views
rest on a moral ideal and above all they show a hatred of evil and of
violence, from whichever quarter they might come. We see here the attitude of the artist as humanist, who, on his own admission, is striving
to leave behind the evils of the world and to reach the world of his own
creativity.

The present work attempts to offer a brief encyclopaedia, as it were, of
Tchaikovsky's views; but it is also an encyclopaedia of his spiritual development. His most important observations on all matters which at any time
engaged his enthusiasm or his interest have been gathered together and
arranged chronologically. But the book is in fact an autobiography since it
is Tchaikovsky who is speaking to us in his own words.

Since the tale is told in the first person, i.e. in the person of Tchaikovsky
himself, it is inevitably a subjective story. Nor are there any scholarly commentaries or assessments. The contents of the book are varied. Some
chapters are thin on events because the relevant letters are not available and
in fact not all the important events in Tchaikovsky's life found their way
into his letters; this applies particularly to his childhood, boyhood, and
youth. In some chapters 'personal confession' predominates (especially in
the early years of his friendship with Mme von Meck), in others it is 'the
chronicle of his life' which predominates. But it is not only the nature of the
material which has determined the arrangement of the book.

The pattern of Tchaikovsky's life varied from one period to another. We
can take several examples for purposes of comparison. Consider the very
different conditions surrounding the birth of two of his greatest works: *The
Queen of Spades* and the Sixth Symphony (the *Pathétique*).

The composer shut himself away in Florence to write the opera, where
nothing could interrupt his work. In his 'autobiographical narrative' we
have a daily chronicle establishing all the stages of its development and,
incidentally, of its composer's frame of mind. The measured tread of his
life at this period, exclusively occupied as it was with composing, is reflected in Tchaikovsky's account.

And how did the Sixth Symphony come into the world? In fits and starts,
in the intervals of his travels and concert appearances, with all the agitation
which they involved. The penultimate chapter alternates the events of his
life with his composing, since this reflects his circumstances at the time.

In this respect the chapter about the writing of *Eugene Onegin* is a close-textured 'patchwork'. The reader will see how the events of Tchaikovsky's private life are intertwined with his composing, how the latter affected what he did, how his enthusiasm for *Onegin* had a fateful influence on his conduct in general.

My concern has not been with quantity of material (as mentioned above, Tchaikovsky's letters run to thousands); I have preferred to try to present the most characteristic aspects of what he had to say and not the fortuitous ones. In doing so I have always had in mind his own admission that letters are hardly ever completely sincere, that they are always in some measure adjusted to the character of the recipient. However, on the basis of a comparison and analysis of a large number of Tchaikovsky's statements, we can assert that if on occasion he did indeed adjust to the character of his correspondent he did so only in practical matters. But as soon as the discussion turned to what was for him the main thing—his artistic outlook, his views on life, and his opinions of people—then Tchaikovsky never said anything which went against his convictions.

The material for this book was selected by comparing and correlating an enormous number of letters and carefully analysing Tchaikovsky's texts. The passages selected are those which constantly recur at different periods of his life and in letters to different people. The most important 'benchmarks' for the 'autobiographical narrative' are the letters to his brothers Anatoly and Modest, and to Mme von Meck.

The work has been compiled on a strictly documentary basis. The texts are entirely Tchaikovsky's own; nothing has been invented or added.

However, in attempting to make the exposition into as fluent a narrative as possible, and not just a selection of quotations, I encountered insuperable difficulties, mainly concerning the inevitable conflict of styles. Sometimes the narrative is in the present tense (when Tchaikovsky is describing current events), sometimes it is in the past (if he is writing about some recent occurrence).[13]

Naturally enough, the style and manner of exposition differs in diary entries, letters, and articles. I trust that the reader will understand the reasons for this awkwardness and will overlook it in the interests of getting to know Tchaikovsky's own texts, without any changes or corrections.

It has been essential in a number of cases (where passages have been cut or there are omissions or several texts have been run into one) to leave out any indication of the omission so that the book should read smoothly as a unified and coherent text. It is always possible to determine the source of a quotation from the footnotes, which also indicate when a passage is made up from a number of quotations. It would have been difficult to maintain the principle of the 'autobiographical narrative' if it had been necessary to cite the letters in full. Whilst carefully preserving Tchaikovsky's text, I

[13] When Tchaikovsky recollected events from the remote past the material appears in the text at the period about which he is writing.

have generally omitted his direct forms of address to his correspondents and have given any necessary information in square brackets (e.g. [Modest], [Mme von Meck] etc.). The names of the addressees are given in the footnotes.

The basic source for the present work has been the Academy edition of Tchaikovsky's letters, which offers the most reliable texts.[14] The volume and page references in the footnotes refer to this edition, unless specified otherwise. However, since this edition is not complete, I have had to include material from other sources. I have, moreover, attempted to reconstruct the omissions in Tchaikovsky's letters to his brothers (up to and including 1879) from the fuller text available in the first volume of *Pisma k rodnym* [*Letters to Relatives*] which is banned in the Soviet Union. The Diaries have been checked against the originals.

Explanatory and additional material is given in the text in square brackets. Essential linking and explanatory passages are in smaller print. I must emphasize that it has been my aim to let Tchaikovsky speak for himself; my linking passages are therefore extremely concise.

For events taking place in Russia, dates are given in the Old Style (i.e. twelve days behind the West); for events abroad, both Old and New Style are given (the New Style was adopted in Russia from 1918).

It is my pleasant duty, in conclusion, to thank the late Professor Gerald Abraham for his encouragement and his interest in my work; Professor David Brown for practical advice in preparing the English edition; R. M. Davison for his excellent translation; Mrs Mary Worthington for undertaking the by no means easy task of copy-editing the typescript, and my son Dr Mikhail Orlov for his practical help in publishing this edition.

Jersey City, USA   ALEXANDRA ORLOVA
February 1988

---

[14] A list of sources is given on p. xxv.

ACKNOWLEDGEMENTS

The publishers wish to thank Professor Chevalier H. M. Gilles, Emeritus Professor at the Liverpool School of Tropical Medicine and Dr Bruce Forrest of the London School of Hygiene and Tropical Medicine for their expert advice on Chapter 26.

Acknowledgements are also due to David Brown's four-volume study of Tchaikovsky, vol. i: *The Early Years: 1840–1874*; vol. ii: *The Crisis Years: 1874–1878*; vol. iii: *The Years of Wandering: 1878–1885*; (vol. iv is forthcoming) (London, 1978, 1982, 1986); John Warrack's *Tchaikovsky* (London, 1973); the article 'Tchaikovsky' by David Brown in *The New Grove Dictionary of Music*, ed. Stanley Sadie (London, 1980); the *Tchaikovsky-von Meck Letters*, translated by Galina von Meck (forthcoming).

The autographs on pp. 107–9 and 112 are taken from the collected edition of Tchaikovsky's literary works, *Polnoye sobraniye sochineniy: Literaturnye proizvedeniya i perepiska*, vol. vii (Moscow, 1962), pp. 125, 126, and 132 (Bodl. 17402 d 788(7)).

CONTENTS

CONTENTS

PART IV

LIST OF PLATES

16. Tchaikovsky's autograph sketches for the second movement of the Symphony No. 6 ('Pathétique'), composed 4 February–19 August 1893; the title 'Pathétique' was proposed by Modest the day after the première in St Petersburg later that year
17. Pyotr Il'yich Tchaikovsky in 1893
18. Death mask of Tchaikovsky

The publishers would like to thank the following organizations who have kindly supplied the photographs used in this book:

Society for Cultural Relations with the USSR, London: 1, 9 (Tretyakov Gallery, Moscow), 11; Novosti Press Agency, London: 2, 3, 4, 13, 14, 15; Private Collection: 5; Tchaikovsky House Museum, Klin (from *Pyotr Il'yich Tchaikovsky,* by K. J. Dawydowa, I. G. Sokolinskaja, and P. J. Waidmann, published by VEB Deutscher Verlag für Musik, Leipzig, 1978): 6, 10, 17, 18; Bibliothèque Nationale, Paris/Robert Harding Picture Library, London: 12; Archiv für Kunst und Geschichte, Berlin: 8, 16.

LIST OF SOURCES

Tchaikovsky, P. I., *Polnoye sobraniye sochineniy* [*Collected Works*], vols. v–xvii: Literary works and correspondence (Moscow, 1958–81). All cited references are to this edition unless otherwise stated. [*CW*]

P. I. Tchaikovsky, *Dnevniki* (Moscow–Petrograd, 1923). [*Diaries*]

Tchaikovsky, M. I., *Zhizn P. I. Chaykovskovo* [*Tchaikovsky's Life*], 3 vols. (Moscow–St Petersburg, 1900–3). [*Life*]

P. I. Tchaikovsky, *Pisma k rodnym* [*Letters to Relatives*], vol. i (Moscow, 1940). [*LR*]

P. I. Tchaikovsky, *Muzykalno-kriticheskiye stati* [*Articles on Music Criticism*], ed. T. Sokolova (Moscow, 1951). [*MC*]

Kashkin, N. D., *Vospominaniya o P. I. Chaykovskom* [*Reminiscences of Tchaikovsky*], in the series Russian Music of the Past, ed. Igor Glebov, vol. i (Petrograd, 1924). [*RMP*]

Regretting the past, hoping for the future, and never being satisfied with the present—there is the story of my life.

PART I

1

1840–1859

I started to compose as soon as I knew what music was.

I was born on 25 April 1840 in Votkinsk in Vyatka province.[1] I really have no precise notion of who my forebears were [on my father's side]. The only thing I know is that my grandfather was a doctor and lived in Vyatka province, but otherwise my family tree is lost in the mists of obscurity.[2] On my mother's side I have a little French blood since her father was André Assier, a descendant of a family which emigrated at the Revocation of the Edict of Nantes [1685].[3]

My mother was a marvellous, intelligent woman who was passionately fond of her children.[4]

Ilya Petrovich Tchaikovsky, Pyotr's father, came from a poor family of landless gentry; after graduating from the College of Mines (now the Plekhanov Mining Institute) he returned there to teach for many years, attracting attention for his abilities both as a teacher and as an administrator. In 1837 he became manager of the factory in Votkinsk, a post which brought about a great improvement in his financial circumstances; he was provided with a finely appointed house complete with a body of servants. Ilya Petrovich was a man of extraordinary kindliness who did not abuse his power; his relations with subordinates were both cordial and solicitous. Having been widowed he made a second marriage in 1833 to Alexandra Andreyevna, née Assier. Ilya Petrovich had a daughter Zinaida by his first marriage. The first child of his second marriage was Nikolay, born in 1838, then Pyotr (Petya); a daughter, Alexandra (Sasha, Sanya), was born in 1842, and a son, Ippolit (Polya), in 1843.

Tchaikovsky's first musical impressions are connected with his mother's singing. He remembered her performance of Alyabyev's *The Nightingale* all his life. He also got to know folk-songs in Votkinsk. The boy's musical development was assisted by an orchestrion—a mechanical organ—which played Zerlina's arias from Mozart's *Don Giovanni* and excerpts from operas by Weber, Bellini, Donizetti, and Rossini.

My musical bent became apparent at the age of four. My mother noticed that listening to music gave me very great pleasure and asked a music

---

[1] xiii. 244 (Felix Mackar).
[2] viii. 229 (Nadezhda von Meck).
[3] xiii. 244 (Mackar).
[4] vi. 253 (von Meck).

teacher, Mariya Markovna [Palchikova], to give me lessons in the fundamentals of music.[5]

I started to compose as soon as I knew what music was.[6]

At the age of five the boy was picking out on the piano arias played by the orchestrion. Even earlier, before his enthusiasm for music became apparent, Petya had written poetry, and his relations called him 'the little Pushkin'. He was four and a half years old when the French governess Fanny Dürbach joined the Tchaikovsky family. She read to the children a great deal and made them write and tell stories. Nobody could think up such fascinating stories as the young Tchaikovsky; his imagination was inexhaustible. But soon his love for music firmly took the place of all his other enthusiasms. Every moment that he was free from his lessons the boy spent at the piano. However these long spells of improvisation had an adverse effect on his health and attempts were made to distract Petya from his musical activities. 'He was something of a hothouse plant,' recollected Fanny Dürbach. The servants called Petya 'the family treasure'. In 1848 Ilya Petrovich retired and the family moved to St Petersburg.

It is a matter of regret to me that the time I spent in Votkinsk went by so quickly.[7]

In St Petersburg Petya and his elder brother Kolya were sent to the Schmelling boarding-school. Petya took music lessons from the pianist Filippov. He did a lot of hard work as well as going to the theatre frequently. He was a nervous child and this all turned out to be too much for him: he fell ill. When he recovered, the doctors would not allow him any activities or amusements for a long time and this ban included playing the piano.

[In 1849] Papa took up a new post in the Urals [as manager of the private factories in Alapayevsk], where he spent about three years. I was only there for a year.[8]

Tchaikovsky's younger brothers, the twins Anatoly and Modest, were born in Alapayevsk in May 1850. In the time which had gone by since his nervous illness Petya had changed a great deal. He had become capricious and irritable. Gradually this passed but he remained very reticent and unsociable.

I am never away from the piano; it cheers me up when I am sad.[9]

[At the end of the summer of 1850] Mama came [to Petersburg] to see me safely into the preparatory department of the School of Jurisprudence.[10]

Whilst Alexandra Andreyevna was busy organizing matters for her son, Ilya Petrovich wrote from Alapayevsk that she 'should, of course, not forget to give a thought to music as well, it would be a pity to abandon a good cause half-way through'; and, he added, 'Go out and go to the theatre as often as you can.'[11]

  5 xiii. 244 (Mackar).   6 Ibid. (Mackar).   7 v. 9 (Fanny Dürbach).
  8 v. 57 (Dürbach).   9 v. 10 (Dürbach).   10 v. 57 (Dürbach).
 11 v. 14 (Ilya Tchaikovsky to his wife).

On 21 August I began work in the preparatory class. [On 22 August my mother and] I went to the theatre to see *A Life for the Tsar*.[12]

At the end of September Alexandra Andreyevna left St Petersburg. 'To the end of his life Pyotr Ilich could not speak of that moment without a shudder of horror. The impression created by this first sorrow of childhood paled only by comparison with an even deeper impression—that created by the death of his mother,' according to Modest Tchaikovsky. The boy spent two years in St Petersburg, longing for those dear to him and hoping to see his parents as soon as possible.

[1851, from a letter to his parents] I congratulate you, my saintly Papa, on your Saint's day and wish you all good things on earth; I also send you good wishes my lovely, precious Marna for this dear anniversary. I like to remember this day last year. I remember we went out on a trip the next day. I remember the tent, I remember the boat, I remember the peasant choir, I remember the Ekaterinburg orchestra, I remember the illuminated monogram, I remember the dancing, I remember Sasha, Malya, Polya, and me. I remember all the visitors, I remember lovely Zinusha and her lovely dance with lovely Lidusha, I remember everybody, and finally I remember that poor creature which has flown from its little nest, which has said farewell to all that it will never see again—I remember Pyotr Tchaikovsky.[13]

[1852] Recently I played the piano at school. I began to play *The Nightingale* and suddenly remembered how I had played this piece before. A dreadful sorrow seized me; then I remembered how I had played it in Alapayevsk, and how I had played it four years ago in Petersburg with my teacher Mr Filippov, and then I remembered how you [mother] used to sing it with me; and in fact I remembered that it always was your favourite piece.[14]

[In May 1852] the whole family left the Urals, never to return. Mother brought the two little twins with her as well.[15]

[1852–1854] In my time the Metropolitan always used to perform the Liturgy on St Catherine's day. Right from the start of the school year we used to prepare for the solemn day. The choristers were very good; my voice was a splendid soprano and for several years in succession I took the first line in the trio which on these occasions was sung by the three boys at the altar at the beginning and end of the service. The Liturgy, particularly when it was performed by the Metropolitan, always made a very strong aesthetic impression on me.[16]

[1854] *13 June 5 o'clock*. On this day my mother died. It was my first experience of profound sorrow. Her death had a colossal influence on the way things turned out for me and for the whole of the family. She died quite

---

[12] v. 37 (his mother).   [13] v. 35 (his parents).   [14] v. 48 (his parents).

[15] v. 57 (Dürbach).   [16] viii. 434 (von Meck).

suddenly of cholera in the full flower of her life. Every moment of that appalling day is as vivid to me as though it were yesterday.[17]

These lines were written twenty-five years after his mother's death.

Mother suddenly fell ill with cholera. She died so quickly that she had no time to take her leave of those around her. On the day of my mother's funeral my father in his turn fell ill with the disease and we expected that he too might die at any minute but, thank God, he recovered after a week.[18]

Father got a place for Sasha in the Smolny Convent. Ippolit was sent to the Naval College.[19]

[In 1856 Sasha] left [the Smolny Institute] and although she is only fourteen she is already a proper young lady. Nikolay is an enormous young man of eighteen. [Ippolit] is doing well [at the Naval College]. Father is well and never seems to get any older. We are now living at my uncle's, my father's elder brother [Pyotr Petrovich], my cousins are delightful girls.[20]

Tchaikovsky's friendship with one of his cousins (Anna Petrovna, whose married name was Merkling) lasted throughout his life.

As soon as I glanced at the envelope [containing a letter from Anna Merkling] my memory took me flying back to times long past, and in a flash I saw before me a picture of the dining-hall in the School of Jurisprudence. The smell of borsch and gruel pleasantly tickles the nostrils (that is what we always had on Thursdays), the spirits rise at the thought of rissoles to follow the borsch and one's heart suffers a pang of delight at the thought that Saturday is only two days off, and then to crown all my joys the porter Golubev comes up to me with his calm and stately tread and with a letter in his hand. I see your beloved writing, open the envelope and read your delightful chatterings.[21]

[1856/7 theatre season] I was sixteen when I first heard Mozart's *Don Giovanni*. Before that I had only heard Italian opera. People of my generation, brought up on a diet of contemporary music from childhood onwards, made the acquaintance of Mozart only after they had got used to Chopin, for instance, in whom the Byronic spirit of despair and disillusionment is still to be seen so clearly reflected. It was my good fortune that fate brought me up in a not very musical family and in consequence I did not suffer in childhood from that poison in which music is steeped after Beethoven. It was that same fate which nudged me towards Mozart when I was still young and through him opened up to me unknown musical horizons of unbounded beauty. And these youthful impressions will never leave me.[22] The music of *Don Giovanni* was the first music to have a really shattering effect on me. It took me through into that world of artistic beauty where

---

[17] viii. 255 (von Meck).   [18] v. 58 (Dürbach).   [19] Ibid.
[20] Ibid.   [21] v. 351 (Anna Merkling).   [22] ix. 255 (von Meck).

only the greatest geniuses dwell. It is to Mozart that I am indebted for the fact that I have dedicated my life to music. He was the first to stir my musical powers and it was he who caused me to love music more than anything in the world.[23] I think that the aesthetic ecstasies which one experiences in one's early years are of enormous significance and leave a trace which lasts throughout one's life . . . It is similarly a matter of chance which explains why, of all the operas after *Don Giovanni*, I am most fond of *A Life for the Tsar: A Life for the Tsar*, it will be noted, not *Ruslan!*[24]

[In 1857 my father] handed over to a female swindler, who promised him millions, the capital which he had accumulated over many years of work. His capital vanished irretrievably inside twelve months.[25]

In the autumn of 1857 Ilya Petrovich and his family set up house with Elizaveta Schobert, sister of his late wife.

In 1858 [my father] took up work again and was for four years Director of the Institute of Technology [until the spring of 1863].[26]

I spent nine years in the School of Jurisprudence. I did not work seriously at music, although at the end of this period my father arranged lessons for me with an excellent pianist, Mr Rudolf Kündinger. I am indebted to this outstanding artist for the fact that I came to realize that music was my true vocation; it was he who brought me to the classics and opened up new musical horizons for me.[27]

I heard the name of Anton Rubinstein for the first time in 1858. I was then eighteen and had just moved into the top class of the Imperial School of Jurisprudence; my musical activities were far from serious. One day Kündinger turned up for the lesson in a distraught condition and paid no attention to my scales and exercises. I asked this excellent artist and nicest of men what was the matter and he told me that the day before he had heard the pianist Rubinstein who had just returned from abroad; this genius had made such a profound impression on him that he could not bring himself back to normal and found it just as insufferable to listen to my scales as it was to play himself. I knew how noble and sincere a man Kündinger was, I had a high opinion of his judgement and knowledge and in consequence my imagination and my curiosity were aroused to the highest degree.[28]

During this, my final year at the School, I had the opportunity to hear Rubinstein and not only to listen to him but also to see how he played and conducted. I emphasize this first *visual* impression because I am firmly convinced that Rubinstein's reputation rests not only on his incomparable talent but also in the irresistible attraction of his personality; it does not suffice just to hear him, for a proper impression he must be seen as well. Like everybody else I was carried away by him.[29]

[23] vii. 181 (von Meck).   [24] *MC* 368.   [25] vi. 253 (von Meck).
[26] Ibid.   [27] xiii. 244–5 (Mackar).   [28] xvi*b*. 104 (E. Zabel).
[29] Ibid.

Although I left school [in 1859] as one of the best pupils of my year, the teaching in those days was such that immediately you left you forgot everything you had ever known. It was only later, at work or in pursuing your private interests, that you could learn things thoroughly. But in my case my musical interests ensured that what little I had learnt at school soon vanished. In my time the School of Jurisprudence only produced precocious legal officials with no academic training. The beneficial influence of lawyers of the old sort was felt only in that they brought the notions of honesty and incorruptibility into a world of intrigue and venality.[30]

[30] vii. 175 (von Meck).

2

1859–1861

They have made a civil servant of me, and a bad one at that.

When I finished my studies in *jurisprudence*, I became an offical of the Ministry of Justice. A little of my spare time was spent on music.[1]

On 6 November 1860 Tchaikovsky's sister Alexandra married Lev Vasilyevich Davydov, whose father took part in the Decembrist uprising of 1825. Early in 1861 her husband took her off to his family estate of Kamenka, where he worked as a manager for his elder brothers who had been born before their father's exile and had inherited the Davydov property.

My way of life has not changed at all. Was wild and stupid during the Shrovetide carnival. Have said goodbye to theatres and masquerades and have settled down now; all the same, I can't just stay at home. I'm just off to the Picciolis—I'll talk Italian there and listen to some singing.[2]

It was through his aunt—his mother's sister Ekaterina Andreyevna Alexeyeva, a famous amateur singer of the 1830s and 1840s—that Tchaikovsky got to know the family of the singer and singing teacher Luigi Piccioli. He was very friendly with Piccioli, learnt Italian from him, and used to go to the theatre with him.

I went to the Picciolis. They are both as nice as ever. Got home early, in time for dinner. Over dinner we talked about my musical abilities. Father insists that it is still not too late for me to take it up professionally. I would like to think that he is right but the trouble is that if I have any ability it's quite impossible to make anything of it now. They have made a civil servant of me, and a bad one at that. I do my best to mend my ways and take my work more seriously—and am I now supposed to start studying figured bass at the same time?[3]

I am going abroad. It turns out that the trip will cost me practically nothing; I will be a sort of secretary and interpreter or dragoman for Pisarev. Of course it would be better if I did not have to carry out these duties but there is no other way.[4]

This was Tchaikovsky's first trip abroad. He had no money to finance his own

---

[1] xvi*b*. 104 (E. Zabel).   [2] v. 60 (Sasha Davydova).
[3] v. 61 (Sasha).   [4] v. 63 (Sasha).

travels so he took advantage of the offer made by the engineer Vasily Pisarev. His father gave him only a small sum to cover his personal expenses.

If ever I have done anything monumentally stupid in my life then it is this trip. Behind that mask of *bonhomie* which had led me to regard him as an uncouth but decent sort there was hidden the most disgusting character; it can easily be imagined what it was like for me to spend three months as the inseparable companion of such a pleasant type.[5]

I was extremely happy when I got back to Petersburg. I admit, I have a great weakness for the Russian capital. It can't be helped. I have got so used to it. Everything that is dear to my heart is to be found in Petersburg and life is absolutely impossible for me anywhere else.[6]

How will I end up? What does the future hold for me? It's terrifying even to think about it. I know that sooner or later (sooner, more likely) I will be powerless to cope with the difficult side of life and will be smashed to smithereens. Meanwhile I enjoy life as much as I can and sacrifice everything for pleasure.[7]

When theory and composition classes were started by the brilliant scholar Zaremba [under the auspices of the Russian Musical Society] I began going to them in 1861.[8] I started working on figured bass and made remarkable progress.[9]

Things go on as before. In my work at the Ministry I hope soon to obtain a post with responsibility for special duties; the salary is twenty roubles more and there isn't much to do. So far as the provinces are concerned, I can't see myself getting out of Petersburg now. I have begun working on music theory, and with great success; it would be foolish not to try my luck in that line when I have quite reasonable ability. The only thing that worries me is my weak character: laziness might well take over and I would not stick it out. I have my strong points and am not without talent but I suffer from the illness known as *Oblomovshchina** and if I do not conquer it then, of course, I could easily come to grief. Fortunately there is still some time left.[10]

* After the hero of Goncharov's humorous novel, *Oblomov*, who was cursed with incurable laziness [trans.].

[5] v. 69 (Sasha).   [6] v. 70 (Sasha).   [7] Ibid.
[8] xiii. 244 (Felix Mackar).   [9] v. 70 (Sasha).   [10] v. 71–2 (Sasha).

3

1862–1865

There is no other road for me now but music.

After leaving his post as Director of the Institute of Technology Tchaikovsky's father was given a small pension. It was also at this time that Elizaveta Schobert acquired a boarding-school and left the Tchaikovskys. Ilya Petrovich was left with his sons Pyotr, Anatoly, and Modest. Nikolay was working in the provinces and Ippolit was still studying. It was also precisely at this time that Elizaveta Mikhailovna Alexandrova (née Lipport) appeared in the Tchaikovsky family in the role of housekeeper and as Ilya Petrovich's *de facto* wife. The children were not at first well disposed towards her but later came to love their stepmother and to value her tactful kindness (Ilya Petrovich married her in 1865).

In 1865 my father married for the third time. My stepmother, a woman only half-educated but very intelligent and extraordinarily kind, managed to instil in all of us the most sincere respect by the tender and whole-hearted devotion which she showed her elderly husband. All of us, i.e. my sister and brothers, love her with all our hearts.[1]

We are now living alone with father and, contrary to expectations, it's not tedious at all. For a start, I have lunch at home every day. In the evening we often go to the theatre (the Russian one) or play cards. Father's housekeeping expenses have been more than halved—and this suits him. I do the ordering for lunch.[2]

It was at this period that Pyotr began to draw closer to his younger brothers. When their sister Alexandra went off to Kamenka he felt responsible for the future of Modest and Anatoly and took an interest in their education.

I might say that my affection for these little fellows [the brothers Anatoly and Modest] grows day by day, particularly (this is a secret) for the former. Deep down inside I am immensely proud of them and I cherish this best of all emotions. In life's unhappy moments I have only to think of them and life is worth living again. I try so far as I can to make my love a substitute for their mother's tender care which fortunately they did not know well enough to remember; I think I manage to do this.[3] We are tied by a mutual affection which is rare even amongst brothers. When our mother died they were four. Even I, of course, was not a mother for them. But from the first

---

[1] vi. 253 (von Meck).　　　[2] v. 74 (Sasha).　　　[3] v. 75 (Sasha).

moment that they were orphans I *wanted* to be to them what a mother is to her children because I knew from my own experience how a mother's tenderness and a mother's endearments have a lasting influence on a child's nature. And right from that time the relationship that has established itself between us has been such that I love them more than I love myself and would make any sacrifice for them, and they are utterly devoted to me.[4]

Little by little my true calling has become apparent.[5] I have enrolled in the new Conservatoire and courses begin in a day or two. Last year I did a very great deal of work on musical theory and I am now absolutely convinced that, sooner or later, I will leave my civil service career for music. Don't imagine [Sasha] that I see myself becoming a great artist: I simply want to follow my true calling. Whether I become a famous composer or an impoverished teacher, my conscience will be clear and I will not have the solemn duty of grumbling at fate and mankind in general. Of course, I will not finally abandon my civil service career until I am finally sure that I am a musician and not a bureaucrat.[6] My professors were Zaremba for fugue, counterpoint, and so on and Anton Rubinstein (the Director) for musical form and orchestration. I was at the Conservatoire for three and a half years.[7]

I cannot help being touched by my recollection of how my father took my escape from the Ministry of Justice to the Conservatoire. Although it pained my father that I had not fulfilled his hopes of an administrative career, although it could not but grieve him to see that I was willing to endure poverty to become a musician, he never so much as by a single word made me feel that he was displeased. He simply took a keen and enthusiastic interest in my plans and intentions and gave me every encouragement. I owe him so very, very much. I do not know what would have become of me if fate had given me a wilful tyrant for a father.[8]

It is impossible to do my work conscientiously when I am spending so much time on music; I cannot take a salary all my life for doing nothing nor would they let me. Consequently, the only thing to do is leave the civil service, particularly since I can always go back to it. So, after a lot of hard thinking, I have decided to remain attached to the Ministry but with neither an established post nor a salary. Of course there is little material advantage in this but I will be giving a few lessons next year. My expenses have shrunk to very small proportions because I have completely given up social activities, smart clothes, and so on. What will eventually become of me when I finish my studies? Of one thing I am sure and that is that I will turn into a good musician and that I will always have my daily bread. All the professors at the Conservatoire are pleased with me and say that I could achieve much.[9]

[4] vi. 253 (von Meck).   [5] xvi*b*. 104 (E. Zabel).   [6] v. 74 (Sasha).
[7] xvi*b*. 104 (Zabel).   [8] vii. 161–2 (von Meck).   [9] v. 77 (Sasha).

For the summer of 1864 Anton Rubinstein set Tchaikovsky the task of writing a big overture. It was Tchaikovsky's own wish to take Ostrovsky's *The Storm* as a programme. The work was published posthumously by Belyayev as Op. 76 (1896).

At the Conservatoire Tchaikovsky became particularly friendly with Herman Laroche who was later to become famous as a music critic. They went to orchestral concerts and the opera and often made music together.

Pyotr and his brothers spent the summer of 1865 with their sister at Kamenka. There he wrote the orchestral Overture in C minor.

Rubinstein is very pleased that I have managed to finish my work. I have heard no music yet; by a curious coincidence they gave the first performance of my *Dances* at Pavlovsk the day after I arrived but I did not see the posters until the evening, when it was too late to go. Laroche was there and was very pleased with the *Dances*.[10]

The *Characteristic Dances* were composed at the beginning of 1865 and first performed in Pavlovsk on 30 August 1865, conducted by Johann Strauss. This was the first public performance of a work by Tchaikovsky. Strauss most probably obtained the music through his friend August Leibrock, the owner of a music shop in The Passage (Leibrock's daughter was in the same class as Tchaikovsky at the Conservatoire). In the early 1860s Leibrock published Tchaikovsky's Italian Romance, *Mezza notte*.

In the autumn of 1865 Tchaikovsky composed two works: a Quartet movement in B♭ and the Overture in F, both of which were received favourably by his teachers and performed in student concerts. The Overture was conducted by the composer, making his first appearance in this role (27 November 1865).

I am beginning to give some thought to the future, that's to say to what I will have to do in December when I finish the course at the *Conservatoire*. I am increasingly convinced that there is no other road for me now but *music*. (I simply cannot live anywhere but Petersburg or Moscow.) It's extremely likely that I will go to Moscow.[11] Despite a few misfortunes I am in quite a rosy frame of mind, mainly, I think, because my consuming vanity (which is my greatest weakness) has recently been flattered by a number of musical successes and I foresee others in the future.[12]

At the Conservatoire Tchaikovsky had to write a graduation cantata on the text of Schiller's *Ode To Joy*. The young composer coped successfully with this difficult task and was awarded the silver medal (the gold was not awarded).

The cantata on Schiller's text was performed in December 1865 at a Petersburg Conservatoire prize concert in the palace of the Grand Duchess Elena Pavlovna; Anton Rubinstein conducted. After that I moved to Moscow.[13]

Tchaikovsky was offered the post of Professor of *Composition* for the music classes at the RMS by Nikolay Rubinstein and left St Petersburg on 5 January 1866.

[10] v. 87 (Sasha).   [11] v. 85 (Sasha).
[12] v. 86 (Sasha).   [13] vii. 505 (von Meck).

4

1866–1871

I have only one interest in life: the success of my compositions.

I am living at [Nikolay] Rubinstein's. He is a very kind and agreeable man, quite lacking that element of unapproachability which one feels in his brother. I have a small room next to his bedroom and when we go to bed at night (which, I might say, looks like being a very rare occurrence) I am, to tell the truth, somewhat embarrassed because I am frightened that even the squeak of my pen will stop him getting to sleep (there is only a thin partition between us) and I really am terribly busy. I have already orchestrated a large part of my summer overture and to my horror it has come out far too long, which is not at all what I expected.[1]

The Rubinsteins did not approve of the Overture in C minor, written in the summer of 1865 at Kamenka, and it was not performed.

I have been to the Arts Circle★ once or twice; I heard Ostrovsky read *The Abyss* and Pisemsky read *The Comedian*. Mostly I stay at home.[2]

I am on excellent terms with everybody but have managed to establish an especially close rapport with Rubinstein, Kashkin (Laroche's friend), and Albrecht. [Rubinstein] looks after me like a nanny and that's certainly what he would like to be so far as I am concerned. He insisted on giving me six shirts, all brand new, and wants to take me off by force to order some new clothes.

I must not omit from the list of my friends here Rubinstein's servant Agafon, a most estimable old man.[3]

My lessons are going very well and I even enjoy the particular favour of the ladies of Moscow whom I teach. My nervousness is gradually going altogether. Now we are always having committees and discussions about the Conservatoire here† and the discussions are very stormy. I helped a few days ago to draw up the Statutes and wrote an enormous *Administrative Memorandum* which was accepted without any changes.[4]

★ The Arts Circle was founded in 1865 by Nikolay Rubinstein and Alexander Ostrovsky. It brought together many artists.
† In the winter of 1865/6 the music classes at the Conservatoire were being reorganized (to start from 1 Sept. 1866).

[1] v. 91 (Anatoly and Modest).   [2] v. 95 (Modest).
[3] v. 97 (Anatoly and Modest).   [4] v. 98 (Anatoly and Modest).

Apart from his lessons at the Conservatoire, Tchaikovsky taught, having been recommended by Nikolay Rubinstein, at the house of Vladimir Begichev, the Intendant of the Imperial theatres in Moscow. He gave composition lessons to his younger stepson, fourteen-year-old Vladimir Shilovsky, who was the son of Mariya Shilovskaya, a pupil of Glinka and Dargomyzhsky and a well-known society singer from the 1830s to the 1850s. Tchaikovsky kept up his friendship with Vladimir and with his brother Konstantin, a talented musician and man of letters who later became an actor at the Maly Theatre under the name of Loshivsky. Begichev was a gifted and cultured man who was to be the co-author of the scenario for *Swan Lake*.

Rubinstein has arranged permission for me to use the Commercial Club, where there is an excellent library; I have taken a lot of good books out of this library and am enjoying reading. When I am on my own I roar with laughter at Dickens's *Pickwick Papers* and sometimes the fact that nobody can hear me laughing makes it seem even funnier. He has much in common with Gogol: the same direct and natural comic gift and the same ability to depict a whole character in a couple of swift strokes, though he lacks Gogol's depth.[5]

I am beginning to get a bit more used to Moscow although my loneliness sometimes makes me sad. To my surprise, my courses are going extremely well, my nervousness has vanished altogether, and gradually I am beginning even to look like a professor. My pupils, particularly the female ones, are always telling me how pleased they are and this gratifies me. My depression is going as well, but Moscow is still an alien town and it will be a long time yet before I can start thinking without horror that I will have to stay here for long or even for good. I am still living at Rubinstein's and will probably stay there right up to the summer. He is an excellent man and in general the people in Moscow are all good somehow, but the musical side here is much worse than in Petersburg. The opera is revolting and the concerts of the Musical Society are also, in many respects, worse than in Petersburg. On the other hand, the Russian Theatre here is remarkably good.[6]

On 4 March 1866 Nikolay Rubinstein conducted the first performance of Tchaikovsky's orchestral Overture in F, at a special symphony concert of the Moscow branch of the Russian Musical Society.

The overture which I wrote was a success, everybody called me out to take a bow and, to express it in exalted terms, I was assailed with loud plaudits. Even more flattering to my vanity was the ovation which I received at the dinner which Rubinstein gave after the concert. I was the last to arrive and when I went into the room applause broke out which lasted for a very long time; I blushed and bowed very awkwardly to all sides. At dinner we drank Rubinstein's health and he then proposed mine himself, which led to another ovation. Really this has been my first public success and for that

[5] Ibid.   [6] v. 101 (Sasha).

reason very agreeable to me (one further detail: the players applauded me at the rehearsal). I make no secret of the fact that this event has made Moscow much more attractive in my eyes.[7]

Tchaikovsky and his brother Modest were invited by Alexandra Ivanovna, the mother of Lev Davydov, to spend the summer of 1866 at the Myatlev dacha on the road to Peterhof (Tchaikovsky's father lived nearby). Anatoly, however, went to spend the summer with Alexandra Ilinichna (his sister) at Kamenka.

Tchaikovsky worked on his First Symphony for the whole of this summer. For the first time (and the last!) in his life he worked at night and this led to a nervous illness.

I ruined my nerves at the Myatlev dacha, slogging away at the symphony, which just would not come.[8]

The First Symphony was written in 1866. On Nikolay Grigoryevich [Rubinstein's] advice I made a few changes before it was performed and in this version it was given a performance in 1868. But then I decided to subject it to a thorough revision. However, I did not manage to get this done until 1874.[9]

I'm gradually getting down to work on an opera. There's a possibility that Ostrovsky will write me a libretto from *The Voyevoda* himself. I have made a number of new acquaintances, including Prince Odoyevsky.[10] [Vladimir Fyodorovich] Odoyevsky was one of the finest people it has been my lot to know. He was the embodiment of genuine kindness which went along with immense intelligence and wide-ranging knowledge, even, incidentally, of music . . . Four days before his death [1869] he was at a Musical Society concert where my orchestral fantasy *Fatum*—a feeble thing—was performed. He gave me his views in the interval with great good humour. The Conservatoire has some *cymbals* which he gave to me, having sought them out himself. He thought that I had a gift for using this instrument in the right place but was not satisfied with the instrument itself. So this splendid old fellow set about exploring Moscow in search of the cymbals which he did indeed send me with a charming letter which I still have.[11]

[The Dean of the Conservatoire Konstantin Karlovich Albrecht] plays a great part in my Moscow life so I must say a few words about him. In the first place he is the nicest man in all Moscow. I became very friendly with him last year but now I have become so fond of him and have got so used to him that I feel myself quite at home in his family and at times that is a great comfort to me.[12]

At the beginning of June 1867 Pyotr and Anatoly made a trip from St Petersburg to Vyborg and Imatra. They wanted to travel the whole summer but did not have enough money so Tchaikovsky settled at Hapsal, near to Alexandra Ivanovna Davydova and her daughters Sofya and Vera.

[7] v. 104 (Anatoly).   [8] v. 388 (Modest).   [9] xiii. 319 (P. Jurgenson).
[10] v. 113–14 (Anatoly).   [11] vii. 501 (von Meck).   [12] v. 114 (Anatoly).

I arrived at Hapsal with a strong prejudice against the place and quite insignificant financial resources. But with every day I find some new virtue in my surroundings and am now entirely reconciled to them. I am working very systematically and have done a great deal already. My opera is getting along very reasonably and I am perfectly content with that side of things.[13]

From Hapsal Tchaikovsky went to St Petersburg by steamer. He spent about a week in the capital and returned to Moscow some time between 20 and 29 August. His sister wrote to Tchaikovsky about Vera Davydova's love for him. He replied:

It is beyond doubt and inevitable that I will always suffer a little from my inability to make her happy, to provide her with an outlet for an emotion which, as she puts it, has taken up the whole of her existence. The question concerns the happiness of someone's entire life and it would be strange if I were altogether indifferent towards her love for me. I am bound to suffer some degree of torment precisely because I am grateful to her and do most sincerely love her. Please assure her that my heart has always responded to her with the warmest friendship and gratitude—in case she is in any doubt on the matter, which would surprise me. As to my coldness, which so distresses her—it has a number of causes, of which the main one is that I love her as a sister but because of the pressure of various social conventions our relationship cannot be sincere; this sets up a wall, as it were, between us, through which we can have no direct relationship with each other. Apart from that there are all manner of psychological subtleties which probably only a Tolstoy or a Thackeray could analyse properly.

To start with, both of us are continually dishonest with each other: she (being afraid, as she would put it, to bore me with her pious expression) pretends to be indifferent; I look as if I don't understand or know anything; meanwhile we both understand and know each other perfectly well, and so a sort of dissonance strikes up in our conversations; this gets on my nerves and I begin to lose my temper and feel that I cannot hide it; I can feel that she is upset; she feels that I feel this; I feel that she feels what I feel, and so it goes on endlessly. There is another reason for all this. It often occurs to me that she loves me as much as she does because she thinks I am a muscial genius, but I often suffer from my (perhaps imagined) creative weakness and am furious that I cannot live up to the ideal that she worships. If in such a moment she begins to praise my compositions or asks me to play something, I am overcome with a terrible feeling of malice towards myself and her. When, on the other hand, I am confident in my own ability (as I was in Hapsal), her high opinion of me flatters and pleases me and for these invisible reasons our relationship grows warmer. In general she should have noticed in me these sharp transitions from ill-concealed malice to the most sincere outpourings. All this is the consequence of various painful sensations, sometimes even without cause, which are characteristic of a

[13] v. 119 (Sasha).

nervous sensibility. It is as if a valve of the heart suddenly closes and when this happens, however hard you try, you remain cold; then, again without any particular cause, the valve opens; now you are touched by the most tender, brotherly feelings, but if remorse appears, or malice, the valve shuts again. Finally, I think that there is some sort of inexplicable law of fate by which, however kind and gentle a man's heart may be, he cannot help tyrannizing and tormenting a little the one who loves him. I can feel how often I am overcome by this power and if I commit acts of malice towards such a gentle and loving person whom I love, this happens against my will.[14]

There's nothing to say about me for the moment except, perhaps, that I must have got quite used to Moscow because it seems far less loathsome a place than it did at this time last year. My opera is now going fairly well; I have written all of the Third Act; the dances from it which I orchestrated at Hapsal will be played at the next concert.[15]

Ostrovsky had written the libretto for the first act and for the first scene of Act II of *The Voyevoda*, but then did no more work on it. Tchaikovsky finished the libretto himself.

The *Entr'acte* and *Dances of the Hay Maidens* from Act II of *The Voyevoda* were reworkings of the *Characteristic Dances* of 1865. Nikolay Rubinstein conducted them on 2 December 1867 at the Second Symphony Concert of the Russian Musical Society.

My *Dances* have had a great success here, and Jurgenson is even planning to publish them in an arrangement for four hands. I had a verbal request from Petersburg to send them but sent a message back that I would only hand them over if I got an official letter signed by all the directors. Zaremba gave instructions through Rubinstein that I should be told that I would get such a letter. These rogues are too cavalier with me. If I show them I don't care about them they'll realize who they are dealing with.[16]

Tchaikovsky's grudge against Zaremba and Anton Rubinstein is attributable to their refusal to perform the First Symphony in St Petersburg. It had its first complete performance in Moscow, at the Eighth Symphony Concert of the Russian Musical Society on 3 February 1868, conducted by Nikolay Rubinstein. On 19 February, at the Bolshoy Theatre, Tchaikovsky made his début as a conductor at a public concert (he had conducted at private concerts in St Petersburg in his student days).

My symphony was a great success, particularly the Adagio. I am setting about orchestrating the Third Act of *The Voyevoda*. I would like to get the opera finished with by the summer. I already have another libretto in mind [probably *Undine*].[17]

10 March 1868. Tchaikovsky made his first appearance in print in the newspaper *Sovremennaya letopis* [*The Contemporary Chronicle*]. This happened almost acci-

---

[14] v. 141–2 (Sasha).   [15] v. 128 (Anatoly).
[16] v. 129 (Modest).   [17] v. 133 (Anatoly).

dentally when he defended Rimsky-Korsakov's *Serbian Fantasy* against the attacks of the Moscow reviewer hiding behind the pseudonym of 'The Stranger' (Alexey Suvorin).

A couple of years ago Rimsky-Korsakov appeared on our musical horizons with a symphony. This work was in the normal German symphonic form; it was the first effort of a young talent still inexpert on the technical side. The first and last movements, remarkable neither for any originality of melodic invention nor for any beauty in the contrapuntal development of the themes, were the weakest movements of this first step on the symphonic road. But one could sense a powerful talent in the Adagio and in the Scherzo. It was particularly in the Adagio that Rimsky-Korsakov's notable talent as a symphonist was immediately apparent. This movement is based on a folk-song about a captive of the Tatars and it astonished everyone with its rhythmic originality (7/4), its charming and, incidentally, natural orchestration, its form, which is innovatory without trying for effect, and above all with the freshness of its purely Russian harmonic colouring. We can boldly say that in all respects this young composer has made marked progress in the last two years. But this is not to say that Mr Rimsky-Korsakov yet strides along his chosen path with the assured tread of a fully mature talent. His style is still not formed; at every turn one can feel the influence of Glinka and Dargomyzhsky and see him imitating Mr Balakirev's methods. Let us not forget that Mr Rimsky-Korsakov is still a young man and that the whole of the future stretches before him: there is no doubt that this remarkably gifted man is destined to be one of the finest ornaments of our art.[18]

I am absolutely fascinated by that quiet life, bereft of cheerful bustle, which is the usual lot of those who live in the country. Despite the fact that old age is still far away I am certainly the sort of man who is *worn out by life*. The people around me are astonished at my taciturnity and frequent depression when life is, in fact, far from bad. Even when a man is well provided for materially, when he has friends, when he has shown himself to be out of the ordinary in his chosen field and it is widely acknowledged that this is so, does it still seem that he needs something else? Because despite all these favourable circumstances I avoid company of any sort, feel incapable of maintaining a host of acquaintances, like to shut myself away and say nothing and so on. All this is to be explained by the weariness which I mentioned above. It is precisely in moments like this, when I feel disinclined not only to talk but even to think, that I dream of some blissful existence, brimming over with gentle delights.[19]

Tchaikovsky went abroad in the summer of 1868 at the invitation of Vladimir Shilovsky and Begichev.

[18] *MC* 26–7.   [19] v. 136 (Sasha).

My material circumstances are very good. I am living with very rich people who are, moreover, nice and very fond of me. I saw the various sights of Paris when I first came here so I have not by any means been leading the life of a tourist, running around churches, museums, and so on. I am living here like a man entirely devoted to his cause and only in the evenings do I crawl out of my burrow. It must be admitted that, for an artist trying to work, the glittering, noisy surroundings of Paris are infinitely less suitable than somewhere like Lake Thun, to say nothing of the banks of my beloved, if stinking, Tyasmin.[20]

Classes at [the Conservatoire] began on 2 September [1868]; I have even more to do there now than I did before. I had got out of the habit of giving classes and during the first lesson I was so embarrassed that I had to go out for ten minutes or I would have fainted.[21]

I will be paid somewhat more but how I have to work for it! My plans for living on my own have come to nothing. When I hinted to Rubinstein that it was not altogether convenient for me to live in his flat and in addition I felt guilty at staying there without payment he took great offence and promised to arrange things so that nobody would disturb me.[22]

They wanted to put my opera [*The Voyevoda*] on in October; they copied out the parts and started the rehearsals, which I had to attend. Of course, they were no more than a read-through. When I realized that the opera could not be put on at such short notice I told the management here that so long as the Italian opera was in Moscow occupying the attention of the chorus and orchestra I would not give them a score and I wrote a letter to [S. A.] Gedeonov to this effect. As a consequence of my action the rehearsals were stopped and the opera postponed until the Italians had gone.[23] The Italian opera is creating a tremendous furore amongst the public here. Artôt is a splendid person; she and I are friends.[24] What a singer Artôt is! What an actress! I have never before felt such a power of attraction from an artist as on this occasion.[25]

I first met Artôt last spring. When she returned this autumn I did not visit her throughout the whole month. Then we met by chance at a musical evening, I promised to visit her, but would not have carried out my promise (because I am never quick to make friends) if Anton Rubinstein, who was passing through Moscow, had not dragged me there. Practically every day since then I have received a note asking me to visit her and I have gradually got into the habit of seeing her every evening. We were soon stirred by the tenderest feelings for each other and mutual declarations thereof followed rapidly. Of course, the question of a legal marriage then arose; we both desire this very much and hope to have the wedding in the summer if nothing prevents it. But that is precisely the problem: there are

[20] v. 137–8 (Sasha).   [21] v. 139 (Anatoly).   [22] v. 141 (Modest).
[23] v. 143 (Anatoly).   [24] v. 144 (Anatoly).   [25] v. 146 (Modest).

certain obstacles. In the first place, her mother opposes the marriage on the grounds that I am too young for her daughter and, in all probability, because she fears that I will make her live in Russia. In the second place, my friends, [Nikolay] Rubinstein in particular, are making the most strenuous efforts to ensure that I do not carry out my proposed plan to get married. They say that if I become the husband of a famous singer I will play the wretched role of my wife's husband, that's to say that I will have to travel all over Europe with her and live at her expense, that I will get out of the habit of working and will not have the chance to do any. Just as she cannot bring herself to abandon the stage, I for my part am reluctant to sacrifice my future for her, for there can be no doubt that if I blindly follow her I will deprive myself of the chance of making progress in my own chosen role.[26]

The Artôt business has resolved itself in the most amusing way. In Warsaw she has fallen in love with the baritone Padilla, who was the object of her ridicule when she was here, and is marrying him! What of the lady? You would need to know the details of our relationship to have any idea of how funny this dénouement is.[27]

The première of *The Voyevoda* took place in the Bolshoy Theatre on 30 January 1869. The opera was given only five performances, the last on 2 March 1869 (at the end of the winter season).

My opera [*The Voyevoda*] went off very well; despite the most awful libretto it had a brilliant success. I took fifteen curtain calls and was presented with a laurel wreath. The performance was quite reasonable. I received a number of letters of thanks.[28]

The Voyevoda is, beyond a doubt, a very bad opera. In saying this I am taking into account not only the qualities of the music taken on its own but all the considerations which in their totality constitute the greater or lesser merit of an opera. In the first place the story is entirely unsuitable; it lacks dramatic interest and action. In the second place I wrote the opera too quickly and thoughtlessly, in consequence of which it emerged in a non-operatic form which was unsuitable for the stage. I simply wrote music to the particular text with no regard at all to the tremendous difference between the operatic style and the symphonic style. In *The Voyevoda* I paid great attention to the filigree elaboration of themes, completely forgetting about the stage and its requirements. Its third weakness is a far too massive orchestra which dominates the voices. All of these weaknesses are the fruit of inexperience.[29]

When he was in St Petersburg a year before this (28 March 1868) Tchaikovsky had attended a musical evening at the house of Balakirev, whom he had previously met in Moscow. Here he met the other members of Balakirev's circle (which has gone

[26] v. 149 (his father).   [27] v. 155 (Modest).
[28] v. 155 (Modest).   [29] viii. 444 (von Meck).

down in history as the Mighty Handful). The members of the group were not very well disposed towards Tchaikovsky's compositions. They thought that he was on the wrong road because in his works he used not only peasant song but urban folklore as well. They called Tchaikovsky an eclectic and a cosmopolitan and could not forgive him his Conservatoire education (they regarded the Conservatoire as being against the folk element).

But Tchaikovsky too failed to understand Musorgsky's attempts at reform and did not like his music, although he acknowledged that the composer of *Boris Godunov* had immense talent. Of all the members of Balakirev's circle Tchaikovsky held Rimsky-Korsakov in most esteem. At the end of the 1860s and the beginning of the 1870s, when Tchaikovsky developed a particular interest in peasant song, he drew musically nearer to the Handful. Consequently, when he came to St Petersburg he always met the composers of the group. He dedicated his symphonic fantasy *Fatum* to Balakirev but the captious and despotic leader of the Mighty Handful was severely critical of it.

I admit I was not in raptures about your [Balakirev's] review [of *Fatum*] but I was not at all offended and in my heart I respected the sincere directness which is one of the most attractive features of your musical personality. I will, of course, not withdraw the dedication but I hope to write something a bit better for you one day. Rubinstein and I were indignant in the extreme to hear of what the beautiful Elena [the Grand Duchess Elena Pavlovna, President of the Russian Musical Society] has done to you and I have even made up my mind to say something in print about her absolutely disgraceful behaviour. I am particularly glad that *la belle Hélène* is arriving in Moscow on the day that the newspaper with my little article comes out.[30]

Balakirev had had an argument with the Board of the Russian Musical Society and in consequence had been relieved of his responsibility for conducting the symphony concerts of the RMS. In his article 'A Voice from the Musical World of Moscow' (*Sovremennaya letopis* [The Contemporary Chronicle], 4 May 1869) Tchaikovsky made an indignant protest and enumerated Balakirev's services to music.

Regardless of Balakirev's significance as a fine composer, let us just mention the following facts. He compiled and published an excellent collection, of Russian folk-songs and revealed to us in these songs a rich store for the future of Russian music. He brought to public notice the great works of Hector Berlioz, who died so recently. He developed and formed the talents of several highly gifted Russian musicians amongst whom we shall single out Rimsky-Korsakov as the most talented. And finally, by putting on Glinka's immortal opera *Ruslan and Lyudmila* in Prague, one of the most musical cities in Europe, he has made it possible for foreigners to see for themselves that Russian music and Russian composers really exist.[31]

In the summer of 1869 Balakirev came to Moscow.

Balakirev is still here, we often see each other and I am more and more con-

<hr />

[30] v. 162–3 (Balakirev).   [31] *MC* 28–9.

vinced, despite all his virtues, that if we lived in the same town his company would become oppressive and burdensome. In particular I find his narrowness of view unpleasant as well as the stubbornness with which he sticks to his enthusiasms. But in some ways his brief stay has been of some value to me. However wearisome he might be, justice compels me to say that he is a good, honest man and as a musician he stands way above the general level.[32]

During this visit Balakirev persuaded Tchaikovsky to write an overture on Shakespeare's *Romeo and Juliet*.

My overture [*Romeo and Juliet*] is getting on quite quickly; the greater part has already been sketched out and a considerable part of what you [Balakirev] advised me to do has been done. In the first place, the layout is *yours*: the introduction portraying the friar, the fight—Allegro, and love—the second subject; and, secondly, the modulations are yours: the introduction in E, the Allegro in B♭ minor and the second subject in D flat. I am certainly in no position to say what is respectable in it and what is not so good. I cannot be objective towards my children; I compose in the only way I know; it is always difficult for me to settle on any one specific musical idea out of those that come into my mind but if I do pick one of them out then I soon get used to it, to its good and bad sides and it becomes incredibly difficult for me to rework it or to recompose it. I am telling you all this so that you will understand why I do not intend to send you the overture in its outline form: I want to show it to you only when it is properly finished. You can tear it to pieces then as much as you want; I will take note of all you say and will try to do better in my next work. But if you are hard on it now, when all the essential composing has been done but has still not emerged into the light of day, I will be discouraged and will achieve nothing. I cherish the hope that I might be able to please you, even if just a little, but goodness alone knows; I have already noticed more than once that things which I have thought respectable you have not liked, and vice versa.[33]

I will soon have to see Artôt again: the rehearsals for *Le Domino noir* [Auber] with my choruses and recitatives will begin when she arrives and it will be essential for me to be there. This woman has done me a lot of harm but, despite that, some inexplicable sense of being in sympathy with her draws me to her, so much so that I am beginning to feel a feverish impatience as I await her arrival. Alas! That is not the same thing as love.[34]

My overture is not only finished but is already being copied for performance at one of the next concerts. Now that it is finished but has still not been performed I know less than ever what it is worth; the one thing I do know is that it is certainly not so bad that I need fear that it will cover me with shame here in Moscow (in marvellous, imperturbably calm Moscow, without its assorted Famintsyns and Serovs!).[35]

---

[32] v. 168 (Anatoly).   [33] v. 180 (Balakirev).
[34] v. 182 (Anatoly).   [35] v. 185 (Balakirev).

Most composers who have had their works published from the start subsequently regret the public exposure of their immature efforts. I had no
such early success and am very glad about it. Some of my first works have
survived but I have burnt most of them, including two operas: *The Voyevoda* (the dances from which have survived) and *Undine*. I offered the latter
work to the management of the Petersburg theatres who rejected it. I was
greatly distressed and insulted at the time by this refusal but subsequently
I was glad that the management had performed this service for me. It was
in fact a very bad opera and I threw it into the fire without the slightest
regret.[36]

Balakirev and Rimsky have been visiting us. We met every day, of
course. Balakirev has taken to worshipping me more and more so that I am
going to end up by not knowing how to repay him for so much affection.
Rimsky has dedicated to me a very pretty little song ['My thoughts fly to
you']. They both like my overture [*Romeo and Juliet*] very much and I like
it too.[37]

I take the maximum advantage of my perfect health and life is, as before,
neither tedious nor especially cheerful but I must say that it is peaceful.
One thing does distress me and that is that there are no people in Moscow
with whom I am on an intimate domestic footing.[38]

My overture was at last performed at the Musical Society. I think it is the
best thing of all that I have written.[39]

Romeo and Juliet was first performed on 4 March 1870 at the Eighth Symphony
Concert of the Russian Musical Society, conducted by Nikolay Rubinstein.

There is nothing special to say about my life here; I am just as busy at the
Conservatoire as before and I do a bit of composing as before. I have begun
writing an opera on the subject of Lazhechnikov's tragedy *The Oprichniki*;
I've barely written a few scenes. Just as before an indescribable depression
descends on me from time to time but it at least does not stop me working;
on the contrary, I find work by far the best antidote.[40]

I received the stupidest letter from [Modest] in which he demanded an
explanation of my coldness; there wasn't any coldness, it was just that when
I was in Moscow it was unpleasant for me to realize that he is the same as I
am. We talked about it when I was in Petersburg and I hope he has calmed
down.[41]

I am very worried about Modest. I can't get used to the idea that he will
have to get on more or less on his own now. Just as I am convinced that
Tolya will work hard to get a decent position, I am equally alarmed by
Modest. I think he will end up as some sort of failure, although not without
interest.[42]

[36] viii. 435 (von Meck).   [37] v. 201 (Modest).   [38] v. 203 (Sasha).
[39] v. 208 (Anatoly).   [40] v. 211 (Lev Davydov, Lyova).
[41] *LR* 130 (Anatoly).   [42] v. 212 (Lyova).

In the summer of 1870 Tchaikovsky went to visit his friend Vladimir Shilovsky who was then living in Paris. He was seriously ill and had asked Tchaikovsky to visit him.

I went from P'burg to Paris non-stop; I was terribly tired and arrived in a state of dreadful agitation. I was afraid that I would find Shilovsky dying. His joy at seeing me was indescribable. We spent three days in Paris and then set off for here. Soden is a nice, clean little village at the foot of the Taunus mountains. The situation is beautiful and the air is excellent, but the enormous number of consumptives gives a somewhat gloomy tone to the place; in consequence, I was so downcast on the day we arrived that I had difficulty in restraining myself from hysterics. My low spirits have now cleared up; I am taking my responsibility for looking after Volodya very seriously. What puts me into ecstasies is the view of the mountains. I have found some things here which deserve not merely one's attention but real enthusiasm. Königstein castle is particularly interesting: it was built in 967 and in 1800 it was still an important fortress. Volodya and I climbed to the top of the tower and the view which opened up before our astonished gaze was truly magnificent. Every morning I set off on foot for a place which they call the Drei Linden, and there, on my own, I read or compose surrounded by the severe mountain scenery and with a marvellous panorama before my eyes encompassing some 130 miles.[43]

There was a big music festival in Mannheim to celebrate Beethoven's centenary. The famous composer Lachner was conducting. Incidentally, I heard for the first time Beethoven's *Missa solemnis*, which is very difficult to perform. It is one of the most outstanding works of musical genius. But other musical pleasures were lamentably few. The orchestra in Soden is small and doesn't play at all badly but the programmes are dreadful. Volodya and I have made them learn Glinka's *Kamarinskaya* which they are going to play.[44]

During this time Tchaikovsky was revising his fantasy overture *Romeo and Juliet*. He wrote to Balakirev:

You [Balakirev] wanted the introduction to be like one of Liszt's religious passages in *Faust*. It hasn't turned out like this. In the introduction I wanted it to express a lonely soul whose spirit reached towards the sky. I don't know whether I have succeeded.[45]

The Franco-Prussian War began on 2 July 1870; Tchaikovsky and Shilovsky moved to Interlaken.

It would be superfluous to say anything about the strong impression which Switzerland has made on me, and especially the delightful place where we are now. This view is so striking, so superb that on the first day we arrived I

---

[43] v. 219, 222–3 (Anatoly and Modest).   [44] v. 226 (Anatoly).   [45] v. 237.

even felt an obscure sense of fear, some sort of oppressiveness, but little by little one begins to get used to these miracles of nature. It is quite beyond me to relate what my feelings are, confronted by the most superb scenery anyone could possibly imagine. There is no end to my raptures and astonishment; I rush about like a madman from morning to night and do not get tired at all. And what I have to look forward to when I go for walks in the mountains, over the glaciers and through the ravines![46]

I spent six weeks in Switzerland where I had some pleasant times; then went to Munich, where I spent twenty-four hours, and from there to Vienna, which I liked almost more than any other town in the world, and at last returned triumphantly to Petersburg 24 August. I spent a week in P'burg.[47]

I spend my time as before and am becoming increasingly attached to Moscow. If only I had some money I could set myself up here incomparably well. But if the financial side were organized rationally it would be possible even with my means to live here very comfortably.[48] I carry on with the long-established arrangements. I am doing a little work on the new opera [The Oprichnik] and still move amongst the same people at the same places. I am settling into Moscow more and more so that now I could not think of living anywhere else.[49]

[46] v. 227 (his father).   [47] v. 229 (Anatoly).
[48] v. 243 (Anatoly).   [49] v. 244 (Sasha).

5

1871–1872

We are getting older.

As before our concerts are attracting large audiences but, to be honest, the programmes are not particularly interesting. *Sadko* [Rimsky-Korsakov] was a great success; my 'Chorus of Insects' a flop; the latter was badly interpreted although the orchestra played excellently. At the last concert they played *Don Quixote*. I find this piece very interesting and cleverly written, although its episodic structure gives it a whiff of pantomime ballet music. The orchestration is better than average and in places very effective. The Finale (which seems to aspire to being a parody on Liszt) is too long drawn out. The love theme is pretty banal; I like the theme of the knight's wanderings. The episode with the windmill is superb. Altogether I think that this is one of the most interesting and most meticulously thought out of Rubinstein's compositions. The next concert will include *1000 years* [Balakirev] which I am overjoyed about.[1]

Tchaikovsky spent the summer of 1871 at his sister's at Kamenka (June and July), at his friend Kondratyev's at Nizy near Kharkov (part of July and of August), and at Shilovsky's house at Usovo in the Tambov province (to the end of August). When he got back to Moscow he moved from Nikolay Rubinstein's house to his own flat (Lebedev's House, Spiridonovka—now 9, Alexey Tolstoy Street).

I am absolutely overjoyed at my decision to move from Rubinstein's. For all that I am friendly with him, his company weighed on me; I have set things up very nicely and am glad to feel that I have the place to myself.[2] Apart from my work at the Conservatoire I am trying hard to finish my opera by the spring and on top of that I have started writing articles about music; this is causing a lot of difficulty because it is something new to me.[3]

In November 1871 Tchaikovsky began to write for *Sovremennaya letopis* [*The Contemporary Chronicle*]. This only lasted for a month. They printed four review-articles about concerts with an evaluation of the works of Wagner, Beethoven, Schumann, and Mozart, together with a critical assessment of the Italian opera venture in Moscow.

In embarking upon musical conversations with the reader I had it in mind

---

[1] v. 249 (Balakirev).   [2] v. 262 (Nikolay Tchaikovsky).   [3] v. 266 (Sasha).

to be of some use to my fellow citizens by moulding their preferences and
furthering their development in the aesthetics of music.[4]

I am willing to agree that no decent, *self-respecting* capital can do without
an Italian opera company. But as I listen to Mme Patti's trills can I, as a
Russian musician, forget for even a moment the way in which our native art
is humiliated in Moscow, where there is no time to spare for it and it has no
place of refuge? Can I forget the pitiful way Russian opera is allowed to
vegetate when we have in the repertoire a number of works which any other
self-respecting capital would proudly regard as its most precious treasure?[5]

During the winter vacation, in the middle of December 1871, Tchaikovsky
travelled from Moscow via St Petersburg to Nice where he spent about a month.

It's extraordinarily strange to come from the depths of the Russian winter
to a place where oranges, roses, and lilac are growing and the leaves are
bright and green on the trees. But I must, incidentally, mention something
very strange. I waited for the moment of my departure from Moscow with
such frenzied impatience that towards the end I couldn't even sleep. But
then on the very day that I left I was seized by a consuming melancholy
which stayed with me throughout the whole of the journey and which has
not left me even now, amidst all the marvels of nature. Of course there are
pleasant moments, especially in the mornings when the sun is scorching
but not uncomfortable and I sit on my own, right by the sea. But even these
pleasant moments are not without a touch of melancholy. What follows
from all this? That this is old age, when nothing pleases any more. One lives
in one's memories or in one's hopes. But what is there to hope for?[6] However much I enjoyed the trip as a whole, my idleness eventually began to get
me down and I was glad to get back to Moscow.[7]

When he returned to Russia Tchaikovsky finished orchestrating his opera.

I am sending the score of my opera *The Oprichnik* to Petersburg.[8]

Tchaikovsky went off to Kamenka on 31 May. From there he went to visit his
friends: first Kondratyev, then Shilovsky. During the summer he wrote the Second
Symphony (and orchestrated it in the autumn in Moscow).

I spent ten days at Kondratyev's and about a month at Shilovsky's. I have
been in Moscow since 15 August. I am moving into a new flat and I am very
busy getting it organized.[9] I am finishing the symphony but it has so
drained me that I am in no state to start on anything else. This work of
genius (as Kondratyev calls it) is nearly finished. I think that this is my best
work so far as perfection of form is concerned—a quality for which I have
not previously been noted. My quartet created a furore in Petersburg.[10]

[4] *MC* 157.   [5] Ibid. 34.   [6] v. 271–2 (Anatoly).
[7] v. 273 (his father).   [8] v. 276 (Nápravník).
[9] v. 286 (Anatoly).   [10] v. 287, 288 (Modest).

Tchaikovsky moved to Kudrinskaya Square, to Kozakov's house (now No. 46 Square of the Revolution [Ploshchad Vosstaniya]).

The First Quartet was performed in the presence of the composer in St Petersburg on 24 October at the Third Quartet Concert of the RMS.

Depression makes all our lives a misery and this is because we are getting older. So far as I am concerned myself I have only a single interest in life: my success as a composer. It can hardly be said that I have been spoilt in this respect. To take an example: two composers offer their operas to the theatre management at the same time, Famintsyn's *Sardanapalus* and my *Oprichnik*. Famintsyn is generally acknowledged to be completely without talent; people say and write about me that I am talented. However, Famintsyn's opera has already been accepted for production whereas my fate is quite unknown, but there is good reason for thinking that my opera will be submerged in the waters of Lethe, like *Undine*, and forgotten. That was all right for *Undine*—water was her element; but imagine my *Oprichnik* submerging in the waters of Lethe and struggling with the waves—the poor fellow is sure to drown and if I go in to save him he'll drag me down with him, that's to say, putting it in plain language, that I solemnly swear that if my opera is rejected I will never set pen to paper again. When the symphony is performed I will write and tell you [Klimenko] what it is like; I can say nothing just now because one moment it seems no good at all and the next I start being far too pleased with it.[11]

Famintsyn's opera *Sardanapalus* was produced a year later than *Oprichnik* and was dropped from the repertoire after its failure.

From September Tchaikovsky started writing regular musical articles for *Russkiye vedomosti* [*The Russian Gazette*] and continued to do so for five years.

The reader should know that if a reviewer goes astray he does so honestly, that it is possible for him not to understand; but he must have *wanted to understand*.[12] Neither music nor literature nor any other kind of art, in the true sense of the word, exists solely for amusement; they all answer to far deeper needs of human society than the common passion for diversions and light entertainment, for the satisfaction of which there are circuses, all manner of acrobatic performances, conjuring tricks, cabarets with their indecent ditties and similar more or less cheering spectacles.[13]

I have finished my new symphony (The Crane) on which I place great hopes.[14]

I quite unexpectedly found myself in P'burg during the holidays: I was called to attend a meeting of the committee deciding the fate of my opera. I was so convinced that they would reject me and was in consequence so distraught that I decided not to go to father's straight away: I was frightened that my air of desperation would upset him. On the day after this wretched

[11] v. 289 (I. Klimenko).   [12] *MC* 26.
[13] Ibid. 65.   [14] v. 293 (Modest).

committee, which had really tormented me despite turning out to my entire satisfaction, I went to father's and stayed there for about a week. I won't claim to have enjoyed the time because I was reduced to a wreck; not a day passed without dinners and musical evenings so that I even became impatient to find a chance to slip away from all these pleasures and get back as soon as possible to my dear mother-Moscow, God preserve her. There is indeed less bustle and more calm here. This present trip has altogether convinced me that I have left Petersburg behind me for good and have, by contrast, come to feel myself at home in Moscow. Whatever sweet words they might say to me, whatever successes might fall to my lot in Petersburg I will now be a thoroughgoing Muscovite to the end of my days.[15]

When I was in Petersburg [in December 1872] I played the finale of the Second Symphony at Rimsky-Korsakov's and the assembled company nearly tore me to shreds in their rapture.[16]

[15] v. 297 (Sasha).   [16] v. 303 (Modest).

6

1873

The times we are living through will occupy a glorious page in the history of Russian art.

Time is going very quickly because I am so busy. I am making an arrangement of my opera and writing articles on music. I stay at home every evening and in general conduct myself like the most peaceful and loyal of Moscow citizens.[1]

In the last decade the cause of music in Russia has made such bold and decisive strides and society has reached such a high level of musical development that, whatever dark sides there might still be to our public musical life, the times we are living through will even so occupy a glorious page in the history of Russian art. In both capitals and in some provincial towns music societies are being formed which pursue the highest artistic aims and familiarize the public with the greatest European works; these same societies in Petersburg and Moscow found conservatoires which offer the musically gifted the opportunity to study and, at the same time, through their pupils disseminate healthy musical principles amongst the masses. Composers, encouraged by the opportunity of having their works performed alongside the best compositions of the West European symphonists, are given a beneficial stimulus to their activity; reviewers are appearing who are equal to the achievements of contemporary music; public interest has been caught by the new spirit of life in music for which there is developing a lively sense of sympathy and support. In brief, music is getting into its stride and is leaving its sleepy stagnation for seething public activity. Many horrors are perpetrated on our opera stages and there is much which sadly testifies to the immaturity of our musicians and of our public; but there are also many consoling features which push the gloomy side of our musical affairs into the background and cause us to remember with gratitude those people to whose energies or gracious support music is indebted for its comparative, though undoubted, well-being.[2]

[The Second Symphony] had a great success and 'the Crane' in particular earned the most flattering reviews. I do not attribute the credit for this success to myself but to the real composer of the work mentioned, Pyotr

---

[1] v. 301 (his father).   [2] *MC* 113.

Gerasimovich [the butler at Kamenka], who all the time I was composing and running through 'the Crane' would come and take up the tune with me. It will be played again in the last concert and they are preparing an ovation and presentation for me on that occasion. Oh, how burdensome it is to submit to the tyrannical demands of the mob! And indeed the time is approaching when Kolya and Tolya and Ippolit and Modya will no longer be Tchaikovskys but just *brothers of Tchaikovsky*. I will not conceal that that is precisely what I would most like my efforts to achieve.[3]

This symphony was first performed on 26 January 1873, conducted by Nikolay Rubinstein.

It was at this time that Stasov, always ready to come to the help of his composer friends in choosing a subject, suggested to Tchaikovsky the programme for a symphonic fantasy *The Tempest*, after Shakespeare's play.

I really do not know how to thank you [Stasov] for your excellent programme which is tempting and inspiring in the highest degree. I do not know how I will cope with it but of course I will carry out your plan in every detail. The subject of *The Tempest* has so much poetry in it and your plan demands so much musical polish and elegance of style that I intend somewhat to restrain my usual impatience when I am composing and to wait for the *propitious* moments.[4]

In 1873 the Maly Theatre in Moscow was closed for repairs. The opera and ballet companies found themselves with nothing to do, and so the management conceived the idea of staging a spectacle which would at one and the same time use the actors as well as the performers from the opera and the ballet. A play was commissioned from Ostrovsky who chose as his subject a 'tale of spring', based on folk legends and called *The Snow Maiden*. Tchaikovsky wrote the music.

The Snow Maiden was written and performed in the spring of 1873 in response to a commission from the management of the theatres and at the request of Ostrovsky. It is one of my favourite children. It was a marvellous spring; my spirits were high, as always at the approach of summer and three months of freedom. I liked Ostrovsky's play and I wrote the music in three weeks, without any effort. I think that you can feel in this music the happy, spring-like mood which possessed me at the time.[5]

First I am going to the south of Russia, to my sister's, then abroad and my main aim is *Switzerland*, where I intend to travel the length and breadth of the country. I am worn out with work and all sorts of agitations; I can scarcely wait for the hour of my departure when I will tear myself away from every kind of work and will indulge in complete idleness to revive myself.[6]

At the time of the 1873 exhibition in Vienna I was going abroad from Kamenka and my route lay through Vienna. Because of my hatred of

[3] v. 302, 303 (Modest).   [4] v. 299.
[5] viii. 434 (von Meck).   [6] v. 321 (Bessel).

crowds I made a terrible detour through Breslau and Dresden so as to avoid the hectic whirl.[7]

I left Sasha's the day before my name-day. I visited Breslau, Dresden, Cologne, Zurich, Geneva, Milan, and Lake Como and finally made my way to Paris. I travelled a lot in Switzerland and, incidentally, went up the Rigi by the newly-built railway which is technically most astonishing. I also paid a brief visit to Vevey. The situation of Vevey is truly superb, although because one is not used to it there is something terrible and fearsome about these towering, crushing masses. From Switzerland I made my way to Italy with the intention of travelling the length and breadth of the country but in Milan the heat was already so unbearable that I decided not to go any further south and after thoroughly reconsidering my plans I bent my steps towards Paris, which is pleasant at any season. I cannot describe how convenient and agreeable life is in Paris and how pleasantly one can pass the time here if one wants to enjoy oneself. Even just walking along the streets and gazing at the shops is extraordinarily fascinating. But apart from that, the theatres, the walks out into the country, the museums—this all fills the time up so that one does not notice how it flies by. I intend to spend about a week here then I will rush home.[8]

I know no greater pleasure than to spend some time in the country in complete solitude. At the beginning of August I went straight from Paris to visit one of my bachelor friends in Tambov province. It so happened that he had to make a trip to Moscow just at that time and so I found myself completely alone in this delightful oasis in the steppes. I cannot convey to you how blissful those two weeks were. I was in some sort of exalted condition of spiritual bliss, wandering on my own through the woods during the day and, towards evening, across the measureless steppe; at night I sat by the open window listening to the solemn stillness of this isolated place, broken from time to time by vague nocturnal sounds. In the course of these two weeks, without any effort, as though moved by some supernatural force, I wrote the rough draft of the whole of *The Tempest*.[9]

Tchaikovsky went to Shilovsky's estate at Usovo.

My life hasn't changed. I have no time to be bored and would be completely happy if it weren't for worrying about the fate of my opera, which I have had no concrete news about up till now. I have just been told that it hasn't been decided whether it will be included in the current season, but I desperately don't want to wait any longer and besides I need the money. As I have no children of my own, I cling with all my heart to the offspring of my musical fantasy and suffer for them, like mothers trying to marry off their daughters, and searching anxiously for suitors.[10]

I have recently been oppressed by the most profound and hopeless sense

[7] vi. 323 (von Meck).   [8] v. 326 (his father).
[9] vii. 232 (Modest).   [10] v. 329 (his father).

of disillusionment about the value and significance of the career which I
pursue as a music critic. When I embarked upon my musical conversations
with the reader, I set about the task with some degree of enthusiasm. In my
youthful innocence and with my firm faith in the power of the printed word
I had it in mind to be of some use to my fellow citizens by moulding their
preferences and furthering their development in the aesthetics of music, by
explaining the merits and deficiencies of whatever the musical world might
offer to the public for its appraisal. There is, in truth, nothing especially
bold about this and the hopes which I placed in the useful effects of my
reviewing activities in no way suggest that I was suffering from any grave
deficiency of modesty. Since I had already acquired a sufficient degree of
skill and expertise in my field, why should I not guide public opinion in
musical matters, especially if using a very widely-distributed organ of the
press would give me the chance to talk to tens of thousands of readers? But
life's experience soon began to pour cold water on the fire of critical fervour
that burnt within me; gradually I sobered up and my ardour cooled for the
critic's task. I began to realize that my fellow citizens were not only not
learning anything from my arguments and protestations and not accepting
my views and opinions, but they were not even paying any attention to me
at all. Since everything that I said was at odds with their hallowed preferences and their ingrained disposition towards all that is coarse and vulgar in
art, they did not go to the trouble of listening to my exhortations, and I
soon realized that mine was the voice of one crying in the wilderness. When
I spoke with genuine enthusiasm of the beauties scattered so generously
throughout their works by the hands of such geniuses as Mozart, Beethoven, Schumann, and Glinka my fellow citizens passed me by with laughter
as they hastened to drink their fill for the hundredth time of the inspirations
of maestro Verdi at the Italian opera or to listen spellbound to the vulgar
tunes of Offenbach. When I set about explaining to them the inexhaustible
riches of music and beauty hidden away in the Russian folk-song and
lashed those charlatans who distort these beauties and play upon the Russian's patriotic sympathies, my fellow citizens, like the sea itself, flooded
into the concerts of the self-styled *Russian* singer Mr Slavyansky. If I
demonstrated that Mme Patti was a great and inimitable artist, then I immediately ran up against dozens of people who denied, in tones of the
utmost conviction, that she had any serious virtues at all. If an article came
off the presses in the morning in which Mr Marini caught it from me for his
lack of musical sense and of style and for his pitiful lack of talent, then that
very same evening I would myself witness the most ecstatic ovations being
lavished on this singer after he had crudely brought off a high note. Like all
my press colleagues, I poured out in reviews my indignation at the spectacle of the shameful humiliation to which Russian opera is subjected in
Moscow, the so-called heart of Russia. But did anybody heed my philip-
pics, seasoned as they were with the most venomous darts of irony, anger,

and indignation? And is the public not still deprived of the chance to see even a barely passable performance of our best Russian operas—*Ruslan, Rusalka, Judith, Rogneda, The Power of Evil*? And is it not still the case that the impresario of the Italian opera has the free run of all the resources of the State theatre? In conclusion, I shall only say that the period is past when I was disillusioned about the extent to which my journalistic activities might be of use and my spirit has now entered that phase when a man, experienced in life and with no faith any longer in the early realization of his ideals, none the less does not lay down his weapons but proposes steadfastly to continue the struggle in the hope that his very persistence will eventually attract attention, that his voice will be heard, if only just, and that the truths which he has propounded to the best of his ability will receive proper consideration.[11]

At the moment I am under the influence of a tragic catastrophe which has befallen a man who was very close to me, and my nerves are severely shaken. I am in no state to do anything at all.[12]

This concerns the suicide of Eduard Zak, a young man whom Tchaikovsky helped a great deal. Zak's cousin, R. Keber, was a pupil of Tchaikovsky at the Moscow Conservatoire.

I have rented a flat and moved into it three days ago. It is in the Malaya Nikitskaya, Vishnevsky's House (on the right-hand side going away from Kudrin's), in a wing in the yard. The flat is not spacious but very comfortable. I am quite well and have completely recovered my normal state of mind.[13].

[11] *MC* 157–60.   [12] v. 333 (Bessel).   [13] Ibid.

7

1874

If I survive I am sure I will write a few good operas.

Although the production of *The Oprichnik* in Petersburg met with every possible obstacle I couldn't wait to hear it; but right from the first rehearsal I was astounded when I saw that it was a great failure as an opera and listening to *The Oprichnik* since then has caused me dreadful suffering. Modesty apart, I know perfectly well that there are fine things in it here and there, but as a whole, as a whole! It is absurd, cold, and tedious![1]

The Oprichnik torments me. This opera is so bad that I fled from all the rehearsals (particularly of Acts III and IV) so as not to hear a single note and at the performance I wished the earth would swallow me. How strange that, when I was writing it, it at first seemed such a delightful piece. But what a disappointment at the very first rehearsal![2] Now that the opera has played to full houses five times in a fortnight I can frankly say that I am firmly convinced *The Oprichnik* will not survive in the permanent repertoire. I am sure it will be given a few more performances, as many as are necessary to cover the costs, but it has no future. However malicious Cui's review may have been, however monstrously biased his response, he was fundamentally fairly accurate in his assessment of its qualities as a musical-dramatic work. It lacks *style* and *action*, the two deficiencies which guarantee that the public will turn cool towards an opera. In any event, I am glad that *The Oprichnik* was performed. It was not a fiasco and at the same time it was an excellent lesson for me in how to compose an opera.[3]

The first performance of *The Oprichnik* took place on 12 April 1874, conducted by Eduard Nápravník. After the production of *The Oprichnik* Tchaikovsky went to Italy. He was planning to attend the première of *A Life for the Tsar* at La Scala, Milan, as the correspondent of *The Russian Gazette*. He first made for Venice.

Venice is the sort of place where, if I had to stay for a week, I would hang myself from despair on the fifth day. Everything centres on St Mark's Square. After that, wherever you go, you get lost in a labyrinth of stinking passage-ways which take you nowhere and unless you get into a gondola and tell them where you want to go you will not know where you are. It's not a bad idea to take a trip along the Grand Canal: palaces, palaces,

---

[1] v. 361 (Korsov).   [2] v. 353–4 (Modest).   [3] v. 355–6 (Bessel).

palaces, all of marble, one better than another, but at the same time one dirtier and more dilapidated than another. In fact, it's just like the decrepit scenery from the first act of [Donizetti's] *Lucrezia*. On the other hand the Doge's Palace is the acme of beauty and fascination, with a romantic flavour of the Council of Ten, the Inquisition, torture, oubliettes, and similar delights. All the same I did rush through the length and breadth of the place again, to clear my conscience, looked into two or three churches with great masses of pictures by Titian and Tintoretto, statues by Canova and all manner of aesthetic treasures. But, I repeat, it is a city which is so gloomy it might be dead. I received a telegram in reply from Milan. They will not be doing *A Life for the Tsar* before 12 May (New Style) and I am making my mind up to going straight to Rome and then to Naples.[4]

My travels are very unfortunate. Naples loses almost all its charm in bad weather and it's more a question of guessing at its beauties than revelling in them. None the less, in these four days I have walked and travelled all over the place to see what one should in the town itself and in the immediate surroundings.[5]

I went to Pompeii. I cannot express in words the force of the sensation which I experienced as I wandered through these ruins. First I went round everything with the inevitable guide but then I got rid of him and went round the whole town again *on my own*, looking into nearly every house, falling into reveries and trying to imagine life in this place that was buried alive. Florence I will pass over for the moment. Rome I did not, to tell the truth, particularly like. The monuments of art and antiquity are, of course, astonishing but as a town it seemed gloomy to me, rather lifeless and boring. In Naples it was very interesting to wander along the streets, observing and scrutinizing the people and their ways. In Rome I tried wandering about but only felt bored. However, I think that to come to like Rome one would have to live there a bit longer.[6]

Because of the letter which I have received [about the opera production] I have decided not to go to Milan. It transpires that *A Life for the Tsar* has suffered such injuries that it would not be fitting for a Russian musician to witness the operations which this opera has undergone at the hands of the conductor. Something should have been done about it but nobody asked me.[7]

Tchaikovsky returned to Moscow in May.

I was shown a copy of the *Augsburg News* with a letter from Bülow about *A Life for the Tsar*. This letter contained an assessment of my music which gave me more pleasure than anything else I have seen in print.[8]

[4] v. 347–8 (Modest).   [5] v. 352 (Anna Merkling).   [6] Ibid.
[7] v. 355 (Bessel).   [8] v. 357 (Bessel).

In the *Augsburg News* (29 May 1874) Bülow wrote:

> Contemporary Russia does not lack powerful creative talents in any branch
> of music: but if these talented people, in blind obeisance to the undoubted
> power of their native resources ... neglect those difficult paths of study trav-
> elled by Glinka, which by no means get you to your destination at top speed,
> then they will scarcely prevail in winning for themselves the position of suc-
> cessors to the founder of their national music. I know so far of only one Russian
> composer who, like Glinka, labours tirelessly and whose works, although they
> do not as yet show a full maturity in keeping with the high degree of his talent,
> none the less offer even now the securest guarantee that this maturity awaits us
> in the future. I am referring to Mr Tchaikovsky, the still young Professor of
> Composition at the Moscow Conservatoire. His excellent String Quartet has
> already been granted civic rights in many German towns; there is good reason
> to pay similar attention to many of his piano works, the two symphonies, and in
> particular the remarkably interesting overture *Romeo and Juliet*, which is out-
> standing in its originality and tunefulness; I am told that it is already available
> from a music publishing firm in Berlin.

At the end of 1873 the Petersburg committee of the Russian Musical Society
announced a competition for an opera to be called *Vakula the Smith* to a libretto by
Polonsky based on Gogol's story *Christmas Eve*. Tchaikovsky feverishly set about
composing the opera, for some reason thinking that the closing date was 1 January
1874 whereas in fact the time allowed did not expire until autumn 1875. He spent
part of the summer at Kondratyev's in Nizy, where he worked on *Vakula*, and
returned to Moscow at the beginning of September (having moved to a new flat—
Poluektov's House, Malaya Nikitskaya).

I have studied *Boris Godunov* and *The Demon* thoroughly. Musorgsky's
music is utterly and damnably awful; it is the most vulgar and squalid parody of music; there are some attractive things in *The Demon*—but a lot of
dead wood as well.[9]

At the moment I am weighed down by the composition of a piano concerto. I want Rubinstein to play it in his concert without fail; it is causing
me great difficulty and is not coming easily. In principle I am forcing myself and making my brain think up pianistic passages; the result is a considerable degree of nervous strain.[10]

In the first place, I am in excellent health, and in the second place, I am
very pleased with my new flat.[11] I am very glad that my admirers liked the
Second Quartet. I regard it as my best work; no other piece has poured
forth from me so simply and easily. I wrote it almost at one sitting.[12] I am
very distressed at the cold reception accorded to *The Tempest*, not only by
the public but by my friends as well ... Laroche's article simply enraged
me. How he loves saying that I imitate Litolff, and Schumann, and Glinka,
and Berlioz, and somebody else as well. As if the only thing I can do is just

[9] v. 372 (Modest).   [10] v. 379 (Anatoly).
[11] v. 366 (Anatoly).   [12] v. 372 (Modest).

stick together anything that comes my way. I am not offended that he does
not particularly like *The Tempest*; I expected that and am glad that at least a
few little things win his praise. But I do not like his general characterization
of my music which clearly suggests that it is full of bits grabbed from every
composer alive.[13]

In an article in the newspaper *Golos* [*The Voice*] (22 November 1874) Laroche
wrote: 'The earlier programme pieces by Mr Tchaikovsky, particularly *Romeo and
Juliet*, were significantly reminiscent of Litolff; their harmonization was a combination of Glinka and Schumann and certain contemporary elements, but not Wagner.
The form of his latest work shows a marked similarity to the symphonic poems of
Liszt. It is constructed (and I mean constructed) almost exactly like Liszt's *Les Pré-
ludes*.'

I have been to Kiev to see *The Oprichnik*. A *magnificent* performance. The
opera was a success; at all events, they created a terrible noise and gave me
far more flattering ovations than I could ever have hoped for. An enormous
crowd of students took me from the theatre to my hotel. I was absolutely
delighted.[14]

The Oprichnik was staged in Kiev on 9 December 1874 by courtesy of Joseph Setov.

In December 1874 I wrote the [First] Piano Concerto. Since I am not a
pianist it was essential for me to refer to a virtuoso, a specialist who could
tell me what might, in the technical sense, be awkward and ungrateful to
play or ineffective and so on. For this purely external side of my work I
needed a critic who was severe but at the same time well-disposed towards
me ... I must state clearly that some inner voice warned me against choosing Rubinstein as one of the arbitrators on this mechanical aspect of my
composition. I knew that he would seize this convenient opportunity to
give a little display of *petty tyranny*. Nevertheless, he is not just the best
pianist in Moscow but is excellent by any standards. So, knowing in advance that he would be deeply offended if he found out that I had passed
him over, I suggested that he should hear the concerto through and let me
have his observations on the piano part. This was Christmas Eve 1874. We
had both been invited to a Christmas party at Albrecht's that evening and
Rubinstein suggested that we should settle ourselves down in one of the
classrooms of the Conservatoire before the party; this we did. I turned up
with my manuscript and then Rubinstein came with Hubert. I played the
first movement. Not a single word, not a single comment! How stupid and
insufferable to be put in the position of someone cooking a meal and offering it to a friend who then eats it and says nothing! Oh for one word, even of
friendly abuse, but for God's sake just one word of understanding, if not of
praise! Rubinstein was brewing up his storms and Hubert was waiting for
the situation to develop so that he would know which way to jump. The

[13] v. 381 (Modest).   [14] v. 383 (Bessel).

most important thing was that I did not need a verdict on the artistic aspect. I needed comments on the virtuoso technique, on the piano. Rubinstein's eloquent silence was of the most pointed significance. I girded myself with patience and played to the end. Silence again. I got up and asked: 'Well then?' A torrent of utterances then poured from Rubinstein's lips; at first he was quiet but then he more and more assumed the tone of Jupiter with his thunderbolts. It appeared that my concerto was no good at all, that it was unplayable, that some passages were hackneyed, awkward, and clumsy beyond redemption, that the work as a whole was bad and vulgar, that I had stolen this bit from somewhere and that bit from somewhere, that there were only two or three pages which could stand and the rest would have to be thrown away or completely revised. 'Now look at that for example! What's that supposed to be? (At which the passage referred to is given a caricature of a performance.) And that! How could anyone do it!' and so on, and so on. I cannot convey the main thing, which is the *tone* in which all this was said. So to put it briefly, an outsider might well have thought that I was a madman, an incompetent and ignorant scribbler pestering the famous musician with my rubbish. I was staggered and dumbfounded that such a dressing-down should be given to someone who had already written a great deal and who taught the free composition course at the Conservatoire. Hubert noticed that I was maintaining a stubborn silence and began to explain Rubinstein's criticisms; he did not disagree with him at all and merely toned down what His Excellency had expressed far too unceremoniously. I was not just astonished by this scene but offended by it as well. I left the room without saying anything and went upstairs. I could not speak from anger and agitation. Rubinstein soon appeared and, noticing how upset I was, called me into one of the rooms some distance away. There he again repeated that the concerto was impossible and, after pointing out a large number of passages which required radical alteration, said that if by a specified time I revised the concerto in accordance with his demands he would do me the honour of playing my piece in one of his concerts. 'I will not revise a single note', I replied, 'and I will publish it in exactly the form it is now!' And I did.[15]

Hans von Bülow was the first to play this concerto and Tchaikovsky dedicated it to him in gratitude for his performance.

In his capacity as a music critic Tchaikovsky went to all the concerts and often to the rehearsals as well.

Your [Rimsky-Korsakov's Third] Symphony has been performed here. I listened to it carefully at the three rehearsals and at the concert itself and came to the conclusions which I have expressed frankly in the enclosed extract from my review. Forgive me for crawling to you with my candid comments; I do it out of sincere affection for you and your works and I feel

---

[15] vii. 64–5 (von Meck).

the need to tell you what my impressions are. I personally am in raptures over the first two movements.[16]

Tchaikovsky's article about Rimsky-Korsakov's Third Symphony appeared on 3 January 1875. And as a sort of counterbalance to the cold, intellectual approach Tchaikovsky cites the works of Mozart, Schumann, and Glinka.

Night in Madrid. What warmth of inspiration, what a wealth of poetic fantasy in this enchanting work by our great composer: the unusual and original introduction depicting the translucent twilight of the southern night as it draws closer, and the passionate, gripping sounds of the dance tune, first heard as a melody in the distance, and all the rapidly changing episodes of the middle section where you can positively hear the mysterious chattering, and a kiss, and embraces, and then again the dark stillness of the starry, fragrant southern night. And at the same time what mastery in the finish, what richness of colouring and what amazing plastic beauty in the form, free and yet organically coherent. I am sure I will not be mistaken if I assert that there was not a single listener who was not transported to the highest degree of rapture by the dazzling outbursts of Glinka's mighty creative genius which shines forth so brilliantly in his Spanish overture. It is characteristic of his massive talent that the melodic line in his music is distinct and always beautiful but he is also in full command of a sumptuous and beautiful harmonic *facture* which would satisfy the most recherché demands of his admirers.[17]

There are a few rare works which have the capacity to afford equal pleasure to the perceptive expert and to the untutored majority. Their beauty is unfading; the more one hears them, the more one loves them; their power and essential originality is such, that one can never take them for granted; they will never become part of our normal musical language because they can be neither imitated nor plagiarized. To the most restricted corpus of precisely such works belongs the famous Allegretto of [Beethoven's] Seventh Symphony which is an abundant source of the highest artistic delight to the whole civilized world. The preceding and following movements of this astonishing symphony are at a level no lower than that of the Allegretto but, I repeat, it is the latter which has the privilege of being especially beloved of the public and this is partly to be explained by the fact that it is captivatingly tuneful, without any complicated development, and partly by the physical beauty of the sound i.e. the superb orchestration.[18]

Glinka's music for the tragedy *Prince Kholmsky*. In this work Glinka shows himself to be one of the greatest symphonists of our time. Beethoven's hand can be seen in many features of *Prince Kholmsky*. There is the same restraint in the resources employed, with no striving at all for external effect; there is the same serious beauty in the basic idea, inspired but not contrived in the clarity of its exposition; there is the same plasticity of form,

[16] v. 387.   [17] *MC* 180.   [18] Ibid. 207–8.

with the most sharply contrasting parts of the work fusing together; and finally that same inimitable orchestration, eschewing the affected and the recherché, powerful but without sound and fury, transparent but without the hazy vacuity of a harmonic sketch. To take just one example, note the skill with which Glinka manages the transition from the introduction to the Allegro in the overture. What a striking impression is made at this point by the extreme dissonance of the triad which, like an ominous foreboding of *Kholmsky's misfortunes to come*, suddenly transports the listener from the martial ceremony of the introduction to the grim and stormy Allegro. Glinka shows no less skill in bringing together the two basic ideas of the Allegro of the overture and then integrating them into a single grouping; and finally, after an exhaustive development, the music gradually fades away on a closing tonic chord. Each of the entr'actes which follow the overture is a little picture painted by the hand of a great artist, a symphonic miracle worth a dozen long symphonies by a second-rate composer. A particularly delightful impression is made by the entr'acte before Act II depicting Kholmsky's amorous languors which are cut short by his growing awareness of his duty to his country and the ensuing conflict with his amorous passions. Creative artistry can go no further than this; confronted with such beauty one simply throws up one's hands with a sense of being utterly powerless to express it all in words.[19]

Reflection has a destructive effect on inspiration. Look at what happened to the latest attempts by contemporary composers to base opera on a realistic reproduction of life, renouncing traditional forms, chasing after the illusion of rationality and truth. Wagner, in taking up the struggle against the misuse of a singer's virtuosity, subjects the singer to a whole orchestral horde, which not only deprives the stage characters of their supremacy but also drowns them. Dargomyzhsky goes a step further: having decided to sacrifice the beauty of the music to imperfectly understood rules about the authenticity of dramatic action, he not only deprives the singer of everything that is captivating about singing, but deprives himself of rich resources of musical expressiveness. His *Stone Guest*, in subject-matter close to Mozart's *Don Giovanni*, is the pitiful fruit of a dry, utterly rational process of invention, being capable only of inflicting a sense of mortal tedium on the audience, who seek in art not the narrow truth like the fact that a real apple tastes better than a drawing of an apple, but the higher artistic truth, which flows from the mysterious depths of a man's creative powers and pours forth into clear, easily understood, and conventional forms. Only the self-satisfied amateurish stupidity shown by those unrecognized innovators who find refuge in the pages of the *St Petersburg Gazette* could, with comical seriousness, proclaim the latest work by the gifted Dargomyzhsky to be a model of the latest kind of opera and put it on a par with the greatest creations of the masters of lyrical dramatic art.

[19] *MC* 222–33.

The music of *Don Giovanni* offers us an unbroken string of such pearls of musical inspiration, before which everything written both before and after this opera pales into insignificance. From whatever side this unique, inimitably beautiful opera is analysed, one can only marvel and bow down before the greatness of human genius. Lovers of the elegant cantilena will pause at the wonderful duet in Act I between Don Ottavio and Donna Anna, who is mourning the death of her father and already calling for revenge, at the duet between Don Giovanni and Zerlina, at the arias of Donna Elvira, Zerlina, and Donna Anna, or at Don Giovanni's famous serenade. The devotee of musical declamation, brought to such remarkable perfection by Gluck, will find in Donna Anna's recitatives such shattering pathos, combined with bewitching beauty of harmony and modulation, such strength and might of tragic expression, that the beauty of Gluck's recitatives fades. If attention is turned primarily to the ensembles, to the broad build-up of weight in the Finales, to the orchestration, to the art of writing vocal music which takes account of the features required to make it rewarding to the performer, if one studies the mastery of musical characterization—then *Don Giovanni* responds more than adequately to all of these demands and will continue to serve as the best possible model so long as art survives.[20]

[20] Ibid. 165.

8

1875

I am very lonely here.

I cannot bear holidays. On ordinary days you work at the appropriate time and everything goes like clockwork; on holidays your pen drops out of your hand, you feel like spending a bit of time unburdening your soul to those you know, and this is precisely when you become aware (albeit to excess) that you are a lonely orphan. And in truth I really do live in Moscow rather like an orphan. It was actually for this reason that I was so deeply depressed at holiday times. In fact I very much wanted to go to P'burg but hadn't enough money. Apart from the fact that I have no *friends* here in the real sense of the word, I was still powerfully under the effect of the blow administered to my self-esteem as a composer by none other than Rubinstein. And Hubert, too, annoyed me in that same affair. These gentlemen simply cannot stop regarding me as a beginner who needs their advice, their exacting comments and their definitive judgements. Taking into account that they are supposed to be my friends and that there is no one in the whole of Moscow who can be expected to give my work any sympathy or attention, I really did feel wretched.

An astonishing thing! The assorted Cuis, Stasovs and Co., although they do sometimes play dirty tricks on me, occasionally make me think that they are far more interested in me than my so-called friends. Cui recently wrote me a very nice letter. I had a letter from Rimsky which touched me very much. I am very, very lonely here. If I did not always have my work to do I would simply lapse into melancholy.[1] Unfortunately, Fate the Joker has so arranged things for ten years in a row that those whom I love most in all the world are far away from me. My friendship with Rubinstein and my other colleagues at the Conservatoire is based solely on the fact that we all work at the same place. I have no one here to whom I can unburden my soul. Perhaps this is in part my own fault; I am not very amenable to intimacy.[2]

I am very, very lonely here and were it not that I work all the time I would simply succumb to melancholy. It is a fact that [my inclinations] create an impassable gulf between the majority of people and myself. They impart to my character a host of features—a sense of alienation, fear of

---

[1] v. 390 (Anatoly).　　　[2] v. 397 (Anatoly).

others, timidity, excessive shyness, mistrustfulness—which make me more
and more unsociable.[3]

(The words in square brackets are supplied from the context since there is an omission in the source.)

I have been constantly depressed this winter to a greater or lesser degree—
and sometimes to the ultimate degree of being so revolted by life that I
would have welcomed death. Now that spring is approaching these attacks
of melancholy have stopped altogether but, since I *know* that every year or,
to be precise, every winter they will recur with extreme severity, I have decided to spend the whole of next year away from Moscow. Where I will be
or might get to I still do not know but I *must* go somewhere else, to different surroundings.[4]

   You [Modest] complain that you find it difficult to write and have to
brood over every phrase. But do you really think that anything comes without labour and effort? I sometimes sit nibbling my pen for two hours
because I don't know how to begin an article; I think that it's going to come
out badly, but—quite the opposite, people praise it, find it easy to read and
even note signs of a lack of constraint in the actual writing. Other things involve much biting of nails, the smoking of a vast number of cigarettes, and a
great deal of pacing up and down before you light upon the basic theme. On
the other hand, writing sometimes comes dreadfully easily; ideas positively
swarm and chase after each other. Everything depends on a particular
frame of mind and disposition. But even if they are not right you have to be
able to make yourself work. Otherwise you'll never do anything.[5] I am
treating as a joke what you say about my antipathy towards you. What mad-
dens me about you is that you have every single one of my faults—that
much is true. I would like to discover that you lacked even just one of my
bad characteristics, but I am quite unable to. You are too like me and when
I get angry with you I am at bottom angry with myself because you are permanently cast as the mirror in which I see all my weaknesses.[6]

   My extreme view is that there is no rational ground, when criticizing the
qualities of a work, for taking into account the greater or lesser productive-
ness of the composer. I have often had to read or listen to the stock phrase
about the composer's *critical attitude* to his own work in connection with
Mr Rubinstein and certain other composers. But everybody knows that
absolute perfection is not to be found under the sun and if we are to take to
its logical conclusion the demand for composers to be self-critical then
there would be more sense in advising all aspiring composers never to pick
up a pen. For what is the criterion, where is the limit beyond which the
composer must be careful not to go if he makes up his mind to submit
himself to a detailed critical interrogation, investigation, and, perhaps,

[3] *LR* 214 (Anatoly).   [4] v. 397 (Anatoly).

prosecution? There is no worse, no more biased, no more partial judge of a work of art than its own creator, at least at the moment when he has just finished his labours. Only with the passage of time, only when the morbidly sensitive special relationship between the artist and his creation has been broken, when the delights as well as the trials and tribulations which inevitably accompany the creative process are long forgotten, only then does the composer become capable of considering his work calmly and objectively, of analysing it critically and pronouncing a just verdict.[7]

I attended the numerous rehearsals of *The Oprichnik* [at the Bolshoy Theatre] and endured with stoic bravery the systematic disfigurement of this ill-fated opera which was hideous enough to start with. However, the performance of *The Oprichnik* was not what I expected in the sense that I had expected something far worse. Everybody was trying hard. It seemed to me that the public was very cold towards the opera, which, of course, did not stop my well-wishers bawling and clapping and presenting wreaths. All my thoughts are concentrated now on my favourite child, my dear *Vakula*;[8] how I love him! I will send this opera to the competition in a day or two and I am most put out at the thought that there perhaps already exist at this moment other *Vakulas*, and better ones than mine. The prize does not interest me at all but the staging of the opera is now a question of life and death for me and if it does not come off I think I will go out of my mind.[9]

I spent the summer at various places in the provinces with friends and relations. I worked quite conscientiously and, apart from the symphony, sketched out two acts of a *ballet*. At the invitation of the Moscow management I am writing the music for the ballet *The Lake of the Swans* [*sic*]. I have taken on this task partly because of the money, which I need, partly because I have wanted to try my hand at this sort of music for a long time.[10] I do my duties at the Conservatoire, I am working hard at my ballet, I keep a record of musical events—I hope I have enough to do. Living arrangements are as before; the only difference is that I am one floor higher, with a little more luxury.[11]

The Italian opera has started. They are doing *The Oprichnik* in a day or two at the Russian opera, in the same disgraceful production. I often see Taneyev—he plays my concerto marvellously![12]

The benefit performance of *Ruslan and Lyudmila* at the Bolshoy for Mme Alexandrova drew an enormous audience, despite the increased prices. . . . One could not but rejoice at the sight of this huge crowd, attracted now solely by the sacred name of that great Russian composer whose music is so

[5] v. 388 (Modest).   [6] v. 398 (Modest).   [7] *MC* 248–9.
[8] v. 403 (Anatoly).   [9] v. 404 (Rimsky-Korsakov).
[10] v. 412 (Rimsky-Korsakov).   [11] v. 414 (Modest).   [12] Ibid.

rarely performed in Moscow, and usually doomed to content itself with the sugary and vulgar devices of the Italian opera. Even more comforting was the delicate tact with which the audience conducted itself, considering the shameful disfigurement which had, as might have been expected, been inflicted upon Glinka's unfortunate opera. It was obvious that those who had come to hear *Ruslan* had known in advance that the performance would only be a sorry parody. Out of respect for the music of the greatest genius amongst Russian composers everybody had, as it were, agreed patiently and indulgently to suffer all those horrors which are a perfectly normal, daily occurrence for us but would be unthinkable on any other stage anywhere else anywhere in the world.[13]

At a meeting of the competition jury on 16 October 1875 Tchaikovsky's opera *Vakula the Smith*, submitted under the motto *Ars longa, vita brevis*, was declared to be the only one meeting the requirements (out of five submitted) and awarded the first prize.

At the First Symphony Concert of the RMS in St Petersburg on 1 November, Nápravník conducted Tchaikovsky's First Piano Concerto with Gustav Kross, a professor at the Conservatoire, as soloist.

I heard [the concerto] in Petersburg where it was desperately mutilated, especially by the conductor (Nápravník), who did everything in his power to accompany in such a way that instead of music we had a continuous and dreadful cacophony. Kross was conscientious but dull, tasteless, and entirely without charm. The piece was not well received at all. It is being played in Moscow in two days' time, where I hope it will be more successful.[14]

And indeed the concerto was performed in Moscow with great success on 21 November at the Third Symphony Concert of the RMS. Taneyev was the soloist and Nikolay Rubinstein conducted.

I went straight from the station to the rehearsal of my Third Symphony. So far as I can see, this symphony has no particularly inventive ideas but in terms of technique it is a step forward. I like the first movement best and both of the scherzos, though the second one is difficult and was not at all so well played.[15]

Because of the unbearable cold I have had to move. I am now living near the Vozdvizhenka in Schlesinger's House, Krestovozdvizhensky Lane. I have three comfortable rooms with an entrance hall, a kitchen, a lavatory, and running water.[16]

I am submerging in a flood of work. Apart from the ballet [*Swan Lake*], which I am hurrying to finish as soon as possible, so that I can get down to the opera, I have masses of proofs and—the most dreadful thing of all—I

---

[13] *MC* 241.   [14] v. 419–20 (von Bülow).
[15] v. 417 (Rimsky-Korsakov).   [16] v. 424 (Anatoly).

am committed to writing articles on music. I find that an intolerably heavy burden![17] I have been having an incredibly furious polemic in the papers about Slavyansky.[18]

Like all the foremost figures of his day in the arts (including Chekhov, for instance), Tchaikovsky strongly disapproved of the activities of Agrenev-Slavyansky, a variety-artist and singer. He performed in a pseudo-folk style and at the same time aspired to the role of propagandist for true folk-song, even claiming to be the first to have discovered it. Slavyansky and his choir performed in national costumes and won a resounding success both in Russia and abroad.

If Mr Slavyansky is regarded as some sort of hero, holding aloft the banner of Russian music, then I assert that only people knowing nothing of music in general and of Russian music in particular can think thus. Russian song, with its originality of structure, with the special features of its melodic outline, with the individuality of its rhythm (for the most part not falling into the accepted bar divisions), offers the educated and talented musician a most precious source which in certain circumstances can be exploited to advantage. And indeed its rich seam of inspiration has been used and exploited by all our composers: Glinka, Dargomyzhsky, Serov, Messrs Anton Rubinstein, Balakirev, Rimsky-Korsakov, Musorgsky and others. A skilled hand is called for in dealing with the Russian folk *bylina*, or tale or song. Just as popular books lie outside the sphere of serious literature, so likewise has the popular singer Mr Slavyansky condemned himself to be ignored on the part of the chronicler of Russian musical life. If Russian song interests us as an ethnographic feature of extreme beauty, as an original product of the creative individuality of the folk, then we must do one of two things: either listen to the songs on the spot i.e. performed by the folk in that characteristic fashion which is so attractive to the Russian ear, or we should send for true folk singers from the depths of their isolation in the countryside. We could also resort to the collections of songs, of which, admittedly, there are not many but they do include a fine piece of work in the shape of Mr Balakirev's collection. The recording and harmonizing of the Russian folk-song, without distortion and with careful attention to preserving its characteristic peculiarities, requires the sort of substantial and broadly-based musical personality, the profound knowledge of the history of the art, and at the same time the great gifts which we see in Mr Balakirev. Whoever sets himself up in print as a recorder and transcriber of folk-song without being Mr Balakirev's equal in musical culture and understanding (to say nothing of talent) has neither respect for himself, for his art, for the folk, nor for his public; his sacrilegious hand desecrates the holy places of our folk culture, he loses all right to be called an artist, for the aims which he pursues have nothing at all in common with art.[19]

[17] v. 417 (Rimsky-Korsakov).   [18] v. 423 (Anatoly).   [19] *MC* 287–9.

The attack on Slavyansky effectively put an end to Tchaikovsky's activities as a critic. He appeared in print only once more—in the pages of *The Russian Gazette*—with an account of the Wagner performances at Bayreuth.

PART II

9

1876

I am now going through a very critical period of my life.

I have four brothers. The eldest is Nikolay, who works for the railways and lives in Kharkov. He is married but has no children. Then there's me, and after me my brother Ippolit, who lives in Odessa and is married, also without children. Then there are the twins Anatoly and Modest. They were both educated at the School of Jurisprudence; Anatoly has done well and is now an assistant public prosecutor. Modest (who has immense resources of character but no special inclination for any one sphere of activity) has not had a notably brilliant career. He was more interested in books, pictures, and music than in writing his reports. One of our mutual friends (Mme Davydova, the wife of the Director of the Petersburg Conservatoire) had the idea of recommending him to a certain Mr Konradi who was looking for a tutor for his only son, a deaf mute. The matter was arranged. Modest soon turned out to be an excellent teacher.[1]

Before he started his teaching, Modest had to go to Lyons to study the phonetic method of teaching the deaf and dumb under a famous specialist, Jacques Gugentobler, with a view to using it when teaching Kolya Konradi. Tchaikovsky went abroad with his brother at the end of December 1875. They first went to Geneva, where their sister Alexandra was then living with her children.

We arrived here exactly a week after leaving Moscow. We are enjoying ourselves but have stayed at home apart from a couple of walks around the town. I don't like Geneva all that much but it really is pleasant to live in a *comfortable little place.*[2]

From Geneva Modest set out for Lyons and Tchaikovsky himself went to Paris where he stayed for a while. Then he returned to Russia via Berlin. And, as always, parting from someone close to him—in the present case for a long time—did not come easily.

One good thing about parting from someone you love is that it gives you an excellent opportunity to measure the strength of your affection.[3]

My stay in P'burg became insufferable towards the end because of the usual business of being pulled in all directions. Nápravník gave a very good performance of my symphony on 24 November; it was notably well

---

[1] vi. 253–4 (von Meck).   [2] v. 427 (Anatoly).   [3] vi. 15–16 (Modest).

received. They called me forward and applauded me in a very friendly way. I have been to two rehearsals of *Angelo*. I do *not* like [Cui's] opera at all. I often see Cui and once had dinner at his place with Taneyev: he was showering compliments. I have seen all my cousins, and Laroche and I had dinner at Annette's [Anna Merkling].[4]

Tchaikovsky then returned to Moscow.

My life is uneventful, as ever. It is full of feelings, worries, work, and impressions but it takes time to give them proper expression and I have none. I am now going full steam ahead to finish the quartet which I began in Paris. It's already done but I haven't scored it yet. I have stopped writing articles altogether. On musical matters there are one or two things to record. First, I have been to *Aida* and my rapture over it was redoubled by Artôt's marvellous Amneris. I have had a letter from Bülow with masses of articles about my First Quartet which has been performed in America. The press, including Laroche, was rather cool about my symphony. Everybody agreed that there was nothing new in it and that I was beginning to repeat myself. Could this really be true? I want to have a rest after the quartet, that's to say I want to finish the ballet and not start anything new until I set about the opera. I am wavering between *Ephraim* [a biblical subject] and *Francesca* but I think the latter will win.[5]

Tchaikovsky misunderstood Laroche's article. His assessment of the Third Symphony was very favourable: 'In the strength and significance of its content, in the rich variety of its form, in the nobility of its style, which is marked by an individual and distinctive inventiveness, in the rare perfection of its technique, Mr Tchaikovsky's symphony is one of the most important musical events of the past decade not only in Russia, of course, but in all Europe.' And he continued: 'Tchaikovsky goes ever onwards. In his new symphony the contrapuntal development and formal skill is at a higher level than in any of his previous works.' (*The Voice* (1876), No. 28.)

Is it not strange to reflect that, of the two most famous musicians of our time, it is not my teacher Anton Rubinstein but [Bülow], who got to know my works only recently, who gives my music that benevolent support which it so much needs? Rubinstein is an Olympian god who has never shown anything but the loftiest contempt for my compositions and I must admit, in private, that I have always found this deeply hurtful.[6]

I have finished the quartet which I began in Paris and it was given its first performance at a soirée at [Nikolay] Rubinstein's. It has been much praised but I am not altogether satisfied with it. I think I have rather written myself out, am starting to repeat myself and am not able to think of anything new. Has my song really been sung already? Am I really at the end of the road? Extremely gloomy.[7]

[4] vi. 20 (Modest).	[5] vi. 24 (Modest).
[6] vi. 22 (von Bülow).	[7] vi. 28 (Modest).

I am up to the eyes in orchestrating the *ballet*. So as to get my work finished without interruption I decided to go away for two weeks (the weeks either side of Easter) to stay in the country with Konstantin Shilovsky.[8]

Shilovsky's estate of Glebovo was in the Moscow area, near to Voskresensk (now Istra).

The first rehearsal of some numbers from Act I of the ballet took place in the Drama School hall. Everybody in the audience was in raptures over my music. My new quartet has been performed three times: first in the Conservatoire and then twice in public. Everybody likes it *very much*. Many of the audience wept (so I am told) during the Andante (Andante funebre e doloroso). If true, this is a great triumph. The piano arrangement has come out. *Vakula* is causing a furore in my immediate circle. Taneyev already knows it by heart from cover to cover. This is a source of great pleasure to me because *Vakula* is my favourite child.[9]

I spent only a day and a half [in Petersburg]. On the day I arrived there was a committee meeting of the theatre management, where, by the way, they discussed various details of the production [of the opera *Vakula*].[10]

At the end of May Tchaikovsky went to Kamenka and from there went on abroad. He first went via Vienna to Lyons to see Modest and then to Vichy.

I cannot describe how glad I was to see Modest and his family. Kolya [Kolya Konradi and his nanny] straightaway swept me off my feet for good and all.[11] He is astonishingly clever. The first day I saw him I only felt sorry for him, and his handicap (the fact that he is a deaf mute), the unnatural sounds which he produces instead of words—all this provoked a sort of overpowering feeling of distaste. But this only lasted a day. Then everything about this marvellous, clever, affectionate, and poor child seemed lovely to me.[12]

I have reached Vichy, a confoundedly disgusting and revolting place. Everything has conspired here to make my stay insufferable. I have to get up at five o'clock to have a *bath*. Then the *fuss*, the crush to get every glass of water from the spring, the high-society style of life, the complete absence of any of the beauties of nature, but above all the *loneliness*—all this absolutely poisons every moment of my life.[13] No wonder I was bored, living on my own in such an unattractive place when Modest and his agreeable entourage were six hours' journey away. [At last] I was reunited with my dear Modya.[14]

In the middle of July the brothers moved from Lyons to Palavas. From here Tchaikovsky went to Paris (26 July), spent two days there and then set off for

[8] vi. 30 (Anatoly).   [9] vi. 33 (Anatoly).   [10] vi. 38 (Polonsky).
[11] vi. 53 (Anatoly).   [12] vi. 334 (von Meck).   [13] vi. 53 (Anatoly).
[14] vi. 60 (Sasha).

Bayreuth where, as the correspondent of *The Russian Gazette*, he was to attend the first performance of Wagner's *Ring* tetralogy.

[On the way to Paris 27 July.] This morning, when I was in the train, I read the Fourth Canto of *Hell* and was seized with a burning desire to write a symphonic poem on *Francesca*.[15] Unrelieved gloom on the way [to Bayreuth]. Spent the night in Nuremberg and only arrived here the day before the performance. Met dozens of people whom I know and immediately got into the whirl which spins me around all day like a madman. I have got to know dozens of new people; called on Liszt, who received me with remarkable kindness; called on Wagner, who now receives nobody, and so on. [Nikolay] Rubinstein is here (we are staying together) and so is Cui, whom I reconciled with Laroche, only for them to quarrel again two hours later, and so on.[16]

Tchaikovsky accidentally wrote 'Fourth Canto'; the story of Francesca is in the Fifth Canto of 'Hell' in Dante's *Divine Comedy*.

The *Rheingold* has been performed: as a scenic spectacle this work interested and fascinated me because of the *astounding* production; as music it is unbelievable chaos through which there flash from time to time remarkably beautiful and striking details. At all events, I am not bored, though no one could say that I enjoyed myself since all my thoughts are concentrated on making off as fast as I can for Vienna *en route* for Russia.[17]

Everyone who believes in art as a civilizing force, every devotee of the aesthetic, divorced from its material purposes, must experience in Bayreuth a profound feeling of joy when confronted by this tremendous artistic enterprise which, in the magnitude of its dimensions and by virtue of the interest which it has aroused, has assumed the significance of a whole historical epoch . . . Whether Wagner is right in taking devotion to his cause to such an extreme, or whether he has pushed beyond the point of equilibrium those aesthetic factors which ensure the stability of a work of art, whether art will take Wagner's starting-point and go further along the same road, or whether *The Ring of the Nibelungs* [sic] marks the point where a reaction sets in—at all events, something has been achieved at Bayreuth which our grandchildren and great-grandchildren will not forget. When I was in Bayreuth I had the opportunity of meeting many great artists who are utterly devoted to Wagner's music. It is my own fault, I willingly admit, that I have not yet risen to a proper understanding of this music; and if I apply myself to a thorough study of it, I too may one day join the wide circle of those who truly appreciate it. For the present, to be honest, the overpowering impression produced by *The Ring of the Nibelungs* came less from its musical beauties, which are perhaps scattered too profusely, than from its duration, from its colossal dimensions. The final impression which

I carried away from listening to *The Ring of the Nibelungs* was a confused recollection of many striking beauties, especially those of a symphonic character, which is very odd, since least of all was Wagner trying to write a symphonic opera; I came away with amazed respect for the composer's enormous talent and for his unprecedented technical resources; I came away in doubt about the validity of Wagner's view of opera; I came away quite exhausted, but at the same time wishing to continue my study of this music, the most complex which has ever been written. Perhaps *The Ring of the Nibelungs* seems boring in places; perhaps much of it is at first sight obscure and incomprehensible; perhaps Wagner's harmony occasionally suffers from excessive intricacy and subtlety; perhaps there is no small element of pointless quixotry—all the same, *The Nibelungs' Ring* [sic] is one of the most significant events in the history of art.[18]

Bayreuth left a painful impression on me, although much occurred there which was flattering to my artistic vanity. It turns out that I am by no means so unknown in Germany and other places abroad as I had thought. The impression is painful because the constant bustle there was indescribable. Eventually it all came to an end and with the final chords of *The Twilight of the Gods* I felt as if I had been liberated from captivity.[19] From Bayreuth I went to Nuremberg where I spent almost a full day, writing my reviews for *The Russian Gazette*; I managed to finish them off all right. Nuremberg is delightful![20]

I arrived at Verbovka in a terrible mental state and with my nerves utterly shattered. Two weeks at Verbovka were sufficient for my spirits to pick up and for me to take a calmer view of my life.[21]

Tchaikovsky returned to Moscow for the beginning of the academic year.

I am now going through a very critical period of my life. I will go into more detail later, but for now I will simply tell you: *I have decided to get married*. It is unavoidable. I must do it, not just for myself but for *you* [Modest] as well, and for Tolya, and Sasha, and all those I love. For *you* particularly! You too, Modya, should think about this carefully. [Your inclinations and your duties as a tutor]* cannot be reconciled.[22]

During this period I have changed many of my ideas about myself, about you and about our future. The result of all this thinking is that from now on I will make serious preparations for entering into a lawful marriage alliance, regardless of the identity of the other party. I think that for both of us our *dispositions* are the greatest and most insuperable obstacle to happiness and we must fight our natures to the best of our ability.[23] You will say

---

* There is a cut in the source so the words in square brackets are supplied from the context. An alternative possibility would be: 'Our inclinations and marriage'.

[18] *MC* 325, 328.   [19] vi. 64 (Modest).   [20] vi. 65 (Modest).
[21] vi. 70 (Lyova).   [22] *LR* 253 (Modest).   [23] Ibid.

that at your age it is difficult to conquer your passions, to which I would
reply that at your age it is easier to direct one's interests to another quarter.
I would have thought that your religion must be a source of considerable
support to you in this. So far as I am concerned, I will do my utmost to get
married this year and if I lack the necessary courage, I will at any rate abandon my habits for ever and will try to stop people regarding me as [one of
the old dears].[24]

Your [Modest's] anti-matrimonial arguments: many of them make no
sense, but many, on the other hand, are in complete agreement with my
own ideas. You predict for me a fate like that of Kondratyev,* Bulatov, and
tutti quanti. Rest assured that if my plans ever come to fruition then I will
certainly not be following in the footsteps of those gentlemen. Then you
say that I mustn't give a damn about *qu'en dira-t-on*! That's true only up to
a point. There are those who cannot hold me in contempt for my vices
simply because they started to love me before they suspected that my reputation is, in fact, ruined. For example, Sasha is one such! I know that she
has guessed *everything* and that she *forgives everything*. Many people whom
I love or respect regard me in the same way. Surely you realize how painful
it is for me to know that people *pity and forgive* me when, in truth, I am not
guilty of anything. How appalling it is to think that those who love me are
sometimes *ashamed* of me! But this has happened dozens of times already
and, of course, it will happen dozens of times again. In short, I seek marriage or some sort of public involvement with a woman so as to shut the
mouths of assorted contemptible creatures whose opinion means nothing to
me but who are in a position to cause distress to those near to me. But in
any event, have no fear on my account. My plans are far from coming to
fruition. I am so fixed in my habits and tastes that I cannot just cast them
off like an old coat.[25] And, anyway, I don't have an iron will by any means,
and after writing to you, I gave in to the power of my natural inclinations
about three times.[26] And so you are quite right when you say that it is impossible not to indulge one's weaknesses, however much one may have
sworn not to. All the same, I am sticking to my intentions and you can rest
assured that I will carry them out one way or another. But I won't do anything suddenly or without careful thought. Whatever happens, I am not
going to put a *millstone* round my neck. I will only embark on a lawful or
unlawful liaison with a woman if I have completely assured my peace and
freedom. But I still have nothing definite in view as yet.[27]

When I am angry with myself it always appears that I am angry with
others. And I am angry with myself for this reason: I could feel that I was

* Nikolay Kondratyev was a homosexual; he married and had a daughter but did not
change his ways.

[24] *LR* 254 (Modest).   [25] Ibid. 259.
[26] von Meck, i. 571 (Modest).   [27] *LR* 260 (Modest).

lying when I said that I had *wholly* made up my mind to bring about a complete *revolution* in my way of life. In fact, I have not decided anything of the
sort. I have no more than a serious intention to do *this* and am waiting for
something to force me to act. Meanwhile I must admit that my nice, comfortable little flat, my evenings to myself, my circumstances in general, the
peace and quiet which surround me—all this now has a special attraction
for me which I have not appreciated before. My flesh creeps when I think
that I must part with it all.[28]

About my proposed marriage. It is, in the first place, no part of my intention to take this step in the near future and in any event it will certainly not
happen in the current year (i.e. the academic year). But during these few
months I just want to get used to the idea of marriage and to prepare for it
because, for various reasons, I think it will be a very good thing for me. I
will not heedlessly fling myself into all the upheaval of an unsuccessful
marriage.[29]

I am very glad that you [Modest] are religious. I don't agree with any of
your ideas but if my theories were to shake you in your faith I should be
very annoyed with you. I am just as keen and ready to argue with you about
questions of faith as I am keen that you should stick to your religious
beliefs. When religion takes the form which it does in you it testifies to the
high quality of the metal from which you are forged.

I probably hate no less than you the beautiful unknown woman who is
going to force me to change my way of life and my entourage. Don't worry
about me. I have no intention of hurrying in the matter and if I do in fact
get involved with a woman I will be very circumspect about it.[30] I repeat: I
seriously intend to *transform* myself, but I just want to prepare for it gradually.[31] But we can't go into all that here.

I have finished my new work: a fantasia on *Francesca da Rimini*. I wrote it
with love and I think that the *love* has come through quite well. So far as the
storm is concerned, I would have liked to compose something close to
Doré's illustration but it did not come out as I wanted. In any case, it is impossible to reach a proper conclusion about the piece until it has been
orchestrated and performed.[32]

There are hours, days, weeks, and months when everything looks black,
when it seems that no one loves you, that you have been flung aside and
abandoned by everybody. Apart from the fact that my nerves are weak and
sensitive, my depression is to be explained by my bachelor state, by the absence of any element of *self-sacrifice* in my life. I do, in fact, live up to my
vocation to the best of my ability but I am no *use* at all to any human being.
If I were swept off the face of the earth today, then Russian music would
perhaps suffer some small loss but it is quite certain that it would not make

[28] Ibid. 256–7 (Modest).   [29] Ibid. 261 (Sasha).   [30] Ibid. 256 (Modest).
[31] Ibid. 257 (Anatoly).   [32] vi. 80 (Modest).

anybody unhappy. In short, I live a bachelor's egoistic life. I work for myself, look after myself, and am concerned only about my own well-being.
This, of course, makes for a nice quiet life; it is, on the other hand, dry,
dead, and narrow.[33]

Of course I would have liked *Vakula* to have been performed earlier. I
always want to hear my favourite offspring as soon as possible. But if fate
decrees that *Maccabeus* is staged first I shall not sink into the depths of despair. I only want an assurance that *Vakula* will be included in the current
season. Actually, if the occasion arises, you can tell Bessel that he is a swine
if he campaigns against *Vakula*. If possible, say to Anton Rubinstein, 'Your
brother asked me to tell you that you are a swine!' Heavens! for how long
have I had a profound loathing for that man! He has never, never treated
me with anything other than condescending disdain. No one has wounded
my sense of my own worth, my justifiable pride (forgive me, Tolya, for
boasting) in my own capabilities, as this house-owner from Peterhof. And
now he conspires with his lousy operas to block my way! Does international
fame really count for nothing with this most stupid and puffed up of
mortals? Are Berlin, Hamburg, Vienna, etc. etc. not enough for him? If it
weren't for the penal code and Volume fifteen, I would go to Peterhof and
set fire to his accursed dacha . . .[34]

The first performance of the opera *Vakula the Smith* took place on 24 November
1876 at the Mariinsky Theatre, conducted by Nápravník.

Vakula was a splendid failure. The first two acts were greeted with the
silence of the grave, apart from the overture and the first duet, which were
applauded. In Golova's scene, and particularly in the Official's, they
laughed a lot but there was no applause and no one was called forward. I
was given a lot of calls after both the third and the fourth acts (the third was
divided into two) but there was loud booing from many of the audience.
The second performance went somewhat better but all the same it is quite
clear that the opera has not been welcomed and will barely manage another
five or six performances. The remarkable thing is that everybody at the
dress rehearsal, including Cui, predicted a tremendous success. This made
my fall the more painful and distressing. I will not deny that I am badly
shaken and discouraged. The main thing is that I have no cause for complaint either about the performance or about the production. In short, the
failure of the opera is my own fault. It is jammed too full of details, the
orchestration is too dense, the voice parts are not sufficiently striking. The
style of *Vakula* is not operatic; it lacks sweep and breadth.[35]

Perhaps you [Stasov] are right in suggesting that *Othello* is beyond my
powers. But it is also not inconceivable that you are wrong. I value your intellect greatly, your fine artistic intuition, your many-sided and enormous

[33] vi. 85 (Sasha).   [34] vi. 73 (Anatoly).   [35] vi. 88–9 (Taneyev).

erudition, but despite all of this (to be entirely frank), your verdicts concerning the power of creative talent are sometimes not absolutely correct. I strongly suspect that the same *power* which you do not recognize in me is perceived by you in Messrs Musorgsky, Shcherbachov, Ladyzhensky, etc. Wasn't it you who said to me in a letter that Shcherbachov had written the best piano piece since Schumann. Schumann and Shcherbachov!!! A man who could in a letter juxtapose two such incommensurable talents, should, it seems to me, allow the possibility of another, at least as bold a juxtaposition, i.e. Shakespeare and myself. But I repeat, most revered Vladimir Vasilyevich, it is also very possible that you are right. Nevertheless, I am not only asking but *demanding* that you fulfil your promise. Now that the seeds of Shakespearean tragedy have been cast on the soil of my musical imagination, I cannot stop myself from composing *Othello*. What would be the point if I devised the scenario myself or turned my attention to the first line that my finger pointed to? I am deeply and firmly convinced that of all the people I know you are the only one who is capable of creating a genuine scenario for *Othello*. On the one hand you are well acquainted with and understand Shakespeare, on the other you have such an excellent knowledge of the musical requirements of an opera scenario. It is obvious that *Othello* has to be changed (as far as the sequence of scenes is concerned), when it is subjected to the conventions of a scenario. It seems to me that you cannot avoid cutting something, perhaps even making substantial alterations. It is a tricky job. I have already spent several sleepless nights trying to visualize my scenario, but could not make anything of it. You could do it, and I am sure, Vladimir Vasilyevich, that you will not refuse to come to my rescue. I waited for your last letter with feverish impatience. I shall await the next one with even more impatience. *Ivan the Clown* is a delight. But just at the moment I cannot turn my attention to anything other than *Othello*. I shall without a doubt use your delightful programme, only not just yet.[36]

A lot of work has piled up for me, including some paid commissions.[37]

It was in fact at this time that Tchaikovsky received commissions for various arrangements from Nadezhda Filaretovna von Meck, a rich music-lover and an enthusiastic admirer of his work. Her house-musician Iosif Kotek, a pupil and a friend of Tchaikovsky, had told her of the composer's difficult financial situation and she paid generously for her commissions. Tchaikovsky and Mme von Meck began a correspondence.

Amidst failures and all manner of obstacles it is consoling for a musician to know that there is a small minority of people who love our art with such warmth and sincerity.[38]

Tolstoy expressed a wish to meet me. He is very interested in music. Of course I made a feeble effort to hide from him *but* with no success. He came

[36] vi. 92–3 (Stasov).   [37] vi. 96 (Sasha and Lyova).   [38] vi. 96–7 (von Meck).

to the Conservatoire and told Rubinstein that he would not go away until I came down to meet him. Tolstoy's colossal talent is one with which I find myself in complete harmony. Most people would consider it flattering and agreeable to meet him, and there was no way of getting out of it. When we were introduced I, of course, gave the impression that I was very flattered and pleased, so I said that I was delighted, that I was grateful, the whole inevitable rigmarole, in fact, none of which was true. 'I want to get to know you better—he said—I want to talk to you about music.' And no sooner had we met than he straightaway started expounding his views on music. According to him, *Beethoven lacked talent*. And that was his starting-point. So, this great writer, this brilliant student of human nature began, in a tone of the utmost conviction, by delivering himself of an observation which was both fatuous and offensive to every musician. What is one to do in circumstances like this? Argue? Well, I did start to argue, but can one really pursue it seriously? After all, the proper thing to have done would have been to read him a lecture. Perhaps somebody else would have done just that. But I just stifled my agony and kept up the act, that's to say I pretended to be serious and good-humoured. He has visited me several times since then. Although my acquaintance with Tolstoy has convinced me that he is a somewhat paradoxical, but good and straightforward man, even, in his own way, sensitive to music, all the same, my acquaintance with him, as with anyone, has brought me nothing but weariness and torment.[39]

When I met Tolstoy I was seized with terror and a sense of awkwardness. It seemed to me that this greatest of students of human nature would, with a single glance, penetrate to the innermost recesses of my soul. I could not, so I thought, succeed in hiding from him all the rubbish lying at the bottom of my soul and just show him the bright side of things. If he is kind, I thought (as he *ought to be* and, of course, is), then, like a doctor examining a wound and knowing all the sore places, he will gently and delicately avoid touching and irritating them, but will by that very fact let me know that nothing can be hidden from him; if he is not especially sympathetic he will poke his finger right into the source of the pain. I was dreadfully frightened of either possibility. But neither the one thing nor the other actually happened. In his works the most profound student of human nature, he turned out in his ordinary dealings with people to be a man of simplicity, integrity, and sincerity, who revealed very little indeed of that *omniscience* which I had so feared. He did not avoid *touching* but he did not cause the pain intended. It was clear that he did not regard me as the subject of his investigations but simply wanted to have a chat about music, which interested him at that time. But I have perhaps never in my life been so flattered and touched in my vanity as a composer as when Tolstoy, sitting next to me and listening to the Andante of my First Quartet, burst into tears . . .[42]

[39] viii. 121–2 (von Meck).   [40] *Diaries*, 211.

This winter I have had several interesting conversations with the writer Count Tolstoy; they have revealed much to me and made many things clear. He has convinced me that the artist who works not in response to an inner stimulus but with a careful calculation of the *effect* which he will achieve, who does violence to his talent with the aim of pleasing, and who forces himself to satisfy the public, that such a man is not truly an artist, that his works will not last, that his success is ephemeral. I am completely converted to the truth of this view.[41]

[41] vi. 171 (von Meck).

10

1877

My heart is full. It craves to pour itself out in music.

To my delight Tolya has been staying with me; he came specially so that he could stay with me and, incidentally, hear the music for my ballet, which has been performed at last. And indeed poor Moscow is flooded with my music at the moment. Never a day passes but something is played and even I recently decided to make an appearance as a conductor. Although I was clumsy, timid, and unsure of myself I recently conducted my *Slavonic March* with great success at the Bolshoy.[1]

The first performance of the ballet *Swan Lake* was given on 20 February 1877 in the Bolshoy Theatre; the first performance of *Francesca da Rimini* was planned for the Symphony Concert of the RMS on 25 February under Nikolay Rubinstein.

If you [Mme von Meck] did but know how pleasant and gratifying it is for a musician when he can be sure that there is another living soul which just as powerfully and just as deeply experiences everything that he himself felt when he conceived his work and brought it to fruition. That you should like my music but make no attempt to get to know its composer is a matter of no surprise to me.[2] My relations with you are marked by the fact that, every time we write to each other, the tricky question of money comes into the picture. Naturally, no artist is ever insulted by being rewarded for his labours but, you know, apart from labour, a work like that which you are at present requesting calls for a certain kind of feeling, a feeling which we call inspiration, and this is not always at my disposal. I would be artistically dishonest if I improved my material circumstances by misusing my technical skill and offered you false coin in return for good. Composing requires a certain disposition, a conjunction of certain conditions which is not always possible. Now, for instance, I am first of all immersed in a symphony which I began last winter and would very much like to dedicate to you because I think that you would find in it echoes of your innermost thoughts and feelings. In the second place, I am at the moment constantly in a state of nervous irritation and fuss which is not conducive to composition and is not having a beneficial effect on the symphony, which makes slow progress.[3] When anyone has been of such immense practical service as you have to

[1] vi. 114 (Sasha).   [2] vi. 116 (von Meck).   [3] vi. 125–6 (von Meck).

me, it needs a vast amount of tact and delicacy to avoid imposing a yoke on the recipient. Our correspondence is nothing but a source of pleasure to me, if only because talking about and around music is always pleasant.[4]

During this time I have changed greatly, both physically and, especially, mentally. I don't seem to have any gaiety or desire to play the fool left in me at all. Not a jot remains of my youth. My life has become frighteningly empty, dull, and trivial. I am seriously thinking about *marriage* or another sort of permanent *union*. But one thing that has remained as before is my desire to compose. If circumstances had worked out otherwise, if in my seeking to create I hadn't met obstacles at every turn, such as my teaching at the Conservatoire, which with every day becomes more and more repulsive to me, then I could have written at one time or another something really worthwhile. But alas, I am tied to the Conservatoire.[5]

Tchaikovsky apparently started composing the Fourth Symphony in March and had finished it by 27 May 1877.

In the winter of 1876/7 Tchaikovsky had the idea of writing a new opera but could not find a suitable subject. He looked through various themes but none of them was satisfactory. He did not even know himself what he really wanted. One thing was clear: the opera should be about perfectly ordinary people, just like everybody else and easy to understand, and the action should take place in Russia.

Tchaikovsky spent the evening of 13 May 1877 at the home of the famous singer Elizaveta Andreyevna Lavrovskaya.

The conversation turned to subjects for an opera. Her stupid husband churned out indescribable rubbish and suggested the most impossible subjects. Lizaveta Andreyevna was silent and smiled good-naturedly, then suddenly said: 'But what about *Eugene Onegin?*' This suggestion was so incredible that I said nothing. Then later, when I was dining alone at the inn, I remembered about *Onegin*, thought it over, began to find Lavrovskaya's idea possible, then was carried away by the idea, and by the end of the meal had decided upon it. I immediately ran to find a copy of Pushkin. I eventually tracked one down, went home, reread it with delight and spent a completely sleepless night, the result of which was a scenario for a delightful opera with the libretto by Pushkin. Next day I went to visit Shilovsky [15 May].[6]

I spent two days at Kostya Shilovsky's. I went to see him to ask him to *deal with* the scenario of the new opera. I intend to write a delightful work which perfectly suits my musical personality. Everyone to whom I have mentioned it has first been astonished and then in *raptures*. And do you know, [Anatoly], who gave me the idea? Lavrovskaya. The opera is going to be *Eugene Onegin*! I have worked out a delightful scenario,[7] not by a cold and rational process but by turning to account a great deal of passionate

---

[4] vi. 128 (von Meck). [5] vi. 132 (Klimenko).
[6] vi. 135 (Modest). [7] vi. 134 (Anatoly).

emotional excitement, painful yet pleasant. I have been walking about in such a state of inspiration that I might well have floated away. Of course I have had to pay for it and I have almost gone crackers since.[8]

Tchaikovsky began composing the opera at Tatyana's letter scene.

You won't believe what a frenzy I have got myself into over this subject. How glad I am to be spared the Ethiopian princesses, Pharaohs, poisonings, and all kinds of stilted mannerisms. What a wealth of poetry there is in *Onegin*. I am not deluding myself; I know that there will not be much theatricality or action in this opera. But the general level of poetry, the humanity, the simplicity of subject-matter, combined with the *brilliant* text, compensates handsomely for these shortcomings.[9]

Sometimes it seems to me that Providence, so blind and unfair in its choice of protégés, deigns to concern itself about me. Truly, I am sometimes beginning to consider certain coincidences as not purely *random chance*. Who knows, maybe this is the beginnings of religious faith, which, if it ever takes hold of me, will do so whole-heartedly, i.e. with Lenten oil and cotton wool from the [Church of the] Iverskaya* Virgin Mary, etc.[10]

Tchaikovsky's story in Nikolay Kashkin's version:

In April or early May 1877 I received a declaration of love in the form of a fairly long letter; it was from Antonina Milyukova who said that she had first fallen in love with me several years before when she was a student at the Conservatoire. Although, since I went to the Conservatoire almost every day, I knew most of the students, my memory didn't tell me anything about Mlle Milyukova. In her letter she said that she had been in Eduard Langer's piano class, so when I met him in the Conservatoire I asked him about his former pupil Milyukova, whom, as it turned out, he remembered and he gave a brief sketch of her (and of me too) using a single unflattering epithet, without giving any explanation. I didn't ask any more about Mlle Milyukova. I was entirely preoccupied at the time with thoughts about *Eugene Onegin*, i.e. about Tatyana, whose letter had originally drawn me to composing the opera. In the absence not only of the libretto but even of some sort of general scheme of the opera, I began writing the letter song, driven to the work by an irresistible emotional need, in the heat of which I not only forgot about Antonina Milyukova but even lost her letter, or hid it so successfully that I couldn't find it. I remembered about it only when, a little while later, I received the second one. I was completely buried in my

---

* There is a measure of irony here, in that Tchaikovsky, an educated man, should accept the customs and beliefs held by the simple peasants. The ikon depicting the Virgin Mary in the Church of the Iverskaya Virgin Mary, not far from the Kremlin, was said to have healing powers. [Trans. note: the church has since been demolished.]

[8] xiii. 49 (von Meck).   [9] vi. 136 (Anatoly).   [10] vi. 139 (Modest).

composition and had grown so close to the character of Tatyana that she and all around her started to seem real to me. I loved Tatyana and was terribly angry with Onegin, whom I saw as a cold and heartless fop. When I received the second letter I was ashamed and even came to hate myself for my attitude to Mlle Milyukova. In this second letter she bitterly complained that she had not received a reply, adding that if the second letter met with the same fate as the first the only course open to her was to take her own life. In my mind this all got associated with my conception of Tatyana and it seemed to me that I had myself behaved infinitely worse than Onegin; I was genuinely angry with myself for my heartless treatment of a girl who had fallen in love with me. Since Mlle Milyukova gave her address in the second letter, I wasted no time in following up that information, and so our acquaintance began. In my new acquaintance I found a modest, sweet-looking young woman, who in general made a pleasant impression on me. At our first meeting I told her that I could not return her love, but that she inspired in me a genuine liking for her. She answered that any sympathetic response on my part was precious to her and that she could be content with that, or something like that. I promised to call on her often and kept my word.

You, Kashkin, probably remember that before this I have discussed with you more than once my intention of marrying someone not young but possessing particular qualities which would enable her to be a good friend and companion to me in my life. Antonina Ivanovna differs from this in that she is comparatively young, but she has expressed such devotion, such willingness to do whatever I want, that she has in some way imposed on me the obligation to answer her in like manner, in spite of my lack of feeling towards her. Besides, I was constantly under the influence of my genuine anger with Onegin for his casual and flippant treatment of Tatyana. It seemed to me that to behave like Onegin would be heartless and quite impermissible on my part. I was in a frenzy. My mind was fully concentrated on the opera and I was almost unconscious or semi-conscious of everything else. I remember perfectly, however, that I was firmly convinced that I must not tell any of you at the Conservatoire anything about my relationship with Antonina Ivanovna and my intentions arising from this relationship.[11]

To my considerable surprise I *got engaged* towards the end of May. This is how it happened. Some time previous to this I had once received a letter from a certain girl whom I knew and had met before. I learnt from this letter that I had long since been the favoured object of her love. The letter was so warm and sincere that I decided to reply, which I had previously been careful not to do in such cases. Although my reply did not give the girl any grounds for hoping that the affection might be reciprocated, a

[11] RMP 118–20.

correspondence got under way. I agreed to her request that I should call on her. Why did I do this? It now seems to me as though some power of fate was drawing me to this girl. When I saw her I explained to her again that my only feelings for her were of sympathy and of gratitude for her love. But when we had parted I began to reflect on my action and all its frivolity. If I did not love her and did not want to encourage her sentiments, then why had I visited her and how would it all end? From her next letter I realized that if, having gone thus far, I suddenly turned away from the girl I would make her truly unhappy and would bring her to a tragic end. And so, one fine evening, I set off to see my future wife and told her frankly that I *did not love* her but that at least I would be her devoted and grateful friend; I described my character to her in detail: irritable, unpredictable, unsociable. Then I asked her, did she want to be my wife? The answer was, of course, affirmative. I cannot put into words the dreadful sensations I went through in the days immediately following. I decided that I could not escape my destiny and that there was something fateful in my encounter with this girl. So be it. God can see that I am filled with the very best intentions towards my partner in life and that if we are unhappy together it will not be my fault. If I am marrying without love it is because circumstances have turned out that way. I have not lied to her or deceived her.[12]

The eldest of the Shilovskys, a most talented and agreeable man, lives some forty miles from Moscow. He is now writing the libretto for the opera in accordance with my instructions. As soon as the examinations are over I am going to see him and will immediately get down to composing the opera. And it is essential that I should write this *opera* because I feel an irresistible urge to do so and must not let the opportunity slip.[13] It will not, of course, have any strong, dramatic action but on the other hand the social side will be interesting and on top of that how much poetry there is in it all! Take the scene of Tatyana with her nurse—what is that alone worth?[14] Perhaps my opera will not be good theatre, perhaps there will not be much action, but I am in love with the character of Tatyana, I am fascinated by Pushkin's verse, and I am writing the music to it because I am so drawn to it. I am absolutely immersed in composing the opera.[15]

Here [in Glebovo] the circumstances could not be more propitious for my work. I have a whole wing to myself and Alyosha to look after me; I have a piano in my drawing-room. In short, nothing more convenient could be imagined. I have divided up the day in a very regular fashion, I work systematically at specific times and since positively nothing at all hinders my work the opera is making good progress; I greatly enjoy writing the music and I am sure that the poetry of the subject and the incomparable beauty of the text will make themselves felt.[16]

[12] vi. 144–5 (von Meck).   [13] vi. 136, 137 (Lyova).   [14] vi. 140 (von Meck).
[15] vi. 141 (Modest).   [16] vi. 142 (Anatoly).

When I recall the month at Glebovo it comes back to me literally like a *dream*, and a very sweet one at that. O, thrice-blessed, lovely, peaceful little spot, I will never forget you!!![17]

I wrote a substantial part of the opera during June and would, of course, have written a great deal more had it not been for my disturbed state of mind. I do not in any way repent my choice of subject. I cannot understand, Nadezhda Filaretovna, how anyone with your strong and lively interest in music can fail to appreciate Pushkin, the genius of whose gifts very often breaks out of the narrower paths of verse into the infinite scope of music. That is not an empty phrase. Regardless of the substance of what he expounds in verse form, there is *something* in the verse itself, in the succession of sounds, which penetrates to the depths of one's soul. That something is music.[18] I have finished my symphony, in sketch, that's to say. I will orchestrate it at the end of the summer. If you [Mme von Meck] are not agreeable to having your name appear with the title of the symphony, then, if you so wish, it need not be done. Let us leave it that only you and I will know to whom the symphony is dedicated.[19]

I approach my marriage not without alarm and agitation but still utterly convinced that it is essential. There will be only two witnesses at my wedding: my brother Tolya and Kotek.[20]

I will tell the story in the right order. When the train set off I could have shouted out because I was so choked with sobs. But I still had to engage my wife in conversation as far as Klin so as to earn the right to settle into my own seat in the dark and be on my own. Meshchersky burst into the compartment at the second station after Khimki. When I saw him I felt that he must take me away somewhere as quickly as possible. And he did. I had to give way to a flood of tears before I said a word to him. Meshchersky showed me much tender sympathy and bolstered my sinking spirits. When I came back to my wife after Klin I was much calmer. Meshchersky arranged for us to have a sleeping compartment and I then slept like a log. The rest of the journey after I woke up was not particularly bad. What amazed me more than anything was that my wife did not understand, was not even aware of my ill-concealed sorrow. She has a perpetual expression of complete happiness and contentment. *Elle n'est pas difficile.* She agrees to everything and is content with everything. We stayed at the Evropeyskaya and dined in our room. In the evening we took a carriage to the islands. We sat through one part [of a concert?] and then went home. [There is a cut in the text about the attempt to consummate a physical relationship which ended in failure.] But there were some conversations which clarified even further our mutual relations. *She agrees to absolutely everything and will never be dissatisfied. All she needs is to pamper me and look after me.* I have

---

[17] vi. 159 (Konstantin Shilovsky).   [18] vi. 146 (von Meck).
[19] vi. 140 (von Meck).   [20] vi. 150 (Vladimir Shilovsky).

retained for myself complete freedom of action. I took a good dose of valerian and, after begging my embarrassed wife not to be embarrassed, slept like a log. I don't think that the time is too far off when I will *finally* calm down. I have guaranteed my own complete freedom of action to such an extent that once my wife and I have got used to each other, she will not embarrass me at all. I am not deluding myself: she is a very limited person, but even that is a good thing. A clever woman might have made me feel frightened of her. I stand so high above this one, I dominate her to such a degree, that at least I don't feel the slightest bit frightened of her.[21]

We have been to Pavlovsk. My father was delighted with my wife, which was to be expected. Lizaveta Mikhailovna was very kind and attentive, but I saw tears in her eyes once or twice. My good stepmother is a shrewd woman and she must realize that I am going through a critical period of my life. I must admit that I found it all very difficult. I am indeed going through a difficult period; yet I feel that I am gradually getting used to my new situation which would be utterly false and unbearable if I were deceiving my wife about anything, but I did warn her that she could count on no more than my love as a brother [. . .] In the physical sense my wife has become *absolutely detestable*.[22]

After a day as dreadful as 6 July, after that everlasting moral torment, a rapid recovery is out of the question.[23] I have got married in accordance with the dictates not of the heart but of some incomprehensible conjunction of circumstances which led me, as though by fate, to choose the most difficult of the options. But as soon as the ceremony was over, as soon as I found myself alone with my wife and realized that it was now our destiny to live together, inseparable, I suddenly felt that not only did she not inspire in me even simple friendship but that she was *detestable* in the fullest sense of the word. It seemed to me that I, or at least the best, perhaps the only good part of me—my musical talent—had perished beyond recall. So far as my future lot was concerned, the picture rose before my eyes of vegetating miserably, of an utterly intolerable, oppressive farce. To pretend for the whole of one's life is the greatest of torments. And how could I think about work? I fell into deep despair. I began passionately, hungrily to long for death. Death seemed to me the only way out, but I could not contemplate killing myself. I knew that if I made my mind up to commit suicide it would be a mortal blow to my family. Apart from that, my weakness (if it can be called a weakness) is that I love life, I love my work, I love the successes awaiting me in the future. And finally, I have still not *said* all that I can and want to say before the time comes to depart for eternity. So, death has not yet taken me and I do not wish, nor am I able, to seek it—what then remains? I do not know how I did not go mad. Then I had to go to see my

[21] *LR* 286–7 (Anatoly).
[22] *LR* 289–90 (Anatoly). The square brackets denote a cut in the text.
[23] *LR* 286 (Anatoly).

wife's mother. Here my torments were increased tenfold. They have a narrow outlook, their opinions are savage, and they are all at daggers drawn.[24]

Tchaikovsky went to Kamenka, leaving his wife in Moscow.

My nerves, my whole spirit are so weary that I can hardly put two thoughts together. However, this does not stop my soul, which is weary but not crushed, from glowing with infinite, with the deepest gratitude to that measurelessly dear friend beyond all price who is saving me. I will prove to you [Mme von Meck] that this friend did not come to my aid in vain. I have still not said a fraction of what I should like to say. My heart is full. It craves to pour itself out in music. Who knows, perhaps I will leave behind me something truly worthy of the reputation of a first-rate artist. I am bold enough to hope so.[25] If I emerge as the victor in this vicious mental struggle, then it will be to you that I am indebted, to you, to you alone, my best friend, my own providence.[26]

I still cannot get down to work at all. Work frightens and oppresses me, whereas it is just what ought to be the most potent cure for my sickly condition.[27] *Our* symphony has made some progress. Orchestrating the first movement will be hard work. It is very long and complicated; at the same time, I think it is the best movement. But the other three movements are very simple and I will enjoy orchestrating them. There is a new instrumental effect in the Scherzo of which I have hopes. First the strings play on their own, pizzicato all the time; the woodwind comes in in the Trio, and also plays on its own; their place is taken by a brass group, yet again on their own; at the end of the Scherzo all three groups exchange brief little phrases. I think that this should make an interesting effect of sounds.[28]

I have finished orchestrating the first scene [of *Onegin*] and am now making the piano arrangement.[29] Now that my first ardour has passed and I can look at the work more objectively it seems to me that [the opera] is doomed to failure and public neglect. The story is very ingenuous, there is nothing in it which is good theatre, the music lacks sparkle and brilliant effects. But I think that a *select* few may, when they listen to this music, be moved by the same feelings as stirred me when I wrote it. I am not trying to say that my music is so good that it is inaccessible to the *contemptible* masses. I cannot understand at all how anyone could write intentionally either for the masses or for the elect; my view is that one should compose in direct response to one's own inclination and with no thought of pleasing this or that section of humanity. I did, in fact, write *Onegin* without pursuing any extraneous purposes at all. But the way it has worked out, *Onegin* will not

[24] vi. 161–2 (von Meck). [25] vi. 164. [26] vi. 160.
[27] vi. 165 (von Meck). [28] vi. 168 (von Meck). [29] vi. 169 (Anatoly).

be *interesting* in the theatre; so those for whom *dramatic action* is the first requirement in opera will not be satisfied. However, those who are capable of finding in the opera the musical re-creation of ordinary, simple emotions, common to all humanity and far removed from the tragic, the theatrical, may (I hope) be pleased with it. In short, the opera has been composed sincerely, and it is in the sincerity that I place all my hopes.[30]

How little does the prospect of seeing [my wife] console me. However, at least she does not evoke horror in me. Just mere misery.[31]

I have arrived in Moscow. I find things difficult: I will say no more. But of course this was inevitable after the complete happiness which I have enjoyed at Kamenka.[32]

In the end death is really the greatest of blessings and I yearn for it with all the strength of my being. To give you an idea of what I am suffering, suffice it to say that my one idea is to find a means of running away somewhere. But how, and where to? It is impossible, impossible, impossible.[33]

[Antonina's] head is as utterly empty as her heart: on not one occasion did she in my presence utter a single idea, nor did she give a single sign of any emotional feeling, though she was, admittedly, kind to me. She never once showed the slightest desire to know what I did, what my work was, what my plans were, what I read, what my intellectual and artistic tastes were. She did not know *a single note of my music*. This put me in a complete quandary. She never went to the Musical Society concerts, whether orchestral or chamber music. How did we spend the time when we were on our own? She is a great talker. She kept up an endless stream of tales about endless men who had harboured tender feelings for her and catalogued with indescribable enthusiasm the vices of her family and their cruel, squalid treatment of her. Wishing to know what sort of maternal instincts she had I once asked her if she liked children. Her reply was: '*Yes, when they are intelligent!*' I spent two weeks in Moscow with my wife. They were two weeks of continual, absolutely unbearable moral torture. I fell into despair. I sought death; it seemed to be the only way out. I began to experience moments of madness in which my mind was filled with such a vicious hatred for my unfortunate wife that I wanted to strangle her. It became impossible to do either my own work or my Conservatoire work. I was at my wit's end. And yet there was nobody to blame but myself.[34]

There was one evening in September when I was very close to that state of blind, insane, pathological rage which can lead one to a criminal act. I was no more than an inch away from it and was only saved by a miracle.[35]

In utter despair, Tchaikovsky decided to take his life. But he determined to do it in such a way than no one would be able to suspect suicide. He contrived a means of dying whereby his immediate circle would conclude that his death was the result of

[30] vi. 170 (von Meck).   [31] *LR* 293 (Anatoly).   [32] vi. 177 (Anatoly).
[33] vi. 175 (von Meck).   [34] vi. 197–8 (von Meck).   [35] vii. 329 (von Meck).

illness. And so, one cold autumn night, he went to the Moscow River, immersed himself in the water and stood there until his body was seized with cramps. When he got home, he explained that he had stumbled and fallen into the river. He was sure that he would catch pneumonia and die. But his nerves were in such an excited condition that he did not even catch a cold. (This incident was recounted by Nikolay Kashkin who had it at first hand from Tchaikovsky.)

Tchaikovsky's story in Nikokay Kashkin's version:

Although no more than a week had gone by since I had got back from my sister's I was no longer in any state to do battle with the difficulties of my position; from time to time I realized that my mind was beginning to wander. I still tried to work at home during the day but the evenings had become unbearable. Because I did not dare to call on any of my acquaintances or even go to the theatre I used to set off for a walk every evening and used to wander aimlessly round the remote and dead streets of Moscow for hours on end. The weather was gloomy and cold and there was a slight frost at night; one such night I went to the deserted banks of the Moscow River and the idea occurred to me that it should be possible to catch a cold which would prove fatal. So with this aim, and unseen by anybody in the darkness, I walked into the water almost up to the waist and stayed there as long as I could stand the aching in my body caused by the cold. I emerged from the water firmly convinced that I was bound to die from pneumonia or some such ailment; when I got home I said that I had been out fishing at night and had accidentally fallen in the water. However, my health turned out to be so robust that my icy bathe passed off without any effects. Before I made any further attempts like this I realized that I could not continue in such circumstances: I wrote to my brother Anatoly and asked him to send me a telegram on behalf of Nápravník saying that my presence was essential in Petersburg, which he promptly did.[36]

I have had a telegram from Petersburg saying that Nápravník needs to see me about the revival of *Vakula*.[37] If I had stayed in Moscow even one more day I would have gone mad or drowned myself in the stinking waters of my nonetheless-beloved Moscow River.[38] I set off for Petersburg, past myself with delight at getting away, even for a single day, from the chaos of lies, dishonesty, and deception that I have got myself into here.[39]

This telegram had been sent by Anatoly at Tchaikovsky's request.

When I met my brother, everything that I had been concealing in the depths of my soul for two interminable weeks poured forth. Something dreadful occurred which I do not recollect. When I started to come round again it turned out that my brother had managed to make a trip to Moscow to talk things over with my wife and with Rubinstein and had arranged to take me abroad; my wife would go to Odessa, but nobody would know

[36] RMP 125.   [37] vi. 178 (Karl Albrecht).
[38] vi. 194 (Albrecht).   [39] vi. 185 (von Meck).

this.[40] She received with quite inconceivable equanimity Anatoly's news of my flight and illness. I formed an overpowering inner conviction that *she had never loved me*. She had thought her wish to marry me was love.[41]

The rumour which has been circulating that I have gone mad is not altogether implausible. When I think of all that I did, of all the crazy things I got up to, I can only come to the conclusion that I was afflicted with a bout of temporary insanity from which I have finally emerged only now. Much of the recent past is like a dream to me, strange and wild, like a nightmare in which someone, who to all intents and purposes seemed to be me, behaved exactly as people do in dreams: senselessly, incoherently, wildly. This was not *me*, conscious of my own personality and exercising the normal resources of my will-power in a reasonable and logical way. Everything I did then bore the stamp of that morbid disjunction between *reason* and the will which is, in fact, the mark of madness. Amidst the nightmares which clouded my brain at that strange and dreadful, though brief, period of my life I reached out to save myself towards the hands of several persons dear to me who helped to drag me out of the abyss. To you [Mme von Meck] and my two dear brothers, *to the three of you*, I am indebted for the fact that I am not only alive but physically and morally well.[42]

I am coming round at last and returning to life. During the time, the terrible time I have gone through, I have been supported and comforted by the thought of you [Modest] and Tolya. It is only this experience which has made me realize how much I love you both. You have both been the straw at which I grabbed and Tolya was the straw which brought me to the bank.[43]

Anatoly took Tchaikovsky abroad at the insistence of his doctors.

Here I am [in Switzerland] amidst marvellous scenery but in the most dreadful moral condition. What will come of all this? Obviously I cannot now go back to Moscow. I cannot see anybody, I am frightened of everybody, and then, of course, I cannot do any work, I cannot talk to anybody about anything now. It's strange, isn't it, that my life has crossed with yours [Mme von Meck] just at this time. I can feel that you are my *real* friend, a friend who can read my soul, despite the fact that we know each other only through corresponding.[44]

[40] vi. 185 (von Meck).   [41] 198–9 (von Meck).   [42] vii. 75 (von Meck).
[43] vii. 179.   [44] vi. 185–6.

11

1877–1878

I am an artist who can and must bring honour to his country. I can feel great creative powers within me. I have still not done even a fraction of what I can do.

[Anatoly] and I are staying in a delightful place on the road between Clarens and Montreux. We have excellent accommodation: two delightful rooms which take up the whole of the mezzanine. The windows look out right over the lake. Here is our daily routine: we get up at seven, coffee at eight, then we read and work till lunchtime. Lunch at one. After lunch we walk till five or even six o'clock, usually somewhere higher up, in the mountains. Dinner at seven, then reading, and writing letters, and bed at ten. As might be expected, this regime is having an extremely beneficial effect on my mental and physical well-being. I have started working, that's to say I have set about orchestrating the opera.[1]

Nadezhda Filaretovna! If you only knew what an enormous amount you do for me! I was on the edge of the abyss. It was your friendship which saved me. I can work now. Life has no meaning for me without work.[2] I am equally astonished by *what* you do for me and by *how* you do it. Every note which pours from my pen from now on will be dedicated to you! I owe it to you that the desire to work has returned to me with redoubled force and as I work I will never, never forget for a single second that you are making it possible for me to follow my artistic vocation. And very much still remains for me to do. I can say, with no false modesty, that everything I have written up to now seems so imperfect, so feeble by comparison with what I *can* and *must* do. And I will do it.[3]

I have finished orchestrating the first act of *Onegin*. I was very keen to do it. To see it produced *actually in the Conservatoire* is my fondest dream. It is designed for modest resources and a small stage.[4] If it is carefully produced, I think that this opera ought, with its guileless plot, its marvellous text, and its simple human feelings and situations, to create a poetic effect.[5] I am gradually getting down to a bit of work and I can now definitely tell you that our symphony will be finished no later than December. May this

[1] vi. 189–90 (Modest). [2] vi. 191, 192. [3] vi. 196.
[4] vi. 193 (Nikolay Rubinstein). [5] vi. 206 (N. Rubinstein).

music, so closely linked to my thoughts about you, tell you on my behalf
that I love you with all the strength of my heart, my best and incomparable
friend.[6]

At the moment when you [Modest] are short of money I have suddenly
become if not rich at least very well provided for, and for some time ahead.
A certain person known to you has sent me 3,000 francs and is going to send
1,500 monthly thereafter. It has all been offered with such amazing tact,
with such kindness, that I am not even conscience-stricken about it. Great
God! How good and generous and tactful that woman is! At the same time
she is remarkably intelligent because in showing me these immense favours
she does it in such a way as to make it absolutely clear to me that it is a
source of pleasure to her. And so I have the means at my disposal not only
to live comfortably and peacefully abroad for several months but also to
repay my debts (including the one to Lyova*), to look after Antonina
Ivanovna, and to send money to Alyosha† to help Kotek to go abroad.
Which reminds me, if he is still in St Petersburg, for goodness sake find
him and tell him all this, but don't tell anyone else. I want your word of
honour that you won't let the secret out to anyone. I am terrified that you
might tell Laroche, for instance. Tell nobody, nobody!!! Tell everyone that
I have been given a grant by the Conservatoire and am living on this.[7]

I unexpectedly found myself in Paris for a day. I left Clarens a day earlier
than I had originally intended in case there were letters waiting for me in
Rome which I had asked to be sent there. During the last days in Clarens I
had been suffering from my old complaint, gastric catarrh. I lost my appetite completely, slept badly, and this had the most unpleasant effect on my
morale. The doctor who treated me a month ago in Petersburg had told me
that the over-sensitivity of the nervous system which I suffer from is due in
considerable measure to this complaint. I underwent a very successful
course of treatment in Vichy last year under Dr Saligoux, in whom I have
the greatest trust. Before I travelled to Naples, to a country whose language
I couldn't speak, I decided to consult Saligoux and to ask him to draw up a
regime for me which I could follow while I was in Italy, and in addition to
indicate some method or course of treatment. I decided to undertake this
journey to Paris, because I had heard from my sister, who had lived a long
time in Geneva, how bad the doctors there were.[8]

I am greatly regretting coming to Paris. I am experiencing nothing but
suffering; the only consolation is that Tolya is pleased that he has been to
Paris, which has always attracted him. I am tormented by pangs of conscience at being in *Paris* at Mme von Meck's expense and at a time when a
Russian has no cause for jollity. We are staying here only until tomorrow,

---

* Lev Davydov, Alexandra's husband, Tchaikovsky's brother-in-law [trans.].
† Alexy Sofronov, Tchaikovsky's manservant [trans.].

[6] vi. 200 (von Meck).   [7] vi. 208.   [8] vi. 216 (von Meck).

i.e. in all only two days. Yesterday I was feeling very ill. Today I am well, although a little weak. Tolya has just come back from the opera, where they were doing *Faust*. He is in seventh heaven about everything but about Carvallo in particular. I wanted to have a laugh and went to the Palais Royal, but walked out before the end. One needs to be in a more peaceful frame of mind to enjoy oneself.[9]

I find it hard to lie to you [Mme von Meck], even when there is every mitigating circumstance. We came here by accident. Around Modena I felt so ill and the following day I was in such distress that I decided to stop in Florence for a day, which is allowed under the terms of our ticket, which we bought in Paris: *avec l'arrêt facultatif pendant trois jours*. It is not that I am ill. Yesterday I took myself sternly in hand and today I am quite all right. The trouble is depression, an all-consuming insane depression, which will not leave me for a moment. When I was in Clarens amidst the uttermost tranquillity, peace, and the simplest but comfortable surroundings, I was sometimes sad and melancholy. I did not know how to explain these attacks of melancholy and I imagined the cause to be the mountains!!! What *naïveté*. The cause of these fits of melancholy, which never lasted long, was purely psychological. I also imagined that once I crossed the frontier into Italy, I would be happy for ever after. What rubbish! Here I am a hundred times sadder. The weather is magnificent, the days are as warm as July, there is plenty to see and to be distracted by—but I am still tormented by a gigantic, colossal depression! And the livelier the place I find myself in, the worse it is. I can't explain it. I think it is impossible to explain. But the main thing is that I don't know what to do! If I hadn't asked all my friends to send letters to me in Rome, I don't think I would have gone any further. At all events I must get to Rome—but what will happen there, I don't know. The mass of *Sehenswürdigkeiten* in Rome alarms me. It would somehow be strange not to see everything that was there, but in order to sightsee, you need to be a tourist travelling for pleasure, and not someone who is suffering from nervous and physical illness. I definitely cannot live the life of a tourist at the moment: this is somehow odd, embarrassing, and laughable in the circumstances, Russia's in general and mine in particular. And also, if you are going to rush around the streets, museums, and churches of Florence and Rome, Baedeker in hand, you need time especially allotted to this occupation; I, on the other hand, have come to rest, and to rest not by means of worthless rushing about, but by working. At the moment I think for some reason that I cannot work in Italy in general or in Rome in particular. On the strength of all this I now bitterly regret leaving quiet, peaceful, dear Clarens, where I would have set to work willingly and successfully. I am thinking that it might be better to return there![10]

I have already explained the *geographical* reasons, so to speak, behind my decision to cross into Italy. There is also another reason. When I arrived here I was still *very ill*. Things are fine here, but each one of the objects which surround me reminds me of my moral torment. By the way, since yesterday the weather too has become gloomy. I have decided to leave in three days. I intend to spend a few days in Rome, where on my last visit I only spent a day. Much of it struck me forcibly and I very much want to see this remarkable city in greater detail. But my heart belongs to Naples hardly less and I think that I will finally settle there for the winter. Whatever happens I will inform you of my peregrinations in the minutest detail, which, anyhow, will be very uncomplicated because from Rome I can only travel to Naples. Meanwhile I will await your letters in Rome at the poste restante.

In reflecting carefully on all that has happened to me I have several times come up against the idea of a Providence which, incidentally, even looks after me. Not only have I not perished, when that seemed the only course open to me, but things are fine now and the future is dawning in happiness and success. I must say that so far as religion is concerned my nature is split and I cannot yet reconcile its two halves.... my reason persistently declines to accept the truth of the dogmatic side of Orthodoxy and the other Christian confessions. For instance, however much I have thought about the dogma of retribution and reward, according to whether a man is good or bad, I have never been able to find the slightest sense in such a belief.[11]

We have arrived in Rome.[12] I am in no state to travel further for the moment. I cannot stand the noise of towns at all. I went around the Vatican museum like a fool because I could think of nothing but how quickly I could get back to my room.[13] I hope to do a bit of work in Venice and then, when I get to Clarens, things will really start moving.[14]

I have turned out to be a complete invalid. I literally cannot stand any noise; both yesterday in Florence and today here, every passing carriage makes me wild with rage, every shout, every sound grates on my nerves. The crowds of people moving through narrow streets annoy me to such an extent that I regard any acquaintance we meet as my sworn enemy. Only now do I fully understand the immeasurable folly of coming here. My brother and I have just been to St Peter's which, earlier, on my first visit, evoked tears of joy, but this time I experienced nothing but unbearable physical exhaustion. To say nothing of the streets, the foul air, the dirt: I didn't notice all this before. I realize that my illness is masking for me all the beauty of Rome and making its shortcomings stand out in sharp focus—but this is small consolation.[15]

The day before yesterday, after a wonderful walk on a warm autumn day, I returned home, overcome by an urgent need to write to you, even if only a

[11] vi. 222 (von Meck).   [12] vi. 225–6 (von Meck).   [13] vi. 229 (N. Rubinstein).
            [14] vi. 223 (von Meck).   [15] vi. 213 (von Meck).

few words, dear Nadezhda Filaretovna! I wanted to tell you that I am completely calm and happy, after arranging my affairs in such a way that all that remains is to set about my work with redoubled energy and to find in it complete oblivion from the endless nightmare which has been oppressing me. But a disappointment was waiting for me at home: two letters from my wife, which distressed me very, very much. In the first letter she threw a mass of the most offensive accusations at me; in the second, written a day later, without retracting anything at all from her first letter, she had, on the contrary, sunk into her habitual tone of grovelling and self-abasement. These letters can serve as an addition to the portrait I drew of her for you. What upsets me most of all is that these letters show evidence of a strong desire on her part for me to return home to her with my tail between my legs. Only she doesn't know how to set about this, whether to be a gentle lamb, prepared to suffer everything out of her love for me, or whether, on the contrary, to act the fierce and angry woman, accusing me of *dishonour* and *deceit*.[16]

The last day we spent in Rome, although I did find it very tiring, was at the same time some measure of recompense for all my misfortunes. On the morning of that day I had to fuss about, getting hold of the draft of my symphony. After all, if the symphony had got lost, I would not have had the strength to write it all out again from memory! The package was found. Calmed down, I set off with my brother for the Capitol where there was much that interested me and touched me to the quick.[17] I must frankly say, though, that I am not the most passionate admirer of the plastic arts and am ill equipped to recognize their finer points. Rapid tours of art galleries soon tire me. Out of dozens of works of art usually only one, just possibly two or three, seizes the whole of my attention; I study them down to the last detail, thoroughly soak myself in their atmosphere and then look at all the rest quite superficially. A judge as poor as I am would need to live there for a year to appreciate the treasures which Rome houses, and then one would have to go around them every day. I looked around the palace of the Caesars in detail and it left me with an astonishing impression of overwhelming grandeur. What colossal dimensions! What beauty! At every step you reflect and try to re-create in your imagination an image of the remote past, and the further you go the more vivid are these images of grandiose elegance. The weather was marvellous. At every turn one had a different view of the city, dirty, like Moscow, but far more picturesque and richer in historical memories. And then the Coliseum, with the ruins of the palace of Constantine beside it. It is all so majestic, huge, and beautiful! I am very glad that I left [for Venice] with such a favourable and unforgettable impression.[18]

The special charm of this city has captivated me. I have been chasing

---

[16] vi. 212.   [17] vi. 233–4 (von Meck).   [18] vi. 234 (von Meck).

around Venice all day in sheer delight.[19] Every day I discover new pleasures. We went to see the church of the Frari, which, amongst other beautiful things, contains Canova's mausoleum. What a miracle of beauty! But what I like best here is the quietness, the absence of the usual commotion that you get in towns. To sit by the open window in the evening and watch the moonlight on Santa Maria della Salute, which is directly opposite our windows, and on the lagoon, to the left, is pure enchantment. It's also very lively if you sit after lunch outside one of the cafés on St Mark's Square and watch the bustling crowds of all sorts of people. I even like the little streets, no wider than corridors, especially in the evenings when the shops are lit by gas. In short, I have taken to Venice.[20] The few days I have spent in Venice have been very good for me. In the first place, I have been working a bit, and with such vigour that my brother will be taking away with him the completely finished second scene of the opera for Rubinstein. In the second place, I can feel an improvement in my health. Thirdly, I have taken a great liking to Venice and am even beginning to fall in love with the beautiful creature and I have decided to come back here when I have seen my brother off. I have even taken some very nice accommodation on the Riva dei [sic]Schiavoni, in the Hôtel Beau Rivage, where I found two rooms that suited me perfectly, with a delightful view of the lagoons, the island of S. Giorgio, the Lido and so on. When I get back from Vienna I will set about the *symphony*, our symphony, and I will not stir from the spot until I finish it.[21]

I am definitely going to write some romances and piano pieces. I have even tried to make a start now, but in vain. I have not yet achieved the peace of mind that I need for composition and it doesn't look as if I will find it in the near future. However, I have started to orchestrate my opera with great enthusiasm; I will also start work on my symphony, as soon as I receive my sketch book, which I asked you to send and which I am awaiting with the greatest impatience.[22]

Do you know what infuriates me about Venice? It's the evening newspaper vendors. If you are wandering about St Mark's Square you hear from all directions, ' "Il Tempo", Signori, "La gazetta di Venezia", di Vittoria di Turchi! . . .' This 'vittoria di Turchi' happens every evening. Why don't they shout about our real victories instead of trying to entice the customers with imaginary Turkish ones? Does peaceful, beautiful Venice, who once lost her power in the fight against these same Turks, really breathe the same hatred towards Russia which is common to all of Western Europe? Yesterday I lost my temper and fixed on one of the shouting paper-sellers, 'ma dove la vittoria?' It turned out that by 'victory' he meant a Turkish communiqué about some reconnoitre, in which several hundreds of Russians were said to have been killed. 'But is this really a victory?' I continued in a threatening tone of voice. I didn't understand his reply fully, but he stopped shouting about victory. At bottom, to do them justice, the Italians are friendly, polite, and ready to be of service.[23]

I like travelling abroad for relaxation; it is the greatest of pleasures. But I could *live* only in Russia. Only by living somewhere else do you realize how much, despite all its faults, you love our dear country.[24]

Anatoly had to return to St Petersburg and Tchaikovsky went as far as Vienna with him.

We have arrived in Vienna. The journey through the Semmering really captivated me.[25]

I think that you [Mme von Meck] feel sympathy for my music because I am always full of a longing for the ideal, just as you are. Our sufferings are the same, your doubts are just as serious as mine, both of us sail over the measureless sea of scepticism, seeking a harbour and finding none. Is this not why you feel such a close kinship with my music?[26]

I felt at my best in Clarens, in Switzerland. The trip to Italy was utter folly. The wealth of dazzling splendours merely enraged and irritated me. For my brother's sake I had to go round the museums and galleries and I was totally incapable of taking in the beauties of art, whatever they might have been.[27]

I heard Wagner's *Valkyrie* in Vienna, which gave me the opportunity to have another look at the first impression I formed in Bayreuth. If music is indeed fated to see in the person of Wagner its chief and greatest representative, then it is a matter for despair. Can this really be the last word of art, are future generations really to delight in this pretentious, ponderous, and ugly rubbish just as we now delight in the Ninth Symphony which in its own time was also considered to be nonsense? If the answer is yes, it is dreadful. But it was also in Vienna that I *heard* Léo Delibes's ballet *Sylvia*; and I did *hear* it because it is the first ballet in which the music constitutes not just the main but the only interest. What charm and elegance, what riches in the melody, the rhythm, the harmony. I was ashamed. If I had known this music before, I would, of course, not have written *The Lake of the Swans*.[28] In recent years I can think of nothing which has caught my attention as seriously as Bizet's *Carmen* and Delibes's ballet.[29]

I heard Wagner's *Walküre*. The performance was outstanding. The orchestra excelled themselves; the excellent singers did everything they could to show the opera off to good effect ... but in spite of all that I was bored. What a Don Quixote this Wagner is! Why does he exhaust himself, chase after the unattainable, when there under his very nose is an enormous talent, from which, if only he would devote himself to it entirely and follow

[23] vi. 243 (von Meck).   [24] vi. 245 (von Meck).   [25] vi. 247 (von Meck).
[26] vi. 248 (von Meck).   [27] vi. 259 (Kashkin).   [28] vi. 294 (Taneyev).
[29] vi. 260 (Kashkin).

its natural inclinations, he could draw a whole sea of musical beauty. In my opinion Wagner is a natural symphonist. This man has been endowed with the talent of a genius, but it is being destroyed by his whims, his inspiration is being paralysed by the theories which he has invented and which he wants to put into practice at all costs. Chasing after *reality, truthfulness,* and *rationality* in opera, he has completely lost sight of the *music,* which in general has been conspicuous by its absence in his last four operas. For I cannot call music the kaleidoscopic, motley musical fragments which constantly follow one another, never leading to anything and never allowing one to settle into some sort of recognizable musical form. There is not a single generously rounded melody, not once is the soloist allowed any breadth. He has constantly to chase after the orchestra, and worry all the time about missing his entry, which in the score has no more significance than an entry by some fourth horn. But there is no doubt whatsoever that he is a wonderful symphonist. I will give you an example of how the symphonist in him dominates the vocal or in general the opera composer. You have probably heard at a concert his famous *Wallkührenritt* [sic]? What a wonderfully grandiose picture it portrays. You can see in your own mind these wild female giants, flying with thunder and lightning through the clouds on their magic steeds. The piece always creates an enormous impression in a concert-hall. In the theatre, against the backdrop of painted rocks and canvas clouds, and the warriors clumsily rushing across the back of the stage, and against the backdrop also of this insignificant theatrical sky pretending to portray the enormous heavenly heights, the music loses all its pictorial qualities. So it follows that the theatre does not enrich the effect here but acts like a glass of cold water. Finally, I don't understand and never have understood why the *Niebelungen* is considered a literary *chef-d'œuvre*? As a national epic maybe, but as a libretto, no. All these Wotans, Brünnhildes, Frickas, and so on are so impossible, so inhuman, so difficult to sympathize with. And how little action there is. It takes Wotan a whole three-quarters of an hour to scold Brünnhilde for her disobedience. What tedium! But nevertheless there is a wealth of wonderfully powerful separate episodes of great beauty, of a purely symphonic nature.[30]

Tchaikovsky met Kotek in Vienna.

Kotek and I have been studying Brahms's new symphony [No. 1]; in Germany they praise him to the skies. I do not see what is attractive about him. My view is that it is sombre and cold, and full of pretensions to being deep without real depth. I think in any case that Germany is on the way down musically. I think that the French are coming on to the scene now. They have a lot of new, powerful talents. But in Germany there is definitely a downward course. Wagner is the great representative of this period of decline.[31]

[30] vi. 261–2 (von Meck).   [31] vi. 262–3 (von Meck).

We stay at home almost all the time. Kotek and I play piano duets or the three of us talk, but in the evening we often go to the theatre. We have seen Cherubini's *The Water Carrier*, Delibes's *Sylvia* (ballet), Wagner's *Walküre*, and *Aida*. The latter was very bad. Out of all those it was *The Water Carrier*, and *Sylvia*, performed as a double-bill, which made the greatest impression. Yesterday and today we are doing without the theatre.[32]

My brother and Kotek have gone to a Grand Philharmonic Concert, where, incidentally, they are playing Schumann's splendid Third Symphony which I like so much. However, I preferred to stay at home. I was frightened that I would have to meet some of the musicians here whom I know and thank them for the attention they give my music and so on (last year they included the *Romeo and Juliet* overture in their programme without any request on my part; it was, however, unanimously booed). It would greatly aid the spread of my works abroad if I visited the *bigwigs* and said complimentary things to them. But my God, how I hate that sort of thing! They are so offensively patronizing to Russian musicians. You can positively read in their faces: *although you are a Russian, I am so good and kind that I will favour you with my attention.* Good luck to them! Last year I had to see Liszt, through no wish of my own. He was polite, nauseatingly so, but there never left his lips a smile which, with the greatest clarity, spoke the words I have given above.[33]

It was exactly this view of the attitude of foreigners to Russian composers which caused Tchaikovsky to decline a suggestion made at that time that he should go to the World Exhibition in Paris as a music delegate.

Rubinstein is right in saying that I am *capricious*. It is true—but indeed my only illness is due to the fact that I am capricious and cannot help it. From a purely physical point of view I am *perfectly* healthy.[34]

The main thing is that I don't want to go to Paris, for it sickens me, it bores me, I want to spend the summer in the country in Russia, and I am tired of wanting to appear to be what I am not, I am tired of straining against my own nature, rotten though it may be.[35]

I see that you [Nikolay Rubinstein] are cross with me for refusing to be a delegate. My dear friend! You know me well enough. Do you think I could really be of some use to Russian music if I agreed to be a delegate? You know how hopeless I am at *arranging* anything. Add to that my *unsociability*, which has now taken on the characteristics of an incurable disease. What would come of it? I would torment myself and agonize, all to no effect, over the petty intrigues of all kinds of riff-raff, French or Russian, and I would not arrange anything. As far as I am concerned, in my defence, it is enough to say that without exaggerating, I would far rather be

[32] vi. 264 (Modest).   [33] vi. 265–6 (von Meck).
[34] vii. 52 (Anatoly).   [35] vii. 57 (Jurgenson).

sentenced to penal servitude than have to go to Paris as a delegate. If my character were different, if I were in a healthier state of mind, I agree that it would be useful for me to go and live in Paris for a while. But not now.[36]

I can live only in absolute quietness, insulated from the noise and bustle of a big city and in complete calm. For my fame and successes abroad I do not give a damn, a damn, a damn. All I want, all I ask for is to be left in peace. I would gladly settle in the most inaccessible backwater if I could only avoid friction with other people. I have no intention of chasing after fame and honours. I will compose if I feel the inner urge to do so; I will compose because I am incapable of not composing. And of course I still do not know if I am up to doing something new. However that may be, I cannot live without working and if I do not *compose*, then I will find some other musical activity. In short, I am not going to concern myself with the propagation of my works for this is not something which I need.[37]

First of all, I want to ask you [Mme von Meck], how you can imagine that your *profession de foi* could alter my relationship to you or detract from my ardent love and devotion to your shining, intelligent, and everlastingly kind personality. Do you really think that an insignificant difference of opinion and convictions could change our feelings of mutual compatibility? I have not cooled in the smallest degree in my boundless sympathy towards you after reading your autobiographical confession, and I hope that your friendly feelings towards me will not cease if I allow myself to answer some points in your letter. One thing is clear to me—that in theory you have irrevocably broken with the Church and its dogma of faith.[38]

I have a quite different attitude to the Church from yours [Mme von Meck]. It has kept for me a very great deal of its aesthetic attraction. I very often go to mass: the Liturgy of St John Chrysostom is, in my view, one of the greatest works of art. If one attends one of our Orthodox services and follows it closely, going carefully into the significance of each stage of the rites, it is impossible not to be spiritually moved. I also dearly love the All-night Vigil. To set off on a Saturday for some ancient little church, to stand in the half-light filled with the fumes of incense, to become absorbed in oneself, seeking there answers to the eternal questions: *why, when, whither, for what*, to be roused from one's reflections when the choir sings 'Many passions contend with me from my youth' and to allow oneself to be carried away under the influence of the enchanting poetry of that psalm, to be infused with a quiet rapture when the royal gates are opened and there rings forth 'Praise the Lord in the Heavens'—oh! how tremendously I love it all! It is one of the greatest pleasures of my life! So on the one hand, I still have strong ties with the Church, on the other, I, like you, have long since lost my faith in its dogmas. I am also like you in having reached the conclusion that if there is a future life it is only in the sense that matter is inex-

[36] vii. 15.   [37] vii. 30 (Karl Albrecht).   [38] vi. 247 (von Meck).

haustible and in the pantheistic sense of the permanency of nature, of which I constitute a microscopic part. In short, I cannot understand personal immortality. And how are we supposed to imagine eternal life after death? As eternal pleasure? But if there is to be eternal pleasure and bliss there must also be the contrary: eternal torment. This latter I reject entirely. Finally, I do not even know if life after death is desirable, because life is only attractive when it consists of an alternation of joys and sorrows, of the struggle between good and evil, of light and dark, of variety in unity, to put it briefly. Can we really conceive of eternal life in the form of unending bliss? To our earthly minds it would seem that even *bliss*, if it remains permanently untroubled, must eventually cloy. So the result of all my thinking is the *conviction* that there is no eternal life. But conviction is one thing, emotions and instincts are another. Though I deny eternal life, I still indignantly reject the monstrous notion that I will never, never see again some of my dear ones. Despite the telling force of my *convictions*, I can never reconcile myself to the thought that my mother, whom I loved so much and who was such a fine person, has vanished for ever and that I will never have the opportunity of saying to her that after twenty-three years of being parted I love her just as much. So, I am a mass of contradictions; despite the considerable maturity of my years I have not come to rest anywhere, I have not calmed my anxious soul either with religion or with philosophy. Indeed, I would go out of my mind were it not for *music*. That is truly heaven's greatest gift to mankind as it blunders about in the darkness. Music alone brings light, and calm, and reconciliation. But it is not merely a straw to be grabbed at: it is a true friend, protector, and comforter, and it alone makes life on this earth worth living. After all, there may not be any music in heaven, so let us live in this world so long as there is life in us![39]

I have received a long letter from Antonina Ivanovna. She keeps asking me to explain why I did not go on living with her, and presses me to be *utterly* frank with her. But, oh Lord, I cannot tell her anything that hasn't been said to her already, many times. I admit that I am to blame, I give her credit for her good intentions, and her sincerity and honesty, but I cannot live with her. She told Tolya that she suspected that after my manservant Mikhaila had lost his job when I got married, he had visited a witch, and under her spell had implanted hatred towards her in my heart. I cannot confirm that! She now imagines that I suddenly changed towards her when I came back from Kamenka. I can only marvel that she has never noticed the perpetual numbness in my fight with my heart. It is true that at the beginning I showed her more tenderness, but I was hoping to come out the winner in this fight. But even then I had occasion to burst into tears in her presence—and now she writes that she was perfectly happy then! But that isn't the trouble. Antonina Ivanovna writes that she loves me more than

[39] vi. 251–2 (von Meck).

anything else in the world. I ask her to prove it by her deeds. And she could prove it by ceasing to poison my wounds in many different ways. Today's letter is written in the most loving tone. It is very long, full of the most noble sentiments, but nevertheless she asks *why I acted so pitilessly towards her, and what she did to deserve this*!

Goodness, from what heights do I have to shout, on what platform must I stand in order to say for the thousandth time: for no reason, for no reason, for no reason, it's my fault, it's my fault, it's my fault. When will all this finally come to an end!

So that's how it is, Sasha. I must overcome my modesty and say something: apart from the fact that I an Antonina Ivanovna's husband, that I have treated her mercilessly, apart from the fact that she is not to blame for anything, that she is a *poor* creature etc., etc., whereas I am a half-crazed merciless tyrant, there is one other factor. I am an artist who can and must bring honour to his country. I can feel great creative powers within me. I still have not done even a fraction of what I can do. And I want, with all the power at my command, to do it. Yet I cannot work now. Look at the saga of Antonina Ivanovna from this point of view. Tell her to stop tormenting me with reproaches and threats that she will commit suicide. Let her be quite clear about this. I must be given a chance to follow my destiny. I am ill, and, I swear to you, close to insanity. I implore her to give me the chance to calm down and start working properly. I know that Rubinstein told her as much in no uncertain terms, but she has forgotten all about it. She has become the most merciless executioner of my . . .* if you want to do this for me. But there is only one way to achieve perfect peace of mind in my case: I need the opportunity to put at least some way behind me everything that I have gone through recently. And to this end, Antonina Ivanovna must stop trying to find the reasons for our separation. She can be my friend, but she really must not keep harping back to the same questions: *why, what for*, etc., etc. Not even I know the whys and wherefores.[40] My sadness at parting with my brother [Anatoly] is much easier to bear since the news of the capture of Plevna. I nearly embraced the waiter when he brought in the coffee yesterday morning and said, 'Plevna ist gefallen'. Judging by the local papers Austria feels a little injured by this victory and is surly towards us because the best Turkish army has been taken captive.[41]

I knew that I would miss my brother but I didn't know I would miss him so much. Venice seemed so attractive when I was with him [but now] it strikes me as gloomy, desolate, and miserable as the grave. I am working at the symphony and I am taking great pains over it. I am hoping that little by little this work will eventually drive out of my heart my longing for my dear brother. I have received the very glad tidings that the first act of *Onegin*

---

* Several words are missing in the original.

[40] *LR* 313–14 (Sasha).   [41] vi. 267 (von Meck).

sent all my colleagues into raptures, starting with Rubinstein. I was very apprehensive about their verdict. This is very, very pleasing.[42]

At the same time a fear arose that the Conservatoire students would not be able to cope with performing the opera. In fact, Albrecht wrote to Tchaikovsky about this.

But here is my reply. If I have to wait for a *real* Tatyana, a *real* Onegin, an *ideal* Lensky and so on then, of course, the opera will never be staged. Whatever Klimentova might be like, she is still better for me than Raab, Velinskaya, Menshikova, and so on [from the Imperial Opera] because she will be rehearsed by Galvani, you [Albrecht], Samarin, and Rubinstein. Gilev is also better for me than Melnikov, and Silberstein than Dodonov because they are pupils, young people still not in the rut of that disgusting banality which is what I fear for my opera above all else. I will *never* offer this opera to the theatre management before it is performed at the Conservatoire. I wrote it for the Conservatoire because I do not need in this work a large theatre with its *dull routine, its conventionality, its undistinguished producers, its nonsensical staging (even if it is opulent), its flapping machines instead of a conductor etc. etc.* This is what I want for *Onegin*: (1) singers of middle rank, but well-drilled and sound; (2) singers who can also act *simply* but *well*; (3) a production which is not opulent but adheres strictly to the period; the costumes must be exactly of the period in which the opera takes place (the twenties); (4) the choruses must not be a flock of sheep, as they are in the Imperial Opera, but people, who take part in the action of the opera; (5) the conductor must not be a machine, nor even a musician à la Nápravník: he only cares about getting a C♯ and not a C but I want someone who will be a true guide to the orchestra. In short, for this production I need neither Kister, not Kavelin, nor Nápravník, nor Merten, nor Kondratyev, nor Dmitriyev, but I do need *Hubert, Albrecht, Samarin, and Rubinstein*, i.e. true artists and, moreover, my friends. Not for all the world will I give *Onegin* to the managements in Petersburg or Moscow and if it is destined not to be put on at the Conservatoire then it will not be put on anywhere. I am prepared to wait as long as you like. So far as Klimentova's unsuitability is concerned, an *entirely* suitable singer will never be found. If we are to wait for this *ideal* Tatyana we shall have to wait for ever more.[43]

I have now set about orchestrating the symphony. It's coming along only with great difficulty. I write from the morning up to dinner time and by the evening I can't go on. You [Jurgenson] are still under the threat of an opera and a symphony before long! Of course I know perfectly well that my works enrich your shelves but not your pocket. But let us just hope that by the time Boris is fifty the odd one of my works might be marginally on the credit side of his account.[44]

---

[42] vi. 271, 280 (von Meck).   [43] vi. 275–6 (Karl Albrecht).
[44] vi. 283, 284 (von Meck).

Tchaikovsky's compositions began to make a profit for his publisher sooner than this. Jurgenson's son Boris was nine at the time.

I like your [Mme von Meck] haughty attitude to public opinion. Before I was as broken down as I am now my contempt for *qu'en dira-t-on* was at least as strong. Now, I admit, I have become somewhat more sensitive in that respect. Even so, I have always hated *publicity* and have always been distressed if I have seen people taking a lot of interest in me. Unfortunately, my activity as an artist entails *publicity* and the role of an outside observer, of no interest to anybody, is not open to me.[45]

What is human beauty? The concept is, of course, entirely relative and has nothing in common with the *absolute beauty* which manifests itself in art; one can like a face even if it is not beautiful. I will go further. Faces which are beautiful in the classical sense are rarely attractive. What pleases us in a person's face, walk, mannerisms, movements, glance is something elusive, not amenable to definition. This something is, in essence, a reflection of spiritual beauty. In this sense, of course, I can easily succumb to the charms of a person's appearance. *Beauty* in a human being means the external reflection of inner qualities.[46]

One thing I can never agree with is your [Mme von Meck] view of music. I particularly dislike your comparison of music with intoxication. I think this is wrong. A man resorts to drink to deceive himself, to obtain for himself the *illusion* of contentment and happiness. And what a price he has to pay for the deception! The effect is dreadful. Be that as it may, drink does, admittedly, momentarily obliterate sorrow and anguish—and that is all. Is that what music does? It is not a deception, it is a *revelation*. And it is precisely in this that we see the triumph of its power: that it reveals to us otherwise inaccessible elements of beauty, the contemplation of which reconciles us with life not just for the moment but for good. It brings light and joy. The processes of musical enjoyment are very difficult to track down and capture but they have nothing in common with *intoxication*. In any event, this is not a *physiological* phenomenon. Obviously the nerves and, in consequence, the physical organs participate in apprehending the musical impression and in this sense music gratifies the body but then it is well known to be very difficult to draw a sharp distinction between the physical and spiritual sides of man. After all, even *thinking* is a physiological process because it belongs to the functions of the brain.[47]

I am living in Venice now, which I chose for a temporary stay because I like its peace and quiet. I don't think I will stay here long. I will probably finish the symphony, which I have taken up with great energy, and then go somewhere in Switzerland. However beautiful Venice may be, however quiet, I cannot stay here very long, and do you know why? I cannot get

[45] vi. 288–9 (von Meck).   [46] vi. 289 (von Meck).
[47] vi. 289–90 (von Meck).

used to the foul smell of Venice at all. One can't breathe *fresh* air here; it is eternally infected with noxious fumes and one can never get used to it. I don't understand how people can live here for the whole of their lives.[48]

It's not just a question of working hard at the orchestration of *our* symphony, I'm immersed in it. None of my previous orchestral works has ever cost me so much effort, but then I have never felt so much affection for one of my works. I had a pleasant surprise when I settled down to work. At first I was writing mainly because I did, after all, have to finish the symphony, however difficult it might be. But gradually I got caught up and now it is difficult for me to tear myself away from my work. Perhaps I am wrong but I think that this symphony is something out of the ordinary, that it is the best thing I have done so far. I am so pleased that it is *ours* and that when you [Mme von Meck] hear it you will know that I was thinking about you in every bar. If it had not been for you, would it ever have been finished? In Moscow, when I thought that it was *all over* with me, I made this inscription on the manuscript draft which I had forgotten about and have only just found when I got down to work. The inscription on the title-page was: *In the event of my death I entrust this sketch book to Mme von Meck.* It was my wish that you should keep the manuscript of my last work. Now I am not only alive and well but can, thanks to you, devote myself whole-heartedly to my work in the knowledge that the composition coming from my pen is not, I think, likely to be forgotten. Of course, I may well be wrong; every creative artist is probably carried away by his most recent work.[49]

I am leaving Venice without regrets. But it is only thanks to the monotony of Venetian life and the absence of all distractions that I have been able to work with such persistent diligence. Writing the opera does not give me the same feeling as does the symphony. With the former it's a matter of guesswork: perhaps it will be suitable or perhaps nothing will come of it. But when I work on the symphony I am firmly convinced that this piece is *out of the ordinary* and that it is the most formally perfect of all that I have written so far.[50]

Today I received the joyful and now definite news that my brother Modest and his dear pupil are coming to join me. Konradi (the child's father) agreed to his son and teacher joining me on condition that I settled in a place whose climate would be suitable for the child's weak constitution. He suggested San Remo, near Menton, where we could arrange matters very comfortably since a lot of guest houses and hotels have been built there recently. It is warm, the air is healthy and clean, the setting is magnificent and life simple, without worldly amusements and noise. I have nothing against this choice. There is only one small unpleasantness in all this: I shall have to tear myself away from my work in which I have buried myself whole-heartedly. I will have to lose three or four days. But on the other

[48] vi. 294 (Taneyev).   [49] vi. 298–9 (von Meck).   [50] vi. 300–1 (Anatoly).

hand what joy, what delight it will be for me to live with my dear brother again, who on his part won't be at all put out. Coming from Konradi, this action is so kind that I don't know how to express my gratitude towards him.[51]

I received your [Jurgenson's] letter and nearly died with shame. The symphony has absorbed me to such an extent that I haven't had the strength to tear myself away, particularly for such a trivial occupation as translating cheap Italian verses with their cheap juvenile music. Let us pray that it is *lucrative*—but even so it is very bad. Nevertheless, today I sat down to it and did as much as I could. Today I am sending you everything that you gave me to do. However, as you will see, I have not done it all. For the sake of greater clarity I have numbered each piece and added notes on what I have done with it.

No. 1 The Quartet 'Come di gloria al nome' is unfinished, and I am not going to finish it, besides which it is very bad and I haven't translated it. Since Balakirev involved you in this, let him finish it if you definitely want to publish it.

No. 2 'La Notte o mai s'appressa'—the same applies.

No. 3 Bass recitative 'Ai quobil core'. Look, however much of a genius Glinka may have been, surely you can't publish his exercises in the art of recitative? And then the recitative has no ending and does not lead to an aria. Also, to my no small surprise, after the solemn words about the tomb, there suddenly appears a chorus of voices who begin to drown him with the words 'As we raise the tsar so we raise everyone', however it also has no ending and tails away. I don't understand what it means.

No. 4 Romance 'Tu sei figlia'—already translated.

No. 5 Romance 'Pur nel sonno'—translated.

No. 6 Romance 'Mio ben recordati'—translated.

No. 7 Romance 'Ho perduto'—translated.

No. 8 Aria—translated.

No. 9 Quartet, which had no words. *This is the only respectable piece.* I have set some words to it although they are nothing special.[52]

Venice, 15 December

I have finished the Scherzo. I am very tired. The whole day was so foggy that you couldn't see further than two paces ahead. I am going to bed now. It is 10 o'clock. Tomorrow I shall have to get up at 6.0. Everything is packed and the bill settled. Oh, how happy I am that I won't have to eat the disgusting food that they give us any more. We are the last guests at the hotel. Tomorrow there will be nobody left.

---

[51] vi. 303 (von Meck).

[52] vi. 305 (Jurgenson). This concerns the translation of the texts of Glinka's early works.

Milan, 16 December

We left at 8 o'clock and arrived at 4.0. We are staying at the Hôtel d'Europe. We went for a walk and dined. I am just off to the theatre and to-morrow I will write down my first impressions. I am feeling in excellent health.[53]

They have been doing Marchetti's *Ruy Blas*. The performance of this opera provoked melancholy thoughts. There is a young queen in it with whom everyone is in love. The singer who took this role was very conscientious; she did all she could. But how little did she resemble a graceful, royal lady with the power to captivate every man she met! And the hero, Ruy Blas! Again, his singing was not at all bad. But instead of a young man, a handsome and elegant hero, we had nothing but a flunkey! No illusion at all. I thought about my own opera. Where am I going to find a Tatyana as Pushkin imagined her and as I have tried to portray her in music? Where is there a singer who even remotely resembles the ideal Onegin, that cold dandy, *comme il faut* to the marrow of his bones? Where will we find a Lensky, a youth of eighteen, with a thick crop of curls and the impetuous, quirkish ways of a young poet *à la* Schiller? How Pushkin's charming picture is vulgarized when it is transferred to the stage with its sacred routine of senseless traditions, and with its veterans like Alexandrova, Komissarzhevsky, and *tutti quanti* who quite shamelessly assume the roles of sixteen-year-old girls and beardless youths! The moral of which is: it is much nicer to write instrumental music because there are fewer disappointments. How much have I not had to suffer from the productions of my operas, particularly *Vakula*? There was nothing in common between what I imagined and what emerged on the stage of the Mariinsky Theatre. What an Oxana, what a Vakula![54]

I have been to the top of Milan Cathedral for the first time. The weather was good but not perfect and the Swiss mountains were not visible. But the mountains of the Tyrol shone forth in all their glory. Milan Cathedral as a whole is one of the most beautiful things I have seen. You cannot know the full grandeur of its beauty until you have been up to the top and have seen all the details.[55]

From Milan Tchaikovsky went to San Remo where he took accommodation for himself and for his brother Modest who was coming from Russia with Kolya Konradi.

The day before yesterday we left Milan at six and at 11.45 we had already reached Genoa and settled in at the Hôtel des quatre nations. The hotel is exactly what I like, i.e. a very old building with thick walls, and doors six inches thick, all badly appointed and *completely empty*. We were shown to a magnificent great suite with an enormous fire already burning. After taking

[53] vi. 306 (Anatoly).   [54] vi. 308–9 (von Meck).   [55] vi. 307 (Anatoly).

tea, we lay down to sleep and for some reason I slept very badly with trem-
blings etc. The whole of the next day, i.e. the 30th, we spent walking about.
Incidentally, we climbed up to the top of one of the churches and had a
wonderful view of the whole of Genoa. We went to the theatre in the evening where we saw [Meyerbeer's] most tedious *L'Africaine*, which was
moreover very badly performed. Today we left at one. The journey is marvellous.[56]

I came upon the Pension Joly tucked away in a very nice spot, right on
the edge of the town; there were four small rooms available. Although they
were badly furnished, they did make up a separate flat. So far as the area is
concerned, it really is quite magical. Yet I went for a walk along the prom-
enade and felt an indescribable urge to go home and straightaway to pour
out in letters my unbearable sense of melancholy. Why should this be?
Why is it that a simple Russian landscape, why is it that a summer walk in
Russia, in the country, through the fields and woods, through the steppe in
the evening, used to bring me to such a state that I would lie on the ground
as though exhausted by an upsurge of love for nature, of those indescribably sweet and intoxicating sensations into which I was plunged by the
woods, the steppe, the rivers, a village in the distance, a modest little
church, in short by everything that makes up the feeble landscape of our
native Russia? Why should this happen? And here! Certainly, you could
imagine nothing more attractive than San Remo, but I swear that neither
the palms nor the orange trees, neither the miraculous blue of the sky nor
the mountains—none of these beauties affected me as one might have expected. I can draw peace and consolation, the sensations of happiness, only
from within myself. So the success of the symphony, the knowledge that I
am writing something good, will tomorrow reconcile me to all my past and
future misfortunes. But I have a somewhat strange attitude even to scenery
as luxuriant as it is here. It dazzles me and irritates me. It annoys me.
Admittedly, I am a bit like the old woman whose fate Pushkin recounted in
The Tale of the Fisherman and the Fish. The more cause I have to be happy
and content, the more I am discontented. Since I left Russia I have had so
many demonstrations of affection from several people who are dear to me
that there is enough affection to keep a few hundred happy and yet for me
there is no happiness, none, none, none. There are only moments of happiness. Then there is also the *préoccupation* with work which, when it is in full
swing, takes such a grip on you that you have no time to think about what
you feel like and you forget everything apart from what has a direct bearing
on the work.[57]

Tchaikovsky received a letter at this time from Mme von Meck with a request that
he should give a characterization of the composers of the Mighty Handful.

All the latest St Petersburg composers are a very talented lot. But they are

[56] vi. 313 (Anatoly).   [57] vi. 315, 316–17 (von Meck).

all infected to the marrow by the most terrible conceit and a purely dilet-
tantish confidence in their superiority over the rest of the musical world. Of
late, Rimsky-Korsakov has turned out to be an exception. He is self-taught
like the rest of them but he has done a complete about face. He has a very
serious, honest, and conscientious nature. When he was very young he got
in with a crowd who first of all convinced him that he was a genius, and
second, told him that there was no need *to study*, that studying kills inspiration, dries up the creative powers etc. He believed this to start with.
His first compositions show a very substantial talent, devoid of any theoretical basis. In the circle to which he belonged they were all in love with
themselves and each other. Each of them tried to imitate one or another of
the pieces which had emerged from the circle and had been proclaimed remarkable by its members. As a result, the whole circle sank into a monotony of approach, into mannered anonymity. Rimsky is the only one of
them to whom, about five years ago, the thought occurred that the ideas
which the circle preached were in reality completely unfounded, that their
contempt for training, for classical music, their hatred of authority and of
precedents was based on nothing other than ignorance. I still have one of
his letters dating from that time. It shook me and touched me to the core.
He was in the depths of despair on realizing how many years he had wasted,
and that he had been going down a blind alley. He asked me then what he
should do. It goes without saying that he needed to study. And he began to
study, but with such zeal that soon academic techniques became an atmosphere which he couldn't do without. During one summer he wrote a
countless number of contrapuntal exercises and sixty-four fugues, of which
he immediately sent me ten to have a look at. The fugues turned out to be
beyond reproach in their own way, but I noticed even then that in his reaction he had gone too far the other way. From contempt for study he had
swung towards the cult of musical technique. Soon after that his symphony
[No. 3] and quartet [No. 1] came out. Both compositions are packed full of
tricks, but as you yourself have rightly remarked, they are permeated by a
feeling of dry pedantry. It is clear that he is now undergoing a crisis, but
what will come out of this crisis is difficult to predict. He will either emerge
a great master, or will be for ever bogged down in contrapuntal trifles.

Cui is a talented dilettante. His music is devoid of originality but it is
elegant and refined. It is too coquettishly smooth, as you might say, and for
this reason you take to it at once, but it quickly loses its charm. This is
because Cui is not a musician by profession, but a professor of *military for-
tification*, who is very busy and lectures constantly at nearly all the military
academies in Petersburg. On his own admission to me, he can only compose by means of playing around and picking out on a piano little tunes
attached to little chords. Having found some nice little idea, he plays
around with it, finishes it off, embellishes it, and touches it up in all sorts of
different ways, and all this takes a very long time, so that for example his

opera *William Ratcliffe* took ten years to write. But I repeat, he does have some talent; at least he has taste and sensitivity.

Borodin is a fifty-year-old professor of chemistry in the Academy of Medicine. Again he has talent, even great talent, but it has been destroyed by a lack of knowledge, because of a blind fate which led him to a chair of chemistry instead of an active life in music. However, he has less taste than Cui, and his technique is so weak that he cannot write a single line of music without help from someone.

Musorgsky. You are very right to call him a has-been. As far as talent goes he could be superior to all those mentioned above, but he has a narrow-minded outlook, with no desire to better himself, and has blind faith in the inept theories of his circle and in his own genius. Apart from that he has a base side to his character, inclined to the coarse, the uncouth, the rough. He is the opposite extreme to his friend Cui, who is always superficial, but always elegant and graceful. Musorgsky, on the contrary, flaunts his illiteracy, is proud of his ignorance, botches things any old how, blindly believing in the infallibility of his own genius. And indeed, he does have the odd flashes of talent, which moreover are not without individuality.

The most powerful personality in the circle is *Balakirev*. But he has fallen silent, after composing very little. He has an enormous talent, which was destroyed as a result of some fateful circumstances which turned him into a religious fanatic after a long period when he prided himself on his complete atheism. He is now constantly in church, fasts, makes obeisance to relics, and does nothing else. In spite of his enormous gifts, he has done much harm. For instance, he destroyed Rimsky by persuading him that it was harmful to study. In general it is he who has invented all the theories of this strange circle, which unites within itself so many undeveloped, misdirected, or prematurely blighted forces.

There you have my frank opinion of these gentlemen. What a sad sight! There is so much talent but, apart from Rimsky, it is hard to think that anything serious will come of it. But isn't everything like that in Russia? Enormous powers which a sort of Plevna fatefully prevents from coming out into the open and proclaiming themselves as they ought. But the power is there all the same. Even in its very ugliness the language of a Musorgsky is new. It is not beautiful, but it is fresh. And this is why we can expect that Russia will one day produce a whole Pleiad of powerful talents who will point to new paths for the development of art. Our ugliness is still better than pitiful feebleness disguised as serious creativity, as in Brahms and other Germans like him. They have faded away irrevocably. We must hope that Plevna will nevertheless fall, and our forces will be allowed to make themselves heard.

Meanwhile very little has been done. As far as the French are concerned, there is apparent at the moment a very strong progressive movement. Of course, they have only now begun to perform Berlioz, ten years after his death. But many new talents have appeared and many energetic fighters against the status quo. And in France it is very difficult to fight the status quo. The French are terribly conservative in the arts. They recognized Beethoven after everyone else. In the 1840s they still regarded him as nothing more than a crazy eccentric. The leading French music critic, Fétis, expressed regret that Beethoven had *transgressed* (?) against the rules of harmony and it is no more than twenty-five years since he obligingly corrected these mistakes.

Of the contemporary French composers my favourites are Bizet and Deslibes [*sic*]. I don't know the overture *Patrie*, of which you write, but I know Bizet's opera *Carmen* well! This is music which has no pretensions to be deep, but is so delightful in its simplicity, so alive, spontaneous, but sincere, that I almost know it by heart from beginning to end. I have already written to you about Deslibes [*sic*]. The French are not so bold in their innovatory efforts as are our innovators, but on the other hand they do not go beyond the limits of the possible, like Borodin and Musorgsky.[58]

The symphony was sent from Milan, addressed to you [Nikolay Rubinstein] on Thursday morning; so it will be in your hands in three days' time. I beg you not to pronounce judgement on it before it has been performed. It is very possible that at first glance you won't like it, but don't be in a hurry to pass your final judgement; write to me with your frank impressions after the performance. I hope you won't refuse to fit it in to one of the last concerts. As far as I am concerned, I think this is one of my best compositions. Of my two most recent offspring, i.e. the opera and the symphony, I prefer the latter. In Milan I wanted to add metronome markings, but a metronome costs 23 francs and I didn't feel it was worth it. You are the only conductor in the world on whom I can depend. After the performance, when the question of publishing it arises, I will put in the metronome markings according to how it was performed. In the first movement there are some very difficult and frequent changes of tempo which I beg you to pay attention to. The third movement is all pizzicato. The faster the tempo the better it will be—but I really don't know how possible it will be to play pizzicato at a very fast tempo.[59]

Our symphony is already on its way at full steam ahead to Rubinstein in Moscow. On the title-page I have put in the dedication *to my best friend*. Has this symphony got a future? Will it survive long after its composer vanishes from the face of the earth or will it immediately fall into the abyss of oblivion? I do not know, but I do know that at this moment, perhaps with the blindness typical of some parents, I am incapable of seeing the deficiencies of my youngest infant. I am still convinced that in matters of form and finish it represents a step forward in my development, which is a very slow business. Despite my maturity in years, I still have a long way to

---

[58] vi. 328–31 (von Meck).   [59] vii. 16 (Nikolay Rubinstein).

go before reaching the point beyond which my abilities will not take me. Perhaps this is why I value life so highly.

We have arrived in Genoa where we are staying so as not to tire Kolya by travelling at night and to show my brother Modest this delightful town. Unlike me, my brother is very fond of pictures and knows something about them. I am very cheerful and in a good frame of mind.[60]

Whatever happens in this coming year [1878] it cannot possibly be worse than the one just past. So far as the present is concerned I could wish for nothing better if it were not for my unfortunate nature with its disposition to see everything bad in exaggerated terms and not to take sufficient pleasure in the present. The last few days, in Milan and Genoa and on the way here [San Remo] have been full of the happiest feelings. I am terribly fond of children. Kolya gives me no end of pleasure. It's remarkably interesting to watch such an intelligent child whose handicap has placed him in a very exceptional position.[61]

The beginning of 1878 was marked by the 'polemic' between Tchaikovsky and Taneyev about *Onegin*.

It may well be that you are right in saying that my opera is not good theatre. My reply to that would be that I don't give a damn for the theatre. It is a fact long since acknowledged that I have not got a drop of theatrical blood in me and I am little disposed to grieve over it now. If it's untheatrical then don't produce it, don't put it on. I wrote the opera because, one fine day, I felt an indescribable urge to put to music everything in *Onegin* that asks to be put to music. And that is what I did, as best I could. I worked at it with boundless enthusiasm and enjoyment, caring little about whether there was any action or stage effects. If that is what you find in your *Aida*, for instance, then I assure you that not for anything in the world could I now write an opera on such a subject: I need people, not puppets. Though it may lack powerful and surprising effects, I will gladly tackle any opera where the characters are like me and have feelings which I too have experienced and can understand. I neither know nor do I understand the feelings of an Egyptian princess, of a Pharaoh, or of a demented Nubian. Some instinct suggests to me that these people must love and speak and, in consequence, express their feelings in some altogether special way, not as we do. And so my music, which is, whatever I may think about them, saturated in Schumannism, Wagnerism, Chopinism, Glinkism, Berliozism and every other modern *ism*, has about as much in common with the characters of *Aida* as the elegant, gallant speeches of Racine's heroes, addressing each other with polite formality, have in common with our notions of the real Orestes, the real Andromache and so on. For me this sort of thing is *a lie*. And it is a lie which I find offensive. I am, incidentally, reaping the fruits of

[60] vi. 340 (von Meck).   [61] vii. 13 (von Meck).

my inadequate reading. If I knew more of various kinds of literature I would, of course, have found something which suited my taste and was theatrically effective as well. Unfortunately I can find nothing for myself and I never meet anybody who could point me towards a subject like Bizet's *Carmen* for instance—one of the most charming operas of our time. You will ask, what do I want? All right, I'll tell you! I want no emperors or empresses or popular revolts or battles or marches, in short, none of what constitutes the attributes of *grand opéra*. I am looking for an intimate but powerful drama resting on a conflict of situations which I have seen or experienced and which are capable of touching me to the quick. I am not averse to an element of fantasy because its absence of inhibitions gives unlimited scope. So, in short, Aida is so far removed from me, I am so little moved by her unhappy love for Radames, which I likewise cannot imagine, that my music would not be heart-felt, as all good music must be. I recently saw [Meyerbeer's] *L'Africaine* in Genoa. Unfortunate woman! Slavery, a dungeon, death under the poison tree, and the victory of her rival in her final moments—all this is her lot, and yet I did not feel sorry for her at all. And, incidentally, there are stage effects as well: a ship, fights, the whole bag of tricks! Well, the effects can go to hell. *Onegin* will never be a success. I know that now.[62]

I will never find artists who can even approximately meet my requirements. The staid routines of our big theatres, their senseless productions, their system of retaining old crocks and giving no openings to the young—all this makes my opera almost impossible to stage. I will not even call [it] an opera—*lyric scenes* or something like that. Yes, it is an opera without a future; I knew it when I was writing it and I wrote it all the same; I will finish it and bring it out if Jurgenson will agree to print it. Not only will I not make any efforts to have it put on at the Mariinsky Theatre, I will do all I can to stop it. I wrote it in response to an irresistible inner urge. I assure you that that is the only way one ought to write operas. Thinking and worrying about theatrical effectiveness comes into it only up to a point. Otherwise it will be effective and entertaining, possibly even beautiful or interesting but it will lack life and the power to captivate. If my fascination with the subject of *Onegin* is testimony to my limitations, my dimwittedness, my ignorance of and unfamiliarity with stage requirements, then it's a great pity but at least what I have written *literally* poured forth from me; it was not contrived or forced out.[63]

I might observe that you are not quite right in maintaining that the characters of Tatyana and Olga are presented through their monologues and dialogues and not through the action. Admittedly, their actions are very simple, ordinary, and untheatrical but all the same they both act in the only way they know how. Olga is fundamentally a very colourless girl so she has correspondingly little to do. Tatyana has more character so she has

[62] vii. 21–2 (Taneyev).   [63] vii. 22–3 (Taneyev).

correspondingly more to do. And incidentally I have already told you that
if, as you maintain, *opera is action* and there is none in *Onegin* then I am
willing to call it not an opera but what you will: scenes, a stage presentation,
a poem, whatever you like. I wanted to write a musical illustration of
Onegin; in doing this I inevitably had to resort to the dramatic form and I
am willing to take upon myself all the consequences of my notorious inability to understand the stage and of my inability to choose subjects. I think
that all the theatrical infelicities are redeemed by the charm of Pushkin's
verse. But I am apprehensive even on that score: I am referring to the sacrilegious audacity with which I have frequently been obliged to add my own,
or, in places, Shilovsky's verses to Pushkin's. That's what I am frightened
of, that's what bothers me! About the music all I can say is that if ever
music was written with genuine enthusiasm, with love for the subject and
the characters, then *Onegin* was. I languished and trembled with ineffable
delight when I was writing it. And if the listener responds to only a fraction
of what I experienced when I was writing the opera I will be well pleased
and will ask no more. Suppose *Onegin* is just a very tedious spectacle but its
music is deeply felt—that's all I want.[64]

I am doing a great deal of work. The symphony is complete and now I
am finishing off the opera. These are two big jobs which will be done by the
time I get back to Russia. About publishing the symphony: there is no need
to print it abroad. I have recently decided to publish my works exclusively
in Russia, with Jurgenson to be precise.[65]

Jurgenson has always been very generous and enterprising, and extremely considerate towards me. He willingly published my works even
before anybody had begun to pay any attention to them. So far as my
foreign reputation is concerned, it does not suffer at all from the fact that
my things are published in Russia. Jurgenson sells a lot of them abroad. In
general, I stick to the rule that there is no need to pursue foreign publishers, conductors, and so forth. I have never done anything to spread my
reputation outside Russia in the firm conviction that if I am destined to
make frequent appearances on their programmes it will happen of its own
accord. In general, one must be patient, not push oneself forward, and *not
go to them* but wait for *them to come* to us.[66]

[I have had] a letter from Rubinstein, the tone of which made me furious.
I got very excited and wrote a reply which Modest regarded as very satisfactory. How right I am not to like this man! How heartless and dry he is,
and how crazy about his role as a benefactor! It is going to be very disagreeable for me to fall under his yoke again in Moscow.[67]

Rubinstein's letter has not survived but its tone and content can be judged from
Tchaikovsky's reply.

[64] vii. 69 (Taneyev).   [65] Ibid.
[66] vii. 38–9 (von Meck).   [67] vii. 44 (Anatoly).

What you [Nikolay Rubinstein] write and *how* you write to me proves that *you know me very badly*, as I have had cause to observe many times even before this. I was again astonished by your inconceivable ignorance and misunderstanding of me in general and of my present crisis in particular. You have many times told me and others that you love me. I see no signs of affection in your letter. Everybody who really likes me took an entirely different attitude to my refusal [to be a delegate in Paris]. In your reply I could find only an attempt to make me feel that you had heaped favours on me and that I had turned out to be ungrateful, lazy, and unworthy of your kindness!!! This will get you nowhere. I know perfectly well how much I owe you but, in the first place, reproaches cool my gratitude and, in the second place, I was not at all pleased that you should see your good deeds even in places from which they are absent. I must tell you that all your *hints* about Mme von Meck could only *spoil* my relations with her and they upset her very much. I cannot refrain from saying about this lady that never have kindness, consideration, generosity, and limitless magnanimity been so perfectly united as they are in her. I owe her not only my life but also the fact that I can continue working, and for me that is more precious than life itself. It was insulting to me on her behalf that you understand her as little as you do me. She is certainly not *dotty*. She is to me simply a sort of hand of providence which never lets me down. One only has to know her as I do to be convinced that there still exist people so incomparably good and trusting. But let us move to matters in which you really have been my benefactor. Since I am completely without talent as a conductor I would, of course, never have made a name for myself if I had not had to hand such an excellent interpreter as you. If you had not existed in Russia my works would have been doomed to distortion in perpetuity. You are the only person who knows how to show my works to advantage. I now expect and ask from you for my opera and symphony that same astonishing ability instantly, by some incomprehensible, instinctual force, to learn and perform a new and difficult work after two rehearsals, without previous study. I am inseparably linked to the Conservatoire for the rest of my life for habit has brought it about that I can now live nowhere other than in Moscow and amongst you. I love you all, including you, perhaps much more than you suppose. But you have never known me or understood me. Your strange letter is a fresh demonstration of this fact.[68]

As far as Nikolay Rubinstein is concerned, you [Mme von Meck] are almost right, i.e. in the sense that he is not at all the hero that he is sometimes made out to be. He is an exceptionally gifted man, clever although not well educated, energetic, and skilful. But he is destroyed by his passion for admirers and his utterly childish weakness for all kinds of expressions of submission and servility. His administrative capabilities and his ability to get on with the powerful ones of this world are remarkable. His nature is

[68] vii. 45–6.

certainly not petty but it has become petty as a result of the senseless serv-ility and admiration which surrounds him. One must further grant him that he is honest in the best sense of the word, and unselfish: he has not busied himself with achieving narrow, material ends, and has not worked for his own gain. He has a passion for reconciling and preserving by all means in his power the inviolability of his authority. He does not tolerate any contra-dictions and if anyone dares not to agree with him over something he im-mediately suspects him of being a secret enemy. He is not above resorting to intrigue and injustice as long as he annihilates this enemy. All this is out of a fear of giving even an inch of ground from his impregnable position. His despotism is very often scandalous. He does not flinch from demon-strating his power and might over pathetic people who are incapable of standing up to him. If he meets with opposition he immediately softens and is then not averse to intriguing a bit. He does not have a particularly kind heart, although he likes to flaunt his paternal kindness and will pretend to be a kind fellow for the sake of popularity. All his faults stem from his mad passion for power and shameless despotism. But what a servant in the cause of music he has turned out to be! One can forgive him everything for the sake of these services to music. Whatever one might say about his Conser-vatoire, which is something of an alien growth in Moscow soil, it neverthe-less propagates sound musical ideas and taste. Twenty years ago Moscow was, after all, a desert as far as music was concerned. I often get angry with Rubinstein, but then when I remember how much his energetic activities have achieved, I am disarmed. Let us suppose that he has acted more than anything else for the fulfilment of his own personal ambition—all the same it is a worthy ambition. Then one must not forget that he is a superb pianist (in my opinion the greatest in Europe), and a very good conductor. My re-lationship to him is strange. When he has had something to drink he becomes nauseatingly tender towards me and accuses me of coldness, of a lack of feeling towards him. When he is normal, he is very cold towards me. He likes very much to make me feel *that I owe everything to him*. In reality he is a little afraid that the worm will turn. Because in general I am not very communicative, he sometimes imagines that I am trying to get the position of director behind his back. He has several times tried to sound out my opinion on this, and when I tell him straight out that I would rather be a beggar than director, for nothing could be more opposed to my nature than that sort of job, he is reassured, but not for long. In general, although he is naturally remarkably intelligent, he becomes blind, stupid, and naïve when he gets the idea that someone wants to take away from him his position of the most important musician in Moscow.[69]

We have returned from a delightful walk. In the hills, an hour and a half away from here there is a little town called Cola. Somehow or other I

[69] vii. 45–6 (von Meck).

walked ahead on my own, settled myself down under a tree, and suddenly felt that sublime sense of pleasure which came to me so easily in Russia, in the country, on all my walks, and which I have looked for in vain here. I was alone amidst the solemn silence of the forest. Such wonderful moments are like nothing else on earth and there is no way of describing them. A necessary condition is that one should be on one's own. I always go for walks on my own in the country. A walk with an agreeable companion has its charms but it is something entirely different. So, to put it briefly, I was utterly happy.[70]

After breakfast I took some music paper and went off alone into the hills in order to finish the duel scene, which isn't yet all written. I managed to find a spot where there were no people and worked successfully.[71]

I have been working hard at orchestrating and completing the composition of everything in the opera that had not been finished. I very much want to get this work behind me as soon as I can so as to try to spread my wings and fly somewhere a bit higher. At last I have well and truly finished the writing and orchestration. I only have to do the piano arrangement of all the new parts. I feel fine and my spirits are good and healthy. I scrutinize and observe myself with pleasure and have reached the undoubted conclusion that I have now recovered completely.[72]

Yesterday at 6.30 in the evening we returned from Nice. This trip made a very pleasant impression on me. I have always feared and disliked Nice because it is the town where all the fashionable world congregates. But this time I have quite reconciled myself to it. First, I didn't go to the places where the fashionable world promenades. Secondly, I don't know why, but in Nice the approach of spring is much more evident than it is here. Although all the travel guides say that San Remo has more favourable climatic conditions than Nice, it seemed to me that the latter was warmer and less windy. Thirdly, I have never seen such a mass of flowers as there were in Nice now. Wherever one looked, wherever one walked there were flowers everywhere and what wonderful ones they were! Now wild hyacinths have come out in the fields: they are delightful, beautiful, and sweet-smelling flowers. We went on some wonderful walks, of which I particularly liked (a) the one to the grotto of St André and (b) the one to the Château. The latter we walked to twice. I don't know whether you have visited it? It is a hill on which once stood a castle. Now they have built a terrace from where you can see an indescribably wonderful view of the whole of Nice and its surroundings. And what weather we had. It was bright, warm and joyful! The birds were twittering in the trees. Even the path itself which we walked up was delightful. How glad I was to see at last the pines, cedars, and cypresses, instead of olives, these eternal olives,

[70] vii. 49–50 (von Meck).   [71] vii. 52–3 (Anatoly).
[72] vii. 59–60 (von Meck).

which here are the only representatives of the tree kingdom. I have taken a real dislike to this olive tree. Imagine, my friend, in San Remo you can't go on a single walk, take one single step without these unbearable, disgusting trees hiding the view. Here there is not one *point de vue*; whichever way you turn, there are always olives, olives, olives. Besides the fact that they are ugly in themselves, they have a further inconvenience in that the whole year round something is being done to them: either they are loosening the soil around them, or gathering the olives from under the trees, or shaking them from the tres themselves, or pruning them, or chopping them down, so that in San Remo it is only on Sundays that one can find a quiet spot in the trees where nobody is working. Admittedly, this tree is a means of support for the inhabitants and it should be held in respect. And I do respect it but at the same time I hate it. I said earlier that the olive tree is the only representative of the forest here. This isn't strictly true because at the foot of the hill are palms, lemon trees, orange trees, and aloes! But all these are planted artificially. Forests—that is what you don't find here, i.e. places where there is somewhere to hide for dryads, nymphs, fauns, hares, and birds.[73]

I have finished the piano arrangement. Now all I have to do is put in the markings and make a clean copy of the libretto. Then the opera will be complete in all respects. But what will be its fate?[74] It seems to me that this opera is more likely to be successful in private houses and perhaps even on concert platforms than on large stages; for this reason the fact that it will be published long before going into the repertoire of the large theatres is not unfavourable. The success of the opera must begin from below and not from above i.e. it is not the *theatre* which will make it known to the public but, on the contrary, if the public gradually gets to know it, it may come to like it and then the *theatre* will put the opera on to satisfy a public demand. Perhaps I am on the wrong track but I think that with a really efficient, careful production it could even work on the stage. But for such a production all the stilted, ingrained, formal conventions would have to go and I *would have to have the right* to demand everything that I considered necessary for the proper staging of the opera. This is why I will not take the first step towards having it produced in a State theatre and will wait until they humbly ask me for it. Then I shall say: with pleasure, but if you want it you must do it like this and like this, not like that.[75] I have never written a work as easily as I did this opera and the manuscript is very clear to read in places; there are not many corrections.[75]

Tchaikovsky gave Mme von Meck the sketches for *Onegin* in the autumn of 1878. Unfortunately the manuscript is lost.

I have heard that my eldest sister Zinaida has died in Orenburg. The news

---

[73] vii. 72–3 (von Meck).   [74] vii. 80 (von Meck).
[75] vii. 97 (Jurgenson).   [76] vii. 321 (von Meck).

made me very sad although my grief was not profound or overpowering. I did not know her well and had not seen her for fifteen years. She got married when I was still in the junior class at school. Thereafter she hardly ever left the Urals where she went to live and I only saw her briefly on a couple of occasions. Even so, her death leaves in its wake a lot of sadness for those close to me. I am very apprehensive about my father. He has grown very weak of late. It is not easy to carry around one's neck the burden of eighty-three years.[77]

I have had a letter from Rubinstein in reply to mine. All these *despots* go quiet when you bare your teeth at them. They are doing my new symphony on 10 February. It will be very interesting to see what happens.[78]

It is a source of great pleasure to know that I have finished two big works in which I have, I think, made progress, and significant progress. I am in a very rosy frame of mind; I am happy that I have finished the opera, happy that spring is coming, happy that I am healthy, free, and insured against meeting people or bumping into them, and happy above all that I have such secure supports in life as your [Mme von Meck] friendship, the love of my brothers, and the knowledge that I have the ability to make progress in my chosen field. If circumstances are favourable, and I am disposed at the moment to think that they will be, I could leave something lasting behind me. I hope that this is not self-delusion but a proper awareness of my powers.[79]

I am reading Schopenhauer very slowly and thoroughly. My head is so arranged that reading philosophy comes only with difficulty.[80] In Schopenhauer's final conclusions there is something offensive to human dignity, something arid and egoistic, unwarmed by love for humanity. I was surprised that a man who did not at all put into practice his theory of strict asceticism should preach to the rest of mankind the total abnegation of all the pleasures of life. How could a man who sets such little store by human *reason*, who assigns to it such a pitiful place, such a dependent role, at the same time believe with such pride and assurance in the infallibility of his own intellect, speak with such contempt of other theories, and regard himself as the sole prophet of truth? What a contradiction! A philosopher who, like Schopenhauer, has got to the point of seeing in man nothing but the instinctive *desire* for the life of one's own race should be the first to admit the utter uselessness of all philosophizing! Whoever comes to the conclusion that the best thing is *not to live* ought himself *not to live*, so far as is possible i.e. he should take himself off and destroy himself and leave in peace those who want to live.[81]

In recollecting the whole seven weeks which I have spent here I cannot come to any other conclusion but that they have been enormously useful. Thanks to the regularity of my life, which is sometimes boring but always

[77] vii. 78–9 (von Meck).   [78] vii. 87 (von Meck).   [79] vii. 89 (von Meck).
[80] vii. 100 (von Meck).   [81] vii. 105 (von Meck).

ruled by unbroken peacefulness, but most of all thanks to time which heals all wounds, I have completely recovered from my *insanity*. I was undoubtedly a little *insane* for several months on end and only now when I am completely recovered have I learnt to regard *objectively* what I did during this short period of insanity. The man who in May took it into his head to marry Antonina Ivanovna, in June wrote a whole opera as if nothing had happened, in July got married, and in September ran away from his wife, who in September was railing against Rome, and so on—this was not me but a different Pyotr Ilich, of whom all that remains now is *misanthropy*, which, really, is hardly likely ever to leave me.[82]

We are going to Florence. I want to see whether I might like Italy now.[83] Goodbye San Remo! You were dull but good for me.[84]

[Pisa.] The cathedral, the famous leaning tower, and the no less famous Campo Santo went far beyond what I was expecting to see. The cathedral is not as massive and grandiose as in Milan but makes a very pleasant impression both inside and outside. I liked the Campo Santo with its dozens of ancient monuments, sarcophagi, and pagan urns. But the most delightfully original and beautiful thing is the Campanile. We went right to the top. The view from the top of the tower is breathtaking. However much I like the sea, I found it extraordinarily pleasant to look upon a broad landscape consisting of an endless green plain fringed by a chain of mountains on the far horizon—and no sea! And the most important thing is that there is not a single olive tree—what could be better than that? At bottom, Pisa is a proper little provincial town; the unpaved square strongly reminded me of a Russian provincial town. This gives Pisa a lot of charm. After lunch we went to Cascina, which has nothing in common with the elegant Cascine gardens in Florence. We spent a couple of hours there entirely on our own. I've had a marvellous day today! I feel so bright and cheerful![85]

[Florence.] After dinner I went for a walk around the town. How pleasant it is! And how enjoyable to be in a crowd where nobody knows you and nobody is concerned with you! Italy is beginning to make herself felt and her magical influence is gradually entering into my soul. But however much I might enjoy Italy, whatever beneficial influence she might now be exercising upon me, I nevertheless remain and always will remain faithful to Russia. I have never met anyone who was more in love than I am with Mother Russia in general and with her Great Russian features in particular. Lermontov's poem ['The Homeland'] gives a fine picture of only one side of our homeland, the indescribable charm of its modest countryside, sparse and poor but broad and expansive. I would go further. I am passionately fond of Russians, of hearing the Russian language, of the Russian cast of mind, of the beauty of the Russian face, of Russian customs. Lermontov says openly that *the sacred traditions of dark antiquity* do not stir his soul.

[82] vii. 98 (Anatoly).   [83] vii. 92 (Anatoly).
[84] vii. 100 (von Meck).   [85] vii. 102 (von Meck).

But I even love them. I think that my sympathies for Orthodoxy, the theoretical aspects of which I long ago subjected to a critique which proved fatal, are directly related to my *infatuation* for whatever is Russian. It would be vain to attempt an explanation of this *infatuation* by reference to one quality or another of the Russian people. These qualities exist, of course, but when one is infatuated one loves not because the object of one's love attracts by its virtues—but because it is in one's nature to love, because it is impossible not to love. This is why I am intensely annoyed by those gentlemen who are willing to starve to death in some place in Paris, who take a peculiar delight in abusing everything Russian, and who can, without showing the slightest sign of remorse, spend the whole of their lives abroad on the grounds that it is more comfortable and convenient than Russia. I hate such people; they trample in the mud what for me is precious and holy beyond words. I would be horrified if I were condemned to live for ever even in so marvellous a country as Italy, but a temporary stay is a different matter. The Italian countryside, the Italian climate, the wealth of artistic resources, the historical associations of every step one takes here—all this has much that is irresistibly attractive to one who seeks in his travels repose and oblivion for the passions. If one's misfortunes are far enough removed for the wound to have stopped smarting there is nowhere better finally to heal the wound than Italy.[86]

I am one of those people who like to finish a thing off at once; if I start a letter I cannot settle down until I have finished it and sent it off straight away.

You [Mme von Meck] ask me whether I have known non-Platonic love. *Yes* and *no.* If we put the question in a different way and ask whether I have known complete happiness in love then the answer is *No, no, and no again!* In any case the question is answered in my music. If you were to ask me whether I understand the full force, the immeasurable power of this feeling I would answer *Yes, yes, and yes again* and I would say yet again that my repeated efforts to express in music the torments and, at the same time, the bliss of love have themselves been efforts lovingly made. I do not know if I have succeeded or, to put it more accurately, I leave it to others to judge. I cannot agree with you at all that music *is incapable of conveying the all-embracing nature of love.* My view is quite the reverse: *that it is only music which can do this.* You say that *words* are needed. No! It is words that are exactly not what is needed and where they are powerless we find a more eloquent language taking over in the fullness of its strength: music. After all, even verse form, to which poets resort to express love, is itself a usurpation of the role which falls entirely to music. When *words* are shaped into verse they stop simply being *words*: they have been musicalized. The best proof that verses attempting to express love are more music than words is the fact

---

[86] vii. 103–4 (von Meck).

that when such poetry (consider Fet, for example, whom I like very much) is carefully read as words and not as music it makes hardly any sense at all. In fact there is not only sense in it but there is *a profound idea* as well; this idea, however, is not literary but musical. I am very glad that you place instrumental music so highly. Your remark that the words often merely spoil the music and drag it down from its remote heights is absolutely true. I have always been deeply conscious of this and perhaps it explains why I have been more successful with instrumental works than with vocal.[87]

I continue to feel very well in Florence and find the town agreeable in all respects. There are masses of flowers in the streets, even my favourite lily of the valley. The lovely sight of these beautiful flowers on my table at this very moment is enough in itself to make me love life. We made a trip out of town to a place called Bellosguardo from where there is a marvellous view over Florence and the surrounding area. From there we went on to the Carthusian monastery [the Certosa]. My goodness, how wonderful it was! To start with there is the wonderful situation of the monastery, which has marvellous views over the valley in which it stands and over the town. Then in the monastery itself there are masses of monuments of antiquity and particularly of ancient tombs. The main church is ravishingly beautiful and graceful.[88]

Nikolay Rubinstein gave the first performance of the Fourth Symphony in Moscow on 10 February 1878. Mme von Meck was at the concert. Afterwards she sent a telegram to the composer.

From the tone and wording of your telegram I can see clearly that you were pleased with the piece I wrote for you. I am still convinced to the bottom of my heart that it is the best of all that I have written. I was present at the concert in spirit: I counted the minutes until the opening phrase was due to ring forth and then followed every detail, trying to imagine what impression the music would produce. The first movement (the most complicated but the best as well) probably seemed too long to many and not altogether comprehensible at first hearing. The other movements are simple.[89]

Has this symphony got a precise programme? Usually when people ask me this question about a symphonic work I answer: '*None at all!*' And it is indeed a difficult question to answer. How can one recount those imprecise feelings which one experiences in writing an instrumental work without a precise subject? It is a purely lyrical process, a personal confession in music which boils up for a long time then, by its very nature, pours itself out in the form of sounds, just as a lyric poet expresses himself in verse. The only difference is that music has incomparably more powerful resources and a more subtle language in which to express the infinite variety of human emotion. Usually the *germ* of a new work appears suddenly and quite unexpectedly. If the ground is fertile, i.e. if one feels disposed to work, this seed

[87] vii. 103, 105–6 (von Meck).   [88] vii. 111 (von Meck).   [89] Ibid.

puts down roots with incredible strength and rapidity, starts to show above the ground, pushes up a stalk, then leaves and branches, and finally flowers. This comparison is the only way I can describe the creative process. The difficult thing is getting the germ and ensuring that this seed falls on fertile ground. All the rest happens of its own accord. There is no point in trying to describe in words the measureless bliss of the feeling which possesses me when I have the main idea and when it starts to grow into distinct shapes. You forget everything, you become almost demented, you tremble and throb inwardly, you can scarcely manage to get the sketches down as one idea piles upon another ... Sometimes in the midst of this miraculous process an external stimulus suddenly rouses you from your somnambulistic state: somebody rings at the door, a servant comes in, the clock strikes and reminds you that you have an appointment ... Such interruptions are troublesome, indescribably troublesome. On occasion inspiration vanishes for a time. One has to go in search of it, sometimes in vain. One very often has to summon to one's aid a way of working, absolutely cold and rational, which relies on technique. Perhaps this is why even in the greatest masters one can sometimes detect a lack of organic coherence, one notices the join, the parts of the whole which have been artificially stuck together. But it cannot be otherwise. If that condition of the artistic spirit known as *inspiration*, which I have just tried to describe, were to persist all the time one would not survive a single day. The strings would snap and the instrument would be shattered to smithereens! Only one thing is essential: that the main idea and the general outline of all the separate parts should not be arrived at by a process of *looking for them*, but should suggest themselves through the supernatural, inscrutable power called *inspiration*, which no one has ever explained. But I am digressing and not answering your question. There *is* a programme in our symphony, that's to say it is possible to put into words what it is trying to express. I can and I would like to indicate the meaning of the separate parts and of the whole, but to you [Mme von Meck] and you alone. Naturally I can only do this in broad terms. The introduction is the *germ* of the whole symphony, unarguably the main idea.

This is Fate, that inexorable force which prevents our aspirations to happiness from reaching their goal, which jealously ensures that our well-being and peace are not complete and unclouded, which hangs over our heads like the sword of Damocles, which with steadfast persistence poisons our souls. It is invincible, you will never master it. One can only resign oneself to fruitless sorrow.

The joyless, hopeless feeling becomes ever more powerful and fierce. Would it not be better to turn away from reality and submerge oneself in dreams?

Oh joy! there is at least a sweet and tender dream appearing! A bright and gracious human form flits by and lures us on somewhere.

How lovely! And how remote the obsessive first allegro theme now sounds! The dreams have gradually taken full possession of the soul. All that was gloomy and joyless is forgotten. Here it is, here is happiness! No! They were dreams and *Fate* rouses us from them.

So life is a constant alternation between grim reality and evanescent visions and dreams of happiness . . . There is no haven. Sail upon that ocean until it seizes you and engulfs you in its depths. That is roughly the programme of the first movement. The second movement of the symphony expresses another phase of depression: that melancholy feeling which comes on in the evening, when you are sitting on your own, tired with work, and you take up a book but it falls out of your hands. Memories come flooding in. It is sad that so much *has been and gone*; it is pleasant to recollect one's youth. One regrets the passing of time yet there is no wish to begin life anew. Life wears one out. It is pleasant to rest and reflect. There are so many memories! There have been happy moments when young blood coursed through the veins and life was good. There have also been difficult times, irreplaceable losses. But now that is all somewhere in the past. There is a sweet sadness in burying oneself in the past . . . The third movement does not express any precise feelings. These are the whimsical arabesques, the elusive images which flash across one's imagination when one has had a little wine to drink and is in the first stage of intoxication. One's spirits are not happy, but neither are they sad. One does not think about anything: one gives free rein to one's imagination, which for some reason sets about painting strange pictures . . . Amongst them one recalls a picture of some roistering peasants and a street song . . . Then somewhere in the distance a military parade goes by. There is no connection between these images which are like those which flash through your mind as you are going to sleep. They have nothing to do with reality: they are strange, wild, and incoherent . . . The fourth movement. If you find no cause for joy in yourself, look at others. Go amongst the common people and see how they know how to enjoy themselves, abandoning themselves completely to feelings of joy. Picture of a peasant celebration on a holiday. But scarcely have you managed to forget yourself and be distracted by the sight of other people's pleasures than inexorable *Fate* appears once more and reminds you of its existence. But you are no concern of anyone else. They do not even turn round, they do not glance at you, and they have not noticed that you are lonely and sad. Oh! what fun it is for them! They are so lucky that all their feelings are simple and direct. Blame yourself and do not say that all the world is sad. There are simple but potent pleasures. Enjoy other people's happiness. One can live despite everything. That, my dear friend, is all I can say by way of explaining the symphony. Of course, it is neither clear nor complete. But it is in the nature of instrumental music that it is not amenable to detailed analysis. As Heine observed: '*Where words end, music begins.*' . . . I am horrified at the obscurity and inadequacy of the programme which I am sending you. For the first time in my life I have had to recast my musical ideas and musical images in words and phrases. It was beyond me to make a good job of it. I was cruelly depressed last winter when this symphony was being written and it serves as a true echo of my experiences at that time. But it is indeed an *echo*. As to translating this into clear and precise arrangements of words—I can't do it, I don't know how to. There are also lots of things that I have forgotten: I am left only with a general recollection of the passion and terror of what I went through.[90]

My brother and I have been to the Uffizi and the Pitti Palace twice. Thanks to Modest, I have had quite a number of artistic experiences. He is simply basking in an ocean of delight over the *chef d'œuvres* of Raphael, Leonardo da Vinci, etc. We also visited a gallery of the most modern paintings and came across some outstanding things. If I am not mistaken, Italy has now been overtaken by a wave of realism in art. All the paintings by contemporary artists, which I have managed to see here, have been notable more for their amazingly realistic detail than for the profundity and poetry of the general conception. The figures are life-like, but the general idea itself is very simple: a page drawing back a curtain, moreover the page and the curtain itself are so real that you expect something to move; a Pompeian lady reclining in an ancient armchair and laughing with such Homeric laughter that you yourself want to laugh—all this has no pretence

[90] vii. 124–8 (von Meck).

at depth of ideas—but both the drawing and the colours are amazingly life-like.[91]

Tchaikovsky started work in Florence on the songs of Op. 38 and the piano pieces of Op. 40.

What a dear town Florence is. The longer you spend here the fonder you grow of it. This isn't a noisy capital in which your eyes don't know which way to look and which tires you with its bustle; at the same time, there are so many things here full of artistic and historical interest that there is no chance of being bored. We are taking our time in looking at the sights of the town, not rushing from one museum to another and from church to art gallery. Every morning we set off to see something and return home at about eleven. From eleven till one I am busy, i.e. I write small pieces.[92]

I was suddenly and quite unexpectedly seized with depression, and such a bad one that I could not drive it away all day. Scrutinizing and observing myself I soon found the cause. I had supposed that all I needed to do was start working. But what at? For a big work I need seclusion and consequently will have to wait till autumn. But there is nothing to stop me writing a whole series of little things and I made a decision to write a small piece every morning.[93] I have tried to write little pieces here in the mornings but in the first place it's somehow difficult to put one's whole heart into work when there are so many temptations about and in the second place all manner of musical sounds reverberate from morning to night. The English women in our hotel practise the piano all the time; opposite my window somebody plays trombone exercises all day; people sing and shout in the street. So far as the fortnight in Florence is concerned, it will stay in my memory as a marvellous, sweet dream. I have had so many marvellous experiences here—the town itself, its surroundings, the pictures, the marvellous spring weather, the folk-songs, the flowers—that I am weary. My nerves have gone to pieces. So it tears my heart to leave this marvellous, charming, and beautiful town and at the same time I am glad it is all coming to an end. I could never make up my mind to settle permanently in Italy and I cannot understand how people can live here all the time, how they do not languish and drown in this sea of varied impressions.[94]

I wrote to you from Florence about the boy whom I heard in the street one evening and whose wonderful voice so touched me. A couple of days ago to my indescribable joy I found this boy again; he sang 'Perche tradir mi, perche lasciar mi' to me again and I simply fainted with delight. I can't remember when such a simple folk-song ever reduced me to such a state. This time he taught me a new local song, which was so attractive that I am going to try to find him again and make him sing it several times over so that I can write down the words and the melody. It goes more or less like

91 vii. 121 (von Meck).   92 vii. 112 (von Meck).
93 vii. 112 (von Meck).   94 vii. 136–7 (von Meck).

this (someone called Pimpinella is singing—what that means I don't know but I am determined to find out):

Allegretto

How I pity that child! He is obviously being exploited by his father, his uncles, and all his relations. Now that it is carnival time he sings from morning till night and will go on singing until his voice is irreparably ruined. Compared to the first time, his voice already has a slight crack in it. This cracking adds a new charm to his phenomenally attractive voice—but it won't last.[95]

It was sad making preparations to leave. Florence had become my favourite amongst all foreign towns.[96]

How endlessly far away we are [Mme von Meck] from each other. You are in the middle of winter and I am in a country where the leaves are already coming out and where I am writing at an open window at eleven in the evening! And yet I think of that winter with both revulsion and love. I

[95] vii. 132 (von Meck).   [96] vii. 137 (Anatoly).

love our long, stubborn winters. You wait and wait for the coming of Lent which brings with it the first signs of spring. But on the other hand how magical is our spring, with its suddenness, its luxuriant vigour. How I love it when the melting snow runs through the streets and there is a life-giving and exhilarating feeling in the air. How lovingly is the first blade of grass welcomed! How glad we are to see the rooks flying in and behind them the skylarks and other summer visitors from overseas! Here spring approaches softly, gradually, so that you cannot accurately pin-point the moment of its arrival. And how can I be moved by the sight of green grass when even in December and January it was still to be seen.[97]

Tchaikovsky and his travelling-companions left for Clarens on 23 February.

I can imagine nowhere (outside of Russia) which is better suited than Clarens to calming the spirits. One never tires of gazing at the deep blue of the lake, fringed by mountains.[98] I have ordered a piano for myself [in Clarens] and would like to spend some time making music. Since I left Russia, apart from playing duets once or twice in Vienna, I have not touched a piano.[99]

May I say something about your wish to continue providing for my financial needs after I get back to Russia? I am not at all ashamed to receive such assistance from you and my pride does not suffer a scrap; the knowledge that I am indebted to you for everything will never weigh upon me. The constraints which affect most human relationships do not apply to us. In my own mind I have set you so far above the normal level of humanity that the *delicacies* of the usual sort of association between two people are incapable of troubling me. In accepting from you the means by which I can live a peaceful and happy life, I experience nothing but love, the most direct, spontaneous feeling of gratitude, and a burning desire to bring about your happiness by all the means in my power.[100]

Nadezhda Filaretovna! I must tell you once and for all that I will accept from you whatever you may wish to offer without any pretence of shame. I have only one request: that you should never look after me to your own disadvantage. I know that you are rich, but then richness is a very relative thing! A great ship asks deep waters.[101]

Lord! how grateful I should be to this marvellous woman and how much I fear starting *to take for granted* as my due all she does for me! I will never, never be able *to prove* the sincerity of my gratitude.[102]

I am deeply distressed, offended, and surprised by the incomprehensible silence of my Moscow friends about the symphony. So far I have had news about it only from you [Mme von Meck] and, indirectly, from Kotek. I expected that this symphony would at least interest my musical friends even if it did not move them or astound them. I had expected that they would realize how impatiently and eagerly I was waiting for a sympathetic

[97] vii. 131.   [98] vii. 140 (von Meck).   [99] vii. 136–7 (von Meck).
[100] vii. 141 (von Meck).   [101] vii. 142.   [102] vii. 145 (Anatoly).

response from them. I do not want their raptures but a degree of friendly attention. When you have put your heart into writing a major work and know in advance that amongst the hundreds who hear it there will be few who appreciate even the half, you can only console yourself with the thought that your friends will understand and appreciate it and will encourage you. Then you hear not a word from them. This is hurtful and offensive beyond all measure![103]

It is exceedingly pleasant for me to talk to you [Mme von Meck] about the way in which I compose. As it happens I have never before revealed these mysterious manifestations of the spiritual life to anyone, partly because so few have asked, partly because those who have asked have not inspired me to want to give a proper reply. But to talk to you about the details of the composing process is especially pleasant because I have found in you a spirit which responds with the utmost sensitivity to my music. Do not believe those who try to convince you that musical creation is a cold and rational business. The only music which can move you, grip you, touch you is that which pours from the depths of an artistic soul stirred by inspiration. There is no doubt at all that even the greatest geniuses of music sometimes wrote without the fire of inspiration. This guest does not always come at the first invitation. However, one must always *work* and the true, honest artist cannot sit twiddling his thumbs on the pretext that he is not in the right mood. If you just wait for the right mood and make no attempt to go and find it, you can easily become *lethargic* and *apathetic*. You have to be patient and have trust, and inspiration will invariably come if you can conquer your *wrong mood*. I do not think that you will suspect me of self-adulation if I say that I am very rarely afflicted with these *wrong moods*. I attribute this to the fact that I am well endowed with patience and have taught myself never to give way to *disinclination*. I have learnt to conquer myself. I am glad that I did not follow in the footsteps of my Russian brethren who suffer from a lack of self-confidence and have no powers of endurance; at the slightest obstacle they prefer to postpone matters and have a rest. This is why, despite their great gifts, they write so little and in such a dilettante way. You ask me how I approach the question of orchestration. I never compose in the abstract, that's to say musical ideas always come to me complete with their external form. This means that the musical idea itself is worked out simultaneously with the orchestration. Consequently, when I was writing the *Scherzo* of our symphony I imagined it exactly as you heard it. It is inconceivable played any way other than pizzicato. If you bow it, then it loses absolutely everything. It would be a soul without a body; the music would lose all its attraction. So far as the Russian *element* in my works is concerned, I can tell you that it has not infrequently happened that I have set about composing with the direct intention of working up some folk-song or other to which I have taken a liking. Sometimes (as, for

[103] vii. 148–9 (von Meck).

instance in the Finale of our symphony) this happens of its own accord, quite unexpectedly. So far as the Russian element in general is concerned in my music, i.e. the melodic and harmonic devices akin to folk-song, this occurs because I grew up in the wilds and was steeped from my earliest childhood in the indescribable beauty of Russian folk music with all its special characteristics, because I am passionately fond of the Russian element in all its manifestations, because, to put it briefly, I am a *Russian* in the fullest sense of the word.[104]

I slept well. We went for a walk. I set to work again without enthusiasm, forcing myself. I don't know and cannot understand why I *don't feel like* working when the conditions are so favourable. Have I dried up? I have to squeeze out of myself weak and paltry little ideas and ponder over every single bar. But I shall achieve what I am aiming for and I hope that inspiration will awaken in me again.[105]

I am very busy with the sonata and the concerto. It's the first time in my life that it has fallen to my lot to start a new piece without finishing the preceding one. So far I have always strictly adhered to the rule of never starting on a new piece of work until the old was finished. The way it worked out this time was that I could not resist the desire to sketch out parts of the concerto, got carried away, and left the sonata on one side. However, I am gradually returning to it.[106]

The Grand Sonata in G major for piano and the Concerto for Violin and Orchestra in D major.

I do not know how to thank you, my dear, for the volumes of verse which you sent me. I am particularly pleased with the Tolstoy, of which I am very fond and, quite apart from my intention to use some of his texts for songs, I will look forward to rereading many of his longer works. Amongst them I am particularly interested in *Don Juan*. The passage which you have marked from *Don Juan* is delightful and I will certainly set it to music.[107] I have greatly enjoyed rereading a lot of Tolstoy. He is not a first-class talent or a genius but he is not without a certain individuality and originality, and is always elegant. I was never very fond of Nekrasov. I can never forget that Nekrasov—this defender of the weak and oppressed, this democrat, indignantly scornful of lordliness in all its aspects—in fact lived well and truly like a lord himself.[108] It is very difficult to find texts to set in Nekrasov. Despite all my lack of enthusiasm for his work I cannot, of course, deny his talent. I like 'Frost the Red-Nosed'; 'The Forgotten Village' is a *chef d'œuvre* of its kind. But there is no material here for music. This is really very significant. *Verse* and *music* are fundamentally so close to each other![109]

An excerpt from A. K. Tolstoy's *Don Juan*, 'Don Juan's Serenade'. (Op. 38 No. 1)

[104] vii. 154–5.   [105] vii. 151 (Anatoly).   [106] vii. 159 (von Meck).
[107] vii. 161. This concerns the poet, Alexey Tolstoy.
[108] vii. 168 (von Meck).   [109] vii. 198 (von Meck).

Tchaikovsky wrote two works to texts by Nekrasov: a choral setting for the jubilee of O. A. Petrov in 1875 ('With heartfelt emotion') and the song 'Forgive!' (Op. 60 No. 8) of 1886.

What wonderful days we have been having! Straight after two weeks of bad weather spring arrived in all its loveliness. The sun shines brightly and gives out warmth, the trees are coming into bud and a mass of meadow flowers have appeared and, to crown it all, moonlit nights. I cannot tell you, my friend, how much I am enjoying all this. I feel so well, I am so peaceful, content with myself because of working successfully, my health is so wonderful, there is so little to be alarmed at or feel threatened by in the future, that I can boldly call my present condition happiness. Could I, in view of this, forget to whom I am beholden for all this, and who is the cause of my being able to breathe freely, of my being able, in spite of Schopenhauer, to be filled every minute of the day with a sense of the joy of life and love of nature? As I am a little superstitious, and since I remember that not very long ago happiness seemed to me to be altogether unattainable, I am sometimes afraid and the realization of the precariousness of happiness flashes through my mind with the speed of lightning; but then I remember you, and my soul becomes joyful and calm again.[110]

The first movement of the Violin Concerto is finished already. From the first moment that the right frame of mind came to me it has never left me. With one's inner life in this condition composing ceases altogether to be work: it becomes unalloyed pleasure. While you are writing you do not notice how time passes and if no one came to interrupt you you would sit there and never leave your work all day. But I am not deviating from my established routine and, thanks to the marvellous weather, our afternoon walks have been very extensive and remarkably pleasant.[111]

The best moments of my life are those when I can see that my music strikes deep into the heart of those I love and whose sympathy means more to me than fame and success with the public at large. I must tell you [Mme von Meck] that you are the one person whom I love with all my heart because I have never met anyone in my life whose feelings were, like yours, so close, so akin to my own, who responded so sensitively to my every thought, to every beat of my heart.[112] The concerto is getting on well. I have already reached the Finale and it will soon be finished.[113]

It was at this time that Tchaikovsky had some good news from Moscow.

Rubinstein is going to play my concerto. It is one of my favourite progeny! I would very much like to think that you [Mme von Meck] would be present on that evening to hear my concerto.[114] Is it not true that you can

[110] vii. 164 (von Meck).   [111] vii. 164–5 (von Meck).   [112] vii. 169.
[113] vii. 175.   [114] vii. 162.

hear the music better from a platform seat than from down below amongst the elegant audience, whose last interest is the music?[115] I was quite sure that he [Rubinstein] would play it splendidly. That concerto was really written for him and it counts upon his immense powers as a virtuoso.[116]

It was very pleasant for me to find in your letter a new proof of our intellectual kinship. Your opinion about our government coincides exactly with mine. Like you, I am a great supporter of our dynasty, I love the tsar with all my heart, and I feel great sympathy towards his heir; like you I am distressed at the way the government rules, which is the source of all the weakness, the dark sides of our political development. Without going into specific details, I will take the treasury. It is so obvious that if our fiscal affairs were managed by national representatives, Russia's credit would not be so low in the European markets. What enormous steps forward would national education be able to take if we ourselves were allowed to be involved with the problem! How Russia would be revived if the tsar ended his remarkable reign by giving us our political rights. Let no one say that we are not ready for constitutional forms. After all people said that we were not ready for judicial reform. When the judicial reforms were introduced how often did we hear complaints that there were no prosecuting or defence lawyers! However both appeared. Both representatives and voters will be found.[117]

Mme von Meck did not like Mozart and expressed this opinion to Tchaikovsky. He put up a spirited defence of his idol.

I do not merely like Mozart—I worship him. For me the best opera ever written is *Don Giovanni*. It is true that Mozart does not thrill us so profoundly as does Beethoven, that his range is not so broad; he was a carefree child to the end of his life so his music lacks the element of personal tragedy which we feel with such power and strength in Beethoven. However, this did not prevent him from creating an impersonally tragic character, the most powerful, the most striking human type ever portrayed in music. I refer to *Donna Anna* in *Don Giovanni*. I simply cannot tell you how I feel at a performance of *Don Giovanni* when Donna Anna makes her majestic appearance on stage, proud, beautiful, and vengeful. There is nothing in opera which affects me so powerfully. When Donna Anna recognizes in Don Giovanni the man who has not only injured her pride but has actually killed her father, when the raging torrent of her fury finally bursts forth in a brilliant recitative and then in that miraculous aria where fury and pride are in every chord, in every note from the orchestra, I shudder with horror and could cry out and weep, so overpowering is the effect. Her lament over her father's body, the duet with Don Ottavio, where she vows vengeance, her arioso in the big sextet in the graveyard—these are unscalable peaks of the

[115] vii. 165.   [116] vii. 179.   [117] vii. 173 (von Meck).

operatic art. I so love the music of *Don Giovanni* that at this very moment as I write to you I could weep from emotion and excitement. I cannot discuss it calmly. In Mozart's chamber music it is the charm and purity of the style which captivates, the astonishing beauty of the way in which the parts are woven together. But sometimes one comes upon things which bring tears to the eyes. Think of the Adagio of the G minor Quintet. No composer has ever expressed so beautifully the feeling of resigned and helpless grief. When Laube used to play that Adagio I always hid in the remotest corner of the room so that no one should see how the music affected me. He was a marvellous, irreproachable, infinitely good, angelically pure person. He was the embodied ideal of the great artist, creating in response to the involuntary urgings of his genius. He wrote music as the nightingale sings i.e. without reflection, without constraint. And how easily he composed! He never wrote draft sketches. The power of his genius was so great that he wrote all his works straight off in score. He put the finishing touches to them in his head down to the last detail. Difficulties simply did not exist for him. The purity of his soul was untarnished. He bore neither grudges nor ill-will, nor was he envious and I think that all this can be heard in his music, which by its very nature spreads calm and light and tenderness.[118] There is something else I wanted to say about Mozart. You say that my adoration of him is in contradiction with my musical character. But perhaps it is precisely because as a man of my times I am broken and morally sick that I so love to seek peace and consolation in Mozart's music, which for the most part serves to express the joys of life as experienced by a healthy, wholesome nature, uncorrupted by introspection. I think that in general an artist's creative spirit and ability are quite independent of his sympathies for one master or another. One can like Beethoven, for instance, but be nearer in character to Mendelssohn. What could be more contradictory than Berlioz the composer i.e. an extreme manifestation of ultra-romanticism in music, and Berlioz the critic, who made Gluck his idol and placed him above all other composers of opera? The absence of any kinship of character between two artistic personalities does not exclude their mutual sympathy.[119]

I have finished the concerto. I have to copy it out yet, play it through a few times (with Kotek, who is still here) and then orchestrate it.[120]

Do not concern yourself, my dear [Mme von Meck], about my reputation abroad. If it is my destiny to achieve such a reputation it will come of its own accord, although it is very probable that it will only come when I have gone. Taking into account that on my numerous trips abroad I have never paid any visits at all to the bigwigs and have not thrust my works upon them, and that I have never made any attempt to get myself better known abroad, one must be satisfied with such minor successes as my

[118] vii. 179–81.   [119] vii. 213.   [120] vii. 182.

pieces have achieved. All my piano works are printed in pirated editions in Leipzig, and all my songs have been translated and printed in Germany, excellently moreover. I don't know about the small towns but there is no difficulty about obtaining any of my major works (apart from the operas) in the big towns, at least in Germany, France, and England. So far as the extremely rare foreign performances of my orchestral pieces are concerned, there are many explanations. In the first place, I am a Russian and in that capacity I inspire prejudice in every Westerner. In the second place, again in my capacity as a Russian, I have in my music an element alien to Western Europe which is not to the taste of foreigners. In musical circles abroad they do know, of course, that I exist. There is no doubt that if I travelled around all the capitals of Europe thrusting my works on the *bigwigs* I could assist the spread of my reputation. But I would sooner deny myself all the pleasures of life than do that. Lord! What humiliations one would have to suffer, what bogus declarations of respect and affection one would have to make, what indescribable damage to one's self-respect—all to secure the attention of these gentlemen. Take an example. Suppose I want to ensure my reputation in Vienna. I must, in consequence, visit Brahms. Brahms is a celebrity, and I am a nonentity. Yet without false modesty I have to say that I think I am better than Brahms. What am I to say to him? 'I do not rate you at all highly and regard you with the greatest condescension. But I need you and so I have come to you!' If, however, I am dishonest and untruthful, then I will say the exact opposite. I can do neither the one thing nor the other. I have a reputation for being modest. My modesty is in fact concealed pride; great, very great pride. Amongst all living musicians there is not one before whom I would willingly bow my head. Yet nature, which has so filled my soul with pride, has not endowed me with the skill and ability to show myself at my best. I am morbidly shy, perhaps from an excess of pride. Since I cannot go out to meet my fame and acquire it by my own initiative, I prefer to wait for it to come to me. I have long since got used to the idea that I will not live to see any general recognition of my abilities. Fame will come slowly, quietly but surely, if I am destined to be favoured by it. History shows that very often when fame is slow to come it is more secure than when it appears all at once and is easily attained. How many names which resounded in their time have now sunk into the abyss of oblivion! I do not think that an artist should be troubled by inadequate recognition from his contemporaries. He must toil at expressing all that he was predestined to express. He should know that a true and just verdict can be reached only by history. Perhaps I accept my modest allocation of fame so indifferently because of my unshakeable faith in the just verdict *of the future*. I am, in my lifetime, savouring in advance the delights of that portion of fame which the history of Russian art will accord to me. I am entirely happy with what I have achieved. I have no cause for complaint. I have in my life met people whose ardent enthusiasm for my music sufficiently rewards me for the indifference, the incomprehension or the ill-will of others.[121]

I have finished copying out the first movement of the concerto and have played it. Modest and Kotik [Kotek] are both in raptures. I was very pleased with the ovation they gave me.[122] I was not satisfied with the Andante when he played it on the violin and I will either revise it radically or write a new one. The Finale, if I am not mistaken, is as successful as the first movement.[123] I have written a new *Andante* which satisfies both of my severe but sympathetic critics.[124] [It] fits better with the two neighbouring movements of the concerto. The first one makes an independent violin piece which I will put with the two other violin pieces which I plan. They will make a separate *opus*.[125]

The original Andante of the Violin Concerto appears under the title of Méditation in the group of violin pieces Op. 42, *Souvenir d'un lieu cher*.

Tchaikovsky received a letter from Taneyev with his views on the Fourth Symphony and entered into a polemical exchange with his pupil.

I really do not understand what you mean by ballet music and why you cannot accept it. Do you mean by ballet music any cheerful tune with a dance rhythm? In that case you ought not to accept most of Beethoven's symphonies where you constantly meet that sort of thing. Are you trying to say that the trio in my Scherzo is written in the style of Minkus, Gerber, and Pugno? But I don't think it deserves that. In fact I cannot understand at all how the expression *ballet music* can include an element of *disapproval*. Ballet music is not all bad, you know; there are some good things. (Delibes's *Sylvia*, for instance.) And if it's good, does it make any difference whether Sobeshchanskaya dances to it or not? All the same I do not understand why a dance tune should not occasionally appear in a symphony, even if only with the deliberate intention of adding a touch of vulgar, rough humour. Take Beethoven again: he used this effect more than once. And I would also add that I am racking my brains to no purpose in an attempt to think of what balletic features you could have found in the middle section of the Andante. That remains a complete mystery to me. So far as your remark that my symphony is programmatic is concerned, I agree entirely. But what I cannot see is why you should regard this as a failing. I fear the opposite, that's to say I would not want my pen to produce symphonic works which expressed nothing and were merely an empty play of chords, rhythms, and modulations. Of course my symphony is programmatic but the programme is such that it cannot possibly be formulated in words. That would provoke ridicule and would have a comic effect. But is this not what a symphony should be i.e. the most lyrical of all musical forms? Should it not express everything for which there are no words but which struggles

[121] vii. 186–9.   [122] vii. 191 (Anatoly).   [123] vii. 192 (Anatoly).
[124] vii. 194 (Anatoly).   [125] vii. 196 (von Meck).

from the heart in search of expression? Incidentally, I admit that in my naïvety I had thought that the idea of this symphony was easy to understand, that its sense could be grasped in broad outline even without a programme. And please don't think I'm trying to put myself forward as a source of deep emotions and great ideas which lie beyond words. I was not even trying to express any new ideas. Fundamentally, my symphony is an imitation of Beethoven's Fifth; that's to say that I imitated the basic conception and not the musical ideas. Do you think that the Fifth Symphony has a programme? Not only does it have a programme but there can be no argument about what it is trying to express. Much the same thing forms the basis of my symphony and if you have not understood it all it means is that I am not Beethoven, about which fact I have never been in any doubt. I would add, moreover, that there is not a single phrase in that symphony (i.e. mine) which is not deeply felt, which is not the echo of some sincere emotion. The only exception is perhaps the middle of the first movement where there are tensions and joins and glueing together; in short, *artificiality*.[126]

I will not try to make up my mind whether a stupid man can possess creative talent, though I do think that the answer would be yes rather than no. But after all, possessing talent—the blind, unexplained power of instinct—is nothing special. One must be able to direct one's talent in the appropriate way. For this reason I am inclined to think that in the end a talented but stupid individual will not get very far.[127]

I have recently had a number of very pleasant reports about my works. *Francesca* was a great success in Petersburg; and Rubinstein performed the concerto with equal success. Bülow played my variations in Dresden with great success.[128] I was very interested to hear about *Francesca*. It wasn't Cui's idea that the first theme is like a Russian song. I told him about it last year. If I hadn't he would never have noticed. The comment that I wrote this under the influence of *The Nibelungs* is *very true*. I felt it myself when I was working on it. If I am not mistaken, it is particularly apparent in the introduction. Is it not strange that I should be subject to the influence of a work of art which in general I find very antipathetic?[129]

Francesca was performed on 11 March. Nikolay Rubinstein played the First Piano Concerto on 16 February. Bülow played the F major Theme and Variations for piano from Op. 19.

You [Taneyev] won't believe how pleased I am that you like *Onegin*. I value your opinion *very, very highly*. And the more frankly you express it the more valuable will it be; don't be frightened of being *blunt*. A blunt expression of the truth is exactly what I want from you; whether it is favourable or unfavourable is neither here nor there.[130]

[126] vii. 200 (Taneyev).   [127] vii. 189 (von Meck).   [128] vii. 205 (Taneyev).
[129] vii. 201 (Taneyev).   [130] vii. 202.

I have finished the Violin Concerto and have played it here many times. On every occasion it has produced a unanimous or, more accurately, duanimous furore because the audience, consisting of Modest and Kotek, sings me hymns of praise in unison after the concert. Kotek assures me that it is not at all difficult.[131] in 1877 I wrote a violin concerto which was dedicated to Leopold Auer. I don't know whether Mr Auer was flattered by my dedication, but in spite of his sincere feelings of friendship towards me, he never wanted to overcome the difficulties of this concerto, and considered that it was awkward to play; such a verdict by this authoritative Petersburg virtuoso relegated my unhappy offspring for many years to an abyss of irretrievable oblivion or so it seemed.[132] At my brother's request I played through *Onegin* from the manuscript drafts. I was very pleased indeed to see that Tatyana's letter scene made a strong impression on him.[133]

We are spending our last days in Switzerland.[134] Looking back over the whole six weeks that we have spent here I must say that, despite the bad weather, they leave me with the happiest memories. The company of my brother and his pupil, the peace, the opportunity to work without any interruption—oh, how I value it all![135]

Leaving foreign countries behind and on the eve of my return to Russia as a perfectly sound and healthy man, full of new powers and energy, I must thank you [Mme von Meck] again, my good and invaluable friend, for all that I owe you and which I will never, never forget.[136]

On the title-page of the symphony must appear: *Dedicated to my best friend.*[137]

[131] vii. 203 (Jurgenson).   [132] *MC* 340.   [133] vii. 205 (von Meck).
[134] vii. 208 (von Meck).   [135] vii. 214.   [136] vii. 220.
[137] vii. 204 (Jurgenson).

12

1878

Inspiration is a guest who does not like visiting the lazy.

My expectations were not fulfilled. I had thought that my emotions on crossing the frontier into Russia would be sweet and powerful. But no! Nothing of the sort. Quite the contrary. The coarse and drunken gendarme would not let us through for a long time because he could not work out whether the number of passports which I handed over corresponded to the number of travellers. The customs official and the porters who smashed our trunks up, the officer of gendarmerie who looked at me suspiciously and interrogated me for a long time before making up his mind to return my passport; the dirty trains, meeting an enormous hospital train full of typhoid patients, the hordes of soldiers, just young lads, travelling on our train, and, of course, at every station the scenes as they parted from mothers and wives—this all poisoned my pleasure in seeing that native country which I love so much.[1]

All the charm of living here consists in the high moral qualities of the people at Kamenka i.e. of the whole Davydov family. Alexandra Ivanovna Davydova, the old lady who is head of the family, is one of those rare manifestations of human perfection which repay with interest the many disappointments which it is our lot to experience in encounters with other people. Incidentally, she is the last living representative of those Decembrist wives who followed their husbands to Siberia. What she bore and suffered there in the first years of staying in various places of detention with her husband is truly dreadful. On the other hand, she took with her consolation and even happiness for her husband. I have the greatest affection and respect for this venerable person. All her children belong likewise to the most select representatives of the human race. So, living in daily contact with a large number of good people is very agreeable.[2] My sister and her husband are a living confutation of the view that there are no absolutely happy marriages. Their happiness is so perfect that one sometimes becomes afraid for them. What if fate is preparing for them one of those surprises which sometimes come like a bolt from the blue in the form of illness, death, and so on?[3]

---

[1] vii. 221 (von Meck).   [2] vii. 235 (von Meck).   [3] vi. 167 (von Meck).

What a joy it is to be an artist! In a sad period like the one we are now
going through only art can distract our attention from unpleasant reality.
When I sit at the piano in my little cottage I am completely isolated from all
the tormenting questions which weigh us down. Is this perhaps egoistic?
But then each of us serves the general good in his own way; and art is, in my
view, an essential requirement for humanity. Outside of the musical sphere
I am incapable of being of service to my neighbour.[4]

The days go by in a steady, unchanging sequence. I find this way of life
very beneficial and calming. I am doing a very adequate amount of work.
The sonata is completely finished already. I have also finished twelve pieces
of moderate difficulty for piano solo; of course all this is just in draft. I am
starting on a collection of miniatures for children. I have long since had the
notion that it would be no bad thing to do what I could to enrich the repertoire of music for children, which is very sparse. I want to write a whole
series of small pieces, very easy indeed, with titles that would be attractive
to children, like Schumann's. Then I will set about some songs, some violin
pieces, and, if my favourable frame of mind continues, I would like to try to
do something for church music. I can see certain merits in Bortnyansky,
Beryozovsky, and so forth, but their music is so utterly out of harmony
with the Byzantine style of the architecture and the icons, with the whole
structure of the Orthodox service. It could well be that I will decide to set
to music the entire Liturgy of St John Chrysostom. I would like to write an
opera. Rummaging in my sister's library I chanced upon Zhukovsky's
Undine and I reread this tale which I was tremendously fond of when I was
a child. The subject is now starting to attract me again and I have asked
Modest to draw up a scenario.[5]

At the invitation of Mme von Meck Tchaikovsky spent some time at her estate of
Brailov in the Ukraine.

Taking advantage of the permission you gave me to have free rein in how I
use my time, I asked Marcel to give me lunch at one, and at nine in the
evening, tea and some sort of cold meal. I very much like this arrangement.
It gives one the chance to devote oneself to enjoying nature during the
hours of the day best for walking, i.e. from five until nine, without an over-
full stomach. In the mornings I will do a little work and walk in the garden;
after lunch until four I will read, write letters, play, etc. and after supper I
will again occupy myself with music, look through your countless albums
and in general devote myself to *dolce far niente*. In general I am happy; I am
deeply grateful to you for the prospect of these wonderful days.[6]

How pleasant and free it is here! The sun had already set and in the broad
meadow in front of the main entrance the scorching heat of the day had

---

[4] vii. 239 (von Meck).   [5] vii. 238 (von Meck).   [6] vii. 255 (von Meck).

given way to the cool of the evening. The air bore the scent of lilac and of the hay that they had been cutting somewhere. The may-bugs broke the silence with a bass note, the nightingales sang, and a song came from far away. Before I went to bed I sat for a long time in front of the open window, breathing in the marvellous, fresh air, listening to all the sounds of a spring night, the charms of which could not be spoilt even by the angry croaking of the frogs.[7] My life at Brailov has already assumed a steady, regular course. After coffee in the morning I go for a walk in the garden and when I have been right round I go through some little wooden gates, go on across a ditch and then, not far in front of me, there opens out a garden which has run wild and has turned into a delightful, quiet, cosy little spot; it is populated by every kind of avian inhabitant and the call of the oriole and the trilling of the nightingale stand out as the most attractive sounds. In places the paths have grown over so thickly, and the greenery is so fresh and clean that you could imagine you were in the depths of a forest. I first go for a walk here and then I sit down somewhere in heavy shade and spend about an hour like that. There is nothing to compare with these moments of isolation, surrounded by greenery and flowers, when you sit listening and observing that organic life which, though it may manifest itself silently, noiselessly, yet speaks louder of infinity in time and space than the rumble of the roads and all the bustle of town life. When I have been abroad, amongst all the striking and luxuriant beauties which nature provides in the south, I have never experienced these moments of holy rapture in the contemplation of nature which are higher even than the delights of art. I like open places at sunset and the meadow [in front of the house], with trees, lilac bushes, and the stream at its edge, makes a charming evening walk. What a marvellous life! It must be some sort of dream, a reverie![8] Unforgettable, marvellous days.[9]

I have found a considerable quantity of mushrooms, which are one of my greatest pleasures in the summer. All night I dreamt of enormous, fat, red mushrooms. When I woke up it struck me that these mushroomy dreams were very childish. And indeed, when one lives alone with nature, one does develop a childlike receptivity to the simplest, most guileless joys which it offers. Yesterday, for instance, it gave me the greatest delight to spend it must have been about an hour by the path in the garden watching how a snail got in amongst a tiny bunch of ants. Even when living entirely on one's own, I do not understand how anybody could be bored in the country for a single moment. Surely there is more interest in that little scene, which shows in microscopic form the whole tragedy of the conflict amongst so many individuals, than in the vacuous chatter, the pathetic and pointless flapping about which is the essence of how most of society spends its time.[10]

[7] vii. 260, 261 (von Meck).   [8] vii. 267, 268, 269 (von Meck).
[9] vii. 280 (von Meck).   [10] vii. 277 (von Meck).

Because of my love for order and routine, my life here is as securely established as if I had been living here for years.[11]

I chanced on a book which attracted me very much. It was the memoirs of Okhotsky, published by Krashevsky and very well translated by someone into Russian.* You, my friend, know about my unquenchable passion for everything to do with the eighteenth century. These memoirs have presented me with a lot of new things of interest, for I did not know much about *daily life* in Polish society in the last century. I don't know whether you have read the whole of this book? It is written in a remarkably lively way, in a style that is naïvely truthful and sincere, giving the facts and information it imparts much reality and at the same time a certain warmth and vivacity. By the way, in Part Two there is a page which touches on the history of Brailov.[12]

I am starting on a collection of children's pieces, then I will copy out the Mass, and after that I will gradually get round to planning something new and big. I have turned cool towards *Undine* for some reason or other. I would like to find a more deeply gripping subject for an opera. What do you [Mme von Meck] think about Shakespeare's *Romeo and Juliet*? It has, admittedly, been used many times already as a basis for operas and orchestral works, but it is a tragedy of inexhaustible riches. When I reread it I was somehow immediately attracted to the idea of an opera which would retain the development of the plot as it is in Shakespeare, without all the deviations and additions you find in Berlioz and Gounod.[13]

All objections vanish when confronted by the enthusiasm with which the subject has fired me. It will be my most important work. I could laugh when I think that I have not realized before that it is as if I was made to set this play to music. There could be nothing better suited to my musical personality. There are no emperors, no marches, none of what constitutes the routine trappings of grand opera. But there is love, love, love. And then the secondary characters are so attractive: the nurse, Tybalt, and Mercutio. Please don't worry [Modest] about monotony. The first love duet will be quite different from the second. In the first all is bright and clear: love, untroubled love. In the second: tragedy. Romeo and Juliet were carefree children, revelling in their love; now they have become *people*, who love and suffer because of the tragedy of the situation in which they are trapped. How keen I am to get on with it![14]

I have played through almost the whole of *Eugene Onegin*! The composer was also the only listener. I'm ashamed to admit it, but all right, I'll tell you as a secret. The music brought tears of delight to the listener's eyes and he

---

* The memoirs of Jan Duklan Okhotsky up to the year 1783, published as *Recollections of Jan Duklan Okhotsky with the manuscript he left rewritten and edited*, 4 vols. (Vilno, 1857). Russian trans., *Tales of Ancient Poland*, 2 vols. (St Petersburg, 1873) [trans.].

[11] vii. 281 (Modest).   [12] vii. 282 (von Meck).
[13] vii. 336 (von Meck).   [14] vii. 281–2 (Modest).

said all manner of nice things to the composer. Oh, if only everybody else who hears this music in the future could be as moved by it as was the composer![15] I spent a long time walking about the garden, saying farewell to it. I am *very, very, very* sad to leave Brailov. One always regrets what passes and when it has been as good as the days spent at Brailov its passing is painful. There was lilac here—and now nothing remains of it! There were good days and they passed; when will they return???[16]

After leaving Brailov Tchaikovsky briefly went to Moscow on business.

I somehow felt quite insufferably weighed down after my trip to Moscow. My meetings with Rubinstein were unpleasant. The vague sense of being out of sympathy with him which had taken root in me managed to grow into quite an excruciating feeling of hostility. It is difficult for me to analyse this psychic phenomenon. It could be felt most acutely during our tête-à-têtes. Something awkward occurred when we were alone together. I could read in his eyes that he was not at all well disposed towards me and that it was only circumstances which compelled him to wear a mask of friendship. In general he does not like people who do not regard themselves as his beneficiaries. So, in short, he does not like me and either could not or would not conceal the fact. And in general, whether it was because it was summer and Moscow is so stuffy, and dusty, and horrible, or whether it was because the recollection of my moral torments early last autumn is still too fresh, whether it was because at every turn I had to go through the same inevitable little farce when I met people who were fishing about for some expression of joy—for whatever reason, the two and a half days I spent there were like two months of torture. And yet I love Moscow and would not wish to live anywhere else, at least not in any other town.[17]

From Moscow Tchaikovsky went to see Kondratyev at Nizy in the Kharkov province. Then he went via Kiev to Kamenka.

I read in the papers the news about the army train colliding with the goods train on the Elets line, where there were fatalities, seriously injured etc. I must tell you that during my last trips I came across an enormous number of military trains. I don't mind admitting to you that the sight of these poor people being conveyed like sheep in goods trucks for days on end, badly fed and badly clothed, distressed me each time I saw them. I talked to many of them and could not listen to their descriptions of their journey without anger. One reserve regiment which I met in Konotop had been travelling for nine days. They have nothing to eat but bread, and that only if the sellers happen to be out on the station platform. The crowding and the stuffiness in the carriages is unbearable. They have no idea where they are going or why, and are unspeakably bored from the inactivity and

[15] vii. 285–6 (Modest).   [16] vii. 289 (von Meck).   [17] vii. 298 (von Meck).

monotony. But as if that wasn't enough, their drunken drivers make them collide with a goods train and people die a horrible death and all to no purpose! . . . The political news is no less depressing. Our dear fatherland has never before found itself in so humiliating a position. But Kiev is nevertheless a wonderful city. I am spending a day and a night here partly because I needed to do some shopping, including some manuscript paper, and partly because I love Kiev as much as you do. Yesterday morning I went to Podol, to the bishop's service in the Bratsky Monastery, and it made a remarkably strong impression both because of its wonderful church and because of the unusually splendid service. When you go to a service of that sort you understand the whole immeasurable power that religion has over the people. It is a substitute for the people for everything that we find in art, philosophy, and science. It allows the poor people to elevate themselves every so often to a recognition of their human worth. Voltaire, the believer, was right when he said that if religion did not exist, *il faudrait l'inventer*.[18]

Because of the phenomenal, the impenetrable stupidity of a certain person,* it is not possible to make any progress with her on the delicate matter of a divorce. She has got it into her head that if the truth were known I am in love with her and that it is wicked people, like my brother Anatoly, and my sister, and so on, who are to blame for the rift between us. She is convinced that I should return and fall at her feet. It is all such a morass of nonsense that one really doesn't know where to start. And if she was absolutely serious in maintaining, both in her letter to me and in discussions with Jurgenson, that *the divorce was planned before the marriage* then we will get nowhere by arguing with her.[19]

And so my dreams of being completely rid of the burden of this heavy yoke have been shattered because of the unbelievable obduracy and stupidity of a certain person. There is only one thing left to do. To shield myself as far as possible from meeting her, and from anything that will remind me of her. One can only hope that some day she will finally understand that divorce is as necessary to her as it is to me.[20]

Do you wish to know about the process of composing? . . . It is not easy to give a detailed answer because the circumstances in which a given work comes into the world vary in the extreme. But I will still try to tell you in broad terms how I work. First of all I must subdivide my works into two types and this is very important in explaining the process of composing: (1) works which I write on my own initiative, consequent upon a spontaneous inclination, an irresistible inner need; (2) works which I write in response

---

* This is how Tchaikovsky referred to his former wife in his correspondence with Mme von Meck.

[18] vii. 300 (von Meck).   [19] vii. 305 (von Meck).   [20] vii. 306 (von Meck).

to an external stimulus, at the request of a friend or publisher, *to commission*, as happened, for instance, at the opening of the Polytechnic Exhibition when they commissioned a cantata and so on. I must hasten to add that I know from experience that the quality of a work is not dependent on the category to which it belongs. It has very often happened that a work of the second category, despite the original stimulus to its appearance having come from outside, has been entirely successful whereas something which I have conceived myself has, for quite incidental reasons, been less successful. These incidental circumstances determine the state of mind in which a work is written and have immense significance. At the moment of creation it is essential that an artist should have complete calm. In this sense artistic creation, even musical creation, is always *objective*. People are wrong when they think that the creative artist can use his art to express what he feels at the very moment he *experiences* it. Feelings of joy and of sorrow are always expressed *retrospectively*, so to speak. Without having any particular cause for rejoicing I can immerse myself in a spirit of happy creativity and, on the other hand, I can produce in cheerful circumstances a piece which is steeped in gloom and hopelessness. In short, the artist lives a double life: the normal human life and the artistic, and, moreover, these two lives do not always coincide. Be that as it may, the most important requirement for composing is, I repeat, the opportunity to get rid of the cares of the first of these two lives, if only for a time, and to devote oneself entirely to the second. For compositions of the first category no effort of will, not even the slightest, is called for. One only has to obey one's inner voice and if the melancholy contingencies of the first life do not overwhelm the second, the artistic, then work proceeds with quite unbelievable ease. You forget everything, the spirit throbs with some quite incomprehensible and inexpressibly sweet excitement, you will certainly not manage to keep up with it as it rushes off *somewhere*, time passes literally unnoticed. There is something *somnambulistic* about this state. *On ne s'entend pas vivre.* It is quite impossible to recount what these moments are like. When one is in this state what comes from the pen or merely sinks into one's head (because such moments very often occur in circumstances where writing or thinking is out of the question) is always *good* and if nothing, no external jolt, takes you back to the other, normal life, then it should emerge as the perfect representation of what the particular artist has it in him to achieve. Unfortunately these external jolts are absolutely inevitable. You have to go to work, dinner is ready, a letter arrives and so on. This is why one so rarely finds works which attain an equal level of musical beauty throughout. This is why you get *joins, patches, unevennesses, inconsistencies*. For a work of the second category you sometimes have *to get attuned*. In such cases you very often have to conquer laziness and disinclination. Then all sorts of things happen. Sometimes victory comes easily. Sometimes inspiration slips away and is elusive. But I consider it an artist's *duty* never to give in because *laziness* is a very strong human characteristic. There is nothing worse for an artist than to submit to it. One must not wait.

Inspiration is a guest who does not like visiting the lazy. She comes to those who invite her. Either I write in response to an inner urge, carried along by the lofty and inscrutable force of inspiration, or I simply *work*, summoning up this force which either comes or does not, and in the latter case my pen produces *work*, untouched by the warmth of true emotion. My appeal to inspiration is rarely in vain. I can honestly say that the power which I have called a capricious guest has for so long been familiar to me that we live together inseparably and it leaves me only when it feels itself superfluous because the circumstances of my everyday life are oppressing me. But as soon as the cloud disperses it is there again. So if I am in a normal state of mind it can be said that I am composing all the time, every minute of the day and in all circumstances. Sometimes I keep a curious watch on the work which continuously and automatically goes on in that part of my head devoted to music, regardless of what I am talking about, regardless of the people I am with. Sometimes it is some sort of preparatory work e.g. polishing the details in the parts of some piece which I have planned earlier; but on other occasions it will be some completely new and independent musical idea which I try to store in my memory. Where it comes from is an impenetrable mystery. I write my sketches on the first piece of paper that comes to hand, sometimes even on just a scrap of music paper. I write in a very abbreviated form. I never conceive a melody without the harmony to go with it. These elements of music, and rhythm can rarely be separated from one another i.e. every melodic idea bears within it its own implied harmony and is invariably equipped with its own rhythmic structure. If the harmony is very complex I might note down details of the way the parts move even at the sketch stage; if the harmony is very simple I sometimes just put in a single bass line or sometimes I mark the figured bass; on other occasions I don't put the bass in at all—it stays in my memory. So far as instrumentation is concerned, if I have an orchestra in mind, the musical idea comes to me already coloured with a particular scoring. But sometimes the original intention changes when I am actually doing the orchestration.

Words can *never* be written after the music because, immediately music is written to a text, the text evokes a suitable musical expression. One can, of course, add or adjust words to a little tune but if the composition is a serious one there can be no question of this sort of picking and choosing of words to the music. In the same way it is impossible to write a symphonic piece and then seek out a programme for it, because yet again each episode of the programme selected will evoke a corresponding musical illustration. This stage of the work i.e. the sketching is extremely pleasant and interesting and sometimes affords quite indescribable delights but at the same time it is accompanied by anxiety, by a kind of nervous excitement. You sleep badly and sometimes you completely forget to eat. But the actual bringing of the project to fruition goes very peacefully and calmly. It is great fun to score a work which has matured fully and has been worked out in one's head to the last detail. One cannot say the same about copying out works for piano, or solo voice, or small pieces in general. That can be boring.

Do I keep to established forms? Yes and no. Some kinds of composition imply adherence to a certain form, the *symphony*, for example. Here I keep in broad outline to the form established by tradition, but only in broad outline i.e. in the sequence of movements in the work. One can deviate as much as one likes in detail if the development of a particular idea requires it. So, for instance, in *our* symphony [the Fourth] the first movement has very marked deviations. The second subject, which ought to be in a related and, moreover, a major key, is in fact in a remote key and in the minor. In the recapitulation of the main part of this first movement the second subject does not appear at all and so on. The Finale is also a whole series of departures from the traditional form. In vocal music, where everything depends on the text, and in the fantasia (*The Tempest* and *Francesca*, for instance) the form is totally unrestricted.[21] When discussing the process of composing I did not make myself sufficiently clear about the phase of the work in which the sketch is developed. This phase is of crucial importance. What was written in the heat of the moment must now be checked critically, corrected, expanded, and, in particular, cut down in the light of formal requirements. Sometimes one has to do violence to oneself, to be merciless and cruel; for example, by completely cutting out passages which have been conceived with inspiration and affection. If I cannot complain of lack of imagination and inventiveness, I have always suffered by contrast from an inability to cope with the demands of form. Only by persistent hard work have I now reached the position where the form of my compositions more or less corresponds to their content. Previously I was too careless and was insufficiently aware of how important it is to examine the sketches critically. For this reason the *joins* have always been noticeable in my music, there has been a lack of organic connection in the sequence of separate episodes. This was a crucial failing and only with the passage of years have I gradually been able to correct it, but my works will never be *models of form* because I can only correct, and not altogether eradicate the essential features of my musical personality. Likewise I am far from thinking that my abilities have already reached the highest peak of their maturity. I have a long way to go yet. But I am pleased to see that I am all the same gradually making progress along the path of improvement and I passionately desire to attain the highest point of that perfection which my abilities entitle me to expect. So I expressed myself inaccurately in saying that I *copy out* my works straight from the sketch. This is not just a copying-out but a

[21] vii. 314–18 (von Meck).

meticulous, critical examination of what has been planned; at the same time I make corrections, sometimes expand and very frequently shorten passages.[22]

Nothing could be more sensible than the advice to rest more and to put less of a strain on my inventive capacities. But what am I to do? As soon as I draft a sketch I cannot settle until I have developed it. And as soon as one composition is finished I immediately feel an irresistible urge to start on a new one. Work (i.e. this sort of work) is as necessary to me as the air I breathe. As soon as I succumb to idleness I begin to feel melancholy, to have doubts about my ability to reach that degree of perfection which is within my powers; I feel dissatisfied and even hate myself. I begin to fall victim to the tormenting thought that I am a useless creature and that only my musical activity redeems all my failings and raises me to the level of a *human being* in the proper sense of the word. The only way to escape from these excruciating doubts and self-recriminations is to get down to work again. In this sense I just go round like *a squirrel in a treadmill*. Sometimes I am seized with almost overpowering lethargy, apathy, and disillusionment with myself—this is a most wretched condition and I fight it in every way. I am very inclined to hypochondria and I know that I must not give way to the attractions of idleness. Work alone can save me.[23]

I am enjoying myself very much but my heart sinks at the thought that 1 September is so near. I love Moscow and I love many of the people there but here follows a large number of various buts.[24]

I have received a long missive from a certain person. I don't want and am unable to conceal from you [Mme von Meck] the fact that during the last few days I have been under the influence of this missive. It consists entirely of outrageous impertinences, of completely incomprehensible absurdities. Her insults of course do not have any effect on me and I am completely indifferent to them; that is not what worries me. But her letter makes it clear that if she hasn't lost her reason yet, she is about to. Who knows to what lengths she is prepared to go! In view of this incomprehensible folly, it is impossible to know what *ligne de conduite* one should take up. It is impossible to make out what she wants and what she is getting at. It would seem that she herself doesn't know. For instance, can you imagine what she suggested: that I should go to her in Moscow so that we could go together *to some people (???) and so that these people could pronounce judgement on us and divorce us*. If this were to happen, she would take it upon herself to prove to *these people* that she was *not to blame*. As if I had ever even once accused this absolutely irresponsible person of anything! However much I write to her that it is time to stop these recriminations and that all that remains is to determine my material obligations towards her, she as before

---

[22] vii. 320–1 (von Meck).   [23] vii. 331–2 (von Meck).
[24] vii. 334 (Jurgenson).

tries to paint in the most vivid colours possible the baseness and darkness both of my soul and of the souls of my brothers and sisters. I replied to her that from now on all her letters would be returned to her unopened and that all monetary transactions would be carried out through Jurgenson.[25] But one thing is clear: *I cannot deal with her now*, because I would have to be fully aware of the role I was playing, and there is no possibility of my achieving that.[26] And so this is how things stand. I have come to the conclusion from her letter that if she isn't already quite insane, she will soon be completely out of her mind. For this reason one can suppose that she will not desist for long. Without going into the details of my financial dealings with her, I can tell you positively that there has never been on earth such *a foul creature* as her (in all senses of those words).[27] I cannot start proceedings for divorce now. My only hope is that one day she will *come to her senses* and take the initiative herself. I cannot ask her to do anything. She must ask herself. I must repay my debt to her. I must give her a conditional allowance, i.e. the more I am guaranteed protection from meeting her, the more she will be paid. Her letters, if she sends any, will be returned unopened. When she finally sees from my behaviour towards her that my sole aim is to avoid seeing her and to ignore her existence, then maybe she will realize that a divorce is the best solution. And only when she realizes that will I be able to approach the delicate matter of divorce proceedings.[28]

What a joy it is for me to go to Moscow completely my own master! How alien and repellent it seemed the last time I was there.

I cannot conceal the fact that I will approach the fulfilling of my duties at the Conservatoire with extreme revulsion. Of course, it could well be that I will soon get used to it and cope, the more so as I will be encouraged by the knowledge of my own freedom. Freedom is indeed an ineffable blessing and joy. Given freedom, one can adjust and reconcile oneself to circumstances of any sort.[29]

My health is excellent; I haven't felt so well for a long time. But, as before, there come over me moments of an unconquerable longing to escape *somewhere*, as far as possible away from everyone and everything. It will be very good for me to be able to be alone for a while at Brailov. I think about Moscow with anguish, fear, and a sinking of the heart.[30]

I am very glad that you like *Romeo and Juliet* as a subject. For the moment I have not lost enthusiasm for these plans. But I won't be starting to write this opera in the near future. At the moment I am working on a setting for the Liturgy which has to be ready before I go to Brailov. Then a rest, then Moscow ... Ugh, Moscow! It will be hard for me there at first. But I must go, it is unavoidable.[31]

I have just finished a whole string of different non-orchestral compositions

[25] vii. 332 (von Meck).   [26] vii. 329 (Jurgenson).   [27] vii. 324 (von Meck).
[28] vii. 330 (von Meck).   [29] vii. 346 (von Meck).   [30] vii. 337 (von Meck).
[31] vii. 342 (von Meck).

and am very glad that I can do nothing for a while. I have written a piano sonata, three violin pieces, twelve little pieces for piano, twenty-four piano pieces for children, six romances, and the complete Liturgy of St John Chrysostom for mixed choir. Our poor Pyotr Ivanovich [Jurgenson]! I have given him a lot of work.[32]

I am writing to you [Mme von Meck], my dear, kind friend, with a light heart, pleasantly conscious of having finished some work more or less successfully. Today I copied out the last page of the Liturgy and so that whole long, boring task of transcription is finished. Now I shall rest and gather new strength. Do you know what has just occurred to me? People who work in a fever of haste like I do are in reality the greatest of lazybones. They hurry in order to win as quickly as possible their right to do nothing.[33]

I played through the whole of *Onegin* to my fellow residents [his sister's family]. Their impressions were extremely favourable. I am ashamed to admit it but I cannot deny that I enjoyed it as much as they did and there were moments when I had to stop from excitement and my voice refused to sing because my throat was full of tears. But then the more I think of performing the opera the more I am convinced that it is *impossible*, i.e. a performance that would correspond to my dreams and intentions. I am at a loss to know what to do about *Tatyana* and *Lensky* in particular. Consequently, I am inclined to think that, apart from the Conservatoire performance, which I regard as a student exercise and a try-out, my opera will never see the stage.[34]

I derive little pleasure from *thumbtwiddling* because of my ridiculous nature which constantly anticipates improbable delights and is constantly dissatisfied. I know that only when I have left Verbovka will I fully appreciate the calm and peace of life here. Regretting the past, hoping for the future and never being satisfied with the present—there is the story of my life.[35]

I make constant efforts to gather up my courage for my forthcoming installation in odious Moscow and am working out how I can best organize my life. I have come to the conclusion that the best thing would be to cut myself off straight away and to live on my own as far as possible. I have a fancy gradually to build up a library because the older I get the more I am convinced that the company of books is more pleasant and conversation with them is more useful than the company and conversation of human beings. Conversation is pleasant only with people to whom you are not obliged to talk i.e. with your intimates. But compulsory conversation i.e. *entertaining a guest* is always a futile proceeding.[36]

Before setting off for Moscow Tchaikovsky again spent some time at Brailov.

I have brought a few good books with me including George Sand's *Histoire*

[32] vii. 343 (Karl Albrecht).   [33] vii. 345 (von Meck).   [34] vii. 355 (von Meck).
[35] vii. 357 (Anatoly).   [36] vii. 366 (von Meck).

de ma vie. It's written rather carelessly, that's to say it lacks coherence, just as an intelligent gossip is constantly distracted by recollections, then runs ahead, then dashes off to one side. On the other hand, it is very sincere, there is absolutely no *showing off* and she is remarkably gifted at re-creating the characters amongst whom she spent her childhood. There are also quite a lot of books on the shelves and when I settle on the floor beside a bookcase to look through them I find it hard to tear myself away. I have, incidentally, found an excellent edition of de Musset who really is one of my favourite writers. As I was looking through this book his drama *André del Sarto* caught my interest and in fact I sat there on the floor until I had read the whole play. I am passionately fond of all Musset's dramatic works. I have often dreamt of making a libretto from one of his comedies or dramas. But, alas, they are for the most part too *French*; they become improbable and altogether lose their charm when translated into a foreign language. On the other hand, those of his works which are less *local* either have no dramatic action or are far too full of philosophizing.[37]

To return to Alfred de Musset, particularly his *Caprices de Marianne, Il ne faut pas badiner avec l'amour*, and *Carmosine*. Don't you think all of that positively begs to be set to music? It is so full of ideas and of wit; it is so deeply felt; and it is stunningly graceful! And yet as you read it you sense that the writing came easily and that it was not done for the sake of some *idea* which had been forcibly inserted into the literary material in advance, thereby crippling the free development of the characters' actions and situations. And then how I like those absolutely Shakespearean anachronisms which permit a discussion of the art of the singer *Grizzi* at the court of some fantastic King of Bavaria who receives the *Duke of Mantua*! Just as in Shakespeare, there is positively no vain pursuit of local *truth* in de Musset, but on the other hand he has, again as in Shakespeare, so much human truth which is eternal and is tied to no time or place. But his focus is narrower and he does not fly so high. His play *Les Caprices de Marianne* has made a special impression on me and I am wondering how it could be adapted for an opera scenario. I really will have to settle on some subject for an opera. I have lost enthusiasm for *Undine*; *Romeo and Juliet* is very attractive but in the first place it's terribly difficult and in the second, although Gounod's opera on this theme is mediocre, it still scares me off.[38]

I have reached the quite unshakeable conclusion that the only way of life which entirely satisfies me is being in the country and, for the most part, on my own. Yes, if it were possible I would agree at once to tie up my boat for ever in a harbour like this and spend all the years of my allotted span somewhere in the wilds but I would see a few close friends from time to time and they would visit me; I would also visit our capitals as well as other villages

[37] vii. 368 (von Meck).   [38] vii. 370 (von Meck).

and other parts of the country. I am made for that sort of life. Glinka was wrong to say he was like mimosa. He is not the mimosa, *I* am. It is only in the spacious peace and isolation of the countryside that I can open my petals and live a normal life.[39]

I have broken my promise to devote some time to relaxation. When I was at Brailov I happened to note down a sketch for an orchestral scherzo. As soon as I had done it there appeared in my mind a whole series of *pieces* for orchestra which must go together to make a *suite*. When I got to Verbovka I realized that there was no question of my being able to resist my inner inclination so I hastened to set down on paper the sketches for this suite. I so enjoyed the work and was so carried away by it that I literally did not notice how the hours went by. I don't think I have any right to resist my nature when it burns with the fire of inspiration.[40]

Eventually the time came to leave for Moscow, but Tchaikovsky first went to St Petersburg for a few days.

I bought a newspaper (*Novoye vremya* [*New Times*]) at Fastov and found that it contained a 'Moscow Diary' given over to a filthy, squalid, sordid *philippic* full of slander about the Conservatoire. There was hardly anything about me personally and it even said that I concerned myself *only with music* and took no part in the intrigues and squabbles. But at one point the article discusses the *amours* of the professors and the girl students, then adds at the end: 'at the Conservatoire there are amours of another kind as well, but I do not intend to discuss these for very obvious reasons' etc. It's obvious what he is getting at. So that sword of Damocles in the form of a newspaper insinuation, which I have always feared more than anything else in the world, has once more struck at my neck. Supposing that this time the insinuation is not directed at me personally—that only makes it worse. My [infamous] reputation is now extended to the whole of the Conservatoire, which makes me even more ashamed and distressed.[41] What an impression the article made on me—you could have knocked me down with a feather! I have the most profound and incurable aversion for publicity in general and for newspaper publicity in particular. There could be nothing worse, nothing more dreadful for me than being the object of public interest. Since I have chosen an artistic career I must, of course, be prepared to see my name in the papers all the time and however much I might dislike it I am in no position to stop people discussing my music in print. Unfortunately, the newspapers do not confine themselves to one's artistic activities: they like to probe further into one's private affairs, and to touch on the intimate aspects of one's life. No sooner had I started to get over the depressing

[39] vii. 372 (Modest).
[40] vii. 375 (von Meck).
[41] *LR* 442 (Modest). There is a cut in the source; the word in square brackets is derived from the context.

effect of this article in the paper than something else happened which utterly shattered me once more. There were various gentlemen in the train of whom one was a musician or something in Petersburg. They were talking about all the squabbles and gossip in the world of music. Eventually they got round to me. It wasn't my music they talked about but me, my marriage, my *madness!* Good God! I was dumbfounded at what I had to listen to. It was such a farrago of nonsense, lies, and absurdities. The point was not what they actually said. What I find insufferable is not that people tell lies and invent cock-and-bull stories about me but that they are interested in me, that they point me out, that I am the subject not just of musical and critical judgements but of pure gossip ... I was seized by a massive, unspeakable, overwhelming urge to run away and hide, to get away from it all. I was also seized by an indescribable terror and horror at the thought of the life in front of me in Moscow. Naturally, I immediately started making plans for a final break with society. From time to time I was taken with a desire, a craving for absolute peace, i.e. death. Then this would pass and again I would have a craving to live so that I could finish my job, so that I could say all that I had not yet said. But how is one to reconcile the one and the other, i.e. how is one to protect oneself from contact with people, to live at a distance from them, and yet to work, to make progress, to bring one's talents to their peak?[42]

Luckily I am not crushed by a sense of my own worthlessness only because nature has endowed me with musical gifts in which I believe, about which I have no doubts, and which I am proud of, if only because my music has brought consolation and pleasure to people such as yourself [Mme von Meck].[43]

Have you [Mme von Meck] been to any of the Russian concerts [in Paris]? I cannot get at the truth. According to some newspapers my compositions were a great success; to others a failure. As far as everything that is written in the papers here is concerned, nothing can surprise me, but I see not without bitterness what a lot of enemies I have. Isn't this a little odd? I have never taken part in *intrigues*, I have always tried to avoid *taking sides*, and I can say in all sincerity that I have never consciously done harm to anyone in the whole world, and meanwhile I have enemies who rejoice at my failures, belittling and poisoning any success I might have. There are times when I not only feel like living far away and apart from everyday life, but when I even feel like giving up composing and doing anything rather than take part in social activities. Of course this feeling passes. I only have to find myself in circumstances where I am shielded from encounters with people who are alien to me and I will write.[44]

What if after a time I were quietly and discreetly to leave the Conservatoire for good? What if I were to spend another year, perhaps two years,

---

[42] vii. 382–4 (von Meck).   [43] vii. 378.   [44] vii. 387.

living far away from the scene of my former activities? I have been in some doubt about where my duty lies. For a start I always have been and always will be a bad teacher if only because I have got into the habit of regarding my pupils as sworn enemies whose job it is to torment and torture me. Then have I not an obligation to devote all my time and all my powers to the cause which I love, which constitutes the whole purpose, the very essence of my life? I cannot say precisely where I would like to settle down for good and all. Not in Petersburg in any circumstances and not in Moscow either. I have never been able to stand Petersburg. I love Moscow with a sort of pain and bitterness in my heart. I like the place, the town, even the climate but Moscow is now less capable than ever of satisfying me. I would like to spend the greater part of the year in the country, at my sister's or at Brailov, to spend some time there in the spring and the autumn. I would also like to spend some time in places like Clarens and Florence. In short, I would for a time lead the same sort of nomadic life as I have done this past year. Good lord! What a liberation it would be for my work, how happy I would be enjoying my *freedom*, how much I would start composing and how good it would be![45]

I came to Moscow with one very firm conviction: to get away from here as soon as I could.[46] Why is it that the three days I have spent here seem to me like three long years? Why do I find the place vile, loathsome and repellent? Why is it in general that what might before have seemed to be very boring but normal and inevitable now seems insufferable and impossible? All my thoughts are now concentrated on one idea, on one feeling: that I must get away from here at all costs.[47] I feel like a visitor at the Conservatoire; all that goes on there has nothing to do with me. Why did I not foresee this? Why did I get settled down here before first making sure that the Moscow air suited me? Alas! It has turned out not to. I have not moved away from my own street and the Zamoskvorechye. My fear of meeting people has become something like a mania.[48]

Rubinstein has returned [from Paris]. We gave a dinner for him at The Hermitage. There were speeches at the dinner. Rubinstein's first speech paid tribute to me. He said that my works had produced an enormous impression in Paris and that the Conservatoire was very happy to have the services of such a celebrity. Everybody congratulated me and, in brief, we went through a farce which I found very disagreeable. After all that I thought it would be inappropriate for the moment to start discussing my intention of leaving very soon. I was sad when I got home and woke [in the morning] with despair in my heart and with the notion that I would have to delay my retirement till next year.[49]

In the Russian concerts at the World Exhibition in Paris Nikolay Rubinstein twice

[45] vii. 385–6 (von Meck).   [46] vii. 389 (von Meck).   [47] vii. 395 (von Meck).
[48] vii. 402, 403 (von Meck).   [49] vii. 407 (Modest).

played the First Piano Concerto; he also played the Romance for piano and conducted the symphonic fantasy *The Tempest,* the *Sérénade mélancolique,* and the
Valse-scherzo for violin and orchestra in which the soloist was Stanislaw Barcewicz.

Imagine my amazement. I had thought that Nikolay Grigoryevich [Rubin-
stein] would be upset, would get angry, and would start assuring me that
for my own happiness it would be better to stay. Nothing of the sort happened. Rubinstein heard it all out with the smile of a man listening to the
words of a capricious and spoilt child, and did not express much sympathy.
He only said that without my name the Conservatoire would lose *a lot of
prestige,* as if hinting that in reality, the students' cause would not suffer at
all from my leaving. Let us suppose that he is absolutely right and that I
really am a very bad, irritable, and incompetent teacher, nevertheless I was
expecting more of an effort to keep me at the Conservatoire. You will
understand, my friend, how glad I was to see that my proposed departure
did not particularly anger or distress Rubinstein. I will not go deeper into
the reasons for his indifference, which are all the more puzzling to me since
the day before I somehow read into his words a firm request on his part for
me to stay. Be that as it may, I feel that a great weight has fallen from my
shoulders. I was expecting a stormy, unpleasant scene; it turns out that
everything will be concluded very peacefully and quietly.[50] Fortunately,
Rubinstein saw me at the Conservatoire and himself asked if we could have
a few moments' private conversation; he started asking me how I was and
what I was doing. Then I blurted straight out that I could not stay beyond
the end of November. I kept the conversation on a very friendly plane; we
chatted for an hour and parted with long friendly embraces. It was a load
off my mind.[51]

However, Tchaikovsky did not even stay as long as this.

I was struck by a thought: why should I stay here a whole month when I
don't have to? My life is in such a mess that it would be difficult to last out
even for a month. I did not want the haste of my departure to indicate how
little I value my *soi-disant* friends here. But in the first place I have good
reason not to be all that tactful and in the second place all these considerations are outweighed by the fact that my life is now such an appalling mess,
is so insufferable, so unbearable that I cannot last out even for a month.[52] I
have told Rubinstein that I am going at the end of the week.[53]

I am unbelievably contented and happy. There is one more circumstance
which is working towards my complete peace of mind. Rubinstein is not
only not upset by my departure but has already taken steps to find a re-
placement. To be precise, he has invited Taneyev to teach at the Conservatoire, and in order that no one should know why at the moment, he will

[50] vii. 408 (von Meck).   [51] vii. 405–6 (Modest).
[52] vii. 416–17 (von Meck).   [53] vii. 418 (Anatoly).

temporarily be a piano teacher but he has been asked to be prepared to teach theory. And so I can leave with a clear conscience at any time.[54]

I am going to Petersburg. And so, I am a *free* man. This knowledge is a source of indescribable delight. And how satisfying it is when this delight is not mixed with any unpleasantness or awkwardness. My conscience is quite clear. I am leaving in the firm conviction that the Conservatoire will not in any way suffer from my absence. On the day I left I had dinner with some of my friends: Rubinstein, Albrecht, Jurgenson, Kashkin, and Taneyev. Despite my joy at my longed-for liberation, I felt rather sad at parting from people amongst whom I had lived for more than twelve years. They all seemed very sorry I was going and this touched me. I found Petersburg already immersed in its autumn slush, mist, and dampness. I never have liked and never will like Petersburg as a town.[55]

Vakula went off just as it did at the first performance: smoothly, fairly cleanly, but run of the mill, feeble, and insipid. I was angry with one man all the time I was listening to it: myself. Lord! how many unforgivable mistakes there are in that work which are mine and mine alone! I did everything possible to cripple passages which could in themselves have been successful if I had restrained my purely musical inspiration and had given more thought to the *visual* and *theatrical* requirements of operatic style. The whole work suffers throughout from *piling on an excess* of detail, from wearying chromaticism, from a lack of polish and finish in the separate numbers. *C'est un menu surchargé de plats épicés.* There are lots of fancy things in it but not much simple, healthy food. I am very acutely conscious of all the deficiencies in the work, which, unfortunately, cannot be put right. But listening to it again has been a good lesson for the future. I think that *Eugene Onegin* is a step forward.[56]

What bliss it is for me to be free from the obligation to have dealings with outsiders. I *count my relations* as outsiders. I have an enormous number of relations and they all live in Petersburg. They are a very heavy yoke to bear. Apart from ties of blood we have, for the most part, nothing in common and their company does nothing for me except impose the tiresome necessity of seeming happy when I don't feel happy at all. What I really can't stand is that they all consider it their duty to talk to me about music and to ask me *to play some new little thing*.[57] Only when I am on my own with my brothers and at my dear old father's cosy little place can I relax and gather up my strength to cope with the tedium of life in Petersburg.[58]

We are living through dreadful times and when you start to think about what is going on it becomes frightening. On the one hand the government stands helpless, and on the other our crazed and unhappy young people are

---

[54] vii. 412 (Anatoly).   [55] vii. 420 (von Meck).   [56] vii. 440–1 (von Meck).
[57] vii. 425–6 (von Meck).   [58] vii. 428 (von Meck).

exiled in their thousands to the back of beyond and with no trial; between these two extremes stands a mass of people, indifferent to everything, wallowing in their own selfish interests, and watching the others with no protest at all. Happy is the man for whom the world of art is a refuge from the contemplation of this melancholy scene.[59]

My retirement from my professorial duties and the appearance of *Onegin* have created something of a sensation in the musical world here. People are talking about me a lot and have concocted all sorts of fantasies. Everybody is convinced I am trying to get a chair in Petersburg. Oh, how far from the truth they are! Of the musical people here I have seen only [Karl] Davydov, where we spent the whole evening getting to know *Onegin*, which, apparently, he likes.[60] My goodness! What bliss it is to be free and not to have to correct sixty harmony and orchestration exercises every day![61]

[59] vii. 387 (von Meck).   [60] vii. 429 (von Meck).   [61] vii. 448 (von Meck).

PART III

13

1878–1879

What a joy it is to be in command of one's own time, to belong to oneself.

At Kamenka my heart was at peace, a feeling which I had sought in vain in Moscow and Petersburg.[1]

Tchaikovsky stayed briefly at Kamenka and then set off, via Vienna, for Florence. Mme von Meck and her family were staying there at the time and she had arranged accommodation for Tchaikovsky at the Villa Bonciani, on the Viale dei Colli.

I came here straight from Vienna, without going to Venice. The journey here from Vienna was as pleasant as the journey from Russia to Vienna was unpleasant and exhausting because of the gumboils and the remains of the ill health I had suffered at Kamenka. The weather was wonderful and there was plenty of room in the carriages—in a word it was excellent. Here Pachulski met me (Kotek's successor with Nadezhda Filaretovna) and drove me to my lodgings which were already warm, lit, and waited only to welcome their amazed and delighted lodger. The flat consists of a whole suite of magnificent rooms, to be precise: a drawing-room, dining-room, bedroom, dressing-room, lavatory, and Alyosha's room. There is a magnificent instrument in the drawing-room and on the writing table are two enormous vases of flowers and everything one needs for writing letters. The furniture is first class. I am utterly delighted by all this, but the main charm is that the flat is outside the town.[2]

I really cannot find words to tell you how absolutely delighted I am with my surroundings. One of the things about the flat that I most appreciate is the enormous balcony where I am at liberty to walk about and enjoy the fresh air without, as it were, going out. For such a passionate lover of the fresh air as I am, this is of prime importance. I cannot begin to tell you how I glory in the perfect peace of the evenings, when all you can hear is the distant sound of the waters of the Arno as they tumble or flow down an incline.[3] One could not imagine anywhere more comfortable or convenient to work. Dear town! There is something welcoming about it which makes me feel at home.[4]

I have settled in a very comfortable and attractive place outside the town,

---

[1] vii. 450 (Anatoly). [2] vii. 463 (Anatoly).
[3] vii. 462 (von Meck). [4] vii. 465 (Modest).

surrounded by absolute quiet. I love this quiet passionately and in the evenings I wander for hours on the balcony, enjoying the absence of any sounds at all. It would seem strange to you [Jurgenson]: you would say, how can one enjoy the negation of sound and in general something that does not exist? But if you were a musician, then perhaps, like me, you would have the gift of being able, in the absence of sound, surrounded by the silence of the night, to hear nevertheless some sort of sound, just as if the earth, in rushing through the heavenly expanses, made some sort of low bass note![5] I am a great lover of walking and am very glad that visiting the town entails walking. If I get tired I can always take the public carriage on the way home. Indeed, I have nothing to wish for beyond what has already been provided in my dwelling and its furnishings.[6]

Inspiration has visited me here and I have already finished the draft of the [First] Suite. But I am worried because I have left the manuscript of the first three movements in Petersburg and it might get lost. I have written the last two movements here. This short and (if I am not mistaken) good little suite will have five movements in all.[7]

I think there must be few people on earth who like me can spend days on end without being bored or depressed in such unbroken solitude. In the evenings Alyosha usually goes to bed at about nine, but I stay up alone until about midnight in such absolute quiet that there is not a single sound to be heard apart from the beating of my own heart. My house is on a hill. The nights are now moonlit; sometimes I go out on to the balcony and enjoy this silence and solitude.[8]

You ask [Mme von Meck] whether I have been to Santa Croce. Yes, more than once. In fact I have seen everything there is to see in Florence and all the wonderful churches are familiar to me. I have also been to Bodoli, Bellosguardo, and the Certosa. I can work peacefully in Florence because my *tourist's* conscience is clear. In Rome, where I had only one day the first time and the second time (last year) three or four days, I looked at almost nothing properly; I have been to Naples once and spent a week there but in such awful weather that I didn't see much there either. So I wouldn't feel comfortable in either of these towns now for I didn't come abroad in order to sightsee, but to work, fully protected from all visits of the kind that in Petersburg poisoned my life. The conditions of life which I am now living in are ideal for me in all respects and I haven't enjoyed myself so much for a long time as I have done here. The Villa Bonciani will remain with me all my life as the warmest and sweetest memory. How grateful I am to you, my friend, for this wonderful month![9]

My brother Tolya has written to say that the manuscript has been found. I will set about scoring the suite with a zeal which will be all the greater because I am beginning to be very much tempted by a new subject for an

---

[5] vii. 475 (Jurgenson).   [6] vii. 462 (von Meck).   [7] vii. 457 (Modest).
[8] vii. 477 (von Meck).
                                                                      [9] vii. 509.

opera: Schiller's *The Maid of Orleans,* to be precise. The idea of writing an opera on this subject came to me at Kamenka when I was browsing through Zhukovsky and he has a *Maid of Orleans* translated from Schiller. It has marvellous potential for music and the subject is not hackneyed yet, although it has already been used by Verdi. I got hold of Verdi's *Giovanna d'Arco* in Vienna. In the first place, it does not follow Schiller, and in the second, it is extremely bad. I have sometimes thought about this subject before but I am now beginning to be attracted by it seriously.[10]

I am beginning to get so used to the Villa Bonciani, to being on my own, to the wonderful peace of my marvellous flat that I never feel downcast at all. The evenings are sometimes so enjoyable! I have plenty of books and music as well. Nadezhda Filaretovna sends them but I also have my own. I have bought Massenet's opera *Le Roi de Lahore* and am playing it with immense pleasure. Damn it all, these Frenchmen have such taste, such style. So, everything is fine here and I have no worries because I know that nobody is stopping me going somewhere else and changing my way of life if I want to.[11]

I had a look at both suites by Ries and the concerto by Lalo. The latter I don't like at all and it is not to be compared with the *Symphonie espagnole.* But the suites are very charming; they are written without pretension but charmingly, elegantly, although, as with all contemporary Germans, there is not much freshness. That reminds me—about freshness in music. I recommend the orchestral Suite by the late Bizet, *L'Arlésienne.* I heard it in Petersburg. It is a small *chef-d'œuvre* of its kind. It has been published in a piano duet arrangement if I am not mistaken.[12]

I am writing a *suite* for orchestra and I am working at it with a degree of vigour. Sometimes I take a walk into this marvellous and lovely town and look in at the picture galleries. I am *perfectly* happy, I am enjoying being on my own and never, not for a single minute, do I regret having left Moscow. I spent my best years in Moscow, I love the place very much, but I could not live there now without languishing and being miserable. I am at peace only in the country or abroad, where nobody knows me. In any case I could not live in Moscow as I did before and in the present circumstances it would be quite insufferable. The only thing I lack here is music.[13]

I was very interested to read some of the articles in *Russky arkhiv* [*The Russian Archive*]. One of them made me feel sad. The article about the bibliographer Sobolevsky several times mentioned Prince Odoyevsky. Only when I was reading this article did I recall that he will have been dead ten years next February. Yet it seems no time since I saw that good and kindly face. I feel sad both because he is no more and because time flies so quickly! I suddenly felt that I had not made much progress in these ten years. I am not saying this so as to provoke people to say the opposite. The point is that

[10] vii. 467–8 (von Meck).   [11] vii. 484 (Modest).
[12] vii. 478 (von Meck).   [13] vii. 491 (Karl Albrecht).

I am as dissatisfied with myself now as I was then. I cannot, for instance, say about myself that even a single one of my works is *perfect beyond question*. Not even the smallest of them! Not one of them matches up to what I am *capable* of achieving. But perhaps this is in fact a good thing. Perhaps it is in fact a stimulus to activity. Who knows? Will I not lose my impulse to work when, eventually, I am completely satisfied with what I do?[14]

I read very quickly but this failing is an aspect of my nervous condition. I do everything with feverish haste as though I was frightened that somebody would take away the book or the music that I am interested in or the paper that I am writing on. But this haste leaves its mark both on what I read and on what I write. I very quickly forget what I have read, so that my reading profits me little.[15]

I read Italian quite fluently, but speak it pretty badly, although I do try. At one time I studied it and spoke it quite well. That was when I was occupied with Ristori.[16]

I read the story by Karnovich with the greatest of pleasure, the beginning of which, more's the pity, I do not know. But what I found particularly interesting was the article by the doctor who treated Nekrasov in his last illness. This article was so painful for me to read because of his endless, unbelievable suffering and in particular because of the dog's life, to use the doctor's phrase, which his illness condemned him to, that I couldn't sleep. I forgave Nekrasov everything that I had against him as a man, because of this suffering.[17]

I have nothing with me apart from *Animal Life* by Brehm. But what a marvellous book it is! I am a terrific lover of animals and yesterday read his article on dogs with the greatest delight.[18]

I much enjoyed reading Daudet's stories, as well as some of the other articles in the most recent issue of *Otechestvennye zapiski* [*Notes of the Fatherland*]. But all that fades into oblivion by comparison with the enthralling interest of Catherine's letters. One cannot but be amazed at the brilliance and flair of a woman who was able to predict Napoleon and who in general formed such an accurate estimate of the character of the French although it only revealed itself fully much later. What a pity that Taine probably did not have sight of these letters when he was writing *Les Origines de la révolution*, otherwise he would have been bound to pay due tribute to this contemporary of the revolution whose colossal intellect led her to assess *historically* an event of her own times. Nor can one grasp how she managed to enter into every detail of ruling her empire, to bring up her grandchildren, to give them written advice, to draw up Edicts and Instructions, and at the same time to gossip with Grimm, Voltaire, Mme Geoffrin, and a host of others. I am a passionate admirer of this remarkable woman.[19]

Allow me, my dear friend, to give you my critical appraisal of Lalo's con-

[14] vii. 501 (von Meck).   [15] vii. 505–6 (von Meck).   [16] vii. 480 (von Meck).
[17] Ibid.   [18] vii. 521 (von Meck).   [19] vii. 498 (von Meck).

certo, which I have played through several times and which I now know fairly well. First of all I must say that Lalo is very talented; of that there is no doubt. But either he is a very young man because all his shortcomings come down to a certain lack of stylistic polish, typical of youth, or, on the other hand, he is going to get nowhere. What I mean is that if he is already mature, then his shortcomings are endemic and incurable. I find his concerto considerably weaker than his Spanish symphony. Everything in the latter which I explained to myself as being deliberately injected into the music to give it a somewhat wild and disconnected rhapsodic character, all the strange characteristics which I put down to the Eastern Moorish cast of Spanish melody, are also in the concerto, which, however, is not Spanish.[20]

I will definitely go to the exhibition of new paintings. I went to it last year but it was in a different place. There was one Roman matron of astonishing beauty and the thought occurred to me that if you had seen this painting you would perhaps have bought it.

Apart from this I will not leave Florence before visiting the Uffizi, Pitti, and San Lorenzo. Do you like the Duomo here? I love it passionately. I like its stern simplicity, and after that in architecture I don't know of anything more captivating than the Campanile. I am very fond of Florence as a whole.[21]

Laroche does not actually call me an enemy of programme music but he thinks I am no good at it and therefore says that I am an anti-programme composer. He takes every convenient opportunity to complain that I often write symphonic works that have a programme. What is programme music? Since you [Mme von Meck] and I do not accept music which consists of an aimless play on sounds, then in our wide sense of the word, all music is programme music. But in the narrow sense of this expression it means symphonic or in general instrumental music bearing the title of the particular subject illustrated, which is given to the audience in the *programme*. Beethoven invented programme music, partly in the 'Eroica' symphony, to be precise, but more especially in his Sixth Symphony, the Pastoral. But Berlioz must be considered the real founder of programme music in that every work of his not only carries a specific title, but is provided with a detailed explanation. I will briefly explain my views on this. I think that a symphonic composer's inspiration can be twofold: subjective or objective. With the first he expresses in his music his feelings, of joy, of suffering, in a word, like the lyric poet, he pours out, one might say, his own soul. In this instance a programme is not only unnecessary but impossible. But it is another matter when the musician reads a work of poetry or is struck by a scene from nature, and wants to express in musical form that subject which set alight his inspiration. A programme is essential here. As I see it, the *raisons d'être* of both kinds of inspiration are on an absolutely equal footing and I cannot understand those gentlemen who accept only one kind to the exclusion of the other. It goes without saying that not every subject is suitable for a symphony, just as not every subject is suitable for an opera, but nevertheless programme music can and must be allowed to exist, just as you can't demand that literature should do without the epic and restrict itself to lyrics alone.[22]

I am not at all convinced that music specialists are infallible. They are very often biased; their *knowledge* often paralyses their *sensitivity*; because they are keeping such a watch on the technique they often lose sight of the very essence of the music. A lover of music such as yourself, i.e. endowed with remarkable sensitivity and understanding, is absolutely worthy of conversing with the most perceptive and erudite musician.[23]

How strange and dark is the human heart! I have always thought, or at least for a long time, that I did not like [Nikolay] Rubinstein. I recently dreamt that he had died and that this cast me into the depths of despair. Since then I have not been able to think about him without deep regret and the most positive feeling of affection. This is very easily explained. With very few exceptions I do not like anybody close to because in general I do not like human company. But I only have to go a short distance away, look at people from there, and it turns out that I like them.[24]

Nadezhda Filaretovna no longer bothers me. I have even got used to our daily correspondence but one must be fair to this marvellous woman because she is also very intelligent. She knows how to organize matters so that I always have masses of things to write about. On the dot of eleven thirty she walks past and peers into my window, trying to catch sight of me and not succeeding because of her short-sightedness. But I can see her perfectly. Apart from this, we saw each other once at the theatre. There is not the slightest suggestion that we should meet so I am not troubled at all in this respect.[25]

I am going to Clarens via Paris. At all costs I want to get hold of the libretto of the opera *Jeanne d'Arc* which was put on in Paris five years ago. Until I have that libretto to hand I cannot get down to my work properly. So far I only have Schiller's drama in Zhukovsky's translation. The opera text obviously cannot strictly follow Schiller's scenario. There are too many characters, too many secondary episodes. It will have to be reworked and not just cut down so I want to know what the Frenchman did because he always has a good feeling for the stage. Apart from that, I would like to rummage through the catalogues and get together a proper little library about *Jeanne d'Arc*. Meanwhile I have taken one scene straight from Zhukovsky: whatever happens I must have it in. It is the scene where the king, the archbishop, and the knights recognize Joan as an emissary from on high.[26]

[22] vii. 513–14 (von Meck).   [23] vii. 498 (von Meck).   [24] vii. 515 (Anatoly).
[25] vii. 516 (Anatoly).   [26] vii. 519 (von Meck).

I have begun the opera!!!—and fairly successfully. What a rich subject![27] I am up to my eyes in the work, so much so that I don't notice time passing. I am in excellent spirits and things are going like clockwork.[28]

I have started on *The Maid of Orleans*. It gave me considerable trouble: the difficulty was not lack of inspiration but, on the contrary, its presence to excess. A sort of mania seized me: for three whole days I was plagued and tormented because there was so much material and so little in the way of time and human resources. I wanted to get everything done in the space of a single hour, as sometimes happens in dreams. I wailed horribly when I was reading the book which Nadezhda Filaretovna gave me about Joan of Arc and I got to the proceedings of the *abjuration* and the execution itself (she cried out dreadfully as she was being led to execution and begged them to cut off her head but not to burn her). I suddenly felt sorrow and pity for all mankind and had a fit of indescribable melancholy. I have given a tremendous amount of thought to the libretto but I still cannot make a firm plan. I like a great deal of Schiller but I must admit that his scorn for historical truth somewhat disturbs me.[29]

I have become frightfully selective and exclusive about what I read. I can categorically say that I have lost the ability to read novels for ever and in general any sort of *belles lettres*. A few days ago Nadezhda Filaretovna highly recommended to me some stories by Daudet. I started them but could not persevere. And in exactly the same way I started to read *Une page d'amour* twice but without success. And so all that remains to read are historical articles—but again not all history interests me, only specifically the eighteenth century and of course the seventeenth. But on the other hand what pleasure I got from reading in two volumes of the *Russian Archive* the correspondence between Catherine the Great and Grimm! Apart from that I am reading, not without pleasure, Brehm on the life of animals. I bought these huge six volumes in Moscow the day before I left. Of the newspapers I get *Moskovskiye vedomosti* [*The Moscow Gazette*] from Nadezhda Filaretovna every day and sometimes also *Golos* [*The Voice*] when it has articles by Laroche. But the book I read with keen interest was the one about *Jeanne d'Arc* which Nadezhda Filaretovna also sent me. I have probably already told you and written to you that for my next opera I have decided on Schiller's *The Maid of Orleans*, but I don't by any means like everything in this tragedy and I want to delve about in history a little and also get hold of the librettos of the two unsuccessful French operas on this subject. This is what is drawing me to Paris more than anything else.[30]

I have been to the theatre. Nadezhda Filaretovna sent me a ticket and was also there with her whole family, and in the interval I watched her through my binoculars with mixed feelings of curiosity, affection, and surprise. She was chatting to her delightful daughter, Milochka, and her face

[27] vii. 519 (Modest).   [28] vii. 520 (von Meck).
[29] vii. 525, 526 (Modest).   [30] vii. 530 (Anatoly).

expressed such tenderness and love (she is her favourite), that I even liked her unattractive but distinctive appearance![31] I can't think of anything more delightful in the whole world than the little face of a sweet child.[32]

Tell Bobik that this music was composed by Uncle Petya and on it is written: dedicated to Volodya Davydov. He, the silly, will not understand what it means to dedicate something. But I will write to Jurgenson and ask him to send a copy to Kamenka. I am more than slightly worried that Mityuk may be a bit hurt. But, you must agree, how can one dedicate musical compositions to him when he says straight out that he doesn't like music? But to Bobik—even if only because of the inimitably delightful way he plays and peers at the music and counts—one could dedicate whole symphonies.[33]

This refers to the *Children's Album*, Op. 39.

Yesterday I sent Modest my verses. Please [Anatoly] read them and enthuse about them. I have never been so proud of any of my musical compositions as I am of this poetry.[34]

However proud I may be of my 'Lilies of the Valley' I still don't think them suitable for publication and therefore I decline your offer to get them published. And moreover you are mistaken, Modya, in thinking that *Vestnik Yevropy* [*Messenger of Europe*] and *Russky vestnik* [*Russian Herald*] will be ready to vie with each other for the honour of printing my rubbish. There are infinite gradations in works of art. My poetry is excellent as far as I am concerned, i.e. for a non-specialist. But what is it like in comparison with Apukhtin's poetry, for instance? No. Broadcast my poetic fame far and wide, trumpet and roar, but don't give it to the printer.[35] Because I am not a poet but only a compiler of verses, it seems to me, though I may be wrong, that poetry can never be completely sincere, and pour freely out of the soul. The rules of poetic composition, rhyme (particularly rhyme) make for *artificiality*. That is why I maintain that music is still infinitely superior to poetry. It goes without saying that music can also have what the French call *remplissage* but it is less obvious. When you look at them carefully you can always find in every poem lines which exist only for the sake of the rhyme.[36]

I will always have the pleasantest recollection of the time which I have spent here. I have been happy and at peace with myself, I have been in good and cheerful spirits, and the proximity of my dear, best friend has imparted a special sort of charm to my surroundings. I have *begun* the opera and have written one of the most important scenes. So I have not been idle all this time and I am leaving with a clear conscience as well as with marvellous memories of this lovely little spot.[37]

[31] vii. 540 (Anatoly).   [32] vii. 538 (von Meck).   [33] vii. 531 (Lyova).
[34] vii. 546 (Anatoly).   [35] vii. 576 (Modest).   [36] vii. 543 (Modest).
[37] vii. 533 (von Meck).

Nadezhda Filaretovna has gone and contrary to expectations, I feel an emptiness and a great longing for her. I walk past her empty villa with tears in my eyes and the Viale dei Colli has become dark and miserable. I had grown so used to being in daily contact with her, watching her every morning walking past with all her company and what at first used to embarrass and confuse me has now become the object of the most sincere regret. Lord, what an amazing, wonderful woman she is! How touching were all her efforts on my behalf, paying attention to every detail, with the general effect of making my life here pleasant in the highest degree.[38]

I suffer from a disease which the Germans call railway fever. For several days before the journey I always fuss about and get bothered, and all because I hate travelling in a crowded train with people who either stare at you or talk to you. I never grudge any expense if it gives me the opportunity to travel without other people.[39]

Leaving a place that you have enjoyed is always sad and I felt awful when I was leaving. But since one has to move some distance away from it in order fully to appreciate a happy period of one's life, I am only now beginning fully to understand just how permanently the pleasant memories of this marvellous month have fixed themselves in my mind. I cannot think of the Viale dei Colli without tears welling up in my eyes.[40]

I am very fond of Paris. But the noise, the bustle! After the peace which surrounded me at the Villa Bonciani I am even more struck by the countless numbers of carriages and pedestrians and even somewhat frightened by them.[41]

I was very unhappy with the music in Paris. There was not a single interesting concert while I was there. At the opera I heard Gounod's *Polyeucte* and I have never heard anything worse in my life. Even Kashperov's *The Storm* is more interesting: it, at least, is sometimes funny because the composer's methods are so naïve.[42] Gounod's artistic arrangements remain a mystery to me. It cannot be denied that *Faust*, if not a work of genius, does show remarkable mastery and a not inconsiderable degree of originality. But everything that he has written before and since *Faust* is feeble and shows no talent. There has never been anything like it in the history of music.[43]

I have been to the Comédie Française twice. The first time I saw *Le fils naturel* and the second *Les Fourchambaults*. I was expecting the same enjoyment from the latter comedy as from *Le gendre de M. Poirier* but was quite wrong. It is very boring. The lead was played by Got, but there is no similarity between the wonderful creation that Poirier is and the part of Bernard in *Les Fourchambaults*, in which he plays a young and unbelievably upright man who receives an insult at the end of the play. What wouldn't I

---

[38] vii. 541 (Modest).   [39] vii. 546–7 (von Meck).   [40] vii. 547 (von Meck).
[41] Ibid.   [42] viii. 23 (Taneyev).   [43] vii. 565 (von Meck).

give for the same hand which delivers the insult to Got to slap me in the face a hundred times every day! This hand belongs to the godlike being whom we both admired in the memorable production in 1876. His name is Boucher. Do you remember him? What charm of personality and what a wonderful actor he has turned out to be! I was so pleased that I saw him in both plays. In *Le fils naturel* he played Worms and was marvellous. It is amazing that both comedies are written on the same theme. In both, illegitimate sons live with their mothers and find out from them who their fathers are and then a whole string of complications follows in which they turn out to be wonderful sons to both parents. They also have in common the fact that in both plays the role of the mother is played by a *jeune première*. In the first play the mother was played by Favart, and in the second by Agar. I have a very poetic memory of both plays thanks to Boucher. What a voice, what a smile, what movement, bearing, gestures![44]

I have got together all the material I need for *Jeanne d'Arc*. I am very glad that I got Michelet's book; it will give me a lot of useful information. As to Mermet's opera, I think the general scenario is very bad but there are two or three effective scenes which I might make use of. I have finally reached the conclusion that although Schiller's tragedy is weak on historical truth it surpasses all other artistic portrayals of Joan in the depth of its psychological truth.[45]

The book by J. Michelet, *Jeanne d'Arc* (Paris, 1853), has not survived in Tchaikovsky's library at Klin.

When he had gathered together the material which he needed for the opera Tchaikovsky left Paris and went to Clarens.

I have decided to go to Clarens. Although all my days here are filled with distractions I always find ultimately that a life of idleness is exhausting. Life constantly goes by in alternating series of good and bad days. I felt astonishingly well in Florence. But here, though I go to the theatre every day and am living in a town which on holidays seethes with happiness, I am not happy.[46]

You [Jurgenson] must never trouble to send me articles which praise me because if there is anything I don't give a *damn* for it is these newspaper reviews, whether they praise or blame. They are all for the most part rubbish and to tell the truth they always rather irritate me: their praise is stupid and their blame is stupid. But this does not mean that I do not give a *damn* for the views of my friends or the opinions of authorities such as Rubinstein. I was *delighted in the extreme* at your news that Nikolay Grigoryevich was in raptures over my opera. On the contrary, nothing has so encouraging an effect as that sort of response.[47]

There has once more unexpectedly risen up before me an appalling

[44] vii. 568 (Modest).   [45] vii. 566 (von Meck).
[46] vii. 557 (von Meck).   [47] vii. 549.

vision of my recent past. *A certain person* is again reminding me of her existence. Occasionally I forget the whole story but when the vision unexpectedly crops up again it weighs me down very much at first.[48]

You [Jurgenson] perhaps read in the papers about the terrible snowstorm which raged in France during the night of the 28th to the 29th old style. It just so happened that I left Paris on the evening of the 27th. It would take too long to tell you all about our sufferings from cold and hunger. For instance at one station where you couldn't get anything to eat apart from bread, and even that with difficulty, we had to wait from four in the morning until one in the afternoon and were frozen stiff! God, how cold we were! The train dragged us to Dijon at three and then immediately began to shunt about, but as we had not been given any warning Alexey and I remained in our carriage. After the shunting had stopped we were left somewhere in the dark amongst a mass of other carriages. It grew completely dark and we were still there. Finally we climbed out and, sinking up to our bellies in the snow, began looking for someone who could tell us our fate. Eventually we came across some sort of railway employee. It seems that all the passengers had been warned long before the shunting started that no trains would be going any further: ours was the only carriage they forgot about and we couldn't see anything out of the frozen and ice-covered window-panes. We had to drag our luggage in the dark through the snowdrifts to the station, the master whereof informing me very politely that *everyone had lost their heads* and so it was not surprising that we had sat in a siding for more than three hours. All the trains had been cancelled until the track was cleared. There was only one thing left to do: to go to a hotel, which I did. My goodness! What a pleasure it was to sit in front of a fire in a comfortable armchair and then sit down to an excellent dinner at the *table d'hôte*. This was yesterday. Today, after a marvellous sleep and warming up by the fire, I walked to the station to find out when we could leave. The station master informed me that we could get a train at two in the morning. I looked round the town which is not large but very attractive. It turns out that there is a very good museum here and a charming little theatre, which I managed to get in to yesterday evening. But what a frost—it is terrible! You can sit in your room only if you are near the fire. The snow is knee-deep in the streets and there are whole walls of snow by the pavements. They say that there has been nothing like this since 1840.[49]

I feel at home here and I am very much looking forward to enjoying some peace after all the noise of Paris. I was very glad to see the lovely, familiar places but I feel sad all the same. I have taken the room where Modest and Kolya stayed last year, every corner, every object reminds me so much of both of them that my heart sinks in pain when I think of how far away they are.[50] Oh memories! How much sweetness and yet how much bitterness![51]

[48] vii. 556–7 (von Meck).   [49] vii. 572–3.
[50] vii. 575 (Anatoly).   [51] vii. 576 (Modest).

I write the music for the opera in the mornings, and before dinner I plug away for an hour or two at the libretto; it won't be at all bad: it is not all based on Schiller. I have borrowed a lot from Mermet and from Barbier and have even invented odd bits myself. There will be some very good scenes. I intend to work at it carefully, not rushing too much. I am working very hard and the opera is gradually beginning to make its way out of my head on to the paper.[52]

The postman turned up unexpectedly and handed me *the suite*! I simply could not believe my eyes when I at last had these precious tatters of dirty music paper in my hand. I am perfectly content. However, there is no question of starting to orchestrate them now. I cannot possibly tear myself away from the opera which completely occupies my thoughts at the moment. I must finish at least two acts before I tackle the suite.[53]

I am up to the eyes in the opera. It's very easy work but what causes endless problems, wears me out, and irritates me is the libretto, which I am concocting for myself. It's not at all a bad concoction, but what an effort it costs me! If I find musical composing pleasant, easy, and a delight, the literary variety comes only at the price of excruciating and exhausting effort. I have surrounded myself with my numerous sources but I am drawing mainly on Zhukovsky-Schiller. Thanks to my work and a strictly organized routine (in this respect I am not artistic at all and I hate lack of order in the way one uses one's time) the days pass unnoticed. The quiet here is ideal and only God alone knows how I love such peace. However, when working at something like composing a large opera, it would be better to live in a big town where one could refresh oneself with the distractions of the place.[54]

I was sitting on a bench and fell into a reverie and suddenly I felt so well, so much at peace! Unfortunately it didn't last long because when I got home I immediately started to worry about the scene between Dunois and the King in Act II, and to give way to despair at the thought of the literary revision of this scene which faced me—as usual, I started fussing. It really is funny—I always work as though it were essential to get everything finished by tomorrow, or my head will be cut off. Rush, fuss, fears about nothing, the appalling thought that you are writing something which one day will be finished and one day will be performed—all this always, not excluding the present occasion, ruins the pleasure of writing something which is to your own liking. While I am writing the music in the mornings I don't notice how time passes, but as soon as it is finished my worries and senseless fears start up.[55]

I am very pleased with my work on the music. As to the literary side i.e. the libretto, it is a toil which will certainly take at least a few days off my

[52] viii. 17 (Modest).   [53] viii. 26 (von Meck).
[54] viii. 30 (Jurgenson).   [55] viii. 31 (Anatoly).

life. It's hard to convey how exhausted I am. How many pens do I nibble away before I squeeze a few lines out of myself! How many times do I get up in complete despair because I can't get the rhythm right, or the number of feet doesn't work out, or because I don't know what a particular character should say at a particular moment.[56]

There are three remarkable people: (1) Mr N. N., a pretty poor versifier who has only written a few texts for some Russian songs; (2) Mr B. L., a former music critic of *The Russian Gazette*, and (3) Mr Tchaikovsky, the composer and ex-professor. Mr Tchaikovsky invited his two fellow residents Messrs N. N. and B. L. to join him at the piano and played them the second act of an opera which he had composed called *The Maid of Orleans*; since Messrs N. N. and B. L. are the most intimate friends of Mr Tchaikovsky he had no difficulty in conquering his characteristic shyness and played his new work for them with great artistry, enthusiasm, and inspiration. The rapture of these two gentlemen had to be seen! One might well have thought that they had themselves had some part in composing the opera (Mr N. N. did indeed compile the libretto, but this does not mean that he is the composer of the opera), so proudly did they start to stride about the room, such airs did they give themselves, so moved were they by the beauty of the music which they had heard! Eventually the composer, who had for long been trying to play the part of a modest man, suddenly got excited as well and it ended with all three rushing around the balcony like lunatics, trying to soothe their shattered nerves in the fresh air and to restrain their impatient desire to hear the other acts as soon as possible (the whole of the first act had already been performed). To no purpose did Messrs N. N. and B. L. reproach Mr Tchaikovsky for thinking that operas could be cooked as quickly as pancakes: he despaired at the weakness of his human nature, which was incapable of getting down on to paper in a single week all that had previously accumulated in his head. Eventually these good people somehow calmed the demented composer.[57]

Tchaikovsky signed his translations of texts for vocal works and the words which he wrote for songs with the initials N. N. He used B. L. for his early articles on musical topics.

Would it not be better to commission a libretto in Russia? But I do not know a single person from whom I would be willing to commission one. The most talented poets disdain such work and if they do take it upon themselves they demand an enormous fee which by no means corresponds to the value of their piece, because it is not sufficient to be a poet—one must understand the stage and these gentlemen have never had anything to do with the theatre. Apart from that, they regard every line they write as holy and get annoyed if the composer alters, expands, or abbreviates to suit his

---

[56] viii. 32 (von Meck).   [57] viii. 44 (Jurgenson).

own purposes;* such changes are unavoidable in composing an opera. Of course there are plenty of middling scribblers who would take the job on for a modest fee but the point is that I will probably make no worse of it than they would. In fact there are advantages in the composer of the music compiling his own libretto in that he is quite free to lay out the scenes to suit himself and can adjust the metre to the requirements of the particular situation. On the other hand, the whole business is very difficult for a musician like me who has problems with the technicalities of verse.[58] It cost me much effort to lay out the action, taking it bit by bit from Zhukovsky, Mermet, Barbier, and from myself. Barbier has been of great service to me because I am taking the last scene of Act IV from him. Joan will die at the stake and not of wounds on the field of battle, as she does in Schiller ... Even if this opera is not a *chef d'œuvre* in the history of music it will certainly be my *chef d'œuvre*! The style is of the utmost simplicity. Formally it is easy to understand. It will, in short, be in the sharpest contrast with *Vakula*.[59] I have now come to the conclusion that opera should in general be the most accessible of all forms of music. The operatic style should have the same relationship to the symphonic and chamber music styles as decorative art has to fine art. This, of course, does not mean that operatic music should be more vulgar and banal than any other. Not at all; it is not a question of quality but of the method of presentation, of style.[60]

Tchaikovsky wrote the cantata *For the two-hundredth anniversary of Peter the Great* (1872) and the opera *Vakula the Smith* (1874) to texts by Polonsky.

I have now collected a lot of reading matter. I have found some good Russian books in the library here. Besides that I am rereading one of my favourite novels—*Little Dorrit* by Dickens, and rereading it with pleasure.[61]

I am committing a great folly in reading a Russian newspaper every day. Every time something angers and upsets me. I don't want to know what is happening in Russia, apart from everything that concerns my nearest and dearest, and I am quite happy when I am occupied either with my own affairs or with yours. As soon as I begin to read about what is happening in our dear fatherland in general (beginning with the terrible rate of exchange and the plague and ending with the curses which the base *New Times* showers on Nikolay Rubinstein), I am inevitably seized by feelings of depression and anger. It would be good if one could just not know about all the unpleasant and base things that go on in Russia and live only in the close circle of family interests.[62]

---

* I know from experience because I have twice set texts by Polonsky (*Tchaikovsky's note*).

[58] viii. 45–6 (von Meck).   [59] viii. 48 (Modest).
[60] viii. 67 (von Meck).   [61] viii. 41–2 (von Meck).
[62] viii. 43 (Anatoly).

My trip to Geneva did not give me the slightest pleasure. The concert which I attended and which had a programme of little interest (a symphony by Spohr, dances from an opera by Spontini and *Euryanthe*) somehow struck me as very comical in its performance and in the whole manner in which it was put on. The conductor was particularly comical, working himself into such a frenzy that sometimes his body looked as if it was in convulsions. The orchestra itself was very bad. In general, much as I love the shores of Lake Geneva, starting at Vevey and ending at Villeneuve, I find the pretty town of Geneva, which always overwhelms me with despondency, quite lacking in attraction. In the hotel where I stayed they behaved towards me like bandits: they were dissatisfied because they had had few guests this season, and so they descended on me with an enthusiasm which should have been directed to a better purpose. Their prices were exorbitant. I returned here with a new wave of love and affection for the Villa Richelieu, where I am so comfortable and where, moreover, it is so cheap. I cannot praise highly enough the tact and kindness of my dear hostess.[63]

I have added a new pleasure to my life. In Geneva I bought various quartets by Mozart and Beethoven in a piano arrangement and I play through one every evening. You won't believe what a delight it is and how it sobers one up! Nadezhda Filaretovna sent me Goldmark's opera *La reine de Saba*; I find it a piece very much lacking in talent and full of pretensions. On the other hand I have completely fallen in love with Massenet's opera *Le roi de Lahore*. I advise you [Modest] to get hold of it and play it through. What wouldn't I give for *The Maid of Orleans* to be no worse than this opera.[64]

I went for my usual walk after lunch today [27 January 1879] and came back home; one or two letters arrived and I sat on the balcony to read them. When I had finished I raised my eyes and saw the whole marvellous scene bathed in warm, quite spring-like sun; I suddenly felt such a rush of that tranquil, utterly incomparable rapture which comes only from nature that I sat there in ecstasy for two hours or so and did not stir. This had an astonishingly refreshing effect on me. I have been too engrossed in the opera recently to pay attention to the beauties of nature; but then today I realized the true extent of the delights which nature can afford.[65] I bear my isolation not only without complaining but with indescribable pleasure. It is, after all, my normal way of life. I can only feel settled and really happy when I am alone. Naturally I am not at all averse to occasionally enjoying the company of the very few people whom I love and appreciate; indeed this is essential. But all the same I feel best when I am entirely on my own.[66]

The poison of pathological shyness is the most terrible of poisons, and there is no cure. But I did not think that your [Anatoly's] veins had already been infected by it and was therefore a little surprised at the strength of the feelings of fear which you experienced. Of course you can console yourself

[63] viii. 52 (von Meck).   [64] viii. 68 (Modest).
[65] viii. 73–4 (von Meck).   [66] viii. 76 (Jurgenson).

to a certain extent with the thought that it is only those who are solid from the neck up who possess that golden self-assurance which makes them not care a fig for anyone else. But all the same it is better not to be shy, better not to be afraid of the mob, for it is always stupid.[67]

I have finished all I planned to do here in Clarens. Now I have gone beyond that and written a grand coronation march which opens Act II Scene 2. I have decided not to break off this work and to try to finish the whole opera in Paris. It will not be especially difficult because I have really not got so very much left to do, only about three weeks' work. I had wanted to relax in Paris and to score the suite but now I have changed my plans.[68] As the time to leave draws near I appreciate the Villa Richelieu even more.[69] It is very nice for me to know that there is one place in Western Europe where they will always be glad to see me and will look after me with kindness, where my habits and needs are well known, where they always manage to arrange things so that I feel at home.[70]

In Geneva I came across an article in the *New Times* in which Nikolay Rubinstein was under attack again. Jurgenson has written to me that he is irritated beyond all measure. I decided to do something for him on my part and, with this in mind, have just written a letter to Stasov (a music colleague), asking him to explain to the editor, Suvorin, that one should not hound a man with such determination and malice, particularly one who has in the past rendered great services to Russian art and continues to do so.[71] I came to the conclusion that there is only one thing left for me to do. Stasov, who in his writings is so vehement, unjust, and harsh, is in reality not malicious but quite decent, although biased and prejudiced. I decided that if I wrote him a letter in which I explained to him that it was the duty of every honest man who loves his native art to defend a public figure such as Nikolay Grigoryevich [Rubinstein], and that one cannot allow a man who has rendered incalculable services to Russian music to be slandered with impunity in the press every week, and finally that we can *never replace* this man and that the whole of Moscow's musical world will perish if he goes, then he would be decent enough to force Suvorin to call off his pack of Moscow curs from Nikolay Grigoryevich. This is what I did. I wrote the letter.[72]

I am far from being an admirer of your [Stasov's] articles on music. I do not like either the substance of your opinions nor the harsh, quick-tempered tone in which they are expressed. But, at the same time, I well know that even those sides to your activities with which I cannot sympathize in any way, have a silver lining in their undoubted sincerity, their passionate love of art, their whole-hearted dedication to the select few who in your opinion are destined to raise Russian art on high. If you are mistaken, your mistakes are, of course, *bona fide*. Everything that you say and write, you

---

[67] viii. 64 (Anatoly).   [68] viii. 86 (von Meck).   [69] viii. 89 (Modest).
[70] viii. 91 (von Meck).   [71] viii. 52–3 (von Meck).   [72] viii. 56 (Jurgenson).

believe yourself. You are an absolutely straightforward man and writer and because of this, a quality as strange as it is rare, I am partly reconciled to you as a critic. As far as your kindness is concerned, your perpetual readiness, in spite of your many activities, to devote your time to those who like myself have turned and still turn to your erudition, your knowledge, and experience, these qualities deeply touch me and this is why, despite everything else, I will always esteem you as a human being. It is all the sadder to find out that between us two lies a bottomless abyss, which neither of us will ever leap across. What I considered and will continue to consider until my last gasp the highest artistic revelation, you call trash. Where I find nothing apart from ignorance, ugliness, and a parody on art, you find pearls of aesthetic beauty. Where I see light, benefit, and immeasurable worth, you see harm, darkness, and even *crime*.

I will not try to alter your unfair opinion of Rubinstein in any way. One cannot change ingrained prejudice. But I will say that not one of your accusations against Nikolay Rubinstein has the slightest shadow of truth. I was a member of his Conservatoire for twelve years and I find it very odd to hear that he has a corrupting influence on young people, when every single student who finished his studies there is known to me and I cannot point to one of them who would uphold your opinion, which is based on those anonymous slanderers who write for *New Times*. I would also like to know where the *talents* are which he is supposed to have hounded? Even his small sympathy for the new school, which you call a crime, has not prevented him from collaborating with and as far as was within his powers from supporting those representatives of the school whose talent no one could doubt. Wasn't it he who stood up for Balakirev when he was subjected to the most august persecution? Isn't he the only pianist who has given several public performances of the excellent but most ungrateful of all piano pieces—*Islamey*? Does a lack of enthusiasm for the works of Messrs Shcherbachov, Ladyzhensky, etc. really amount to *hounding and persecution*? Are not the works of Balakirev, Rimsky, and Cui performed every season in Moscow? I am inclined to think, Vladimir Vasilyevich, that, basically, all Nikolay Grigoryevich's crimes stem from the ill-starred Paris concerts. I admit that you can regret and complain that the programmes of the Paris concerts did not include excerpts from Musorgsky's operas; I readily share your anger that, for example, not one of Balakirev's marvellous overtures was played. But here there is neither premeditated malice, nor calculated neglect, nor hounding, nor persecution. As I see it, Rubinstein tried to display in Paris what in his opinion would have the best chance of showing our music in a good light. He might have been wrong in his choice—but it was without spiteful intention. If his particular partiality for me played a certain part here, this is because he has indeed a very high opinion of me, even if it is mistaken. Imagine, Vladimir Vasilyevich, that you were the delegate and that you had to make up the programme. There is no doubt at all that at least a modest share would be granted to that majority of writers who are not among those that you like. I am even very much inclined to think that you would be much more selective in your point of view than Rubinstein was, because I know that he is much more tolerant and charitable in his musical judgements than you are. But that is enough of trying to justify him in your eyes. I know that it won't be of any use.

If I want you to stand up for Nikolay Grigoryevich, it is not because I fear for him. His reputation as an honest man, an honest artist, will not be shaken by the pages of *New Times*. His integrity is self-evident. But this man, in spite of all his good qualities and some significant faults, has the unfortunate weakness of feeling insulted and injured by newspaper opinion. The result of all this spreading of slander and gossip might be that he throws his hand in. If you look at it from the point of view of his career then he can only gain from doing this, as did his brother when he left the Conservatoire. But I am reduced to tears and to despair at the thought of how much would be lost. You don't know what Moscow is like! There you need to behave *à la* Peter the Great, i.e. forcibly to shine light on a society which has sunk into darkness. No one could ever match Rubinstein's skill in fighting against ignorance and obscurantism. You are mistaken, Vladimir Vasilyevich, if you think that I am an out-and-out, an unconditional admirer of Rubinstein, blinded to such an extent that I can't see *le revers de la médaille*. I was often annoyed and irritated by him. But what do all his faults matter in comparison with his immeasurably beneficial activities. That element of petty tyranny, which manifests itself in the way in which he sometimes, quite unnecessarily, raises thunder and lightning—which, moreover, frightens no one, for in reality he is very kind—cannot interfere with or cancel out the good which his activities bring about. Especially now, standing back from him and all that is going on in our musical life and regarding it objectively, I am overcome with amazement at his qualities and willingly forgive him his weaknesses, which in your character sketch of him appeared with such terrible exaggeration. To reply in print to any slander, as you suggest, is impossible, and anyway, I know from experience that if you enter into an argument in print with these journalist gossips, you are only adding fuel to their fire.[73]

I found myself in Paris all for the sake of [. . .] Mme von Meck, who very much wanted me to come here. I admit I do long for my dear Clarens where I happily spent a month in perfect peace. Things are fine here and very convenient but the trouble is that I have altogether lost the capacity for properly enjoying life in a town, even in a town as splendid as Paris. The remoteness of the countryside is essential to me, without the noise and bustle of town life. My health (touch wood) is all that I could wish for. My work is going so well that I will be coming to you [Sasha] with the finished sketches of a whole major opera, which I will orchestrate in the summer.[74]

[73] viii. 77–9 (Stasov).   [74] viii. 111 (Sasha).

I do not remember ever in my life having such a marvellous spell of happiness and well-being as I have had on this trip abroad. Living in Florence, in Switzerland, where I got on so well with my work, my arrival now [in Paris]—it has just been one happy, placid, carefree day after another. I am often frightened that *I will get used to it, will get hardened to it, and will come to take for granted* the limitless blessings I am now enjoying.[75]

I went to the Comédie Française and saw three plays: (1) *Le mariage forcé* by Molière (2) *Le petit Hôtel*, a new and very sweet little play and (3) one of the best of the plays in the French repertoire, *Le gendre de M. Poirier*. How annoyed I am that I did not write and tell you [Mme von Meck], my friend, that you should have seen this excellent play in the wonderful production at the Comédie Française! It gave me the greatest delight. Got, who plays the part of Poirier, is particularly outstanding. This is not acting but simply *une incarnation*. At Christmas I saw this actor in another part (*Les Fourchambaults*) where he seemed such a different character altogether that I even thought: are there two actors called Got in the company? This is the real triumph of the actor's art—to implant in a member of the audience a suspicion about the identity of the same person! I will take the liberty of advising you to visit this theatre when the production of Dumas's *Le fils naturel* is on, in a few days' time. The play is not bad and it is also excellently acted.[76]

I have experienced a great aesthetic pleasure. I have heard Berlioz's *Damnation de Faust* in its entirety—it is one of the miracles of art.[77] I am in general far from being an uncritical admirer of Berlioz. There was something incomplete about his musical make-up, some deficiency of sensitivity in his choice of harmonies and modulations. There is, in short, an element of ugliness in Berlioz to which I cannot reconcile myself at all. But this did not stop him having the spirit of an artist, one of the most distinguished and subtle, who on occasion reached unscalable heights. There are parts of *Faust*, especially that striking and marvellous scene on the banks of the Elbe, which are among the pearls of his art. I had difficulty in holding back the sobs which rose in my throat during this scene. Mephistopheles' recitative before Faust's sleep and the subsequent chorus of spirits and dance of the sylphs are splendid. As you listen to this music you can feel how deeply its composer was moved by his task, how he was seized by poetic inspiration. There are many other marvellous details but I do not particularly like the famous *menuet des feux follets*. The ending is rather boring and there is nothing special about the climax.[78] I have just played through *Etienne Marcel* [Saint-Saëns]. I can honestly say that this opera is a completely insignificant work, quite without talent. It is shallow, dry, tedious, without style or character. I think he was trying to worm himself into

[75] viii. 91 (von Meck).   [76] viii. 106 (von Meck).
[77] viii. 104 (von Meck).   [78] viii. 105 (von Meck).

public favour with its calculated simplicity but not everything that is simple is good. What could be simpler than *Don Giovanni* or *A life for the Tsar*! But the thing is that these operas are not just simple but are also amazingly good, because they have been imbued with a lot of inspiration and creative genius! Saint-Saëns' opera has neither. He has dexterity, knowledge, taste. These three qualities are enough for those small symphonic pictures, some of which are very successful. But for the opera—he has not enough material. The poverty of melody is particularly striking.[79]

I went to the opera. They were doing *Freischütz* and *Yedda*, a new ballet. I enjoyed *Freischütz* very much; in Act I my eyes were wet with tears in several places. In the second act Krauss gave me great pleasure with his beautiful performance of Agathe's aria. 'The Wolf's Glen' was not nearly as brilliantly staged as I had expected. The third act was curious because of the way in which the French unceremoniously permit themselves on the one hand to interpolate *Invitation à la valse* with the most idiotic dances, and on the other, to eliminate the role of the hermit who comes on at the end in the denouement. As far as the ballet *Yedda* was concerned, neither the notorious dancer, San-Galli, nor the notorious music of M. Métra, nor the notorious opulence of the production could satisfy me, and I walked out after two scenes. I have never seen such an ugly mug as San-Galli's. Vazem is a Venus de Milo compared to her. In general I must admit that the Grand Opéra has gone downhill in a big way.[80]

I am at the moment very much under the influence of Dostoyevsky's story *The Brothers Karamazov*. As always in Dostoyevsky the characters are a peculiar crackbrained lot of morbidly nervous types, more like creatures from the realms of dreams and fevered delirium than real people. As always there is in this story as well a sense of oppression, misery, hopelessness, but, as always, there are momentary flashes almost of genius, incredible revelations of his power of analysis as a novelist. The scene where the Elder Zosima receives the sick who have come to him to be cured staggered me, it shook me with sobbing and an attack of hysteria. Amongst the sick is a woman who has come more than three hundred miles to seek comfort from him. Her children have all died one after the other. When she had buried the last one she had no strength left to do battle with her grief; she abandoned her home and her husband and became a wanderer. The simplicity with which she describes her unrelieved despair, the striking power of the artless phrases in which she pours forth her infinite sorrow that *never, never, never* will she see him or hear him again and particularly when she says: '*I wouldn't go up to him, I wouldn't say anything, I would hide in the corner just to be able to see him for a single minute*'—even now I am still racked by the indescribable emotion of it all. And indeed it is better to die oneself twenty-four times a day for a thousand years than to lose loved ones

---

[79] viii. 107 (von Meck).   [80] viii. 102 (Modest).

and to seek consolation in the dubious notion that *we will meet in the next world*. Will we meet? Happy are they who can be certain.[81]

Why do I not visit Turgenev? The question provokes me to give a very thorough and detailed answer. All my life I have been a martyr to the relationships which I have been obliged to keep up with people. I am an unsociable person by nature. I have always found knowing people and meeting new people a source of acute mental strain. I even find it difficult to explain what the real nature of the strain is. Perhaps it is shyness taken to the point of mania, perhaps it is the utter and complete absence of any need for sociability, perhaps it is the misguided fear of appearing other than I am, perhaps it is the inability to say what I don't think without forcing myself to it (and without this ability one will never get to know anybody), in short I do not know what it is but what I do know is that, when my situation did not permit me to avoid meeting people, I did meet them, pretended that I enjoyed it, was compelled by sheer necessity to act out my part (because if one lives in society there is no possibility of avoiding this), and suffered agonies. Only God knows what I went through. I am so happy and relaxed now precisely because I can, at least here and in the country, live without seeing anybody apart from those with whom I can be myself. *Never in my life* have I made so much as a move to get to know somebody or other interesting. And if it has happened of its own accord, by force of circumstances, all it has brought me has been disappointment, sadness, and exhaustion. What I mean is, in broader terms, this: *in my opinion one can enjoy someone else's company only when, after knowing them and sharing their interests (especially family interests) for many years, one can be oneself with them.* Without this, any form of association is a *burden* and my mental make-up is such that it is a burden which I am unable to bear. That is why I do not go to see Turgenev or anybody else. There are plenty of people I could go to see here. Saint-Saëns is here and when he was in Moscow he made me promise that whenever I was in Paris I would visit him. Anybody else in my position would have got to know all the people to do with music here. And I very much regret not having done so—I miss a lot because of my unsociability. How I have struggled with this failing of mine and how much I have suffered in the battle with my peculiar character! What a torment it has been! How hard I have worked at trying to change myself! But it does not worry me now. I have finally convinced myself that there is no point in keeping trying to re-educate myself. Turgenev has several times expressed a sympathetic interest in my music. Viardot has sung some of my songs; so it would seem that I ought to have gone to see them and it would probably even have been useful. But I am now reconciled to the notion that my unsociability paralyses my chances of success and have stopped worrying about

[81] viii. 116–17 (von Meck).

it altogether. I have been very happy since I have been able to hide away in my burrow where I can always be myself; I have been happy since books and music have been my constant and almost my only companions. As to actually knowing famous people, my experience has led me to stumble upon the truth that their books and their music are more interesting than they are themselves.[82]

Tchaikovsky heard Berlioz's *Symphonie Fantastique* at one of the Pasdeloup concerts on 18 February.

Berlioz's symphony makes very interesting listening but I would not say that it is one of my favourite pieces by him. There are many unartistic, purely external effects in it: the depiction of the storm, for instance, using only *timpani*. But the waltz and the march are beautiful. And the main theme, which runs through the whole work and portrays the beloved, is weak.[83]

Completely to my own surprise *I have finished the opera altogether*. What an immense relief it is to get such a load off my mind. Whatever you may say, sitting down at a particular time every day for almost two and a half months and squeezing music out of one's head, sometimes very easily, sometimes with an effort, is an exhausting business. But how I am going to relax now! The scoring, after all, is only brain work! It is like embroidering on a canvas over a ready-printed design.[84] I wrote it really quickly. The whole secret is working systematically every day. In this respect I have an iron grip on myself and when I don't especially feel like working I can always make myself overcome my disinclination and develop some enthusiasm.[85]

I have been walking round Paris like quite another man, like *an idle flâneur* in fact, and perhaps this is why all the love which I have nurtured for this city over the years is making itself felt with the force which it used to have in my youth. This process has, incidentally, been aided by another circumstance: my *Tempest* has been announced for one of the Châtelet concerts. Meeting my name on the advertising pillars and in the windows of music shops has made me feel at home in Paris.[86]

It will be an entirely new feeling for me to hear one of my own works in the audience, which will have no suspicion of my presence. This feeling could be remarkably pleasant if the performance turns out to be good. As far as success or failure is concerned, I assure you that I am not even thinking about it, so convinced am I in advance of its failure. The French public has got thoroughly stuck in a musical rut, and if it chooses to recognize its own native musicians only many years after their death, what can foreigners expect. I will not be at all surprised and will be very little hurt by failure: I am an old hand at this.[87]

[82] viii. 121–3 (von Meck).   [83] viii. 123–4 (von Meck).
[84] viii. 129 (Modest).   [85] viii. 124 (von Meck).
[86] viii. 129 (Modest).   [87] viii. 131 (von Meck).

The torments I have gone through are the clearest possible proof that I should not live anywhere but in the country. Even listening to my own works, which previously gave me the greatest pleasure, has become nothing but a source of agony. One would have thought that the conditions under which I heard *The Tempest* would have assured my complete tranquillity. Not at all. From the morning onwards, and right up to the opening chords, my agitation was crescendo all the time and when they started playing I was in such a state of perturbation that I thought I would die, right there, on the spot. And I was agitated because for some time every fresh hearing of one of my works, whatever it may be, has been accompanied by the most acute sense of disappointment in myself. As if on purpose, they played Mendelssohn's 'Reformation' Symphony before *The Tempest*; though it did move me very much, I was constantly astonished by his marvellous craftsmanship. I lack *craftsmanship*. I still write like a promising *young man* of whom much can be expected but who gives very little. What surprises me most of all is that my orchestra sounds so bad. Of course my reason tells me that I am rather exaggerating my faults, but that is small consolation. *The Tempest* was performed not badly at all, although it was not first-rate either. The tempi were absolutely right. I thought that the musicians played diligently but without enthusiasm or love. One of them (a cellist), whom for some reason I could not take my eyes off, was smiling and looked as if he was exchanging glances with someone, as if to say, 'Forgive us for offering you such strange fare, but it isn't our fault: they order us to play and we play!' When the final chords had been played, reasonably warm applause broke out, then it was as if another round was in preparation, but at this point there were three or four very loud whistles, whereupon the hall was filled with cries of 'Oh! Oh!', signifying a well-meant protest against the hissing, and then the hall fell silent. I withstood all this without any particular feelings of hurt, but I was devastated by the thought that *The Tempest*, which I have grown used to regarding as my most brilliant composition, is in fact so worthless! I left immediately. The weather was wonderful and I walked for about two hours without stopping, after which I went home and wrote a note to Colonne in which I lied that I had only been in Paris for one day and therefore could not be there in person. The note expresses sincere gratitude, and indeed, he had learnt *The Tempest* very well. After that I felt notably calmer. I have adjusted to this situation by deciding that after the opera and the suite I will, at last, write a model symphonic work. And so it seems that until I draw my last breath I will only strive for mastery and never attain it.[88]

Today I discovered from the newspapers that in actual fact only one man hissed *The Tempest*. He also hissed Saint-Saëns. I am sending you the newspaper cutting which confirms this piece of information. In general,

[88] viii. 138–9 (Modest).

with my usual capacity for seeing all my smallest adversities in a very exaggerated light, I also exaggerated the failure of *The Tempest*.[89]

I have been to see *L'Assommoir* [Emile Zola] and will tell you what I think of it. As a play it is at least interesting to watch because everybody likes to see the washerwomen at their work in Scene 2, and in Scene 6 all the characters are drunk and there is an orgy of gluttony, and in Scene 8 a drunkard dies of *delirium tremens* with the most dreadful writhing convulsions. This is all interesting in its way, but none the less *L'Assommoir* as a play is a double offence to any decent person's sense of good taste. In the first place, it is based on a novel written by a man who, although he is gifted, is a cynic and likes to spend his time amongst all sorts of human squalor, both physical and moral. In the second place, in adapting the play from the novel they have tried to make it more striking by inserting into the story an altogether improbable element of melodrama so as to satisfy the vulgar demands of the public. In consequence, when seen in the theatre, *L'Assommoir* lost its sole merit: its remarkably faithful depiction of life.[90]

For the first time in my life I am reading Rousseau's *Confessions*. One cannot but be astonished, first at the amazing strength and beauty of his style, and then at the depth and truth of his analysis of the human heart. That apart, it gives me indescribable pleasure to find, in his admissions, aspects of my own character which I have never seen described with such incredible accuracy in any work of literature. For instance, I read his explanation of why, although he was a clever man, he never gave the impression of being one when he was in the company of other people. In this context he expatiates on his unsociable nature and on *the unbearable burden of being obliged to maintain a conversation,* to which end one has to utter empty words, devoid of feeling, and expressing no real mental process or emotion. My God! How profoundly true and accurate are his thoughts on this scourge of social life![91] What an incomparable book it is! There are parts which simply astound me. He says things which I find astonishingly easy to understand and which I have never discussed with anybody because I have not known how to express them and then I suddenly come upon them given the fullest possible expression in Rousseau![92] The interest of the book lies in the fact that one cannot decide which are the more astonishing: the agreeable sides of Rousseau's character or the repulsive sides. His most disgraceful act was to send to a *foundling hospital,* as *enfants trouvés,* his *five* children by the beautiful woman whom he loved; then he lived for years and years, apparently not in the least concerned about this and not making any effort to find out what had happened to them!!! There is something so offensive and disgusting about this action that I spend hours trying to work out how such phenomenal heartlessness can go with the clear evidence of a kind and loving heart to be seen in other episodes of his life. The

[89] viii. 143 (Jurgenson).   [90] viii. 131 (von Meck).
[91] viii. 142–3 (von Meck).   [92] viii. 145 (Anatoly).

book as a whole has made a tremendously strong impression on me. Sometimes I find descriptions of emotional experiences which are familiar to me but which I have never before seen in any work of literature. All the same, there is a lot in the *Confessions* which I cannot understand so I would like to read quite a lot of books describing this strange, impenetrable eighteenth century. I would like to know how his contemporaries regarded Rousseau; and by comparing his autobiography with other views I would like to find the key to understanding this extraordinary character who interests me because some of his weaknesses are astonishingly like my own. Of course, this similarity does not extend to the intellect, which in his case may have been paradoxical but was certainly great, to which I can and do have positively no pretensions.[93] Towards the end of his life Rousseau was just a trivial and peevish gossip. I am somewhat disappointed in him.[94]

I forgot to thank you for Liszt's book about Chopin. I knew it already and I don't like it. Far too wordy, too much empty blather and condemnation of the Russians.[95]

The desire to hear *Onegin* has overcome my inclination to hide myself away and so I have decided that I will definitely be in Moscow on 17 [March], but only if I can be incognito i.e. nobody is to know apart from a small circle at the Conservatoire.[96] At first I wasn't sure whether to go to Moscow on this occasion but now I so much want to see my dream realized on the stage that there is no doubt at all about my trip to Moscow.[97] So, I am setting off for Russia. I will take with me the happiest memories of these months which have been immensely enjoyable as well as being useful. It is a long time since there has been in my life such an extended period of unbroken happiness.[98]

Of everything I have seen in Berlin I like the aquarium most of all. Yesterday I saw the crocodiles being fed, and today it will be the feeding time for the snakes and boa constrictors, and I wanted to go and watch, but I am afraid of the impression the boa constrictors will have on me when they are fed live rabbits.[99]

Admittedly you can hear Bilse's excellent orchestra and a good programme here every evening and I have been two evenings in a row, but I couldn't at all get used to the German habit, while listening to a Beethoven symphony, of drinking beer, coffee, eating sausages and sauerkraut, and similar delights, as a result of which, towards the end in particular, the atmosphere was completely impossible. One can say much in defence of this strange custom, and most importantly, that while the music is being performed, this whole noisy audience was quiet, and absolute silence reigned. On the first evening they performed, incidentally, the Andante

---

[93] viii. 147–8 (von Meck).   [94] viii. 151 (von Meck).
[95] viii. 135 (von Meck).   [96] viii. 140 (Jurgenson).
[97] viii. 142 (von Meck).   [98] viii. 141 (von Meck).
[99] viii. 150 (von Meck).

from my First Quartet, and listening to this piece gave me great pleasure. All the strings played it, but with such good ensemble and with such elegance that it was as if each part was being played by one colossal instrument. In general the orchestra is excellent, but it is a pity all the same that while listening to it you have to inhale air laden with tobacco smoke and the smell of cabbage and roast meat.[100]

[100] viii. 146 (von Meck).

14

1879–1881

*How little it takes to satisfy me: reasonable progress in my work, the chance to
have a walk through the woods every day, the small world of the close family
circle—that's all.*

I will not go into detail about my impressions here in Petersburg. Suffice it
to say that despite the presence of my father and my brothers I really am
the *unhappiest* of men so long as I live in this revolting town. I find everything here disgusting, starting with the climate and ending with the chaotic
way people live. More distressing and insufferable than anything else is my
total inability to avoid the necessity of seeing and meeting endless people
who are of no interest to me, whom I do not especially like or, at best,
regard with indifference; but I have to talk to them, to keep up a conversation, and at the same time to stifle my boredom and displeasure.[1]

Tchaikovsky then went to Moscow for the première of *Eugene Onegin* on 17 March
in a performance by students of the Conservatoire.

I arrived in Moscow just before the rehearsal started. It was being done
with costumes and full stage lights but there were no lights in the auditor-
ium. So I was able to sit in a dark corner and listen to my opera without
being pestered. I enjoyed it very much. The performance was very satisfactory on the whole. The chorus and orchestra did their bit beautifully. The
soloists, of course, left a very great deal to be desired. Gilev was very conscientious as Onegin but his voice is so feeble, so dry and charmless.
Klimentova as Tatyana comes nearer to my ideal and this is largely
because, despite her marked lack of ability as an actress, she sings with
warmth and sincerity. Lensky was sung by some Medvedev fellow, a Jew,
with not at all a bad voice but still a complete novice and his Russian pro-
nunciation is poor. Of the secondary roles, Triquet and Prince Gremin
were well done. The staging was extremely good and in my view some of
the scenes (particularly the dance in the country) were beyond criticism in
this respect. The same might be said of the costumes. These few hours
spent in a dark corner of the theatre were the only ones that I enjoyed in the
whole of my stay in Moscow. During the intervals I met all of my former

---

[1] viii. 154 (von Meck).

colleagues. I was very glad to see that they were all, without exception, remarkably enthusiastic about the music for *Onegin*. Nikolay Grigoryevich, who is very sparing with his praise, told me that he was *in love* with the music. After the first act Taneyev wanted to tell me how much he liked it but broke into sobs instead. It's hard to put into words how touched I was. In fact everybody without exception was so enthusiastic and sincere in telling me how they liked *Onegin* that I was surprised and gratified.[2]

My brothers and a few other people including Anton Rubinstein and Alexandra Panayeva, the object of Anatoly's affections, arrived on Sunday morning (the day of the performance). I was in a very agitated state of mind all day, in particular because I had had to agree to Nikolay Grigoryevich's insistent request that I should appear on the stage if there were any curtain calls. My worries rose to a pitch of extremity during the performance and got to the point where they were an excruciating torment. Before it began Nikolay Grigoryevich called me on to the stage. When I got there I saw, to my horror, the whole Conservatoire assembled and Nikolay Grigoryevich at the head of the professors with a wreath which he presented to me to the accompaniment of loud applause from everybody present. I had to say a few words in reply to his speech. The Lord alone knows what an effort it cost me! I was given a lot of curtain calls at the intervals. I did not, incidentally, observe that the audience was exactly in raptures. I conclude from this that it was me the public was calling on to the stage and not the performers; the performance was interrupted by vigorous applause only twice: after Triquet's couplets and Gremin's aria. It was noticeable that they did not like Onegin and Lensky. They gave Klimentova a very warm reception. And there was vigorous applause for the chorus after the two choral numbers in the first act. After the performance there was a supper at The Hermitage and Anton Rubinstein was there. I really don't know whether he liked *Onegin* or not. At any rate he didn't say a word to me. There were speeches and I for my part was compelled to get up and say a few words. Making speeches at dinners and suppers is one of the most disagreeable things I have to do. Towards the end everybody livened up and Anton Rubinstein spoke once or twice.[3]

I want to tell you [Mme von Meck], my dear friend, about the scene which a certain person unexpectedly made this morning. Hardly had the servant you sent left when a woman rang the doorbell and asked for me. Since, as the doorman explained, this woman had come several times yesterday as well and had wandered about near the entrance waiting for me, I had an intuition that this could be none other than a certain person. So, as I went into my brother's study, where she was waiting for me, I was to a certain extent prepared for this interview and was even convinced that everything would happen as it indeed did. I had hardly appeared than she threw

[2] viii. 155–6 (von Meck).   [3] viii. 156–7 (von Meck).

herself on my neck and began to repeat ceaselessly that I was the only person in the world that she loved, that she could not live without me, that she would agree to any conditions provided that I would live with her and so on. She probably wanted to touch my feelings and by her outpourings of tenderness achieve what she was unable to achieve by her refusal to grant me a divorce. I cannot possibly go into all the details of the succession of scenes which she tormented me with over the next two hours at least. This scene shook me to the core. It demonstrated to me that only abroad and in the country am I guaranteed against being pestered by a certain person. As far as *divorce* is concerned, there is no point in thinking about it. Evidently nothing on earth is going to shake her out of her delusion that in reality I am in love with her.[4]

At last I am at Kamenka. The nightingales and larks are singing, there are lots of violets in the garden, the sun is warm and welcoming; all my near ones are in good health.[5] Though I do sometimes complain that Kamenka is not a very attractive-looking place and is not quite the country, all the same I have completely revived here. From time to time I am seized with those moments of ecstasy which only nature can provide.[6] They have arranged a permanent little flat for me here: they have made three very nice little rooms out of the former laundry which will be my permanent *pied-à-terre* so long as my sister's family lives at Kamenka. My quarters consist of a small study, a little room for Alexey, and my bedroom. All my things—books, music, pictures—have arrived here and my new flat now looks quite enticing. I feel very well and my mind is at peace with a feeling of calm, tranquil happiness. I started working two days after I got here and my famous, long-suffering suite will soon be finished.[7]

The time passes in the following way: I get up at eight o'clock. After drinking tea I work in my dear little study. Lunch is at twelve. Then I work again. At three I go for a walk. Dinner is at five, after which I wander about near the house and enjoy the wonderful twilight—my favourite time of day. Tea is served at eight and then they sit in the drawing-room, chatting, playing cards, and finally go to bed at twelve. I am sleeping marvellously well at the moment. Yesterday all my things arrived, i.e. books, music, pictures and so on. Now everything is already standing and hanging in its proper place. Tanya is exceptionally sweet. I don't remember her ever before making such a good impression on me. Sasha worries me a little. She looks somehow tired and exhausted. However, it's nothing very serious.[8]

I have been working on the Suite for two weeks now. At Brailov I want to give myself up altogether to my ever-increasing love for nature. There is nowhere in the whole world which would give me such scope in this respect. To be entirely free and alone, to be able to visit the woods every

[4] viii. 159–60.   [5] viii. 166, 167 (von Meck).   [6] viii. 169 (von Meck).
[7] viii. 170 (von Meck).   [8] viii. 171 (Anatoly).

day, to be amongst greenery and flowers all the time, to listen to the night-ingale at one's windows at night, and, moreover, still to have the use of books and musical instruments, to be able to wander through the lovely house—such an unheard of conjunction of circumstances conducive to pleasure could not be found elsewhere. If on top of all this I stay on until the flowering of the lilac, which is the most sumptuous glory of the grounds, then it would, I think, be impossible to imagine a more tempting form of existence. I will never forget how happy I was at Brailov last year, especially on my first visit. One of the pleasures of country life is finding oneself far away from all the hideous monstrosities that are now taking place in towns and cities. I cannot pick up a newspaper without a feeling of horror![9]

From now on Tchaikovsky for several years organizes his life into a strict 'cycle'. He spends the spring, summer, and early autumn in the country, where his sister's houses at Kamenka and Verbovka become his home; he stays at Brailov and Simaki as the guest of Mme von Meck, and goes abroad for the winter.

Here I found everything in its place. It was strange! This time I did not want to come here at all, although in my heart I knew that a few days' solit-ude amidst the wonderful surroundings here would be very good for me. But when I arrived and smelt the house's characteristic smell as I walked in, and seeing all the familiar objects and faces which last year had wit-nessed the wonderful peace of mind which I found on both my visits to Brailov, I immediately felt happy.[10]

I have at last finished the Suite and have earned the right to turn to the opera, which I will do in the next few days.[11]

[At Kamenka] spring makes colossal progress by the hour. The lilac is beginning to blossom and *the lily of the valley* (!!!) is starting to show. This present time of year is marvellous in every way: lily of the valley, lilac, nightingales, and, to crown it all, marvellous weather and moonlit nights.[12] I can think of no more perfect form of happiness than lying on the grass drinking tea on a fine day in the woods. The walk to Trostyanka is the only one which reconciles me to the actual location of Kamenka. I go there nearly every day.[13]

This woodland quiet and cool evokes wonderful sensations. One of the pillars of contemporary music, Raff, tried to express the delights and wide expanses of the woods in his symphony, 'Im Walde', and he succeeded very well in some places; in the first movement particularly there is a wonderful harmonic sequence with echoing horns, repeated three times, which always takes me straight back to the woods with all their charms.[14]

You [Mme von Meck] have several times asked me about boating, and I, with unforgivable absentmindedness, have not answered you at all until now. No, my friend, I am not a great lover of this activity. In general I only

[9] viii. 173 (von Meck).   [10] viii. 196 (Anatoly).   [11] viii. 186 (Anatoly).
[12] viii. 181 (von Meck).   [13] viii. 188 (Anatoly).   [14] viii. 202 (von Meck).

of *The Tempest*. But what makes me inexpressibly happy is that I discovered from the newspaper *Kievlyanin* [*The Kiev Citizen*] that my
Liturgy has been sung there several times at the University Church. And
there I was thinking that it was probably doomed to eternal oblivion![24]

Brailov, Kamenka, Nizy, Kamenka again . . . At the end of the summer Mme von
Meck invited Tchaikovsky to spend some time at the farm of Simaki, near to
Brailov.

My first impressions of this place. They are astonishingly pleasant. The
little house is positively ancient; there is a densely packed garden with cen-
turies-old oaks and limes, very neglected and delightful for that very
reason, a river at the end of the garden. Our distance from the factory, and
from the little town, the absolute peace, the exceptional comfort of my
accommodation, which consists of a drawing-room, a huge study, a dining-
room, a bedroom, and Alyosha's room—all this answers perfectly to my
tastes and preferences. All around there are farmsteads, fields, and copses
where one can wander without meeting anybody. But alas! There is always
a fly in the ointment. The *fly* here is the proximity of Nadezhda Filaretovna
with her family and entourage. Although I am quite sure that no one will
disturb me, this proximity bothers me a little all the same.[25] I really am
bound to say that my feelings are of utter bliss; life here is like a marvellous
dream, the realization of all my most sacred visions of the ideal. Only when
one is alone in the warm bosom of nature can one experience moments of
true happiness. Not even art can provide those moments of ecstatic rapture
which nature gives.[26]

Why did I call the second movement of the suite a Divertimento? That
question takes me back vividly to the *unforgettable, incomparable, blissful
days* which I spent at Simaki. I was working on the orchestration of the
opera at that time. I was sitting on the veranda after lunch one day, revelling in my happiness and the marvellous sight of the lovely little garden, all
densely overgrown, when I thought of my suite and suddenly realized that
all five movements are in duple time. I was horrified and decided straight
away to add a sixth movement, not too long, and in a gentle waltz rhythm.
Since I was in exactly the right mood my intention was very soon carried
out. I did not know what to call the new movement and chose Divertimento
as the first name I thought of. I did not think it had any particular significance amongst the other movements and it was only inserted into the suite to
save it from rhythmic monotony. I really did write it in just one sitting and
gave it far less thought and polishing up than the other movements. Apparently this does not stop people liking it the best of all. It only goes to show
me for the thousandth time that the composer can never be the judge of his
own works.[27]

[24] viii. 265 (von Meck).   [25] viii. 309 (Modest).
[26] viii. 311 (von Meck).   [27] ix. 54–5 (von Meck).

I am terribly fond of these nice, greyish days. And indeed the beginning of autumn can only be compared with spring for its attractions. I even think that the tender melancholy of nature's colouring in autumn has the greater power to fill my soul with a gentle sense of joy. There are charming places near Simaki which one can enjoy at sunset in the evening or on a day when there is no sun. I am very fond of these places. When it is sunny during the day the sun prevents you from seeing the countryside which spreads so picturesquely before you. It's very pleasant to sit somewhere rather higher up and look at the enormous willows which grow down below, mixed in with the poplars, at the village with its little church (a little country church does so much for any village scene), at the woods in the distance. I sat in such a spot for about an hour and experienced one of those marvellous moments when all one's cares and concerns just vanish. You abandon yourself instead to all sorts of half-digested ideas and fantasies. Flocks of swallows circle overhead and you immediately start to wonder: why are they gathering, are they going to fly off, where will they fly to? You look at the ancient trees and try to work out how old they are.[28]

I am intending to orchestrate the last act of my opera here and will get down to work tomorrow. I want to cast from my shoulders the burden which has been somewhat troubling me; here I am bringing to completion a major and complex work, on which I am pinning a lot of hopes; here I can breathe freely and experience the pleasure second to none of realizing that the end of a difficult task is in sight.[29]

Tchaikovsky made a short business trip to Moscow and St Petersburg.

It is very difficult for me to describe to you [Mme von Meck] my troubled state of mind, which does not clear up for a single minute, to such an extent that I have to make a tremendous effort just to write the simplest letter. It is as if I had been hit over the head with a poker and my intellectual capabilities had become dim. This is how I have reacted to the sharp transition from country life to the chaos of Petersburg. One thought never leaves my mind, and one desire has taken possession of my soul—*to get out of here as quickly as possible*! I am ashamed to admit this not only to you but to myself as well. Here I have my father and my brother, whom I love dearly; but my hatred of Petersburg overcomes my warmest and most heartfelt attachments. The hardest thing of all is that I have as far as possible to hide my secret intentions so as not to hurt my nearest and dearest. Up till now I have hardly dared to utter the word *departure*: I so much wanted to avoid making them sad! But really, I cannot stand it any longer! I think, however, that I shall be able to leave in a week's time.[30]

Yesterday I went to a sympony concert in Pavlovsk. I was interested in hearing the Scherzo from our symphony which was on the programme.

[28] viii. 347–8 (von Meck).   [29] viii. 307 (von Meck).
[30] viii. 360.

The performance was unremarkable, but I enjoyed hearing it all the same.[31]

In Moscow I was just as exhausted and bored as I was in Petersburg—even more so. It is very strange. My friends from the musical world of Moscow greet me with expressions of great joy, and for the first few minutes I am glad to see them; but as soon as these first moments have passed and we have asked each other how we are and what we are up to, a sort of tedium and a kind of awkwardness set in. A great gulf has appeared between us which gets wider and wider. Their way of life, which is just the same as I led with them before, in which abundant libations to Bacchus play all too large a part, their petty personal concerns and relationships, reproaches, and misunderstandings, all this has become so alien to me! And yet, I sincerely love and respect many of them. I think that our vague mutual feeling of alienation from each other stems from the fact that, although they are all my *friends* in the ordinary sense of the word, none of them has ever been a real *friend* to me, has never been really *close* to me. Our friendship has been purely on the surface, and now that destiny has made our paths diverge, the lack of real feelings of friendship makes itself felt.[32]

Tchaikovsky spent the autumn at Kamenka.

I go for lots of walks, read a lot, and even do *just a tiny bit of composing*. I have started a Piano Concerto [The Second Concerto (G major)]. I have had a letter from my brother Anatoly. Incidentally, he mentions the performance of *Vakula*. The theatre was packed but, as before, the audience was cool. Anatoly attributes this to the appalling performance. But I can see with astonishing clarity that this coolness is the consequence of my *clumsy* mistakes. I am glad to think that *The Maid of Orleans* shows no traces of my former, misguided operatic style, which consisted in exhausting the listener with a superfluity of detail, complexity of harmony, and an excess of orchestral effects. That apart, I did not know how *to let the listener rest*; I gave him too much spicy musical food all at once. The operatic style must be marked by spaciousness, simplicity, and a certain decorative element. The style of *Vakula* is not operatic; it is a symphonic, even a chamber-music style. It is a matter for astonishment that it was not a complete failure and that it continues not only to hold its ground but even to attract large audiences. It may well be, indeed, that in time the public will even come to like it. As to my own attitude to *Vakula*, I must say that, whilst I am acutely aware of its deficiencies *as an opera*, I none the less place it in the first rank of my works. I wrote that music with affection and with delight, just as I did *Onegin*, the Fourth Symphony, and the Second Quartet.[33]

[31] viii. 361 (von Meck).   [32] viii. 369 (von Meck).
[33] viii. 389–91 (von Meck).

When writing an opera the composer must constantly have the stage in mind, he must remember that the theatre requires not only melodies and harmony but *action* as well; that one must not take up too much of the attention of the opera audience which has come not only *to listen but also to look*; and, finally, that music for the theatre should correspond in style to decorative art, which means that it should be *simple, clear, and colourful*. Music overflowing with harmonic subtleties is wasted in the theatre where the listener needs clearly defined melodies and a transparent harmonic texture. The requirements [of the stage] paralyse the composer's purely musical inspiration to a considerable extent and this is why symphonic and chamber music is of a far higher order than operatic music. In a symphony or sonata I am *free*, without restriction or constraint. On the other hand opera does have the advantage of making it possible to speak in the language of music to *the masses*. The mere fact that an opera may be performed forty times in a season gives it an advantage over a symphony which will be played once in ten years! Yet, despite all the allure of opera, I derive infinitely greater pleasure and enjoyment from writing a symphony, or a sonata, or a quartet. One must pass through a series of unsuccessful experiments in order to reach whatever level of achievement one is capable of and I am not at all ashamed of my operatic failures. They were useful lessons from which I have learnt much. [I used to be] so stubborn in my refusal to see where I had gone wrong, to see that I could not understand the requirements of opera: after all, *Undine* (the opera which I burnt) and *The Oprichnik* and *Vakula*—none of them is what is needed. It is a skill which does not come to me at all easily. *I think* that at last I have got it right in *The Maid of Orleans* but I may indeed be mistaken. If so, if it turns out that *The Maid* still does not satisfy the requirements of the operatic style, then it will be clear to me that those who maintain that I am by nature exclusively a symphonic composer who ought not to clamber on to the stage are right. In that case I will never attempt again to write an opera.[34]

My new musical offspring is beginning to grow and the traits of its character are gradually becoming clear. I am composing very enthusiastically, but a little at a time, and I am trying to contain my usual feverish haste which always reflects badly on my work. We are all well and happy here; only the elderly Alexandra Ivanovna Davydova, Lev Vasilyevich's mother, has often been unwell recently; *c'est le commencement de la fin*, but, God willing, the end will come as slowly as possible. The whole family, with its many members, adore the head of the family and this truly saintly woman is worthy of it. She is the last surviving wife of the Decembrists who followed their husbands into penal servitude. Several of her children were born in the Petrovsky factory *at the penal settlement*. She generally had to bear a lot of grief in her youth. But her old age has been full of peaceful family happi-

---

[34] viii. 445–6 (von Meck).

ness. And what a marvellous family it is. I count myself lucky that fate has brought us together and so often gives me the opportunity of seeing in their faces the spiritual heights of which man is capable. Fate generally spoils me in that respect. I am a misanthropist not in the sense that I hate people but in that I feel oppressed when I come into contact with *a crowd* of people. But there are separate individuals who are near to me (for instance that best of friends to whom my Fourth Symphony is dedicated), and who make me love mankind and wonder at the perfection which its moral beauty can attain.[35]

Have you [Mme von Meck] read, my dear friend, the philosophical articles by Vladimir Solovyov (the son of the late Dean and historian) in *Russky vestnik* [*The Russian Herald*]? They are *excellently* written in the sense that they are entirely accessible to the non-specialist and the ideas are expounded with great talent and acuity. I do not know what conclusions he will eventually reach but in the last issue (August) he gave a remarkably convincing and acute proof of the deficiencies of positivism, a negative school of thought which regards metaphysics as mere imagination but is powerless to do without philosophy. Solovyov makes a remarkably telling criticism of the materialists who think that in denying metaphysics they are dealing only with *what really exists* i.e. with matter, whereas matter does not have an objective existence and is only a *phenomenon* i.e. the result of the activities of our feelings and of our intellect. The only thing which has *any real existence* is our power of cognition i.e. our *reason*. I am only giving a poor exposition of his ideas. That apart, I have started on Chicherin's book *Science and Religion*. As you can see, I have launched out into philosophy. My cast of mind is not at all philosophical and such reading does not come easily to me but at times when my attention is not completely engrossed in a difficult piece of work I like to do a bit of philosophizing.[36]

My thoughts are confused and the pen is slipping from my hand. I have found at my sister's some enormous bundles of my letters to my father and mother, written from Petersburg some time when I was ten or eleven and completely alone in the big, strange town. It's difficult to explain how disturbing it was to read these letters which took me back almost thirty years and vividly reminded me of how I suffered as a child from missing my mother, whom I loved with a sort of morbidly passionate love. It is twenty-five years since she died! As a result of reading the letters I spent an entirely sleepless night.[37]

Tchaikovsky went abroad for the winter of 1879/80. He spent some time in Paris and then settled in the Hôtel Costanzi in Rome with Modest and his pupil Kolya Konradi.

How interesting Passek's memoirs are and how grateful I am to you for the

[35] viii. 393 (von Meck).   [36] viii. 396 (von Meck).   [37] viii. 402 (von Meck).

book. I like the warmth, the liveliness of expression and the accuracy, and also the complete objectivity with which she depicts the young people of her day and in particular Herzen. He was an amazingly clever and talented person, but how much triviality and vanity there was in him! In general when we see great people intimately, *chez-soi*, they come down from the pedestal on which we, in our imagination, have placed them, and turn out to be exactly the same simple mortals as the rest of us poor sinners. The only exception (at least among musicians) is Mozart. He had a great spirit, as pure as a dove's, on all occasions and in whatever circumstances. He had no great intellect, but not once did any of those feelings creep into his heart which perpetually torment people of a certain profession in their dealings with society in general and with people belonging to the same profession in particular. His was a remarkable personality![38]

I do not entirely agree with your opinion of Cui, my dear friend. I do not see any great creative power in him, but he has elegance, beautiful harmony, and taste, in which he stands apart from the other representatives of this circle of musicians and in particular from Musorgsky, who is more naturally gifted, but who is spoilt by the coarseness of his methods and his leaning towards musical ugliness. Do you know Cui's opera *Ratcliff*? There are some delightful things in it, but, unfortunately, it suffers from a certain sickliness and oiliness in the vocal writing. It is evident that the author sat over each little bar for a long time and lovingly finished it off, and in consequence the picture is not free enough, the touches are too artifically contrived. Besides that, the thing that destroys him is what you call *originalizing*. The nature of Cui's talent inclines him towards a light type of music, with the piquantly rhythmical characteristics of the French. But the demands of the circle to which he belongs force him to distort his talent and to impose on himself those pseudo-original harmonic tricks which make his style sound artificial and strained. You are not quite correct in calling him prolific. Cui is now forty-four, but he has written in all two operas and about forty romances. He took ten years to write *Ratcliff*! It is obvious that the opera was composed piece by piece, each very painstakingly polished but in the work as a whole this manifests itself in a lack of unity and an unevenness of style.[39]

I found Modest and Kolya utterly enchanted with Rome. It would have caused the greatest sorrow to both of them to have to go anywhere else at the moment. So we are staying here, but as the Hôtel de Russie is very uncomfortable and very expensive, and besides they have nowhere where we can all be together, we set out today to find either a furnished room or another good hotel. Our efforts were rewarded with success. We found some very attractive rooms with a magnificent view of Rome in the Hôtel Costanzi, on a corner so that we won't have any neighbours, and the price is

[38] viii. 435 (von Meck).   [39] viii. 439–40 (von Meck).

comparatively modest. We move there tomorrow and my address will now be: Hôtel Costanzi, Via S. Niccolo di Tolentino.[40]

I have finished the rough draft of my concerto and I am very pleased with it, especially the second movement, the Andante. Now I am going to start revising the Second Symphony, in which I am going to leave only the last movement untouched. An extraordinary thing happened with this symphony: I handed it over to Bessel in 1872 and as a reward for the trouble he took over the production of *The Oprichnik*, did not take any royalties, but it was agreed that he would print the score of the symphony. He deceived me for seven years, continually assuring me that the score would soon be ready when he had not even started to engrave it. I was very angry, but what a service he did me by being so dishonest. Since I have been looking at the symphony again I have found, side by side with the successful parts, such weak places that I have decided to rewrite completely the first and third movements, revise the second, and just to shorten the last. And so if I succeed in working well in Rome, instead of an immature and mediocre symphony, I shall have a good one. You never can tell when you are going to win and when you will lose.[41]

In the evening the moon rises and a wonderful picture of Rome unfolds from our windows. Yesterday we walked to S. Pietro in Montorio. You have probably been there and I will not describe the delights of the view which you get from the terrace below the church. Today I went inside S. Giovanni in Laterano and experienced deep artistic pleasure from the sight of this church's grandiose façade. I also saw the Scala Santa. A service was taking place in the church. A Cardinal was officiating and the choir sang the Mass *a cappella* with the organ. The music was contemporary and was not at all suitable for a church service, but it was wonderfully performed. What voices the Italians have! The tenor soloist sang a bad, utterly operatic aria, but his voice was so marvellous that I was completely captivated. The service itself has nowhere near the same poetically solemn fascination that the Russian Orthodox service is steeped in.[42]

It is Christmas Day today. In the morning we went to St Peter's and heard a solemn Mass. What colossal grandeur this cathedral has! There were a lot of people, but compared with the enormous dimensions of this astonishing temple the crowd seemed nothing more than an insignificant handful of people moving about. In all the countless side chapels there were silent masses being said, and priests with donations, accompanied by small processions, kept on walking across in all directions: all this was full of movement, picturesque, and beautiful. But nevertheless I would a thousand times rather have our Orthodox Liturgy, where everyone present within the building sees and hears the same thing, where the whole congregation stands together instead of darting from corner to corner. It is less

---

[40] viii. 460 (von Meck).   [41] viii. 457 (von Meck).   [42] viii. 463 (von Meck).

picturesque but more moving and more solemn. What weather! What sun! What a view from our windows![43]

Yesterday we went to the Monte Testaccio, from where you have a wonderful view of Rome and of the Campagna di Roma. From there we walked to S. Paolo fuori le Mura, a basilica of huge proportions and enormous wealth, outside the town. This is a strikingly beautiful hall, but it is just a hall and not at all like a church. Today I looked at the Forum Romanum in detail for the first time. My interest in this has increased threefold at the moment since I am reading Ampère's excellent *L'histoire romaine à Rome*, which goes into the greatest detail about everything which went on in this very place. I have quite a respectable piano; I equipped myself with some volumes of Bach in Ricordi's music shop and a few arrangements for piano duet (to play with Modest) and I am playing a great deal both by myself and with my brother, but I am getting no ideas at all for composing. Rome and Roman life are too characterful, too full of variety and noise for me to be enticed to my writing table. However, I hope that I will gradually settle down and then my work will go well. Yesterday I heard a delightful folk-song in the street which I will definitely make use of.[44]

Today I visited the Villa Borghese for the first time. It is a delightful place to walk in and, most importantly, was completely deserted; there were some magnificent carriages with opulently dressed ladies, but there are some little avenues for pedestrians only, where it is easy to find solitude.[45]

Today I started reworking the Second Symphony, the first movement of which I want to rewrite completely, and my work went so well that by lunchtime I had managed to sketch out almost half of the first movement. How grateful I am to fate for prompting my publisher Bessel to deceive me for years and not to print the score. If it had been printed I would not have been able to get the revisions published and my poor symphony would have remained in its original version. Seven years mean a lot in the life of someone who works hard and makes progress. In seven years time will I see my present works through the same eyes as I now see a work written in 1872? It may well be, because the road towards the ideal does not come to an end and in seven years I will still not be old.[46]

I have just come back from a long walk. I went to S. Maria Maggiore, S. Pietro in Vincoli (which has Michelangelo's *Moses*) and to the Coliseum, where I admired the sunset from the top row. In general we have been fortunate in chancing upon the best weather people here can remember for a long time for this time of year. Last year there was persistent rain at the same time of year.[47]

Today Modest and I walked to the Capitol and spent at least an hour and a half in the hall where the busts of the emperors are. Since I am reading

[43] viii. 465 (von Meck).   [44] viii. 466 (von Meck).   [45] viii. 471 (von Meck).
[46] Ibid.   [47] viii. 475–6 (von Meck).

Ampère's book about the emperors' rule in Rome at the moment, this hall held the greatest interest for me. How full of character these busts are! How revolting and obtuse is Nero's face with its bestial sensuality! How enchanting is Marcus Aurelius! How beautiful is Agrippina the elder! And how disgustingly repulsive is Caracalla! Some of the faces do not correspond at all to the picture which one has created for them from books. For instance, the face of Julius Caesar is devoid of all majesty and power—he looks like some sort of privy councillor in the Russian civil service; or Trajan? Who would have thought from looking at this narrow forehead, the prominent chin and general air of insignificance, that the original from whom the portrait was made was a great man! As always, after looking round a museum in great detail, I felt throughout the day (and still feel now) utterly exhausted. It is strange. I can walk for several hours on end without feeling tired. But I only have to spend one hour in a museum to feel exhausted beyond measure. I have started to copy out my corrected and transformed Second Symphony.[48]

We are spending the time very idly, that's to say we just enjoy ourselves all day. We have been to the Capitoline Museums and then we saw the ruins of the Palace of the Caesars in the Palatine gardens. It was an extremely interesting excursion, particularly since I had just read a detailed history of these magnificent ruins.[49]

Modest and I went to the Vatican and in a single visit we saw the Picture Gallery, the Loggia, the Stanze,* and the Sistine chapel. Michelangelo's frescos no longer seem incomprehensible to me. The athletic muscles of his figures, the sombre grandeur of his painting is no longer a mystery to me; it interests me, even staggers me, but I am still not carried away by it, it does not excite me or move me. My favourite is still Raphael, the Mozart of painting. I also find very much to my taste the paintings of Guercino, the Endymion of Florence; some of his madonnas are so angelically beautiful that they fill my heart with a sort of quiet rapture. However, I must admit that nature has not endowed me with much sensitivity to the plastic arts and only very few paintings or statues make any real impression on me. I think that museums are generally fatal to widening one's knowledge of art because they offer more food than can be swallowed in one go. It would, for instance, take more than a lifetime to give all the artistic treasures of Rome the attention they deserve. Every picture needs at least a whole day. I have also discovered how important it is to look at a picture intently and for a long time. I sat in front of Raphael's *Transfiguration* and at first I thought there was nothing special about the picture; then gradually I began to understand the expressions of each of the Apostles and of the other figures and the more I looked at it, the more I was attracted by it both as a whole

* The Loggia and the Stanze were painted by Raphael.

[48] viii. 480 (von Meck).   [49] viii. 485 (von Meck).

and in detail. Alas, I had just begun to enjoy it when Modest reminded me that it would soon be three o'clock and we still had to see the Sistine chapel. So I have only had a foretaste of Raphael's artistic delights; when am I going to be able to appreciate him properly? One simply cannot go to the Vatican every day when there are so many other interesting things to see. And after all I also have to do a bit of work every day, to read a bit, to have a walk. I don't think I could live in Rome for long. There is *too much* that is interesting. There is no time to daydream, no time to ponder your inner-most thoughts, and in the end you constantly feel tired. For somewhere to live permanently I would prefer Florence if I had to choose. Things are calmer there, it's quieter, there's less variety. Rome is grander and has more to offer but Florence is nicer and more pleasant.[50]

I went for a walk on my own today and spent about two hours in St Peter's. I am impressed most of all by the grandeur and beauty of the architecture. Of the funerary monuments, Canova's mausoleum for the Stuarts is amazingly good. Most of the others did not appeal to me particularly. But the famous bronze statue of St Peter is no good at all: it is like a pagan idol.[51]

The last few days have been notable for the considerable pleasure that I have derived from visiting certain museums. In the Vatican I was struck by certain paintings (Raphael's *Transfiguration* and Domenichino's *Last Communion of St Jerome*). Michelangelo's frescos in the Sistine chapel have ceased to be double Dutch to me and I am beginning to be filled with wonder at his original and powerful beauty. I also visited the *Casino* of the Villa Borghese which has some remarkable statues, and I was pleased with what I saw. My feelings towards Rome as a city have not changed however. I cannot stop myself from feeling an indefinable antipathy towards it. But what really is becoming intolerable is dinner at the *table d'hôte*.[52]

We greeted the New Year [1880] in very good shape. As I look back over the past year I have to sing a hymn of thanks to fate for all the good days it has sent me, both in Russia and abroad; I can honestly say that throughout the year I have enjoyed a sense of unclouded well-being and have been happy, in so far as happiness is possible. Of course, there have been bitter moments, but only moments, and even then I have only been reflecting the misfortunes of those near to me; personally, I have in fact been entirely content and happy. This has been the first year of my life as a free man.[53]

Michelangelo's *Moses* is a tremendous work! On a number of occasions I have stood gazing at this statue for a long time and on each occasion I feel even greater reverence for it. The conception and execution truly are of the first order of genius. It is said that some things about it are wrong! This

---

[50] viii. 485–6 (von Meck).   [51] viii. 487 (von Meck).
[52] viii. 488–9 (Anatoly).   [53] viii. 490–1 (von Meck).

reminds me of old Fétis who looked for mistakes in Beethoven and triumphantly announced that he had found in the 'Eroica' Symphony an inverted chord which *le bon goût* did not permit. Do you not think that Beethoven and Michelangelo are very similar types?[54]

I have started making sketches for an Italian fantasy on folk themes. I want to write something like Glinka's Spanish fantasies.[55]

I have had a most pleasant experience. I have been to the Villa Ludovisi. Nothing could be more delightful. There is a remarkable sculpture gallery with many remarkable statues; there is also the *Casino* with Guido's famous ceiling frescos (*Aurora* and *La Renommée*), and with a marvellous view over Rome and its surroundings. But the best thing at the villa is the garden— astonishingly grand, extensive, picturesque, and deserted. I spent two hours entirely on my own in the shady pathways. This walk did me a great deal of good.[56]

We took advantage of the absolutely marvellous weather to go to Tivoli. It is one of the most enchanting places I have ever seen. When we arrived we went to the Albergo della Sibilla to have lunch. The table was set at the edge of a steep precipice at the bottom of which one could hear a waterfall. There were hills and crags all round, covered with pines and olive trees. The sun was as hot as though it were June. After that we went for a long walk and then visited the famous Villa d'Este where Liszt spends three months every year.[57]

I have been to the gallery of the Palazzo Borghese where there are several *chefs-d'œuvre*. The ones which most impressed me were Correggio's sumptuous *Danäe* and some pictures by Raphael.[58] The more I see of Michelangelo the more he astonishes me. I went to San Pietro in Vincoli and stood looking at *Moses* for a long time. The church was empty; nothing disturbed me in my rapt contemplation of the work. It began to frighten me. Moses is depicted rising and turning his head towards the place where sacrifice is made to Baal. His face is filled with awful wrath; he is a majestic and commanding figure. You feel that he has only to rise, to utter a word, and the erring mob will fall on its knees before him. Nothing more perfect than this mighty statue can be imagined. You can see that this genius of an artist was able to express the *whole* of his idea in the form, there is no striving for effect, none of that *posturing* which one sees, for instance, in all Bernini's statues of which there are, unfortunately, so many in Rome. It was only gradually that I realized that even something as effective as the Trevi fountain offends by being too elegant, by lacking simplicity and truth. Rome is indeed a good school for developing one's taste for the plastic arts and I have made immense progress in this respect.[59]

It's true what they say: you can only get to like Rome if you have lived

[54] ix. 29 (von Meck).   [55] Ibid.   [56] ix. 29–30 (von Meck).
[57] ix. 44–5 (von Meck).   [58] ix. 45 (von Meck). [59] ix. 46 (von Meck).

there. In this respect it has much in common with Moscow. Rome is not altogether a suitable place for me to stay. It is too noisy, too abundant in its historical and artistic riches; you cannot live here in your burrow, quiet and unnoticed, you keep having to crawl out, and I have not even been able to keep up my incognito. All the same, I am having a good time, thanks to the company of my brother Modest. The state of my work is: (1) The Piano Concerto has been finished in draft for some time; I had already finished it before I left Paris. (2) At the moment I am busy revising the Second Symphony. I have written a new first movement, apart from the introduction and coda which remain as they were. I have written a new first subject for the Allegro and what was the first subject is now the second. This movement has now come out compact, nice and short, and not difficult. If anything deserved the description *impossible* it was the first movement in its original form. Goodness me! It was difficult, noisy, incoherent, and muddled. The Andante is unchanged. The Scherzo has been radically revised. I have made a big cut in the Finale; to be precise, after the big pedal-point before the recapitulation of the first subject I have gone straight to the second subject. I have nearly finished all this.[60] Now I can put my hand on my heart and declare that this symphony is a good[61] piece of work. I have burnt the old score.[62]

The score (first edition) of the Second Symphony was reconstructed from the orchestral parts, which had been kept in the library of the Moscow Conservatoire; it was first published in the *Complete Works of Tchaikovsky*, vol. 15b (1954).

Memory is one of heaven's most precious gifts. I know no greater pleasure than to bury myself in the past. Like a shaft of moonlight, memory has the gift of illuminating the past so that the bad side is not noticed and the good side seems even better.[63]

A day or two ago I received a telegram from Colonne in which he told me that my Fourth Symphony had been a success in Paris, particularly the Andante and Scherzo. This makes me very happy but what a pity that I could not hear it. There will be another chance some time.[64] I don't need to tell you how pleased I was that my symphony was well received. It would have been very unpleasant for me if all the trouble you took to get a Paris performance had been crowned with a failure! Of course, one does not have to believe all Colonne says. I think he has somewhat exaggerated its success in his usual tactful way, i.e. he described it not as it actually was but how he wanted it to be. But all the same it is good if the symphony only had a success *of sorts*—which is a great deal by French standards. I think that we will find out the true extent of success from Colonne's letter which I am expecting. You ask, my friend, why I am so pessimistic with regard to the news of *great* success? It is because I absolutely cannot imagine the French

[60] ix. 15–16 (Taneyev).   [61] ix. 17 (Jurgenson).   [62] ix. 24 (Jurgenson).
[63] ix. 19 (Karl Albrecht).   [64] ix. 28 (Anatoly).

public being happy with my symphony when they are hostile even to their own composers (Saint-Saëns for instance), as they are to anything new. I think that the first movement must have filled them with a certain amount of horror; the Andante may have been received without signs of dispproval, the Finale must have seemed vulgar and trite (this is the impression always made on them by works based on a Russian folk-song, e.g. 'Kamarins-kaya'), and only the Scherzo could have really pleased them thanks to the effective orchestral sound. But what I am absolutely convinced about is that my symphony must have evoked a spark of sympathy towards my music in certain people's hearts. This is all that I need. I cannot and do not know how to appeal to the massed public. I have noticed that those of my compositions which I have written with the greatest love and effort are doomed at first to failure or to partial success, and it is only gradually that they progress from *certain chosen people* to being understood by the public.[65]

Tchaikovsky's father died on 9 January 1880. Anatoly sent a telegram: 'Father has died peacefully, without any great suffering. No need to come.'

I bore my family sorrow without too great a shock. Time hardens people and accustoms them to losses. But I am dreadfully sad to think that I will never see my dear kind old father again.[66]

I am still in the same nervous and irritable state of mind as I described to you before. I am sleeping badly and have generally fallen apart. However I have been working successfully for the last few days and I have already completed the sketches for an Italian Fantasia [*Italian Capriccio*] on folk tunes, for which I think I can foresee a rosy future. It will be effective thanks to the delightful tunes which I succeeded in collecting partly from albums and partly with my own ears from the streets.[67]

Thank God the Carnival is over. On the last day the frenzy broke all bounds. My general impression of the carnival is most unfavourable. All this noise made me feel despondent, exhausted, and irritated, though I could not but appreciate the sincere jollity which the whole native population shows during the carnival. Just imagine, I didn't see one drunkard, and no uproars, quarrels, or brawls at all. Jokes often entail someone getting hurt or something getting damaged, but I didn't once see anyone lose their temper. As I have said before and always maintain, this shows the extraordinarily kind and gentle nature of the Italians. The weather was marvellous for the whole time; spring is definitely making itself felt. I can say without exaggeration that every bright, warming ray of the sun reminds me of you, my friend. My thoughts constantly fly to you and I am sorry that circumstances prevent you from enjoying the beneficial effects of the Italian climate.[68]

[65] ix. 28–9 (von Meck).   [66] ix. 39 (Jurgenson).
[67] ix. 35 (von Meck).   [68] ix. 42–3 (von Meck).

Tchaikovsky left Italy in the spring of 1880 and went via Paris and Berlin to St Petersburg where he had to busy himself with the arrangements for getting *The Maid of Orleans* accepted for production.

I am leaving Rome in the knowledge that this is a town which does not entirely fit my requirements but it has the effect of gradually endearing itself. I am beginning to understand why many people who have come for a short stay remain here all their lives.[69]

In Paris Tchaikovsky visited the Comédie Française.

I [have seen] a wonderfully performed *Polyeucte* and *Les femmes savantes*. Modya, I am completely in love with Racine or Corneille (which of them is the author of *Polyeucte?*). What poetry, what beauty and power and, I will go further, how much artistic truth of the *highest* order there is in this tragedy, which at first glance is so false and so improbable. When Felix suddenly becomes a Christian in the last act after suffering the pangs of conscience and being illuminated by the rays from the light of Christ, I felt shaken to the core. And as far as the performance was concerned, the actors were not first class, but *very* good. In *Les femmes savantes* the cast consisted of Madeleine Brohan, Got, Coquelin, Lloyd (a delightful jeune-première), Jouassin, Barré and really I have never seen the like of this production anywhere except perhaps in the Maly Theatre fifteen years ago. How can one not love Paris! How can you put a price on the Comédie Française alone! Each time you leave with a replete feeling, as if you had not eaten for ages and had at last satisfied your hunger properly. So far as theatres go, the Comédie Française is the closest to the ideal. Of course it has no actress like Rachel, nor an actor like Sadovsky, i.e. there are no *geniuses* there, but an ensemble of several first-class talents and superb middle-rankers leaves nothing to be desired.[70]

I spent a day without particular pleasure [in Berlin] but some moments were far from boring. In the morning I visited the Aquarium and was absolutely enchanted with a chimpanzee which lives in the greatest friendship with a dog. They played and behaved delightfully together all the time; it did amazing leaps and laughed delightfully when it got to a place out of the dog's reach. It has a remarkable mind; it behaves towards the keeper like a child towards its nurse. It gave me great pleasure. At twelve o'clock I lunched on coffee and pies. Then I went to the museum. You [Modest] would not recognize it now. Do you remember how untidily the pictures were hung and without any sort of system? Now the system and order is magnificent. I am sure I have taken a significant stride forward so far as my understanding of painting is concerned. There was much that gave me real pleasure, particularly the Flemish school; but I liked Teniers, Wouwerman, and Ruysdael better than the vaunted Rubens, whose Christ even has

[69] ix. 61 (von Meck).   [70] ix. 70 (Modest).

fat pink thighs and an unnatural glow on his cheeks. One thing actually started me thinking *I was a great expert: I recognized a Correggio by the style before I had seen his name in the catalogue*!!! What do you think about that!!! But Correggio must have been a very *stylized* painter because all his male faces and figures remind one of his *Christ* in the Vatican, and all the women of his *Danäe* in the Palazzo Borghese. I didn't look at the sculpture—I will go today. At four we had the usual dinner, just the same as ever; I was in a bad mood, for a man who was sitting opposite kept staring at me and this made me furious and embarrassed [...] I thought *The Dutchman* horribly noisy and boring. The singers were very bad, the Prima donna (Mallinger) had no voice and was generally worse than mediocre. I didn't even wait till the end. I went to hear Bilse and then went for a walk.[71]

I went to Bilse's concert. The enormous, magnificent hall made a strange impression on me, steeped as it is in the smell of filthy cigars and of food, full of ladies knitting stockings and gentlemen drinking beer. After Italy where one could say that we lived with fresh air all round us, this seemed revolting. But even so, there is a *wonderful* orchestra, magnificent acoustics, and a good programme. I heard Schumann's *Genoveva*, the overture to *Mignon*, some sort of very witty pot-pourri, and I was well pleased.[72]

I like the [violin] concerto by Brahms just as little as everything else he has written. He is of course a great musician and even a master but he has more mastery than inspiration. There are all sorts of preparations for something, a lot of hints at something which is about to appear and delight everyone, but nothing ever comes of it apart from boredom. His music is not fired by genuine feeling, he has no poetry, but on the other hand he has great pretensions to depth. However there is nothing in these depths—just empty space. For instance if we take the opening of the concerto: it is fine for an introduction to something, it is an excellent pedestal for some columns, but the columns themselves don't exist, and immediately behind one pedestal there is another. I don't know whether I am expressing my thoughts well, or rather the feelings Brahms's music evokes in me. I mean that he never makes a statement or that if he does begin to say something, he never *finishes* it; his music consists of little pieces of something, artificially glued together. The brush strokes are without definition, colour, or life. But I think that apart from all specific accusations, I should have said first and foremost that I am simply *antipathetic* towards Brahms as a musical personality. I cannot stomach him; however hard he tries, I remain cold and antagonistic. This is a purely instinctive feeling.[73]

The weather is wintry and the transition from Rome to Petersburg is deadly. I went to see my stepmother today. It was indescribably sad to see that flat which I know so well without its principal tenant. What marvellous

---

[71] ix. 71–2 (Modest).   [72] ix. 71 (Modest).   [73] ix. 56 (von Meck).

women there are in the world! Although her life with my eighty-four-year-old father was far from easy, my stepmother is consumed by inconsolable grief! Only women can love like that. My visit left me with many sad impressions but with some happy ones as well.[74]

I am deeply touched by the care you are taking of poor Wieniawski in his dying days,* which will be lightened by your concern for him. I am very sorry for him. We are losing in him a violinist who, in his way, is inimitable, and a very gifted composer. Wieniawski is in this latter respect very highly talented, in my view, and if fate had prolonged his life he could have achieved as much for the violin as Vieuxtemps. His charming *Legend* and parts of the D minor Concerto are evidence of a serious creative talent.

Yesterday I visited my father's grave for the first time. So far it only has a modest wooden cross on it. In the near future we will be putting up the monument on it which we have ordered. The weather was bright and sunny but there was a very hard frost. I hadn't expected at all that I could suffer so much from the cold; three winters spent in warm climates have spoilt me. Petersburg generally has an appallingly depressing and gloomy effect on me. Poor Russia![75]

Today Bessel spent a long time with me in the morning. He brought only half my royalties and I got tired of his interminable chatter. Then suddenly a letter turned up from Nápravník in which he said that the Grand Duke Konstantin Nikolayevich had invited me to dinner that day. But I had promised Konradi and Apukhtin to have some oysters with them; I have no tails and my throat is sore. On the other hand Nápravník says bluntly that I have to go for the sake of my opera. I had an agonizing and lengthy period of indecision. Finally I write saying that I cannot go today but that I will go the following Friday. Feeling distracted by all this I go for a walk. I call in for lunch at Palkin's; I drink more than I should; as a result I have heartburn, feel tired and sleepy. I am going to loaf about. My legs hardly drag themselves along. I cross the bridge over the Neva towards Peter the Great's little house. The wind blows mercilessly; there is a considerable frost and the sky is grey. At the Church of the Saviour I find prayers in progress. The praying women, the smell of incense, and the reading of the Bible all instil some sort of peace in my soul. I pray very earnestly and then cross over the Neva again. I go home, suffering from heartburn all the while. At home I try to work but sleep overcomes me to such an extent that I throw myself on my bed and fall instantly asleep, but with a palpitating and thumping heart. I overcome my sleepiness and feel refreshed.[76]

It is snowing heavily. The streets have become silent because the layer of snow muffles the sound of the carriages. I am so bored at home that I go to

* When Wieniawski was dying of cancer, Mme von Meck took him into her house in Moscow.

[74] ix. 73 (von Meck).   [75] ix. 76 (von Meck).   [76] ix. 82 (Modest).

the Alexandrinsky Theatre. I come in at the third Act of *La Dame aux
camélias*. Savina is repulsive; the actors who are supposed to be French
gentlemen look like servants. I meet Pylyaev and Averkiyev in the interval
and talk to them. I go home. There is no one there. I ask sleepy and gloomy
Akim to put on the samovar. I sit down to write to you [Modest]. Don't you
think life is delicious?[77]

Having gone to see Vera [Butakova], I immediately found myself in a
peculiarly unpleasant situation. She says that the Grand Duke Konstantin
Konstantinovich wants to spend an evening with me at her house. I was
indescribably horrified at this; Apukhtin suggested that Vera Vasilyevna
should invite him straight away to come after dinner. I managed to persuade her to put it off.[78]

I am making great sacrifices for the sake of the opera. It has even got to
the point where, on Nápravník's advice, I *am paying calls*!!! At his insistence I have to call on the Grand Prince Konstantin Nikolayevich. Isakov
has organized a concert here consisting entirely of my works; Panayeva will
perform, with the orchestra of the Russian Opera. I was invited to the
Chamber Music Society where Auer and Davydov played my Second
Quartet; I was given an ovation and presented with a wreath. This is very
flattering but God, how tired I am, how disgusting everything is here! I
dream of leaving Petersburg as of some unattainable joy. What a fool I was
abroad not to appreciate the immense blessing of being free! Here I always
have to go somewhere to see *somebody* from morning far into the night.[79]

My concert, so-called, went off well. *C'était très aristocratique* and quite a
furore.[80]

Nápravník conducted a concert on 25 March 1880 for the St Petersburg Conserva-
toire Student Hardship Fund. The items performed were the First Suite, the Letter
Scene from *Eugene Onegin* (Alexandra Panayeva), the Overture-Fantasia *Romeo and
Juliet*, a selection of songs (Vasily Isakov), and the Andante cantabile from the First
Quartet in a violin arrangement (Achilles Alferaki).
Tchaikovsky left St Petersburg for Moscow.

I arrived today and am intending to spend at least three days incognito, in
order to finish my work. Besides I need to rest. Imagine, my dear and good
friend [Mme von Meck], the last few days I haven't changed out of white
tie and tails and have spent my time with various elevated and even august
personages. All this is very flattering, at times touching, but extremely
exhausting! I feel so good in my room at the Kokopevsky Hotel, so happy
that I am alone and that I don't need to go or drive anywhere!!! And it is so
pleasant for me to know that you are here and that today I will have news
about how you are! Isn't that so, dear friend, you will send me a word or
two about how you are? Now I am going to have a stroll across at the other

---

[77] ix. 83 (Modest).   [78] ix. 82 (Modest).
[79] ix. 86 (Modest).   [80] ix. 91 (Modest).

side of the river, have lunch, and at about three o'clock I will come back and work until late in the evening.[81]

My plans to spend yesterday alone were shattered in the strangest way. I had some lunch at two, and then went for a walk across at the other side of the river, in the hope that I would not meet anyone. As I was walking along the embankment a carriage suddenly appeared and in it an admiral who was greeting me in a friendly way, whom I immediately recognized as the Grand Duke Konstantin Nikolayevich. It turned out that after the performance at the Conservatoire he had gone out for a drive, and, as if on purpose, fate had brought us together. After calling out to me he expressed astonishment at meeting me on the wrong side of the river, and surprise that I was not at the performance and warned me that at dinner with the Governor General he would tell Rubinstein about our strange meeting. And so my incognito was broken.[82]

Moscow and Petersburg have tired me very much; there were many difficult and unpleasant moments but as things have turned out in the end I don't think I have any cause for complaint. It is sometimes good for someone who is happy always to work in the same field, who is exclusively occupied with one thing, to be dragged out of his rut, whether he likes it or not. Strange though it may seem, I am beginning to think that *my captivity in Petersburg and Moscow* will refresh me and give me new strength. The freedom which I enjoy in the country will now seem all the more enticing. What vigour I will bring to my work![83]

Eventually Tchaikovsky was able to get away to Kamenka.

I found all the family *almost* in good health. I say *almost* because my sister is still not really well and keeps to her bed. My niece Tanya is much thinner and is very pale—but she is much prettier. Vera is charming. Tasya is more cheerful than ever. My nephews are growing up and getting bigger; Volodya, my favourite, has made great progress with his music, and little Yury can already speak English fluently. Lord! what a marvellous and delightful family they all are and how lucky I am to be with them![84]

I have been studying two new operas at the same time: Rubinstein's *Kalashnikov* and *Jean de Nivelle* by Deslibes [*sic*]. The former is a remarkably feeble work. Rubinstein is just like a singer who has lost her voice and yet still attempts to charm the ear of the audience. His talent is long since *played out* and has *lost* all its attractiveness. He should have stopped and contented himself with what he had already achieved. I pray God that I do not fall into the same error with the passage of time. The opera by Deslibes [*sic*] is quite another matter: fresh, graceful, and talented in the extreme.[85]

As to our plans to marry Kolya [von Meck] to one of my nieces, I would

[81] ix. 97 (von Meck).   [82] ix. 98 (von Meck).   [83] ix. 104–5 (von Meck).
[84] ix. 108 (von Meck).   [85] ix. 109 (von Meck).

be equally happy whichever one he chose because I love them equally, all four of them (though each in their own way).[86]

Modest is a wonderfully pleasant person to live with and I have the happiest memories of all the occasions when we have shared accommodation abroad. His equable temperament, his quietly philosophical way of looking at life, his remarkable mind, and extraordinarily kind heart make him the most precious friend. I love Anatoly just as much but his character presents many obstacles to tranquillity; he is for ever anxious, over-excited, and worried, and often without any particular reason. He is too nervy to act as a support for such a highly-strung person as I am.[87]

I have decided to arrange the Italian Fantasia for piano duet myself because if I give it to Taneyev I shall have to write out the score and then Sergey Ivanovich will put it to one side and the whole thing will drag out, whereas I would definitely like this Fantasia to be performed during the present season. I am dedicating this Fantasia to Karl Davydov and the opera to Eduard Nápravník.[88]

Kolya's parents have divorced and after careful thought Modest decided to explain the forthcoming change to Kolya. Although the poor boy had been long expecting this fateful news, it had the most devastating effect on him. He is completely crushed with grief. We hope that he will gradually get used to the idea that he has lost his mother for good, although one can guess that after this catastrophe his soul will be irrevocably scarred for life. If he had been a normal child he would not have taken the news so hard. In his natural isolation from people it will be more difficult to accept the idea that *his mother* deserted her home and children of her own free will.[89]

I have finished the corrections and sent them to Moscow together with the Italian Fantasia. Now I have no urgent work for the moment and this suits me very well because I shall have to help Modest in his lessons with Kolya. There is another reason why I cannot leave here in the near future. My sister has engaged for the summer a student from Kiev, for her boys. He will arrive at the end of next week and I would like to take the place of their absent parents when he is first getting to know the children and supervise his first steps in looking after them. Both my sister and brother-in-law would *very much* like me to do this. The grandmother and aunts of my nephews and nieces are here as well and have temporarily taken over the overall responsibility for them in the absence of their sister, but they are staying in a separate house.[90]

I am coming to the conclusion that I write too much and I want to write nothing for a year, apart from small things.[91]

I have finished orchestrating the Italian Fantasy. I don't know what the strictly musical value of this work will be, but I am already certain that it

[86] ix. 112 (von Meck).   [87] ix. 115 (von Meck).   [88] ix. 125 (Jurgenson).

[89] ix. 138 (von Meck).   [90] ix. 139 (von Meck).   [91] ix. 110 (Jurgenson).

will sound good, that the scoring is brilliant and effective.[92] I have begun composing some little vocal pieces and I started with a duet to words by [A.K.] Tolstoy, 'Passion spent'. Tolstoy is an inexhaustible source of texts to set to music; he is one of the poets I like best. The Moscow poet Surikov, who died of consumption this spring, was self-taught; his real job was sitting in a scruffy little iron booth selling nails and horse-shoes. And *a shop-assistant* he remained to the end of his life but he had a serious talent and his writings are infused with genuine emotion. I want to use some of his verses for works which I intend to write.[93]

Tchaikovsky had begun to write the Six Duets Op. 46. He wrote the duets 'Evening', 'In the garden, near the ford', and 'Dawn' to words by Surikov. He later set words by Surikov in 'Was I not a little blade of grass?' (Op. 47 No. 7) and the children's song 'The Swallow' (Op. 54 No. 15).

My dear [Jurgenson], you seem to think that composing ceremonial pieces for an exhibition is in some way the highest form of bliss which I will hasten to enjoy and that I will immediately get down to pouring out my inspiration, not even knowing properly where, how, why, when, and so on. I will not lift a finger until I get a *commission* for something. If they want me to set some words to music let them send me whatever text they want (if commissioned I am prepared to set to music even the pharmacist Tchaikovsky's advertisement for corn lotion). If they want me to write something instrumental, let them write to me explaining *what exactly*, in what form, and to fit what occasion. It is also essential that (1) a fixed price is named with exact details of where and from whom I should receive it (2) they should state a time limit. And so find all this out, talk to whoever you need to, and give me your decision. I am demanding all this not out of capriciousness but because I cannot compose such things in any other way, i.e. ceremonial pieces, except when I am told accurately and clearly what is required of me, for what price and how quickly. There are two sorts of inspiration: one comes uncompromisingly from the heart after the free choice of some creative motif; the other is commissioned. For the latter you need incentives, encouragements, some means of stimulation in the form of exact orders, definite time limits, and the promise in the more or less distant future of (a lot of) big banknotes. You present me with the choice of several festive occasions as if I could be tempted by any one of them![94]

Tchaikovsky now received an invitation to write music for the opening of the Industry and Art Exhibition in Moscow in 1881, which was timed to coincide with the Silver Jubilee of Alexander II, and with the dedication of the shrine of Christ the Saviour in Moscow.

The suggestion filled me with extreme revulsion. And how could one not feel revulsion at writing music which is destined to glorify something

[92] ix. 125 (von Meck).   [93] ix. 146 (von Meck).   [94] ix. 157 (Jurgenson).

which, to tell the truth, does not attract me at all? Neither the jubilee of the highly-placed person (for whom I have always nourished a pretty fair distaste) nor the *shrine*, which I do not like at all, has anything which might stir my inspiration. Meanwhile I have so many plans in my head, so many enterprises of all sorts that I would gladly make a start on if I did not have to hold myself in because I can feel that I am beginning to write too much.[95]

Today I received a letter from Anatoly with some reassuring news. You [Mme von Meck] know, dear friend, that I was in some doubt whether my opera would be performed in Petersburg next season. Now I can be sure that it will. The members of the Mariinsky Theatre came to Moscow for Pushkin's anniversary celebrations and told Anatoly that the opera has been cast and that the chorus will start rehearsing in the summer, in other words the production has been decided on. I am glad about this. My brother said in his letter that during the evenings of the Pushkin celebrations Klimentova twice sang Tatyana's letter song in costume and with stage scenery, and was a great success.[96]

Do you [Mme von Meck] take *Otechestvennye zapiski* [*Notes of the Fatherland*]? If you do, I strongly recommend you to read the story by Krestovsky (a pseudonym) called 'Family and School' which is in the April issue. This Krestovsky (in case you didn't know already) is none other than Madame Khvoshchinskaya, a very talented woman and author of the well-known novels *Waiting for Something Better*, *The Great Bear*, etc. I am very fond of this writer, in spite of the slight morbidity which permeates all her works. She has great sensitivity in psychological analysis and sometimes the depth of understanding of the human soul is truly remarkable. Her female characters are particularly successful and mostly negative. In the story which I mentioned there are some situations which are amazingly true to life. She paints a very desolate and sad picture but with a masterful touch.[97]

The feature which has most characterized recent days has been my devotion heart and soul to the cause of *picking mushrooms*. It really is one of the things I enjoy doing more than anything else. I have started concocting some little vocal things.[98]

Printing the score of *Onegin* is, in my view, a gross folly, which could only have been committed by a publisher carried away by the ardour of his friendly enthusiasm. Who needs it? Who will gain by it? Is it a *chef-d'œuvre* which has been seen on stages throughout the world? It has, in short, brought Jurgenson considerable expense to no purpose, and to no pleasure or purpose for anybody else either. There is no question of being modest here. I am proud of *Onegin*, I love it, but I still think the *score* is a folly and a wild example of Russian recklessness.[99]

[95] ix. 171 (Jurgenson).   [96] ix. 150 (von Meck).   [97] ix. 150–1 (von Meck).
[98] ix. 147 (Anatoly).   [99] ix. 160 (Karl Albrecht).

Tchaikovsky went to Brailov as he had done in the previous year.

Such are the joys of life in society and circulating amongst people!!! At Fastov I saw (fortunately not for long) the three tenors Setov, Orlov, and Bartsal. The last-named talked to me about *The Oprichnik* and reproached me for some of the failings of that opera. Setov advised me to become a conductor, and Orlov interrogated me from on high about my new opera. I was somewhat humiliated by this and, assuming the unnaturally sweet smile of the *other Petya*, asked him to take the main role in it. As I was talking to them and letting the other Petya put on the most horrible airs, I thought to myself: 'Jump in the river for all I care, but go away.' They did go away, eventually.[100]

This is a jocular reference to the 'two Petyas' which Tchaikovsky felt within himself: the real one was sincere and said what he thought; the 'other' one appeared when Tchaikovsky was in strange surroundings where he had to be pleasant and make pretences.

Apart from some extremely kind letters from Nadezhda Filaretovna, there was waiting for me [at Brailov] a valuable present which she had left when she went away. She had ordered a *watch* for me in Paris last winter and it had just been sent. The purpose of the present is to ensure that I will always have something about me to remind me of her, as though I ever could forget this marvellous woman who appeared in order to ease and smooth my life in every way, to protect me from misfortunes and difficult times. Brailov is as luxurious, peaceful, and comfortable as ever but I would like to get to Simaki as soon as I can—it's more cosy there.[101]

On the front cover of the gold watch which Mme von Meck gave to Tchaikovsky was depicted in relief a representation of Joan of Arc, and on the back cover, Apollo and the Muses. This watch was stolen from Tchaikovsky on 29 July 1891 when he was living at Maydanovo.

Everything is fine here: spacious, peaceful, and quiet; it's even a bit frightening in the evenings. By the way, Nadezhda Filaretovna has acquired masses of new music, some separate numbers from *Judith* (I enjoyed playing them through and recalled my raptures very vividly), *Le Roi l'a dit* by Delibes, Rubinstein's *The Maccabees* and lots of other interesting things. There's heaps to read as well, but what a strange fellow I am! I am so used to rushing to get things done all the time that even now, when I have an idle life, I still start worrying as soon as I get up and sometimes the thought that there will not be time to read something, to play something, to write to somebody actually *torments* me. How short the days really are and how little one can get done! But that is the complaint I suffer from: always rushing and fussing, and reproaching myself for not getting things done.[102]

[100] ix. 173 (Modest).   [101] ix. 167, 168 (Lyova).   [102] ix. 179 (Modest).

1. Tchaikovsky's parents, Ilya Petrovich Tchaikovsky and Alexandra Andreyevna

3. Tchaikovsky's nieces Natalya (left) and Vera Davydov

2. Tchaikovsky's nephew Vladimir (Bob) Davydov

СОСТАВ ПРОФЕССОРОВ
МОСКОВСКОЙ КОНСЕРВАТОРИИ в 1872г.

4. Staff of the Moscow Conservatoire in 1872: the founder, Nikolay Rubinstein, is in the centre (top) with Tchaikovsky to his right

6. Pyotr Il'yich Tchaikovsky, c.1869

5. Nadezhda von Meck

7. *Vakula the Smith*, title-page of the vocal score (first edition, Jurgenson, 1876) of Tchaikovsky's opera. Despite its initial failure the work remained a favourite of the composer; the revised version, *Cherevichki* (1885), was more successful.

8. Tchaikovsky and his bride Antonina Milyukova in 1877, the year of the ill-fated marriage

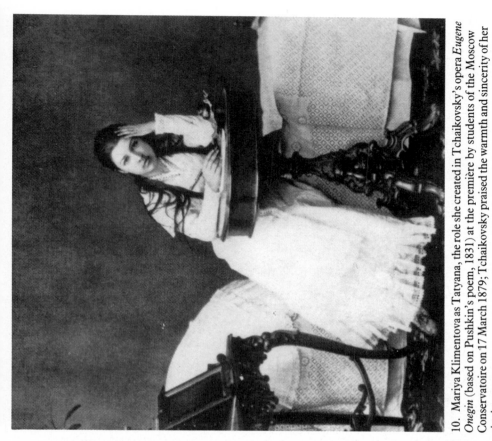

10. Mariya Klimentova as Tatyana, the role she created in Tchaikovsky's opera *Eugene Onegin* (based on Pushkin's poem, 1831) at the première by students of the Moscow Conservatoire on 17 March 1879; Tchaikovsky praised the warmth and sincerity of her singing.

9. Alexander Pushkin, portrait (1827) by Orest Kiprensky

11. The main living and working room at Tchaikovsky's house in Klin, where he settled in February 1885

12. Tchaikovsky with the cellist Anatoly Brandukov for whom he composed the *Pezzo Capriccioso* (1887)

13. The Tchaikovsky brothers in 1890: (left to right) Anatoly, Nikolay, Ippolit, Pyotr, and Modest

15. Nikolay Yakovlev as the Old Woman who Lived in a Shoe, with two children, in the Act 2 *divertissement* of *The Nutcracker* at the first production of Tchaikovsky's ballet at the Mariinsky Theatre, St Petersburg, on 6 December 1892

14. Tchaikovsky in his Cambridge doctoral robes, 1 June 1893

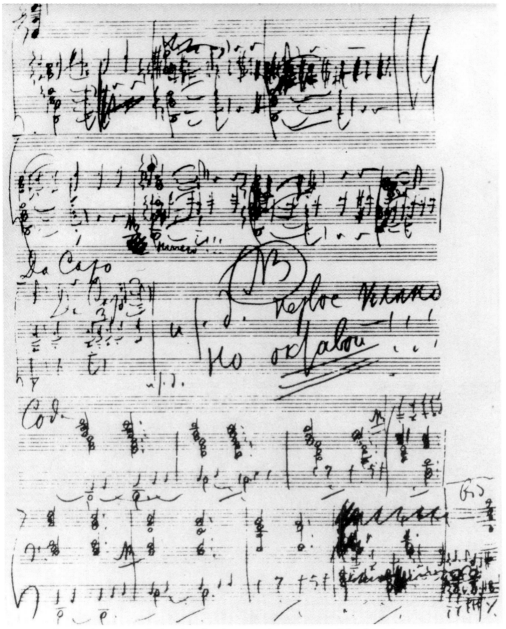

16. Tchaikovsky's autograph sketches for the second movement of the Symphony no. 6 ('Pathétique'), composed 4 February–19 August 1893; the title 'Pathétique' was proposed by Modest the day after the première in St Petersburg later that year

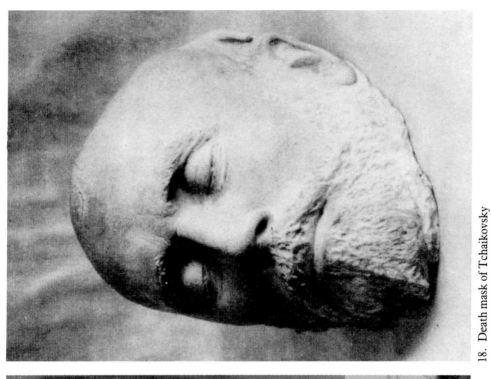

18. Death mask of Tchaikovsky

17. Pyotr Il'yich Tchaikovsky in 1893

I have had a look through all the music in the library. And incidentally I found a separate, bound volume consisting of Glinka's dances. Almost all these polkas, waltzes, and polonaises were new to me and I was very interested in them. What a remarkable phenomenon Glinka was! When you read his memoirs, which show him as a good and kind man, but empty and even banal, when you play his little pieces—it is impossible to believe that they were written by the same man who, for instance, composed *Slavsya*, a work of superlative inspiration which stands alongside the loftiest manifestations of the creative spirit in the great geniuses. There are so many other things of astonishing beauty in his operas and overtures. *Kamarinskaya* is a work of amazing originality; all subsequent Russian composers (including me, of course) have continued to draw on it quite blatantly for patterns of harmony and counterpoint whenever they have had to incorporate a Russian theme with a dance quality. This is unintentional, of course, but it happens because Glinka was able to concentrate in this small work everything that dozens of second-rate composers might have *contrived* and *devised* with great expenditure of effort. And then a man like that, at the peak of his maturity, can suddenly go and write such dismal, dreary rubbish as the Coronation Polonaise and the Children's Polka! Yet he also wrote *Slavsya*.[103]

I have found a complete collection of my works. Good Lord! what a lot I have written, but how feeble and poorly finished it all is still, how lacking in *technique*.[104]

I had expected that I would greatly enjoy Simaki but the reality far surpassed my most fevered imaginings. I simply cannot put into words what I feel. My happiness is so complete that it frightens me! It's just like a dream from which you will soon have to wake up. When I arrived I inspected every corner of the house and garden (a thousand thanks for all the magnificent flowers, for the new wallpaper, for arranging everything); I went out of the garden and down the familiar path to the ravine, then I went up the hill and stopped to take in the whole view of this lovely place which I know so well. The sunset was magnificent and the full moon was already quite clear in the east. In the distance the woods, Brailov, the fields, green everywhere. For a moment I could not hold back tears of ecstasy.[105]

I was so seized with rapture that I fell to my knees and thanked God for the intensity of my bliss. I was on a slight rise in the ground: not far away I could see my house peeping through the dense foliage of the trees; in the distance, in all directions, were low hills covered with woods; beyond the river was a village, whence there drifted up the lovely sounds of country life—children's voices, the bleating of sheep, the lowing of cattle coming home; there was a magnificent sunset in the west and in the opposite direction the full moon was already to be seen in all its glory. Space and beauty

---

[103] ix. 176–7 (von Meck).   [104] ix. 174 (Modest).   [105] ix. 181 (von Meck).

everywhere! Oh! Oh! Oh! that there should be such moments in life! They can make one forget everything! . . .[106]

Dear Nadezhda Filaretovna has herself made all these marvellous arrangements for me down to the last detail. There's no concealing the fact that I am living in clover here but of course such a fabulously marvellous life cannot last for long: ultimately I still belong to Kamenka, which may not be much to look at but is dear to me.[107] What a night I had last night [9 July]! I had to drag myself away from the window at two o'clock in the morning. The moon was shining in all its glory, the peace, the scents of the flowers, those marvellous, vague sounds of the night—Good Lord! how wonderful it all is! I am floating on waves of unalloyed pleasure.[108]

Thank you for sending *Sakuntala* and the programme—I have received both. How boring *Sakuntala* is! I will nevertheless have the patience to read a little of it, although I can see already that it is no good for an opera.[109]

The older I get the more my rapturous love for the friend I mentioned earlier [nature] grows and strengthens within me. And it is strange that I enjoy it nowhere more than in Russia, amidst modest country surroundings. I love Switzerland and Italy as well but in quite a different way: almost like a beautifully drawn illustration rather than living nature. I would be truly blissfully happy here if my belonging to human society and all the obscenities associated with this great honour didn't make themselves felt even here. You can never escape from the life of the herd. However hard you try you still have to be a member of the flock and join in with its dirty tricks—otherwise you might just as well not live, which of course I do not want, for there is still a lot that is extremely attractive about life. And moreover we will all manage to die in the end.[110]

I have played through the first two acts of *The Maid of Orleans* which are now finished and ready for the printer. Unless I am very much mistaken you were quite right to have the heroine of my latest opera portrayed on the watch which you gave me. I don't think that *The Maid* is the best or the most deeply felt of all my works but *I do think* that it might just be the one which could make me popular. I have the feeling that progeny of mine like *Onegin* and some of the instrumental compositions are closer to me and are more deeply rooted in my own nature; I put less of myself into writing *The Maid* than I did, for instance, into our symphony or the Second Quartet but on the other hand I paid more attention to aural and visual effects, and after all that's the main thing in opera.[111]

So as to have a rest from my own music (I eventually got a bit fed up with the proofs), I played through Bizet's *Carmen* from beginning to end. It is, in my view, a *chef-d'œuvre* in the full sense of the word, i.e. it is one of those few works which are destined to reflect in the highest degree the musical

[106] ix. 184 (Modest).   [107] ix. 181–2 (Lyova).   [108] ix. 185 (von Meck).

[109] ix. 182 (Anatoly).   [110] ix. 204–5 (Taneyev).   [111] ix. 188 (von Meck).

aspirations of an entire epoch. I think that the characteristic feature of our age which distinguishes it from earlier ones is that composers chase (*they chase, be it noted*, which neither Mozart, nor Beethoven, nor Schubert, nor Schumann did) after *pretty* or *piquant* effects. What is the so-called *new Russian school* if not the cult of various spicy harmonies, original combinations of instruments and all manner of purely external effects. The musical content has moved to the background; it has become not the end but the means, the excuse for devising some particular grouping of sounds. Previously people *composed* or *created* but now (with very few exceptions) they *select* or *devise*. A process of musical fabrication like this is, of course, purely rational and for this reason contemporary music—which is witty, piquant, and odd—is cold, is untouched by the warmth of emotion. And here we have a Frenchman in whom all the piquancy and spiciness are not *contrived* but pour freely forth in a stream which, whilst it charms the ear, also moves and excites. It's as though he said to us: 'You don't want anything majestic, or powerful, or grandiose, you want something *pretty*. Well, here's a *pretty* opera for you.' And indeed I know of nothing in music which has a better right to stand for the element which I call *the pretty*, *le joli*. It is fascinating and delightful from beginning to end; there are plenty of piquant harmonies and completely new combinations of sounds, but that is not the exclusive aim; Bizet is an artist who pays due tribute to his age and his times but he is fired with true inspiration. And what a marvellous subject for an opera! I cannot play the last scene without weeping; on the one hand, the popular rejoicing and coarse merriment of the crowd watching the bullfight; on the other, the terrible tragedy and death of the two main characters, pushed and dragged by an evil fate (*fatum*) through a succession of sufferings to their inevitable end. I am convinced that in ten years or so *Carmen* will be the most popular opera in the world.[112] Of course, I will never write an article about it because I have not got the skill or the knowledge, in short, all the things that Laroche has got. One needs to show, after all, that it is not only the Russian school but really Wagner and Liszt as well who chase after the pretty and the tasty; that the last of the Mohicans of music's golden age were Mendelssohn, Chopin, Schumann, and Glinka, in whom, however, one can observe a transition *from the great and the beautiful to the tasty*!* One needs, in short, to do very many things that I cannot.[113]

I was praising Bizet yesterday and today [19 July] I intend to go into raptures about another Frenchman, Massenet. I found that Nadezhda Filaretovna had his oratorio *Marie Magdeleine*. The text depicts Golgotha and the resurrection as well as Christ's relationship to Mary Magdalene and to Judas; when I read it I was filled with a prejudice against the work.† But

---

* Dargomyzhsky, however, was quite exclusively *tasty* (*Tchaikovsky's note*).

† Because I thought it was too bold (*Tchaikovsky's note*).

[112] ix. 196–7 (von Meck).   [113] ix. 199–200 (Modest).

when I got down to playing it I immediately realized that it was something quite out of the ordinary; in my opinion the duet for Christ and Mary is a *chef-d'œuvre*. Massenet has succeeded here in expressing in sound the infinite goodness of Christ and I was so moved by this deeply-felt music that I burst into floods of tears. Marvellous tears! All praise to the Frenchman who knew how to call them forth. The French have indeed taken the first place in music without a doubt. I have been obsessed with this duet all day today and under its influence I have written a song to words by [A.K.] Tolstoy: 'Softly the spirit flew up to heaven'; the tune was suggested by Massenet. I have written a few songs and I am so inordinately fond of one of them* that I cannot play it without dissolving in tears.[114]

Have I told you [Mme von Meck], dear friend, that I have started learning English a little? This aspect of my work is going very smoothly and successfully here. I am hoping that in about six months' time I shall be able to read English fluently. This is my one aim; I know that at my age I cannot learn to speak it with any confidence. But to read Shakespeare, Dickens, Thackeray in the original would sweeten my declining years.[115]

I think that all circumstances have conspired together to make my last days spent here perfectly happy. I haven't received any disquieting news; I have finished with the opera; I feel a great upsurge of inspiration, and I am writing romances which I am pleased with; the weather is magnificent; and finally even my health leaves nothing to be desired.[116]

How quickly this month has gone by! Perhaps it is in fact a good thing that circumstances prevent me from staying here too long. I am in a permanent condition of ecstasy and this must, in the end, have an effect on my nerves. I have become acutely receptive to impressions of all sorts; I have become tearful; I am constantly weeping when there is no need to: perhaps about a book, or music, or simply because of the beauty of nature. I am driven along here by some abnormal life force, as though it were four times stronger than usual. Sometimes I get carried away so far and so high, in thought and in feeling, that I scarcely feel as though I am on earth. At such moments I am offended and irritated by any sharp reminder that I belong to the real world. This condition is very pleasant but it is certainly not normal and if a month spent like this has a beneficial and reviving effect, a longer stay amongst all these things which constantly send me into spiritual ecstasies might be too much for me! Be that as it may, the fact remains that I will be sorry to leave. I very much want to avoid the hackneyed expression '*There's no question*'. But there *is* no question: I have been happy here and I have constantly blessed in my thoughts the one to whom I owe these happy days.[117]

* To marvellous words by Mickiewicz (*Tchaikovsky's note*). 'Dusk fell on the earth', words by Mickiewicz, translated by Nikolay Berg.

[114] ix. 201 (Modest).   [115] ix. 211 (von Meck).
[116] ix. 211 (von Meck).   [117] ix. 216–19 (von Meck).

'MONOLOGUES' ABOUT FAME

You [Taneyev] rather stung me when you said that '*I was being hypocritical when I said that fame was a burden*'. In the first place, that is not what I said because my fame is as yet so light that it could not be a burden. In the second place, *I venture to believe* that I am not, in fact, a hypocrite. I compose, i.e. through the language of music I pour out my moods and feelings and, of course, like everybody who talks and has or claims to have something to say I need people to listen to me. The more people listen to me the better I am pleased. In this sense, of course, I do like fame and aspire to it whole-heartedly. It is quite possible that in describing my sufferings in Petersburg I involuntarily gave expression to the pleasure which I take in the knowledge that people are beginning *to listen* to my music. It does not, however, follow that I liked the way in which *fame* expressed itself in the form of dinners, suppers, and musical evenings, where I suffered as I always do suffer in strange company. If I liked attracting the attention of the public and of society to myself, to my personality, then it would cost me no effort to spend the whole of my life in society of one sort or another. But I have never aspired to that; on the contrary, I have always been at pains to hide myself away somewhere and stay outside of society. *I wish, desire, and love* people to be interested in my music, to praise it, and to like it but I have never sought that they should be interested in me *personally*, in my appearance, in my conversation. It would be silly and stupid not to put my name on my works because of my unsociability; I have to mark myself out in some way from others who are speaking at the same time as I am. So I could take a pseudonym; what difference does it make? I want my name, whatever it might be—my own or a borrowed one—to be the *label* which marks my goods out from others and I want this label to have its value, its reputation, I want it to be in demand in the market. But what has this got to do with my revulsion from spending time in *society*? I have always suffered from that and always will.[118]

    Fame! What contradictory feelings it arouses in me! On the one hand, I want it, I aspire to it, I strive for it; on the other, I hate it. If the whole meaning of my life lies in my composing, then I am bound to desire fame. After all, if I always find I have to speak in the language of music there will, naturally, have to be people to listen to me and the larger and more sympathetic the circle of my listeners the better. It is my passionate desire that my music should be widely known and that the number of those who like it, who find comfort and support in it should grow. It is not just a question of liking *fame*; in this sense, it is the aim of anything serious that I undertake. But alas! I have only to reflect that parallel with the growth of my reputation as a composer there is a growth in the interest in my private personality, that I am in public view, that the idly curious are always ready to

[118] ix. 222 (Taneyev).

draw aside the veil with which I try to screen my intimate affairs, and I am
immediately overcome with distress and revulsion, I want to fall silent for
good, or at least for a long time, if only I can be left in peace. The thought
that some day I might indeed achieve a crumb of fame, and that an interest
in my music will stimulate interest in me personally is very burdensome. It
is not that I fear the light of day. I can declare with my hand on my heart
that my conscience is clear and that I have nothing to be ashamed of. But
the notion that some day people will try to probe into the private world of
my thoughts and feelings, into everything that throughout my life I have so
carefully protected from contact with the mob, is very sad and unpleasant.
There is even an element of tragedy in the conflict between the aspiration to
fame and revulsion from its consequences. Like a butterfly, I rush into the
flames and always get my wings burnt.[119]

Dear friend [Jurgenson]! If, as for all I know it may be, I become famous
one day and people start to collect material for a biography after my death,
they would come to a completely false conclusion about me from your letter
today. You might think from reading it that I am in the habit of thrusting
my compositions forward and crawling to influential people and generally
making whatever overtures are necessary in order to get them performed.
But this is completely untrue. I can put my hand on my heart and say that
not only have I never taken any steps but that I have never even lifted a
finger to ensure that some Bilse or other should favour me with his attention.
My pride is precisely of this *passive* sort. But it is another matter when they
make the first move. Then I melt, soften, and am ready (of course by letter
from far away) to grovel before them. This was what happened with Bülow,
with Colonne in Paris, etc. I just cannot forget that on several occasions
Bilse had the courage to withstand whistles and all sorts of signs of disapproval on behalf of one of my works. As far as your advice to copy Rubinstein is concerned, I must say that our relative positions are so different that
no comparison can be made. If you take away Rubinstein's *virtuosity* he immediately falls from his greatness to the level of my insignificance. I would
like to know then which one of us showed more pride as a composer. You
really don't know everything about what Rubinstein did in Paris in order to
get his opera performed; however many insults he received, he still kept on
trying; and there are a lot of other things you don't know, as I can see![120]

I don't altogether understand your [Taneyev] explanation of how you
isolate Russian music from European music, and I find a certain inconsis-
tency in your words. If you accept that Western musicians are fatally
attracted to their present path, Russian music is equally fatally following
them, and you can't do anything about Fate. If I am not mistaken one needs
to read not just the lines of your letter, but *between* them. From your argument between the lines, you can deduce, I think, that we are walking in
darkness, but the dawn of a new sun, which will rise over the isolation of

[119] ix. 233–4 (von Meck).   [120] ix. 235–6 (Jurgenson).

Russian music, is just beginning. Its whole future lies in the painstaking search for a Bach from the nearby fire station who by means of an infinite number of contrapuntal writings, fugues, and canons on themes from Russian folk-songs and Orthodox chants will lay the foundation stone for the future greatness of Russian music. This may be so, but I fear, Sergey Ivanovich, that our Bach is a bit of a Slavophile Don Quixote. For you cannot change history and if, thanks to Peter the Great, we have fatally been relegated to the tail of Europe, then it is in Europe that we will at any rate remain. I value highly the richness of material which the *dirty* and *suffering masses* create, but we, i.e. those who make use of this material, will always rework it into forms which we have taken from Europe, for, even if we are born Russian, at the same time we are even more European and their forms have been so firmly and deeply established and assimilated that in order to break free from them you have to distort and strain yourself but nothing artistic can come out of such distortion and strain. Where there is distortion there is no inspiration, and where there is no inspiration there is no art. It is very probable that in music as in science we don't say anything of our own, but this only means that either by nature or by historical circumstances we have been deprived of creative powers. In any case we can hardly correct this deficiency by harking back to the past, and you have to go a painfully long way to get away from Europe. Songs are written by people who have been Europeanized and have forcibly adapted the melody to a major or minor key, and Europe has made itself felt even in the clefs used to notate everyday tunes!!! Generally speaking, Seryozha, to my way of thinking at any rate, a musician should avoid clever philosophizing, and should take inspiration as it comes. The whole question is whether it comes or not. All the extremes, the absurdities, the confused cacophony of the new Russian school are the result of clever philosophizing. Wagner's tetralogy, that grandiose monument to artistic self-delusion, is also the result of philosophizing, although the thinking is deeper than ours. I know that you are too intelligent and serious not to have extracted for all of us some useful lessons and explanations from your efforts in this boring genre. Perhaps the fruit of all this will be some sort of interesting monograph on Russian music. I admit that I see, not without regret and sadness, that you are falling prey to analysis, and the artist working in the sphere of creativity is giving way more and more to the painstaking seeker after musical subtleties. Perhaps I am mistaken and you have set out on your true path; your ideas are bold and you are obviously well-intentioned but don't forget the hero of Cervantes' novel.[121]

European music is in my view a treasure-house to which every nation contributes something of its own for the general good. Every West European composer is first of all a Frenchman, a German, an Italian, or whatever—but then he is also a European. *Nationalism* makes itself felt in

[121] ix. 222–4 (Taneyev).

Glinka to pretty much the same extent as it does in Beethoven, Verdi, and
Gounod; and if you [Taneyev] hear Russian overtones in my works, I can
smell something peculiarly French in every bar of Massenet and Bizet. If
our seed is destined to grow into a splendid tree with its own distinctive
characteristics, so much the better; I like to think that this tree will not be
so frail as the English one, or so puny and sterile as the Spanish but that it
will, on the contrary, be comparable in height and beauty with the German,
the Italian, and the French. But however hard we may try we cannot get
away from the European garden, for fate has decreed that our seed should
fall upon ground cultivated before us by the Europeans; it is now some time
since it put down quite deep roots there and we no longer have the strength
to uproot it. In general terms what I would like to see, and it is a heartfelt
wish, is that Russian music should stand on its own feet and that Russian
songs should infuse *a fresh spirit* into music, as other folk-songs have done
in their time.[122]

I am very fond of Kiev and although I wouldn't like to live there I am
always delighted to go there for two or three days. There are places in the
Tsar's gardens where you can sit for hours on end with indescribable
pleasure, admiring the beauty of the views. And the Botanical gardens, the
Vydubetsky Monastery (near the main monastery), and countless other
places are a delight.[123] Unfortunately I have had to rush around the shops
for days on end and only had time to go to the Tsar's gardens and the
Botanical gardens. I have spent the evenings in the Château des Fleurs and
enjoyed the music!!! Imagine—the orchestra there is small and by no means
first class. What it means to be deprived of the pleasure of listening to
music for a long time: as I entered the gardens I heard the sounds of the
well-known introduction to *Robert* [*le Diable*, by Meyerbeer] and I nearly
fainted from the powerful effect it had on me. Indeed, I am generally going
through a stage of particular receptivity to musical impressions. My stay in
Simaki and the abundance of wonderful happy moments conversing with
mother nature has filled my moral being with a sort of indefinable and
unquenchable longing for *beauty*. And at each encounter with the beauty in
the arts I can hardly stop myself from bursting into sobs. Oh Simaki,
precious spot! How much happiness and ecstasy I experienced there. How
I love it![124]

I have finished copying out my new vocal works and have already sent
them off to Jurgenson. Besides that I have done a major revision of my
overture *Romeo and Juliet*, which will be republished.[125]

It appears that on the occasion of Pushkin's Jubilee a book was published
in Moscow consisting of a collection of verses in praise of Moscow. I think
it is called *Moscow in the works of the Russian Poets*. I badly need this book
because I am hoping to find in it a theme for my music for the exhibition,

[122] ix. 239–40 (Taneyev).   [123] ix. 227 (von Meck).
[124] ix. 228 (von Meck).   [125] ix. 248 (von Meck).

the composition of which I am preparing to start, with, if I am truthful, unspeakable revulsion.[126]

Even at Kamenka I can enjoy the delights of autumn. My walks are longer now because I am doing absolutely nothing at all and spend nearly all day wandering through the woods and fields. I want to hold back from working for a time so as to have a rest from my own music which I have had to fiddle about with for ages because of the endless proofs. I'm going to play other people's music as much as I can and I have begun by starting to make a careful study of Mozart's *Zauberflöte*. Never was a subject of such senseless stupidity seen in the company of such entrancing music. How grateful I am to the circumstances of my life and of my musical career which have ensured that, for me, Mozart has not lost a shred of his artless charm and fascination. What marvellous sensations I experience when I immerse myself in his music! They have nothing in common with the agonized ecstasies provoked by Beethoven, Schumann, Chopin, and in general all Beethovenian and post-Beethovenian music. This alarms, excites, thrills us, but it does not soothe and caress like Mozart. When I read or play Mozart I feel more lively and vigorous, almost a young man again![127]

I do not like to settle for too long in one place and I feel a strong attraction now towards the place *wo die Citronen [sic] blühen*.[128] I am by nature a *tourist* because only someone who likes being on his own can really and truly enjoy travelling.[129]

On the subject of Kamenka, do you [Mme von Meck] get *Russkaya starina [Russia of the Past]* abroad? They published some of Pushkin's letters in one of the recent issues, including one to Gnedich from *Kamenka*. Pushkin wrote *The Prisoner of the Caucasus* here; Lev Vasilyevich Davydov's mother, Alexandra Ivanovna, who is now an old lady, remembers him very well.[130]

I am studying Ponchielli's opera and a work by Bussy [Debussy] with great interest.[131]

My intentions of spending a long period in relaxation are never very firm. I had scarcely embarked on a few days of doing absolutely nothing when I began to experience a vague sense of ennui, even of not feeling well; I began to sleep badly, I felt weary and weak. I couldn't hold out and I started doing a bit of work on sketching out my next symphony—and then? And then I immediately felt healthy and fit, and my mind was at rest. It seems that, apart from when I am travelling, I am incapable of spending even two days without doing something. Of course, this has its good and its bad side. I am dreadfully frightened of turning into a scribbler like Anton Rubinstein, for instance, who seems to regard it as his duty to treat the public to new compositions every day. The consequence is that he has converted his enormous creative talent into small change and the majority of

[126] ix. 253 (Jurgenson).   [127] ix. 255 (von Meck).   [128] ix. 272 (von Meck).
[129] ix. 280 (von Meck).   [130] ix. 274 (von Meck).   [131] ix. 275 (von Meck).

his recent works are copper rather than the pure gold which he could have produced if he had written in greater moderation. I have kept trying to think of something to do which would temporarily distract me from music altogether but would still seriously engage my interest. Unfortunately I have not been able to settle on anything. There is no guide at all in our literature to the history of music and it would be a very good thing if I worked on the compilation of such a book; I do sometimes give some thought to it. But then, of course, I would have to stop composing altogether for two years—and that really is too much. Do some translating?—that's not interesting enough. Write a monograph about some composer or other? But so much has already been written about the great musicians of the west; I could not write enthusiastically about Glinka, Dargomyzhsky, or Serov because my assessment of their works is as high as my assessment of their personalities is low. How much I would enjoy, by contrast, working on a monograph about Mozart, but there is nothing left to write about him since Otto Jahn devoted the whole of his long life to his critical biography. So it seems there is no way to occupy my time and satisfy my inner need to work—*apart from composing*. The result is that I am now planning a symphony or a string quintet; I still don't know which I will settle on.[132]

The work which Tchaikovsky began was the *Serenade* for string orchestra.

I have had official notification from the management of the Imperial Theatres that my opera [*The Maid of Orleans*] has been accepted and will be staged in January. They also sent me a copy of the libretto as approved by the *Censor's Office* but with the following qualifications: '*that the Archbishop should be called A Pilgrim (?), that all talk of the cross should be removed, and that there should be no crosses on the stage*'. How stupid! The problem comes at the end of the opera when Joan is being led to the stake: she asks for a cross and one of the soldiers ties together two pieces of stick to make a cross which he gives to her. The whole of this scene has been banned. I have also had to change words and scenes in other places. But the most absurd thing of all is that I have been *ordered* to call the *Archbishop 'A Pilgrim'*, which makes no sense at all. Who would think that such instructions issue from a central body supervising everything that is printed in Russia and which ought, therefore, to consist of educated people! It was no good—I had to submit.[133]

I have heard that *Eugene Onegin* will be on at the Bolshoy in Moscow at the same time as *The Maid* is on in Petersburg. How unfortunate I am in the performances of my operas! I known that for *The Maid* there will not be a singer equal to the role of Joan and I am equally certain that they will not find a Tatyana or a Lensky in Moscow.[134]

Nikolay Rubinstein has approached me with a request to write for the Moscow Exhibition, where he will be the Head of the Artistic Section,

---

[132] ix. 262–3 (von Meck).   [133] ix. 279 (von Meck).   [134] ix. 284.

some large composition for chorus and orchestra or for orchestra alone. He suggests that the music should illustrate one of the following three subjects: (1) the opening of the exhibition (2) the Tsar's Silver Jubilee or (3) the consecration of the Church of Christ the Saviour. I can think of nothing worse than to have to compose something for some ceremony or other.

Just think, dear friend [Mme von Meck], what for example can one write on the occasion of the opening of an exhibition that isn't just banalities and noisy platitudes? However, I don't feel like refusing the request and so whether I like it or not I shall have to get down to this uncongenial task.[135]

We are all very gloomy here. My sister is better but she is very weak and her drawn, exhausted face makes one think sad thoughts. I don't think she will ever be completely well again. Yet the well-being of the whole family depends on her well-being. When she is ill the remaining members of the family are unhappy, such is the fanatical feeling of love and devotion that she inspires in them all. It is an incomprehensible business! This family has all the attributes for complete, universal happiness, they are all so nice, all so fond of each other, there is nothing lacking, yet some evil spirit dogs them and there is hardly a moment when they are all peaceful and happy. Now, for instance, not counting the disasters of the housekeeping, which can easily be rectified, there are no misfortunes threatening the family. Meanwhile my sister is ill, and evidently ill in mind, not body; the weakness of the latter is merely a reflection of her state of mind. I have no idea why she is suffering, what she is afraid of and what is troubling her. My eldest niece, Tanya, is a wonderful, intelligent, kind girl, who is passionately fond of her parents and passionately loved by them in return. One would expect her to be the happiest of creatures and yet she is constantly sad, constantly anticipating some kind of disaster, constantly tormented by a sense of dissatisfaction and of vague sadness. It only takes these two, in their broken mental state, to ensure that the rest of the family suffers from an obscure sense of sadness as well. What is the reason for it? I often ponder this question and am tormented by the knowledge that I am powerless to help them.[136]

I have received *La Gioconda* [Ponchielli] and *Danse bohémienne* [Debussy]. I warmly thank you and Julia Karlovna, who so kindly packed them and wrote my complicated address, for them both. I played through *La Gioconda*, not without pleasure. If I am not mistaken Ponchielli has no true creative gift, but he is a sensitive musician, not a hack, and not without taste, in which he differs from the majority of his colleagues. There are passages which are quite fine and effective, although without any sort of originality. There is strong evidence of Verdi's influence (his later period, i.e. the composer of *Aida* and the Requiem), and also of the French school of opera. This opera is written on the same subject that Cui chose for his opera *Angelo*. If you compare the two operas, you cannot but accord

[135] ix. 286–7 (von Meck).   [136] ix. 293 (von Meck).

supremacy to the Russian composer. In any case Cui has incomparably more talent and taste. *Danse bohémienne* is a very *sweet little thing*, but too short. Not a single thought is worked through to its conclusion; the form is excessively constricted and lacks completeness.[137]

My muse has been so well-disposed towards me of late that I have written two works very quickly: (1) a grand Ceremonial Overture [1812]. I have done this for the exhibition at Nikolay Grigoryevich's request; (2) a Serenade, for string orchestra, in four movements. I am scoring both of them little by little. The overture will be very loud and noisy, but I wrote it without warmth or love so it will probably not have any artistic merit. But the Serenade, by contrast, I wrote from an inner compulsion; it is deeply felt and for that reason, I venture to think, is not without real merit.[138]

It is not for me, of course, to decide the value of my works, but I can say with my hand on my heart that (with very few exceptions) I have *lived through and experienced them all myself* and they come straight from my heart. It is the greatest joy to me to know that there is a kindred soul in the world who responds to my music with sensitivity. The knowledge that she will experience everything that was in my mind when I wrote a particular work always warms and inspires me. You must not think that I have lots of such *souls*, even amongst the people with whom I live; I have a close spiritual kinship only with my brothers, and particularly with Modest. As to professional musicians, I have met with less positive sympathy amongst them than anywhere else.[139]

You [Mme von Meck] ask why I do not write a trio. It is beyond my powers. The difficulty is that the construction of my accoustical apparatus makes it impossible for me to stand the piano playing in partnership with either a solo violin or a solo cello. It seems to me that these sounds repel each other. Listening to a violin or cello trio or sonata is pure torture for me. I do not presume to explain this fact but simply affirm it. The piano with an orchestra is an entirely different matter: again there is no tonal blending, indeed the piano has no capacity for blending with anything because its sound has an elastic quality which, as it were, bounces off any other body of sound. But here we have two equal forces: the orchestra, powerful and inexhaustibly rich in its colouring, and its small, insignificant, but strong-minded rival which, given a talented performer, triumphs after a struggle. There is much poetry in this struggle, as well as endless combinations of sounds to tempt the composer. But the violin, the cello and the piano—what an unnatural grouping of three individuals! The singing tones of the violin and cello, with their marvellously warm timbre, have a quality all their own when set alongside the *king* of instruments, which latter vainly tries to show that it too can *sing* like its rivals. In my view the piano can be used only in three situations: (1) on its own; (2) in a contest with the orchestra; (3) as an accompaniment, i.e. as a background to the

[137] ix. 295 (von Meck).   [138] ix. 294 (von Meck).   [139] ix. 305 (von Meck).

picture. But a trio, of course, implies equal rights and homogeneity and where is that to be found between solo stringed instruments on the one hand and the piano on the other? It is not to be found, and I'll tell you why: there is always something artificial about a *piano trio* and each of the three instruments is constantly playing something which is not natural to it but has been imposed upon it by the composer who often encounters difficulties in distributing the parts and in arranging the constituent elements of his musical idea. I am full of admiration for the art and miraculous skill with which composers like Beethoven, Schumann, and Mendelssohn overcome these problems; I know that there are many *trios* which are musically of the highest quality, but I do not like the *trio* as a form and for this reason I am incapable of bringing any real warmth of feeling to writing for this combination of sounds. Even thinking about the sound of a trio is a source of actual physical discomfort to me.[140]

To my surprise I have written a serenade for string orchestra in four movements. Whether it is because it is my most recent child, or because it really isn't bad, I really do love this serenade.[141]

I am excessively pleased that you liked the places in *The Maid of Orleans* which I love best of all. But allow me to ask you, my friend, to bring the same sensitivity to one more heartfelt scene: Joan's narration and the Finale which closely follows it. Please note the variation on the theme of the angels' chorus from Joan's lips. Perhaps I am mistaken, but I think that this theme, translated from heaven to earth and now no longer imparted by angels but by a human being, i.e. by the vessel of suffering, must touch people's hearts here. Of course the piano arrangement only gives a very superficial idea of all this.[142]

From Kamenka Tchaikovsky went to Moscow.

I had a strange experience in Moscow. For all its faults, my love for this dear old town has in no way diminished; it has, on the contrary, become stronger and more intense but it has taken on a sort of morbid aspect. I felt that I had died a long time ago, that everything which had been there before had vanished into the abyss of oblivion, and that I was some quite different person, from another world and another time. It was an extremely morbid and dreadful experience which I find difficult to put into words. But there were some pleasant moments. I'll tell you about one of them. The people who run the Musical Society in Moscow were very interested in my *Liturgy* and one of them (Alexeyev) gave it to the best Moscow choir to learn. The result of their work was a performance of the *Liturgy* in the Hall of the Conservatoire. The choir sang excellently and I had one of the sweetest moments of my career as a composer. Everybody present enjoyed it as much as I did and it has now been decided that there should be a public

---

[140] ix. 306–7 (von Meck).   [141] ix. 308 (Jurgenson).
[142] ix. 305 (von Meck).

performance at a special concert of the Musical Society. So, my *Liturgy*, which has been so persecuted, at last becomes public property. Apart from that, they played on the same evening, as a surprise for me, the *Serenade*, for string orchestra which I had just written at Kamenka. At the moment I consider it the best of all that I have written so far. It was played very competently by the professors and students of the Conservatoire and gave me no small pleasure.[143]

The 'persecution' consisted in a ban on the performance of Tchaikovsky's *Liturgy* imposed by the Director of the Imperial Choir.

Eugene Onegin is going to be done in Moscow in a very good production at the Bolshoy. I am glad about this because it is very important for me to know whether this opera can establish itself in the repertoire. We will now see if *Onegin* can be transferred to the public boards or whether it is to remain the uncontested property of private societies.[144]

Tolichka! You say that there should be a change in the last scene of *Onegin*. Although I personally do not agree with you and consider that Pushkin with his few hints and suggestions gives me the right to conclude this scene as I have done, I have hearkened to thy voice and have tried to change the scene, as you will see from the enclosed notes. (1) On p. 242 instead of the direction for Tatyana to fall on Onegin's breast, etc. I have written: 'Onegin moves closer.' Then he sings what is written on this page, still addresses her formally;* then the rest is as before; right at the end I have changed Tatyana's words: she will not falter or weaken any more but will continue to tell Onegin of her duty. Onegin will not clasp her to him but will simply implore her with his words and then, instead of 'I will die', Tatyana says, 'Goodbye for ever' and disappears, while he, after standing dumbstruck a few moments, will make his final speech. The General should not enter. I am entrusting these changes to you. Take them to Klimentova, go to see Begichev or Bevignani or ask Nikolay Grigoryevich [Rubinstein] to do it all for you. I expect everyone will be pleased with these changes.[145]

The longer I stay in Moscow the less I can see an end to my suffering. It appears that I shall not be able to get away before the beginning of next week: on Friday evening there will be a ceremonial performance of my Mass at the Conservatoire and I have promised to be there. On Saturday I have to have a discussion with Bevignani about *Onegin* which he is putting on at his Benefit concert. On Sunday Klindworth has organized a ceremonial dinner in my honour; next week my *Italian Capriccio* is being performed and I want to listen to at least one rehearsal. Then the rehearsals for *Onegin* are beginning, and so on and so on. So, in short, either I will get to

* The Russian formal 'Vy' is equivalent to the French 'Vous' [trans.].

[143] ix. 319–20 (von Meck).   [144] ix. 320 (von Meck).   [145] ix. 301 (Anatoly).

Petersburg in some spare gap, for instance at the beginning of next week, or not until much later. However, I haven't decided anything yet. The corrections keep mounting up. *Alyosha has been taken for military service.* Life is endurable only because I have to drink a lot! If it were not for these constant lunches and suppers with drink, this life would have literally driven me out of my mind.[146]

My stay in Petersburg turned out to be far more disastrous than Moscow. There's a terrible upheaval going on in the theatre world about *The Maid of Orleans*. In the spring I allocated the part of Joan, in the absence of other singers, to Mesdames Raab and Makarova. Meanwhile a new claimant to this role appeared, Mme Kamenskaya, whose voice, although it is a mezzo-soprano, has such an enormous range that she turned out to be capable of taking the soprano role of Joan. Since the beauty of her voice and of her figure make her far more suitable for my requirements than the other two singers, I, of course, had to do everything possible to have the principal role assigned to her. Meanwhile Mesdames Raab and Makarova had heard that there was some talk of taking their roles from them and had managed to set the senior management of the theatre against Kamenskaya and me. In the event I still used my legal right as the composer to allocate roles and Kamenskaya was allowed to sing Joan, but on condition that she did not take the role on the first night. I have vowed never to write another opera for the Petersburg stage. What a dreadful town! The permanent fog and lack of sun are quite enough in themselves! They are all very well-disposed towards my opera at the theatre, and Nápravník (to whose friendship I am in general very much indebted) predicts a great success. And indeed the quarrel amongst the prima donnas is in itself evidence of interest in the work. They all find that part effective and grateful to sing.[147]

Then Moscow again.

My successes. Monday [15 December]—the third performance of *The Oprichnik*, great enthusiasm: insistent curtain calls for me, but I wasn't there. The same evening a performance of my First Quartet at the Musical Society concert: the Andante was repeated and there were curtain calls. Today [18 December] a *concert spirituel* of the Musical Society with my Liturgy. The hall was full and, despite the ban on applause, there was a tremendous and unexpected ovation and an anonymous donor presented a sort of lyre made of greenery. The rehearsal for the concert was in the morning and I heard the *Italian Capriccio*. It sounds wonderful.[148]

My poor, poor Alyosha! I went to see him in the Pokrovsky barracks. Oppressive, dirty barracks, Alyosha's downtrodden miserable appearance, in his military uniform already, without his freedom and obliged to drill from morning till night—it was all so depressing and dispiriting.[149]

---

[146] ix. 317 (Modest). [147] ix. 322, 323 (von Meck).
[148] ix. 337 (Modest). [149] ix. 334 (von Meck).

A couple of days ago in the evening at the Huberts I suddenly had a frightening attack of nerves, worse than I have ever had before. I think that the direct cause must be Alyosha, whom I had visited on that day and whom I am so sorry for, that I cannot find words to express it.[150] And for so many years yet! I don't think I will ever get used to being without him; I constantly have cause to think about him and to realize what an invaluable friend I have lost in him. He was so familiar with all my ways, he had such an ability for making himself both necessary and useful at every turn, that no other servant, however diligent, could replace him. When Alyosha was here I knew that every paper I needed, every item I might require in the course of my work, would be meticulously laid out in its proper place. Because I am dreadfully absent-minded and am constantly absorbed in my musical goings-on I need someone around to look after me and all my possessions. Now I am completely at a loss. Half of the clothes and linen which were brought from Kamenka six weeks ago are now missing. I haven't the remotest notion what has happened to the rest. I will have to get a grip of myself and pay attention to these things but unfortunately it would be easier for me to write forty symphonies than to keep my paltry few possessions in order.[151]

[21 December]—the *Italian Fantasia* has been performed, with great success.[152] Being a composer brings with it the finest moments of earthly happiness—*but at the price of a lot of unpleasantness and much suffering.* I speak from experience.[153]

Onegin has had its first performance. I was under great pressure from the most varied emotions both on the night and at all the preceding rehearsals. The audience was very cool towards the opera at first but things got better as it went along and it all ended more than satisfactorily. Of course, the success of an opera is not apparent on the first night but only later when it is possible to establish what its drawing power is. However that may be, I have every reason to be entirely satisfied with the marks of encouragement which greeted it. I am very pleased with the performance and with the production. Onegin (Khokhlov) and Verni (Tatyana) were particularly good. Bevignani conducted with great skill and I am indebted to him more than anyone for the success of the opera.[154] The *press* took a very peculiar attitude. There is far more blame than praise, which is of no importance, but what is sad is that even the papers which praise me do so in terms which are, in effect, insulting. One paper said that Triquet's couplets were the best thing in the opera and that the part of Tatyana was arid and insipid. Another said that I had no inspiration but that I was very learned and so on. There is a chorus of gutter abuse from the Petersburg press for the *Italian Capriccio*. They regard it as an impermissible vulgarity and Mr

---

[150] ix. 339 (Modest).   [151] ix. 347 (von Meck).   [152] ix. 339 (Modest).
[153] x. 14 (Modest).   [154] x. 16 (von Meck).

Cui foresees that *The Maid of Orleans* too will be banal from beginning to end. I find it astonishing and incomprehensible that most of the organs of the press, which serve as a reflection of public opinion, are somehow ill-tempered and disapproving when they write about me. Why should this be? What have I done to deserve it? Incidentally, the worst thing about it is not that they are unanimous in their abuse, but that they concern themselves with me, that they point to me, and that I am just now generally in public view.[155]

The first performance of *Eugene Onegin* in the Bolshoy Theatre in Moscow took place on 11 January 1881. The conductor was Enrico Bevignani.
  The premiere of *The Maid of Orleans* was to take place in St Petersburg.

The journey did me good, as always; I slept the whole way and arrived [in Petersburg] in good shape both physically and mentally. I have not been anywhere yet; I have only been to see Kuindzhi's picture, about which so much is being written and said at the moment. It really is an astonishingly skilled work in the genre of landscape painting; the utterly faithful reproduction of nature can go no further than this![156]

A.I. Kuindzhi's picture *A Birch Grove* was exhibited on 15 January 1881 at the premises of the Society for the Encouragement of Artists.

I have been to rehearsals of the opera every day. One must give Nápravník his due: my music has been studied thoroughly and I can be certain that in this respect everything that can be done will be done. But the production is poverty-stricken; the theatre management, which has just spent thousands on producing a new ballet [*Zoraiya* by Minkus] has declined to spend even coppers on the new opera. Instructions were given that all the scenery and costumes should be got together from old stock. What can you do? I can only hope that a good performance of the music will save the opera. What pleases me very much is that all the artists performing in the opera like it and are doing their job not just out of duty but with affection and sincere enthusiasm. The success of the opera will now also depend on the fact that the role of Joan has been entrusted to two singers: Mesdames Kamenskaya and Makarova. The former, in voice, in appearance, and in acting ability is nearer to my ideal than Makarova, who has talent but neither voice nor power. I, Nápravník, and the producer want Kamenskaya to sing in the first performance; but the management, in the person of a Mr Lukashevich, has personal reasons for wanting Makarova to sing. It is not difficult to foresee what the end of our disagreement will be. Mr Lukashevich's wish will be granted, because, unfortunately, once having handed the opera to the management, I have no legal right to make any demands at all. Oh God! how squalid it is! How glad I will be to escape from this world of squabbles, petty niggling, and bureaucratic obtuseness![157] Just how far this niggling

[155] x. 19 (von Meck).   [156] x. 22 (von Meck).

goes is hard to believe. At the rehearsal yesterday [6 February] he accidentally discovered that at one point in the opera I had transferred a melody
from Joan's part to that of Agnes, for reasons to do with the voices and the
production; he declared that *I had no right to do this and must seek permission
from somebody*!!! For a moment I thought I would take my score back and
leave the theatre. Nápravník persuaded me not to. It's infuriating and
squalid! I would like to run as far as I can from this confounded town which
is ruled by bureaucratic whim.[158]

Mariya Kamenskaya took the part of Joan at the first performance.

I had a difficult day on 13 [February]. I was agitated and tormented with
fears from the morning onwards and by evening I was simply crushed by a
heavy burden of distress and anxiety. But the success of the opera was clear
from the very first act. Kamenskaya sang the whole scene with the angels
magnificently and I took eight curtain calls at the end of Act I. They also
liked the second act very much. Scene 1 of [Act] III provoked a storm of
applause. The second scene was much less successful; the staging of the
march, in fact of the whole scene, was so wretched, dirty, and pathetic that
one could expect nothing else. But then they liked the fourth act very much
again. In all I took twenty-four calls. Kamenskaya was outstanding; even
her acting was excellent, which has not previously been the case. Of the
others the best was Pryanishnikov [Lionel]. After that I spent a sleepless
night and went [abroad] next morning.[159]

This was the day of the premiere of *The Maid of Orleans*. The conductor was
Nápravník.

[In Vienna], they were giving Weber's *Oberon*. What a wonderful production! It is funny to think back to the Mariinsky Theatre! The music is a bit
boring but there are some delightful parts. I did not stay to the end but
went home; I am writing to you [Anatoly] and Modya and drinking tea. On
the way here I read in the *Neue Freie Presse* a dispatch from Petersburg
which said that my opera had a *huge success* but that nevertheless it is *bad,
boring*, and *monotonous*.[160]

I stopped in Florence for a day instead of Venice. I wanted to get to the
real Italy as soon as possible, to see the green grass and, above all, the warm
spring sun. And here, straight away, as soon as I heard the sounds of Italy,
as soon as my eyes lit upon the typical features of these lovable people, I
realized how much I was infatuated with Italy. I was already in raptures as
I approached Florence early in the morning and saw the bright spring sun
shining on the lovely Italian landscape. It all seemed to be some sort of
magical dream![161] After breakfast I went to the Viale dei Colli and walked

[157] x. 24–5 (von Meck).   [158] x. 28–9 (von Meck).
[159] x. 32–3 (von Meck).   [160] x. 34 (Anatoly).

the full length of it, from the Porta Romana to San Miniato and beyond, right up to the hotel. I went past the Villa Oppenheim and looked in at the Villa Bonciani for a few minutes. Lord! how sweet are my memories of autumn '78! Indeed, they are *sweet, and painful as well*. But that could not happen again. Or if it did the circumstances would be different; it was, after all, two and a half years ago. We are older now. Yes, painful and sweet. What light! The sun is superb! What a pleasure it is to sit by the open window, with a bunch of violets on the ledge, breathing the fresh spring air. O marvellous, blessed country! I am overwhelmed with so many different feelings. It's so good to be here yet it's so sad as well, for some reason. One wants to weep and does not know what the tears are for: there is emotion in them, and gratitude, and regret. In short, only music could express it.[162]

Tchaikovsky left Florence for Rome.

Five minutes before I arrived I woke up and first saw the Lateran Cathedral, lit by the red light of the rising sun, then Minerva, then Rome itself at last. My feeling was that I had come home; it was as though I had left just a week ago. They greeted me at the hotel with open arms. Then I walked around the town on my own and *savoured Rome*. It looks as if I love the place but the main thing is how much I feel *at home* here.[163]

I can truthfully say that I have literally not taken off my white tie and tails in Rome and spent my last day until late into the night at the Bobrinskys, flirting with the ambassador's wife, and charming some Roman princes and marquises with my music.[164]

It turned out that many of Tchaikovsky's Russian acquaintances were in Rome and he fled to Naples to avoid social encounters.

A Russian sailor of my acquaintance came to see me and told me the terrible news about the death of the Emperor. I was so stunned by the news that it almost made me ill. It is distressing to be abroad at such a dreadful moment of national disaster, in circumstances which are such a disgrace to Russia. I wanted to rush back home, to find out the details, to be amongst my own people, to take part in the demonstrations of sympathy for the new Emperor, to howl for vengeance along with everybody else. Is it possible that this foul cancer of our political life will even now not be torn out from the roots? It is dreadful to think that this most recent catastrophe is perhaps still not the epilogue to the whole tragedy.[165]

I am spending the time here like a real tourist. I have been right to the top of Vesuvius. I walked from Resina to the observatory; then I took the funicular to the top and after that I went with two guides right up to the crater, which is a sight of hellish magnificence; I am glad to have seen it. I was planning to go to Sorrento but I did not feel like a *partie de plaisir* at

[161] x. 35–6 (von Meck).   [162] x. 39 (von Meck).   [163] x. 40, 41 (Modest).
[164] x. 56 (Modest).   [165] x. 54 (Modest).

such a dreadful time so I have confined myself to going to the museum, which is very interesting.[166]

Of all I have seen I was most impressed with Sorrento; if there is a place on this earth which one can call paradise, it must be this very wonderful corner of the world.[167]

From Naples Tchaikovsky went to Nice. But he was not destined on this occasion to enjoy the pleasures of the south.

I have heard from Anatoly that Nikolay Grigoryevich [Rubinstein] left Moscow for Nice on 28 February. Here, however, no one knows anything. I fear that he has not been able to stand the exhausting journey and is lying ill somewhere! My brother writes that his condition is very serious! It is terrible to think what would happen if the Conservatoire were to be without him.[168]

In Nice I learnt, first through a telegram from Jurgenson, that Nikolay Grigoryevich was in a bad way, then, through telegraphic communications with the Grand Hôtel, that (1) his condition was hopeless, and (2) he had died. I left Nice the next day. The journey was a hellish mental torture. To my shame I must admit that I was suffering less from a sense of terrible, irreparable loss than from the fear that in Paris, in the hotel, and in the Grand Hôtel moreover, I would see poor Rubinstein's corpse, disfigured by his excruciating suffering. I feared that I would not be able to cope with such a shock and that I would collapse or something, despite my determination to conquer my shameful fear. Be that as it may, my fears on this score were unnecessary. Nikolay Grigoryevich's body had already been taken to the Russian church.[169] The funeral took place [the next day]. The church was full. Then the coffin was taken down to the crypt, where I saw him for the last time. He had changed beyond recognition. My God! My God! how dreadful are such moments in our lives! I am utterly crushed by sorrow. I hastily dashed off a report for *Moskovskiye vedomosti* [*The Moscow Gazette*] about Nikolay Grigoryevich's last days.[170] My mind is in confusion, and it could not be otherwise, a feeble intellect faced with such insoluble questions as *death, the aim and meaning of life, and its infinity or its finitude*. But yet the light of faith penetrates deeper and deeper into my soul. Yes, dear friend, I feel that I am leaning more and more towards that only bulwark that protects us from all disasters. I feel that I am beginning to be able to love God, which I was unable to do previously. I am still visited by doubts: I still sometimes try to attain the unattainable with my feeble and pitiful mind but, ever louder and louder, the voice of divine truth is beginning to reach me. Already I often find an indescribable pleasure in bowing before God's inscrutable yet, for me, unquestionable wisdom; I often pray

[166] x. 55 (von Meck).   [167] x. 60 (von Meck).   [168] x. 61 (von Meck).
[169] x. 64 (Modest).   [170] x. 68 (von Meck).

to Him with tears in my eyes (where is He, who is He?—I don't know except that I know that He exists) and ask Him to grant me humility and love, ask Him for forgiveness and enlightenment—but most important of all, I find comfort in saying to Him: Lord, Thy will be done, for I know that His will is holy. I will say this also, dear friend, that often, thinking about my life I begin to see the finger of God, clearly showing me the way and shielding me from harm. Why it is God's will to shield me in particular, I do not know. I want to be humble and not to count myself one of the chosen few, for God loves all His creatures equally; but all I know is that God protects me and I often shed tears of gratitude for His infinite kindness. But this is only a beginning. I want to teach myself to accept that if disasters befall me they are in reality for the best; I want to love God always: both when He sends me happiness and when I am being tested. For somewhere there must be the kingdom of everlasting happiness which we vainly strive for on earth. The hour will come when all the questions which are beyond the reach of our minds will be resolved, and when we will understand why God finds it necessary to test us. I want to believe in a life after death. When my desire turns into reality then I will be happy in as much as it is possible to be happy on this earth.[171]

I was at the church for the requiem and the dispatch of the coffin with Nikolay Grigoryevich's body to the railway station. From there I went to the Gare du Nord and saw them nail up the lead coffin in a wooden box and put it in the luggage van. It was terribly painful and distressing to know that our poor Nikolay Grigoryevich was lying there in that wooden box and would go to Moscow in the luggage van. Yes, it was *painful*.[172] Fortunately I have a grain of *faith* and I console myself with the thought that such is the *inscrutable* but *holy* will of God. I always had a high opinion of Nikolay Grigoryevich's professional activities, though I did not, particularly in recent times, entertain any warmth of affection towards him as a person. Now, of course, all is forgotten apart from his good side and there is more to that than there was to the bad, and this is to say nothing of his *significance as a public figure*. One is simply seized with horror at the thought of trying to replace him.[173]

For Russian music as a whole and for me it is a great, irreparable loss. In all probability I will now have to face a sharp alteration in the course of my life. Mme von Meck has admitted to me *that she is almost ruined*. With the astonishing delicacy which is typical of this marvellous, but poor, woman, she tries to assure me that my allowance counts for nothing amongst the millions she has lost and begs me not even to mention it; but I do not want to abuse her generosity and cannot do so.[174]

I am going to Petersburg. I will stay there a few days and then, avoiding Moscow as far as I can—because at the present sad time I think of it as a

[171] x. 70 (von Meck).   [172] x. 70–1 (von Meck).
[173] x. 73 (Anatoly).   [174] x. 72 (Lyova).

sort of miserable graveyard—I will go to Kamenka, probably for some time.[175]

I did not go to Moscow for the burial of Nikolay Grigoryevich. There are two reasons for this: (1) I want to be on my own more than ever, and (2) I would constantly be in a position to observe the behaviour of Anton Rubinstein towards the loss of his brother; his behaviour is *strange and incomprehensible, and it offends my feelings.* I do not want to cast stones at him, for how can we enter into someone's heart? We cannot know how far the inner, emotional state corresponds to external appearances. But [in Paris] he conducted himself as though he were not only not distressed by his brother's death but was *pleased* about it. Incomprehensible and unbelievable—but sad to see.[176]

[175] x. 74 (von Meck).   [176] x. 76 (von Meck).

15

1881–1882

Either I have sung myself out or I will strike up again better than before.

I have arrived safely [at Kamenka]. The children gave me a wonderful welcome. In general, although I am a little sad, I am pleased to feel at home again, in my own place, and above all to be surrounded by these dear children.[1] Because my sister is ill and is away with her husband I have had in a way to be the head of the family and to spend the greater part of my time with the children. I would have found it strange and onerous if I did not love these children as my own. I am doing nothing at all and take a pen into my hand only to write letters. Nor do I feel like composing. Do you [Jurgenson] not need anything? Have you no plans which I could help you to bring to fruition? That sort of external stimulus might stir my stagnating energies. Can I be getting old? Is my song already sung?[2]

The Davydov children were Tanya, Vera, Anna, Natasha (Tasya), Mitya, Volodya (Bob), and Yura (Uka).

This request prompted Jurgenson to ask Tchaikovsky to edit Bortnyansky's church music.

I am not writing anything at the moment but I am preparing to start on a setting of the *All-night Vigil* as a *pendant* to my Liturgy. If I find a subject I will perhaps start on an opera later. Apart from church music this is the only kind of music which attracts me. Since Rubinstein's death I have lost all interest in symphonic music.[3] I am dragging out a grey and joyless existence at the moment and have no inspiration, but I am perfectly healthy physically and have even started working. I am now arranging for full choir the basic chants of the *All-night Vigil* from the Ordinary. The work is difficult but quite interesting. I want to preserve the ancient ecclesiastical chants quite untouched but they are constructed on scales of a very special type so that they do not easily lend themselves to the most modern harmonization. However, if I do manage to emerge victorious from all my difficulties, I will take pride in being the first contemporary Russian musician to have worked on re-establishing the original style and structure of our church music. I still do not feel the remotest inclination to write anything of my own. It sometimes occurs to me that *my song is sung*, that the source

[1] x. 88 (Anatoly).　　　[2] x. 100 (Jurgenson).　　　[3] x. 108 (Anatoly).

of inspiration has dried up. But then I recall that I have had to go through periods completely devoid of creative impulse before. Probably when my mental horizons are brighter the urge to compose will appear as well. But will things get brighter? At the moment I seem to see misfortunes on all sides, threatening me and all those dear to me.[4]

It would seem that I have found something to do. In my present religious mood I will enjoy delving into Russian music. I have begun studying the *Ordinary*, i.e. our basic ecclesiastical chants, and I want to make an attempt at harmonizing them.[5]

My time has been occupied recently in busying myself with the *Ordinary*, with arranging the traditional chants for full choir, and indeed everything that is sung during the All-night Vigil. I have already done a little but I am still feeling my way. I have no proper knowledge either of the history of ecclesiastical singing, or of the service, or of what relationship there is between what is in the Ordinary and what is normally sung in churches (such as Kamenka), and so on. In all this complete chaos reigns. Many people want to change ecclesiastical singing completely and to restore it as far as possible to its primeval purity and individuality. Alas! I am becoming convinced that would be impossible. In the last century Europeanism invaded our church in the form of a number of *vulgarities*, such as dominant chords and so on, and its roots have penetrated so deep that, even in the heart of the countryside, deacons who have trained in seminaries in the towns sing something which is infinitely far removed from the genuine chants which were written down in the music for the Ordinary, but is, on the contrary, very close to what is sung in Kazan Cathedral in Petersburg. If we take the eight principal tones, each deacon knows them and confidently sings for the appropriate day the troparion, the Ave Maria, the psalms, etc. in the appropriate voice. But these modern tones remind one of the originals only intermittently and the harmony, which is formed haphazardly by whatever clergy happen to be gathered together (as for example in Kamenka), is nothing more than the most shockingly vulgar dregs of European musical platitudes. In view of all this, I think that for my part I would be being Quixotic, like Potulov or Odoyevsky, if I composed new forms of ecclesiastical chants which had their roots in the spirit of former times. You cannot rewrite history; it is just as impossible to recreate the singing that Ivan the Terrible heard in the Cathedral of the Assumption as it is to change the contemporary congregation in that cathedral, dressed as they are in tails, uniforms, chignons, and German clothes, into boyars, the local garrison, etc. Why am I writing all this to you, by the way? I just wanted to say a few words, but something like an *avant propos* of my future composition has come out instead: an All-night Vigil set to music by P. Tchaikovsky. I want, but only to a certain extent, to *retrieve* ecclesiastical music from its excessive Europeanism not so much by means of *theory* as by

[4] x. 110–11 (von Meck).   [5] x. 101 (von Meck).

artistic *sensitivity*. I will be an eclectic, i.e. something mid-way between Bortnyansky and Potulov. But my All-night Vigil will be much less European than my Liturgy; this, of course, is partly because here (in the All-night Vigil) there are fewer occasions when you can get carried away and compose. Here I will be more of an *arranger* of the Ordinary than a freely creative artist.[6]

Everything that is happening here is so joyless and so difficult that it is hard for me to write. Though as far as the health of the two most important characters is concerned, i.e. Sasha and Tanya, everything is tolerable enough. The first few days after Tanya arrived were terrible. She seemed to be in a state close to insanity and was filled full of ether, morphine, and all kinds of horrors.[7] But I have the same anxieties, the same depression and worry. My sister and niece have begun to alternate their illnesses in the most regular pattern but sometimes, as for instance today, they are both ill together. The difference between them is only that my poor sister is really ill and is suffering from a very complicated organic disorder, whereas Tanya is suffering only from nerves, or rather, *nervous behaviour*. I am often angry with the poor girl, because I know perfectly well that it would only take a little strength of will for her to concern herself more with her mother, and then she could more often conquer her own nervous suffering. Alas! She is too spoilt by her adoring mother and all those who surround her, she is too used to sacrifices being made for her and regarding them as somehow her due. But while I am angry with her, I also recognize at the same time that all this is the result of many mistakes of upbringing on the part of her too lenient parents. Be that as it may, the fact remains that at the moment living at Kamenka is the purest and cruellest torment for me, mainly because one has to restrict oneself to the desire to be useful and the conviction grows by the day that one is helpless to contribute to a moral and physical cure for the two invalids.[8] Nothing more cheerless could be imagined than life at Kamenka just now and it is a matter for astonishment that I can bear it. However, I am not leaving. Anywhere new frightens me because in new circumstances and new surroundings I have to change things in my routine and this is always very difficult for me. On the other hand it would be rather awkward to go away just now—as though I were abandoning them when things are difficult. How curious is the fate of man! Thanks to Nadezhda Filaretovna I am completely free. But here now is the proof that even material security does not purchase *freedom*. I know of no place on earth more disagreeable than Kamenka (in the sense of natural beauty). What previously constituted the sole attraction of life here i.e. beholding with my own eyes the happy family life of those close to me, has now turned into quite the opposite. And *yet it is precisely here that I am fated to spend the greater part of my life* because it seems I am not looking so much for *enjoyment of life* as *peace*. And peace I do have here, despite the constant alarms,

---

[6] x. 119–20 (Modest).   [7] x. 125 (Modest).   [8] x. 136 (von Meck).

because I am *at home* here, sitting on a well-warmed seat. I am doing very little work. I don't know why it should be, but at the moment I am lacking something which would enable me to take pleasure in work or to find in it any satisfaction of my needs. On the contrary, I am working only because I have to. No inspiration at all.[9]

I am busy with the *All-night Vigil*. When I am finished I want to do *some children's songs*, and then, if I still have inclination and inspiration, I will set about the opera. I have to hand a very decent libretto which I got from K. Yu. Davydov who had started to write an opera on it himself but then abandoned it for lack of time. The libretto is based on Pushkin's *Poltava* and was compiled by Burenin. So if I do write anything big it will be an opera.[10]

I have received Bortnyansky's works, have looked through them, and have started the editing, which has turned out to be quite laborious and tedious work mainly because most of his compositions are exceedingly dismal tripe. I have even begun to have doubts about giving my name to an edition with which I can have no sympathy. I am working at the moment on a piece of religious music which is an attempt, albeit a very modest one, to oppose the bad style established by Bortnyansky and *tutti quanti*; then am I suddenly to present the public at the same time with everything of which my own work is the negation? The simpler view, of course, is that I am a musician living by my work and there is nothing reprehensible in editing any bilge my publisher takes it into his head to publish so as to earn my living; but my pride suffers all the same.[11]

Tchaikovsky regarded as 'bad style' Bortnyansky's departure from the folk treatment in his religious music and the presence of a large amount of ornamentation. In the first volume of Bortnyansky's works he wrote a note about the performance of the ornaments, adding that 'the abuse of devices of this sort gives Bortnyansky's music an excessively refined and mannered quality . . .'.

Bortnyansky had talent but he was very second rate, and quite incapable of treading new paths. He was an excellent musician and had superb technical mastery and for this reason if you [Jurgenson] won't be doing a great service to art in publishing his complete works, you won't be doing anything to be ashamed of either. He has become hateful to me not because what he wrote was *bad* but because he was a prolific mediocrity, in whose ocean of compositions there is not one passage which is really alive; it is all smooth, clean, nice, but monotonous and bare, like the Steppes in Kherson province.[12]

I return to Bortnyansky for the last time to remark on the huge difference between a major talent and a mediocre one. Glinka, like Bortnyansky, learnt from the infidels and also almost slavishly imitated their forms, but

---

[9] x. 145–6 (Anatoly).   [10] x. 132 (Jurgenson).
[11] x. 149–50 (Jurgenson).   [12] x. 200 (Jurgenson).

only their forms. The inner spirit of what he created, the content of his music is completely individual. Bortnyansky wrote characterless little motets to a Russian text; Glinka wrote genuine *Russian* operas and created a completely new, if not school, at least a minor school of music, the influence whereof reaches even unto me, for I am the progeny of Glinka.[13]

Life here gets more difficult every day. Relations are difficult between Tanya and me. I am constantly annoyed with her, try to hide it, try to *forgive* her, but cannot. I can excuse my sister resorting to morphine after several hours of excruciating pain. But when a *perfectly* healthy girl, out of caprice, because she lacks character, to spite herself and those around her, of her own free will ruins herself like a drunkard drinking his fill: that I do not understand, and it infuriates me. When, after all her shouting and fits of nerves, I look at the anguished face of her father as he wrings his hands in despair, when I recall that the illness of my poor sister is entirely due to the worries and alarms caused by Tanya, I am furious with her, and in vain do I try to suppress my feelings of anger towards her.[14]

There is nothing more sterile than *trying* to be original or independent. The great creative artists never give it a thought. They seek *beauty* and whether it is original or borrowed becomes apparent later. The things that theories do to a man! You [Taneyev] want me to spend my time on contrapuntal treatments of [chants] from the Ordinary, imitations, figurations. But how can I, by the very nature of my musical make-up, do things like that? And even if I did, nothing would come of it but arid groups of notes. After all, to write like Palestrina and to achieve what he achieved one has to be a man of his time. One has to be filled with a warm naïve faith, one has to forget all about the poison which has laid low the sickly music of our time. But this is impossible! I am more infected by this poison than anybody![15]

I cannot think of Moscow and my Moscow friends without a sense of aching sadness. One of them, and a *very distinguished one* moreover, is no longer to be counted amongst our number, others have aged, have got a bit past their best, or have been much battered by the blows of fate. The only one I can contemplate with pleasure is Taneyev. The whole future of the Conservatoire lies with him.[16]

Don't be too modest [Taneyev]. Have confidence in your abilities; they are such that you can and ought gradually to come to take the place of Nikolay Grigoryevich. You have an obligation to realize this and to go straight to your goal for the good of the whole cause of music in Moscow which has been orphaned. You might have been made to uphold Rubinstein's cause. I think that in the piano class, in the Director's office, at the conductor's desk—everywhere, you *must* take the place of Nikolay Grigoryevich.[17]

I am reading *The Karamazovs* and I am dying to finish it as quickly as I

[13] x. 201 (Jurgenson).   [14] x. 166 (von Meck).   [15] x. 203 (Taneyev).
[16] x. 194 (Jurgenson).   [17] x. 204–5 (Taneyev).

can. Dostoyevsky is a writer of genius but I don't like him. The more I read of him, the more he gets me down.[18]

Tchaikovsky made a short business trip to Moscow.

During the last days of my stay in Moscow, and particularly on the way back, I was worried sick by the doubts about what is going to happen to *The Maid of Orleans*. But one evil drives out another, so on the way back I constantly turned over in my mind the question of a subject for a new opera (I don't like Mazepa, it doesn't attract me) and after much thought I came to the conclusion that the subject best suited to my abilities was the old but ever new one of *Romeo and Juliet*. So I have taken the plunge: I am going to write an opera on this theme. My feeling is that if I make an effort it will be a success and this has completely reconciled me to the thought that *The Maid* will not last.[19]

Apparently Tchaikovsky wrote the duet for Romeo and Juliet in October–November 1881. (It remained unfinished; Taneyev completed it after his death.) In Tchaikovsky's private library at Klin there has been preserved a volume of Shakespeare with the composer's sketches for this scene.

Tchaikovsky returned to Kamenka just at the time of the engagement and marriage of his niece Vera.

[Her fiancé Nikolay Alexandrovich] Rimsky-Korsakov made an agreeable impression on me from the start with his pleasant face, not handsome, but intelligent, and the simplicity with which he treats his bride, making no attempt to conceal the fact that he is head over heels in love. We got on to good terms remarkably quickly; only an hour after we had met we were, at his request, talking to each other without any formality and he immediately started calling me 'uncle'; it all happened in an incredibly simple and natural way. Verusha looks as if she is perfectly happy.[20]

What poor creatures you and I are Modya: we are, after all, going to go to our graves without having known even for a single moment the full happiness of love.[21]

Before Vera's wedding the whole family went to Kiev.

Since I am very interested in all kinds of singing in churches I have attended the churches here very assiduously and in particular the Monastery of the Caves.[22] On Sundays solemn services are sung for the bishop in both the Mikhailovsky and Bratsky monasteries. The singing in these two monasteries is famous but I found it unbearably awful, pretentious, and with a repertoire of something like concert pieces which were as banal as they were inelegant. The Monastery of the Caves was another matter; they sing there in their ancient way, observing the thousand-year-old traditions,

---

[18] x. 202 (Modest).   [19] x. 231 (Anatoly).   [20] x. 243 (Anatoly).
[21] x. 244 (Modest).   [22] x. 264 (von Meck).

without music and as a result without any pretensions to being like a concert, but nevertheless this is individual, original, and sometimes majestically beautiful devotional singing. Yet most people consider the
monastery's sacred music to be awful and admire the honeyed choral singing of the psalms which is heard elsewhere. This offends and irritates me to
the utmost degree. It is hard to acknowledge one's inability to help this sad
state of affairs. My attempts to work for the cause of Russian sacred music
have met with persecution. My All-night Vigil has been banned. Two
months ago in Moscow when the All-night Vigil for the departed took place
for Nikolay Grigoryevich [Rubinstein], the organizers wanted my setting
to be performed. Alas! I was deprived of the pleasure of hearing my service
in a church because the Moscow Episcopal Council decisively opposed it.
Bishop Ambrose called it *Catholic*; last year he wrote an article in the
journal *Rus* [*Russia*] about the unsuitability of singing my All-night Vigil at
concerts as the Music Society had done. So—I am powerless to fight
against this wild and senseless persecution. Against me are people with
power behind them who stubbornly refuse to allow a single ray of light to
reach this sphere of ignorance and obscurantism.

I heard *Ruslan* at the opera—and very respectably performed.[23] The
wedding of my niece Vera is fixed for 4 November. I had always suspected
that your [Mme von Meck] idea and my dream of linking the fates of this
marvellous girl and Kolya would be difficult to bring about in view of the
fact that she is already nineteen. But it is difficult for me to abandon the
hope of becoming related to you so I venture to offer another candidate—
Anna. She really is a lovely girl and has just turned sixteen; she is not as
pretty as her two elder sisters, but she has a very nice nature and is remarkably intelligent.[24]

Tchaikovsky went abroad after Vera's wedding. He went to Rome to join his
brother Modest and Kolya Konradi.

Yesterday I heard by telegram the news that my Second Symphony was a
great success in Moscow in a performance under the new conductor Zike.
It is terribly sad to think that new performers have already appeared in the
place of Nikolay Grigoryevich. I have been informed that my *Maid of
Orleans* is going to be put on in Prague. This is pleasant news.[25]

Venice somehow affects me in an altogether special way. Apart from the
fact that it is in itself poetic, beautiful, and at the same time somehow sad, it
also evokes in me memories that are both melancholy and at the same time
sweet.[26]

I am enjoying Venice very much indeed on this visit. Today I got up,
opened the window and discovered it was a wonderful day; the air is somehow soft and caressing. I got dressed, went for a walk, and had breakfast in

[23] x. 265 (von Meck).   [24] x. 249 (von Meck).
[25] x. 276 (von Meck).   [26] x. 268 (von Meck).

the same little inn where you and I used to go, then wandered along the comically narrow streets, and at every meat or vegetable stall the stench reminded me of how angry it made you; I went into Santa Maria dei Frari (where Titian and Canova are buried, you remember?), then sat in the square and enjoyed the wonderful day and the animated crowd filling the square to hear the military band that was playing in the middle of it. I am so happy and feel so well here that I have decided to stay one more day and not to travel to Florence until tomorrow evening. I will also stay there for two days.[27]

Florence has never seemed so enchanting as it did yesterday. But I am afraid that it will be difficult to fight Modest's passion for Rome, which, however, I can understand well, for Rome is also dear to my heart in many ways. But whatever happens, I will come to stay in Florence for a while, if not in winter, then in the spring (in February) and if necessary alone.[28]

I am full of various projects and feel in exactly the right mood for composing but have not settled on anything as yet. I think that one of two things will happen now: either I will write better than before or it will turn out that, although I have plenty to say, I am no longer up to it. I have lost my enthusiasm for my earlier works; they all (there are no exceptions now) seem immature, formally unsatisfactory, empty. Reason tells me that I am exaggerating my deficiencies at the moment, but I cannot force myself to think about a single one of my works with pleasure. In short: either I have sung myself out or I will strike up again better than before.[29]

I went to a Gala Concert in honour of Liszt who is now seventy. The programme consisted entirely of his works. The playing was less than satisfactory. Liszt was at the concert in person. One could not but be moved at the sight of this brilliant old man, who was himself touched and affected by the ovations of the ecstatic Italians. But the works themselves leave me cold; there is more of poetic intention about them than real creative power, more colour than line. In short, his works are effective in their external appearance but they offend by the vapidity of their inner content. This is the exact opposite of Schumann, the fearful power of whose creative talent is not matched by the greyish, colourless presentation of his ideas.[30]

I do not altogether agree with the advice to publish my operas with French titles. I do not like all this chasing after *abroad*. Let them come to us and not vice versa. If the time comes that they want our operas, then we will translate not only the titles but the whole text as has already been done with the German translation [of *The Maid of Orleans* for a production] in Prague. Until an opera leaves Russia there seems no point in translating it into the language of people who are not interested in it.[31]

In spite of the pouring rain I have been taking long walks every day and in the intervals between showers have been enjoying the beautiful sights of

[27] x. 270 (Anatoly).   [28] x. 272 (von Meck).   [29] x. 272–3 (von Meck).
[30] x. 277 (von Meck).   [31] x. 278 (von Meck).

this city to which I am growing more and more attached. At first Rome is not as entrancing as Florence but it has the same characteristic as Moscow of attracting you to it little by little and gradually bewitching you. Now I am totally bewitched in spite of the bad weather. Tell me, dear friend, where else but in Rome could one go on a walk such as the one we did yesterday? We walked past S. Maria Maggiore to Pietro in Vincoli, and then along the delightful path to the Coliseum, then to the incomparable Baths of Caracalla, then to the Lateran Cathedral, and then finally home along new roads near the railway. And every day you can think up an endless selection of walks. On Sunday Modest and I succeeded in getting into a solemn Mass at which the Pope officiated in St Peter's (on the portico where the rites for a canonization took place). This was remarkably interesting. One could not imagine anything more impressive than the procession of the Pope, preceded by his bishops, cardinals, and chamberlains in medieval costume, and all this to the accompaniment of Palestrina, a capella, i.e. without organ. The moment when the Pope entered, sitting under his canopy, was remarkably impressive. The service itself wasn't particularly interesting and the heat became so intolerable that I couldn't even stick it out to the end.

Our living quarters are not just good but almost luxurious. My room is comfortable and convenient to the highest degree. I immediately started to compose as soon as I arrived. I don't know what will come of it but I started with the music for the scene with Mariya and Mazepa from Pushkin's *Poltava*. If I get carried away, perhaps I will write a whole opera on this theme.[32]

I must admit that the scenery here, the bright sun sometimes has too much of a stimulating effect on me. In the life we lead here it is fairly difficult for me to find a few hours of the day when I can cut myself off completely from reality and lose myself in my work, without keeping track of time. I feel like being outside all the time, going to look at something, or even just strolling idly about, seeking the sun in the morning and the shade after midday. I think that in spite of my new-found desire to compose and the fact that I devote several hours to it every day I will not write much while I am here. However, why does it have to be much? All I need is for it to be *good* and I hope that it will be.[33]

Jurgenson wrote to tell me that our dear, good Brodsky has played my concerto in Vienna. The news gave me great pleasure and I am touched by Brodsky's heroic act. The thing is that this concerto, which I wrote four years ago, has been declared completely unplayable by various Russian authorities on the violin, and if I am not mistaken nobody has ever played it yet. However, I knew that the opinion of the afore-mentioned authorities was much exaggerated and was waiting for the appearance of some heroic violinist who would prove that the impossible had become possible. I am

[32] x. 283 (von Meck).   [33] x. 285–6 (von Meck).

extremely pleased that the someone turned out to be Brodsky for whom I have always had the warmest sympathy and in whose debt I am glad to be. He has not yet fully established his position in Vienna and I know very well that it was difficult and nerve-racking for him to appear before a Viennese audience with a concerto by an unknown composer, and a *Russian* one to boot. For that reason I am doubly grateful to him for the service he has rendered me.[34]

Adolf Brodsky first performed the Violin Concerto in Vienna on 22 November 1881; this was the first European performance because the first performance of all had been given under Leopold Damrosch in New York in 1879.

In the reading room of the hotel I chanced on a copy of the *Neue Freie Presse*, in which Hanslick writes the music column. He writes about my Violin Concerto that, in general, in so far as he knows my works, they are notable for their unevenness, their complete absence of taste, their coarseness, their barbarity. So far as the Violin Concerto is concerned, the beginning is bearable but it gets worse as it goes along. At the end of the first movement, he says, the violin does not play: it howls, shouts, and roars. The Andante also begins well but it soon shifts to portraying some wild Russian festival, where everybody is drunk and they all have coarse, revolting faces. 'As I listened to Mr Tchaikovsky's music it occurred to me that there is such a thing as . . . *stinking music (stinkende Musik)*.' An odd review, is it not? I have no luck with the critics. Since Laroche left there is not a single reviewer in Russia who would give me a warm and friendly review. And in Europe they call my music '*stinking*'!!![35]

Kotek, my closest friend, got cold feet and went back, faint-hearted, on his intention of introducing my concerto to Petersburg (and in any case this was his plain duty, because he was responsible for the *Spielbarkeit* of the violin part); Auer, to whom the concerto is dedicated, plays all sorts of dirty tricks on me. In such circumstances, how could I not be touched, how could I not be grateful to dear Brodsky, who now suffers the abuse of the Vienna papers on my account?[36]

The foreign press also carried favourable reviews of the concerto and the Russian papers reported this.

Then an unexpected admission, to Mme von Meck.

Do you know, my dear, what I have started writing? You will be very surprised. Do you remember, you once advised me to write a trio for piano, violin, and cello, and I replied frankly that I did not like that combination of instruments? And now, suddenly, despite my antipathy, I have decided to try my hand at this genre which I have never touched before. I have already written the beginning of the trio; I don't know whether I will finish it or whether it will be a success, but I would very much like to bring to a

[34] x. 280 (L. Kupernik).   [35] x. 291–2 (von Meck).   [36] x. 294 (Jurgenson).

successful conclusion what I have started. The main, indeed the only, thing which has reconciled me to the combination of piano with strings which I so much dislike is the thought that I can give you pleasure with this trio. I have to make a conscious effort to fit my musical ideas into a new, unaccustomed form. But I intend to emerge victorious from all these difficulties, and the thought that you will be pleased constantly encourages and inspires me.[37]

I have finished my Trio and have started working hard at copying it out. Now that the piece has been written, I can say with a fair degree of certainty that it is not at all a bad work. But coming so late to the new genre of chamber music and having written for orchestra all my life I am only frightened that I have erred in employing this particular combination of instruments in my music. In short, I fear that this may be symphonic music adapted to the trio, rather than originally written for it. I took great care that this should not be so, but I don't know how it has worked out.[38] I am dedicating this *Trio* to Nikolay Grigoryevich. There is a certain lamenting, funereal quality to it.[39]

Tchaikovsky was living abroad, but he was acutely conscious of the joys and sorrows of his friends and relations. Jurgenson's five-year-old son Alyosha died.

I have received your letter with the news of your terrible loss. Not only do I actively share your grief: for me as well this is not just a sorrow, but real grief. As someone who passionately loves *life* (despite all its misfortunes) and just as passionately hates *death*, I am always deeply shaken when some dear creature whom I know dies. But death is never so monstrously dreadful and senseless as when it strikes a lovely, sweet, healthy child. When Sofya Ivanovna's sorrow abates somewhat please tell her that I must surely be amongst those who have most keenly and deeply sympathized with your parental grief.[40]

I have had a telegram from my brother Anatoly telling me that he has got engaged to the Konshina* girl.[41]

I am terribly glad that you [Anatoly] are happy and although I have never experienced anything like that myself it seems to me that I can understand very well all you are going through. There is a particular kind of need for affection and being looked after which only a woman can satisfy. I sometimes have a crazy desire to feel the affectionate touch of a woman's hand. Sometimes I see women with kindly faces (not young women, however) and I would so like to rest my head on their knees and kiss their hands. But it is difficult for me to put this into words. When you have quite

---

* Praskovya Vladimirovna Konshina, the niece of S. M. and P. M. Tretyakov.

[37] x. 292 (von Meck).   [38] xi. 24 (von Meck).   [39] xi. 47 (Jurgenson).
[40] xi. 22 (Jurgenson).   [41] xi. 41 (von Meck).

settled down, after the wedding, read *Anna Karenina*, which I recently read
for the first time with an enthusiasm verging on the fanatical. What you are
experiencing now is superlatively expressed there in connection with
Levin's marriage.[42]

I am flourishing in all senses of the word. By means of the most cunning
politics I have won complete freedom for myself here; I don't see anyone
except for my own immediate circle; I am working successfully and am in
the very best of spirits. If all had been well in Russia and if we had received
good news from there I could not imagine a better way of life. Unfortunately all is not quite well there. Very dark times have come to our fatherland which is dear to our hearts, sad though it is. Everyone feels an
indefinable anxiety and dissatisfaction; it is as if they were all walking on
top of a volcano which was about to burst open and erupt; everybody feels
that there is a certain precariousness in Russia's affairs and that change is
necessary, but it is impossible to foresee what will happen. Oh, how I wish
there was a tsar on the throne of Russia at the moment who was strong both
in mind and spirit, who had definite aims and a clearly defined plan! Alas!
We are ruled by a kind, agreeable man whom nature has endowed with
little in the way of brains, who is badly educated, and is, in short, ill fitted to
take into his feeble hands the shattered mechanism of government. As a
matter of fact there is no government at all at the moment. The tsar is in
hiding in Gatchina; from there he issues contradictory measures and
instructions; they say he is influenced by Katkov's opinions—at least all of
the foreign newspapers write a lot about Katkov's strong influence on
affairs, but at the same time it is common knowledge that Pobedonostsev
also has the role of a close adviser. But Ignatyev is there and they even write
that some lady-in-waiting or other has a decisive influence on affairs. But
all this is '*des on dit*', but nobody has a clear idea of the spirit and aims of
our rulers.

In my opinion (now or never), in view of the absence of outstanding
personalities, advice and support should be sought from the people at large;
to call upon us all for our guidance and assistance is the only way to re-
establish power and strengthen it. What Russia needs now, I think, is the
Zemsky sobor [the Council of the Land]. The tsar can learn the truth from
us; we can help him to eradicate sedition and jointly decide what is necessary to make Russia strong and happy.

It is exceedingly likely that I am a very bad politicker; perhaps everything that I have said is very naïve and frivolous, but when I think about all
that is happening to us I cannot find any other solution, and it seems to me
simply incomprehensible: how can this idea be inaccessible to those who
hold our fate in their hands? I think that Katkov, who refers to parliaments
as *talking shops* and hates such words as *popular representation* and *constitution*, confuses the idea of the *Zemsky sobor*, which even in the old days

[42] xi. 55–6 (Anatoly).

would be summoned on occasions when the tsar needed advice, with European chambers, parliaments, etc. Perhaps a constitution in the European sense of the word is precisely what the *Zemsky sobor* would reject; the point is not that we should immediately be assured of representative ministers and the whole procedure of English institutions, but that we should uncover the truth, that the people should put their trust in the government and give it guidance as to how and where to lead us.[43]

Have you read Taine? [Whilst reading the volume *La Révolution* of Taine's major work *Les Origines de la France contemporaine*:] No one else has portrayed with such skill those senseless idiots of extreme anarchists and revolutionaries. Much of what Taine says about the French in 1793 and about the significance of that petty gang of anarchists committing unheard of crimes before the very eyes of the vast majority of the population, astounded and powerless to stop their foul deeds, much of this is entirely applicable to our nihilists.[44]

Tchaikovsky and his brother Modest decided to leave Rome for Naples.

One thing I can say: in truth, *Vedei Napoli e poi morire!*[45] It is impossible in Naples to work steadily and persistently, at regular hours, as I did in Rome. I do practically nothing here and am not even ashamed of my idleness. Naples offers no possibility of working; it distracts the mind from such things with its noise, its beauty, the brightness of its colours. For this reason I would never agree to spend a long time here; I find it unbearable to spend a long time doing nothing. But anyone coming here for a few days must abandon all idea of work if that work requires any mental effort. Can one think about the best way of harmonizing the settings of the Ordinary (which is what I planned to do here), or choose a subject for an opera, or plan the form of a new symphonic work, when for hours on end one cannot tear oneself away from the window, from looking at that marvellous blue sea, gently rippling, at Vesuvius, flaunting its grandeur, in short—at the whole incomparable, beautiful picture. We have made a few very interesting excursions; we have been (1) to Herculaneum, (2) to Pozzuoli, Baia, and Miseno, and (3) to Camaldoli. This is an abandoned, deserted monastery with a magnificent and stupendous view of the whole bay, its shores and its islands. But even apart from the view, the excursion itself was remarkably pleasant, as was our walk afterwards along a little path where we found masses of violets and other spring flowers in the grass on either side. I have been to Pompeii and enjoyed it very much.[46]

In spare moments when I am not working or going for a walk I have been reading a very interesting book about Bellini which came out recently. This book is written by his friend, the eighty-year-old Florimo. I have always had a lot of time for Bellini. Even as a child I burst into tears at the strength

[43] xi. 297–8 (von Meck).   [44] xi. 28 (von Meck).
[45] xi. 69 (von Meck).   [46] xi. 79, 80 (von Meck).

of emotion which his elegant melodies, always steeped in melancholy, evoked in me. And ever since, in spite of his many imperfections, his dull accompaniments, the crass banal strettos in his ensembles, the coarseness and vulgarity of his recitatives, I still feel a liking for his music. I didn't know anything about his life except that he died young and was a sensitive, kind man. In Florimo's book his fairly extensive correspondence is also included with the biography. And so it was with great pleasure that I embarked on the description of the life of this composer who from a long way back had been surrounded in my imagination with a special, rather poetic, aura. In life I thought Bellini must have possessed the same sort of childlike good nature as Mozart. Alas! I was doomed to disillusionment. It appears that in spite of all his talent, Bellini was a very ordinary person. He was consumed by self-adoration; he admired every single bar and would not tolerate any criticism of his music whatsoever, everywhere suspected enemies, intrigues, jealousies, although success scarcely forsook him for a single day from the very beginning of his career right to the end. Judging by his letters, he did not love anyone, never ever concerned himself with anyone else, and in general it was as if nothing existed apart from what touched his interests. It is remarkable that the author of the book has evidently not noticed at all what an unpleasant impression Bellini's letters make—otherwise he would not have published them. The other book which I am reading with great pleasure is *On the Hills* [*Na gorakh*] by Melnikov. He has a wonderful knowledge of Russian life, and such a calm, objective attitude to the huge number of characters he portrays.[47]

I am sick and tired of Naples. It is an utterly impossible town to live in. Imagine what it is like having barrel-organs playing under one's window from morning until night without a minute's break and never fewer than two or three at once. I sometimes feel I am being driven to a frenzy, to despair. One forgets all the beauty of Naples because of this accursed music.[48]

Sorrento. In spite of continual rain, wind, and bad weather, I am nevertheless charmed not just with the beauty of the area but with the quiet, the peacefulness, which it was so pleasant to find after the noise of Naples. I have promised myself that if I am still among the living I will spend several weeks here next year, and particularly in spring when the oranges and lemons are in blossom, when the smell of spring flowers permeates the air and the fresh spring green colours the mountain-sides.[49]

I was very angry recently with a certain Mr Flerov, a journalist from *Moskovskiye vedomosti* [*The Moscow Gazette*] who arrived in Rome just before I left. There is nothing I like less than being put on show before the public. Meanwhile this gentleman, in recounting to his readers of *The Moscow Gazette* his walks in Rome, took it into his head to portray me winning pickles on the Piazza Navona and praising these pickles the day after. First, this never happened. Secondly, even if it had who would be interested in

[47] xi. 86 (von Meck).   [48] xi. 89 (Anatoly).   [49] xi. 90 (von Meck).

pickles which I won in a lottery? Thirdly, is it permissible so unceremoniously to expose to public view a man whose only thought is that no one should take any notice of him! Of course this is so trivial that it will have passed unnoticed but I was all the same extremely irritated at Mr Flerov's familiarity.[50]

Tchaikovsky had to attend the wedding of his brother Anatoly and for this reason had to leave Italy earlier than planned.

I will have the most pleasant recollections of the four months which I have spent in Italy. I have had a good rest and feel fit and healthy both mentally and physically. I am sorry to leave. There is nothing especially cheerful waiting for me in Russia; my brother's wedding and all the fuss connected with it frighten me.[51]

To answer your question about my plans: I will spend about two weeks in Moscow and then go to Kamenka, where the whole family will meet immediately after Easter. I know in advance that I won't be as happy at Kamenka as I was before. This is because my niece is worse than ever, is poisoning herself with morphine, and poisoning her parents and everyone else living in her company with her attacks of illness, which are repeated daily because of the morphine. This unfortunate girl seems to live on earth solely in order to torment herself and others. That ideal spirit of family peace and happiness which used perpetually to reign, and which made my stays there happy and pleasant, has long since abandoned the house of my sister and brother-in-law. I know already that it will be sad and bitter for me there. But I love them all so much and on their part they love me so much in return and so cherish my staying with them that I have no option but to settle in with them for the whole of the summer and part of the autumn just as I used to. If I didn't do this I would deeply hurt the whole family.[52]

I am coming to the conclusion that however much you love your country, however much you feel for it, there are certain circumstances which make preferable a stay of several months abroad. It will be enough to recount two instances which happened to me to show you how unbearable life in our dear Russia is. Here is the first instance. A concert of Glinka's works was given in the Manezh and the proceeds were earmarked to add to the sum which is being collected in order to build a monument to him. I set off to it and, after hearing the first half, made my way to the exit in order to leave, but near the exit itself stopped and turned round to look at the view of the Manezh as a whole. At that very moment some steward came up to me and asked me for my ticket. 'But I am going and I have already thrown my ticket away.' 'Your ticket please, or be kind enough to pay.' I tried to protest further when suddenly a policeman came up and shouted in a loud voice, 'Please accede to the request of the steward and do not make a

[50] xi. 88–9 (von Meck).   [51] xi. 91 (von Meck).   [52] xi. 92 (von Meck).

scandal.' I again began to protest but the policeman and the organizer shouted at me in threatening official voices, as if I did indeed look like a swindler trying to gatecrash. What was I to do? I paid and left, extremely irritated and insulted by this incident. The second instance: I was walking back from Jurgenson's at two in the morning along Varvarka Street with Fitzenhagen, and we were talking when suddenly some yard keeper shouted at us in a stentorian voice, 'Hey you devils, get lost, what are you shouting at the whole street for!' When I in my turn shouted at him to shut up and not be insolent, he showered on us a whole heap of swear words, curses, and threats to take us to the police station . . . I sent Fitzenhagen to fetch a policeman so that we could explain what was going on and report the yard keeper but this guardian of the peace took sides with the yard keeper and there was nothing left for us to do but to retire with ignominy. The next day I wanted to complain but I was advised to drop the idea. Of course both these incidents are trivial but they give you an idea of how difficult it is at present for even the most peaceful citizen to live in Russia. You can't help longing for countries where life is freer and where similar incidents would be unthinkable.[53]

My brother's wedding was an extremely wearisome affair. Unless I am very much mistaken Anatoly is very lucky.[54]

I have had a very brief telegram from my niece Vera: '*The lily of the valley is in flower. Vera.*' I will go and stay at Kamenka with the company at the moment only of Lev Vasilyevich and Vera, who has settled there with her husband for the duration of her pregnancy. I saw in the papers that Admiral Butakov, Lev Vasilyevich's brother-in-law, had died. His death saddened me very much because Butakov was one of the nicest people you could meet.[55]

Ivan Butakov died suddenly on 18 April 1882. He was the husband of Vera Vasilyevna, Lev Davydov's sister.

[53] xi. 106 (von Meck).   [54] xi. 99 (von Meck).   [55] xi. 107 (von Meck).

16

1882–1883

The nest at Kamenka *is no longer my* home.

Tchaikovsky spent the spring and summer at Kamenka. But things here were now very different from what they had been.

There was a time when this family basked in imperturbable, boundless happiness. But since Tanya grew up and first started languishing *of something* and pining *for something*, then started ruining herself with this confounded poison, since then their happiness has deserted them. And my sister's illnesses are a direct result of the anxieties caused by Tanya.[1] There has been a big change in Modest's circumstances. The father of his pupil has died suddenly and now, together with the fortune which he has inherited from the father, Modest is also left with all the father's obligations and responsibilities, which rest on him in their entirety.[2]

As I write this letter the tears have not yet dried in my eyes. Fear not [Modest], nothing terrible has happened. But I have just finished reading *Bleak House* and I have been crying a bit (a) because I am sorry for Lady Dedlock, (b) because I am sorry to part company with all these characters, with whom I have been living for precisely two months, and (c) from emotion and gratitude to a writer as great as Dickens. Although the end of the novel is (as usual in Dickens) rather contrived, I still enjoyed it so much from the first page to the last that it seemed to me I would not be doing my duty if I did not pour out my gratitude on paper.[3]

It is in general difficult to get down to work properly at Kamenka (and I never have been able to write anything substantial here; I have only orchestrated things which I have written elsewhere), but this year, because there are so many people here, because of the noise of the children who come for their holidays and play all day under my windows, and for various other reasons, I can hardly do any work at all.[4] Then Blumenfeld* has had the next room to mine, and that's the worst thing that could happen to me: for a musician to hear everything I sing and play. Why have Sasha and Lyova let Blumenfeld come here for the whole summer, or so it would seem? Of course, he is in love with Tanya and they have such long and peculiar

---

* Stanislav Mikhaylovich Blumenfeld, pianist, and music teacher to the Davydov children.

[1] xi. 125 (von Meck). [2] xi. 122–3 (von Meck).
[3] xi. 125–6 (Modest). [4] xi. 129 (von Meck).

tête-à-têtes or whatever that it sends me into a cold sweat. This causes Sasha suffering but Tanya said it was fun for her and poor Sasha just screwed up her eyes.[5]

It's a year ago since Davydov (the Director of the Petersburg Conservatoire) sent me a libretto for *Mazepa* which Burenin had compiled from Pushkin's poem *Poltava*. I didn't like it much then and although I tried setting one or two scenes to music the thing did not really get going, I did not warm to the subject, and I eventually stopped even thinking about it. I made frequent attempts throughout the year to find a new subject for an opera, but to no purpose; and it was an opera that I wanted to do. Then one fine day I reread the libretto, reread Pushkin's poem, was touched by some fine scenes and lines and began with the scene between Mariya and Mazepa, which has gone unchanged from the poem into the libretto. Although I have so far not once experienced that profound pleasure in composing which I got for instance when I was writing *Eugene Onegin*, although the work as a whole makes only modest progress and I feel no special enthusiasm for the characters—I still keep writing, now that I have started, and because I know also that despite everything some of it has come out well.[6]

I am doing a bit of writing on an opera, or at least some scenes from *Mazepa*—the ones which have captivated me to a certain extent. I am having difficulty in writing, and to tell you the truth, you can't write a serious composition like an opera here. There is everlasting bustle and noise under my windows; I have been deprived of my dressing room and it is being prepared as the room for the tutor, who will be arriving any day now and then I am always having to go off somewhere, whether it is to the big house or to the woods during the hours when I usually work ... However, one or two quite respectable things have emerged.[7]

A trip to see Modest (at the Konradis' estate of Grankino) was something of a relief for Tchaikovsky.

Grankino has no special attractions. It's a tiny oasis in the endless steppe. The garden isn't bad but it's still very new. There is no woodland for miles and miles around. On the other hand it is so quiet here that even during the day not a single sound breaks the silence, apart from the rustle of leaves. After the hordes and bustle of Kamenka it was very nice for me to come to this rural isolation. There is quite decent bathing. It will be very convenient for working. Kolya Konradi's father is buried in the garden, close to the house. This gives the estate a somewhat melancholy air.[8] I am working very hard and very systematically. I have gradually developed, if not a passionate enthusiasm for the subject, at least a degree of warmth for the characters. Like a mother whose love for her child increases the more trouble,

[5] xi. 133 (Modest).   [6] xi. 135–6 (von Meck).
[7] xi. 126 (Modest).   [8] xi. 143 (von Meck).

worry, and disturbance he creates, I now feel a paternal tenderness towards my new musical offspring which has given me so many difficult moments of disappointment in myself and almost of despair but is now, despite everything, putting on good, healthy growth.[9]

Tchaikovsky had to interrupt his work on the opera. Various matters, mainly connected with Jurgenson, required a trip to Moscow though not, admittedly, a long one.

I love Moscow with a love that is, in a way, painful and the pain lies in the fact that there, more than anywhere else, I am conscious of the transitoriness of all earthly things. I love Moscow because that is where I spent my best years and I enjoyed living there, but, now that everything which made it attractive for me then has gone, staying there is a painful experience. Consequently, whenever I am in Moscow, I always feel like a visitor from beyond the grave.[10]

Unless I am in the countryside or abroad, life is unthinkable for me, but why this is, I can't for the life of me understand—it's just that I am almost going out of my mind. I will probably one day go to a better world just because of this indefinable, venomous, tormenting and terrible illness, which I am incapable of defining, but which has the effect that I cannot spend one single day or even hour in the Russian capitals without suffering cruelly. And the more indefinable it is, the less can I pour out my causeless grief, the less right have I to complain and the worse do I suffer. I often think that all my discontent and troubles stem from the fact that I am very egoistic and incapable of sacrificing anything for the sake of others, even if they are my nearest and dearest. But I have just had the consoling thought that of course I would not submit myself voluntarily to the poisonous moral torment which I undergo here if I did not consider it more or less obligatory to be here in order to please not myself but others. This consoles me a little. But really, the devil alone knows! I only know that however little Kamenka attracts me, however awful it is there now, I still think of my own refuge there in terms of indescribable happiness.[11]

Then Tchaikovsky returned to Kamenka.

I have never had so much trouble with a major work as I am having with this opera. I don't know whether my powers are declining or whether perhaps I have become more severe with myself, but when I recall how I worked previously without the slightest effort, how I never knew even the briefest moment of self-doubt or despair of my ability, then I cannot but remark that I am a changed man. Formerly I used to give myself up to the labour of composing just as simply and by virtue of the same natural circumstances as cause a fish to swim in the water or a bird to fly in the air. But

---

[9] xi. 158–9 (von Meck).   [10] xi. 220 (Anatoly).   [11] xi. 184 (Modest).

not now. Now I am like a man who bears a heavy burden, albeit one which he values, and must carry it right to the end, come what may.[12] I have finished composing the opera and am getting down to orchestrating it. *I think* it will be a good opera. *I think* that the public, and the singers, and I, and Jurgenson will be pleased, but the devil alone can tell.[13]

I have begun to orchestrate my opera. How well my introduction will sound (in which Mazepa and the famous frenzied gallop is portrayed)! I am convinced that you [Modest] will like this introduction.[14]

The directorship of the Petersburg theatres, in the absence of an operatic soprano, have asked me to rewrite the part of Joan for a mezzo-soprano. At first I thought that I would only have to arrange for the transposition of some of the arias a tone lower. But Nápravník sent me the score with detailed indications as to which numbers had to be altered. He is a practical and experienced man, and I realized that I would have to re-orchestrate almost half the opera. This horrified me, because there is nothing more boring or more unpleasant than having to work again on a piece which was finished long ago and towards which the feelings of authorship have long since grown cold. But there was no alternative; the interests of my opera demanded that I should overcome my reluctance, and so I did. I spent ten days over it, chained to my desk, to this exhausting work, and indeed I had to exert heroic efforts of will in order to achieve everything that I did achieve over this short period. But it was essential to hurry to give time for the orchestral parts to be copied out in Petersburg, for a lot of it to be learnt again, and for the opera to be set up on the new stage of the Bolshoy theatre, where the Russian opera has now found a home.[15]

My *Trio* has been performed in Moscow. Taneyev, whose opinion I greatly esteem, played it at the first concert of the chamber music series and has written me a rapturous account of its virtues. I was terribly pleased about that. He said in fact that all the musical people in Moscow are full of praise for the Trio.[16] I have read Flerov's article. I cannot believe that anybody (from the musical world) can have told him that the Variations in the Trio portray episodes from the life of Nikolay Grigoryevich. I think this brilliant idea must be his own. But how funny! One writes music without the remotest intention of portraying anything and one is suddenly told that it does in fact portray something or other—one has the same sensation as Molière's *bourgeois gentilhomme* who discovered that he had been talking prose all his life.[17]

Flerov's review 'Music Chronicle' (over the pseudonym Ignotus) appeared in *Moskovskiye vedomosti* [*The Moscow Gazette*] for 22 October 1882.

I am having a rather curious correspondence, which he began, with Bala-

---

[12] xi. 216 (von Meck).   [13] xi. 218 (von Meck).   [14] xi. 221 (Modest).
[15] xi. 230–1 (von Meck).   [16] xi. 268–9 (von Meck).   [17] xi. 266(Taneyev).

kirev. He is fired with the idea that I should write a big symphony on the subject of *Manfred*.[18]

I do not want to give you [Balakirev] a final answer about your programme until I have reread Byron's text. In any case, I want to tell you what my feelings are now, before reading Byron. Despite the fact that you say *The Tempest* and *Francesca* were my *apogee* (with which I do not at all agree), I for some reason imagined that your programme would arouse in me a burning desire to reproduce it in music, and I was very impatient to get your letter. But when I got it I was disappointed. In all probability your programme could indeed serve as a canvas for a composer disposed to imitate Berlioz; I agree that, following its indications, one could construct an effective symphony in the style of that composer. But so far it leaves me quite cold and if the imagination and the emotions are not warmed there is little point in starting to compose. To please you I might, as you put it, *have a go* at it and wring out of myself a succession of more or less interesting episodes: there would be conventionally gloomy music to portray Manfred's hopeless disillusionment, masses of sparkling orchestral effects in the 'Alpine Fairy' scherzo, sunrise at the top register of the violins, and Manfred's death with pianissimo trombones; I could supply these episodes with some piquant and peculiar harmonic effects; I could then launch the whole thing upon the world with the sonorous title *Manfred, symphonie d'après* . . . and so on; I might even receive praise as the fruit of my efforts, but that sort of writing has not the slightest attraction for me. It is very difficult for me to explain to you just why your programme fails to kindle the spark of inspiration in me. Despite my venerable age and my considerable experience of writing music I must admit that up to now I have been blundering around the broad acres of composing, trying to find my true path. I have the feeling that this path exists, and I know that once I find it I will write something really good, but I am fated to be afflicted with a blindness which constantly knocks me off course and God alone knows if I will ever get where I ought to. Probably not. I think that geniuses and talents of the first order differ from failures like me precisely in that they get straight on to the highway and stride boldly along, without a backward glance, until they have expended all their energies. I have occasionally chanced to get near to the *path*, and then works have come forth of which I will not be ashamed to the end of my days, which give me pleasure, and which sustain in me the drive to work. But this has happened rarely, and I by no means count *The Tempest* and *Francesca* among these exceptions. It is not at all a question of thinking that programme music *à la* Berlioz is in general a mistaken form of art. I merely observe as a fact that I have not achieved anything of note in that line. It could well be that Schumann is to blame for my incurable lack of enthusiasm for your programme. I am passionately fond

[18] xi. 277–8 (Modest).

of his *Manfred* and I have got so used to seeing Byron's *Manfred* and Schumann's *Manfred* as one indivisible whole that I do not know how to
approach the subject so as to elicit from it any music other than that with
which Schumann has already supplied it.[19]

Until Tanya's arrival I was completely happy with my lot here. Although
I got very tired, nothing outside my work disturbed or irritated me. But
now that Tanya has come I am only at peace when I am sitting in my own
room and cannot see or hear her. There was one point when if only I had
had 100 roubles in my pocket I would have left because I did not know how
on earth I should conduct myself or how to hide my indignation and
horror. Once, after returning from the woods, I sat down in the carriage
beside her with Blumenfeld opposite her. On the pretext of the damp (!!! we
haven't had any rain for a whole month) she spread a thick rug over
Blumenfeld's knees and her own; then they started a game with their legs
under the rug, which I not only *felt but saw* and this went on right up to the
house, with Tanya meanwhile occasionally breaking the silence with some
remarks about the weather or about the places we were passing. I can't
understand their brazenness in behaving as they did in my presence. She
probably regards me as so innocent that she is not afraid of me. Two days
after this, but more particularly on another day, when there were guests on
the occasion of her birthday, I constantly became so distressed, indignant,
and horrified that I nearly went out of my mind ... To descend to such
depths as to allow herself without the slightest embarrassment to do things
which only prostitutes do! From birth I have always lived exclusively
among women who were beyond reproach, and it is because of this I found
her behaviour so monstrous.[20]

I cannot get away from Kamenka without using lies and deceit. We
agreed at lunch the other day that I would leave in the middle of
November. Suddenly Tanya said: 'Can I go with you?' I mumbled something but to myself I thought: not at any price. And I immediately started
making plans to get rid of her.[21] I announced that I was going to Prague
with Jurgenson for the revival of *The Maid of Orleans* (there really is going
to be one). I will hurry to finish the first act and as soon as it is finished I
will say that Jurgenson has left and is expecting me at Zhmerinka; I will
leave and then I will write from Kiev that the revival of *The Maid* has been
postponed. Floundering about in a swamp of lies is not altogether pleasant
but what else can I do? How else could I have got rid of Tanya?[22]

I have left this *little spot* of mine without any regrets; as soon as I started
to be surrounded by people on all sides the place lost its attraction for me,
and I must admit that I have absolutely no desire to return to Kamenka—
and that is a pity. I have no home anywhere, I can settle nowhere else in

[19] xi. 280–2(Balakirev).   [20] xi. 212 (Modest).
[21] xi. 274–5 (Anatoly).   [22] xi. 277 (Modest).

Russia, I am afraid of loneliness abroad; now I really am a sort of nomad and the thought weighs me down.[23]

[In Moscow] I experienced a profound aesthetic pleasure: I heard *Don Giovanni* at the Bolshoy. I can say with all sincerity that no one can delight my spirit, can astound me, can touch me as can this radiant genius![24] I have been to three orchestral concerts and have now got to know Erdmanns-dörfer well enough to make an accurate assessment of him. He is very adroit as a conductor, very experienced and skilful, but it canot be denied that the Muscovites exaggerate his virtues. There is a fashion for him at the moment which is not likely to last for long. His faults are: (1) he is too concerned with external effect and rather indulges the public taste for the exaggeration of nuances. Thus, for example, he at times takes *pp* to such a point that both harmony and melody are entirely inaudible and all that reaches the ear is a bare shadow of sound. This is terribly impressive but scarcely artistic; (2) he is too much a *German*; his programmes are too German, and French music, for instance, he does not play at all; he is slipshod with Russian music (apart from mine). Taneyev's overture, for instance, was given a very rough performance, but a bad piece by Wagner [the *Siegfried Idyll*] was played excellently. He barely played through the former at rehearsal but worked on the latter with affection.[25]

About my life here from day to day, I can tell you that it is exhausting, that, as I should have expected, I have to put up with a lot of unavoidable confrontations with masses of people, but there are also some very pleasant moments. Most importantly, I am glad that Tolya and Parasha have made the most pleasant impression on me; I was not expecting to find them so full of happiness and mutual love, and Tolya has altogether become quite unrecognizable.[26]

Levushka! I have a request to make. Clould you ask Stepan to find my *yellow notebook* which I took with me on my walks all summer? It contains almost the whole of my opera [*Mazepa*] and is essential to me. Send the notebook to Jurgenson who will forward it to me wherever I move to, since I myself don't know yet where I shall be. Please do this as soon as possible; without the notebook my opera will be lost.[27]

From St Petersburg Tchaikovsky went abroad. He deliberately delayed in Berlin to see Wagner's *Tristan und Isolde*, which he had not previously seen.

I did not like the opera at all, but I am still glad I saw it because the performance enabled me to clarify even further my view of Wagner about whom I have long had a definite opinion, but, not having seen all his operas on the stage, I feared that my opinion was not altogether well founded. To put it briefly, my opinion is that, despite his immense creative gift, his

[23] xi. 285 (Modest).   [24] xi. 287 (von Meck).   [25] xi. 293 (von Meck).

[26] xi. 289 (Modest).   [27] xi. 296 (Lyova).

intelligence, his poetic talent, his erudition, Wagner's services to art in general and to opera in particular are negative. He has taught us that the former conventional types of operatic music have neither aesthetic nor logical *raisons d'être*. But if we may not write operas as before, do we have to write them like Wagner? My firm answer is: *no*. Making us listen for four hours on end to an interminable symphony, rich in sumptuous orchestral beauties, but deficient in the clear and simple expression of ideas; making the performers sing, for four hours on end, not tunes in their own right but an assortment of notes adjusted to fit this symphony, which notes, high though they might be, are not infrequently swamped altogether by the thunder of the orchestra—this is scarcely the ideal to which contemporary composers should aspire. Wagner has moved the centre of gravity from the stage to the orchestra; since this is a manifest absurdity, his famed operatic reform, if we discount the negative contribution mentioned above, amounts to nothing. As to the dramatic interest of his operas, I find them all quite insignificant in this respect and on occasion childishly naïve. I have never been so bored anywhere as I was at *Tristan und Isolde*. It is the most wearisome, vacuous rigmarole with neither action not life; it has positively no capacity for engaging the audience's interest nor for evoking emotional sympathy with the characters.[28]

Tchaikovsky's plan on this trip was to spend some time in Paris working on the scoring of *Mazepa*. Then Modest was to come to Paris, without Kolya Konradi this time, and the two brothers planned to travel in Italy.

I am in Paris. Apart from Rome, this is the only town abroad where I can bear to be entirely on my own without being melancholy or fearful.[29]

The Hôtel Richepanse has turned out to be a nice, clean little place.[30] The day after I arrived in Paris I organized a very strict, precise routine; I have been sticking to it so determinedly, and I am so completely protected from all disturbances that I have the feeling that it has been established for ages. My work is getting on very well.[31]

I am looking forward to a great musical pleasure: they are doing Mozart's *The Marriage of Figaro* at the Opéra Comique. I am savouring in advance a whole host of delights. How much majestic beauty there is in this ingenuous music and, by contrast, how little true art in the complex score of *Tristan and Isolde*.[32]

I am continuing to work a lot and am still perfectly healthy and in a settled frame of mind. But I am a little fed up with the theatres and, to tell the truth, I have sometimes been a bit bored in the evenings and have longed for a game of cards which I think is the ideal way of spending the time for someone who has been working a lot during the day. But when Modest

[28] xi. 304 (von Meck).   [29] xii. 15 (von Meck).
[30] xii. 13 (Kolya Konradi).   [31] xii. 26 (von Meck).
[32] xii. 17 (von Meck).

comes I will be happy to spend the evenings at home as well, because although he might be out at the theatre, living with him will make fruitful, will warm, and will, so to speak, lighten my crepuscular loneliness.[33]

Tchaikovsky's plan—to stay in Paris with his brother and then to go to Italy together—unexpectedly had to be changed.

Modya has brought Tanya. Needless to say it was like a thunderbolt for me. I was very upset at first, but I must be fair to Modya. He did the right thing. I have already got used to the idea now that I will have to spend a little time in Tanya's company. We will not go to Italy.[34] The mystery has now been cleared up about why I did not know for so long that Tanya was coming. The point is that Modest had decided to bring her with him some time ago but said nothing to me about it in Petersburg so as not to upset me any sooner than was necessary and indeed I suspected nothing until Tanya actually turned up. Naturally enough, I was very unpleasantly surprised by her unexpected appearance in Paris, but there's nothing to be done.[35]

Tanya Davydova's arrival in Paris was connected with her pregnancy, which the Tchaikovsky brothers concealed from her parents, relatives, and friends. The ostensible reason for her trip was to receive treatment from Professor Charcot. Modest soon had to go back to Russia, to his pupil Kolya Konradi, and Tanya was left in Tchaikovsky's care, though she lived separately in a nursing home, with a female companion engaged by Tchaikovsky.

You [Anatoly] ask 'and what about your Tanya?' For God's sake no—don't call her mine. She can be anybody's you like but not mine. I am willing to help her in any way and to be what use to her I can, but I do not want to regard her as mine. The whole purpose of my life at the moment is to get as far away from her as possible. She is a person who inspires fear and dread in me.[36]

I will not be going to Italy. If I were to follow my own egotistical inclinations I would of course set off for Rome which I long for, and leave Tanya and the girl who is looking after her here with Modest, but I could not abandon poor Modest who will have to endure many difficult moments in the company of my unhappy niece, the sight of whom alone upsets and poisons every minute of one's life. I have not yet grown accustomed to the new way of life demanded by Tanya's presence and my work is going very badly during all this, and my health is not too good either.[37]

The scoring of *Mazepa* is going at snail's pace. In five weeks I have just managed to orchestrate three-fifths of one act. I hope to heaven I finish by the summer. All the same I'll have to leave the opera so as to turn *Slavsya*

[33] xii. 32 (Anatoly).   [34] xii. 39 (Anatoly).
[35] xii. 35 (Praskovya Tchaikovskaya, Panya).
[36] xii. 100.   [37] xii. 37 (von Meck).

from a rich operatic Finale into stanzas. I was asked to do this, and I promised, when I was still in Moscow.[38]

The arrangement of Glinka's *Slavsya* was commissioned from Tchaikovsky for the forthcoming coronation celebrations.

I have sent off *Slavsya* in the strophic arrangement. The work was very straightforward but I think I have done all that was needed, i.e. I have simplified the chorus, orchestrated it in the most *popular* fashion, and have made what I think is a very simple and natural transition to the anthem. I use the expression *popular fashion* not in the pejorative sense but in the literal one, i.e. I have made it as simple and powerful as I could. In all of this I have myself composed only a few transitional bars and the third verse of the text; the city of Moscow is preparing to stump up a fortune and I should receive in total the following: for simplifying the choral parts and orchestrating sixteen bars, repeated three times, 3 roubles; for writing eight bars of transition to the anthem, 4 roubles; for writing four lines for the third verse at 40 kopecks a line, 1 rouble 60 kopecks. Total: 8 roubles 60 kopecks. This sum of 8 roubles 60 kopecks I shall donate to the City of Moscow. Seriously though, it is absurd even to raise the question of payment for work like this and it will be disagreeable for me. One does such things for nothing or not at all.[39]

   Two unexpected and very burdensome tasks have descended upon me. The City of Moscow has commissioned a ceremonial march to be performed at a festivity for the Emperor at Sokolniki and the Coronation Commission has sent me the text of a big cantata (the words are by Maykov) and is most insistent that I should write the music. I had just reconciled myself to the idea of leaving the opera for the march when I suddenly got the letter from the President of the Commission about the cantata. My first thought was to refuse, but then I decided that I must at all costs make an effort and try to produce both of the works on time. Both works, particularly the cantata, will have to be produced with a rapidity which horrifies me. For six weeks I am going to have to wear myself out in sleepless nights and drive myself to the point of exhaustion. The President of the Commission says in his letter that only I can extricate them from their difficulties because Anton Rubinstein has declined on the grounds that the notice was too short and has recommended me.[40]

   I have been much aided by the fact that the words of the cantata, by Maykov, are very fine and lyrical. There is some petty patriotic boasting, but on the other hand the whole piece is deeply felt and written with originality; there is a freshness and sincerity about it which made it possible for me not merely to dispatch my difficult task just anyhow, so long as duty

---

was done, but actually to bring to my music a degree of emotional commit-
ment, stimulated by Maykov's marvellous verse.[41]

I have never written anything as quickly as these two pieces. I think I can
objectively evaluate these two works by saying that the March is noisy but
bad (don't say this to Jurgenson or to anyone else), but the Cantata is far
from being as bad as you might think, judging by the speed with which it
was written. As far as *Mazepa* is concerned, it is progressing gradually and
I hope to have it all finished by the summer.[42]

I have heard absolutely nothing in Paris—I haven't even been to a single
one of the Sunday concerts. Nor have I yet heard Saint-Saëns's *Henry
VIII*. On the other hand I have been four times to an excellent production
of Mozart's *The Marriage of Figaro* at the Opéra Comique. Oh! how divine
the music is! It's so undemanding and simple! I went by chance to Gounod's *Romeo and Juliet* and quite unexpectedly enjoyed it very much. I had
previously known the work from a piano arrangement and from a single
performance in Moscow a long time ago. I had no high opinion of it, when
lo! Oh miracle! I was moved to tears! I don't know whether it was Shakespeare, whose presence can still be felt despite the constraints of the
libretto, or whether Gounod's music really is so good, or whether my mood
was such that taken all together it had a perhaps fortuitous attractiveness
for me, but it is a long time since an opera gave me such pleasure as did this
one. It should, incidentally, be added that Gounod is one of the few in our
day who compose not in accordance with preconceived theories but in response to their emotions. He is, moreover, an inveterate admirer of Mozart,
which proves the unspoilt integrity of his musical character. Since then,
apart from barrel-organs furiously grinding out for hours on end an aria
from [Flotow's] *Martha* and some fashionable waltz or other which drives
me to a distraction verging on lunacy, I have heard nothing. What a
nuisance they were when I was in a hurry to finish my commissions![43]

I will set down my views on French music. It is not all the works being produced by the new French school, and by each of its composers in particular,
which attract me so much as the general air of innovation and freshness
which is apparent in French music nowadays. I like their efforts to be eclectic, the way they keep a sense of proportion, their willingness to get away
from worn out conventions, whilst still remaining within the bounds of good
taste. There is none of that *ugliness* which some of our composers have
achieved because they imagine that *innovation* and *originality* consists in
trampling underfoot all that has previously been regarded as essential to
beauty in music. And if we compare the new French school with what is now
being written in Germany then we really cannot deny that German music is
in a terrible state of decline: they do nothing but mess about endlessly with

[41] xii. 97 (von Meck).   [42] xii. 102 (Taneyev).   [43] xii. 102–3 (Taneyev).

features introduced by Mendelssohn and Schumann on the one hand and by Liszt and Wagner on the other. By contrast, there is something new to be heard in France, and sometimes it is very interesting, fresh, and powerful. Of course, Bizet is head and shoulders above everybody, but all the same Massenet, Delibes, Guiraud, Lalo, Godard, Saint-Saëns, and others are men of talent and the most important thing is that they are at least far removed from the arid, conventional style of the contemporary Germans.[44]

A burning desire to take my *completely* finished opera with me when I return to Russia not only takes up all my time but all my thoughts as well, and I am beholden to all this work, which I am sick of, for the fact that I tolerate these unfavourable circumstances.[45]

How strange things are! Regardless of the masses of things which do not suit me there, I am sorry that Kamenka is, as it were, closed to me. Habit, no doubt. It was not for nothing that Tanya had long since inspired a superstitious fear in me, as though I had a premonition that her fate would affect me personally. On the one hand, I am incapable of trying to build my own nest, as I had dreamt of doing, and on the other hand, the nest at *Kamenka* is no longer my *home*.[46]

I have been looking at a book of Maupassant and greatly enjoyed the first story *Mlle Fifie*. I have read another two little stories by Maupassant and find him quite delightful.[47]

It looks as though I will have to get my opera properly finished before Tanya finishes hers. I will be glad to have the weight off my mind but fear that the waiting will be more difficult if I have nothing to do.[48]

[25 April] I am forty-three, and it looks as though today, or tomorrow at the latest, the number of my nephews and nieces will be increased.[49]

[26 April] It's all over and things couldn't have gone better. The baby was born at one o'clock in the morning. Even yesterday I started feeling a tenderness towards this child who has caused us so much trouble, a desire to be his protector. Now I feel it ten times more and I have told Tanya that so long as I live she need have no worries on his score. Things in general are fine. Thank God that worry is off my mind![50]

The whole of *Mazepa* is finished. I have been working at it for two years and it has cost me a great deal of effort.[51]

When he had arranged for Tanya's son Georges to be taken in by a French family, Tchaikovsky left for St Petersburg.

My niece Tanya will probably ensure that I will no longer be a regular inhabitant of Kamenka. I do not claim the right to blame her for anything. Everyone behaves in life according to one's natural qualities, upbringing, and circumstances. But one thing is certain: my only wish is to be as far

[44] xii. 52 (von Meck).   [45] xii. 108 (Modest).   [46] xii. 119 (Modest).
[47] xii. 125 (Modest).   [48] xii. 134 (Modest).   [49] xii. 137 (Modest).
[50] xii. 139–40 (Modest).   [51] xii. 146 (Jurgenson).

away from her as possible. I can feel sorry for her but I *cannot* love her. It is a *torment* for me to live with her because I have to force myself to hide my true feelings and to lie—but *to live a lie* is beyond me.[52]

I like Petersburg this time, thanks to its emptiness, to the absence of those masses of people whom I find it tiresome to meet, and above all thanks to the absolutely astonishing weather which we are having here. My brother Modest and I, together with his pupil, have made some delightful excursions in the area, to Peterhof, Pavlovsk, and so on. I am abandoning myself entirely to idle relaxation. So far I have not the slightest desire not even to work but to so much as think about it.[53]

The 'emptiness' of St Petersburg is to be explained by the coronation ceremonies which were then proceeding in Moscow.

Tchaikovsky spent the summer of 1883 at Podushkino, near to Moscow, at his brother Anatoly's dacha.

This is a most attractive area, hilly and wooded; the bathing is excellent and the silence is utter and complete. I am enjoying all these delights like a child and yesterday I spent literally the whole day wandering through the woods surrounding the estate where we are living. It was a great pleasure to see my brother and his wife. Their happiness is perfect.[54] Their daughter [Tanya] is a most delightful, lovely little child; she is very funny, very sweet and nice, but she has inherited her father's restless nature and whines quite a lot.[55] The more I get to know this area, the more enthusiastic do I feel about it. But I must admit, unfortunately, that on my walks I am never without a slight fear of *wolves*, which are found in these parts.[56]

My idleness is already beginning to oppress me a little; I have rested long enough and am thinking about some new composition: I will probably write something symphonic. I could work very comfortably here but I have one complaint: there is a constant stream of visitors and they are not always congenial or close friends.[57]

The corrections have worn me out. The more I do the more negligent and the worse Jurgenson becomes, and it is true, I sometimes get exasperated with him in my thoughts and wish that I dealt with some foreign publisher. Besides this, instead of resting from composition I have taken it into my head to write *a suite come what may*. Inspiration has not come; every day I start something and then get disillusioned; I am afraid that I am played out, I am tormented by this thought; I force it out of myself instead of waiting for inspiration to come and as a result am perpetually dissatisfied with myself. Meanwhile all conditions for perfect contentment are at hand. The marvellous weather, Tolya's and Parasha's company, Tanya, who grows more delightful with each day, and finally Alyosha, who is so wonderfully kind and attentive towards me that I cannot find words to express my

[52] xii. 161 (von Meck).   [53] xii. 161 (von Meck).   [54] xii. 170 (von Meck).
[55] xii. 176 (Lyova).   [56] xii. 180 (Kolya).   [57] xii. 178 (von Meck).

pleasure at knowing that he is around.[58] How stupid I was imagining that I could rest in the summer. But these corrections are worse than the most horrific penal servitude. I am not reading anything apart from the eternal journals and the like. My plans to study English, to play through unfamiliar works by Mozart etc. have all had to be postponed. When I eventually live like a free man I will work towards the broadening of my intellectual horizons which are so restricted.[59]

I must tell you [Mme von Meck] about the great unpleasantness which befell me a day or two ago in Moscow. I should explain that recently I had to send a large sum of money to Paris—you can guess to whom. I had to borrow the money and was going to repay it with the money which I was expecting for the commission of the Coronation Cantata. Instead of money I was sent a diamond ring. As I very much did not want to part with this present from the tsar for good I decided to pawn it and with this in mind set out a couple of days ago for the department of the Credit Society for the Pawning of Personal Property. There I received 375 roubles which I put in my wallet. Several hours later the wallet with the money and the receipt had disappeared. I cannot tell you how upset I was about this. All my searches were in vain. The only thing to do was to forestall the redemption of the ring by whoever found my wallet by completing certain formalities— which I did. This was one of the most unpleasant days I have ever spent. Quite apart from the fact that the procedure of pawning the ring was extremely unpleasant in itself, losing the wallet, the fruitless searching, the business of saving the ring—all this made me feel as if I had committed some shameful act. And to add to all this I have had my *first* misunderstanding with Jurgenson in our relationship as composer and publisher. Until now I have never had occasion to be dissatisfied with him. Now it has come about that I really have every justification for thinking that he has seriously insulted me as far as money is concerned. And yet, our longstanding and friendly relationship is holding me back from standing up for my rights. There is nothing more hateful than quarrelling over money.[60]

You know [Jurgenson] that I have never argued with you about the fees which you have fixed, and indeed there has been nothing to argue about: not only have I had no cause to feel aggrieved, but rather has it seemed to me that you should have been aggrieved because I have sometimes felt that you were paying me too generously. Now quite the opposite has happened: the fee which you have fixed for *Mazepa* is so little in accord with justice that I cannot let it pass without protest. Even for *The Maid of Orleans*, if I am not mistaken, you paid me more than 1,000 roubles. But suppose it was in fact a thousand. That was four years ago! How is it that my price has not gone up a penny in all that time? And anyway then I did not carry out the transcription myself, but Messer and Kotek did (for 100 roubles an act),

---

[58] xii. 186 (Modest).   [59] xii. 189 (Modest).   [60] xii. 198–9 (von Meck).

and I did not do all the three stages of the proofs. When you started to engrave *The Maid*, its production was still in question; its fate was unknown. And now when both theatres in the two capitals are competing with you for the voice parts, the orchestral parts, and the piano reduction for *Mazepa* you allocate me 1,000 roubles for an opera to which I have devoted two years and three months of assiduous work. This is as ludicrously *small* an amount as the sum you proposed to pay me for the Cantata was large and unnaturally generous. I will not accept one kopeck from you for the latter. It was written for an occasion, took me less than twenty days' work and has no future and I had no wish whatsoever for it to be printed. *Mazepa* is another matter. It is quite possible that it will be restricted to the two Russian capitals and won't go any further; perhaps it will not be a great success or won't even be a success at all, but however the contrary could happen. Who knows? However that may be, it's funny, unfair, and peculiar that Büttner or Bernard or anybody like that would gladly have taken the work for a far higher fee solely for the pleasure of not letting you get it, and yet you value it at about the same level as a dozen of my rotten songs. I would have thought there were hundreds of songs in *Mazepa*; there is a whole symphonic poem in it, and another orchestral number of some lasting value, so that if we are to be logical about it I ought to be recompensed for it at least ten times more than for a dozen songs or a dozen rubbishy piano pieces. On the other hand I know the difficulty of selling large works in comparison to small ones and for this reason I don't think it would be unfair if I named the following price for *Mazepa*:

For the copyright	2,000 roubles
For the transcription at 100 roubles per act	300
For reading the proofs	100
Total	2,400 roubles

I don't want anything for the Cantata.[61]

Jurgenson replied: 'My dear fellow! I have never liked my job as a valuer of your works and I am very glad that you are exercising your right to determine the level of fees due to you. That is infinitely more agreeable to me.' (Jurgenson, i. 305)

This time I haven't had to make any efforts at all, I haven't even had to offer my opera to the theatre managements for production. The managements themselves made the approach and it even worked out in such a way that the Moscow people were arguing with Petersburg in their desire to get the first performance. I preferred to begin in Moscow on this occasion, in the first place because the members of the opera company here are now in

[61] xii. 200–1 (Jurgenson).

no way inferior to Petersburg, and in the second place because I want to remove the necessity for a long stay in Petersburg.[62]

The management of the [Moscow] theatres arranged a meeting to discuss the production of *Mazepa* and I was invited to attend. Everybody was there: the designer, the conductors, the producers, the costumiers and we sat in the General Manager's office about two hours discussing the details of the production. The vigour, the effort, almost the enthusiasm which the whole theatrical world brings to my new opera is a pleasant surprise, but it also puzzles me. Previously I had to rush around, and beg people, and pay the most insufferable visits on theatrical bigwigs to ensure that the opera was accepted and staged. Now, without any approach from me, both managements—Petersburg and Moscow—are making incredibly vigorous attempts to get hold of my opera. I heard yesterday that the Petersburg management even sent the designer Bocharov to study the effects of moonlight in the Ukraine for the last act of *Mazepa*. I really have no idea why the theatrical world should be so well-disposed towards me.[63]

The explanation of the change in attitude to Tchaikovsky was very simple: not long before this Ivan Alexandrovich Vsevolozhsky had been appointed Director of the Imperial Theatres. He was a widely cultured man who was able to appreciate Tchaikovsky's genius.

I have finished the proofs [of the piano arrangement of *Mazepa*]. I really ought to relax now and spend some time doing nothing. But the demon of composing has got an unbreakable hold on me and I am devoting every free minute to my new symphonic work—a suite [The Suite No. 2].[64]

Tchaikovsky went to Kamenka in the autumn.

I have now set about orchestrating the suite. My life has got into the right groove. It's very pleasant on the whole. I was very pleased indeed to see my niece Vera and her daughter Rina.[65] I am very glad that I do not now feel at all *bad-tempered* towards Tanya as I did last year. On the contrary, I feel a great deal of friendliness towards her, though without the slightest touch of tenderness. The touch of *tenderness*, and a very powerful one at that, is aroused in me by Verusha, and I think that it is she who is the main reason why I feel so happy and cosy here.[66]

As far as my opera is concerned, I can tell you [Mme von Meck], dear friend, that at first go you picked on the number which I consider to be the best. Thanks to Pushkin's wonderful verses, I think the scene with Mazepa and Mariya will be effective on stage as well. Unfortunately you will not see *Mazepa* in the theatre. Allow me, dear friend, to point out some other individual places in the opera which you can most easily get to know from the piano arrangement. In the first Act you can take (1) Andrey and Mariya's

[62] xii. 187 (von Meck).   [63] xii. 208 (von Meck).   [64] Ibid.
[65] xii. 227 (von Meck).   [66] xii. 229 (Modest).

duet (2) Mazepa's arioso; in the second Act (1) the prison scene (2) the scene with Mariya and her mother; in the third Act the final duet.[67]

Of course, I will never write another opera in my life, but if I do, because of some chance attraction to the subject, I should prefer the opera not to be staged at all so long as I am alive. The unpleasantness has already started in connection with the production of *Mazepa*. They wanted to make me give the main role to Raab, whom I dislike both as a singer and as a remarkably crafty person, who made a lot of trouble for me when we were doing *The Maid of Orleans*. I refused outright and wrote to Nápravník that I would make official representations to ensure that my opera was not put on unless my requests were acceded to in the assigning of roles. I don't know what will come of all this, but I am sure that my stay in Petersburg will be torture again.[68]

All the same, the pleasantest form of life is being in the country, the real country, remote from the capitals. I am greatly enjoying scoring the suite; I can tell that it will sound nice. I am having very pleasant walks. Reading a lot.[69]

Kolya Meck is staying here and this has occupied our attention all the week. The official betrothal was on Thursday 22 [September]. Kolya and Anna make a very nice pair. I envy them as I look at them and reflect that this really is true happiness and I have never known it.[70]

My suite makes very slow progress; but I think it will be a success on the whole, and I am almost certain that people will like the Scherzo (with the accordions) and the Andante ('A Child's Dreams'). My enthusiasm for [Serov's] *Judith* has given way to a rush of passion for *Carmen*, which I have been playing right through for three days on end. Playing [Rimsky-Korsakov's] *May Night* has also not been without its pleasures.[71]

Despite the fact that I like listening to some operas, and even write them myself, I still have some sympathy for your [Mme von Meck] apparently somewhat paradoxical view of the bankruptcy of music for the stage. Exactly the same view of opera is taken by Lev Tolstoy, who strongly advised me to abandon my pursuit of success in the theatre; in *War and Peace* the heroine is made to suffer and to be puzzled by the artificial conventions of operatic behaviour. Someone like you, who lives aside from society and has, in consequence, renounced all *conventionality*, or like Tolstoy, who has spent long years buried in the country, concerned exclusively with family matters, literature, and his schools, must be more acutely aware than other people of all the artificiality, the dishonesty of opera. And I, too, feel that I am not free, that I am constrained when I am writing an opera, and in fact I think I will never write another. None the less, it must be admitted that the dramatic genre contains many fine examples of first-rate music and that it

[67] xii. 227 (von Meck).   [68] xii. 234–5 (von Meck).   [69] xii. 236 (Modest).
[70] xii. 243 (Modest).   [71] xii. 245–6 (von Meck).

was indeed dramatic motives which inspired their composers. If there were no opera at all there would be no *Don Giovanni*, no *Marriage of Figaro*, no *Ruslan* and so on. Of course, from the point of view of simple common sense it is silly and absurd to make actors *sing* and not *speak* on a stage which is supposed to be a reflection of reality. But people have got used to this absurdity, and when I listen to the sextet in *Don Giovanni* I no longer think about the fact that something is happening which does not conform to the requirements of artistic truth: I simply enjoy the beauties of the music and wonder at the amazing skill with which Mozart contrived to give a distinctive character to each of the *six* parts of the sextet, to touch in each character with contrasting colouring, so that I forget the absence of any fundamental *truth* and am astonished at the depth of the *conventional* truth, and this fascination causes my reason to fall silent.[72]

Despite the fact that I have written six operas, I am very glad that you [Mme von Meck] regard opera as a lower form of art than either symphonic or chamber music. I have always felt that myself at bottom, and I have probably now abandoned music for the stage for good, though it cannot be denied that opera has the advantage of making it possible to influence the musical sensitivities of the *masses*, whereas the symphonic composer deals with a small and select public. You say that in *Eugene Onegin* my musical patterns are better than the canvas to which they are applied. But I would argue that if my music for *Eugene Onegin* has any qualities of warmth and poetry then it is because my emotions were stirred by the charm of the subject. I also think, incidentally, that you are wrong to see only verbal beauty in Pushkin's text. Tatyana is not merely a young lady from the provinces who has fallen in love with a dandy from the capital. She is a girl full of pure, feminine beauty, still untouched by contact with the realities of life; she has a dreamy nature, vaguely seeking her ideal, and passionate in her pursuit of it. Seeing nothing which answers to her ideal she is not satisfied but neither is she disturbed. But all it needed was for a person to turn up whose appearance marked him off from the dreary provincial milieu and she imagined that he was her ideal; passion took an overpowering grip of her. The power of a young girl's love is portrayed brilliantly, superbly by Pushkin, and from my earliest years I have always been deeply moved by the profoundly poetic quality of Tatyana's character after Onegin appears. So, if I burnt with the fire of inspiration when I wrote the letter scene, it was Pushkin who kindled the fire, and I can tell you frankly, with no false modesty, and I am well aware of what I am saying, that if my music contains only a fraction of the beauty which I found in the subject itself then I will be very proud and well pleased. I can also see very much more than you do in the duel scene. Surely there is something profoundly dramatic and touching in the death of a richly gifted young man because of a fateful clash

[72] xii. 245–6 (von Meck).

with society's view of *honour*. Surely there are dramatic elements in the bored lion of the capital taking the life of a young man for whom, in truth, he has much affection, out of *boredom*, out of trivial irritation, without really thinking about it, because of a fateful coincidence of circumstances! All right, perhaps this is all very simple, even mundane, but the simple and the mundane do not exclude either poetry or drama.[73]

I am enjoying myself very much just now and there is something special about it. Perhaps this is because my work [on the suite] is almost finished and consequently, since I am in a perfectly settled state of mind and not yet embroiled in new composing enterprises, I have the chance more fully to savour the delights of these marvellous autumn days. I am, in sum, very, very pleased with this work, but it is, incidentally, the same old story: I am full of tender love for each of my children as soon as it makes its appearance in the world, whilst it is still all mine and nobody knows it, but as soon as it becomes public property I turn cool towards it.[74]

I probably told you when I finished the suite that I had earned the right to a rest and intended to exercise my right to the full. I always say this when I put a big work behind me and when I am enjoying thinking about a spell of idleness. But it always turns out to be just talk; no sooner do I start resting than I find my idleness bears down on me, I think up a new piece of work, get carried away by it, and once again I begin rushing to finish my new task with a haste which is excessive and quite unnecessary. It looks as though I am fated all my life to be in a hurry *to finish something*; I know that this has a bad influence on my nerves, and, indeed, on my work, but I cannot help myself. Only when I am travelling do I really relax, whether I want to or not, and for this reason I will probably never live a settled life anywhere and will be a nomad till the end of my days. I am writing a collection of *children's songs* which I have had it in mind to do for some time. I am much taken by the work and I think the little songs will turn out all right.[75]

The weather all this time has been so heavenly and marvellous that I cannot remember anything like it at Kamenka: clear sunny days without wind and with a light morning frost. I feel I have a right to a proper rest after two years of unremitting toil and am making wide use of this right, but because I cannot be completely idle I have begun to study English seriously and am making respectable progress; besides this I am composing some little songs for children at the rate of one a day. I find this easy and pleasant but what would poor Jurgenson do if I wrote a song a day for a whole year and next November sent him 365 songs to publish?[76]

The weather for the last few days in Kamenka has been quite summery, and I have delighted in it all the more because masses of mushrooms have appeared and I love picking them just as much as the red and white

---

[73] xii. 246–7 (von Meck). [74] xiii. 255 (von Meck).
[75] xii. 268 (von Meck). [76] xii. 267 (Anatoly).

toadstools, etc. Every day I bring a basketful of them to our house as well as to the big house. I don't think I have ever received such gratitude for my compositions as I have for these mushrooms.[77]

Tchaikovsky left Kamenka for Moscow in November 1883.

The night in the train from Kamenka to Fastov I spent partly in tears and partly in a heavy feverish sleep, for the following reason. After dinner before my departure we were sitting in Lev's study. Sasha was very sad and behaving somehow oddly. Suddenly she said in a kind of *unnatural* voice, 'You will probably meet Blumenfeld. He is always at Kreshchatik.' At first I felt I couldn't restrain myself from expressing displeasure at the prospect of this meeting. But it suddenly came to me that Sasha was *testing* me with this question and I immediately started to talk enthusiastically and warmly about Blumenfeld and his lessons, and Lev was glad of the opportunity to express his natural affinity towards Blumenfeld. Sasha said nothing. Soon afterwards I departed and all evening and all night I was haunted by the idea that Sasha suspects, that she is almost sure, but it is just that she cannot altogether bring herself to believe it. Oh, how sorry I am for her; once more the whole saga seemed so terrible and full of tragedy.[78]

I went to a Musical Society concert where they played my [First] Symphony, which has not been performed for sixteen years. I was given a very enthusiastic reception which was, as always, pleasant and flattering, as well as being excruciatingly disagreeable. I played my new suite to a gathering of the leading musicians here and earned myself great praise.[79]

Max Erdmannsdörfer conducted the First Symphony at the Fifth Symphony Concert of the RMS on 19 November 1883.
Then Tchaikovsky made a brief trip to St Petersburg to see his brother Modest.

I cannot describe how Petersburg depresses my spirits. There are more or less serious reasons which make it unpleasant, almost insufferable for me to be in this capital of the bureaucracy, and add to that the dreadful climate! The marvellous Russian winter set in in Moscow some time ago; there's not so much as a snowflake here, but it's cold, windy, and gloomy, and it's so dark in the mornings that even sitting by the window one can scarcely write.[80]

Tchaikovsky returned to Moscow after a few days.

One day goes by after another, tedious and tiresome; it's now more than a month since I have been in Moscow without doing anything, without even the chance to do any reading. From morning till night I either have to go out visiting or to receive visitors who require something of me. I haven't sufficient character to turn invitations down firmly and take the risk of

[77] xii. 259 (Panya).   [78] xii. 260 (Modest).
[79] 282, 283 (von Meck).   [80] xii. 283–4 (von Meck).

offending or annoying people—the result is that I waste heaps of time, fruitlessly and miserably. I am certainly not made for town life.[81]

An enormous amount of time is taken up by various people who have pretensions to compose and seek my approval and encouragement. Without exaggeration I can say that every day not less than two or three composers turn up to play me their numerous works. In all this mass of people, afflicted by writer's mania I have, with very few exceptions, met no examples of serious creative promise. It is so boring to listen to all this and so unpleasant to have to tell them the unflattering truth![82]

I was very touched by the ovation which I received at the Fisher Girls' High School. The Headmistress of this establishment has written to me several times, expressing a warm interest in my music. This time she persuaded me to accept an invitation to a musical evening at the school and I went there a day or two ago. Mme Fisher met me, surrounded by the teachers and their pupils. After that the choir sang a whole selection of my works. The girls sang charmingly and, although it was a little unpleasant to be the object of everybody's attention, I could not help being touched by the unusual warmth of interest which was shown throughout the evening by everybody who was there.[83]

However tiresome I might find my disordered and compulsorily idle life here, the warmth and strength of my affection for Moscow is undiminished. There is something specially attractive about this strange and peculiar town; once a love for the place has taken hold, it never lets go, despite all the dirt and inconvenience.[84]

On 8 January I am going to Petersburg [with Modest] for the wedding. So, our dream will be brought to pass in a few days! The most astonishing thing about all this is that the plan which we conceived when the young people did not even know each other has come to fruition as though you [Mme von Meck] foresaw that they were made for one another.[85]

[81] xii. 288 (von Meck).   [82] xii. 290 (von Meck).   [83] xii. 289 (von Meck).
[84] Ibid.   [85] xii. 291.

17

1884

I want to go home. *But where is home?*

1883 had been a busy year and a difficult one for Tchaikovsky. It finished with preparations for the production of *Mazepa* in both capitals and with a family pleasure:
the forthcoming marriage of his niece Anna Davydova to Nikolay von Meck.

The new year, 1884, was to be the one in which Tchaikovsky won for himself a
secure and growing reputation. And fame came from St Petersburg too—a town
which Tchaikovsky apparently did not like, but which was deeply attached to him
... 1884 can be described as crucial from every point of view. It was, admittedly,
difficult at the beginning. Tchaikovsky returned to Moscow after Anna's wedding.

Here I found waiting for me an official document from the Imperial
Theatres which so annoyed and upset me that I went about all day like a
lunatic and didn't sleep all night; even today I am feeling completely worn
out. Of course it is ridiculous and shameful to get so worked up over trifles
but how actually can you remain indifferent when your feelings of fairness
and self-respect are affected? The reason is that when I appeared at the
office of the theatres (in November) after an invitation from the Directorate
in order to sign the contract for the production of *Mazepa* I discovered that
the performance fee for this opera had been fixed much lower than it should
have been, on the basis of its being in three rather than four acts. When I
protested that, regardless of being in three acts, my opera took up a whole
evening, just as if it had been in four or five acts; that, in order to make large
quantities of roubles, it would cost me no effort to divide it even into ten
acts but that I was keeping to my original divisions because of the artistic
demands of the words and the music, they suggested that I put all this
down on paper, assuring me that my request would undoubtedly be fulfilled. And so I did. Now I have received official notification, without any
explanation of the reason, that the Imperial Minister, his excellency, etc.
has been *pleased to decline my petition,* as if I had been requesting some sort
of tip. Both the refusal itself and the form in which it was expressed
offended and injured me deeply. I remembered how last year the same
minister was attentive, friendly, and kind to me when *I was needed* for the
Cantata and how he then found words with which to bolster my self-
esteem. I remembered how meanly he rewarded me (for, to tell the truth, it
would have been better not to have rewarded me at all than to have given
me a ring), I remembered how extravagant this minister is towards for-

eigners and how comparatively harsh and unattentive towards Russian composers—and all this wounded me very sorely. At first I wanted to withdraw my score and I went to seek the advice of Jurgenson, who explained to me that I had no legal right to do this. Then I drafted several letters which were so severe as to be insolent, could not decide on any one of them, and only today felt relatively calm and finally wrote a letter to the Director of Imperial Theatres in which I protested against the insulting way in which I had been treated.[1]

The rehearsals for *Mazepa* began on 15 January and for two days in a row I have been accompanying at the theatre from twelve to four. This is such an utterly exhausting experience that I can see that I will be in no state to go through the whole thing again and am not very likely to go to Petersburg.[2]

I am very pleased so far with the way the rehearsals of *Mazepa* are going. The singers are going about it with unusual zeal and I am deeply touched by the heartfelt enthusiasm of some of them, particularly the prima donna, Pavlovskaya. However, in spite of all this zeal, the opera will nevertheless only just be ready by the beginning of February. I realize with horror that, after the intense nervous strain which is going to go on for another two weeks or so, I shall still have to go to Petersburg and experience all over again the anxiety and suffering which an author has to go through at a production of his own opera. Modest is advising me not to go to Petersburg after the Moscow production, but to go somewhere to rest as soon as possible, and I shall probably do this. My nerves are *terribly* strained, and recently I have often thought that the strings are too taut, and that they might suddenly snap without warning; some indefinable fear of death oppresses me. Of course all this is rubbish and in actual fact I am just tired, and perfectly well. However one should not push fatigue to the ultimate limits of toleration.[3]

The opera is beginning to take shape, though I am still very far from being entirely satisfied with it. But at least I cannot complain of a lack of vigour and interest. Everybody loves the opera and they are completely sincere in their enthusiasm. This is the more touching because when all my previous operas have been put on in Petersburg I have got used to encountering intrigues, annoyances, and insults at every turn. Sometimes I am so exhausted that I become almost incapable of speaking, thinking, or understanding. By the hour, almost by the minute, I tell myself that this will be my last opera, that it is not in my character, that I have not got it in me to go through the complex machinations of putting on an opera.[4]

Ippolit Altani conducted the premiere of *Mazepa* at the Bolshoy Theatre in Moscow on 3 February 1884.

[1] xii. 297 (von Meck).   [2] xii. 299 (Modest).
[3] xii. 300 (von Meck).   [4] xii. 304 (von Meck).

The strains that I have been through have so tired me that I could go mad. There's no other solution than to go abroad this very day. My thanks to you [Altani] for all that you have done for me. Please convey my infinite gratitude to all the performers. I am *deeply, beyond words deeply* moved by their interest and involvement.[5]

Mazepa is a success in that the performers and I were given a lot of ovations. I will not describe all that I went through on that day, except that I nearly went out of my mind with anxiety and fear. Amongst the cast I was particularly pleased with Pavlovskaya [who sang the part of Mariya]. She is a remarkably gifted and intelligent artist.[6] Straight after the performance the artists gave a supper for me; despite my appalling tiredness I had to stay until five in the morning, and I had scarcely come round the next day when the time came for my departure.[7]

Nápravník conducted the St Petersburg première of *Mazepa* on 6 February. The performance was not notably successful but Modest did not want to upset his brother, who was worn out after the Moscow production, and sent him a telegram about the favourable reception of the opera.

I have arrived in Paris. The Béliards [the owners of the Hotel Richepanse] were delighted to see me and triumphantly announced that my own room, No. 21, was vacant. Went to see Tanya, who was not expecting me. Both of them [Tanya and her companion Elizaveta Molas] were absolutely delighted. I spent an hour and a half or so with them, then went up to my room to have a wash. The room affected me both pleasantly and sadly as well. What many and varied excitements I had experienced there, how much ink and music paper I had got through, and now—it had all vanished into the mists of the past. Then I went for a walk along the boulevard.[8]

Paris strikes me in general as a town in which I feel at home. I did not feel any particular pleasure at being on the streets of Paris, nor the slightest astonishment at their glitter—it was as if I had just left yesterday. And indeed everything down to the last detail goes on exactly as it did last year.[9]

I have heard Massenet's new opera *Manon Lescaut* here. Going by the reviews in the papers, I prepared myself for a *chef-d'œuvre*, especially since the subject, so it seemed to me, was very well suited to Massenet's particular talent. But I was to be disappointed. The music had been written carefully, gracefully, and with considerable thought. But nowhere is there a single flash of real inspiration. Despite the *excellent* performance, I was getting so bored by the end that I could barely sit it out. And yet I could not cast off a feeling of envy. What a production, what playing, what first-class singers! How far we have to go to catch up with the French in this respect![10]

I can imagine how difficult it was for you [Modest] to lie to me about the

[5] xii. 306 (Altani).   [6] xii. 309 (von Meck).   [7] xii. 309 (von Meck).
[8] xii. 314 (Modest).   [9] xii. 314–15 (Modest).   [10] xii. 316 (von Meck).

grand succès of *Mazepa* in Petersburg. All the same, you did the right thing
with your lies, because the *truth* might well have killed me if I had not been
prepared for it by various signs and by what people did not write in their
letters. I got to know the truth only in a letter from Jurgenson (who was
cruel enough not only to tell me the truth straight out but even to *reproach*
me for not going to Petersburg). It came to me like a thunderclap and I suffered as dreadfully as if there had been some colossal, irreparable disaster.
Of course one always exaggerates, but really, at my age and in my position,
when there is no longer much to hope for from the future, every failure,
however *relative* it may be, assumes the proportions of a disgraceful fiasco.
But above all, it is annoying that if I had not been myself and had taken the
trouble to go to Petersburg, I would probably have left crowned with
laurels.[11]

Now for the most interesting bit. I have been to Bisètre to see Georges.
Although I had been warned that he had grown and was a healthy child, the
reality surpassed all my expectations. I went as a surprise. Georges was shy
at first but then he was quite content to let me hold him and played with me
very happily. As to his looks, he really is altogether remarkable. Fleshy,
brawny (like the children in Rubens's paintings), lively, strong, so heavy
that I could hardly hold him, in short—he should be put on show. However, *unfortunately* I must admit that one thing yesterday did prevent me
from being altogether carried away by him. He is *dreadfully* like his father
[Blumenfeld]. His eyes remind one of Tanya, and in general he is like his
mother, in his solid build, in the colour of his hair. All the same, I was more
struck for some reason by his resemblance to his father than to her. Even
so, I was very glad to see him and I was still very moved by the thought that
he is *mine* and that his situation is so pathetic. What is to be done with him?
Surely he can't stay here for ever? What could I arrange for him in Russia?
What name should he bear? All these questions torment me incessantly.[12]

La joie de vivre [Zola] is disgusting both in its tendentiousness and its
affectation; but there is a spark of genius in the portrayal of Lazare. In
places I simply shuddered at how *true to life* some of the details were which
I know well from experience but about which no one has ever written
before.[13]

I have grown sluggish and am frightened at the thought of long trips,
particularly now when I am so lonely. For the moment at least I think I am
only capable of sitting tight *in my own home* somewhere. Travelling has
ceased to refresh me and distract me pleasantly as it did once. This is why
the idea of settling down keeps occurring to me.[14]

I have had a letter from Nápravník telling me how surprised and sorry
the Emperor was that I wasn't in Petersburg, how remarkably fond he
is of my music, how he takes an interest in me, how he commanded the

[11] xii. 321–2 (Modest).   [12] xii. 318 (Modest).
[13] xii. 323 (Modest).   [14] xii. 331 (von Meck).

production of *Eugene Onegin*, saying that it was his favourite opera etc., etc. Nápravník assures me that I must go to Petersburg and appear before the Emperor. I feel that if I do not do it I will be tormented by the thought that the Emperor will consider me ungrateful, so I have decided to go straight to Petersburg. It's a terrible burden and I am having to make an incredible effort to deny myself the chance of some peace and rest in the country and to subject myself instead to these new alarms and anxieties. But what else can I do?[15]

Tchaikovsky returned to St Petersburg and went to a performance of *Mazepa*.

What a fool I am! Anything that looks remotely like a misfortune has such a disproportionate effect on me. I am ashamed to recall the despair which assailed me in Paris merely because I perceived in the newspaper reports about the Petersburg production of *Mazepa* a disparity between its actual achievement and my expectations. Despite an obscure sense of ill-will from very many of the musicians here, despite a very bad performance, I can see now that people still liked *Mazepa* and that there was no scandal at all (as I thought there had been, looking at it from a distance). Nor is there any doubt that the local critics (who as a man trampled my poor opera into the mud) do not reflect public opinion, and that even here there is still a considerable number of people very sympathetic to my cause.[16]

But what I find most gratifying of all is that the Emperor himself is at the head of all those people who support me. It seems that there was no need for me to have grumbled at all, but that, on the contrary, I should only be giving thanks to God for pouring down on me so much mercy.[17]

The Emperor has ordered *Onegin* to be produced next season. The parts have already been cast and the chorus is already rehearsing.

I feel an access of vigour and I am burning with impatience to come to grips with some new, big task. Of course, it is only at Kamenka that I will be able to carry out my intentions.[18]

Count Lev Tolstoy's *Confession* is circulating in manuscript and has not yet become public property because of the requirements of the censorship; only here have I at last managed to read it. The impression which it made on me was the stronger because I too know the torments of doubt and of tragic perplexity which Tolstoy has been through and which he describes with such astonishing skill in his *Confession*. But my *enlightening* came much sooner than Tolstoy's, probably because my head is constructed more simply than his and I am indebted to my constant need to work for the fact that I have suffered and been tormented less than Tolstoy. Every minute of every day I thank God that He has given me faith in Him. I am so faint-hearted, and my spirits are so prone at the slightest discouragement to

---

[15] xii. 332 (von Meck).   [16] xii. 336 (von Meck).
[17] Ibid.   [17] Ibid.

make me wish that *I did not exist*—what would I do if I did not believe in God and submit to His will?[19]

I am in Moscow and working with feverish haste on a few scenes from *Mazepa* which I have decided to alter and shorten for reasons to do with the staging ...[20] I have finished the three revisions of *Mazepa*. They are: (1) at the end of the first scene of the first act I have put in just a short closing passage in E major, after Mazepa's words 'Now, men, to your horses', so as not to complicate the scene, which suffers at this point from an excess of music; (2) in the second scene of the second act I have made an enormous cut in the scene between Mazepa and Mariya*, (3) in the last number of the third act I have somewhat extended the aria and have made it finish the opera. As to *the drunken cossack*: this will not seem out of place in a good performance and in any case I would not want to change anything at that point because the whole number is so hemmed in that if I started to alter things and make cuts nothing sensible would emerge.[21]

It's annoying that fate is not allowing me to spend this marvellous springtime somewhere in the country. I have had an ecstatic letter from Taneyev who has gone off to greet the spring in the country. How I envy him![22] To be buried in the countryside in spring, the wilds of Russia, the Russian spring—there is nothing I love more.[23]

I am, for the time being, still firm in my intention not to write any more operas; apart from anything else, the knowledge that we have no really good singers is liable to cool the most ardent enthusiasm for opera. I have done nothing for ages! I do want to get down to something new as soon as I can.[24]

This week I have been to a lot of church services and have experienced great, you could say, *artistic* pleasure. The Orthodox service has a wonderful effect on the soul, if it is observed as for example here in the Church of Christ the Saviour.[25]

I only got to Kamenka a couple of days ago. What a joy to be master of my own time, to belong to myself alone, to live how I like and to be able to do what I like![26]

I haven't started work yet; I am just gathering material for my next orchestral composition, but I have not yet decided what form it will take. Perhaps it will be a symphony, perhaps it will be a suite again. I have been particularly fond of the latter form for some time because of the freedom which it offers a composer not to be inhibited by any traditions, by conventional methods and established rules. My only regret is that there is no

---

* I have not only shortened Mazepa's part here but I have put something new in as well, so the scene will have to be relearnt; there is also some new material for Mariya, but very little (*Tchaikovsky's note*).

[19] Ibid.   [20] xii. 337 (von Meck).   [21] xii. 340 (Nápravník).
[22] xii. 342 (Modest).   [23] xii. 341 (Taneyev).   [24] xii. 343 (von Meck).
[25] xii. 344 (von Meck).   [26] xii. 350 (Taneyev).

Russian word which could replace *suite*; we use the French word, which sounds horrible in Russian. I have put my mind to this but have not been able to think of anything.[27]

I have still not started work and there is no real inspiration, but on my walks I put one or two passing ideas down in my sketchbook. They are somehow thin and insignificant and I am altogether going through a period of losing confidence in my own creative powers. But even if I am losing my powers, it no longer has such a dispiriting effect on me. I have worked enough and it would not be surprising if I had finally dried up a little. I eat my meals with Lyova; the rest of the time I go for walks, read, study English assiduously, and also make visits to the big house and other visits as well. I am very pleased with the English periodical which Miss Eastwood has made me subscribe to. As far as reading is concerned, I have masses, for besides a lot of books I have bought but not yet read, I have all the issues of the *Russky arkhiv* [*Russian Archive*] and *Istorichesky vestnik* [*Historical Messenger*] which have so far come out this year. In the evenings we have a daily game of vint.*[28]

I have begun a new composition in the form of a suite. I find this form very congenial because there are no restraints and no requirements to observe any traditions or rules. This suite will be in five movements, of which the last will be a theme and variations.[29]

Kamenka has come alive; our Petersburg dwellers arrived a couple of days ago. And it is a strange thing, we are all together but there is a sort of emptiness. I think that the cause is the absence of the three older daughters; all three, counting Tanya, have fled the nest; nevertheless you never get used to their absence and all the time it feels as if you were waiting for someone so that things could be as they were. One of the greatest charms of family life is the presence of young girls; they lighten the daily circumstances of the family in a wonderful way with their girlish charm and innocence; and without them, however well things might be going, the warmest element of happy family life is missing. Of course one cannot regret the absence of Tanya for she has long since brought nothing but grief to the family, but there was a time when she gave joy and pleasure with her beauty, intelligence and talent. And there is no point in talking of Vera and Anna either; they are very much missed.[30]

The complete happiness of my life at Kamenka did not last for long. When Sasha arrived the usual bustle started up and the peace, which I found so relaxing immediately after I got here, turned into an agitated existence, full to overflowing with irritating trivia. I am beginning to realize that I am too old now to sponge on people. Oh! how I would like to get away to Moscow, to Petersburg, abroad, anywhere!!![31]

* A card game based on whist and preference [trans.].

[27] xii. 352 (von Meck).   [28] xii. 354 (Anatoly).
[29] xii. 360 (von Meck).   [30] xii. 359 (von Meck).

[The night of 24/5 April 1884]. I will soon be forty-four. I have experienced so much, and in truth, without false modesty, I have achieved so little! Even in *my own line*; after all, I can say with my hand on my heart that there is nothing *perfect*, there is no *masterpiece*. I am still searching, hesitating, wavering.[32] I regret the passage of time, of course, and no one likes to immerse himself in memories more than I do, no one is more acutely aware of the vanity and transitoriness of life, but even so, it is not youth that I want. Every age has its attractions and its good sides and the point is not to be permanently young but to suffer as little as possible, both mentally and physically. I don't know what I will be like as an old man but for the moment I cannot but be aware that the sum of the blessings which I now enjoy is far greater than what I was endowed with in my youth and for that reason it does not distress me at all that I am forty-four; I don't care if I am seventy or eighty so long as I am healthy in mind and body. One other thing is essential—not to be frightened of death. I have nothing to boast of in this respect.

I am not so steeped in religion that I can confidently see death as the beginning of a new life, and not enough of a philosopher to become reconciled to the abyss of oblivion, in which one will become engulfed. There is no one I envy more than those who are wholly religious.[33]

The *suite* is coming on. But I am coming to think more and more that I have written myself out, and even if I am not thieving from other people I am doing it a very great deal from myself. Bobik, the suite, and the English language are the three ornaments of Kamenka and constitute its powers of attraction for me; but all the same I would often like to be somewhere else and, curiously enough, that somewhere is Petersburg. The fact is that my stay in Petersburg during the coronation last summer made a marvellous and unforgettable impression and I really feel drawn to the banks of the Neva, now that the second half of May is approaching. I am working quite hard, on the suite in fact, the third in order of writing but the first, I hope, in quality.[34]

Although I do not like Kamenka I was still rather sad to leave because after all I have spent two very pleasant months there and I am terribly fond of the little room that they give me. Of the people who make up the company of Kamenka residents, I most regretted parting with Bobik. He has always been my favourite, almost from the day he was born, but now I find my affection for him increasing all the time.[35]

I am at Grankino. I like it very much here; I am doing a lot of walking and an equal amount of work. Apart from orchestrating the suite I have also made a start on a new work: a piano concerto.[36]

Tchaikovsky has started writing the *Concert Fantasia* for piano and orchestra.

---

[31] xii. 360–1 (Modest).   [32] *Diaries*, 14.   [33] xii. 362, 363 (Anna Merkling).
[34] xii. 365–6 (Modest).   [35] xii. 389 (von Meck).   [36] xii. 391 (von Meck).

I have finished writing the suite and am resting for the moment but when I am in Grankino, staying with my brother Modest, I will start orchestrating it.[37]

My English studies are going so well that I can almost read fluently and this occupation is becoming easier and more pleasant with every day.[38]

I probably ought to give myself a long rest and spend some time in idleness without any pangs of conscience, but the more I doubt myself the more I feel somehow bound to work and to overcome my lack of inclination. What will emerge from all this I don't know. I thought I would distract myself from composing by writing some sort of musical-critical work, for instance by compiling a guide to the history of music or something along those lines, but this would require many months of background reading in German, which I don't know very well, and I am lacking in determination about it all.[39]

As far as *Figaro* is concerned, my view is that it is a great pity that you [Jurgenson] did not publish Breitkopf's arrangement, because it is much better. As regards the disparity between my recitatives and the original, I must explain why this is. You see, I arranged the opera for a production at the Conservatoire and had (I forget whether on Nikolay Rubinstein's order or on my own initiative) to leave out all the indecent passages, while in the original there is, for example, a lot of talk about the *droits de seigneur*; besides this, in view of the difficulty of translating this sort of recitative into Russian I simply cut superfluous details here and there. *Recitativo secco* is not music, but speech with musical accompaniment and you can cut it completely without worrying about it, as long as you preserve the original sequence of modulations. On the other hand in the genuinely musical numbers I didn't allow myself to change the rhythmic groupings once, as is normally permitted in translations, and indeed I am proud of the artistry with which I carried out this task (forgive me for boasting). Whatever happens please print on the first page the proposed preface, explaining the reason for the fact that the translated recitatives do not correspond closely to the original.[40]

Tchaikovsky's 'translator's' preface for P. Jurgenson's edition of the opera *Le nozze di Figaro* (1884), is as follows:

> The first version of the present opera was completed by me in 1875 at the request of N. G. Rubinstein, who intended to perform *Le nozze di Figaro* at the Conservatoire's annual public performance. In undertaking this task I of course approached Mozart's sacred music with due respect, and, in consequence, I undertook that I would not in any way ease my task by resorting to changing or even distorting the rhythm of the original (as opera translators often allow themselves to do). But this strictness in observing the inviolability of the original was applied only to the musical numbers in the opera. As far as

---

[37] xii. 379 (von Meck).   [38] Ibid.
[39] xii. 367 (von Meck).   [40] xii. 383 (Jurgenson).

the musical dialogue is concerned (*recit. secco*), which links the separate numbers, here, bearing in mind that on the one hand the performers in this opera would be students from the Conservatoire, for whom this kind of recitative is very difficult, and on the other the fact that the text of these recitatives, adapted from Beaumarchais's comedy, often contains details which it would be improper to put on the lips of young performers, I allowed myself a few insignificant cuts. Since it is more than likely that even in the event of *Le nozze di Figaro* being performed on our major stages it would be considered embarrassing to preserve the original recitatives without any cuts, I considered it justifiable on publication to leave my translation in the form in which it was presented by me to the late Director of the Moscow Conservatoire. P. Tchaikovsky.[41]

Life here continues so monotonously: today is so like tomorrow and yesterday that you lose the capacity to measure time by days and weeks. Even feast-days deep in the countryside, where there isn't even a church, do not differ at all from any other days. I love this kind of life and nothing has a more beneficial effect on me than spending some time in the depths of the country. The scenery is like the steppes and although the forest is the main source of pleasure in nature, every so often even the steppe has its own special charm, particularly in the evenings.[42]

I have set myself the task of completely finishing the suite before my departure for Moscow, so that I can leave and relax on the journey with the pleasant knowledge of having completed a task successfully. I don't know how much I am influenced at the moment by paternal feelings towards this new offspring and how lasting this feeling will be, but I consider this new Suite to be far superior to its predecessor and that all in all it is not a bad work. I also think that you [Mme von Meck] will like it. Sadly, you will only get to know it through the piano arrangement, and all my compositions lose a lot in this form.[43]

Tchaikovsky had been visiting Modest on the Konradis' estate of Grankino. From there he went to see Anatoly at his dacha at Skabeyevo, near Moscow.

My work is going very well. The piano concerto is almost finished in draft, and I will make a start on scoring it before long. My general faith in my powers as a composer, which did waver, is now on a firm footing again. If God sends me good health I hope I might yet write something good.[44]

We are living here in delightful surroundings which have had all the more charming an effect on me in that I have just come from an area of bare steppe. Laroche is in the room next door. We are writing an article on Mozart together. I find the subject so attractive that the role of writer is remarkably congenial.[45]

I have not started any work yet; I have got to go to Moscow first. And I

[41] xii. 384–5.   [42] xii. 394 (von Meck).   [43] xii. 402 (von Meck).
[44] xii. 417 (von Meck).   [45] xii. 408 (von Meck).

won't particularly force myself to work. In the mornings from half past ten until half past twelve I write the article on Mozart to Laroche's dictation. I may be mistaken but to my horror I am beginning to notice that his talent and imagination are fading. Everything that he has dictated to me up till now is pretty empty-sounding rubbish, which I would have found very colourless if I had read it in a journal.[46]

I am not surprised by your [Modest's] disappointment in the play verging on disgust and making you want to tear it up. This feeling is *terribly familiar* to me, and there is not a single writer or author who has not felt the same. Only mediocre people without talent never lose faith in themselves.[47]

I have long since grown cool towards Daudet but now, in spite of his undoubted and strong talent, he has irretrievably fallen in my estimation. If Daudet had not put a dedication to his sons at the front of his book, giving one to believe that it was designed to instruct someone and warn them against something, then on reading *Sapho* I would have simply said that Daudet described the sensuousness and debauchery of the main characters in a lively and vivid way, and, moreover, with great understanding towards the hero and heroine of the novel. But now, remembering to whom the book was dedicated, I am outraged at the hypocrisy and the feigned virtuousness of the author. In reality, in pandering to the debauched taste of his public, he is describing with cynical frankness the debauchery that goes on in Paris, while pretending that he is teaching his sons a *lesson*; and he wants people to think that he is guided by moral aims and highminded impulses to dissuade young people from debauchery. He had only one impulse: to write a book which would be alluring to the debauched French public, and to earn as much money as possible. And one must admit that he has achieved his goal. The book will enjoy an enormous success, like Zola's *Pot-bouille*, the novels of Gui [sic] de Maupassant and all the works by the adherents of the new French school. If you thoroughly investigate the circle of people portrayed by the author, and their way of life, it becomes apparent that beneath an outer coating of veracity and realism the essence of the novel is *false*. Sapho is an impossible creature; at least I have never met in anyone such a hectic mixture of honesty and baseness, of noble feelings and turpitude. But even so, the author evidently sympathized with his heroine, and although, judging by the dedication she should in the end repel and horrify Daudet's sons, in reality she will be attractive to them. On the other hand the *virtuous* characters in the novel cannot be agreeable either to Daudet's sons or to anyone else in the world.[48]

Then Tchaikovsky went to stay at Pleshcheyevo, Mme von Meck's estate near to Moscow.

The house is magnificent but a little too luxurious. My bedroom is cosy and so is the study. There are no servants apart from Alyosha. I like it very

---

[46] xii. 411 (Modest).   [47] xii. 415 (Modest).   [48] xii. 403 (von Meck).

much that way. The grounds consist only of a fairly narrow but extremely long stretch of river bank, planted with ancient limes, firs, and pines. The river itself is sheer delight. The disadvantage of Pleshcheyevo is that it is rather too closed in, although this does, of course, give it a quality of cosiness. There are masses of books, music, and instruments.[49] Nadezha Filaretovna continues to look after me; she has sent me a magnificent harmonium. I am studying *Parsifal* in the evenings. My God! how wearisome it is! Regardless of the brilliance of Wagner's talents, what a monstrous load of dishonesty, artificiality, and *nonsens* [sic] it all is![50]

Amongst my other activities here I have fulfilled two intentions which I have had in mind for a long time: I have got to know two previously unfamiliar works—Musorgsky's *Khovanshchina* and Wagner's *Parsifal*. I found in *Khovanshchina* exactly what I expected: pretensions to realism, in his own peculiar understanding and application of the word, wretched technique, póverty of invention—with some gifted passages from time to time—but all in a wash of that harmonic bilge and affectation which is characteristic of the musical circle to which Musorgsky belonged. The impression which *Parsifal* produces is quite different: here we are dealing with a great master, with an artist of genius, albeit on the wrong track. The richness of the harmony is astounding, extraordinary, too sumptuous, and, ultimately, exhausting even for the specialist—so what must it be like for ordinary mortals who are treated for three hours to a relentless torrent of the most complicated harmonic tricks? I have always felt that amateur Wagner-lovers force on themselves an ecstasy which deep down in their hearts they do not feel. In my opinion Wagner destroyed his deep creative powers by theorizing. Each preconceived theory which he adopts cools the spontaneous creative feeling. Could Wagner have given himself up to this feeling, when with his intellect he had developed a particular theory of musical drama and musical truth and, for the sake of this so-called truth, had willingly rejected everything which constituted the musical power and beauty of his predecessors? And if the singers are not singing, but, to a thunderous orchestral accompaniment, are speaking insipid sequences of notes which have somehow been fitted in against the background of a splendid but shapeless and incoherent symphony—then what sort of an opera is that? But what really astounds me is the seriousness with which this German-turned-philosopher illustrates in music the most incredibly stupid subjects. Who can be moved by the subject of *Parsifal* where instead of people, whose characters and emotions are familiar to us, you have fabulous creatures suitable for adorning the content of a ballet but certainly not a drama? I find it astonishing that anyone can listen without laughing, or indeed on the contrary, without being bored, to their interminable monologues about the various spells, under the burden of which all these

[49] xii. 430 (Panya).   [50] xii. 434 (Modest).

Kundrys and Parsifals and so on suffer. Is it possible *to suffer with them*, to become emotionally involved with them, to love them or to hate them?! Of course not, because their sufferings, their emotions, their triumphs, and their misfortunes are completely alien to us. And what is *alien* to the human heart cannot be the source of musical inspiration.[51]

I am reading *Wilhelm Meister for the first time* in my life. It has been an absolute *révélation*: I had always thought it would be dreadfully boring, but goodness! what a delight it is! I am grateful for the chance which prompted me to read it.[52] Amongst my other activities here I am able to give quite a lot of time to the English language and I am making very substantial progress; I can now read Dickens without difficulty and without constantly looking words up in the dictionary. Reading his novels in the original has given them a new charm for me. I am greatly enjoying reading *Copperfield* at the moment.[53]

This volume of Dickens is preserved in Tchaikovsky's library at Klin. It is liberally bespattered with pencil notes referring to Tchaikovsky's study of English. There is a note on the last page: 'Finished reading 1885, 28 Apr., and started August 1884. Total of *nine* months; whether this pregnancy has given birth to a knowledge of the English language we shall see.'

It is a long time since I have done so much reading and have found such enjoyment in reading as I have here. Soon I want to invite here for the evening three partners for a game of vint: probably Laroche, Hubert, and Kashkin. I am finishing my concert piece for piano. Now I am faced with a mass of corrections.[54]

How quickly does time fly! I have hardly had time to look round and a whole month has gone by since I arrived here. I am growing more and more accustomed to my solitude, learning more and more to enjoy it, and am becoming convinced that my intention to live out my time in the country is the most sensible and suitable one. I don't feel like going to Moscow one bit; on the contrary, it is somehow unpleasant to have to move. Nevertheless the knowledge that a large familiar city is near at hand is very pleasant.[55]

I am reading a great deal, playing a great deal, wandering about the surrounding countryside (which appeals to me more and more) or the house, enjoying my solitude and the quiet more than ever and more than ever dreaming of settling in the country for good. The weather has deteriorated; it has already been raining for two days in a row. I admit I am not particularly upset by this; as far back as I can remember I have always had a sort of pathological love of gloomy autumn weather, of bare and yellowing trees, of the peculiar delights of autumnal scenery. I have read an enormous quantity of books and in particular I have reread many of the old Russian

[51] xii. 435–6 (von Meck).   [52] xii. 434 (Modest).   [53] xii. 437 (von Meck).
[54] xii. 446 (von Meck).   [55] xii. 447 (Modest).

belletrists and I have noticed that my leaning towards Leo Tolstoy has strengthened as much as I have noticeably cooled towards Turgenev. Why is this? I can't account for it.[56]

I have received a letter from Nápravník in which he tells me that *Onegin* will probably be put on around 20 October.[57]

After a month of complete isolation it's not all that easy to find oneself in the whirl of Petersburg life. How often when I am in Petersburg will my mind go back to that nice, peaceful house![58]

Tchaikovsky did not know then that fame awaited him in St Petersburg ... The first Petersburg performance of *Eugene Onegin* was given in the Bolshoy Theatre there on 19 October.

I am well pleased with the enthusiasm of all the performers for my opera, and in general people in theatrical circles here are much more encouraging now than in times past—when they were doing *The Maid of Orleans* for instance.[59]

Eugene Onegin went off successfully. They gave me a lot of calls. I received an ovation and was presented with a wreath. I was very pleased with the performance and with the way the management and artists treated me. The best performances were Pavlovskaya [Tatyana] and Pryanishnikov [Onegin].[60]

Eugene Onegin was a success: there was a huge house. Tomorrow the Emperor will be present and I shall have to stay here until he has seen *Onegin* for I hear from all quarters how well disposed he is towards me.[61]

Eugene Onegin has provoked if not delight at least great interest here. The tickets for today's performance which were on sale from Monday were sold out by one o'clock. Today they are announcing the sale of tickets for the third and fourth performances.[62]

Of all my operas the biggest success has been *Eugene Onegin* in Petersburg; for seven years it has been thought that this opera lacked dramatic interest and could not be produced on a large stage. In the event Petersburg gave me many happy moments and a sweet sense of real success.[63] I don't know how things will go on, but judging by the first four brilliant performances the Petersburg public likes my *Onegin*; it is a real success, which, I admit, I had not expected.[64]

I have heard that Kotek really has got consumption and that he is painfully anxious to see me. I cannot settle until I see him and find out how much longer he will be with us. So I have decided to go abroad straight from here, to Switzerland, to Davos, where Kotek is at the moment. He is all on his own and apparently hasn't much longer to live. I simply must go.[65]

[56] xii. 454 (von Meck).   [57] xii. 448 (Modest).   [58] xii. 454 (von Meck).
[59] xii. 460 (von Meck).   [60] xii. 465–6 (von Meck).   [61] xii. 467 (Anatoly).
[62] xii. 468 (Jurgenson).   [63] xiii. 245 (Mackar).   [64] xii. 473 (von Meck).
[65] xii. 467 (Anatoly).

I will call at a bookshop and buy a copy of *Manfred*. At this very moment I am setting off for the summits of the Alps, and circumstances would be very favourable for the musical re-creation of *Manfred* if I were not going to see a dying man. At any event, I promise you [Balakirev] *to do my utmost* to carry out your wishes.[66]

Oh! how much it means to know that *Onegin* is a success! (Have I really grasped it?) I feel more lighthearted than I have done for a long time, and it is also a long time since I so much enjoyed being on my own as I am doing now.[67]

I had a pleasant time in Berlin: I went to the opera and heard [Weber's] *Oberon*. I had always been told that it was terribly boring and was prepared to suffer, but to my surprise I thoroughly enjoyed myself instead. Some of the music is enchanting; the story is nonsense, like *The Magic Flute*, but it's fun to watch and at one point I even gave a mad guffaw when the entire *corps de ballet* fell down in contorted convulsions under the influence of the magic *horn*. Musically, Oberon himself is remarkably attractive: whenever he appears the music is lyrical and inspired. Went to one of Bilse's concerts and heard the Andante from my quartet. He gave only the Andante— nobody wants to hear anything else. On the day I was leaving there was an advertisement for another concert, also with the Andante.[68]

I have stayed in Berlin for such a long time because I wanted without fail to compose the Cherubic Hymn as soon as possible for the Emperor and the entr'acte for Samarin's performance. The latter I have finished and sent off. I have also composed the Cherubic Hymn, even two of them, but have not copied them out yet.[69]

At last I have got to Davos. Davos lies very high, in a grim, mountain landscape.[70] I am in a fairly melancholy state of mind; my surroundings are extremely gloomy and depressing, and on top of that I listen from morning to night to the consumptive coughing of my patient. I have read *Manfred* and have given it a great deal of thought, but I still have not started planning either the themes or the form. I have no intention of hurrying, but I give you [Balakirev] my firm promise that, if I live to tell the tale, the symphony will be finished no later than this summer.[71] My stay in Davos was not very cheerful. The surroundings themselves depressed me, as did living in the hotel, which meant that I met a lot of people ... and then, finally, my patient, who never stopped coughing from morning to night— it's all rather gloomy, of course. The day before I left I saw the doctor who is treating Kolya and we had a long talk. It is now the condition of the throat which is worse than the lung, and the greater fear is of consumption of the throat rather than of the chest.[72]

This visit to Davos has in any case has been of great service to Kotek and

[66] xii. 470 (Balakirev).   [67] xii. 476 (von Meck).   [68] xii. 478–9 (Modest).
[69] xii. 478 (Modest).   [70] xii. 481 (von Meck).   [71] xii. 488 (Balakirev).
[72] xii. 491 (von Meck).

I am glad to know this. On the way back I travelled half the journey on sledges and the other half in an excellent stage-coach, with the carriage to myself, and enjoyed the beauty of the Swiss winter landscape.[73]

Kotek died after Tchaikovsky had returned to Russia.
  From Davos Tchaikovsky went to Paris.

I have been in Paris for a few days now, in my beloved Hôtel Richepanse. I am seeing nobody and going nowhere, apart from the theatre, and I must say I am very glad to be on my own, which I have not been since I left Pleshcheyevo. I work a little in the mornings, in fact I am thinking about the changes I intend to make in *Vakula the Smith*. It is one of my favourite offspring, but I am not so blind that I cannot see that it suffers from major faults which have prevented it from staying in the repertoire. So removing these faults is what I would like to do for the next few months.[74] I have still not seriously made a start on *Manfred*, but I think about it a lot.[75] I have been fed up and depressed for the last few days. Most likely it's homesickness, for which going to Russia is no cure, because even there I have no *home*. I have taken a general dislike to abroad, Paris attracts me no longer. But it cannot be said that I am bored from having nothing to do. I have managed to plan all the main changes in *Vakula* while I have been here, to write three new songs, and one church piece. But somehow or other I must have a *home*; it is becoming odd and barbaric to live like a planet in orbit. Where is my home to be?[76]

Tchaikovsky wrote three of the Op. 57 songs in Paris: 'Sleep!', 'Death', and 'Only thou'. The church music was 'To Thee we sing'.
  Thinking about his home, Tchaikovsky returned to Russia. The years of wandering were over. His life had entered a new phase.

---

[73] xii. 493 (Anatoly).   [74] xii. 498–9 (von Meck).   [75] xii. 504 (Balakirev).
[76] xii. 508–9 (Modest).

PART IV

18

1885–1886

To be free *and to have my own* refuge—*that is what I have always wanted and now I have it.*

At present all my thoughts are concentrated on finding a place to live permanently, somewhere in the countryside near to Moscow. I can no longer content myself with living like a nomad; I must at all costs have somewhere that I can call *my own*. There was an advertisement in *Politseyskiye vedomosti* [*The Police Gazette*] for 1 January: 'Single person seeks dacha/country estate to rent.' That's *me*, and I have already had one offer.[1]

I have got back from Petersburg, where I spent eight days in feverish activity. The first days were spent in rehearsals for the concert at which my new suite was performed [under Bülow] and in preparing myself for the severe emotional experience which faced me. A secret premonition told me that people were going to like my *suite* and that it was going to touch the audience to the quick. I was glad, and frightened as well. But the reality far surpassed my expectations. I have never before had such a triumph; I could see that everybody in the audience was deeply moved and was grateful to me. Such moments are the richest rewards of an artist's life. They make life and work worthwhile.[2]

The Suite No. 3 was first performed in St Petersburg on 12 January 1885 at the Fifth Symphony Concert of the RMS.

The house which I was offered to rent or buy turned out to be quite unsuitable. I had almost made up my mind to go abroad but I was so violently seized with inexpressible fear at the journey which faced me, I was so mercilessly crushed by an incomprehensible sense of anguish, that I made a heroic decision and sent Alexey to rent a dacha, about which I had heard that it was in a pretty area, and that it was provided with furniture, crockery, and all necessities. It's in Maydanovo, a village just over a mile from Klin.[3] My first impression of the area was a pleasant one; the house is on high ground on the bank of the river, in a fine position, and there are extensive grounds behind it. But the house itself rather cast me into despair at first. I have got used to living in establishments which, if they are not

---

[1] xiii. 17 (von Meck).   [2] xiii. 25 (von Meck).   [3] xiii. 31 (von Meck).

always luxurious, are at least clean and decent. In the house here, though, I found nothing but pretensions to luxury, clashing colours, lack of taste, dirt, and appalling neglect. On top of that, the house is enormous and cold, not at all cosy. Somehow or other Alexey and I have fixed up three rooms for ourselves. I am already getting used to my surroundings and reconciled to them. But what a delight, what a marvellous relief it is for me to have solitude, peace, and freedom!!! What a joy it is to be in my own place! What bliss it is to know that nobody will come, nobody will interrupt my work, my reading, my walks! I have now realized once and for all that my dream of settling in the Russian countryside for the whole of the rest of my life is not a passing whim but an essential requirement of my nature. Of course Maydanovo is not the answer to my dreams. But I can settle even here for a year or so until I find something more suitable.[4] I have started taking newspapers and periodicals, which makes life a lot more agreeable. I am reading a lot; I am enjoying studying English, my work is going fine, I am eating, walking, sleeping, when I want and as much as I want—in short, I am *living*.[5]

I can't put into words the attractions of the Russian countryside, the Russian landscape, and that peace which I needed above all else. I am working with fervour and with love. *Vakula the Smith* is going to be a jolly good opera. I have written some completely new scenes, have thrown out everything that was no good, have kept what was good, have lightened the massive, ponderous harmony, in short, I have done everything that was needed to save the opera from the oblivion which it does not really deserve.[6]

There was another event in Tchaikovsky's life: he was elected a director of the Moscow branch of the RMS on 10 February 1885.

I have got back from Moscow, where I spent four days, not too disagreeably. I attended two meetings of the Musical Society in my capacity as a director. Heard an excellent performance by Taneyev and the orchestra of my *Fantasia* and am very pleased with it. It was a big success with the public, better than the Suite [i.e. in Moscow].[7]

The *Concert Fantasia* was performed in the Bolshoy Theatre on 24 February 1885 at a concert conducted by Erdmannsdörfer in aid of students.

I am glad to get back home, but all the same Maydanovo will never be my *home*.[8] Having property is still inhibiting to a greater or lesser degree, and only someone who has none can consider himself free. On the other hand I really must have *a place of my own*, *a home* somewhere. As to the wilds of Russia, they don't frighten me. One has to get in good stocks of books and

---

4 xiii. 35 (von Meck).   5 xiii. 36 (Modest).
6 xiii. 38–9 (Emiliya Pavlovskaya).
7 xiii. 39 (Modest).   8 xiii. 40 (Modest).

paper and so on from the town, but so far as food is concerned I am extremely undemanding. What I certainly cannot accept is the view that everything is *awful, and gloomy, and dead* and so on. Just as *the Eskimo* or *the Samoyed* loves his icy north, I love our Russian countryside more than any other, and for me the Russian landscape in winter has an incomparable charm. This, incidentally, in no way stops me loving both Switzerland and Italy, but somehow differently. I find it particularly difficult to agree today [5 March] that the Russian countryside is unattractive. It's a marvellous day, sunny, the snow is glistening like myriads of diamonds and is thawing slightly, my window gives me a wide view right into the distance. It's wonderful and spacious, you can breathe properly in these immense horizons![9] I am now putting my revised score of *Vakula* into order: I am orchestrating the new numbers and correcting the old ones. The opera will be called *Cherevichki*. I am changing the name because there are other *Vakulas*, Solovyov's, for instance, and Shchurovsky's, and others.[10]

There is all sorts of dishonesty and disorder in our country. But is there any country where everything is all right? There was a time when I believed in all sincerity that to get rid of *tyranny* and to establish order and legality we needed political institutions like Land Assemblies, parliaments, chambers, and so on, and that if we only got something of the sort going everything would be splendid. Now it's not that I have gone over to the camp of the ultra-conservatives but I do at least have my doubts about the entire suitability of these institutions. When I look carefully at what is going on in other countries I can see that everywhere large numbers of people are dissatisfied, everywhere the parties are in conflict, there is mutual hatred, and there is just the same *tyranny* and the same *disorder* to a greater or lesser degree. My conclusion is that there is no *ideal* form of government and that in this matter we are condemned to be disillusioned to the end of time. Sometimes great men do appear who are benefactors of mankind. But they are rare exceptions. At all events I am convinced that *principles* and *theories* will bring us no benefit; what matters is the individuals who, by chance of birth or some other reason, are in charge of ruling us. In short, *mankind* is served by *man* and not by the principle which he embodies. But perhaps all my thoughts about politics are just the naivety of someone who lives far from the prose of life and is incapable of seeing further than his own narrow specialization.[11]

It was at this time that a teacher from Rybinsk, P. Pereletsky, suggested to Tchaikovsky that he should write an opera on Turgenev's novel *On the Eve*.

The subject which you suggest from Turgenev is not suitable. The period is too close to us. It is true that the time at which the action of *Onegin* takes place is not so very far off either, but the Crimean war, the emancipation of

---

[9] xiii. 44–5 (von Meck).   [10] xiii. 49 (von Meck).   [11] xiii. 45 (von Meck).

the peasants, the reign of Alexander II in general have drawn such a sharp division between the first half of the century and the second that the twenties have receded into the realms of the remote past. Moreover, the principal merit of Turgenev's tale is that it vividly reflects a particular moment of history with all its social and political ferment, conflicts, tendencies etc. It is not in the nature of music to illustrate literary works like this.[12]

By this time an idea for a new opera had finally taken shape. As his subject Tchaikovsky had chosen Ippolit Shpazhinsky's play *The Sorceress*, which had been a success at the Maly Theatre.

In *conception The Sorceress* bears witness to Shpazhinsky's great dramatic talent, and if the conception is not quite fully carried through it is because he did not give enough thought to the form, to the finish of the work. I do not see Nastasya, I do not understand her at all as he does. Of course she is a *loose* women, but her charm is not only what she says is *fine and pleasing to all*. This would be enough to attract to her inn *le commun des mortels*. But would *this alone* be sufficient to compel the young Prince to change from being a bitter enemy, come to murder her, into her passionately devoted lover? The fact is that there is *a moral power and a beauty* buried at the bottom of this loose woman's heart which have not previously had any occasion to express themselves. *It is the power of love*. She is a strong feminine nature who can love only once (and then for good), and who can sacrifice *everything* to this love. Whilst her love was still in embryo Nastasya converted her *power* to small change i.e. she amused herself by making everyone who crossed her path fall in love with her, one and all. At that stage she is just a pleasant, attractive, though dissolute woman; she knows that she is *charming*, is happy in the knowledge, and having the benefits neither of faith nor, because she is an orphan, of a good upbringing, she sees her whole purpose in enjoying herself. But then the man appears whose role it is to touch the finer strings, hitherto silent, of her *depths*, and she is transformed. Life for her is *as nothing* beside the achievement of her goal; *the power of her charm* has previously been elemental, unconscious, but now it becomes an all-conquering weapon which in an instant smashes the hostile force i.e. *the hatred* of the young Prince. Then both of them abandon themselves to a wild torrent of love, which carries them to inevitable catastrophe—her death, and this death leaves the audience with a sense of resigned compassion. Of course, I am talking about what it will be like in my libretto and not about the existing play. Shpazhinsky has grasped exactly what I need and will adjust the main characters to suit my interpretation. *As I* understand this role i.e. as it will be in *the opera*, I am *sure* you [Pavlovskaya] will like it. In falling for *The Sorceress* I have not at all betrayed the fundamental need of my soul to illustrate in music what Goethe spoke of: '*Das Ewig-Weibliche zieht uns hinan.*' The fact that *the*

[12] xiii. 71 (Pereletsky).

powerful beauty of the feminine is for long concealed in Nastasya within the shell of *a loose woman* tends rather to intensify her dramatic attractiveness. Why do you like the role of Traviata? Why *must* you like Carmen? Because beneath the coarse exterior of both of these characters you can feel *beauty* and *power*. I don't want to say very much about the other characters. One thing I will say is that my Princess will also be a powerful personality in her own way. She is *jealous*, not of the *Prince* as a person, but of his noble standing; she is, in short, a rabid aristocrat, fanatical in defending the honour of *the house*, willing to sacrifice her life for it or to resort to crime.[13]

I have received a long letter from Pavlovskaya in which she urges me *not* to write an opera on this subject. I know that you too [Modest] are against it. But neither of you know to what extent the libretto will be *different* and how the characters and situations will be changed. The heroine will be completely different. The last act of the play is awful; in my version it will be *magnificent*; the whole theatre will be in tears when Pavlovskaya herself dies in this act.[14]

Vsevolozhsky really has been very good: he has given instructions that no expense is to be spared in staging *Cherevichki*, and I have attended a meeting which he chaired to discuss the production. They are sending Waltz [the designer] to Tsarskoye Selo to reproduce the *amber* drawing-room and some other special room in the palace. I am terribly pleased.[15]

I am going to Moscow and will be spending every weekday at the Conservatoire right up to the end of the examinations. I must admit that after so many years of complete freedom even these three weeks, which will take me away from my work, are a considerable burden. But what else can I do? If my directorship of the Musical Society is to be of any use at all then it will be precisely in things like this external supervision of the teaching in the Conservatoire.[16]

My endless and exhausting attendance at the Conservatoire examinations is over at last. I am leaving with the agreeable feeling of having done my duty and certain that I have been of some use to the Conservatoire. This is what use I have been: I realized that Albrecht was quite incapable of serving as the head of the institution so I decided that I must at all costs get a new and proper Director appointed. Since I knew of no Russian musician apart from Taneyev who was competent and worthy of the post I took steps to see that Taneyev was elected. I first had to spend a long time persuading him; when I had obtained his agreement, I then had to win over all the directors of the Russian Musical Society one by one to Taneyev's cause; then I felt obliged to prepare Albrecht for the forthcoming change; in short, I found the energy to bring the whole affair to a satisfactory conclusion. Of course some people had their vanity hurt and their ambitions

13 xiii. 63–5 (Pavlovskaya).   14 xiii. 68 (Modest).
15 xiii. 74 (Modest).   16 xiii. 84 (von Meck).

bruised. I had to smoothe it all over, to pacify people, to convince them, to beg with them, even to resort to cunning.[17]

Tchaikovsky found nothing suitable in the Moscow area and spent the summer at Maydanovo.

Fine grounds, pretty views, marvellous bathing—but it's all ruined by the people coming to their dachas for their holidays. I daren't show my face in the grounds so they might as well not be there. You can't feel free and at home; I constantly reproach myself for being too hasty and incautious last winter when the idea of taking a dacha came to me. It was nice in the winter, but I should have foreseen these insufferable holiday-makers in the summer.[18]

I am immersed in a big new symphonic work. Shpazhinsky was not able to deliver the first act by the promised time and so as not to waste time I began back in April to make *sketches* for my long-planned programme symphony on the theme of Byron's *Manfred*. I have now got so carried away with this work that the opera is probably going to have to be put to one side for a long time. This symphony will need an enormous amount of concentration and effort because it is a very serious and complex task.[19]

I am finishing the task to which I have devoted the whole summer. This task has caused me extraordinary effort and strain as it was a very complex assignment. I am at last coming to the end of it and the nearer I get to finishing the lighter my spirits become and the easier I breathe. I have been in a state of melancholy and nervous strain all summer under the influence of this depressing subject for a symphony (Byron's *Manfred*).[20]

I don't know what it will be like, but I am not satisfied so far. Oh! it's a thousand times more enjoyable to write without a programme! When I am composing a programme symphony I feel like a charlatan swindling the public, paying it not in honest coin but in tatty paper money.[21]

I have not written a single note of *The Sorceress*. The explanation is not idleness at all but the fact that Shpazhinsky is three weeks late. So, to avoid losing three weeks with nothing to do, I started on the sketches for the symphony and as often happens I got carried away and couldn't stop. The symphony has turned out to be an enormous, serious, difficult work which absorbs all my time and which is, on occasion, extremely exhausting; but an inner voice tells me that my labours are not in vain and that this might perhaps be the best of my symphonic compositions. Once I had started on the work and it had caught my enthusiasm it was beyond my powers to put it aside.[22]

I am in a gloomy frame of mind all the time just now. I am working on a very difficult, complex symphonic piece, which is, moreover, of such a tra-

[17] xiii. 90–1 (von Meck).   [18] xiii. 98–9 (von Meck).
[19] xiii. 99 (von Meck).   [20] xiii. 147 (Anna Merkling).
[21] xiii. 101 (Taneyev).   [22] xiii. 118 (Pavlovskaya).

gic nature that I too have temporarily turned into a Manfred. And on top of that I am, as always happens, bursting myself to get on with the work. I am desperately anxious to finish it as soon as I can, so I am straining every nerve. I am inescapably caught in the same old *cercle vicieux*.[23]

I have sat over *Manfred* without, as you might say, stirring from the spot for almost four months. The work was very difficult but very enjoyable, particularly when my enthusiasm took over after a rather laborious start. Never before have I put so much effort into a piece of work and never have I been so exhausted by it. It's a very difficult piece and calls for a huge orchestra i.e. a large number of strings.[24]

That summer Tchaikovsky's brother Anatoly obtained a new post: he was appointed Public Prosecutor in Tiflis.

So it is Anatoly's fate to go to Tiflis and not to some miserable little provincial town. We are all very glad about this; I have long wanted to go to the Caucasus and at last I will have an excuse.[25]

At long last the question has been resolved of where I am to live more or less permanently. After endless and fruitless searching I have accepted the suggestion of the owner of the estate here to stay in Maydanovo. However, I will not be living in the inconvenient and unpleasant house which I have had up to now but in another one where she has been living herself. It stands apart from the others; a considerable part of the garden will be fenced off for me and will be entirely at my disposal, and the house itself was freshly decorated in the summer. I am not particularly fond of this area, but because the main station is nearby, and so is the town, with its shops and post office, and telegraph office, and doctor, and chemist, and above all because of my extreme reluctance to start searching and putting off again, I have decided to take the house which has been offered to me for two years. It's very pleasant and comfortable, and I think it will put me in a good, settled frame of mind.[26]

With the onset of the present awful, overcast autumn weather my health has recovered entirely and now, apart from being tired from working, I have no symptoms of anything. I am coming to the conclusion that for my constitution the *summer* is the most unfavourable time of year and that the *heat* has an adverse effect on me. So long as I am in the country or abroad I always feel better in winter than in summer, but in any case I have finally decided not to work in the summer: I will travel and rest instead.[27]

I have moved into my new house and think it's charming. It's all cosy, and clean, and nice and pleasant. The only thing is that I am not altogether pleased with the bedroom, but that's nothing. On the whole it's excellent!

[23] xiii. 122–3 (von Meck).   [24] xiii. 146 (Balakirev).
[25] xiii. 109–10 (Anna Merkling).   [26] xiii. 136 (von Meck).
[27] xiii. 145 (von Meck).

Heavens! what a pleasure it is to have some peace, to be away from the bustle, to have one's own place, and, moreover, to be on one's own!!! No one is fonder than I am of his near ones and dear ones, but all the same the true *pattern* of my life is to have no company other than books, music, ink, and paper.[28] One thing I do regret: I have always dreamt of having a fine broad view from my windows, and I have not got it here. My windows look out on to the garden, and the trees, young ones at that, prevent me from seeing anything else.[29]

I have finished the first act of *The Sorceress* which lies before me, and I am already beginning to feel the attractions of the task which faces me. There is one thing about opera which all composers find irresistibly enticing: it alone offers us the chance of communicating with *the masses* of the public. My *Manfred* will be played once or twice and will then vanish for ages; apart from a handful of specialists who go to orchestral concerts, nobody will get to know it. Whereas opera, and in fact only opera, draws you closer to people, gives the real public some affinity with your music, makes you the property not just of separate little groups but, if circumstances are favourable, of the world at large. I see nothing reprehensible in this aspiration: Schumann was not moved by vanity when he wrote *Genoveva*, nor was Beethoven when he was composing *Fidelio*; they were moved by a natural impulse to widen the circle of their listeners, to influence the feelings of as many people as possible. One should not merely pursue external effects to achieve one's end but should select subjects of artistic merit which will engage the interest and touch the emotions.[30] So far as the higher significance of symphonic and chamber music by comparison with opera is concerned, I think that abstaining from writing operas is a sort of heroism and there is such a hero in our time: Brahms. Unfortunately his creative talent is weak and does not match the extent of his aspirations. None the less he is a hero. I lack that heroism, and the stage, for all its tinsel, attracts me.[31]

It has been autumn here for quite some time; the cold north wind blows ceaselessly and howls in the chimney at night. Not that it is without its attraction in its own way, especially if you live in a delightful, comfortable house like mine; but then I like to walk for two hours every day and that is not particularly pleasant. Another thing which somewhat spoils my pleasure in walking is the local people and their way of life. The cottages in the local village are wretched, small, and dark, and when you think that they have to live in there, cramped and gloomy, for eight months, the heart sinks. I don't know why, but the people here are especially poor. There is no school. It is pitiful to see the children, who are condemned to live both mentally and physically in constant, stifling gloom. One would like to do something but one feels helpless. This aspect of life in the Russian country-

---

[28] xiii. 151 (Anna Merkling).   [29] xiii. 153 (von Meck).
[30] xiii. 159–60 (von Meck).   [31] xiii. 171 (von Meck).

side is not attractive. However, things are going so well for me personally that I often think that no matter how much contemporary pessimists might deny the possibility of happiness, I can serve as a living refutation of their supposed axiom, because I am in fact happy living like a hermit. To be *free* and to have my own *refuge*—that is what I have always wanted and now I have it—which means that I am happy. To wish for more would be folly and ingratitude.[32] So far my isolation does not at all oppress me and my heart even sinks when I think that I will soon have to go to Kamenka. I always find it dreadfully difficult to leave a place when I have got used to it.[33]

Tchaikovsky was planning to go to Kamenka to celebrate the silver wedding of Lev and Alexandra Davydov.

Damn Zola! I chanced upon *Germinal*, began reading it, got carried away, and it so worked out that I read the ending very late at night. I was so agitated that I got palpitations which stopped me sleeping and the next day I was *really* ill. When I think of that novel now it's like some dreadful nightmare.[34]

I was surrounded by people in Moscow from morning to late at night: I was crazy with tiredness and longed for the freedom of my life in the country. I am overwhelmed with various young composers who want advice and guidance from me. For the most part they are young men who have misjudged the extent of their own abilities. But this time I chanced upon a young man gifted with a powerful creative talent. He is the son of Catoire, who is well known in the commercial world in Moscow. I persuaded him to take up his studies seriously. In Moscow I heard a very decent performance of Rimsky's *Snegurochka* [*The Snow Maiden*] in the Private Theatre.[35]

From Moscow Tchaikovsky went to Kamenka.

It's very pleasant to be here [at Kamenka], but on the other hand things jar on me at every turn, and, apart from that, my room is itself the source of a sort of depression. I feel that I am now a stranger here and that all my inner ties with the past are broken. It has vanished into the abyss and is gone.[36] All my books, pictures, possessions, everything that formerly made this room my only *chez-soi* has already been packed up and sent to Maydanovo. As I look at the empty walls and shelves it is sad to think of the years which have disappeared into the past never to return, but not for a single moment do I repent of my decision to live on my own. Of course my love for my relations here will never die, but for many reasons I can only be a guest here now.[37]

Yesterday I returned home after a month's absence and realized more

[32] xiii. 170–1 (von Meck).   [33] xiii. 176 (Kolya).   [34] xiii. 164 (Modest).
[35] xiii. 181 (von Meck).   [36] xiii. 185 (Modest).   [37] xiii. 188 (von Meck).

than ever how much I needed to possess a little place of my own and how pleasant it was to find myself *at home* after my travels and all the hustle and bustle of the days spent away. In spite of being in the depths of winter, and the gloomy landscape, and the cold (for my little house has turned out to be quite cold), I am utterly content and happy to have returned home. I spent about a week in Moscow. I went to three concerts. The first of them was given by Ziloti, who had just returned from abroad to do his military service. He was a great success. Then there was a concert of the Musical Society and a quartet morning, in which the excellent Parisian violinist, Marsick, took part. I enjoyed these three concerts all the more since it was such a long time since I had heard good music. For a musician who writes as much as I do, it is very necessary, useful, and relaxing to hear other people's music from time to time. I find nothing more inspiring than hearing an excellent work by someone else: it makes one immediately want to try to write something equally good.[38]

I am back at Maydanovo after being away for a month. Much has changed. All the things have come from Kamenka, the pictures have been hung, the books have been put on the shelves, the place is fuller and cosier. Oh! how glad I am to be at home! Haven't heard a murmur about my opera [*Cherevichki*]. Altani is ill.[39]

Unfortunately, thanks to the peculiar way I am put together, to the complete absence of any capacity for showing myself in a favourable light, to that morbid reserve which constantly compels me to seek seclusion, I could not be a conductor. Those few attempts which I have made have not been crowned with success. This results from my shy nature, my reserve, and the lamentable state of my *nerves*. There is only one consolation in all this. *I have never at any stage made any effort to push my works, whether in Russia or abroad*, and yet they are gradually making their way; this shows that they have at least some value.[40]

If Altani soon recovers I could wish for nothing better than that *he* should be the one to learn *Cherevichki* and to conduct it. But if his ill health continues and *so long as nobody at all has any objection whatsoever*, I am not at all averse *to trying, for the last time in my life to learn the opera myself and to conduct it for the first three performances*. I would very much like to help both *the management* and *myself* by making my way on to the podium. I have no right to do this; I am a very poor conductor, but I could try.[41] Where has my boldness sprung from? I do feel that in the present state of my health and nerves I *could* do it.[42]

They played my Third Suite at the last concert [in Moscow] and the audience gave me an ovation.[43]

[38] xiii. 194 (von Meck).   [39] xiii. 192 (Panya).   [40] xiii. 202 (Mackar).
[41] xiii. 212 (Pchelnikov).   [42] xiii. 221 (Panya).   [43] xiii. 219 (von Meck).

At the Fourth Symphony Concert of the RMS on 30 November 1885, conducted by Erdmannsdörfer.

In December 1885 the Academic Council of the Conservatoire elected Tchaikovsky an Honorary Member of the Moscow Conservatoire 'taking into account the great gifts shown in his musical compositions . . . and the services . . . which he has rendered to the development of the art of music in Russia'. This was the first time the Moscow Conservatoire had done such a thing and Tchaikovsky was very touched. He was also worried, as he wrote to Taneyev:

I have been wondering for days how to reply to my election as an Honorary Member. I can't make myself write in a formal way because I am sure it would look comic; I really am touched and don't want to make a joke of it. I will, therefore, confine myself to a personal expression of my very lively sense of sincere gratitude.[44]

At the end of December Tchaikovsky went to St Petersburg where he greeted the New Year, 1886.

My stay in Petersburg this time was particularly onerous and wearing. Apart from being unwell, which lost me several days, I was, as usual, worn out with endless visits and visitors. At last I am back home in the country, enjoying the peace and the freedom again. I have noticed how the village children at Maydanovo never have anything to do and loaf about aimlessly so I started discussions a long time ago with the local '*Father*' about organizing a school. It transpired that it could be done if I would donate a certain sum every year. I declared my willingness to do so, the 'Father' started making applications a couple of months ago, and now we have received *authorization* to open the school; lessons begin this week. I'm very pleased about it![45]

After several days of fierce wind with snowstorms which kept even me indoors, today we are having the most wonderful winter weather, one of those sunny winter days which with its inexpressible charm can make one forget that somewhere in the south there are sun, flowers, and almost perpetual summer. I was moved to tears and my walk had a wonderfully beneficial effect on me. I must tell you that I am now completely immersed in my new work (the opera *The Sorceress*), and, as is my terrible wont, I am straining myself to such an extent and am so tired by the evening that my exhaustion has reacted on my nerves and yesterday I felt ghastly. To add to that, because of the awful weather I have taken little exercise and have breathed little fresh air. But today has resurrected me entirely, and I am feeling well again and full of energy for work. Unfortunately I have to go to Moscow tomorrow on business and stay there several days.[46]

I have come to the conclusion that *The Sorceress* must have four acts, not five. It's a pity that I have come to that conclusion now and not last year,

[44] xiii. 220 (Taneyev).   [45] xiii. 238–9 (von Meck).
[46] xiii. 253–4 (von Meck).

but what can I do about it? It was only through writing the first two acts that I really got to know my subject and became acutely conscious of the fact that it was *absolutely impossible* to spread the opera over the same five acts as the play. Act I has a neat exposition of the story, a splendid, realistic picture of folk life, plenty of vigour and interest in the action; Act II—here the drama, for which we have been prepared in the first act, unfolds; the relationships of the characters and their personalities are presented in suitably clear and powerful terms; the action rapidly proceeds to a climax. Act III is in fact the *climax* of the drama; the composer must be tuned to a very high pitch at this point; his concentration must be extreme; this high pitch of concentration must also be sensed by the listener; he must feel the inevitability of a complex and dreadful catastrophe. It is to this catastrophe that Act IV must then be devoted, after which the listener/spectator leaves the theatre, profoundly moved, but resigned and satisfied. After the two magnificent, terrible, and *passionate* scenes of Act III I *feel* that I can *successfully* write only *one* more act. I haven't got enough colours or enough inspiration to illustrate with music a succession of powerfully dramatic scenes for two whole acts. I am quite *certain* that it would damage the opera. However much he might in general be fond of music, no listener can go away after five such acts without a feeling of surfeit and extreme exhaustion which is fatal to the success of an opera. In a play it is possible to stimulate flagging interest with a few realistic scenes, with flashes of style, with neatly inserted little episodes which have no direct bearing on the action. This is possible only to a limited extent in opera, where one must have conciseness and speed of action, otherwise the composer/author runs out of strength to write, and the listener out of strength to listen attentively to the end. I am not saying that no opera should have *five acts*. But the story of *The Sorceress* is such that a five-act opera cannot be made of it. The question now is what to do about it. Various notions have occurred to me, such as running Acts IV and V together. But in any event I cannot avoid the necessity of devising something quite new, quite different from what it is in the play. The Princess *must, of course*, kill Nastasya; between the Prince and his son there *must, of course*, be hostility, a struggle, and death. But this must happen somewhere on neutral ground, not in the Prince's mansion, and not at Nastasya's. Would it not be possible for all the main characters to come together at the old man's to whom the Princess will go for the poison? Could Nastasya not be cunningly lured by the Princess (with Mamyrov acting as her agent)? Could it be arranged so that there is a public ending to the tragedy, so that the people should be there?[47]

Shpazhinsky carried out Tchaikovsky's request and ran Acts IV and V together; he also followed the composer's advice for the Finale.

I went to Rubinstein's *Schumann* concert. I have never liked him so much

[47] xiii. 263–5 (Ippolit Shpazhinsky).

as I did on this occasion. Because I noticed that he was touched that I had
at last honoured his fourth concert with my presence, and because he was in
general somehow particularly nice and kind to me, I now feel obliged to go
to the rest of the concerts, to the festivities in his honour, and to the various
other dinners and jollifications which have been arranged for him. Life is
going to be hectic.[48]

Anton Rubinstein gave a famous cycle of historical concerts in Moscow which were
intended, in his own words, 'to present . . . a clear history of the gradual development of piano music' (*Avtobiograficheskiye vospominaniya A. G. Rubinshteyna,
1829–1889* [St Petersburg, 1889], 62, 63; see also: L. Barenboym, *Anton Rubin-
shteyn* [Leningrad, 1962], ii, 457.).

I am back from Moscow, where I now go every week and will do a few
times yet for Rubinstein's weekly concerts. If it were just a question of listening to this astonishing pianist the trips would not worry me, despite my
dislike of leaving my abode too frequently; but, every time, I have to go to
all manner of dinners and suppers in Anton Grigoryevich's honour, and for
the most part this is unbearably tedious, as well as having a ruinous effect
on my health. At his last concert Rubinstein played *virtuoso* works i.e. Hen-
selt, Thalberg, Liszt, and so on. There is little artistic merit in all that stuff,
but the playing really was astonishing. At the previous concert he played
Schumann, and at the next it will be Chopin. Then there will be a concert
devoted to Russian music which will close this cycle of concerts unprecedented in the extent of the repertoire and in the difficulty of its execution.[49]

I have been in Moscow for a few days again. I went to Anton Rubinstein's last concert and to all the farewell festivities organized in his honour.
His programme was devoted to Russian music this time. He played four of
my pieces, incomparably of course, but I must admit that his choice could
have been better and more interesting. On the day before the concert there
was an evening of church music at the Conservatoire when one of the best
Moscow choirs performed a programme, which I had compiled, of various
new items of church music. It included some new pieces of mine which
they sang very well.[50]

In his 'Russian' concert Rubinstein played Tchaikovsky's Song without words
Op. 2 No. 3, the Valse-scherzo Op. 7, the Romance Op. 5, and the Russian Scherzo
Op. 1 No. 1. The Precentor Vasily Orlov conducted a *concert spirituel* which in-
cluded the Cherubic Hymn in F major and 'To Thee we sing'. Other contemporary
Russian composers represented were Rimsky-Korsakov, Taneyev, and Azeyev.

I have been playing [Anton Rubinstein's] *Nero*. I still cannot get over my
astonishment at how the composer could be so brazenly slapdash. When I
look at the score I really am furious. I am playing this ghastly stuff, by the

[48] xiii. 262 (Modest).   [49] xiii. 268–9 (von Meck).
[50] xiii. 285 (von Meck).

way, because at least in the sense that I am conscientious it gives me a feeling of superiority which sustains my energies. You think you are writing
rubbish, then you look at this drivel (which was, however, given a serious
performance)—and you feel better. I am ashamed to be so furious about a
thing like this, but why should I pretend in my diary?[51]

At the beginning of March Tchaikovsky went to Moscow for the rehearsals and first
performance of *Manfred* under Erdmannsdörfer at an RMS concert on 11 March
1886.

I will give you my impressions from hearing *Manfred* at rehearsals (I did
not hear it at the concert, i.e. I heard it from a distance). In actual performance there can be no doubt that the first movement is the best. The Scherzo
was played at a very quick tempo and I was not disappointed when I heard
it (which is often the case with me), but, unless I am mistaken, it is written
in such a difficult and impractical way that probably no orchestra will want
to play it or be able to, apart from here in Moscow where the players are in
general very well disposed towards me. The Andante doesn't sound bad.
The *Finale* gains *a lot* in performance; from *the audience's* point of view it is
the most successful movement. I had the general impression that even the
Moscow public, which is particularly kindly towards me, *did not like
Manfred*. On the other hand, the players grew more and more enthusiastic
at every rehearsal and at the final rehearsal they tapped loud and long with
their bows and instruments after each movement. Of my closest friends,
some are solidly behind *Manfred*, others do not like it and maintain that I
am not *myself* in this work, that I am hiding behind some sort of façade. My
own view is that it is my best orchestral work, but that its difficulty, its
impracticality, and its complexity will condemn it to *failure and neglect*.[52]

I think we should not apply modern artistic requirements to Byron in
general and to *Manfred* in particular, i.e. we should not seek a true and
accurate reproduction of everyday life, of events familiar to us from our
own experience, which the narrator illuminates in one way or another by
his talent. Manfred is not an ordinary human being. Byron, so it seems to
me, embodied in him with astonishing power and profundity all the tragedy of the conflict between our insignificance and our aspiration to understand the fateful questions of existence. One English critic says that
Manfred, who was born in the mountains and spent his life in solitude, in
sight of the majestic peaks of Switzerland, is himself like a colossal mountain peak, dominating all that surrounds it, *but lonely and sad in its
grandeur*. You [Mme Shpazhinskaya] are quite right to maintain that every
honest craftsman is more useful in his own narrow sphere of activity than
this *Elbrus* amongst men, whose life is consumed with despair from the
knowledge of his inability to rise above the level of men and forget the sins
of his past; but then Byron does not seek to instruct us, as might a repentant

[51] *Diaries*, 41.   [52] xiii. 298–9 (Balakirev).

sinner, to make his peace with his conscience; his purpose is quite other, it is the one which I have indicated above, and it is achieved brilliantly. But there is no point in my trying to explain the meaning of *Manfred* to you. You say yourself that you have now come to accept the work and attribute this to my music. That is very flattering but in all fairness I must say that my role is confined to being the musical *interpreter* or *illustrator* of an outstanding work of art.[53]

Tchaikovsky's correspondence with the dramatist's wife began at the time of their domestic crisis, when Shpazhinsky left his family. Tchaikovsky was very concerned for Yuliya Shpazhinskaya, and tried to give her moral support.

The same thing happened to *Manfred* as to many other works. After a few years Tchaikovsky turned cool towards it.

So far as *Manfred* is concerned, I can say, with no pretence at being modest, that I find the work disgusting and loathe it heartily, *with the sole exception of the first movement*. However, I intend in the near future to destroy the other three movements entirely—their music is of little value (the Finale in particular is appalling)—and out of the whole great symphony, which is quite impossibly prolix, I will make a *Symphonische Dichtung*. Then, I am sure, my *Manfred* will have the capacity to please; it was inevitable that it would be like this: I enjoyed writing the first movement, but the other three are the fruit of an exertion which, I recollect, made me feel very ill for a time.[54]

None the less Tchaikovsky did not revise the score and the *Manfred* Symphony retained its original form.

Tchaikovsky made a trip to the capital in March.

I had a busy time in Petersburg, but it had its pleasant moments. I was given a rapturous reception at the concert of the Musical Society. There was a great musical rout at dear Yuliya Abaza's* where I was regarded as a fashionable society lion. What a joke![55]

Bülow was the soloist in a performance of the First Piano Concerto on 15 March at the Seventh Symphony Concert, conducted by Karl Zike.

Tchaikovsky went to the Caucasus for the first time.

I saw to my passport in Moscow, and bustled about saying goodbye to everybody; I left on 23 [March]. Arrived in Taganrog on the 25th. Ippolit and Sonya met me. Spent a day and a half with them. Ippolit took me to sea in his ship and around the town in his cabriolet, where he showed me all the sights. I was very interested in the palace where Alexander died. It really is like a page from my beloved *Russky arkhiv* [*The Russian Archive*] recreated in stone. I was much taken by Rostov, as well as by the journey

---

* Yuliya Fyodorovna Abaza was an amateur singer and an admirer of Tchaikovsky.

[53] xiii. 317–18 (Yuliya Shpazhinskaya).
[54] xiv. 542–3 (Grand Duke Konstantin Romanov).   [55] xiii. 303 (Panya).

there (along the sea shore and the branches of the Don). The road from Rostov to Vladikavkaz stretches over the typical, endless steppe, and the nearer one gets to the Caucasus the more does it smell of the East and of Mahomet. One can see Elbrus long before reaching the resort of Mineralnye Vody, which is where the real Caucasus starts, and from there the road is always in sight of the mountains. The weather is miraculous and clear. Mount Kazbek rises up in all its glory, and the little town itself is a nice, lively place.[56]

The Georgian Military Highway, about which one has read and heard so much, surpassed all my expectations. The famous Daryal Gorge, the climb into the mountains, above the snow line, the descent to the valley of the Aragva—it is all quite astounding, and, moreover, the beauties of the scenery on the journey are so varied! At one moment you feel something like fear and dread as you drive between immensely high granite crags, with the Terek rushing noisily at their foot, then you find yourself in a roadway which has just been cleared between two walls of snow and you huddle in your fur coat from the bone-chilling cold; then you arrive for your night halt at a lovely spot in the mountains, where you can enjoy your rest in clean rooms in the village; then, at last, as you make your descent, distant views open up which are so staggeringly beautiful that you could cry with delight. In short, it is hard to imagine a journey which offers more in the way of powerful and enjoyable impressions. I also like Tiflis itself very much. The change to this southern climate from Maydanovo, where it is no time since I was up to my knees in snow, is a fascinating experience. In its situation and, to some extent, in the style of its buildings Tiflis reminds me of some of the Italian towns, particularly of Florence.[57]

I have got to know Tiflis well and have seen all the most important sights. I have been to the local baths, which are run in the eastern fashion; I have been to the most notable churches, including, incidentally, the Armenian one, where I was very interested in the special features of the service in general and of the singing in particular; I have also been to the Monastery of St David, on the hill, where Griboyedov is buried. I went one evening to a concert of the Musical Society, where a thin and extremely bad orchestra played a very complex programme to an almost non-existent audience. There are a few good, prominent musicians in Tiflis. The most outstanding are Ippolitov-Ivanov, a talented composer, and Korganov, the Armenian pianist, who was a pupil at the Moscow Conservatoire. They show me every attention, and, although I would prefer to be here incognito, I cannot help being touched by my artistic colleagues' expressions of interest and affection. Nor had I expected that my music would be so well known in Tiflis. My operas are performed here more than anywhere else, and *Mazepa* in particular is a great success. All this is very nice for me and dis-

[56] xiii. 304–5 (Modest).   [57] xiii. 308–9 (von Meck).

poses me even more towards Tiflis, which I like in any case.[58] I have been
for dozens of walks. In short, I am enjoying myself, but, unfortunately,
quite unproductively, because I can find no time at all to do any work,
although I would very much have liked to make a little progress with *The
Sorceress* whilst I was here.[59] I have read Sarcey's article about Tolstoy and
could hardly restrain *sobs* of joy that a Frenchman had such an understanding of our Tolstoy.[60]

My stay in Tiflis is coming to an end. Were it not for the fact that I have
had to live a more or less social life, I would say that the whole month
which I have spent in Tiflis has been one of the best in my life. It gives me
particular pleasure to see my near ones, Anatoly and his wife, basking in
unclouded happiness. And I continue to find Tiflis itself an extremely
pleasant place, with its great distinctiveness and its marvellous southern
climate. I cannot but be touched by the attention and respect paid to me by
the musicians here. A great celebration in my honour was organized in the
local theatre on Sunday 19 [April]. It started with representatives of the
Musical Society, the theatre, the public, and so on coming to my flower-
bedecked box to make speeches and present me with wreaths, as well as
with a valuable gift of silver. Then there was a concert of my works, with
countless bows and ovations. After that there was a subscription supper. It
was all terribly exhausting, but my recollection of this celebration, with the
like of which I have never been honoured anywhere, will always be a happy
one.[61]

Oh heavens! One is parting from people all one's life and suffering from
the awful sense of not knowing what will happen after the parting. It is the
not knowing which is so unpleasant. I have been twice to the opera here.
The production and performance were more than adequate. They are
doing *Mazepa* on my birthday. I am giving a lunch on the morning of that
day for all the prominent members of the Musical Society. I have met so
many new friends here![62] I have the most happy recollections of Tiflis and
the month which I spent there. It is a long time since it fell to me to be so
cheerful, healthy, and happy when living in a town, and despite the irri-
tations of the social whirl. The fact is that, by some remarkably fortunate
coincidence, the people with whom I had to deal have been exceptionally
nice and undemanding. They left me in peace as much as possible and I was
even able to do a little work.[63]

We left Tiflis on the morning of 29 [April]. A lot of people came to see
me off. We had a very pleasant journey and did not stop till evening. The
Suram pass is very fine. The situation of Batum is absolutely superb; in the
foreground are elegant wooded hills, and in the distance—snow-capped
mountains. The sea is deep blue and the vegetation is almost tropical.[64] My

[58] xiii. 309–10 (von Meck).   [59] xiii. 316 (Modest).   [60] *Diaries*, 48.
[61] xiii. 325–6 (von Meck).   [62] xiii. 327 (Modest).   [63] xiii. 336 (von Meck).
[64] xiii. 331–2 (Modest).

voyage from Constantinople lasted exactly a week and can be regarded as a great success. The most interesting part of the journey was the passage through the Straits of Messina. We reached the Straits at one o'clock in the morning, but for ten hours or so before that we had seen a vertical cloud of smoke in the distance on the absolutely cloudless horizon which turned out to be a powerful eruption from Mount Etna. After sunset we could see fire as well. When darkness fell completely it became an extraordinarily majestic and somewhat frightening sight. I stayed up as we went through the Straits, which took until sunrise, and watched the remarkable, awesome spectacle of the eruption. The passage through the Straits of Bonifacio was also very interesting. My general conclusion is that travelling by *steamer* in good weather is extremely pleasant and not at all tiring.[65]

I arrived in Paris on 16 May and I am staying in the same hotel where I spent almost the whole winter three years ago. It's strange! Nothing particularly pleasant happened that winter, on the contrary, in fact. And yet it is pleasant to stay in a room which vividly brings back memories of that time, which, one realizes sadly, has vanished into the realms of the past and which one would, for some reason or other, like to bring back. One always regrets the loss of the past, probably because the good moments stay longer in one's mind and everything unpleasant is forgotten, or at least you try to forget it. I will have to meet my publisher here, M. Mackar (I have promised to do so), and through him various people from the world of music in Paris. This goes very much against the grain and I want to postpone for a little the inevitable burden of visits and calls and just enjoy Paris, i.e. wander about this delightful town completely alone and without constraints. However this in no way stops me from dreaming about returning to Russia as soon as possible. During the last few years I have grown particularly fond of our dear Rus and feel that every year I shall be more difficult to dislodge. It is so pleasant to see with one's own eyes the success our literature is enjoying in France. All bookshop *étalages* are adorned with translations of Tolstoy, Turgenev, Dostoyevsky, Pisemsky, Goncharov. In the newspapers one is always coming across enthusiastic articles about one or another of these writers. Maybe it will soon be the turn of Russian music.[66]

... The day of Alyosha's departure. Ascension Day. Got up in a bad mood, because I had to have lunch with Mackar. Wandered along the Rue St Honoré, Palais-Royal, and the streets in between. At Mackar's. Lunch. I was revived. At half past two I went home. Met *Brandukov*. Thank heavens, I have shaken off Mackar, otherwise it would have been hard to part with Alyosha. I must admit that because of his mania for eternally quarrelling about everything he *à la longue* becomes intolerable and his company gives no pleasure. These defects also make parting easier. As a

[65] xiii. 343–4 (von Meck).   [66] xiii. 348–9 (von Meck).

general rule I value and love Alyosha whole-heartedly only in the country where everything runs smoothly and there is nothing to argue about.[67]

Tchaikovsky undertook the journey to Paris for two reasons. First, he wanted to improve and strengthen his business acquaintances with French musicians; secondly he had to help his sister-in-law (the wife of his brother Nikolay) Olga Sergeyevna complete the formalities for adopting Georges, Tanya Davydova's son.

Overcoming my extreme reluctance and my unbelievably intense distaste for the task, I decided to go to see M. Mackar and since then, of course, I have started visiting, going out to dinners, going to restaurants and theatres with friends etc. However, I must give Mackar his due. Knowing my aversion to company, he is taking me under his wing very cautiously and gradually.[68]

I am not complaining about my life in Paris but there is not very much that is pleasant. If I had been free and alone, if I had been able to work, it would have been a different matter. Paris is really charming at this time of year. But alas! I have to see my publisher and discuss business with him and visit people and be visited. I have already promised so many dinners and all kinds of visits that I will soon have to choose between some of them. But the point is that it is very important for my musical career for me to have a lot of friends and admirers in Paris, and so I am reconciled to the unpleasantness of having to come into contact with people and will tolerate it while my money and patience last, and then go either to Vichy or straight home. My health is so excellent at the moment that I can defer the trip to Vichy until the autumn, but we shall just have to see. There have been all the same some very jolly times. For example a few days ago Brandukov dragged me off to the operetta *Joséphine vendue par ses sœurs*.* I went very unwillingly but it turned out to be such a charmingly gay and amusing thing that I haven't laughed or enjoyed myself so much for a long time.

I have sent Alexey back to Maydanovo since I don't need him at all in Paris. He is probably already there.

Today I went to the famous Grand Prix. It was the first time in my life that I had seen a horse race. It was very boring, I must admit, and I will never again be lured to any such time-wasting activity. What's more it poured with rain.[69]

I have at last seen *Patrie*. The first thing I must say is that the production was simply amazing. However much money was spent, you would never see such a wonderful, *realistic* production in Russian, elegant down to the last detail. Sometimes you were simply transported in your imagination to a medieval town and it was as if you were seeing real life. The play is remarkably effective, but too powerful and heavy. There are masses of shootings.

* Tchaikovsky saw V. Roger's 3-act operetta at the Théâtre Bouffe.

[67] *Diaries*, 61–2.   [68] xiii. 351 (Modest).   [69] xiii. 350 (Panya).

At every move I started and was altogether in such a nervous state that my companions were simply amazed at my involuntary movements and convulsive jerks.[70]

My circle of acquaintances is widening all the time and my stay here is becoming more and more sickening and impossible. However there are some pleasant moments. Yesterday [31 May], for instance, I went very reluctantly to have lunch with Mme Viardot, but she turned out to be such a sweet, delightful motherly soul that in the course of the next three hours I kissed her hand ten times and I am very much looking forward to going there for dinner the day after tomorrow. I have had to set aside three periods a week for being *at home*. Yesterday was the first, from four to six. I had a dreadfully hard time of it. But some of the worst guests came outside the appointed time: Colonne, for instance, and Lamoureux, and Ambroise Thomas. I was invited by Thomas to attend a very interesting examination at the Conservatoire.[71] I had got dressed ready to go out when an agreeable man called who turned out to be Bourgault-Ducoudray. He talked enthusiastically about Glinka, and Tolstoy, and about Russian art in general.[72]

Old Mme Viardot fascinates me. *I have seen the score of Mozart's Don Giovanni written* IN HIS OWN HAND!!!!!!!!!![73] On the question of whether Viardot remembers Turgenev I might say that not only does she remember him but that we talked about practically nothing else; she told me in detail how they had written *The Song of Triumphant Love* together. I spent two hours at Viardot's leafing through Mozart's *original score*. I cannot describe the feelings which gripped me as I examined this *sacred object*. It is as though I had shaken Mozart's own hand and chatted with him.[74]

Olya has arrived. Georges was shy of her at first but is gradually getting used to her. She has a very strong character for such an insignificant-looking lass. I am astonished and admire her for it. Apart from seeing to the business with Georges, my affairs with various new acquaintances got so complicated and so numerous that I simply did not know *où donner de la tête*. I attended a Conservatoire examination at the invitation of Ambroise Thomas. He's a very nice old chap. A Mme Bohomoletz, a rich, half-Russian lady, gave a dinner and a soirée in my honour; they played my Quartet [Marsick, Brandukov], and sang some of my songs. Léo Delibes called on me before I called on him and I found that terribly touching. It seems in general that I am by no means so unknown in Paris as I had thought. I am crazy with tiredness and sometimes I do in fact go into a stupor.[75] I think that I have now achieved much to secure the reputation of my works in *France* by ceasing to be some sort of remote and mythical figure to

[70] xiii. 354 (Modest).   [71] xiii. 357-8 (Modest).   [72] *Diaries*, 68.
[73] Ibid. 64.   [74] xiii. 383 (von Meck).   [75] xiii. 365-6 (Modest).

the musicians there and becoming a live human being. I found a great deal of sympathetic interest there.[76]

I am in Petersburg at last. Lord! how apprehensive I was about the journey! However it turned out not to be too bad at all. What was tiring was the fact that he [Georges] is a very lively child and he has to be constantly amused and occupied. But he is very, very gentle and likeable in the extreme. Olga is beyond praise; but I have always felt that she was one of those insignificant little women who have great strength of will and character. [Georges] is peremptory with me and just gives me straight orders, but there is always more than a touch of tenderness about it.[77]

After Paris it's very strange suddenly to find oneself in Petersburg in June. It's an absolute desert. As for the *white nights*, they are very beautiful but I haven't been able to get a wink of sleep. One cannot sleep with this peculiar combination of daylight and nocturnal silence.[78]

Georges was christened at two o'clock in the afternoon on the day I left. I was his godfather.[79]

I am immensely glad to be back home at last! How attractive and nice my little house seems to me! The three months I have spent away from home have been a complete waste of time so far as work is concerned; but I do feel that I have gathered new strength and can devote all my time to working without getting exhausted. I want to finish the draft of the opera by autumn at all costs so that I can give the whole of next winter to orchestrating it.[80]

I have been to the Shpazhinskys to get *the most marvellous* fourth act of the libretto. Oh! what a terrible domestic drama is going on in the dramatist's own family, and what a fine subject their own affairs would make for a drama or a novel! I am gradually beginning to see what sort of a man Shpazhinsky is. He drops ever lower in my estimation as his wife rises ever higher. She is a most excellent woman, and a dreadfully unfortunate one.[81]

I am very pleased and happy to be at home. I started working very energetically but I have decided that from now on I will generally not do so much work without a break. So after lunch and a long walk I do nothing now, apart from some reading, writing letters, and so on.[82]

The peace of his working life was unexpectedly interrupted.

Antonina Ivanovna is bombarding me with letters. She has devised a new ploy: she announces that she loves me madly, arranges a *rendez-vous*, and simultaneously tells me that she has a lover who adores her passionately. I think she is completely mad. Her letters have upset me beyond all measure: I haven't written anything for a week, I haven't felt well, I have lost my appetite, I have been depressed and so on. The main thing is that one does

[76] xiii. 370 (von Meck).   [77] xiii. 367 (Modest).   [78] xiii. 370 (von Meck).
[79] xiii. 372 (Modest).   [80] xiii. 370 (von Meck).   [81] xiii. 381 (Modest).
[82] xiii. 384 (von Meck).   [83] xiii. 387 (Jurgenson).

not know how to reply to such a madwoman.[83] But the main thing is that, *despite everything*, I feel sorry for the poor woman. She is, after all, so mad that in reply to my first letter, where I told her to abandon any hope of living with me, she sent me an invitation to go to see her, to ask the hall porter if her lover was there, whom she has left but who is supposedly in love with her and might unexpectedly turn up and start to make love (she thinks she can instil passion in me by this) and conversation. 'Then we will have a good talk about everything, everything!' So, exactly as if I had once loved her and evil people separated us, now she is ready to be, in her own words, 'all mine'. In the end I wrote her a suitable letter, fixed a sum for her allowance, and I think that she will finally leave me in peace. After this letter, which I took *exactly two days* to write and I think I tore up at least twenty-five unsuccessful drafts, I have calmed down and have settled down to composing the fourth act of the opera.[84] After Antonina Ivanovna's last letters there was (despite the strictest prohibition) yet another one, in which she informed me that she had three children, *all in a foundling hospital*, one of them apparently called Pyotr after me, and suggested that I should bring up one or all of them (???). In addition she sent me an embroidered shirt and asked me to dedicate something to her. She really and truly has gone mad.[85]

Tchaikovsky was proved right. Antonina Ivanovna Tchaikovskya-Milyukova spent the last twenty years of her life in a mental hospital; she died in 1917.

When I am writing a large work I am constantly troubled by the thought that death will prevent me from finishing it.[86] I always used to think that there was no need to pay much attention to *the dramatic side*, and that the music could fend for itself regardless of a poor libretto. Experience has now taught me that the lasting success of an opera can only be ensured by the most careful consideration of the details of the drama.[87]

I was in Moscow on business not long ago and was, incidentally, very pleased to hear some of my pieces sung at Mass in the Cathedral of the Assumption. It was the first time in my life that I had heard one of my religious compositions during a service.[88]

Tchaikovsky was in Moscow on 5–6 July. On 6 July he heard his Cherubic Hymn in the Cathedral of the Assumption.

I hope to see you in August which is why I will not say much now about the thing which occupies at least half my thoughts. The tale concerns one of my acquaintances in Tiflis, an officer in the Engineers called Verinovsky; we became close friends astonishingly quickly and I took a great liking to him—three days after I left he shot himself. This was kept from me for a

[84] xiii. 388 (Modest).   [85] xiii. 429 (Modest).
[86] xiii. 393 (Yuliya Shpazhinskaya).   [87] xiii. 391 (Ippolitov-Ivanov).
[88] xiii. 401 (Shpazhinskaya).

long time and I found out about it by accident. His death affected me *dread-fully*. I am always powerfully moved by the death of any good young person, the more so when it is death by suicide. I can't help thinking that if I had stayed another week in Tiflis he would still be alive. All the same I am glad that there was at least some external cause for suicide: he had failed his examinations. Otherwise it would be simply impossible to live with the sad knowledge that he had perished from a lack of that sympathetic response which his good and gentle nature needed and which he did not find where he sought it.[89]

Because of my ill health I have done appallingly little work all this summer; I am appalled to realize that autumn is upon us and I have not done the half of what I planned. But I have done a very great deal of reading, and, incidentally, I am enjoying rereading Tolstoy immensely. The less I like him as a thinker and as a preacher, the more I venerate his mighty genius as a writer.[90]

When you read the autobiographies of our outstanding figures, or reminiscences about them, you constantly come across feelings, impressions, a general artistic sensitivity, which are familiar from your own experience and are easy to understand. But there is *one* who is not to be understood, who is unattainable, who stands alone in his inscrutable grandeur: *Lev Tolstoy*. Quite often I rage inwardly when I read him, I almost hate him. Why, I ask myself, has this man, who is able as no one else ever has been before to inspire in us the most lofty and miraculous sense of harmony, this writer who was freely endowed from on high with a power granted to no one before him to make our feeble intellects reach into the most impenetrable, innermost recesses of our moral being—why has this man become so manically addicted to *teaching* and *preaching*, to *bringing light* to our clouded and limited minds? Formerly, his descriptions of what were apparently the most simple and everyday scenes would leave an unforgettable impression. Between the lines one could read a lofty love for man, a lofty *pity* for his feebleness, his finitude, and his insignificance. You would weep, without yourself knowing why. Now he writes commentaries on texts; he claims an exclusive monopoly on understanding questions of faith and *ethics* (it would seem), but all the writing he does now has a coldness about it; you can sense *fear*, and you can obscurely feel that he is *a man* i.e. a creature who, when it comes to dealing with questions about our purpose on earth, about the meaning of life, about God and religion, is just as perversely independent and at the same time just as insignificant as any ephemeral insect which appears on a warm midday in July and has already run the course of its existence by evening. Tolstoy used to be a demigod, but now he is a *fanatic*. And fanatics, of course, are *teachers because of the role which they have assumed, and not by virtue of their vocation*. And yet I cannot bring

---

[89] xiii. 405–6 (Modest).   [90] xiii. 413 (Kolya).

myself to condemn his present activity. Who knows? Perhaps he is doing
the right thing and I am simply incapable of understanding and appreciating as I ought this greatest of all artistic geniuses, who has left the path of
the novelist for that of the preacher.[91] I have been finishing an absolutely
superb thing by Tolstoy, his *Kholstomer*; I settled down to *The Death of
Ivan Ilich* and I have finished it. *The Death of Ivan Ilich* is an excruciatingly
brilliant work.[92] More than ever am I convinced that the greatest of all
literary writers who have ever existed anywhere is *Lev Tolstoy*. He alone is
sufficient to ensure that the Russian need not bow his head in shame when
he is being told of all the great things which *Europe* has given mankind. Nor
does *patriotism* play any part at all in my conviction of the colossal, almost
god-like significance of Tolstoy.[93] I took it into my head to read Tolstoy's
The Wood-felling and wept.[94]

Tchaikovsky frequently returned to his reflections on Tolstoy. Three years later he
wrote:

I would not say that my soul was running over with love and forgiveness for
everybody; I have very frequently had to parry blows, yet I cannot but
admire the strength of spirit, the loftiness of view of those exceptional
people who, like Spinoza and Count Tolstoy, draw no distinction between
the good and *the bad*. I have not read Spinoza and what I say about him is
second-hand; as to Tolstoy, I have constantly read and reread him, and I
regard him as the greatest writer in the world, past or present. Quite apart
from the artistic impact, reading his works also evokes in me an altogether
special and distinctive emotional response which I get with no other writer.
The emotion comes to me not only when something happens which really is
moving, such as death, suffering, partings and the like, but also in episodes
which are apparently quite prosaic, mundane, and trivial. I remember, for
instance, that once when I was reading the chapter where Dolokhov beats
Rostov at cards I burst into floods of tears which I could not check for ages.
Why should a scene where both characters behave in a most unpraise-
worthy way have the power to evoke tears? The reason is, of course, very
simple. Tolstoy looks at the people whom he portrays from such a height
that to him they seem poor, insignificant, pitiful pygmies who squabble
with each other blindly, aimlessly, fruitlessly, and *he pities them*. Tolstoy
never has villains; he loves and pities all his characters equally, everything
that they do is a consequence of the general constraints from which they
suffer, of their naïve egoism, their feebleness, their insignificance. So he
never punishes his heroes for their misdeeds, as Dickens does (another
author, incidentally, of whom I am very fond), nor does he ever depict
absolute villains, but simply people who blunder in their blindness. His
humanitarianism reaches infinitely higher and wider than the sentimental

---

[91] *Diaries*, 210.   [92] Ibid. 78.
[93] Ibid. 211.   [94] Ibid. 79.

humanitarianism of Dickens and rises almost to that view of human folly which we see expressed in the words of Christ:'for they know not what they do'.[95]

In the summer of 1886 Mme la Mara, the writer on music, asked Jurgenson to send her one of Tchaikovsky's letters for a collection of letters from great composers which she was preparing for publication.

I understand perfectly the difficulty of your [Jurgenson] position. You are asked for some letter or other of mine for publication; you have hundreds, yet there is not one that would suit the present purpose. That's to be expected: our correspondence has always been too concerned with business or too intimate. But what can I do to relieve the pain? I would be telling a lie if I argued that I was not flattered by Mme la Mara's wish to count me among the outstanding musicians of our time. On the contrary, I am very touched and flattered to receive such attention from this well known writer and I can say with all sincerity that I would be glad to be seen in the company of Glinka, Dargomyzhsky, and Serov. It is odd, isn't it, that there are problems in finding a letter from someone who had and has an enormous correspondence? I am constantly exchanging letters with my four brothers, my sister, several cousins, innumerable friends and acquaintances, and on top of that I have masses of occasional correspondence with people who are very often quite unknown to me. I frequently suffer so much from the need to give an excessive proportion of my time to correspondence that I sincerely curse every postal institution in the world. The post very often brings me problems, but it also brings me the greatest joys. There is a person who has played a leading role in the story of my life for the past ten years; this person is my good genius; I am indebted to her for my well-being and for the possibility of devoting myself entirely to the work I love—and yet I have never seen her or heard the sound of her voice, and without exception all my relations with her have been by post. The only thing you can do is send Mme la Mara the present letter. Even if it casts no light at all on me as a musician it at least gives me the opportunity to satisfy the flattering wish of Mme la Mara to add me to the company of her outstanding figures.[96]

Mme la Mara included this letter, in a German translation by Jurgenson, in the second volume of her book.

I have now entered a good stretch for my work; I have settled down after the various things that were tormenting me, I am in good health again, and I am finding it very easy to work—I am frightened to interrupt my stride. I am not depressed now and I am greatly enjoying my walks; every blade of grass, every little cloud fills me with delight again, and my solitude does not trouble me at all.[97]

[95] xva. 204–5 (K.R.).   [96] xiii. 407–8 (Jurgenson).   [97] xiii. 429 (Modest).

18 August. I have today completely finished the draft sketches for the opera. I thanked God for this favour.[98] What a pleasure it was to close the manuscript book I was using and think that all that I have to do now is score the work; for me that does not involve effort so much as pleasure. When I had finished the opera I immediately set about writing some songs.*[99]

Now that all the holiday visitors have made their way back to town I am very pleased with Maydanovo.[100] I ought to begin by complaining about the disgusting weather, but in truth I *ado-o-ore* bad weather, and I never feel fitter, healthier, and happier than on a nasty autumn day. But the wind is always an enemy of mine; if only it would go away.[101]

So as to get a round figure I have now written another two songs and there is a round dozen. For the last two I have taken texts from Khomyakov. What a *poet* he was! The two poems I have chosen are sheer delight! They are so original and delightful that I can feel how my music has come out better and more successfully than in all the others.[102]

Two songs to poems by Alexey Khomyakov: Op. 60 No. 1 'Last night', and No. 11 'Exploit'.

I am going out now *to fly a kite.* That is my passion at the moment. At the age of forty-six! But what a marvellous kite!!! With rattles![103]

I have got back from Moscow where I had five full days. I went to the theatre and saw a very good performance of *Don Giovanni.*[104]

The day before I left for Moscow I played right through *The Sorceress.* To my horror I discovered that all four acts last an hour each, and the first is even longer. Obviously I will have to make enormous cuts, which is very unpleasant. I have had a charming letter from Konstantin Konstantinovich† with a volume of his poems. Many of them are very pleasant.[105] As I read through this anthology I immediately decided to use it for my next set of songs.[106]

I could find out absolutely nothing in Moscow about when they are going to do my opera [*Cherevichki*]. On such occasions I always think of two people who are hostile to opera: *you* [Mme von Meck] and *Lev Tolstoy*, and I promise myself never to write any more operas; but the irresistible attraction of the theatre then takes over and I feel that so long as I can hold a pen I will still write more operas than symphonies or quartets. But how nice

---

* The set of twelve songs, Op. 60.
† Grand Duke Konstantin Romanov wrote poems under the pseudonym K. R. From 1892 he was vice-president of the Russian Musical Society [RMS] [trans.].

[98] *Diaries*, 88.   [99] xiii. 439 (von Meck).   [100] xiii. 445 (von Meck).
[101] xiii. 448 (Modest).   [102] xiii. 448–9 (Modest).
[103] xiii. 451 (Anna Merkling).   [104] xiii. 454 (Modest).   [105] xiii. 455 (Modest).
[106] xiii. 453 (K.R.).

and peaceful it is to have nothing to do with the theatre and all its unpleasantness![107]

The Philharmonic Society wants to give a concert entirely of my works; of course I am glad, but I can't deny that I am also frightened. After all, the aims of the Philharmonic Society are charitable as well as musical. It is not at all false modesty which leads me to say that although the concert which they plan will be a great honour for me it will not provide any money for the widows and orphans. The great mass of the public *never goes* to a concert for what is *performed but for the performers*. In the present instance the exclusive nature of the programme indicates that the Philharmonic Society is placing its hopes on the interest which my music will arouse. Of course such an interest does exist up to a point, but it will not *fill* the hall, which is extremely important, because what the widows and orphans need after all is money, not a wider public knowledge of my works. So, the hall will probably be half empty, and I will be *extremely unhappy* to think that it is *because of me*. Interest in the concert could be considerably increased if I conducted myself, because that would be a new spectacle for the public. But, to my great sorrow, I am *absolutely no good whatsoever* at conducting and can certainly not undertake to contribute to the success of the concert in that respect.[108]

One can see 'between the lines' here a hint at the possibility of appearing before the St Petersburg public as a conductor, perhaps even a secret subconscious wish to do so.

I have always suffered torments throughout my life from the knowledge that I am *incapable* of being a conductor. It seems to me that there is something shameful and disgraceful about being so unable to control myself that at the mere thought of appearing before an audience with a baton I tremble with fear and dread.[109]

From the strain of my work or from some other cause I intermittently get a headache of a quite peculiar nature. As soon as I have been concentrating on my work for half an hour I experience a sensation as though someone were driving a nail into my brain, and the pain is so excruciating that there is no point in thinking about work; there is only one cure—abandon it, and go away for a time. I decided to go to Petersburg. As always, I suffer very much here from the bustle of life in the capital and long for my solitude; I could weep at the amount of time I am wasting away from my work, but on the other hand, the pain has stopped altogether. I often go to the theatre and the opera, and try to distract myself as much as I can. I have been to see *Ruslan and Lyudmila* in a new and remarkably sumptuous production. Opera flourishes here, i.e. it gets very good audiences, though the members of the company leave a lot to be desired.[110] Although I get very tired, I must

[107] xiii. 460–1 (von Meck).   [108] xiii. 471–2 (Yevgeny Albrecht).
[109] xiii. 472–3 (von Meck).   [110] xiii. 482–3 (von Meck).

say that I am touched by the very sympathetic attitude which I meet everywhere here, in all the groups and circles with which I have dealings. I attribute this to the fact that they like my music very much here and this, of course, is profoundly gratifying to me. How distant are the days when I had to rush around and beg to get a new opera produced![111]

I cannot help noticing how I or, to be accurate, my music has advanced in Russian public opinion in recent years. At every turn I met from everybody in Petersburg so many expressions of encouragement and affection that I was frequently moved to tears. This reached its peak with a celebration concert in my honour at the Chamber Music Society [on 5 November]. The programme consisted of two large works (the [Second] Quartet and the Trio) and some small items. The enthusiasm was sincere, and I left weighed down with emotion and gratitude. I experienced the pride of an artist who has won general recognition in his own lifetime.[112]

I have a particularly special patron in the highest circles apart from the tsar and tsarina who are well disposed towards me—this is the Grand Duke Konstantin Konstantinovich. During this visit to Petersburg I have seen him frequently and have visited him at home. He has an unusually captivating personality. He is a talented poet and recently a volume of his poetry came out under the signature K. R.; it was a great success and praised by all the critics in the newspapers and periodicals. He also composes music and has written several very pleasant romances. His wife is a very agreeable young woman, who, among other things, is remarkable for having learnt to talk and read Russian absolutely fluently in two years. In spite of all my shyness, particularly with people belonging to exalted circles, I felt completely at home amongst these most kind and most august personages and truly enjoyed my conversations with them.

The whole theatre directorate has also expressed at every possible opportunity and in every possible way its support and readiness to take up my operas. It was never like this before.[113]

But I cannot complain of a lack of sympathy in Petersburg towards me, or rather towards my music. It is apparent everywhere at every possible opportunity. I was moved to tears on several occasions and felt the pride of an artist who has already won general recognition in his life. The highest manifestation of this was the celebration arranged in my honour last Wednesday, 5 November. I will not describe it because you probably already know about it from the papers.[114]

When he returned from St Petersburg Tchaikovsky spent some time at Maydanovo.

I have just returned to Maydanovo. What a joy it is to be at home, on one's own, without this unbearable mask which one involuntarily puts on when

---

[111] xiii. 489 (von Meck). [112] xiii. 493 (von Meck).
[113] xiii. 493 (von Meck). [114] xiii. 496 (Shpazhinskaya).

one circulates in society, forcing oneself to be worldly, to speak when one wants to be silent, to smile in a friendly manner when in one's heart one has no cause to smile, to chatter meaninglessly when one needs to work, and so on and so on. But then how can one avoid sinking up to the eyes in the social maelstrom every so often? How can one arrange it so that when one is an artist who addresses this crowd with outpourings of musical thought, striving to make them share these ideas and emotions, one can also turn away from this same crowd when it is trying to express its sympathy towards one by all the means at its disposal? One must be grateful and I try to express my gratitude forcefully, and I do not decline any invitations, meetings, etc. if I see in them a manifestation of real understanding. But how I pay for all this!!![115]

My return to Maydanovo did not bring me much joy. Instead of having a healthy active life I was poorly all the time. And I can't make out what it is. Firstly, at the slightest mental effort, not just when I am working but reading also, I immediately start to get a sort of ache inside my head which there is no other way of describing than as if a nail had been driven into the centre of my brain. Secondly my digestive system has begun to be troublesome again.[116]

My headaches became dreadfully intense. I was not free of them even at night. I couldn't sleep properly, I couldn't work, or read, or go for walks, and I was beginning to despair entirely. Then I suddenly got a telegram saying I was needed in Moscow for the opera rehearsals. My first reaction was to say that I would not attend the rehearsals and that I was going abroad. But at the same time I had the feeling that I was suddenly very much better, either from the anxieties I had gone through or for some other reason. Half an hour later I felt sleepy; I went to bed and had an excellent night's sleep, felt fine when I got up, went to Moscow, and straight to the rehearsal at the Bolshoy. Since then my health has been excellent.[117]

An event has occurred which is very significant for me. I *conducted* at the first orchestra rehearsal and conducted in such a way that (unless it's just flattery) everybody was astonished, because they had expected that I would be covered in shame. I cannot begin to tell you all the torments I underwent when Altani eventually fixed the rehearsal. My sufferings became unbearable as the dread day approached and I was frequently on the point of giving up the idea. But at last I somehow got a grip on myself, arrived, was given an enthusiastic reception by the players, made a fairly confident speech, and very confidently started waving my stick. Now I know that *I can conduct*, and I don't think that I would be frightened even at a performance.[118] The future will show whether I have done the right thing. If I emerge the victor from this painful struggle with myself then innumerable advantageous consequences for the success of my music could flow from it,

[115] xiii. 495–6 (Shpazhinskaya). [116] xiii. 507 (von Meck).
[117] xiii. 508 (von Meck). [118] xiii. 517–18 (Modest).

including an irresistible urge to prove to myself that my conviction of my utter incapability as a conductor is ill-founded. But who knows, perhaps it will all turn out all right. I am very pleased with the attitude towards me of all who are taking part and with the genuine encouragement which I meet at every turn, both from the singers and from the orchestral players. The décor of the opera will be very good. The scenery is excellent and so are the costumes. I owe all this to the former Director [Vsevolozhsky], who had made arrangements for the sumptuous décor of *Cherevichki* two years ago.[119]

It was at this time that the managements of the St Petersburg and Moscow Imperial Theatres were 'split' and Vsevolozhsky took charge of the St Petersburg theatres.

[119] xiii. 532 (von Meck).

19

1887

What a profound, powerful, indescribable pleasure a conductor feels when he stands at the head of a fine orchestra.

I greatly enjoyed spending the [Christmas] holidays at home; I was badly in need of a rest and these twelve days spent in the peace of the countryside have refreshed me very much. None the less I have been working extremely hard, that's to say I have kept on writing *The Sorceress*.[1]

I have rehearsals every day from 7 [January]. I will have to go through a lot of upsets and fears and all manner of alarms and anxieties. Then I will return to Maydanovo and get down to *The Sorceress* again. I often complain that I have to work without resting!!! But what would I do without work!!! The truth is that I cannot live a single day without it.[2]

Of course conducting does not come easily to me and demands a great effort from the whole nervous system. But I cannot deny that it also gives me great delight. First, I have the pleasure of realizing that I have overcome my innate and unhealthy shyness; secondly, it is remarkably pleasant for the composer of a new opera to be able himself to guide the course of his composition and not to have continually to approach the conductor, asking him to correct this or that mistake; thirdly, at every stage I see such genuine signs of support for me on the part of the performers that I am deeply touched and moved. Do you know, dear friend, I am *much less* anxious about the new opera than I used to be when I had to attend the rehearsals without having anything to do. I think that if it all goes well, the end result will be an improvement in my failing nerves rather than a breakdown.[3]

Fortified by the ardent enthusiasm of my friends, by the invaluable advice and guidance of Altani, and by a firm belief in the goodwill of the Moscow public, which encouraged me in my first steps as a composer and has never since denied me its vigorous support, on 19 January 1887 at eight o'clock in the evening I mounted the conductor's rostrum before the orchestra of the Imperial Bolshoy Theatre and successfully conducted the first performance of *Cherevichki*.[4]

Let me describe in brief how the first performance went off. There was a dress rehearsal two days before the performance. I had got so used to

[1] xiv. 16 (von Meck).   [2] xiv. 16–17 (von Meck).
[3] xiv. 18 (von Meck).   [4] *MC* 334–5.

conducting during the rehearsals that I had scarcely any nerves before the final one and thought it would be the same on the first night. But on the day before I started feeling almost ill with anxiety and when I woke on the morning of the 19th I really was ill and even considered withdrawing. I don't know how I got through that dreadful day; I suffered agonies. I turned up at the appointed time in a state of semi-consciousness. When the fateful hour came, I went out to the orchestra like an automaton. Thunderous applause crashed forth, they started sending wreaths down from the stage, and the orchestra played a flourish. Things were better already. I began the overture very confidently and I got calmer the further we went. I came out for Act II as calm as an Altani who has been conducting all his life. There were more than enough presentations, wreaths, bows, ovations, and the like. Everybody is unanimous in saying that I have gifts as a conductor. If this is true it is strange that I have been mistaken all my life and have imagined that I was, on the contrary, quite incompetent in this respect. Be that as it may, everything went off very well. I am very pleased with the performance. Unfortunately Krutikova fell ill (an excellent Solokha), and Svyatlovskaya sang in her place; she is a good singer but quite unsuited to the role. Of the others the best were Klimentova [Oxana], Korsov [Devil], and Usatov [Vakula]. My relatives who were there, apart from Modest, were my brother Kolya and Nix Litke. I will conduct another two performances.[5]

I was almost forty-seven at that time. At that age a real, true, born conductor has, apart from those qualities which depend on the degree of his innate ability, many years of experience; if one takes into account that I did not have this, my début can be considered entirely successful. I continue to be of the opinion that although I have no real gift as a conductor and although I know that I do not have that combination of physical and mental requirements which make a man who is a musician *in general* into one who is *primarily* a conductor, even so, this experience and all subsequent experiences showed that I can more or less successfully direct a performance of my own works, and that is exactly what I needed for my greater happiness.[6]

On the day after the first performance of *Cherevichki* we received news here of the sudden death of my poor niece Tanya. Though I had, in truth, often thought that death was the best and most desirable way out for the unfortunate girl, all the same I was deeply shocked by the news. She died in Petersburg at a *bal-masqué* in the Hall of the Nobility. Morphia destroyed her, and one way or another a tragic outcome was inevitable. I am going out of my mind at the thought of how my poor sister and brother-in-law will bear their sorrow. After all, the less joy their unfortunate, sick daughter gave them, the more her *parents* loved her.[7] The second performance of *Cherevichki* went more smoothly and evenly than the first. Krutikova was

[5] xiv. 25–6 (Panya).   [6] *MC* 335.   [7] xiv. 23–4 (von Meck).

not in good voice but she is still better than Svyatlovskaya. The audience
was quite cool at first but gradually roused itself and by the end there was as
much noise and shouting as you could ask for. I found the conducting
much more difficult than the first time; there were occasions when my fear
and dread made me feel that at any moment I might be unable to wield the
stick any longer. However, nobody noticed. My own explanation of this is
that I was generally *too* exhausted by all my recent experiences. It is time to
go home! It is indeed! My heart aches and swoons with delight whenever I
think that I will soon be in the country on my own.[8] The third performance
also went off very well. Again, as on the first two occasions, I was crazy with
nerves at the beginning, then soon calmed down and my confidence, so they
say, grew. I am under no misapprehensions that so far people do not so
much like the opera as find it interesting. The audience is particularly puzzled at the beginning and is really quite cool, but it warms up as things go
on and Act IV is always a great success. I think that, like *Onegin*, *Cherevichki* will not create very much fuss but gradually people will come to like
this opera as well. From the affection which I cherish for it myself, I am
sure that the public too will come to love it one day.[9]

I cannot find words to describe my joy when at last, on the morning of
the 29th, I set off for home. Unfortunately I am not resting but am working
with feverish haste, sometimes like a madman, on *The Sorceress*. There
stretches before me such an endless string of planned and promised work
that I am frightened to look into the future. How short our life is! Now that
I have probably reached the highest point of perfection of which I am capable, I must inevitably look back, and as I think of how many years I have
lived I look nervously at the road ahead and wonder: can I manage it, is it
worth it? And yet it is perhaps only now that I can write without self-doubt,
with faith in my powers and my skill.[10]

Imagine, my dear friend [Mme von Meck], I am being earnestly
requested to conduct a big concert in Petersburg in the third week of Lent
which will be devoted entirely to my own works, and I want to try myself
out as a symphonic conductor. Once I have started, why not continue? If,
God willing, the concert goes as well as the opera, that means I will have
the opportunity, when a suitable occasion arises, of personally contributing
to the success of my compositions—this is very important, and if I had had
the courage in the distant past to appear as a conductor, who knows how
much more decisively and rapidly my reputation as a respectable composer
would have been established? I am already beginning to dream of arranging
some concerts abroad in due course, but who knows what I will be thinking
of next? . . . Oh! If only I were twenty years younger!!! One thing is certain
and that is that my nerves have improved marvellously and that things that
I could not contemplate before have now become possible. Of course it

---

[8] xiv. 30 (Modest).   [9] xiv. 34–5 (Modest).   [10] xiv. 37–8 (von Meck).

goes without saying that for all this I am beholden to the freedom of a life relieved of financial cares. And who is it, if it is not you, my dear, who is the source of everything good that providence sends me![11]

Six weeks after experience had shown that I was competent to direct an orchestra in an opera I had to try myself out on the concert platform as well. The Philharmonic Society gave a concert on 5 March 1887 in the Hall of the Nobility in Petersburg; the programme consisted entirely of my works and I conducted the performance myself. This experiment too was crowned with success.[12]

I probably have already told you [Mme von Meck] that I did want to make my début in Petersburg as a conductor but at the same time it was very frightening. Sometimes this fear grew so great that I was thinking about refusing to conduct and leaving, because I considered that I was incapable of conquering my timidity. The first rehearsal was the most terrible business of all; I spent the night before in a state of great torment and agitation and turned up to the rehearsal looking almost ill. But, oddly enough, no sooner had I gone up to the rostrum, taken up the baton (at which the members of the orchestra enthusiastically applauded me), than all my fear instantly vanished, and in everyone's opinion, I performed my task well. At the following rehearsals my confidence was complete.[13]

The composer's own concert took place on 5 March 1887. The programme consisted of: the Suite No. 2 (first performance in St Petersburg), an aria and the Dance of the Mummers from *The Sorceress*, the Andante and Waltz from the *Serenade* for string orchestra, *Francesca da Rimini*, some songs, and the *Overture 1812*.

At the concert itself, of course, I was very agitated before I went on but this was not so much fear as a foretaste of that intense artistic delight which a composer feels when he stands at the head of a fine orchestra which is performing his works with enthusiasm and affection. Pleasure of this order was unknown to me until recently; it is so powerful and unusual that I cannot put it into words. Even if my attempts at conducting have cost me an immense and difficult struggle with myself, if they have taken several years off my life, I have no regrets. I have experienced moments of unalloyed happiness and bliss. During the concert the audience and the players frequently expressed their warm enthusiasm for my work and the whole evening of 5 March will always be one of my pleasantest memories.[14] One thing I will say: I had never imagined what a profound, powerful, indescribable pleasure a conductor feels when he stands at the head of a fine orchestra. It is an incomparable feeling which rises at moments to a tremulous rapture. At that concert I felt as though I really did command the wills of all one hundred people who were following my baton. And where did I get this power from? Ah! what a mystery is man! I have never considered myself

[11] xiv. 42–3 (von Meck).   [12] *MC* 335.
[13] xiv. 58 (von Meck).   [14] Ibid.

particularly expert on my 'inner being' and suddenly that 'inner being' shows sides of me that I did not know I had![15]

To my immense astonishment I have heard from the mouths of people whose views I trust entirely such flattering reports of my conducting that my heart beat in my breast with joy, and I could not stifle a sense of pride at knowing that I had conquered myself as well as that savage, vicious, tormenting mental illness which I have suffered from so long and so much throughout my life and which is called *shyness*. One very well-known music critic [Cui], who is always quite unrestrained in his criticisms of me, the same who greeted my début as a composer with the words: 'Mr T. is altogether bad; he has not got a spark of talent'—this same dread, wrathful, but incorruptible critic of the printed page said of me, again of course utterly distorting the truth with his exaggerations, that I am a *'superb'* conductor. I didn't believe him this time either, any more than I did when he condemned my absolute lack of talent earlier. A forty-seven-year-old man making his first appearance with the conductor's baton cannot be 'superb', cannot even hope to become so, even if he has the essential natural attributes; and I know perfectly well that my innate timidity, weakness of character, and lack of self-confidence prevent me, and always will prevent me from competing as a conductor with Wagner, Bülow, and Nápravník. I repeat, all I cared about was that I should be no worse than any other conducting mediocrity when I stood in front of an orchestra playing my own works. I foresaw that thanks to this victory over my incapacity I would now have the opportunity to propagandize my works both at home and abroad and what I had foreseen very soon became reality. The very natural desire to widen the circle of my reputation as a composer as much as possible did not prevent me from entertaining the hope that I would also be able to serve the cause of Russian art by means of propagandizing the works of other Russian composers.[16]

I eventually tore myself away from Petersburg; I am at Maydanovo now. I settled down to work as soon as I arrived and, as always, I am working too hard, to the point of exhaustion.[17]

My impressions of *The Power of Darkness*. One could say a very great deal about this. I regard Lev Tolstoy as the most powerful and profound genius which literature has ever known. Usually, when people want to indicate the measure of an artist's genius they compare him with somebody. Another admirer of Tolstoy might say, for instance, that he is 'the equal of Shakespeare' or 'greater than Pushkin'. But for me Tolstoy is beyond all comparisons and is as isolated in his unassailable grandeur as any Everest or Dhaulagiri amongst the other summits. I will not, I am not capable of launching into explanations of why I find him so lofty and so profound; this

---

[15] xiv. 66 (Shpazhinskaya).   [16] *MC* 335–6.   [17] xiv. 61 (von Meck).

astonishing power is something which I *feel* rather than *know*. But the main feature, or, better, the main *note* which sounds on every page of Tolstoy, however apparently trivial its content, is—*love*, compassion for humanity *at large* (not just for the *insulted* and the *injured*), pity for its insignificance, its feebleness, for the transitoriness of life, for the vanity of its aspirations. Take, for instance, the chapter where the young people are playing cards:* now what could be more mundane, more trivial than that? And yet you weep!!! This is precisely because so much is between the lines, and this *so much* has an astonishing and unfathomable effect on the heart and soul. So Tolstoy is for me the most precious, profound, and greatest of artists. But this is the former Tolstoy who has nothing in common with the present importunate moralist and theoretician. I can see his masterly skill in everything that he writes now, but I do not find that source of deep delight and rapture, that mysterious, irresistible attraction exercised by his earlier works. As to *The Power of Darkness*, leaving aside the message, which you can praise or blame, I can find only one major virtue in it: *mastery of language*. Everything else, if you think about it, is remarkably false and strange, and on occasion infuriating. Suffice it to say that incorrigible villains like *Matryona* belong in cheap melodrama and not in a serious play. To think that *Tolstoy* could create this character, who is as loathsome as she is *untrue*!!! It is beyond understanding! And the revolting girl, *potty* and *deaf*, who becomes the object of the hero's passions, and that *hero*, full to overflowing with improbable contradictions and incomprehensible contrasts! There are, of course, scenes which are moving, as when the old man talks to the girl. In sum, *The Power of Darkness* is in my view the work of a great craftsman, but not of a great artist. In the *artist* we see absolute truth, not in the banal, legalistic sense, but in a higher sense which opens up unknown horizons, areas so inaccessible that only *music* can penetrate them, but no writer has gone further into them than Tolstoy as he used to be.[18]

I was very taken by Chekhov's story [*The Laymen*] in *Novoye vremya* [*New Times*]. He is very gifted, isn't he? I am writing to nobody, seeing nobody, and have got so engrossed in *The Sorceress* that I feel like one of the characters myself.[19]

I should have gone away about a month ago and here I am still [24 April] here. It's my work that has kept me, scoring the opera. It isn't really particularly difficult work but it's very laborious. And it's odd: the older I get, the more problems I find in my work. I am getting stricter with myself, more careful and discriminating in choosing colourings and nuances. How-

---

* Here Tchaikovsky seems to be talking about the episode in *War and Peace* where Dolokhov beats Rostov at cards (see p. 300) [trans.].

[18] xiv. 74–5 (Shpazhinskaya).   [19] xiv. 95 (Modest).

ever, it turns out that I must let them have three-quarters of the whole opera before I leave so I have decided to stay at my desk until I have done what they need. On occasions like this living in the country is an absolute boon. I have no hindrances from anybody or anything. Now that spring is coming my health is fine again. The nearer you get to old age the more lively is your pleasure in living close to nature. Never before have I so revelled in the delights of spring, the appearance of the new shoots, the return of the birds, and everything else that comes with the Russian spring, which really is something especially beautiful and joyous.[20]

I am very pleased that I have at last managed to finish my opera; I felt that one more week and my cup would have been running over. At the moment [14 May], of course, I have no notion at all of writing anything else. It has been particularly nice at Maydanovo this spring but I have left without any regrets because the holiday visitors turned up recently and the charm of the place instantly vanished. In all probability I will not go back there any more, because I would dearly like to spend the first half of next winter abroad and then look for somewhere else to live after that.[21] When I had finished *The Sorceress* I went to Petersburg where I spent ten days or so with my friend [Kondratyev] who is ill and doomed.[22]

From St Petersburg Tchaikovsky went via Moscow to Nizhny Novgorod, thence down the Volga to Astrakhan, by sea to Baku, and by train to Tiflis.

I have no regrets at all about choosing such a long way round because I have seen much that is new and interesting. I left Moscow on 20 [May] for Nizhny Novgorod. After a struggle I managed to get a second-class ticket for the steamer, the *Alexander II*, which was bursting with passengers. I was very uncomfortable and cramped, but on the whole I still very much enjoyed my trip on the Volga. The river is in full flood just now. Our 'Mother Volga' really is grand and majestically poetic. The right bank is hilly and frequently offers very fine landscapes, but, of course, the Volga cannot even be compared in this respect with the Rhine, or even with the Danube and the Rhône. The beauty, however, is not in the banks but in the limitless expanse, in the sheer extent of the water, which, without seething or rushing, peacefully rolls down to the sea. We stopped long enough at the various ports of call to get an idea of what they were like. The towns I liked most were Samara and another little place called Volsk, which has one of the best parks I have ever seen. It took us five days to get to Astrakhan. The Caspian Sea turned out to be very perfidious. We started rolling so much during the night that I was quite frightened. I thought that at any minute the waves were going to smash the boat up altogether. There was such a noise that I didn't get a wink of sleep all night. However, I wasn't seasick.[23] I enjoyed the journey very much because the very nature of our broad

[20] xiv. 98 (von Meck).   [21] xiv. 112 (von Meck).
[22] xiv. 115 (Shpazhinskaya).   [23] xiv. 116–17 (von Meck).

Mother Volga is so much in tune with the Russian spirit, which has an inherent leaning towards all that is broad, majestically calm, and unvarying. And I am so fond of the sea that even the stormy *Caspian* puddle seemed delightful to me.[24] I eventually arrived in Tiflis after a journey lasting ten days. Much to my surprise, Baku turned out to be attractive in every way: the buildings are handsome and laid out on a regular pattern, it is clean, and, moreover, has a lot of character, because the eastern element (the Persian element to be precise) is so predominant that you could think you were somewhere on the far side of the Caspian. The only thing wrong is an absence of greenery. The bathing is magnificent. The day after I arrived I went to see the area where they extract oil. It's an impressive sight, but a gloomy one.[25]

The heat in Tiflis was unbearable and I was very glad to get away. The road to Borzhom is very good, and picturesque too. Borzhom itself seemed a gloomy and depressing place for the first few hours after I got there. I think that any Russian, used to space and broad horizons, would feel the same as I did if he found himself in a narrow valley hemmed in by enormous mountains. But this feeling of *eeriness* went the next day, after my first walk. This place is heaven on earth for anyone who likes going for walks. The parks are splendid and they all lead directly into thick, shady woods. On the very first morning I was so carried away by a marvellous walk along a little path which lead me into the woods and then into an open space which gave a view over the most incredibly beautiful landscape that I fell well and truly in love with Borzhom. There is a remarkable variety of walks and you hardly meet anybody, which I particularly like. I have decided to take a cure here and to have warm baths every day. The water is very like that at Vichy.[26] I don't know whether it is the effect of the waters, or the air, or my way of life (I am walking a tremendous amount), but up to now I have felt no urge at all 'to create' and am therefore doing practically nothing at all. I say 'practically' because for about an hour a day I work at scoring some of Mozart's piano pieces which should form a suite by the end of the summer. I think that this suite will have a great future, especially abroad, thanks to the happy choice of pieces and its *novelty* (*the past in modern dress*).[27]

I am leaving with the next steamer from Batum to Odessa, and from there to Aachen because of Kondratyev's telegram from Aachen. He wired: 'Supplie venir, votre arrivée peut me ressusciter.' I must go.[28] I left Borzhom on 6 July, got the steamer on the 7th and took five days to get to Odessa. I left Odessa on the 12th, stopped in Vienna for just an hour or two and arrived [in Aachen] on the evening of the 15th. I was terribly gloomy all the way and couldn't even think about Borzhom without tears; I had so much enjoyed everything about my stay there and now I had had to leave so

---

[24] xiv. 121–2 (Jurgenson).   [25] xiv. 117–18 (von Meck).
[26] xiv. 122–3 (von Meck).   [27] xiv. 132–3 (Jurgenson).

suddenly. But my gloom has gone now because there are other things to think about. I have had to be so constantly with a very difficult patient, for whom my company is not just a pleasure but a simple necessity, that I have had no time to distract myself from my worries and torment myself with reminiscences and regrets about the past.[29]

I was captivated by Yalta; I had a good walk around. I admired the remaining beauty spots of the southern coast from the steamer. We didn't stop anywhere after Sebastopol. At night it was quite rough. This morning we have arrived in Odessa.[30]

It's strange: I am crushed by *horror* and *misery*, but not by pity!!! Perhaps this is because N. D. is showing fear and faint-heartedness in the face of death and though I am probably just as cowardly myself about death, when he starts *wailing* in despair like a woman or a child I find it terrible rather than pitiful. I cannot understand why I should be so hardened. But I *do* know—I am not wicked and heartless, it is my nerves and my *egoism* which keeps whispering in my ear, louder and louder: 'Go away, don't torment yourself, take care of yourself!' But I dare not even think about leaving yet.[31]

I am no longer in a fit state to relate the saga of Nikolay Dmitriyevich's illness and am altogether incapable of doing anything else, writing, etc. I have but one thought and one feeling: to make the time pass as quickly as possible until the 25th and then to leave. Every minute lasts as long as a whole day did a month ago. You cannot imagine how terrible and exhausting is this long drawn-out process of a man gradually dying, when you have constantly to assure him that he is getting better. I am now deeply convinced that Nikolay Dmitriyevich will not recover.[32]

The six weeks which I have spent in Aachen in the constant company of a man who is doomed, who is suffering terribly and yet cannot die have been an indescribably excruciating experience for me. It has been one of the most sombre periods of my life. I have aged a great deal and lost a lot of weight during this time. I feel a tiredness of life, a sad apathy, as though I too have to die soon, and because death is near everything in my personal life which was important and essential now seems trivial, insignificant, and quite pointless. Probably this will soon pass and I will settle down again as a musician who works and strives for the ideal.[33]

I left Aachen on 25 August. The last fortnight was so dreadful that I don't know now how I could bear it. Kondratyev was in indescribable pain the whole time. I was in Petersburg on the 29th, where I had to see Kondratyev's relatives, and I came here [Maydanovo] on the 30th just to get a bit of rest. I only needed a week in the country on my own to recover. On 7 [September] I went to Petersburg to be at the first read-through of *The Sorceress* and to resolve various doubts and misunderstandings. At the

[28] xiv. 141 (Jurgenson).   [29] xiv. 154 (von Meck).   [30] xiv. 146 (Kolya).
[31] *Diaries*, 170.   [32] xiv. 194 (Modest).   [33] xiv. 202–3 (von Meck).

read-through I realized that some of the scenes are so drawn-out and tiring for both singers and audience that I immediately decided to thoroughly revise some parts of the opera. These revisions are what I am doing at the moment.[34]

Kondratyev died on 21 September, when Tchaikovsky had already returned home.

How short life is! How much one wants to do, to think about, to say! One puts things off, thinking that there is so much time left, but death is already lying in wait around the corner. How much has changed! How strange that three hundred and sixty-five days ago I was still frightened to admit that, for all the warmth of the sympathy aroused in me by Christ, I still dared to doubt his divinity. Since then my *religion* has taken a much clearer form; I have thought much about God, and life, and death throughout this time, and in Aachen particularly the fateful questions why? how? what for? frequently exercised me and passed alarmingly before me. I would like to set down my *religion* in detail some time, if only to clarify to myself once and for all my beliefs and the point at which they begin and my philosophy ends. But life rushes on with all its cares and I do not know if I will have time to give expression to that *creed* which I have evolved of late. It has evolved in very clear terms but I still give it no practical application in my prayers. I always pray in the old way, as I was taught to. In any case God hardly needs to know how or why we pray. He does not need our prayers, but *we do*.[35]

I arrived in Petersburg [on 29 September] for the first orchestral rehearsal. As usual, I was very agitated, but everything went off all right. I am very pleased with the performers and particularly with the care which Nápravník has brought to learning the opera.[36] The first performance of *The Sorceress* is on the 20th. My exhaustion is extreme. There have been days when I have come home from rehearsals so utterly drained that I have refused my dinner and have gone straight to bed until the next morning. None the less, as last year during the rehearsals for *Cherevichki*, I feel incomparably calmer and more content than during previous productions of my operas, when I have not been conducting myself. The position of the composer of an opera which is being learnt is very awkward and peculiar if he is not directly participating in the general effort; it's a different matter now, because when I stand on the conductor's rostrum I know I am really in charge and in control of everything that goes on in the theatre. In general I am satisfied with the performance of the opera, but, unfortunately, my principal singer, Mme Pavlovskaya, is not a success. She has lost her voice entirely and is barely audible. But about two years ago, when she was far better, I promised her that the role of the Sorceress should be hers, and I cannot break my word. The scenery, the costumes, the whole *mise en scène* is splendid.[37]

[34] xiv. 212–13 (Shpazhinskaya).   [35] *Diaries*, 213.
[36] xiv. 234–5 (von Meck).   [37] xiv. 244 (von Meck).

On the day of the performance I was very agitated, as was to be expected. When I made my appearance in the orchestra I was greeted with friendly banging on the desks. Act I did not go too well. Pavlovskaya [Kuma] was so late with her exit in one scene that people got muddled and confused and I had to stop the orchestra. Fortunately Koryakin prompted her with the music and words where we had stopped and everything sorted itself out. After Act I the artists presented me with a silver wreath. The second act went very well. In the third, Pavlovskaya overplayed and sang very poorly; the effect was cold. Many of the numbers in the fourth act were well received, and the storm, with Melnikov's excellent acting [as the Prince], was very effective. The second performance went more smoothly and cleanly, but it was colder, apart from the ending. In sum, I would say that *The Sorceress* is not very popular and the fault lies both with me and, principally, with Ippolit Vasilyevich [Shpazhinsky]. He has an excellent knowledge of the stage but has still not made much adjustment to the demands of opera. He has too many words; *conversation* predominates too much over lyricism. However much I shortened his text, however many *cuts* I found myself obliged to make, I still found that on the whole the scenes were coming out too long. But I am to blame for a lot. I am not despairing by any means; I think this is an opera one has to get used to; later, when the public has had the chance to hear it a few times, it will be accepted into the repertoire.[38]

I am going through a very stormy period in my life and am constantly in a nervous condition. When I had conducted my opera four times I came [home] in a very melancholy frame of mind. Despite the ovations which I was given at the first performance the public does not really like my opera and it was not, in truth, a success. I was met with such malice and ill will on the part of the Petersburg press that I have still not come round and I cannot explain to myself—why? what for? I have never put so much work and effort into any other opera and yet I have never before been the object of such persecution by the press.[39]

For two years I worked on *The Sorceress*, exerted myself to the utmost so that the opera might turn out to be my greatest achievement, and then what happened? This unfortunate *Sorceress* has turned out to be a real fiasco.[40]

Whilst he was in St Petersburg Tchaikovsky heard Rimsky-Korsakov's *Spanish Caprice* at a rehearsal; he was also present at the first performance (Russian Symphony Concert on 31 October, with Rimsky-Korsakov conducting) and presented a wreath to the composer. In a letter to Rimsky-Korsakov he wrote: 'Your *Spanish Caprice* is a tremendous *chef-d'œuvre* of *orchestration*. You may boldly regard yourself as the greatest of contemporary craftsmen.'[41]

Here I am rehearsing every day for a big orchestral concert which I will

---

[38] xiv. 250 (Shpazhinskaya).
[40] xiv. 273 (von Meck).
[39] xiv. 255 (von Meck).
[41] xiv. 252 (Rimsky-Korsakov).

conduct tomorrow, the 14th. I am terribly tired and sometimes fear that I will ruin my health with all these excitements and alarms. I have refused a trip to Tiflis but I will only just have time to rest a little at home in Mayda-novo for on the 2nd January (new style) I have to conduct in Leipzig, then in Dresden, Hamburg, Copenhagen, Berlin, and Prague. Then I will give my own concert in Paris in March and from there I have been invited to London for a concert of the Philharmonic Society. In short, a wealth of new and powerful impressions lies ahead of me. My fame will probably in-crease greatly after all these travels—but wouldn't it be better to stay at home and work? God only knows. One thing I can say is that I miss the time when I was left quietly in peace to live in the solitude of the country-side.[42]

Both of the concerts I conducted in Moscow were very successful, and the second one particularly (where the audience wasn't up to much) left me with the most pleasant impression, the like of which I have never experi-enced before. I cannot describe the rapturous enthusiasm which was expressed to me.[43]

Tchaikovsky conducted the Symphony Concert of the Moscow branch of the RMS on 14 November. The programme consisted of: *Francesca da Rimini*, the *Concert Fantasia* (with Taneyev as soloist), the *Overture 1812*, an arioso from *The Sorceress*, and some songs (Skompskaya). The programme was repeated at a matinée open to the public on 15 November. These were the first occasions on which Tchaikovsky appeared in Moscow as an orchestral conductor.

Not long ago I wrote six romances to the words of the poet K*** R*** [the Grand Duke Konstantin Konstantinovich] who is full of lively poetic feel-ing and congenial to me. I wrote them in particularly unfavourable circum-stances and am afraid that you will not like them. Nevertheless may I take the liberty of requesting your permission to dedicate them to your High-ness. The romances are being engraved at the moment and I take the liberty of asking your Highness to order official permission to be granted to my publisher (P. I. Jurgenson, Moscow, Neglinny Proyezd, No. 10) for them to be dedicated to your Imperial Highness.[44]

The six romances Op. 63 were composed between November and early December 1887 and were dedicated to the author of the texts.

I have been yearning for you [Mme von Meck]. Circumstances have fallen out so that communications between us have not been so constant of late, and on occasion it has seemed that I had become something of a stranger to you. And yet I have never thought of you so much and so often as I have in the days just gone by. I have come away to Maydanovo for a short rest; the abnormal state of my mind and body make it impossible for me to work,

[42] xiv. 255 (von Meck).   [43] xiv. 262 (Shpazhinskaya).
[44] xiv. 290–1 (K.R.).

but frequently I ponder a lot and reminisce. At precisely this time ten years ago I was going through the most tragic period of my life and God knows what would have come of me if you had not appeared with moral and material support. The smallest details of that now remote past are still clear and vivid in my mind. My heartfelt gratitude fills me with veneration for you. What moral strength I derived from your letters then, from your innumerable expressions of friendship and concern! Much water has flowed under the bridge since then and much has changed. Much work, too, has been done in these ten years and I have, so it seems to me, constantly moved forward in my activities, though alas, just as before, I even now have to contend with inaccurate and unfair criticisms on the part of the so-called *mob*.[45]

Mme von Meck replied to Tchaikovsky: 'How could you think, my dear, that you had become more of *a stranger* to me than you were before? On the contrary, the more time passes, the more disappointments and sorrow I suffer, the *nearer and dearer* you are to me.' (von Meck, iii. 508)

It was especially pleasant to see your writing again, to read your kind words about my music, in short, to be in touch with you.[46] I spent about a week in Petersburg; I took part, successfully, in one of the Musical Society concerts; I was terribly depressed all the time I was in P'burg because I am going abroad only with the greatest reluctance.[47]

Tchaikovsky conducted *Mozartiana* at the III Symphony Concert of the St Petersburg branch of the RMS on 12 December 1887.

[45] xiv. 273 (von Meck).   [46] xiv. 279 (von Meck).   [47] xiv. 291 (Anatoly).

20

1887–1888

In honouring me, the whole of Russian music is honoured.

Amongst the innumerable benefits arising (from my conducting) there was also my three-month concert tour of Western Europe; I cannot but be proud of the success which I enjoyed. If we discount Glinka, who gave only one concert in Paris, and Anton Rubinstein, who has long been known abroad because of his brilliance as a virtuoso, then I am the first Russian composer personally to have acquainted foreign audiences with his works.[1]

Tchaikovsky made his first foreign tour in a professional capacity at the end of 1887 and the beginning of 1888. This tour firmly established his reputation in Europe.

It is very difficult to give a precise and detailed description of all that I have experienced and will experience in the near future.[2] Leipzig, with its famous Gewandhaus, is regarded as the musical centre, the capital of Germany. The audience for these concerts is very conservative, and very prejudiced against any novelty, particularly if it is Russian. I was very anxious. The local musical bigwigs were very attentive to me; the orchestral players were soon fired with enthusiasm and the performance was more than excellent. It was a real success, which came as a complete surprise to many. This is very important because it gives me great authority in the eyes of all other *audiences* in Germany. The tendency is different at the other musical institution in Leipzig, the Liszt Verein; they organized a real triumph for me here, with countless bows and wild applause in the Russian fashion.[3]

Tchaikovsky conducted the Suite No. 1 in Leipzig, and the Trio in memory of a great artist and the First Quartet were performed at the Liszt Verein.

After these two very important days for me, I stayed on in Leipzig for another whole week and later visited this town twice more, spending a few days each time. In order not to have to return to the subject of Leipzig again I will describe some of the interesting people I met there and set down some other facts worthy of mention. Leipzig opera boasts a young conductor of genius, Nikisch, who is a specialist in Wagner's music drama of the later period. I heard there *Das Rheingold* (the first part of the famous tetralogy) and *Die Meistersinger von Nürnberg*. The theatre orchestra is the

[1] *MC* 335. [2] xiv. 296 (Modest). [3] xiv. 326 (Pogozhev).

same as in the Gewandhaus and consequently excellent, but however irreproachable its concert performances under the baton of Karl Reinecke, a real conception of what heights orchestral perfection can achieve under the direction of a conductor of genius can only be attained in a performance of Wagner's difficult, complex score, with an incomparable master of such things conducting like Mr Nikisch. His conducting has nothing in common with the effective and in its own way inimitable conducting of Hans von Bülow. Just as the latter is mobile, restless, and effective in his way of conducting, which is sometimes very distracting, so Nikisch is elegantly calm, sparing of unnecessary gesture, but at the same time wonderfully masterful, powerful, and full of self-control. He does not conduct but it is as if he surrenders himself to some mysterious sorcery; you hardly notice him, he does not at all try to attract attention to himself, but meanwhile the effect is that the huge corpus of the orchestra, like an instrument in the hands of an amazing master, is completely and helplessly under the control of its chief. This chief, a small, very pale young man of about thirty, with beautiful, radiant eyes, must indeed have some sort of magic power, making the orchestra now thunder like a thousand trumpets of Jericho, now coo like a dove, and now die away with breathtaking mystery. And all this is achieved without the audience noticing the diminutive conductor, quietly ruling his orchestra, who slavishly obey him.[4]

I have neither time nor opportunity to describe in detail all my experiences here. What I feel more than anything is an insane, agonizing, despairing longing for my own country. It is only in circumstances like this that you realize how much you love your motherland. If it were not for Brodsky, with his sweet Russian wife, and Ziloti, who looks after me like a nanny, I would throw everything up and leave. On the other hand, my artistic vanity has cause for nothing but joy. So I constantly veer from despair and insane melancholy to pleasure and even happiness. I have been on the booze with Brahms. He's very nice, and not at all proud, as I had imagined. But the one who is really charming is Grieg. He and his wife are a delightful and attractive pair. I made a speech in German before the first rehearsal. 'Meine Herrn, ich kann nicht deutsch reden, aber ich bin stolz das ich mit einen . . . so . . . so . . . das heisst . . . ich bin . . . stolz . . . ich kann nicht . . . !!!' That was my speech.[5]

Brahms is remarkably straightforward, without the slightest arrogance; he has a very cheerful disposition and the few hours I spent in his company have left me with very pleasant memories. Unfortunately, I have to admit that in spite of my reasonably lengthy stay in Leipzig at the same time as Brahms, I did not succeed in getting closer to this most outstanding representative of contemporary German music. There is a reason for this. Like all my Russian musician friends, without exception, I respect Brahms only as

[4] *MC* 353.   [5] xiv. 298–9 (Jurgenson).

an honest, single-minded, and energetic figure, but however much I might wish it, I have never been able and am still not able to love his music. In Germany *Brahmsianism* has an enormous following; there are masses of authorities and whole musical establishments specifically devoted to the cult of Brahms, holding him to be a talent of the highest order, almost equal to Beethoven. But there are also anti-Brahmsians in Germany; and outside the frontiers of Germany, the most complete ignorance and lack of knowledge about Brahms reigns supreme everywhere, with the possible exception of London where thanks to the energetic propaganda of the violinist Joachim, who is remarkably popular with the English, Brahms's greatness is to a certain extent recognized. But he has nowhere managed to establish himself less than in our country. In the music of this master there is something dry, cold, misty, and undefined, which is alien to the Russian soul. From our Russian point of view Brahms has no melodic invention at all; his musical ideas are never developed to a conclusion; hardly have you heard a hint of a recognizable melodic phrase than it has already fallen into a whirlpool of insignificant harmonic sequences and modulations, as if the composer had set himself the specific task of appearing incomprehensible and deep; he seems to tease and play on our musical sensibilities, he does not wish to satisfy their demands, and is ashamed to speak in a language which will reach our hearts. When you hear his music, you ask yourself: is Brahms deep or is he only trying to cover up his extreme poverty of invention with an imitation of depth? And this question is never fully resolved. Listening to Brahms it is quite impossible to say to yourself that this music is weak or utterly insignificant. His style is always lofty; unlike all of us contemporary composers, he never resorts to superficial effects, doesn't try to surprise, or amaze us with some new and brilliant orchestral combination; nor will you ever meet in his music banality or imitation; it is all very serious, very noble, and, seemingly, even original—but despite all this it lacks the most important thing: beauty! That is my response to Brahms's compositions and as far as I know all Russian musicians and the Russian public in general have exactly the same opinion as I do. Once, several years ago, when I spoke frankly of my opinion of Brahms to Hans von Bülow, he replied: 'Wait a little, there will come a time when the depth and beauty of Brahms will be revealed to you; like you I didn't understand him for a long time, but gradually I was rewarded with a revelation of Brahms's genius and the same thing will happen to you.' And so I wait and wait but revelation does not come. I deeply respect Brahms as an artist; I bow down before the virginal purity of his musical aspirations; I admire his constancy and haughty renunciation of any relaxation in the spirit of triumphant Wagnerianism, or even Lisztianism—but I do not like his music.[6]

I went to a chamber-music concert where they played a quartet by a re-

6 *MC* 342–3.

markably gifted Italian, Ferruccio Busoni. We soon got to know each other
and became friends. Brodsky gave a musical soirée where I was delighted to
hear Grieg's new sonata. In my view Grieg has immense gifts. His music is
infused with a captivating melancholy which reflects the beauties of the
Norwegian landscape, at one moment grand and majestically broad, at the
next sombre, undramatic, lean—but always immeasurably captivating to
the spirit of a northerner; it is somehow closely akin to us and readily finds a
warm and sympathetic response in our hearts. Perhaps Grieg has much less
mastery than Brahms, the sphere of his music is less elevated, his aims and
aspirations are not as broad, and he has absolutely no pretensions to
plumbing the depths, but on the other hand he is closer to us, more accessible, he is our kin, for he is deeply human. On hearing Grieg we instinct-
ively recognize that the music is written by a man who is moved by an
irresistible impulse to pour out in sound the surging moods and sensations
of a deeply poetic nature which obeys no theory, no principle, no slogan
coined by the chance circumstances of the times—but which does obey the
thrust of a vital, sincere artistic sensitivity. Perfection of form, strictness,
and irreproachable logicality in the development of themes (which, it
should be said, are always fresh, new, and stamped with the characteristic
features of Germano–Scandinavian nationalism) are not things that we will
diligently search for in this famous Norwegian. But on the other hand what
delight, immediacy, and richness of musical invention does he give us! How
much warmth and passion there is in his singing phrases, what pulsating
life in his harmony, how much originality and delightful individuality in
his witty, piquant modulations, and in the rhythm, like everything else,
there is always something interesting, new, and distinctive. If we add to all
these rare qualities utter simplicity, devoid of the slightest artifice or pretensions to unheard of depths and novelty (and many contemporary composers, including Russians, suffer from unhealthy aspirations to find new
paths, without having the slightest true calling or natural talent) then it is
not surprising that Grieg is so much loved and that he is popular everywhere. And let it not be thought self-praise that my eulogy of Grieg's talent
was preceded by a declaration that his nature and mine have a deep inner
kinship. In going on to speak of Grieg's most excellent qualities I did not at
all want to give the reader the impression that I possess all these qualities in
equal measure. I suggest others decide how much I am lacking in what
Grieg possesses in such abundance, but I cannot avoid pointing out that the
attraction which I have always felt for this highly gifted Norwegian has
been and continues to be reciprocated in some measure by him. I will have
occasion below to furnish proof of this but meanwhile I will simply say that
I cherish Grieg's kind feelings most highly, and I am sincerely grateful to
fate for enabling me to meet him and get to know him personally.[7]

[7] *MC* 345–6.

I have successfully dispatched my concert here [in Hamburg]. There were three rehearsals. As in Leipzig, the players were very enthusiastic, even rapturous. The concert went off well. I played: (1) the *Serenade* [for string orchestra], (2) the Piano Concerto (Sapelnikov was the soloist and he played superbly), and (3) the Variations from the Third Suite. It was a great success. After that there was a big reception and supper at Bernuth's—he is the chairman of the Philharmonic Society. My speech in reply was in German!!![8]

They had a celebration in my honour at the Tonkünstler-Verein. Endlessly meeting people, visiting, calling. I am crazy with exhaustion! I have been reading some favourable reviews in the papers; there are, of course, some very peculiar criticisms, but on the whole the press is just as sympathetic as the musicians and the public.[9]

My Berlin concert was very successful. I was dealing with a quite superb orchestra and with players who showed themselves to be entirely in sympathy with me from the very first rehearsal. The programme was: (1) Overture *Romeo and Juliet*; (2) Piano Concerto (Ziloti was the soloist); (3) Introduction and Fugue from the First Suite; (4) Andante [cantabile] from the First Quartet; (5) songs (the soloist was Mme Friede); (6) *Overture 1812*. The audience gave me an enthusiastic reception. Naturally enough I find this very agreeable, but I am getting more and more exhausted and simply do not know how I can face up to all that lies ahead. My life in Berlin was sheer torture. I didn't have a minute to myself; from morning till night I had either to receive visitors or go out paying calls. Do you recognize in this musician travelling round Europe the same man who only a few years ago hid from social life and lived in solitude, whether abroad or in the country?!![10]

The last days of my stay in Hamburg and the day in Berlin were dreadful. In Berlin I heard some works by a new German genius, Richard Strauss. Bülow makes much of him, just as he did of Brahms and others.[11]

After Vasya's [Sapelnikov] departure (whom I simply worship), I spent the night in Berlin and next morning travelled to Leipzig. I visited the opera in the evening—it was *Die Meistersinger*. It was very interesting. Next day I dined with Grieg at the Brodskys' and spent the evening with Ziloti and all the same company of people. On Sunday the 12th I set off for Prague with Ziloti.

From the very frontier I already had the feeling of impending triumphs. The conductor of the train asked whether I was Tchaikovsky and was dancing attendance all the time. At Kralupy, the station before Prague, a whole crowd and a deputation were waiting to accompany us to Prague. At the station—masses of people, deputations, children with bouquets, two

[8] xiv. 325 (von Meck).   [9] xiv. 325 (von Meck).
[10] xiv. 357 (von Meck).   [11] xiv. 336–7 (Modest).

speeches: one in Russian and the other, a long one, in Czech. I replied. Walked to the carriage between two walls of people and cries of 'Hurrah'. Magnificent accommodation at the hotel. In the evening, *Othello* at the opera. A mass of introductions and greetings. Riger and his daughter spoke to me in Russian. After the opera, supper in our hotel room. Yesterday morning Dvořák visited, stayed for two hours; a trip around the town, saw some of the sights, accompanied by curator of the museum and Russian priest (who sends best regards to Sasha and Natya), supper with Valaček (well-known bookseller and Russophile), ball in best ballroom in Prague, at which I sat in full view in a box and was stared at by everyone. Today— service at 10.30 in Russian church, visit to student group, lunch with Dvořák, excursion round the town with same museum curator (speaks excellent Russian), and a grand evening in my honour at the 'Umělecká Beseda'. All this is very pleasant, very flattering, but you can imagine how tired I am getting and, in truth, how much I am suffering. I am going round in a fog and the only thing that keeps me going is the dawning of freedom which is beginning to glimmer in the distance, and also Sasha Ziloti, who never for one moment leaves my side. Obviously the point of my stay here is not that I am generally a good composer but that I am a Russian one.[12]

I spent ten days in Prague. From the very first minute I arrived it was an endless succession of all sorts of celebrations, rehearsals, sightseeing and so on. They received me as though I were the representative not just of Russian music but of all of Russia. My position was awkward because the honours accorded to me were not really mine, but Russia's. As to the concerts, there were two. They were an enormous success. After the first concert there was a banquet for a large gathering at which I made or, rather, read a speech in Czech. The Czechs found this terribly touching and it was an indescribable success.[13]

The first Prague concert took place on 7 February in the Rudolfinum. The programme consisted of *Romeo and Juliet*, the First Piano Concerto (with Ziloti as soloist), the Elegy from the Suite No. 3, the Violin Concerto (with Karel Halíř as soloist), and the *Overture 1812*. The second concert took place in the National Theatre on 9 February. The programme included the *Serenade* for string orchestra, the *Overture 1812*, and Act II of *Swan Lake*.

In his speech in Czech Tchaikovsky said:

It is no false modesty but honesty which compels me to admit that the honours accorded to me so far exceed the measure of my services that they would have stunned and overwhelmed me, were I not capable of distinguishing in them that portion of respect which concerns me personally from that which is paid to me as the representative of something much loftier and more important than I. Rest assured that in that country whose people have close and brotherly ties with you they will respond intelligently

---

[12] xiv. 359–60 (Modest).   [13] xiv. 363 (von Meck).

and sincerely to that part of your hospitable welcome which is not for me alone.[14]

I have brought away with me unforgettable memories from Prague and in spite of monstrous fatigue, I left with tears in my eyes and utterly convinced that the Czechs are a remarkably congenial people, and also deeply devoted to us.[15]

It looks as though in Paris too they are proposing to regard me not just as Pyotr Ilich Tchaikovsky, but as *a Russian* and I will get a very warm reception.[16]

Both the Colonne concerts were a brilliant success and my fame has grown terribly, but I have received no money and I won't get a penny, on the contrary, I spend more than ever. On this trip I have expended a very great deal of my money and even more of my health and strength, and in return I have acquired a little fame, but I constantly ask myself: 'Why? Is it worth it?', and I come to the conclusion that a peaceful life without fame is far better than this demented existence.[17]

Tchaikovsky conducted at the Châtelet concerts in Paris on 21 February and 28 February. The first concert included: the *Serenade* for string orchestra, the Theme and Variations from the Suite No. 3, the Andante cantabile from the First Quartet (for string orchestra), and the Nocturne for cello and orchestra (with Brandukov); the songs were 'None but the lonely heart' and 'Does the day reign?'. The second concert included the Theme and Variations from the Suite No. 3, the Violin Concerto (with Marsick), *Francesca da Rimini*, the Andante cantabile and the Nocturne for cello and orchestra (with Brandukov); the piano pieces were *Song without words* Op. 2, and *Humoreske* Op. 10 (played by Louis Diémer), then the Polonaise from *Eugene Onegin* and the Elegy and Waltz from the *Serenade* for string orchestra, followed by the songs 'A tear trembles' and 'Don Juan's Serenade'.

I have had my London concert. It was a very great success, and the String Serenade in particular called forth a lot of noisy approval; I had to take three bows, which means a very great deal with the reserved London audiences. They did not like the Variations from the Third Suite so much, but there was very friendly applause all the same. Thus ended my torments, fears, and anxieties, but one must be *truthful*: it was the end of my *joys* as well. The trouble is that if the tour had consisted just of rehearsals and concerts, despite the strain on my nerves, my feelings would have been of pleasure rather than of exhaustion. The success which I have enjoyed everywhere is very pleasant. But what was dreadful and unbearable was meeting people, invitations to dinners and parties, the necessity to receive visitors and to pay calls, the obligation constantly to talk or to listen to others, and the utter impossibility of getting away on one's own, of resting,

[14] *Life*, iii. 221.   [15] xiv. 366 (Shpazhinskaya).   [16] Ibid.
[17] xiv. 379 (Jurgenson).   [18] xiv. 385 (von Meck).

of reading, of doing anything at all, apart from this insufferable slavery to the social round.[18]

After Paris, where my concerts were a great success and the trip to London where I also enjoyed a great success, I am now going to rest in my own country, first of all in Tiflis, where my family and friends are waiting for me.[19]

I think I will probably act on the advice to write a detailed account of my travels. Since I belong to no musical party and have no close friends amongst the reviewers or editors I have been doing things on the quiet. But there is no doubt that the trip was interesting, and one could say that in my person was travelling not just myself but Russian music; I think that the Russian reader would like to know how foreigners treated me. They took an even more elevated view in Prague, where they honoured me not as a Russian *musician* but simply as a *Russian* and I was the focus of very significant demonstrations of Russophilism. So I have decided to blow my own trumpet a bit. I assure you it's not to advertise myself.[20]

Tchaikovsky did in fact write an *Autobiographical Account of my Travels Abroad* but did not have it printed because he did not wish to advertise himself. It was only after the composer's death that it was published by Modest Tchaikovsky as an appendix to Tchaikovsky's *Articles on Music* (1898).

All abroad is like a dream to me and I still can't wake up.[21] I have arrived at Taganrog at last, after an interminable journey. I spent six nights in the train. As though on purpose, the weather was splendid all the time and I very much regretted that I had not had the nerve to travel by sea. I so much prefer a sea journey to the train, and in general I am coming to be very fond of the sea. I would love to go on a long voyage and intend to try to get myself invited to conduct some concerts in America next year or the year after. It's strange, isn't it, that after wearing myself out travelling abroad for more than three months I should be thinking about travelling again? But such is man. I dreamt of my return to Russia as the greatest bliss, and as soon as it has become a fact I immediately start hoping that I will have to travel again next year! But that by no means prevents me from rejoicing at the thought that in a month I will be living in my own place again, somewhere in the wilds of the countryside. At the moment Alexey (who, incidentally, got married at the end of February) is busy looking for a dacha for the summer and, if possible, for permanent occupation.[22]

I am enjoying Tiflis very much but I will not stay here long since I have an inexpressible longing to be at *home* in my own place. I know the village of Frolovskoye very well, where Alexey has taken a house; it is a delightfully picturesque spot and you have seen it hundreds of times from a distance travelling from Klin to Moscow. It is just beyond Klin on some

[19] xiv. 390 (Valaček).   [20] xiv. 398 (Pogozhev).
[21] xiv. 396 (Modest).   [22] xiv. 395 (von Meck).

wooded hills to the left.[23] How *exhausted* I am and how I want to *work*, for it is only work and the realization that I am doing something constructive that can get me back on an even keel again.[24]

The Emperor has granted me *a pension for life of 3,000 roubles*. I am not so much overjoyed by this as deeply touched. Indeed I cannot avoid being eternally grateful to the Emperor who attaches importance not only to military and government service, but to artistic activities as well.[25]

[23] xiv. 400 (Modest).   [24] xiv. 401 (Modest).   [25] xiv. 324 (von Meck).

21

1888

In truth, two lives are not enough to do what one wants!

In the past year I really have done nothing and have just idled around Europe and Russia. And I am doing nothing at all now, I am not even trying to start any new work because I still haven't come round, and I think that I will only start wanting to work when I am *at home, at Frolovskoye.* I am thinking about a new symphony, a string sextet, and some small piano pieces.[1]

I am in my new abode [at Frolovskoye]. It is very much to my taste; the house stands on a hill, the view is wonderful, the garden runs straight into the woods, there are no holiday visitors, the rooms are high, with old furniture—in short, I am entirely satisfied with my new surroundings. In the space of a month Alexey has made of an abandoned, uninhabited house a pleasant and agreeable refuge for a wanderer wearied by all manner of experiences and anxieties![2]

I have great sympathy with your [Mme von Meck's] passion for dogs, which I also love very much; but I think that my kind of dog-loving is unique. First, I like simple mongrels best of all and secondly I cannot bear to keep a dog in the house and in all my life have only had one pet dog some long time ago in Moscow. I don't like keeping them because I always feel sorry for them; I imagine that they must be hungry or that they need something that they can't express, that there is something the matter with them, etc. etc. Besides which, Alexey doesn't like them and if a servant does not look after them properly and can't tolerate them, they can't be happy.[3]

I have quite fallen in love with Frolovskoye; after Maydanovo this whole area seems to me like heaven on earth. Indeed, it's so nice that I sometimes go for half an hour's walk in the morning and get so carried away that I don't come back for a couple of hours. There are woods all round and in places there is proper coniferous forest, marvellous and mysterious. Alas! They are already starting to cut a lot of it down in places. At sunset in the evenings I go for walks in the open country, with magnificent views. I still haven't started working yet. And to tell the truth I still have no inclination to do anything *creative.* What does this mean? Have I really written myself

[1] xiv. 408–9 (von Meck).   [2] xiv. 415 (von Meck).
[3] xiv. 403 (von Meck).

out at last? I have no ideas or inspirations. But I hope that I can gradually gather together material for a symphony.[4]

[From some advice to Mme Shpazhinskaya.] Sit down and write. You will retort that you cannot write if you do not feel the urge; but I know from experience that you will never get anything done if you give way to your *lack of inclination*. Every artist, writer, and musician is a craftsman as well and only dilettantes or idle people with weak characters wait for inspiration. If one just lets oneself go, it does not come.[5]

Because I had to see to the printing of the orchestral parts of my Fourth (*our*) Symphony, I renewed acquaintance with it, and I might otherwise rather have forgotten it. It was a great and very pleasant surprise to me to find that not only had I not turned cool towards it, as I do towards most of my early works, but that on the contrary, this child of mine infused me with a strong and lively enthusiasm. I don't know how things will turn out later, but at the moment I think that this is *my best symphonic work*. It is worthy of the person to whom it is dedicated.[6]

I couldn't write from Petersburg at all. I spent ten days there and gained nothing except exhaustion and depression. Of course it was pleasant to see my family, but really I hardly saw them—I had to spend the whole time being entertained. The Emperor held a reception in the Winter Palace. He was of course very gracious but I did not manage to talk to him for very long as he was in a great hurry. It was more like an official introduction and not at all like the heart-to-heart talk we had at Gatchina. My meetings with my family also only gave me mixed pleasure for (1) I saw them little and rarely (2) many of them were unwell and in particular my poor sister, who is a perpetual sufferer. This really is a tragedy! This woman had and still has everything you could ask for and yet one can imagine nothing more terrible than the life she leads. Firstly, she has an agonizing disease of the liver (stones) from which every so often she suffers to such an extent that she cannot help crying out in pain for days on end. Secondly, she is a confirmed morphine addict and with every day gets more and more dependent on this peculiar and terrible form of intoxication. I had not seen her for two years and was longing to see her, but this meeting brought me nothing but grief. This morphine!!![7]

I have no regrets at all that I am not going to write *The Queen of Spades*. I *am definitely going to write a symphony* and I will write an opera only if a subject crops up which is capable of firing my imagination. Something like *The Queen of Spades* does not move me and it would just have come out any old how.[8]

Modest Tchaikovsky had prepared a libretto on Pushkin's *The Queen of Spades* for the composer Nikolay Klenovsky, who did not, in the event, write the opera.

[4] xiv. 430–1 (Modest).   [5] xiv. 405 (Shpazhinskaya).
[6] xiv. 435 (von Meck).   [7] xiv. 425 (Panya).   [8] xiv. 400 (Modest).

Everything that they write in the papers about my new works is *lies*. I really have sometimes thought and still do think about an opera on *The Captain's Daughter*; I really have thought also about accepting the suggestion made to me *by the Director of the theatres* that I should write the music for a ballet on *Undine*, but these are all possibilities, and by no means realities. After a trip to Petersburg and a few visits to Moscow for the Conservatoire examinations I intend first of all to start work on composing *a symphony*, and then we'll see.[9]

I am intending to devote this summer to composing a symphony, and then, God willing, I will turn to the opera. As far as the subject of *The Captain's Daughter* is concerned, something rather strange happened recently: I suddenly and I fear irrevocably cooled towards it. It happened after I reread the story in Tiflis and from that moment I could not feel the slightest bit fired or inspired by the characters in *The Captain's Daughter*. And without that warmth of feeling and inspiration, nothing will come of it. And what's more, Shpazhinsky alarmed me when he wrote that you can't make a libretto from *The Captain's Daughter* except in *five long acts*!!!![10] I reread the story again not long ago and found that it has no characters who actually demand to be re-created in music, and that the heroine in particular is painfully colourless. When I was originally thinking about *The Captain's Daughter* I was probably most attracted by the setting in the last century and the contrast between the gentlemen in European dress and Pugachov and his wild band of followers. But contrast alone isn't enough for a subject for an opera; you need live personalities, touching situations . . . I feel like writing a small-scale opera in three acts, whose subject would be of an intimate character, where there would be plenty of scope for lyrical outpourings.[11]

I am not writing *The Captain's Daughter* and it's not likely that I ever will. Upon mature reflection I have come to the conclusion that the subject is not operatic. It is too fragmented and requires too many conversations, explanations, and actions which are not suitable for being set to music. Apart from that the heroine, Mariya Ivanovna, is not sufficiently interesting, hasn't sufficient character; she is an honest girl of blameless virtue and nothing else, which is not enough for setting to music. When I tried to lay the story out I found that it needed a tremendous number of acts and scenes however much I tried to keep it short. But the most important obstacle (for me, at any rate, because it's perfectly possible that it might be no hindrance at all to somebody else) is Pugachov, with the Pugachovshchina, Berda and all those Khlopusha and Chika fellows. I feel that I am incompetent to reproduce them artistically in musical colours. Perhaps it is a feasible proposition but it is not to my liking. Also, I don't think that it would be

[9] xiv. 416 (von Meck).   [10] xiv. 429 (Vsevolozhsky).
[11] xiv. 427 (Shpazhinskaya).

possible, even in the most favourable circumstances, to have Pugachov appearing on the stage. Naturally one could not do without him and he would have to be portrayed as he is in Pushkin. However kindly the censorship might be, I think it would have difficulty in passing a stage performance which would leave the spectator utterly captivated by Pugachov. This is possible in a story, but scarcely in a play or an opera, at least not in our country.[12]

I have definitely decided not to do *The Captain's Daughter*. I don't know why myself, but I have lost enthusiasm, not especially for *The Captain's Daughter*, but for all these *terre à terre* subjects. For some time now I have had an inclination to subjects not of this world, where they don't make jam, they don't hang people, they don't dance mazurkas, they don't get drunk, they don't submit petitions.[13]

I am going to work intensively now; I desperately want to prove to myself as well as others that I am not yet *played out*. Quite often I have doubts about myself and I wonder: is it time to stop, have I not always put too much strain on my imagination, has the source dried up? After all, this is bound to happen some time if I am to live another ten or twenty years, and how is one to know that the time has not come to lay down one's weapons? I decided to write a symphony. It was rather sticky at first, but now inspiration seems to have descended upon me. We shall see.[14]

I have been working so much, and my life here follows such a regular pattern that when I was writing the day and the month just now it came as a great surprise. It's the end of June already! I have been working well all the time and I have already finished the draft of a symphony and an overture to *Hamlet*, which I have long been planning to do. I'll start on scoring both of them next week. It's difficult to say for the moment how the symphony compares with its predecessors and particularly with *ours*. I do not seem to have the materials so easily and readily to hand as I used to; as I recollect, I did not use to feel so worn out by the end of the day. Now I am so tired in the evenings that I am not even in a state to read.[15]

A strange change has come over me: I have begun to get bored and depressed by solitude, frequently to long for society and distraction. In June I often went to visit Novichikha and Simon or invited them over, because this new little worm, or whatever it is, only stopped gnawing at my insides when I had company. This is strange, is it not? I myself don't understand what is going on. Probably it will pass.[16]

I am working quite steadily, in particular at this symphony, which, if I am not mistaken, will be no worse than its predecessors. But perhaps I just think so; God forbid that it should be true, but recently I have been haunted by the idea that I am played out, that my head is empty, that it is time to stop, etc. etc.[17]

[12] xiv. 442 (K.R.).   [13] xiv. 505 (Vsevolozhsky).
[14] xiv. 452 (von Meck).   [15] xiv. 466–7 (von Meck).
[16] xiv. 479 (the Huberts).   [17] xiv. 451 (Vladimir Nápravník).

I am very occupied at the present moment with questions about flowers and horticulture; I would like to grow as many flowers as possible in my garden, but I have no knowledge or experience at all. But I have plenty of enthusiasm.[18]

DIARY ENTRIES: SELF-ANALYSIS; RELIGIOUS REFLECTIONS

I think that letters are never altogether sincere. At least I am judging by myself. Whoever I write to and whatever it's about I always take care about the impression the letter will make, not only on the recipient but on any chance reader as well. When I read the letters of famous people which have been published after their death, an obscure sense of insincerity and dishonesty always jars on me.[19]

What an infinitely deep chasm there is between the Old and the New Testaments. I am reading the Psalms of David and don't understand (1) why they are so highly esteemed as regards their artistic worth and (2) how they can have anything in common with the Gospels. *David* is completely *of this world.* He divides the whole of mankind into two unequal parts: in one category are the *godless* (and this includes the vast majority); and in the other are the *godly* and he puts himself at their head. In each Psalm he calls down God's wrath to chastise the ungodly, and the godly shall be rewarded; but chastisement and reward are of this earth. Sinners will be destroyed; the godly will enjoy all the delights of earthly life. How unlike Christ all this is, Christ who prayed for sinners, and promised those near to him not *earthly rewards*, but his *heavenly* kingdom. There is infinite poetry and a feeling of love which reduces one to tears, and pity for mankind in the words: 'Come unto me all ye who labour and are heavy laden'. All the Psalms of David are nothing compared to these simple words.[20]

Probably when I am dead people will find it not without interest to know what my musical preferences and prejudices were, all the more so since I have rarely mentioned them in conversation. Let me take it a little at a time. I will begin with *Beethoven* whom it is customary to praise without stint and before whom we are ordered to bow down as before God. So, what do I think of Beethoven? I do bow down before the greatness of some of his works, but I do *not love* Beethoven. My attitude to him reminds me of what I used to feel in my childhood about the Lord of *Sabaoth*. He used to fill me with a sense of astonishment and dread at the same time (nor have my feelings changed even now). He created the heavens and the earth and He created me too, and yet, though I grovel before Him, there is no *love*. *Christ*, on the contrary, specifically and exclusively evokes our *love*. Although he was *God* he was at the same time man. He suffered as we do. We *pity* him and we love in him what represents the ideal of *humanity*. And if *Beethoven* occupies a place in my heart analogous to that of the Lord of

[18] xiv. 451 (von Meck).   [19] *Diaries, 2.*   [20] Ibid. 209.

Sabaoth, I love *Mozart* as a musical Christ. Incidentally, he lived just about as long as Christ. I don't think there is anything sacrilegious in this comparison. He was such an angelic creature, of such childlike purity, his music is so filled with a beauty which is unattainably sublime that if anyone can be mentioned in the same breath as Christ then it is Mozart. In talking about Beethoven I have stumbled upon *Mozart.* It is my profound conviction that *Mozart* is the loftiest peak of perfection which *beauty* has attained in the sphere of music. No one has his ability to make me weep, to make me tremble with rapture from the knowledge that I am close to *something,* to something which we call the *ideal.* Beethoven too makes me tremble, but rather from a sort of dread or painful anguish. I cannot *analyse* music and will not go into details, though I would like to make two points: (i) I like *Beethoven's* middle period and some of the first period, but the truth of the matter is that I *hate* the last period, particularly the late quartets. There are *flashes* there, but no more. The rest is *chaos,* over which there broods the spirit of this musical Lord of *Sabaoth,* swathed in impenetrable mists; (ii) I like *everything* in *Mozart* because we like *everything* in someone whom we really love. *Don Giovanni* most of all, because thanks to it I discovered what *music* is. Until then (when I was seventeen) I had known only Italian *semi-music,* which, incidentally, I quite liked. Of course, though I *love* all Mozart, I would not argue that every trifle he wrote is a *chef-d'œuvre.* Not at all. I know, for instance, that none of his *sonatas* is a great work, and *yet* I *love every one* of them because they are *his,* because this musical Christ marked them with the grace of his touch. Of earlier composers I would add that I like playing *Bach* because it is *interesting* to play a good fugue, but I do not regard him, as some do, as a great genius. *Handel* seems to me to be altogether fourth-rate and isn't even interesting. Though there is nothing special about him I quite like *Gluck.* There are things in *Haydn* which I *love.* But all four of these *bigwigs* were fused in *Mozart.* If you know your Mozart, you know whatever was good about these four: because he was a great *Creator,* the most powerful in all music, he did not disdain to take even them under his wing and save them from oblivion. They are the rays outshone by the sun of Mozart.[21]

What are my views on Russian composers? *Glinka.* An unprecedented, astounding phenomenon in the world of art. A dilettante, who played a bit on the violin and on the piano; who wrote utterly insipid quadrilles and fantasies on popular Italian themes, who also tried his hand at serious forms (the quartet and the sextet) and at songs, but who wrote nothing apart from banalities in the taste of the thirties; and who then suddenly, at the age of thirty-four, produced an opera which, in its inspiration, its scope, its novelty, its immaculate technique, stands alongside all that is greatest and most profound in art. One's astonishment is only increased when one

[21] *Diaries,* 212–13.

recalls that the composer of this opera is equally the author of those memoirs which were written twenty years later. The author of the memoirs impresses one as a nice, decent person, but empty, insignificant, and commonplace. I sometimes have nightmares of anxiety trying to work out how such a colossal artistic gift could be combined with being such a nonentity, and how Glinka, having long been an insipid dilettante, could suddenly, with a single stride, place himself alongside (yes—alongside!) Mozart, Beethoven, and anyone else you like. This can be said without any exaggeration of the man who wrote *Slavsya*! But let other people solve that problem who are more capable than I am of penetrating the mysteries of the creative spirit. I will only say that nobody could love and appreciate Glinka's music more than I do. I am not a fanatical Ruslanite and am even disposed on the whole to prefer *A Life for the Tsar* though it may well be that *Ruslan* really has more that is of musical value. But *the elemental force* makes itself felt more in the first opera, and *Slavsya* is something quite overwhelming and gigantic. And of course there was no precedent for this, not in Mozart, not in Gluck, not in any of the masters. It's astonishing and amazing. No lesser a manifestation of his remarkable genius is *Kamarinskaya*. So, with no intention of exceeding the requirements of a simple, light-hearted trifle, this man offers us, almost *by the way*, a small work in which every bar is a product of the power which creates (from nothing). Almost fifty years have gone by since then; many Russian symphonic works have been written and it could be said that there is a proper Russian symphonic school. And so? It is all in *Kamarinskaya*, just as all the oak is in *the acorn*. And Russian composers will long draw on this rich source for much time and effort will be needed to exhaust all its riches. Glinka is indeed a true creative genius![22]

Tchaikovsky made a mistake: Glinka was born in 1804 and *A Life for the Tsar* was first performed in 1836.

Dargomyzhsky? Yes, of course he was talented. But *the type of the dilettante* in music has never been so clearly seen as in him. Glinka too was a dilettante but his colossal genius saved him from the consequences of his dilettantism; were it not for his disastrous memoirs we would not be talking about his dilettantism. Dargomyzhsky is another matter; his dilettantism is in the very form and content of his works. For a second-rate talent, without technical expertise moreover, to imagine that he is *an innovator* is the purest dilettantism. Towards the end of his life Dargomyzhsky wrote *The Stone Guest* firmly convinced that he was breaking up the old foundations and building something new and colossal on the ruins thereof. What a sad misapprehension! I know of nothing more off-putting and *false* than this unsuccessful attempt to introduce *truth* into the sphere of art, where everything is based on *the false* and where *truth* in the everyday sense of the word

[22] Ibid. 214–15.

is not required at all. D[argomyzhsky] had no craftsmanship, not even a fraction of what Glinka had. He did have a certain piquancy and originality. He was particularly successful with his harmonic *peculiarities*. But *the essence* of artistic beauty is not *in peculiarities*, as many of us think.[23]

I went to Petersburg with the almost exclusive purpose of fulfilling a promise which I gave a long time ago. Mr Laube's orchestra is playing at Pavlovsk at the moment. They took this Laube on on my recommendation (I met him during the winter in Hamburg) and he has been most insistent in asking me to go and hear his performances. So I undertook a trip. My recollection of it is pleasant. I had a very enjoyable time, thanks to the marvellous weather and the excursions which I made to Tsarskoye [Selo], Pavlovsk, and Peterhof. I enjoyed hearing some good music in Petersburg: there is a very great deal of it there in the summer. Moscow has fallen terribly behind her rival in this respect. Laube's orchestra at Pavlovsk is excellent.[24]

The real summer weather didn't last long, but how much pleasure it gave me whilst it did! By the way, my flowers, a lot of which I thought had died, have all or almost all recovered and some of them are even blooming luxuriantly; I cannot describe the pleasure I have derived from watching them grow and seeing more and more new flowers appearing every day, sometimes even by the hour. I think that when I am really old and can no longer write I will take to growing flowers.[25]

At this time Tchaikovsky started an intensive correspondence with the poet K. R. (the Grand Duke Konstantin Romanov). This is one of the richest sources amongst the composer's letters. Apart from musical questions there are vigorous discussions of the problems of writing poetry.

In the matter of versification I am a dilettante. Many questions interest me and nobody has ever been able to give me an entirely clear and precise answer to them. For instance, when I read Zhukovsky's *Odyssey* or his *Undine*, or Gnedich's *Iliad*, I suffer from the unbearable monotony of the Russian hexameter, by comparison with which Latin (I do not know Greek) is, on the contrary, full of variety, strength, and beauty. I am also extremely interested in the question of why German verse, by comparison with Russian, does not adhere so rigidly to the succession of one foot after another in the same rhythm. When you read Goethe you are astonished at his daring with feet, caesuras, and so on; it goes so far that to the unaccustomed ear odd lines seem scarcely to be verse. And yet this merely surprises the ear, it does not offend it. If something comparable happens in a Russian poet it feels unpleasant. Is this a consequence of the particular nature of the language, or simply *of tradition*? I do not know whether I am expressing myself properly but I am trying to establish the fact that infinitely more is required of the Russian poet by way of accuracy, workmanship, musicality,

[23] *Diaries*, 215.   [24] xiv. 482 (von Meck).   [25] xiv. 491 (von Meck).

and above all *polish*, than is required of the German. Until somebody explains it to me I shall continue to be a demanding and carping dilettante in the matter of stress, caesuras, and rhythms in Russian verse.[26] Ultimately, of course, I am wrong, because even such an amazing master of verse as Fet justifies concealing the caesura. From which it probably follows that I approach verse as a musician and see the laws of rhythm being broken when in fact from the point of view of versification they are not, or if they are, it is excusable.

I am not at all surprised that your highness has written fine verse without knowing the technicalities of versification. Many of our poets (Pleshcheyev, for instance) have said the same thing to me. I think, however, that Russian poetry would gain much if our talented poets would take an interest in the technique of their craft. Russian verse suffers, in my view, from a certain monotony. '*I am bored with the iambic tetrameter*', said Pushkin, but I would add that the reader is a little bored with it too. Inventing new metres, devising original rhythmic groupings—surely this should be very interesting. If I had the smallest spark of poetic talent I would certainly do this, and I would try first of all to write as the Germans do, in a mixture of metres.[27] The alternation of varying feet in German verse *stings the ear*. My explanation of this is that the laws of euphony are different in German from Russian and our Russian ears therefore suffer somewhat in places where a German would not notice any roughness. None the less I have for some time come to like precisely this roughness, and at the same time it has seemed that our Russian verse is too rigid in its adherence to the regular repetition of the rhythmic unit, that it is too soft, symmetrical, and monotonous. I would like to see more frequently the sort of deviation from normal verse techniques which we find in Fet. As Turgenev rightly observed in one of his *Poems in Prose*, the Russian language is, after all, something immensely rich, powerful, and great, and I am far even from being certain that, like German, only tonic verse is appropriate to it. I am, for instance, extremely fond of Kantemir's syllabic verses. And what of the metre of the ancient Russian songs and byliny? What of *The Lay of Igor's Host*? Could it not come about that one day people will write not only in tonic and syllabic but in ancient Russian verse as well?

I not only agree with all that you [Grand Duke Konstantin] say about Fet but would go further and regard him as a poet of unqualified genius, though there is about his genius an incompleteness, an imbalance, a peculiar consequence of which is that Fet's writing is sometimes terribly weak and unbelievably bad. Fet is an altogether exceptional phenomenon; it is quite impossible to compare him with other first-class Russian or foreign poets, to find affinities between him and Pushkin, or Lermontov, or Alexey Tolstoy, or Tyutchev (who is also a talent of some considerable magnitude). It would be more accurate to say that in his best moments Fet goes

[26] xiv. 440–1 (K.R.).   [27] xiv. 453–4 (K.R.).

beyond the appointed limits of poetry and takes a bold stride into *our sphere*.* For this reason Fet often reminds me of Beethoven, but never of Pushkin, Goethe, Byron, or Musset. He, like Beethoven, has the power to touch those strings of our hearts which are not accessible to artists, mighty though they be, who are confined to the limits *of the word*. He is not so much a mere poet as a poet-musician, and seems even to avoid those themes which are easily amenable to verbal expression. For this reason, of course, he is often not understood, and there are even gentlemen who laugh at him and maintain that a poem like 'Carry off my heart to the echoing distance' is nonsense. To a limited mind, and particularly to someone who is not musical it may well be nonsense, but it cannot be without significance that Fet, despite what is for me his unarguable genius, is not at all popular, whereas Nekrasov, whose muse crawls along the ground, is the idol of the enormous majority of the reading public.[28]

Grand Duke Konstantin passed on Tchaikovsky's views on Russian versification to Fet, who wrote in reply: 'Now that music has become an independent art and has moved so far away from the word, poets of the word are in our day sometimes quite indifferent, not to say hostile to music. Could one not say the same of musicians? After the genius of Lomonosov has once and for all broken through our Common Slavonic syllabic versification, after Pushkin has given us diamonds of the purest water, it would scarcely be acceptable to the Russian ear that we should once more reach out towards syllabic chaos. That Russian verse is capable of astounding variety is proved by the immortal Tyutchev, if on no other evidence than his poem "Oh, in the decline of our years, how much more fondly and superstitiously we love".' The Grand Duke cited these words of Fet's in a letter to Tchaikovsky, as well as the poet's opinion that 'everything which does not contribute to the main idea must be discarded'.

It was interesting in the extreme to read Fet's comments on my dilettante fantasies about Russian versification. Despite his crafty insinuation about musicians 'indifferent and even hostile to poetry', it was an immense pleasure to me to read his reply. In the first place, Fet's attitude to Tyutchev is touching, and in the second place, Fet's quotation from Tyutchev entirely resolves my doubts. The line 'how much more fondly and superstitiously we love' [*nezhnéy my lyúbim i suyevérney*] is a perfect demonstration of the fact that Russian verse can accommodate that alternation of duple and triple rhythm which so captivates me in German verse. It only remains to hope that such instances will not always be the exception but will become the rule. I really must say about Fet that some of his poems seem to me to be the equal of anything that has ever been written. One such poem is 'On a hayrick on a southern night' which I intend to illustrate in music some time. Fet is quite right to argue that '*everything which does not*

---

* i.e. music (*Tchaikovsky's note*).

[28] xiv. 513–14 (K.R.).

*contribute to the main idea, however good and sonorous it might be, must be dis-
carded*. But it by no means follows from this that only *short things* are fully
artistic. Everything depends in the first place on what *the main idea* is, and
in the second place on what sort of an artist is expressing it. Of two equally
gifted poets or musicians, the distinguishing artistic characteristics of the
one may be his broad sweep, the abundant resources which he brings to his
treatment of the main idea, a tendency to develop it in a rich and many-
sided way; and of the other, on the contrary, conciseness and brevity.
Something which, even if it is good, is superfluous is so-called *remplissage*.
But can it be said that there are *remplissages* in Beethoven? Definitely not, in
my opinion. On the contrary, when you study him you are astounded at the
way in which *everything* in this giant amongst all musicians is equally important, equally full of significance and power, and at the same time you are
astounded at the way in which he was able to control the incredible thrust
of his colossal inspiration and never lose sight of balance and formal perfection. But could anybody find in the 'Eroica' Symphony, which is unusually
long, even a single superfluous bar, even one short passage which could be
discarded on grounds of *remplissage*? So not everything which is long is
drawn-out. *Multiplication* of words is by no means a *reduction* of sense, and
brevity is by no means, as Fet says, a condition of perfect formal beauty.
The same Beethoven who in the first movement of the 'Eroica' Symphony
erects on the simplest and, it would seem, most unpromising subject an
impressive edifice, with an endless succession of new and strikingly beautiful architectonic features, can sometimes astonish the listener with his
brevity and formal conciseness. The Andante in the G major Piano
Concerto—I know of nothing more brilliant than this short movement, I
always turn pale and chill when I hear it. It is, of course, obvious that there
is immense value in the classical beauty of the masters who preceded Beethoven. But then it must also be said that there was no need for Haydn to
restrain himself because he had Lord knows how much material available;
as to Mozart, if he had lived another twenty years, if he had reached the beginning of this century, who can say whether even his genius might have
sought another outlet for his amazingly rich inspiration in less classical
forms than those with which he in fact contented himself. But if I am willing to defend Beethoven from charges of prolixity, I must admit that music
after Beethoven offers many examples of excess and of a verbosity which
amounts to *remplissage*. Beethoven was a composer of genius who liked to
express himself broadly, majestically, powerfully, and even harshly, and he
had much in common with Michelangelo in this. Just as the abbé Bernini
inundated Rome with statues in which, without having his genius, he
attempted to imitate the manner of Michelangelo and in reality reduced to
caricature those elements of his model which astound us by their strength
and their power, in just the same way in music have people over-egged the
cake, and they still do it, when they imitate the style of Beethoven. Is not

Brahms essentially a caricature of Beethoven? Such pretensions to depth,
strength, and power are surely detestable when the content which is poured
into the Beethovenian form is so pitiful and insignificant. Even in Wagner
(an undoubted genius, by the way), all the places where he overreaches
himself can, in their essentials, be traced back to the spirit of Beethoven. So
far as your most obedient servant is concerned, he has suffered all his life
from an awareness of his general incompetence in matters *of form*. I have
long struggled with this organic deficiency and can say with some pride that
I have achieved significant results, but I know that I'll die without writing
anything that is *perfect* in respect of form. My works are full of *remplissages*
and the experienced eye can always see *la ficelle* at the seams; there's
nothing you can do about it.[29]

The regularity of Tchaikovsky's working life was interrupted from time to time
when he was sent works from amateur composers with a request for his opinion.
However busy he was, not only this summer but at any time, he never refused help
and always criticized the works which were submitted to him. He hated dilettantism, was always frank, and did his best to help by word and deed. Tchaikovsky
received a weighty package in the summer of 1888 when he was working on the
scoring of the Fifth Symphony and *Hamlet*. The dilettante composer Achilles
Alferaki had written *St John's Eve*—something midway between a cantata and a
concert version of an opera—and sent it to Tchaikovsky for his opinion. The criticisms which Tchaikovsky made of this amateur work can be taken as typical of those
which he made of all composers (and, indeed, artists of any kind) who lacked professional skill.

Since you have expressed the wish that I should give you a frank opinion
about *St John's Eve* I must warn you that you will not like this letter. It is a
pity that before starting your work you did not seek advice from me or some
other musician about whether you ought to take on such a difficult task.
Anybody would have advised you not to. It was your wish to make a setting
for soloist, chorus, and orchestra of a text which is very suitable for musical
treatment but requires all the resources of the most fertile compositional
technique. Unfortunately, this is what you lack altogether. You have an
undoubted facility of invention, but of course this is far from being sufficient for the task which you have undertaken. I remember that even the
pleasant little songs which you showed me had been written without proper
regard for musical orthography and before they were printed needed to be
looked through by someone who was a musician by trade. But what is a
song by comparison with a large cantata or even a whole opera with
choruses, dances, recitatives, arias, and so on??? After all, to write such a
work properly, you need: (1) to command a thorough knowledge of harmony and counterpoint, (2) to have a perfect grasp of form, (3) to be able to
write for voices, (4) finally, to have a perfect knowledge of orchestration.

[29] xiv. 539–42 (K.R.).

You regard yourself as too old to start getting to know the orchestra and think that you can get round this by entrusting the orchestration to someone else. This is a big mistake. Apart from the fact that it is never too late to learn, why should you imagine that it is possible to write for the orchestra without knowing it? Of course there have been cases of the post-humous works of certain composers being orchestrated by their friends, but these pieces were actually written by people who had the orchestra in mind as they composed and knew how to write for it. Your accompaniment is written in such a way that it could not be orchestrated into anything. But even if we suppose that it were possible to compose an orchestral work without knowing the orchestra—what about harmony? and counterpoint? and, especially, form? In writing an opera or any other complex work, can one get by without a sound technical knowledge of these various branches of the composer's craft? Certainly not! This is why, because you have at your disposal only one undoubted and even very notable gift, you have wasted your time on a work which has no future. Your harmony is very life-less, it has no sense of movement. Some of the details of the harmony are delightful but you have no conception of part-writing—it's angular, and above all, it's dead and monotonous in the extreme. Apart from that, your harmonic sub-structure is too unyielding and unvarying. There is scarcely a bar without complete full chords. There is not a trace of contrapuntal decoration—just chords and more chords. There are no unison accompani-ments, nor even occasional two-part counterpoint. At every turn one comes upon the forbidden fifths and octaves. There is no reason why this rule should not be broken, but it is immediately obvious when it is being done consciously and when it stems from incompetence. Your modulations are for the most part forced and sometimes it is not apparent why they are there at all because when you have completed a very difficult and prolonged modulation you suddenly go into another key than the one to which it has led; and yet, despite all this, you are constantly hitting upon real little gems of harmony: you have a particular talent for piquant harmonic combina-tions. You also have some melodic inventiveness, but your inability to cope with form spoils all the pleasure which these things might afford. You never pursue an idea to the point where it stands out on its own, quite clearly and distinctly. There are some attractive melodic ideas which come to nothing because they are not treated properly. My advice is: start study-ing seriously and then you should not confine yourself to amateurish ex-periments.[30]

I have no definite plans for the winter. There are suggestions for a con-cert tour in Scandinavia and even America. But the timing of the first has not been fixed and the second I regard as somehow fantastic and can't quite believe that it was a serious proposal. Besides, I have promised to conduct

[30] xiv. 489–91 (Alferaki).

in a few places abroad, for example in Dresden, Berlin, Prague—but nothing is fixed yet.[31]

So much work has descended upon me and I have so little time to do all that I have to. On the other hand, the main thing is done already: my symphony is finished and I don't think I have made a hash of it, I think it's good. I'm happy in general, but I can't help complaining about my health. I have been constantly unwell throughout the summer, and when I was scoring the symphony I inevitably overworked and subjected myself to the most extreme pressure. Although I still have masses of things to do, I now find myself compelled to take a short rest, and to this end I am going off to the country for a few days, to the Kiev province, to my sister's. The trip won't last more than a week or ten days, then I'll come back and get down to work again.[32]

I have got back from my trip to my sister's in the Kiev province, with very unhappy feelings. They have a terrible misfortune in the family.[33]

Tchaikovsky's niece Vera Rimskaya-Korsakova was mortally ill with tuberculosis.

Whilst I have been away the house has undergone various improvements: new window-frames have been put in everywhere and a fireplace has been put in the study. Thanks to this I am not suffering from the cold and would feel fine if it were not that I am, as usual, overstraining myself with work. To keep a long-standing promise I have started orchestrating an overture which Laroche wrote ages ago; he is in no state to do it himself, partly because he has got out of the way of it, partly because of his pathological laziness. It is a remarkably talented piece of work which shows how much music has lost because this brilliantly gifted man suffers from an illness of the will which completely paralyses his creative activity. This overture cost me a lot of hard work, and scarcely had I finished it when I had to start straight away on the score of my own Overture Fantasia *Hamlet*. And on top of that I am doing the proofs of the Fifth Symphony with feverish haste. I am dreadfully tired, I work like a slave, with a sort of passionate intentness arising from the fact that I always think I must hurry or I will be too late. But thank heaven! for me, work is the greatest and most incomparable blessing because without it I feel that I would be immeasurably cast down by sorrow and melancholy. And there is something to be sorrowful and melancholy about: my poor niece Vera is dying.[34] One of my closest, oldest, and dearest friends [Hubert] has died; I went to the funeral.[35]

I am extremely pleased that you [Grand Duke Konstantin] approve of my Fourth Symphony, for this is one of my most favourite children, one which was written from beginning to end under the impetus of true inspiration, with love and genuine enthusiasm. There are not so very many

[31] xiv. 506 (von Meck).   [32] xiv. 507 (Shpazhinskaya).
[33] xiv. 522 (Shpazhinskaya).   [34] xiv. 534 (von Meck).
[35] xiv. 350 (Shpazhinskaya).

of which this is true. I do not say this out of any desire to show off my modesty as a composer. *I literally cannot live without working*, because no sooner is one piece of work finished and I feel like a rest i.e. the pleasures of an exhausted toiler who has earned the right to the enticements of *dolce far niente*, no sooner does this happen than instead of rest there appear ennui, depression, thoughts about the vanity of all earthly things, fears for the future, fruitless regrets over the irretrievable past, tormenting questions about the meaning of life on earth, in short, everything that ruins the life of someone who is not immersed in work and is also inclined to hypochondria, and there then arises in consequence a desire to get straight down to some new piece of work. It is obvious that in circumstances like this the new work is not always the fruit of a true creative impulse. On the other hand I am so constructed that once I have started something I cannot settle until I have finished it; so compositions emerge which have been written not by an artist but by a craftsman who only pretends to be an artist. Not a few of my works are, I repeat, of this nature, which only leads me to feel even more parental tenderness for those like the Fourth Symphony which are full of true feeling.[36]

I think that in insisting on *brevity* and *conciseness* as essential conditions for artistic perfection in the lyric your Highness has in mind not so much lyrical verse in general as so-called *minor works*. For we find in Pushkin and Lermontov *chefs-d'œuvre* of the lyrical genre which far exceed the limits which you indicate. This is to say nothing of *odes*, which, although they are not written now, still exist as superb models from a former age. Even two or three of Derzhavin's odes (which, incidentally, I do not like) must be accounted superb models in the lyric genre. 'Literal repetitions',* which are possible in literature only up to a point, are absolutely essential in music. Beethoven never repeated entire sections of his works unless there was some particular need to do so and very rarely did he fail to introduce something new at the repetition, but he realized that his ideas would be fully understood only if he expressed them several times over in one and the same form and even he, therefore, resorted to this technique which is characteristic of instrumental music; I admit that I really cannot understand what you have against the many repetitions of the theme of the Scherzo in the Ninth Symphony. Every time it comes round I always wish he would keep on repeating it again and again. It really is so sublimely good, so powerful, so original, so full of meaning! The length and repetitions which we find in Schubert, for example, are another matter, because for all his genius he really does go too far in endlessly returning to his first idea (as in the Andante of the C major symphony, for instance). This is quite another matter. Beethoven first fully develops his idea, then repeats it; but

---

* In this respect music is nearest to architecture (*Tchaikovsky's note*).

[36] xiv. 552 (K.R.).

Schubert is too lazy, as it were, to develop his ideas and, perhaps because of his remarkable thematic fertility, hastens to put what he has started into some sort of shape so that he can go on to something else. The pressure of his unbelievably rich and inexhaustible inspiration effectively precluded him from devoting himself with affection to the subtle and carefully considered working out of his themes. Would to God that I had been in Petersburg for the performance of Mozart's *Requiem* in the Marble Palace. That requiem is one of the most sublime works of art and one can only pity those who are incapable of understanding or appreciating it.[37]

I have worked myself to a standstill. This work is a strange thing! While you are working you dream all the time of the unbelievable bliss you will feel when it is finished. But as soon as it is finished you get bored, depressed, melancholy, and you seek to cure it by working again. It is really a very good thing that I have begun to be invited all over the place and that I have to travel throughout Europe. I complain about it but in actual fact it is my salvation, for otherwise I would have eventually broken under the constant strain.[38]

I am coming to the end of my time in the country; I will soon have to start my wanderings. I have completely finished off all my work and am busy preparing for my conducting. My house has become delightful and cosy in its winter guise.[39] My Moscow friends are in ecstasies over the *symphony* but it remains to be seen how the public and the Petersburg musical world will take it.[40]

I have just received your dear letter [Chervinkova-Rigerova] and the translation of the libretto of *Eugene Onegin*. I thank you from the bottom of my heart for carrying out such a difficult task and am glad that thanks to the exceptional charm of Pushkin's poetry this task also brought you a certain amount of pleasure. I have a great favour to ask of you. I would like you to write a short Preface to the libretto so that the Prague public should know the circumstances in which my opera became part of the repertoire of our theatres both in the capital and throughout the country. I have had a special, indescribable passion for Pushkin's poem since I was a boy, and as soon as I began to write music my most cherished dream was to write something on Pushkin's wonderful theme. I knew that there was little dramatic interest in this subject and so when I started to work on it I was not thinking of the *theatre* at all. This music of mine was written in the summer of 1877 and, as far as I remember, not one of my works gave me so much enjoyment in composing it, so much pleasure and artistic delight. After that, I did not even imagine that *Eugene Onegin* would ever be staged, did not make any arrangements for it, but simply rejoiced in the hope that my music, which was written with such love and delight, would find an echo in the hearts of

---

[37] xiv. 553–4 (K.R.).   [38] xiv. 562 (Anna Merkling).
[39] xiv. 568 (Panya).   [40] xiv. 572 (Anatoly).

my compatriots, who like me love Pushkin's poetry in general and *Onegin* in particular. My expectations were realized. *Eugene Onegin* gradually became more widely known and some extracts from it became almost popular. But then something happened which I had not expected at all. The present Emperor, who took a great liking to the music for *Onegin*, expressed the wish that this opera (which I called 'lyrical scenes') should be staged at the Imperial Theatre. It was performed in Petersburg in 1884 and, exceeding all my expectations, was a great success.

This is the brief history of my 'lyrical scenes' and I would like it to be known to the Prague audience: they cannot approach the subject in the same way as a Russian audience, who know Pushkin's verses by heart and can forgive the lack of dramatic action and visual interest for the sake of Pushkin's delightful poetry. It is essential that it should be known in Prague that I don't regard *Eugene Onegin* as a real opera, but as an attempt to illustrate the substance of Pushkin's poetry in music; in doing this, however, I had no choice but to use the dramatic form. The audience, knowing all this, will be more charitable towards the opera, and if the music chances to touch their hearts, they will be reconciled to its dramatic deficiencies.[41]

I am writing [13 November] an hour before leaving Petersburg for Prague. I have had a fortnight of feverish activity here. My concert at the Philharmonic Society took place on 5 November and yesterday, the 12th, I conducted my two new pieces, *Hamlet* and the symphony at the Musical Society. Both were well received by the public. I must admit that they like me, my music that's to say, more in Petersburg than anywhere, not excluding Moscow, and everywhere here I meet a warm and sympathetic attitude.[42]

I spent eleven days in Prague. Concert rehearsals started on the very first day I arrived, and then rehearsals for *Eugene Onegin*. The whole of the days was taken up with them and in the evenings I had invitations to visit people and to attend celebrations. The performance [of *Onegin*] was not so much good as, in some respects, simply superlative. I never dared dream of a Tatyana like I had in Prague. There was no end to the ovations.[43]

The part of Tatyana was sung by Berta Foerstrová-Lautererová.

The Prague concert included the Fifth Symphony and the Second Piano Concerto (with Sapelnikov as soloist). The first performance of *Eugene Onegin* was given on 24 November in the National Theatre.

I came [to Vienna] to have a day's rest, but a very sad piece of news awaited me here. I chanced upon a copy of *Novoye vremya* [*New Times*] in a café and read of the death of my beloved niece.[44] The news of Vera's death was by no means unexpected, but even so I was deeply shaken. I shudder

---

[41] xiv. 532–3 (Chervinkova-Rigerova).   [42] xiv. 590 (von Meck).
[43] xiv. 596–7 (Shpazhinskaya).   [44] xiv. 597 (Shpazhinskaya).

whenever I think of Sasha and Lev. Oh what a swine death is, so pitilessly cutting down the life of a young and good human being![45]

Vera was a remarkably likeable, gentle, sweet person. You [Mme von Meck] write, my dear, that you are most sorry for her husband. I am much more sorry for her mother and father, for I have never in my life seen parents more devoted to their children than they. This blind love has led them to make many mistakes in the upbringing of their children, but their punishment is too terrible! To lose one after the other two grown-up daughters, to both of whom life held promise only of joy and happiness—is terrible.[46]

I am tormented by the thought that I manage to write to you so rarely [Mme von Meck]. My life is not now organized at all as it used to be! For instance I have just now had to go to Moscow: rehearsals, two concerts, meetings of the Board, and all the fuss of life in a town gave me no opportunity at all to touch a pen. The same thing happened in Petersburg where I appeared at a so-called *Russian Symphony Concert*. In addition I had a lot of discussions there with the Director of the theatres and the ballet-master Petipa about the ballet I am going to write (*La Belle au bois dormant*) and in general had a hectic time. The two Moscow concerts (one in the ordinary Symphony Concert series, and the other a public one, with the same programme) went off well, but all the same I was left with an unhappy feeling. Every time I play it I am increasingly convinced that my last symphony is not a successful work, and this knowledge of a chance failure (and perhaps of a decline in my abilities) distresses me very much. The symphony has turned out too florid, massive, insincere, and prolix—very disagreeable altogether. With the exception of Taneyev, who stubbornly insists that the Fifth Symphony is my best work, all my honest and sincere well-wishers have a low opinion of it. Have I, as they say, written myself out? Has *le commencement de la fin* started? It's dreadful if it has. The future will show whether or not my fears are mistaken, but it is at all events a pity that a symphony of 1888 should be worse than one written in 1877. Of the fact that *our* symphony is infinitely better than this last one I am utterly convinced.[47]

My participation in the *Russian Symphony Concert* created something of a sensation in the Petersburg musical world. These concerts are organized by one Belyayev, a business man and a passionate admirer of that musical party which calls itself 'The New Russian School', at the head of which stand Balakirev and Rimsky-Korsakov. Up to now this party, in the persons of its most distinguished representatives, has taken a sympathetic interest in me but has not regarded me as *its own*. I have always tried to place myself *outside* of all parties and have constantly affirmed that I like and respect any honest and gifted musician, whatever his tendency. I am

[45] xiv. 596 (Panya).   [46] xiv. 600 (von Meck).   [47] xiv. 609–10 (von Meck).

equally fond of Balakirev, and Rimsky, and Anton Rubinstein, and Nápravník, because they are all talented and conscientious men. I detest anyone who has no talent, who is a mediocrity and claims to be gifted, neglecting no opportunity to advertise himself. For this reason people like Messrs Cui and Solovyov and *tutti quanti* will always be alien and antipathetic to me. So I was very glad to take the opportunity to state in public that although the utterly detestable Mr Cui belonged to the school known as 'The New Russian' or 'The Mighty Handful', this in no way prevented me from liking and respecting such members of the school as Balakirev, Rimsky-Korsakov, Lyadov, and Glazunov and from being flattered to appear on the same concert platform with them. I conducted *The Tempest* there and had an enormous success.[48]

The young pianist Alexander Ziloti had helped Tchaikovsky a great deal with proof-reading and offered him his own edition of the Second Piano Concerto.

I am immensely grateful to you for your concern and interest, and for your desire to make my works more grateful and welcome to performers. But . . . I *certainly* cannot agree with your cuts, particularly with your reshuffling of the first movement. With my changes, the sequence, the logic in the succession of the movements is preserved. Your plan to move the cadenza to the end made my stomach turn over and my hair stand on end.[49]

[48] xiv. 610–11 (von Meck).   [49] xiv. 614 (Ziloti).

22

1888–1889

I am needed, and so long as I live I must satisfy this need.

The manuscript [of the libretto] for *The Sleeping Beauty* has arrived at last. [By 22 August 1888]. I have managed to look through the scenario and I would like to say straight away that I am delighted with it, I am thrilled beyond words. It suits me perfectly and I could wish for nothing better than to write the music for it. This charming story could not have been better adapted for the stage and I hope you, the author [Vsevolozhsky], will accept my heartiest congratulations. I am looking forward to this work. The libretto for the ballet is superb.[1] I *will get down* to it with the greatest pleasure. I have emphasized *will get down* because I have not yet written a single note. Before I start the composing I must discuss it thoroughly with the ballet-master.[2] I have been making so much effort and working so persistently of late that I have already written two whole acts of the ballet. Vsevolozhsky has worked up the story. It is taken from Perrault's famous tale *La Belle au bois dormant*. It's a really charming and poetic story.[3]

Tchaikovsky started work on *The Sleeping Beauty* in October 1888 and continued in early 1889.

I have been a positive slave all this time: I have had to exert myself to the utmost with this present work because I knew that if I did not finish the draft sketches of the ballet before leaving for abroad I would not be in time to get my score to the management. But I am bound to say that my years are making themselves felt: my former facility has gone, and if by an effort of the will I do succeed in working quickly, then it has a marked effect on my nerves. Perhaps I ought now to withdraw from my foreign trip and work on the ballet very calmly and *coolly*, but it would be rather awkward to decline the invitations from abroad; after all, in my person it is not only the writer of these lines who is being honoured but the whole of Russian music. Since they ask me and are interested in me I think I *must* take advantage of it.[4]

As in the previous winter, Tchaikovsky again set off on a concert tour of Europe. The two trips had very much in common. The same insane homesickness and the same triumphant progress. There were new 'ports of call' for his concert appear-

---

[1] xiv. 509–10 (Vsevolozhsky).   [2] xiv. 548 (Pogozhev).
[3] xva. 19 (von Meck).   [4] xva. 26 (Shpazhinskaya).

ances, new towns, new people to meet, but in essence it was the same. Despite his tremendous success Tchaikovsky could think of only one thing: getting home as quickly as possible.

During the last eight days I have had three concerts and nine rehearsals! To be precise, on Sunday 10 February I left Berlin for Cologne. The next day I had rehearsals in the morning and evening, and the following day a rehearsal and a concert. The day after I went to Frankfurt and there I again had to have two rehearsals in the same day and then a rehearsal and concert, then the same thing repeated in Dresden. I simply don't know where I get the strength for all this. It must be one of two things: either this new kind of strain will have a very harmful effect on me, or the opposite, like an antidote to my labours of composition, which involve sitting down all the time, this crazy, unending activity is good for me. There can be no middle way, in other words I must return to Russia either in death or in glory. But I rather think that in spite of difficult moments and the constant battle with myself, all this is good for me! I have had great success in all three towns but especially in Cologne and Frankfurt. In Dresden I played our symphony, but unfortunately this was a bad choice, because I did not know that the orchestra which I would be working with is very bad and this difficult symphony was too much for them. Nevertheless, I was given a very good reception.[5]

From Dresden I went to Berlin. Here I was invited to conduct two pieces in a concert given by the Philharmonic Society. After a lot of debating the *Serenade* for strings and *Francesca* were chosen. I have already spoken of the Berlin orchestra. It is magnificent and in character reminds me very much of the Petersburg orchestra. The concert was yesterday. I wouldn't say that it was an enormous success. After *Francesca* I clearly heard some very vigorous whistling. However, in general it still all went off well. The Waltz from the *Serenade* was encored.[6]

The Berlin concert has taken place. I performed only two pieces: the *Serenade* for strings and *Francesca*. The hall was packed; it was a great success except that *Francesca* really did not have the effect that I had expected, for the orchestra played so marvellously that I thought that the audience would go into raptures from the performance alone. I clearly heard two or three whistles. They particularly liked the Waltz from the *Serenade*. I don't think I have had such a tediously exhausting time since Aachen as I am having here now.[7]

One could say that Russian music is travelling around the centres of Germany in my person.[8]

In Hamburg my new symphony was a great success and I was greeted there like a long lost friend. But all this is only pleasant at the time; as soon

[5] xva. 46–7 (von Meck).   [6] xva. 49 (Glazunov).
[7] xva. 51 (Modest).   [8] xva. 57 (K.R.).

as a rehearsal or a concert is over, I immediately sink into gloom and long for my homeland to the point of despair.[9]

The concert in Geneva was an enormous success in spite of the bad orchestra. The theatre was packed. I was presented with a huge golden (i.e. gilded, of course) wreath from the Russian colony and, in a word, it all went as it should. The next day I left with great reluctance since it was wonderful spring weather.[10]

Here's a short account of my experiences over this period. I began with Cologne, where I had a great success. Then I went to Frankfurt, then Dresden, Berlin, Geneva, Hamburg. At every stop there were several rehearsals, endless invitations, and exhaustion.[11] I decided to play the Fifth Symphony in Hamburg.[12] Each time through the players liked it better and better; at the final rehearsal there was a great show of enthusiasm, a flourish from the orchestra, and so on. The concert, too, went off excellently. The best thing is that I no longer find the symphony horrible and have started liking it again.[13]

Wherever I have appeared I have had a great success.[14] But nobody reads about me in the papers in Russia. It's a great pity. I have no friends in the Petersburg press and those in Moscow have forgotten me. I can scarcely write advertisements for myself.[15] The point after all is not that I personally have been favoured with the attention of the European public, but that in my person attention has been paid and honour has been accorded to the whole of Russian music, to all Russian art. I have come to the conclusion that my foreign successes are ignored in consequence of some hostility aroused by I know not what. If this is so, then I repeat yet again that it has absolutely nothing to do with me as a person. The Russian public ought to know that a Russian musician, regardless of who he might be, has carried the banner of his native art with honour and distinction in the great centres of Europe.[16]

My concert in London will be on 11 April, new style. Early in the morning of the next day I go straight to Marseilles and on Saturday 13 April I catch a steamer which will take me to Batum. From Tiflis I will arrive in Moscow at the beginning of May. Three days ago my Suite No. 3 was a great success at a concert (it was not I conducting but Colonne himself).[17]

First of all I must tell you that I have discovered at last what a London fog is. I enjoyed London fogs last year as well but I could not have imagined one such as we had today. When I walked to the rehearsal this morning it was about as foggy as it gets in Petersburg. But when Sapelnikov and I left St James's Hall at 12.30 *in the afternoon* it was absolutely dark, like 8 o'clock in the autumn on a moonless evening in Petersburg. We

[9] xva. 71 (von Meck).   [10] xva. 68 (Modest).
[11] xva. 75–6 (Shpazhinskaya).   [12] xva. 76 (Ziloti).
[13] xva. 74 (Modest).   [14] xva. 62 (Anatoly and Panya).
[15] xva. 69 (Jurgenson).   [16] xva. 96 (Suvorin).
[17] xva. 83 (Jurgenson).

were both greatly struck by this. I find London quite dreadfully disagree-able without this (for God's sake don't tell Miss Eastwood), but now I feel deep down as if I were sitting in a dark underground prison. It is four o'clock at the moment. It has begun to get a little lighter but it is still dark. What is so surprising is that this should have happened half-way through April. Even the Londoners are surprised and annoyed.[18]

I declined the Russian concerts in Paris. Neither the Exhibition com-mittee nor the French government have agreed to guarantee the expenses and I cannot take the risk on my own account, nor do I want to. However, the Russian concerts will still take place in Paris. The wealthy merchant Belyayev, the admirer of Glazunov, Rimsky-Korsakov, Borodin etc. is arranging *en grand* two concerts at the Trocadéro consisting of their works.[19]

This trip abroad seems to have been particularly exhausting and I have felt quite ill. It took an incredible effort to last out until the London con-cert, which was on 11 April/30 March. I flew in a tremendous rush from there to Marseilles so as not to miss the steamer direct to Batum. I arrived safely after a very enjoyable voyage of twelve days, then spent three weeks in Tiflis. Both on the voyage and in Tiflis I felt idle as I have never done before and couldn't face work, least of all writing letters.[20]

After four months of travels, crammed with all manner of anxieties, wor-ries, sufferings, and homesickness, I am home at last. My dream, passionate to the point of being painful, is a reality. And ... ? I don't know how or why, but instead of unalloyed pleasure and calm what I feel is a vague sad-ness, a sense of dissatisfaction, even melancholy, and (most peculiar of all) I constantly find myself thinking it would be nice *to get away somewhere.* What could be odder than that? I have work to do, the weather is marvell-ous, I have always liked solitude and have always sought it, and yet despite all this I am not exactly unhappy, but wistful, craving for something. So let's just hope I get distracted with my work and it passes.[21]

26 May. I have finished *composing* the ballet.[22] I haven't stirred from the country all this time. As always I have been working very intensely under great pressure because I am tied to a particular date and will have to spare no effort to get the score in on time. We have had cool weather throughout June, I have had complete peace, and I like the story so the work has not particularly tired me and I have felt very well in general of late.[23]

I have decided to look for a flat in Moscow for the winter. In the first place because I will have a very great deal to do there organizing our con-certs and in the second place because with living in the country in the winter I have started suffering from severe headaches in recent years. When you have worked the whole day some sort of entertainment is

[18] xva. 87 (Bob Davydov).
[19] xva. 89 (von Meck).
[20] xva. 105 (Shpazhinskaya).
[21] xva. 119 (Shpazhinskaya).
[22] *Diaries*, 240.
[23] xva. 138 (von Meck).

essential in the evening, perhaps a small party for cards or just a walk, which is impossible in the country. So I have decided to try to find somewhere to settle in Moscow. In any event I can't stay at Frolovskoye because my landlady has cut down all the woods and the whole attraction of my surroundings here has gone.[24]

Tchaikovsky took an active part in organizing the concerts for the 1889/1890 season of the Moscow branch of the RMS.

I continue to lead a quiet, busy, country life. The ballet is coming on gradually but gradually is the word: I can no longer work as fast as I used to. One good thing is that I am happy with my new work and have realized that I need not worry yet about the falling off in inventive capacity which must be a more or less imminent threat. I can feel that the decline has not yet started, and the thought that I am not yet senile is gratifying to me. I know that I am not nearly old enough for my faculties to dim, but when I was young I worked too much and overtired myself too often, so there are grounds for fearing that the decline might set in earlier than it should.[25]

I think that the music for this ballet will be one of my best works. The story is so poetic and so grateful to set to music that I have been quite carried away by composing it and have written it with that warmth and enthusiasm which always determine the value of a work. The scoring is proving considerably more troublesome than these things used to be and work is going much more slowly, but perhaps this is a good thing. Many of my previous works have borne the marks of haste and insufficient consideration.[26] I have devoted particular care and affection to the orchestration and have devised some quite new instrumental groupings which I hope will be very fine and interesting.[27]

After more than ten weeks of work, on 20 [August] I finally wrote the longed-for closing chord of the last act. I was so tired that I felt a need to get away somewhere immediately, for some distraction and relaxation, so I came to stay with my sister in the Kiev province. I have been here for a week now, and the day after tomorrow I am going off into the country, not very far, to my niece [Anna], and then to Moscow. Rehearsals and conducting the first performance of *Onegin* with new décor await me there. Soon after that the preparations for our concerts will start, then conducting in Petersburg at Rubinstein's jubilee concert in November, then the production of the ballet, Moscow again and concerts, in short, a period of complicated and seething activity lies ahead. I scarcely recognize myself! Only six or seven years ago I was a complete recluse, I was anti-social, and very much a cloistered toiler. Now I am caught up in the social whirl. I must

[24] xva. 138–9 (von Meck).   [25] xva. 155 (von Meck).
[26] xva. 160 (von Meck).   [27] xva. 169 (von Meck).

admit that I much prefer my former way of life. But I do what I consider to be my duty.[28]

I went to Kiev and heard *Onegin*. The décor was excellent and the ensemble was good, but apart perhaps from Medvedev none of the singers was outstanding. They *weren't bad*, but no more than that.[29] The audience unexpectedly gave me a very flattering ovation. I left for Moscow the next day. Here I had to deal with some very complex matters to do with the Musical Society as well as with the rehearsals for *Eugene Onegin*, which they did on 18 September, with new, and exceedingly sumptuous décor. I conducted this performance. It was a great success and I was extremely pleased with the performance. I left for Petersburg the next day and spent ten days there.[30]

My Moscow flat is now in proper order because Alexey moved in with all my goods and chattels whilst I was on the way to Petersburg. The flat is very small, but it's very nice and cosy. Now I will have to prepare myself for conducting two concerts in Moscow and three in Petersburg. I am especially scared of the two jubilee concerts of Rubinstein's music. It will be a very complicated and difficult programme and because this triumphant occasion is so unique I am already beginning to suffer agonies of anxiety. [After all] I have never conducted anybody else's works. So my task will be an especially difficult one.[31]

Tchaikovsky took a flat on the Prechistenka, 6, Troitsky Lane.

Tchaikovsky met Chekhov in Moscow; he had been enthusiastic about his works before this.

What do you [Mme Shpazhinskaya] know about Chekhov, our great new Russian literary talent? In my view, he will be a pillar of our literature.[32] Chekhov wrote that he wanted *to dedicate to me* his new collection of stories. I went to see him to thank him. I am immensely gratified and proud.[33]

He is referring to Chekhov's *Gloomy People* which appeared in 1890. Chekhov's letter of 12 October 1889 has survived: 'These stories are tedious and tiresome, like the autumn, they are uniform in tone, artistic and medical elements are mixed thickly together; and yet I still venture to address to you a humble request to permit me to dedicate this book to you; such a dedication would go at least some way towards satisfying that profound sense of respect which makes me think of you every day. The idea of dedicating a book to you took a firm grip on me on the day you told me that you had read some of my stories.' Before the volume was published, Chekhov wrote to Modest Tchaikovsky: 'I am willing to stand day and night as an honorary watchman at the door of Pyotr Ilich's house, so great is my respect for him. If we are to talk in terms of rank, he now occupies the second place in

[28] xv*a*. 175 (Shpazhinskaya).   [29] xv*a*. 177 (V. Zarudnaya).
[30] xv*a*. 190 (von Meck).   [31] Ibid.
[32] xv*a*. 124 (Shpazhinskaya).   [33] xv*a*. 201 (Modest).

Russian art, after Tolstoy, who has long occupied the first place. I accord Repin third place and myself ninety-eighth.' Chekhov sent Tchaikovsky his photograph and wrote: 'I would even send you the sun if it were mine to send.' (A. Chekhov, *Collected Works, xi* (Moscow, 1956, pp. 384–5; 422; 387).

Nor have I thanked you [Chekhov] properly for the dedication of *Gloomy People*, of which I am terribly proud. I have kept meaning to write you a long letter; I even made an attempt at explaining just what it was about your talent which has such a fascinating and enthralling effect on me, but I did not have sufficient time, and, more importantly, I was not up to it. It is very difficult for a musician to put into words just what or how he feels about anything artistic.[34]

I never cut out articles about myself, I never bother about them; the cuttings which I sent you [Jurgenson] and my brother Modest were sent to me by various well-wishers, and mostly by the authors themselves. I feel somehow that it would be awkward and disagreeable to buy papers with articles about myself, to arm myself with a pair of scissors, and then distribute the cuttings to my friends.[35]

My nature is such that I would most ardently wish to live in constant isolation from the mass of humanity, but in recent years the circumstances of my life have fallen out in such a way that I am compelled to live not at all as I would wish. The trouble is that I regard it as my *duty*, so long as I have the strength, to struggle with my fate, not to shun people, but to let them see my activities, so long as they want to. For instance, so far as the Moscow Musical Society is concerned, I am bound to say that I am of considerable use to them by remaining as a director and taking an active part in their affairs. If the forthcoming season is a success I will be very proud because it was my idea that each concert should have an influential conductor and I have arranged this through my personal contacts and correspondence. This will give the concerts a unique and unprecedented interest. But my God! how much I will have to do, how much work I will have right through the winter!!![36]

I am at present completely immersed in the concerts here and in the preparations for Rubinstein's jubilee. I conducted the second Musical Society concert successfully.[37]

This was Tchaikovsky's first appearance as a conductor of someone else's music. The programme of the concert on 28 October was: Mozart's Symphony No. 38, Tchaikovsky's Violin Concerto (with Brodsky as soloist), two dances from Mozart's *Idomeneo*, the overture to Taneyev's opera *Oresteia* (first performance), and Glinka's *Jota Aragonesa*.

What I am living at the moment is not life but servitude: I haven't even five minutes, never mind for letters or reading but just to think. I rush around

[34] xvia. 250 (Anton Chekhov).   [35] xva. 84 (Jurgenson).
[36] xva. 197 (von Meck).   [37] xva. 265 (K.R.).

in all directions like a lunatic, I wear myself out in the course of the day to the point of utter stupefaction; I get home and collapse in a heap on the bed, and the same thing the next day. You will ask why I take such a burden upon myself when previously I lived in such freedom and peace. The answer is simple: I am going through all this because I consider it my duty. I am needed, and so long as I live I must satisfy this need. Of course, I cannot even think about composing!!! It's horrible and disgusting, I can feel that I'm getting older and ruining my health but there's nothing I can do about it. Besides, there are good moments as well: when something comes off successfully.[38]

I got back from Petersburg utterly exhausted with the work which fell to me in connection with Rubinstein's jubilee concerts. There were moments when my strength fell so low that I feared for my life. Learning *The Tower of Babel* with a choir of seven hundred was particularly difficult. At the end of the first part of the concert, before I had to begin this oratorio, I had such a severe attack of nerves that for several min᠁tes it was feared that I would not be in a state to go on to the platform but, perhaps precisely because of this crisis, I was able to get myself under control and in the end everything went off entirely satisfactorily . . . I might add that from the 1st to the 19th of November I was a real martyr, and I am astonished now that I was able to bear it all.[39]

Tchaikovsky's success at the Rubinstein jubilee concerts was so great that the audience gave him a better reception than it did Rubinstein himself.

[In Moscow now] rehearsals are beginning for the concert which I am conducting on the 25th ([Beethoven's] Ninth Symphony), then I am going to Petersburg for the ballet rehearsals. God knows when I will eventually manage to get a proper rest.[40]

For nearly three weeks I have been *idling* in Petersburg. I say *idling* because I regard composing as my proper work and all my activities conducting concerts, attending ballet rehearsals, and so on as incidental, pointless, and serving only to shorten my life, because a terrible effort of will is required to put up with the sort of life I have to live in Petersburg. The most dreadful thing is that I am never alone and am permanently in an abnormal and agitated condition. During these three weeks I have constantly had to attend the rehearsals of my ballet, and, on top of that, I have had to conduct at a Russian Symphony Concert. I am having to stay here so long because of the ballet, which is put off from one day to the next because the scenery is not ready. However, I have all sorts of things to do in Moscow and I have decided to go there tomorrow, the 18th [of December]; but I'll come back here for the first performance of the ballet. I have to be in Moscow again on 6 January, to conduct a Musical Society concert at which

---

[38] xv*a*. 210 (Shpazhinskaya).   [39] xv*a*. 212 (von Meck).   [40] Ibid.

Anton Rubinstein will play his new work, and then I will conduct a public concert again in Petersburg on the 14th.[41]

I have spent a week [in Moscow] in a very wretched frame of mind. I have had a very unpleasant experience and the cause of it all is the lady whom at one time I used to call *a certain person*. I must get away, get away somewhere as soon as I can. I want to see nobody, to know nothing about anything, to work, work, work—that is what my soul craves.[42]

Saw the New year in with Modest, Guitry, and Angèle in Leiner's restaurant [in Petersburg].[43]

Rehearsal of the ballet attended by the *Emperor* [Alexander III]. 'Very nice'!!!!! His Majesty was very haughty with me. Pity about him.[44]

The very successful première of *The Sleeping Beauty* took place in the Mariinsky Theatre on 3 January.

I have no strength left; I have decided to refuse all invitations at home and abroad and to go away somewhere in Italy for four months or so to rest and to work on my next opera. I have chosen the subject for this opera: Pushkin's *Queen of Spades*.[45]

[41] xva. 218–19 (von Meck).   [42] xva. 220 (von Meck).
[43] *Diaries*, 250.   [44] Ibid.
[45] xva. 219 (von Meck).

23

1890

I think that I really have a gift for faithfully, sincerely, *and* simply *conveying in music the emotions, the atmosphere, and the characters suggested by the text.*

For the first half of this winter I have had to submit to strains which have been quite inhuman, constantly travelling between P'burg and Moscow, spending all day at the rehearsal, then at the concert, straining my nervous resources to the utmost. It all ended with me falling into an absolute stupor of fatigue, and I began to fear something very horrible, such as madness or even worse. On the other hand I gradually began to feel a pressing urge to get on with my proper work, i.e. composing, as a form of *relaxation*. And then, just as if it had been planned, Vsevolozhsky took to asking me if I would write an opera on *The Queen of Spades*. The libretto had already been done by none other than my brother Modest for a Mr Klenovsky (who did not, however, write anything). I read it through, I liked it, and then one fine day I decided to abandon everything—Petersburg and Moscow, and lots of towns in Germany, Belgium, and France to which I had invitations for concerts—and go away somewhere abroad so as to work without interruption.[1] We fixed a meeting of an *ad hoc* committee and my brother read through his libretto; then we had a thorough discussion of its theatrical virtues and failings, planned the décor, even assigned the parts, and so on. Consequently there is already talk amongst the theatre management about producing this opera of which not a single note has yet been written. I very much want to work, and if I can manage to get settled down in some nice little spot abroad I think I will be able to cope with my task, send the short score to the management by May, and orchestrate it in the summer.[2]

On 14 January Tchaikovsky left St Petersburg to go abroad. He took with him Modest's servant, Nazar Litrov, since the wife of his own servant, Alexey Sofronov, was dying of tuberculosis.

All the way here I couldn't decide where to go, because in truth I didn't want to go anywhere. But eventually I did settle on Florence. Oh, I am so fed up and out of sorts and I don't even know why. Work will probably rescue me from this insufferable condition.[3] Italy, Florence—nothing gives

[1] xvb. 26 (Shpazhinskaya).   [2] xva. 219–20 (von Meck).
[3] xvb. 19 (Modest).

me the slightest pleasure so far. I don't want anything, except to get away. I
have got settled into the hotel here very comfortably [Hotel Washington]. I
have a suite which is entirely separate. The windows look out on to the
Lungarno. It will be fun to watch people going to the Cascino in fine
weather. I'll see what happens tomorrow when I get down to work. If it
doesn't go well I'll go back to Russia. I cannot live outside Russia.[4]

January 19/31. Started working—not bad.[5] *January 23/4 February.* I
have been here for six days now, my routine is established, I have got back
to my norm, and I can write without complaining of ennui. I am fixed up
very well. Although the furnishings are staggeringly dismal (just like somewhere in the provinces in Russia), my suite is very comfortable and
pleasant, and above all it is quiet and absolutely cut off from the intrusion
of any noise at all, except what comes from the street. Nazar wakes me at
quarter to eight; I have a cup of tea and read the papers (*Nazione* and
Figaro). Then I work till twelve thirty. I get dressed to go for lunch, then
go for a walk. I come back at three for a cup of tea, and Nazar and I watch
the procession of carriages go by till four. I work from four till seven. I go
for dinner at seven. I have dinner and lunch at a separate table. After dinner I go for a walk or to the theatre. And that's my routine every day. If I
don't go to the theatre I write letters or read . . . Nazar either is very happy
or he is pretending to be, but he seems to be positively glowing. For my
part I too am extremely pleased with him and am delighted that he is with
me, otherwise that sense of sadness which I always carry with me would be
nagging me infinitely more. Now, about my work. I set to straight away,
and very diligently; I have already done quite a fair amount. The libretto is
very good but its failing is that it's too *wordy*. I am leaving bits out. The
verse is sometimes very good, sometimes a bit (and sometimes very) stiff.
But on the whole I can say with my hand on my heart that the libretto is
superb.[6] *January 25/6 February.* I have got as far as [Tomsky's] *ballad*.
That's not bad for seven days' work. I think it's turning out all right.[7]

Things have changed completely and though I am experiencing no
pleasure from being in Florence, my former morbid gloom has vanished.
My work has got under way, and to some effect, and this has completely
transformed my morale. Whatever happens I must finish the opera by the
spring; the question is, do my surroundings and my way of life measure up
to what is needed for me to work successfully? In reply I can say yes, completely. Nothing and nobody bothers me; in the evenings I can relax, the
walking is very good—in short I have everything I need to be able to exert
myself without damaging my health. I am completely indifferent to where I
am as long as my work goes well.[8]

January 26/7 February. I am enjoying the work immensely now that I
know that I haven't written myself out, as I thought, and that the opera is

[4] xib. 20–1 (Modest).   [5] *Diaries*, 251.   [6] xvb. 22–4 (Modest).
[7] xvb. 25 (Modest).   [8] xvb. 24 (Modest).

going to be good.[9] *January 27/8 February*. The Finale of the first scene did
not come too easily.[10] I have got over a merlerncolly bout thanks to my
work, which, praise be, is going well. But I couldn't say that I have been
happy. It's a good thing that I have excellent facilities here for writing
undisturbed because I do want to bring off an improbable trick: to write an
opera for next season. Such is the wish of the management, which is extremely well disposed towards me. And on top of that, I must admit I like
working in a hurry, I like it when people are waiting for me and urging me
on. Nor does it have the slightest effect on the quality of my works. *The
Sleeping Beauty* may well be the best of all my works and yet I wrote it
incredibly quickly.[11] *January 29/10 February*. I began the second scene this
morning. Worked well. Read some old scores borrowed from the [theatre]
management.[12] *January 30/11 February*. A letter from P. I. J[urgenson]
with news of A[ntonina] I[vanovna] upset me dreadfully. I was out of my
mind all day. Did not work.[13] I am going through a very mysterious stage
on my road to the grave. Something is going on deep inside me which I myself cannot understand: a weariness of life, a disillusionment; at times an
insane melancholy, but not the sort which hides in its depths a hint of a new
upsurge of love for life, no, this is something hopeless and final, and even,
as is characteristic of finales, banal. And at the same time a passionate desire
to compose. God knows what's going on: on the one hand I have a feeling
that my song might have been sung, on the other an overwhelming desire to
strike up the same or, even better, a new song. But, I repeat, I don't know
myself what's happening to me.[14] *January 31/12 February*. Work has gone
better; real inspiration came to me in the evening, before dinner.[15]

February 1/13. Worked well.[16] *February 2/14*. Worked well today, but a
strain.[17] The scene [the Countess's death] is excellently, and very musically
constructed; I am very pleased with my librettist all round. I have thought
a lot about the scene on *the embankment*. Despite my wish to have as few
scenes as possible and to keep it concise, I fear that without this scene the
whole of the third act will have no women, and that's boring. Apart from
that the audience needs to know what has happened to *Lisa*. I can't put an
end to her part in Scene 4. I am already finishing the second scene. If the
work goes on as it has done up to now then there are hopes that I will in fact
finish it in time. I don't know whether it will be good or bad. Sometimes I
am very pleased and sometimes I am not, but I am no judge.[18] *February 5/
17*. The scene of the old woman's death is proving troublesome.[19] *February
6/18*. What can I devise to give poor Figner a role that isn't too much for
him? *Seven scenes* and he has to do something all the time! For that reason
alone should I not leave out the scene on the embankment? I am horrified

[9] xv*b*. 26 (Shpazhinskaya).   [10] *Diaries*, 252.   [11] xv*b*. 29–30 (Jurgenson).
[12] *Diaries*, 252–3.   [13] Ibid. 253.   [14] xv*b*. 30 (Glazunov).
[15] *Diaries*, 253.   [16] Ibid.   [17] Ibid.
[18] xv*b*. 38 (Modest).   [19] *Diaries*, 254.

when I think how much I have already written for him and how much I have yet to write. I'm frightened that the poor chap will just run out of steam. And it's not only Figner, any performer would be cast into fear and trembling at the thought that he had to be on the stage and singing almost all the time. Will he even have to have a lot of singing during the ball? I am impatient to get the ball scene, otherwise I'll be left without a text, because I am bold enough to hope that I'll finish the fourth scene in a week. Sometimes it comes very easily, sometimes not without an effort. But that doesn't matter. The effort is perhaps the consequence of wanting to write as well as I can and not to be content with the first idea that comes to me.[20] *February 7/19.* My work has made me very nervous. It's funny, but even my inspiration drives me crazy and creates difficulties.[21] I have been writing the scene today where Herman comes to the old woman. It was so dreadful that the horror of it still affects me.[22] I'm terribly pleased with the way [Modest] has adapted Herman's words in the crucial scene of the old woman's death. Pushkin's text is almost unchanged but there's a rhythm to it.[23] *February 11/23.* I have finished Scene 4 and have started the interlude. It was troublesome at first, but then it started going well.[24] *February 12/24.* Still doing the interlude. I occasionally feel as if I am living in the eighteenth century and nothing has happened since Mozart.[25] I began straight away with the interlude because it was giving me the most problems. There must be a chorus at the end and I have written the words for it. I have done this because the chorus is there and it's odd if it doesn't sing anything at the end. When I get to the point in the third scene where the Prince declares his love for Lisa I may find it necessary to add a little so as to make the Prince's role more prominent. I'll write the words then. I have finished the interlude today (I am writing this at eleven thirty) and will start writing Scene 3 this afternoon. I don't think it should take more than five or six days.[26] If, God willing, I finish the opera it will be a stylish piece of work; I think Scene 4 will be stunningly effective.[27] Modya is a splendid fellow—he has made a first-rate libretto.[28] Very tired. Health and everything all right, but sad all the time. *February 15/27.* Writing went well today. Prince's aria.[29] *February 16/28.* Got masses of letters and they kept coming in dribs and drabs. This annoyed me, which meant that work didn't go so well. I couldn't get on at all before dinner.[30] *February 17/1 March.* Made a great effort with my work today.[31] Sent a formal letter to the Board [of the Moscow branch of the RMS] saying (1) that I was withdrawing from conducting six concerts, and (2) that I was resigning as a director.[32] The reason for this is that when Fitzenhagen died the vacancy for the Professor of the cello

[20] xvb. 43 (Modest). [21] *Diaries*, 254–5. [22] xvb. 44 (Anna Merkling).
[23] xvb. 70 (Modest). [24] *Diaries*, 255. [25] Ibid.
[26] xvb. 48–9 (Modest). [27] xvb. 49 (Modest). [28] xvb. 48 (Modest).
[29] *Diaries*, 255. [30] Ibid. [31] Ibid. 255–6.
[32] xvb. 57 (Jurgenson).

fell vacant. I expressed a wish that Brandukov should be appointed, our own pupil and a fine cellist. Safonov, the present Director, firmly refused to take Brandukov. In consequence I had two choices: either (1) go to Moscow, get rid of Safonov and get myself made Director, or (2) since I greatly value Safonov as a businesslike and intelligent Director, resign from the Board of directors myself and give him a completely free hand. I chose the latter course.[33] *February 18/2 March*. Have been working hard.[34] Sometimes it comes easily, at others not without an effort, particularly after the letters from Russia, particularly from Moscow. If I finish it it will be a glorious opera.[35] *February 19/3 March*. Have finished Scene 3 and played it through.[36] I have completely changed the end of the third scene because the way you [Modest] had it it wasn't effective—there was no real ending. On top of that it's not really a good idea to finish with a polonaise—better to start with one. Of course it's not at all *the words* I'm insisting on, it's the scene. I've already written it this way and very much don't want to change it. I think it would make a good ending. The words seem to be fine in the [Prince's] aria, but I'm afraid that in places they don't make sense. For example: 'And I weep with your tear'. What does that mean? Nothing that I can see. It isn't clear what the Prince really means, which is that his love is selfless and that he is ready to sacrifice anything for her. Do you think you could alter it to make the sense clear but keeping the number and pattern of the words exactly the same, because I have already written the music?[37] *February 20/4 March*. I finished Scene 3 last night and was wondering what I should do today, then just as I was starting work I got a letter with Scene 5. I started work on it straight away.[38] It was remarkably hard going. But then it *is* difficult.[39] To say nothing of the fact that Lisa addresses herself to the night in April and says to it '*She is doleful, like you*'. Do you get *doleful* nights in Petersburg?[40] *February 21/5 March*. Alyosha writes that Feklusha '*is now begging God to take her away quickly*'. The poor, poor suffering creature!!! I have started writing the start of Scene 5; I worked the end out in my head yesterday and actually wrote it down this morning. I worked well before dinner.[41] I didn't start writing Scene 5 from the beginning but from the point where there is a knock on the window and I have finished it already. You [Modest] write: '*funeral singing off stage*' but you haven't sent any text. After all I have to have some words and they must be a free translation from the requiem; I don't actually need the tune of that, but I must give some sort of indication. I need the words for the singing off stage today. I'll have to write something myself.[42] *February 22/6 March*. Have finished Scene 5. Not altogether satisfied with it. There are parts which I don't feel are acceptable and yet I can't change them either.[43] I am working

---

[33] xv*b*. 115–16 (von Meck). [34] *Diaries*, 252. [35] xv*b*. 59 (Anna Merkling).
[36] *Diaries*, 256. [37] xv*b*. 62–4 (Modest). [38] xv*b*. 64 (Modest).
[39] *Diaries*, 256. [40] xv*b*. 64 (Modest). [41] *Diaries*, 256.
[42] xv*b*. 65 (Modest). [43] *Diaries*, 256.

hard and I think that *The Queen of Spades* will turn out to be a very interesting opera. It is a little bit on the frightening side as it sometimes even frightens me.[44]

All the advice and guidance which you [Modest] and Laroche have sent has always come too late. For example, you advised me not to put in 'Rest in the saints'; nor had I done, even before I got your letter—I had put something else in. Vsevolozhsky asks for the Countess to make two appearances—once again, I had done that already.[45]

February 23/7 March. Laboured all morning up to lunch time writing the words for Lisa's arioso. I am certainly no poet. Had a walk in the Cascine gardens; really enjoyed my walk today. I have written *the arioso*.[46] *February 24/8 March.* Heard from Alyosha that Feklusha has died. Wept. Sad morning all round. But I did do some work. Had a wonderful walk in the Cascine gardens. One act of *I Puritani* in the evening. Terrible stuff this Bellini, but delightful all the same.[47] *February 25/9 March.* Working on the end of Scene 6, but haven't finished it yet. *February 26/10 March.* Finished Scene 6; went for a walk and then started the overture. As soon as I have finished the draft I'll start straight away on the full piano score. That will be very easy work but tedious and I want to move to some other town to do it, but I don't want to go home. I'll go home when I've finished the piano score. I'll be very annoyed if the seventh scene doesn't come tomorrow. I hate having to interrupt my work, particularly when it's the draft. I think that Scene 6 has come out well and I'm very glad now that I put it in—it wouldn't have been properly rounded out otherwise.[48] *February 27/11 March.* I've got Scene 7. Modest is marvellous[49]—he's made a splendid job of it. I must have another verse in the *brindisi*. Many thanks Modya! You deserve my deepest gratitude, not only for the virtues of your libretto but for the remarkable accuracy of your timing. It's astonishing that I finished Scene 6 last night and Scene 7 arrived today![50] *February 28/12 March.* Work has gone well. Made excellent progress after tea. Sat for a very long time by the open window wondering where to go from here, nerves in a poor state, thinking about the last scene of the opera.[51] Will finish the opera in three days.[52]

Apart from Eletsky's aria, Tchaikovsky wrote the words for Lisa's arioso, and the chorus 'Now, sweet Mashenka'; he also reworked the Finale of Scene 3 and made additions and alterations in practically every scene. Modest left unchanged everything in the libretto that Tchaikovsky had written himself. At the head of the sketch for Lisa's arioso there is a note: 'Oh! what a nuisance these lines were!' In accordance with operatic tradition this is what Tchaikovsky called the tenor's (Herman's) 'bravura' aria 'What is our life?'. The words for this aria were by Modest.

March 1/13. Slept badly. Even had a terrible nightmare early in the night

[44] xv*b*. 66 (Nikolay Tchaikovsky).   [45] xv*b*. 72 (Modest).   [46] *Diaries*, 257.
[47] Ibid.   [48] xv*b*. 77 (Modest).   [49] *Diaries*, 257.
[50] xv*b*. 81 (Modest).   [51] *Diaries*, 257.   [52] xv*b*. 82 (Modest).

(rustling of papers and movements in my room). Have worked diligently. Enjoyed my solitude (???) over my tea. Worked hard.[53] *March 2*. I am sleeping badly, probably because my work is tiring me. Finished Scene 7 today (there's an aria left to do). Wept dreadfully when Herman breathed his last. Result of tiredness, or perhaps I really have made a good job of it.[54] I must have a second verse for the *brindisi*; I haven't telegraphed because it's not holding me up at all. How could you [Modest] think that I would permit women in the last scene? It's absolutely out of the question, it would be stretching things to the point of scandal. And anyway, the only women you would find in a gambling club would be *whores*.[55] *March 3/15*. Fiddled about with the *brindisi* till dinner time. Finished the Introduction after tea. *Finished everything* before dinner. I give thanks to God that he gave me the strength to finish the opera.[56] Wrote the *brindisi* today (I had it planned out before), and *properly finished the Introduction*. I wrote the very end of the opera yesterday before dinner and when I got to Herman's death and the closing chorus I felt so *sorry* for Herman that I suddenly started sobbing violently. This went on for a terribly long time and turned into a minor fit of very agreeable hysterics, that's to say I found the crying immensely pleasant. Then I realized why (because I have never had sobbing like that before on account of my hero's fate and I was trying to work out why I should have such an urge to cry). What had happened was that Herman had not just been the pretext for me to write some music or other: he had throughout been a real living person, and one, moreover, whom I liked very much. Since I like Figner too, and I constantly saw Figner as Herman, I felt very much involved in his misfortunes. I now think that the warmth and sensitivity of my attitude to the hero of the opera has probably been reflected to advantage in the music. My present view is that, all told, *The Queen of Spades* is a jolly good opera.[57]

I don't completely agree with you [Modest] that you need to make the first two scenes into two acts. First, the length of the first act does not mean anything, provided the interval before the second scene is short. It is not a good thing when the following acts are long. In the piano arrangement the opera will be divided into three acts. You can divide that how you like and it won't matter that the piano arrangement will have *three* acts and the posters will announce *four*. It won't always be the Mariinsky theatre, you know; another theatre will be built with new equipment and then, believe me, it will be much easier to make a quick scene-change (as they do in Vienna and Paris) even with the complicated sets that we have in the first two scenes. After all, I wrote it so that the first scene comes to an end and the second begins not like two acts but like two scenes. There is a difference![58]

Laroche wrote and told me that he and Nápravník are *grumbling* about

[53] *Diaries*, 257–8.   [54] Ibid. 258.   [55] xvb. 83 (Modest).
[56] *Diaries*, 258.   [57] xvb. 87 (Modest).   [58] xvb. 97 (Modest).

my having written it so quickly. How can they not understand that speed of working is one of my *fundamental* characteristics; I can't write in any other way except *quickly*. But because it was written fast, it does not mean that it is a *carelessly* written opera. There have been pieces which I have written slowly, for instance *The Sorceress*, the Fifth Symphony, and they were not a success, but I composed the ballet in three weeks, and *Eugene Onegin* also unbelievably quickly. The secret is to write with *love*. And I certainly wrote *The Queen of Spades* with love. Lord, how I wept yesterday when my poor Herman sang his last gasp! Meanwhile I am firmly convinced that *The Queen of Spades* is a good, but more importantly, a very original work (I am talking not about the music but in general).[59]

I have decided to stay in Florence on the basis of the incontrovertible truth that 'only good can come out of good'. I work well here and my accommodation is excellent.[60]

4/16 March. It's very tedious here, very monotonous, but one couldn't imagine more suitable conditions for working. So I am staying here until I finish the *piano score*.[61] *March 6/18*. I am very pleased with the opera so far and sometimes I think everybody else will like it too. But when it comes to the fruits of their own imagination composers are never the best judges. We shall see![62] If I am spared and all goes well with the scoring then I think the end result will surpass anything I have previously written for the stage. I did not find the composing too tiring, but I am doing the piano arrangement now and that work does tire me a lot.[63] I started composing the opera exactly two months ago! I have almost finished the short score of Act II today [19/31 March]. I have only one thing left to do, and for me it is the most dreadful and unsettling work of all. It was a pleasure to get immersed in the writing of the opera; I know I will enjoy orchestrating it. But the piano arrangement! That's dreadful! After all you are constantly having to distort things which were conceived for the orchestra. I'll plod on for another week or so with Act III, and then I would like to get away somewhere for about three weeks so as to try to orchestrate if not the whole of the first act at least the first scene. The last thing I want to do is go back to Russia without taking at least a bit of *the score* with me. Only when part of the score exists will I be sure that the opera *exists*. Unless I am making a dreadful and unforgivable mistake *The Queen of Spades* really will be my masterpiece. In some places, in Scene 4 for instance which I have been arranging today, I experience such a sense of fear, dread, and shock that the audience too is *bound* to feel the same, at least in some degree.[64]

I have written *The Queen of Spades*. I would like to be able to say definitely that the music is a success, but I am frightened to because experience shows that, particularly after they have just given birth, composers have an exaggerated and frequently unjustified weakness for their offspring. All I

[59] xv*b*. 88 (Modest).   [60] xv*b*. 90 (Modest).   [61] xv*b*. 90 (Modest).
[62] xv*b*. 93–4 (Kolya).   [63] xv*b*. 106 (Kolya).   [64] xv*b*. 103–4 (Modest).

can say is that I was passionately carried away by it and put all my heart into it.[65] Whilst I have been in Florence recently there has been something wrong with me all the time and although I have had all the signs of a cold I think that the real cause has been exhaustion, from making *the piano score*, to be more specific. It would have been quite impossible to ask anybody else to do it because apart from me nobody can understand my drafts.[65]

I am leaving Florence at long last. I hesitated about where to go because, to tell the truth, I don't want to go *anywhere* apart from Russia. All the same, I did eventually decide to try going to Rome. I have done nothing for the first time, after working for nine weeks. I spent the whole morning in the Uffizi and enjoyed myself enormously, but in a quite different way from everybody else. No matter how much I urge myself on I have to admit that painting, particularly old painting, is really quite beyond me and leaves me cold. All these masterpieces mean terribly little to me. But I did find there a source of pleasure answering to my tastes in the passage leading through to the Pitti Palace. I spent two whole hours there looking at these old portraits of all manner of princes, kings, popes, and various historical figures. Apparently nobody ever looks at them, apart from me, yet they are extremely interesting.[67]

I have come to Rome. I don't know what I'm going to do later but I am very content for the moment.[68] I chose the Hotel Molaro on the recommendation of the owner of the Hotel Washington and also because I am generally very fond of small hotels. There was a nice small suite available on the upper floor. I am very pleased with my accommodation. The happy feeling which seized me as soon as I went outside and sniffed the familiar air of Rome, and saw the places which were once so familiar too made me realize that I had done the most stupid thing in not settling in Rome from the start. However, I must not abuse poor Florence, which has done me no harm but which, for no good reason, I have taken a dislike to; yet I ought to be grateful to Florence for letting me write *The Queen of Spades* without interruption. I have been in St Peter's Cathedral and the Pantheon. I still haven't seen the Forum. I will stay here for three weeks exactly. With luck I'll finish Act I. Lovely, lovely Rome! Then I intend to go to Petersburg where I have promised my relations to spend my fiftieth birthday with them. I'll be half a century old on 25 April. After this family celebration I will then go back to Frolovskoye, which I have rented again, because I have given up for good and all trying to settle permanently in a town anywhere. The experience of this present winter has proved decisively that I can live in a large town only as a temporary visitor.[69]

Rome has *changed* terribly. Much of it is completely unrecognizable. For instance, that part of the Via del Tritono which used to take you right to the

[65] xv*b*. 109 (Vsevolozhsky).   [66] xv*b*. 121 (Anatoly).
[67] xv*b*. 111–12 (Modest).   [68] xv*b*. 116 (Anna Merkling).
[69] xv*b*. 117–18 (Modest).

Trevi fountain has been made wide and opulent and now runs straight into the Corso. But in spite of all these changes, I feel remarkably pleased to be in my beloved city again. This feeling is mixed with a melancholy awareness of the years slipping by.[70] I haven't been to any museums, except the Capitol, and probably won't. Nazar is sight-seeing a lot thanks to his friend Karl. Next Sunday I will take him to the Via Appia. On my last day I will go to the Vatican for the sake of Antinous.* I am in a much better frame of mind here; but I can tell you frankly that I live only in anticipation of the utterly unbelievable happiness and bliss of returning home!!! Two more weeks of voluntary exile from my homeland. I dare not think seriously about it yet! . . .[71]

With the prospect of my imminent return home after a voluntary exile from Russia of three months, I am in excellent spirits, which have been helped tremendously by the knowledge that I have completed a great task. It could very well turn out that *The Queen of Spades* is a very bad opera; it is all too likely that in a year's time I shall hate it, as I hate many of my works, but at the moment I think it my best work, and that in writing it I have achieved something significant.[72]

You [Mme von Meck] cannot imagine, my dear friend, how I am longing for Russia and with what feelings of bliss I think of my solitude in the country. Meanwhile things don't seem to be going right in Russia. Those near to the Emperor are pushing him into reaction and this is very sad. This spirit of reaction has reached the point that the works of Count Lev Tolstoy are hounded as being some kind of revolutionary proclamations. The young are in revolt and truly the atmosphere in Russia is very threatening. But none of this stops me from loving it with something like passionate love. I am amazed at how I could formerly live abroad for long periods of time, even find pleasure of a sort in being far away from Russia. Did you know, dear friend, that Nikolay Alexandrovich Rimsky-Korsakov is marrying my niece Tasya? The wedding (which at first Tasya's parents looked on unfavourably) will take place very soon, and immediately after the wedding the doctors are sending them to the mountains for the sake of Rina's health which is giving cause for alarm. I find it very touching that Nikolay Rimsky-Korsakov should have chosen the sister of his dead wife when he needed to find a wife for the sake of the children; and I am also touched by Tasya's marrying him out of love for her sister's children.[73]

I am having to run away from Rome, dear friend [Mme von Meck]. I could not maintain my incognito here. Several Russians have aleady visited me in order to invite me to lunch, for the evening, etc. Of course I refused all these invitations, but my freedom has already been poisoned, and all pleasure at being in my dear Rome is at an end.[74]

* There is a statue of the boy Antinous, Hadrian's favourite, in the Vatican [trans.].

[70] xvb. 118 (Modest).   [71] xvb. 125 (Modest).   [72] xvb. 131 (K.R.).
[73] xvb. 128–9 (von Meck).   [74] xvb. 128 (von Meck).

I have spent three weeks in Rome, and three very good ones, but only because I had the not too distant prospect of soon going home.[75] Living abroad in complete solitude has produced a good harvest. But it could well be that this is just my imagination and that *The Queen of Spades* faces an even more pitiful fate than *The Sorceress*.[76]

The history of the world is divided, so it seems to me, into two periods. The first period contains everything that happened from the creation of the world up to the creation of *The Queen of Spades*. The second period began a month ago when *The Queen of Spades* was created.[77]

This was no more than a joke from a composer who was modest and severe on himself; but so far as the history of music is concerned Tchaikovsky was not so far from the truth.

I had a very pleasant time in Petersburg. I went to Tasya's wedding. I have warm feelings towards this wedding and it has raised Tasya in my estimation, of whom I did not have a very high opinion before. I celebrated my birthday at the Davydovs, and all my relations were there. On your [Anatoly] and Modest's birthday we had a lunch (for all those who had signed the congratulatory telegram) and I left for Moscow at eight o'clock.[78]

The furniture has made the house [at Frolovskoye] unrecognizable; the main room (which is a dining-room and study, as before) now looks remarkably good as a result of adding *Ziloti*'s furniture to my own. On the other hand, outside is—horror! *All the woods, literally all*, have been cut down, and they are now busy cutting down what is left. There is *nowhere* to go for a walk!!! Heavens above! how the loss of the woods completely changes the character of the area, and how sad it is! All those nice shady little spots which were still there last year are now just bald, bare patches. I am busy twice over, because I work during working hours and read proofs for the rest of the time.[79] My work is not getting on especially quickly because what I am scoring at the moment (Scenes 4 and 5) demands a tremendous amount of attention and effort.[80]

Alexander Ziloti gave Tchaikovsky some of his furniture, which is still in the study of the museum at Klin.

I am going through a period of feeling great love for life. I have the knowledge of a great task having been successfully accomplished. However, maybe I only *think* that *The Queen of Spades* is a successful opera. I don't know, but for the moment I am convinced that it will have a brilliant future. I managed to finish orchestrating the first half of the opera in Rome;

[75] xvb. 135 (Anatoly and Panya).   [76] xvb. 141 (Ippolitov-Ivanov).
[77] xvb. 114 (Bob).   [78] xvb. 143 (Anatoly).
[79] xvb. 144–5 (Modest).   [80] xvb. 146 (Modest).

here I have started the second half. Then I want to write a rough sketch for a string sextet.[81]

About the *craftsman*'s approach to the job in the field of art. Ever since I started composing I have taken it as my aim to emulate in my activities the greatest masters of music: Mozart, Beethoven, and Schubert, not, that is to say, to be as great as they were but to compose, as they did, in the fashion of *a cobbler*, and not in the fashion of *a lord*, like our Glinka, whose genius, incidentally, I am not at all minded to deny. Mozart, Beethoven, Schubert, Mendelssohn, Schumann all created their immortal works exactly as a cobbler makes boots, i.e. just working from one day to the next, and, for the most part, *to commission*. What emerged was something tremendous. If Glinka had been a cobbler rather than a gentleman, instead of writing two (admittedly excellent) operas he would have written fifteen, and a dozen or so marvellous symphonies on top of that. I could weep with rage when I think of what Glinka could have given us if he had not been born into a gentry family in the pre-Emancipation days. All he did was give an indication of what he could do but did not in fact achieve even a fraction of it. In the field of orchestral music, for instance, (in *Kamarinskaya* and *the two Spanish overtures*) he just *plays about* like a dilettante—and even then one is astonished at the strength and originality of his creative gift. What could we have expected of him if the circumstances of his life had led him to work in the same way as those leading lights of Western music whom I mentioned earlier?!! Though I am incurably convinced that if a musician wants to reach that level of achievement which the extent of his gifts entitles him to expect he must encourage the craftsman in himself, I am by no means of the opinion that this is necessary in other fields of art. In lyric verse, for instance, it is not just a question of *mood* but of an *idea* as well, and this idea is provoked by some event, some incident. *The will* can have no influence on an event or an incident. But for music on the other hand it is sufficient to summon up more or less the right mood; so I can, for instance, put myself in *a melancholy mood for an elegy*. In a poem, however, this melancholy must express itself *concretely*, so to speak, and for this some sort of external stimulus, some outside impetus is essential. But variations in the individual's creative character have a tremendous importance in all this, and what suits one person perfectly will be useless for another. The majority of my colleagues, for example, do not like writing to *commission*, whereas I am never so inspired as when I am asked to do something, when a specific date is set, and when people are waiting impatiently for me to finish my work.[82]

The accommodation for the copying office and the library has all been altered, so before I left to go abroad Vsevolozhsky and Pogozhev asked me for the *manuscript* of The Queen of Spades, to be kept in the library, which they have just got into exemplary order. How could I refuse? I owe all my

[81] xv*b*. 143 (Anatoly).   [82] xv*b*. 148–9 (K.R.).

prosperity to the Petersburg theatre. Not only does it give me a yearly income of four or five thousand roubles, not only does it now give me a pension of three thousand roubles, but I am particularly indebted to the Petersburg theatre for my reputation as a composer. I do not personally ascribe the slightest value to my manuscripts and it is so easy for me to show at least some gratitude for all I owe the theatre and Vsevolozhsky personally by giving them a manuscript. So there is no way that I can go back on my word to give them a manuscript. If in law (I know nothing about this) I have no right to dispose of my manuscripts without consulting my publisher, then I ask you [Jurgenson], as a friend, to waive your rights on this one occasion. But if you insist on your rights and will not permit me to give the theatre the manuscript I will have to spend about three months copying out the score with my own hand. I am not in the least concerned *about the Public Library*. For decades Stasov has been getting them all manner of rubbish as though it were something precious—the works of Shcherbachov and *tutti quanti*. It's not at all flattering for me to be in that company. But Stasov is a decent old fellow all the same and I should have given him the score of something ages ago and that would have done for him.[83]

Jurgenson's reply is worthy of note.

'My dear friend! I am very sorry that you have so taken to heart my request about the manuscript of *The Queen of Spades*. Of course it grieves me, but that's all there is to it. I know your own views about your manuscripts, nor do they surprise me; but I cannot resist my own passion for collecting them. Not for one second did any question of rights come into my request. As to the Public Library, I regard that as a depository accessible to the public for centuries, for millennia, God willing. Who the hell cares about Stasov and his Shcherbachov? Just remember that Glinka is there as well.' (Jurgenson, ii. 168).

The autograph score of *The Queen of Spades* is in the Central Music Library of the Kirov Theatre. In the Public Library in Leningrad there is a score of *The Tempest* dedicated to Stasov; it was given to the library by Tchaikovsky at Stasov's request. Jurgenson fully appreciated the value of Tchaikovsky's manuscripts and carefully preserved his autograph copies. This invaluable collection, together with the whole archive of Jurgenson's firm, is now in the Glinka Central Music Museum, Moscow.

I have finished the opera off altogether and then I spent another two days finally sorting it out i.e. putting in the letters, the page numbers, stitching it up and sewing it together. Alexey did the sewing. Then I took it to Jurgenson in Moscow on 8 June. So I have been writing the opera from 19 January to 8 June, i.e. four and a half months.[84] I have written it with unbelievable passion and enthusiasm, I have vividly experienced all the sufferings and emotions of the story (to such an extent that at one stage I feared that the ghost of the Queen of Spades might make an appearance),

---

[83] xvb. 172 (Jurgenson).   [84] xvb. 179–80 (Modest).

and I hope that all my raptures, excitements, and enthusiasms will find a response in the hearts of responsive listeners. All the same I am sure the opera has masses of failings which are typical of my musical personality, [including] mistakes in setting the words. I am incorrigible in this respect. I don't think I have made too many blunders of this kind in the recitatives, in the dialogue but when I concentrate in the lyrical passages on faithfully conveying the general atmosphere I simply don't notice the mistakes and I need somebody to point out exactly where they are so that I can see them. But to tell the truth people are too finicky about these details. Our music critics overlook the fact that the main thing in vocal music is the faithful re-creation of emotion and atmosphere; they look first for wrong accents which do not correspond to the pattern of the spoken language, surges in the melody, and in general all sort of trivial oversights in the setting which they gather with a sort of evil delight and then reproach the composer with them when their enthusiasm might be directed to better ends. Mr Cui is especially notable in such matters. So far as the repetition of words and even whole phrases is concerned, I must say that there are occasions when such repetitions are entirely natural and reflect reality. Under the influence of strong emotion people very often repeat the same exclamation, the same phrase. I don't find anything that rings untrue in the old, dim-witted governess constantly repeating her *refrain* about the proprieties whenever she finds a convenient opportunity to deliver reproofs and reprimands. But even if nothing like this ever happened in real life I would have no hesitation in departing from literal truth to the advantage of artistic truth. These two truths are quite distinct and I do not wish, nor am I able to pursue the former at the expense of the latter, because if the pursuit of realism in opera is taken to its ultimate conclusion then you inevitably arrive at the total denial of opera itself. People who sing instead of talking—what could be a greater *lie* than that, in the lowest sense of the word? Naturally, I am a man of my own times and do not wish to return to the outmoded conventions and nonsense of opera, but I certainly have no intention of submitting to the theory of realism, with its despotic demands.[85]

Only a specialist could understand what an incredible feat I have achieved. Now I am terribly, indescribably tired!!! And what do I need now to get back to normal? To enjoy myself, to go on the binge? Not at all! I am going to start straight away on a large new work, but of a completely different kind: a string sextet.[86]

All my friends are in ecstasies over *The Queen of Spades*. I think that the opera has, in fact, worked out successfully, but it must be added that the libretto too is splendid in the full sense of the word.[87] I admit that I also like it the best of my operas and there are lots of passages in it which I cannot

[85] xv*b*. 237–8 (K.R.).   [86] xv*b*. 177 (Anna Merkling).
[87] xv*b*. 215 (Shpazhinskaya).

play properly because I am overcome with emotion. It takes my breath away and I want to cry. My God! could I be wrong? We shall see.[88]

I have started writing the sextet and the composing is not going at all well so far; this new form for expressing myself is causing dreadful difficulties; I constantly feel as though I have not got six real parts but that I am in fact writing for the orchestra and just rearranging it for six string instruments. But perhaps it will go better when I get the hang of things. At any event I want to bring the enterprise to a conclusion, whatever it costs me by way of effort.[89] I very much like being on my own in circumstances like this . . .[90]

I have been to see Figner [in the country].[91] He's in raptures over his part; he talks about it with tears in his eyes—a good sign. He knows some of the part already, which convinced me that he is intelligent and quick to grasp things. All his intentions correspond to my wishes. One thing troubles me: he insists on having the *brindisi* transposed a whole tone.[92] Since it's very likely that other tenors too will find this *brindisi* too high I will have to have it printed as a supplement at the end of the piano score with the addition of a modulation in the key in which Figner is going to sing it.[93] I have asked Khristoforov [the music librarian of the Imperial theatres] to be sure not to paste in the transposed number because, who knows, there might be performers who can sing it in the proper key.[94]

It was a very, very miserable business to have to transpose the *brindisi* for Figner, but there was no alternative. I had already put some of the very low tessituras up an octave after seeing Figner. I hope that in the storm scene the orchestra won't drown the singer, but at least I have given the matter my attention. If I have got it wrong I will cut it down a bit where necessary during the rehearsals.[95]

How I hope, Ivan Alexandrovich [Vsevolozhsky], that you will take *The Queen of Spades* to your heart. Judging by the enthusiasm and bliss which I experienced while I was composing it, I truly believe that you will. I am everlastingly grateful for the trouble you took in getting the opera put on. I think about my return to Petersburg, about the rehearsals, and about the realization of my dreams with great pleasure. As far as the production of the opera is concerned, I can foresee that thanks to you, the reality will far exceed my wildest dreams. As far as the music is concerned, I already know that Figner will be excellent. What a valuable artist Figner is and what a brilliant exception to the general truth that 'les ténors sont *bétes*'! [*sic*] In the most powerful scenes, particularly the one by the banks of the Neva, Medea will also be very good. I hope that the other members of the cast will also be good, and as for the orcheatra and chorus, I have no doubts about this side of things being fine.[96]

[88] xv*b*. 190 (Anatoly).   [89] xv*b*. 182–3 (Ziloti).   [90] xv*b*. 187 (Anatoly).
[91] xv*b*. 207 (Jurgenson).   [92] xv*b*. 206 (Modest).   [93] xv*b*. 216 (Jurgenson).
[94] xv*b*. 235 (Nápravník).   [95] xv*b*. 250 (Nápravník).
[96] xv*b*. 250 (Vsevolozhsky).

I have been [in Petersburg] for five days. The main purpose of my visit has been that Figner cannot sing some of the numbers in the key in which they are written. I have had to transpose them and this has involved some reorchestration; since they are now busy copying out the parts from the score in the copying office in the theatre here I have had to work in Petersburg myself. I will finish this work today [30 July] and tomorrow I'll go home to Frolovskoye. Then I will abandon the north for a long time. I want to be in Tiflis at the beginning of September, and on the way there I want to stay with my brothers Nikolay, Modest, and Ippolit, as well as at Kopylovo* and Kamenka. A whole Odyssey awaits me. I am very much looking forward to the journey which will be an excellent relaxation for me after many months of work.[97]

What a musical city Petersburg is by comparison with Moscow! I hear music here every day. I have been to the Aquarium Theatre, to Peterhof, to Pavlovsk; I have heard good performances of good music everywhere; today I am going to Ozerki and again I will enjoy listening to music. There is nothing like this in Moscow. Apart from this summer advantage of the northern capital, I am also delighted in Petersburg by the purity of *the air* by comparison with Moscow, which is quite uninhabitable in the summer because of the appalling hygienic and sanitary conditions. And what a beautiful river the Neva is! I am staying here with my friend Laroche on the Admiralty Embankment. The windows look out on the Neva and an incomparable view. On the whole, although I was previously a fanatical Muscovite, I have recently come to like Petersburg more and more and I am turning unfaithful to Moscow. The neglect and insulting lack of attention which I got from the Board of the Moscow Musical Society was, I think, the final blow to my attachment to Moscow.[98]

It might be added that Tchaikovsky's own works were invariably played in all the concerts which he mentions.

Of my stay in Kamenka I must say that I brought away rather sad feelings. They have all aged a lot there; there's a melancholy note in everything, and not a trace of the former happy existence. My sister worries me greatly. The attacks which she suffers are of a very nasty nature and are a result of the morphine and all manner of other narcotics which she cannot do without. Alcohol has now been added to the morphine. My sister resorts to this new poison in ever-increasing amounts. God alone knows how it will all end!!! I have been doing nothing but rest all the time, but I am now starting to suffer a little from the knowledge of my idleness and I will probably start working on something in Tiflis.[99]

Tchaikovsky began work in Tiflis on the Symphonic Ballad *The Voyevoda* (after Pushkin).

* Kopylovo—the estate of Anna and Nikolay Meck.

[97] xvb. 222–3 (von Meck).   [98] xvb. 223 (von Meck).
[99] xvb. 254–5 (von Meck).

I have a tendency to hypochondria and I fear that it might at some stage develop into something unpleasant. What have I got to complain about? The
present is fine, and I can look forward to the production of an opera of
which I am proud; in fact everything is fine, yet I am somehow dissatisfied
and depressed, I succumb to a secret but sometimes excruciating merlerncolly. Why should this be?[100]

As a matter of fact everything was not fine, and there was a serious cause for his
'secret, excruciating merlerncolly'. Tchaikovsky suffered a heavy blow while he was
staying in Tiflis.

[When I was at Kopylovo] I talked about you [Mme von Meck] a lot to
Anna and Kolya. Incidentally, Kolya told me what a burden you find it to
write letters. I have known for a long time that you find this difficult
because of your frequent headaches. The idea that you should trouble and
upset yourself on my account is insufferable. I implore you, my good and
dear friend, never to worry about answering my letters. However much I
might enjoy getting yours I prefer that you should never trouble and upset
yourself for my sake. I hope that Wladislaw Albertovich [Pachulski] will be
willing to give me news of you from time to time.[101]

Mme von Meck replied from Sokolniki to Tchaikovsky's letter and told him that
she had postponed her departure abroad. The letter is full of complaints about the
shaky financial state of her children, especially her son Nikolay. She blamed Lev
Davydov for this because he had recommended Kolya to buy Kopylovo. 'You
devote all your life and your abilities to ensuring that your children have a good life
and are well provided for; no sooner do you achieve your aim than you see the whole
building, which you have raised up with such toil and effort, collapse like a house of
cards.' The letter ends up in the usual way: 'Think of your ever loving Nadezhda v.
Meck.' And in a PS: 'Please send letters to my Moscow address.'[102]
    There then followed a letter in which Mme von Meck told Tchaikovsky that she
was ruined financially and was stopping his allowance. But this letter has not survived and its contents can only be guessed at on the basis of Tchaikovsky's reply.

My very dear friend! Your news in the letter which I have just received
profoundly grieved me, *not for myself* but for *you*. Those are no empty
words. It would, of course, be untrue to say that such a radical curtailment
of my budget will have no effect on my material prosperity. But it will affect
it very much less than you probably think. The point is that my income has
increased substantially in recent years and there is no reason to suppose
that it will not go on increasing at a rapid rate. So if I occupy even the smallest place amidst your innumerable worries then I beg you, for goodness
sake, to rest assured that I was not in the slightest, even momentarily, distressed at the thought of the material deprivation which faces me. Please
believe that this is the plain truth: I am no good at striking poses and

---

[100] xv*b*. 266 (Anna Merkling).   [101] xv*b*. 255 (von Meck).
[102] von Meck, iii. 604.

thinking up fine words. So the point is not that I will have to reduce my expenses for a time. The point is that you, with all that you have got used to, with your grand style of life, are going to have to suffer deprivations. I cannot tell you how terribly sorry I feel for you. I was rather offended by the last words of your letter but I don't think that you can really have meant what you said. Do you seriously believe that I would think about you only when I was having the benefit of your money? Could I forget for a single moment all that you have done for me and how much I owe you? It is no exaggeration to say that you saved me, that I would certainly have gone out of my mind and perished if you had not come to my aid and supported with your friendship, your concern, and your financial assistance (my sheet-anchor at that time) my desperately flagging energies and drive to go further along my chosen path. No, my dear friend, rest assured that I will remember that until I draw my last breath and will bless you for it. I am glad that it is now, when you are no longer able to share your resources with me, that I can tell you with all the force at my command of my boundless, ardent gratitude which it is quite impossible to put into words. You probably do not even suspect yourself the full extent of your kindness. It would not otherwise have occurred to you, now that you are poor, that I would think of you *sometimes*!!! I can say without any exaggeration that I never have forgotten you and never will forget you even for a single moment, because when I think about myself my thoughts always and inevitably lead me to you.[103]

For Tchaikovsky the break came unexpectedly because he had more than once been assured by Mme von Meck that she would provide for him whatever her financial state. However, a careful study of the letters of the preceding years shows that the catastrophe came on gradually.

In the summer of 1889 Mme von Meck asked Tchaikovsky if she might send him his allowance a year in advance because it was more convenient to change the time of payment to a period when she was herself living in Russia. She wrote about her financial problems in November 1889, expressing a fear that there would be a change in her circumstances. In a letter of May 1890 she delayed paying the allowance for a few days because she wanted to send a cheque as soon as she got back to Russia and not entrust it to anyone else. Mme von Meck did not send this sum to Tchaikovsky by cheque but a trusted servant took it in cash to Frolovskoye, and it was, moreover, a whole year's payment in advance.

On the other hand, the content of Tchaikovsky's letters to Mme von Meck at this time gives no ground for supposing that they had drawn apart emotionally. He is as frank with her as ever. He did write less frequently, but this applies to others as well. His correspondence had increased and he had less time. From having been a recluse Tchaikovsky had turned into a concert conductor who had to meet innumerable people, had a huge number of acquaintances, and many other duties. And not only did he not cut down his composing: he worked at it even more intensively. It is this which explains the reduction in the number of letters, and not any coolness. Moreover, he had already said all there was to say about himself; he had fully

[103] xv*b*. 263–4 (von Meck).

disclosed his inner self. Informative letters now predominate over the confessional variety. However, the termination of the financial assistance caused Mme von Meck also to stop the correspondence. It is true that she was already very ill at this time and had lost the use of her hand. But she was not ruined; her difficulties were only temporary and, as before, she remained a rich woman.

I am very, very, very *offended*; and *offended* is the word. My relations with Mme von Meck were such that I was *never* embarrassed by her generous hand-outs. Now I am embarrassed in retrospect; it is an insult to my pride, and my belief that there was no limit to her willingness to support me financially and to make any sacrifice for me has been betrayed. What I would like now is that she should be so definitively ruined that she needed my help. And after all, I know perfectly well that from *our* point of view she is still immensely rich. It has, in short, all turned out to be a sordid, stupid affair which makes me sick and ashamed.[104]

Tchaikovsky's attempts to get the correspondence going, even through third parties, came to nothing.

It is quite true that Nadezhda Filaretovna is weak and ill, that her nerves are upset and that she cannot write as she used to. What distresses and troubles me, and, to be frank, is deeply insulting, is not the fact that she doesn't write but that she has completely stopped taking an interest in me. I *wanted*, I *needed* my relations with N.F. to continue quite unchanged after I stopped receiving money from her. Unfortunately this has proved impossible because it is perfectly obvious that she has turned cool towards me. The consequence is that I have stopped writing to N.F. and have cut off practically all relations with her *since I have been deprived of her money*. Such a situation humiliates me in my own estimation and constantly torments and burdens me beyond all measure; it also makes it insufferable for me to recollect how I used to accept her payments. I have been rereading N.F.'s old letters. One would not have thought that her illness, or her misfortunes, or her financial problems could have changed the feelings which were expressed in those letters. And yet they did change. Perhaps it is precisely because I never knew N.F. *personally* that she seemed to me to be the ideal of a human being; I could not have imagined inconstancy in such a demigoddess; I would have thought that the world would fall apart before N.F. would change in her attitude to me. But this is what has happened and it turns upside down my view of people and my faith in the best of them; it disturbs my peace of mind and ruins that portion of happiness which fate has allotted to me. Without, of course, meaning to do so, N.F. has treated me very cruelly. I have never before felt so humiliated, so wounded in my pride, as I do now. The worst of all is that because N.F.'s health is in such a bad way I am frightened of distressing and upsetting her and cannot,

---

[104] xv*b*. 268 (Jurgenson).   [105] xvi*a*. 131-2 (Pachulski).

therefore, tell her all that is tormenting me. I cannot give expression to my feelings and that alone would be a relief.[105]

Tchaikovsky did not in fact get any relief; he harboured a sense of injury to the end of his days. Mme von Meck did not long outlive Tchaikovsky: she died two months after he did.

As soon as the first performance of *The Queen of Spades* has taken place in Petersburg I can go straight to Kiev, but the question is this: should I conduct? I gave up conducting operas a year ago and I will not conduct in Petersburg. The point is that a conductor-composer, particularly such a nervous and inexperienced one as I am, could ruin the opera or at least cause a scandal. This very nearly happened to me in Moscow last year. But scandals aside, I think that composers who conduct can communicate to the performers a very undesirable element of nervousness, lack of confidence, and precariousness. The singers, chorus, and orchestra will perform with that much more calm and confidence if they are directed by the familiar and confident hand of their usual conductor.[106]

[Petersburg], the Hotel Russia. I have a wonderful suite, quite separate. Rehearsals have begun; things are moving and I think they'll go well. Life goes on amidst perpetual bustle. At one stage I fell so ill with nervous exhaustion that a doctor had to be sent for. The opera is not going badly. The production will be remarkably sumptuous, and the performance excellent.[107]

Nápravník conducted the première of *The Queen of Spades* on 7 December 1890 in the Mariinsky Theatre. The part of Herman was sung by Nikolay Figner, of Liza by Medea Figner, and of the Countess by Mariya Slavina. The audience gave the opera a rapturous reception, the composer took innumerable bows, tickets were sold out for several performances ahead. But the critics, as had become usual for Tchaikovsky, made mock of it: 'He has put a large amount of good music on such an uninteresting subject in an attempt to make a fortune', 'a question of cards'—such were the assessments of the opera by the reactionary and unperceptive quibblers who unanimously came to the conclusion that they could scarcely predict a success for *The Queen of Spades*. These 'prognoses' were at complete variance with the reality of the matter: the triumphant success of *The Queen of Spades* increased from one performance to the next, despite press ranting.

After the Petersburg première Tchaikovsky went to Kiev so as to supervise the preparation of the opera there as well.

There are rehearsals every day. It's difficult to describe what strange feelings I experience when I am once again present at *the launching* of the opera, and in such a small and comparatively poor theatre. But everybody is trying dreadfully hard and the production looks as though, *so far as it can be*, it will be brilliant. The best of the singers is Medvedev. The others are not as good as in Petersburg. Of course, even Medvedev isn't Figner, but

---

[106] xv*b*. 290 (Pryanishnikov).   [107] xv*b*. 297 (Panya).

his great virtue is his *musicality*.[108] All the performers are poorer and weaker than those in Petersburg to a greater or lesser extent. But there was one exception: for the boys' choir in the cantata and the requiem Pryanishnikov engaged Kalishevsky's well known choir and they have turned out to be simply superb. The boys' voices, either because of their natural qualities or as a result of Kalishevsky's training, achieved such beauty of sound as I would never have dreamt of. Particularly in the requiem the sound of these voices always brought tears to my eyes. It would be comical even to compare Kiev with Petersburg in the rapturous nature of the reception. It was something incredible. Both productions—the unheard of luxury in the capital, and the modest but elegant provincial version—satisfied me entirely and I am perfectly content with all the performers. But the most staggering thing of all is Figner and the Petersburg orchestra who achieved positive miracles.[109]

I have been commissioned to write a one-act opera and a two-act ballet. Vsevolozhsky is ever more kindly disposed towards me and refuses even to consider a season without a new work from me.[110]

It was at this time that Pogozhev wrote to Tchaikovsky about the characteristics and the significance of his works. He explained that though he could recognize various composers by their distinguishing features he could still make mistakes but 'there is one composer whom I can always pick out in all his works, and that composer is Tchaikovsky'. Pogozhev goes on to say, taking as his starting-point his impressions of Tolstoy's *Childhood* and *Boyhood*: 'This talent consists primarily in gathering together and then inferring the general sense of those trivia of life which would not of themselves detain us.' 'You and I', writes Pogozhev, 'are both a product of our time: you as the honoured producer, and I as the modest consumer of that same dramatic truth in music. It is for this reason that I prefer Tchaikovsky's music to any other. I have finally come to the conclusion that it is Tchaikovsky's music which will win for itself the dominant position in the future.' (*Reminiscences*, 390–1).

I think that I really have a gift for *faithfully*, *sincerely*, and *simply* conveying in music the emotions, the atmosphere, and the characters suggested by the text. In this sense I am *a realist* and a thoroughgoing Russian. What artistic merit, what degree of creative capacity has fallen to my lot—this is another question. I have not the slightest pretension to brilliance. I know only that my musical nature has that feature which you [Pogozhev] have confirmed: you reveal a remarkable sensitivity in formulating your opinion about me. I assure you that the judgements of a sensitive music-lover are infinitely more true and accurate than those of well-worn musicians. Do you know that the entire Russian press has for long *denied that I have any ability at all as a vocal composer* and stubbornly sticks to the view that I cannot progress beyond the symphony?[111]

---

[108] xv*b*. 303 (Modest).   [109] xv*b*. 311–12 (Pogozhev).
[110] xv*b*. 308 (Ippolitov-Ivanov).   [111] xvi*a*. 17–18 (Pogozhev).

At about the same time Taneyev wrote to Tchaikovsky: 'The question of how operas are written interests me in the highest degree and I have long wished to exchange ideas with you on the subject. In so far as they are given concrete expression in your operas, I frequently do not find your views altogether satisfying. But it is precisely that aspect of the business which most engages my attention in each new work that you write. The creative gift, the charming turn of the melody, the delicate sensitivity in the harmonic groupings, these are all individual features of a talent; they cannot be taken over from an artist if they have not been given by nature itself. On the other hand, his views on his art, on the technicalities of creation, *the rational side of the matter* as it were is, in truth, of more significance for the specialist interest (Taneyev, 168). Taneyev was writing his opera *Oresteia* (after Aeschylus).

I have always solved, do solve, and always will solve the problem of *how one should write an opera* extremely simply. One should write it (and exactly the same applies, incidentally, to anything else) *just as it comes*. I have always tried to express *as faithfully and sincerely as possible* in the music what was in the text. But *faithfulness* and *sincerity* are not the result of cogitation, they are the immediate product of an inner feeling. So that this feeling should have the breath of life I have always tried to choose subjects to which I could warm. And I can only warm to subjects in which the characters are real living people whose feelings are my own. For this reason I find Wagner's subjects insufferable: there is no *humanity* in them. Nor would I choose a subject like yours with its monstrous misdeeds, its Euménïdes, and Fate cast as one of the characters. So when I have chosen a subject and have set about composing the opera, I have given my emotions free rein, resorting neither to Wagner's prescription, nor to imitating classical models, nor to striving for originality. In doing so I have made no attempt to avoid the influence of the spirit of the times. I realize that if Wagner had not existed I would write differently; I even admit that in my operatic works there is a touch of *handphulitis*; no doubt Italian music, too, of which I was passionately fond when I was a child, and Glinka, whom I adored when I was a youth, have had a powerful influence on me, to say nothing of Mozart. But I have never summoned up one of other of these idols and allowed them to dispose of my musical being as they pleased. It is perhaps a consequence of this attitude to the matter that my operas give no clear indication of belonging to any particular school. Perhaps it has frequently happened that one influence or another has been dominant and I have lapsed into imitation, but, be that as it may, it has all happened of its own accord, and if I am sure of anything it is that in what I have written you see me as God created me and as I have been shaped by my upbringing and by the circumstances and characteristics of that age and country in which I live and move. I have never been untrue to myself. As to whether I am good or bad, let others judge.[112]

[112] xvia. 29 (Taneyev).

24

1891–1892

I see it as my duty to support the prestige of Russian music abroad in every way I can.

Wolff sent me a letter from America from the same gentleman who has arranged my invitation. This is so well paid and so easy, that I would be mad to miss the opportunity of going to America, which I have long dreamt of visiting.[1]

I have been invited to conduct three concerts to celebrate the opening of a new concert hall in New York [the Carnegie Hall]; I will conduct a symphony at the first one, the Piano Concerto at the second, and some choral work or other at the third.[2]

I have agreed with the management to write a ballet and an opera for next season but I have warned them that my travels may prevent me from carrying out such a large undertaking. I will try to work on the ship. Even on the way here [Berlin] I did a little work on the ballet. The main thing is to get the ballet off my hands because the opera interests me so much and I so like the subject that if I just get two weeks of peace I am sure to get it written on time. But we shall see.[3]

The Nutcracker and *Yolanta*. The story of *Yolanta* is taken from Henrik Hertz's play *King René's Daughter* (libretto by Modest Tchaikovsky).

After the Paris concert on 24 March Tchaikovsky went to Rouen to rest for a few days on his own before leaving for the United States.

I am suffering agonies from all that is going on and I have promised myself never again to undertake any foreign trips with the aim of displaying myself to the public. It's quite another matter to spend a few months of peace in Italy, or even in Paris, with the aim of working. If I am spared I will do that on many more occasions. But to do concerts—never, never, never![4]

There was a continuous crescendo in my torments and agonies which culminated in *a crisis* and I wrote a long letter to Vsevolozhsky. It's a load off my mind and I have now recovered after three days of madness. The principal cause of my despair was that my efforts to work were fruitless. All I produced was disgusting. In addition *Casse Noisette* and even *King René's Daughter* turned into dread-inspiring, feverish nighmares, so abominable

---

[1] xvia. 33 (Jurgenson).　　[2] xvia. 54–5 (Anatoly).
[3] xvia. 67 (Anatoly).　　[4] xvia. 76–7 (Kolya).

that I don't think I have the strength to put it into words. I was simply tortured by the knowledge that I was utterly incapable of making a *good* job of what I had taken upon myself. And the prospect of being under constant strain on the way to America, while I was there, and on the way back became a terrible, fatal spectre. It is difficult to convey what I went through but I do not recollect ever being so unhappy. And at the back of all my torments as a composer you can add that *homesickness* which I foresaw and which I can now never avoid when I am away from Russia.[5]

I went to Paris. On the way to Sophie Menter's I called in at the *Cabinet de lecture* which I know in the Passage de l'Opéra. I picked up a copy of *Novoye vremya* [*New Times*] and saw on the last page that Sasha had died. I rushed out as though I had been stung. It was much later when I got round to see Sophie Menter and Vasya [Sapelnikov]. It was a great good fortune that they were here. I spent the night at their place. At first I thought it was my duty to abandon America and go to Petersburg, but then I realized that that was pointless. So I will go to America. My mental sufferings are great. I fear dreadfully for Bob, though I know from experience that at his age such misfortunes are borne comparatively lightly. But I am particularly sorry for Lev and Nata;* their sufferings must be quite unimaginable. So I am going to Rouen today [5 April], to le Havre tomorrow, and to sea at five o'clock in the morning on Saturday. Even more than yesterday and the day before do I feel how utterly incapable I am of re-creating *Konfitürenburg*† in music.[6]

Alexandra Ilinichna Davydova died in Petersburg on 28 March 1891. Modest was in Paris at the time and went to Rouen to tell Tchaikovsky about the family tragedy before himself setting off for the funeral in Petersburg. But he could not bring himself to deal his brother such a blow before his departure for America and concealed the death of their sister from him.

I feel that I am not myself but somebody else, sailing over the ocean and living for the interests of the moment. Sasha's death, with all its painful associations, is like a recollection from some very remote past which I can drive away without any particular difficulty, and then once more I think of the passing interests of that creature who is not *me*, but who is travelling to America *inside me*.[7]

I had thought that I was invulnerable to seasickness. It turns out that I am vulnerable. The nearer I approach New York the more do I get agi-

---

* Nata: Nataliya Andreyevna Plesskaya, friend and companion of Alexandra Davydova; Tchaikovsky had friendly relations with her for many years; he dedicated to her the famous Nata Waltz for piano.

† Konfitürenburg is the name of the imaginary town where the action of *The Nutcracker* takes place.

5 xvi*a*. 86–7 (Modest).   6 xvi*a*. 88 (Modest).
7 xvi*a*. 93 (Modest).

tated, depressed, and fearful; and more than anything else do I repent this crazy trip. Perhaps when it's all over I will think back on it with some interest, but, for the moment, nothing but misery.[8]

New York, American customs, American hospitality, the very appearance of the town, the remarkable comfort of my accommodation—this is all very much to my taste and if I were younger I would probably be greatly enjoying my stay in an interesting new country. But I am *enduring* all this, as though it were a mild form of punishment which the agreeable circumstances make less rigorous. My thoughts and aspirations are as one: home, home!!! People here could not be kinder, they honour me, they entertain me. It seems that I am *ten times* better known in America than I am in Europe. When they first told me that I thought it was exaggerated kindness, but now I can see that it's true. There are some pieces of mine which they still don't know in Moscow; here they play them several times in a season and write whole articles and commentaries about them (*Hamlet*, for instance). They have played the Fifth Symphony two years running. Isn't this funny?!!! At the rehearsals the players gave me a very enthusiastic reception.[9]

All told, I am a much bigger fish here than in Europe. American life, their customs, their ways—I find all this extraordinarily interesting and novel; and at every turn one comes upon things which are staggeringly impressive in their colossal dimensions by comparison with Europe. The place is bubbling over with life, and though the main interest is profit the Americans are also very attentive to art. Proof of this is the huge hall which they have just built and the opening of which was the cause of my being invited here. This building cost millions and it was paid for by music-lovers. These wealthy enthusiasts maintain a permanent orchestra. We have nothing like this! I must admit that the scale and impressiveness of all the Americans undertake is tremendously attractive. I also like *the comfort* about which they take so much trouble. My room, just like every other room in all the hotels, has gas and electric light and a private bathroom and lavatory; there is heaps of extremely comfortable furniture; there is an apparatus for speaking to the reception desk and all sorts of things to make one comfortable which do not exist in Europe. In short, there is a great deal about the country which I like very much and find remarkably interesting.[10]

I won't describe any particular details since I will bring back with me my diary which has all the details. I will talk only of my feelings. To be honest, I now have only a single thought and a single feeling: to last until 21 April/9 May when, having fulfilled all my obligations, I will embark on the steamer *Fürst Bismarck* and set off for Hamburg. I will try to bear the remaining time as patiently as possible. The only pleasant hours or rather minutes are

[8] xvia. 94, 97 (Modest).   [9] xvia. 99, 101 (Bob).
[10] xvia. 101 (Nápravník).

when I am alone in my room in the evening and have the prospect of the
night and morning, guaranteed against visits. The rest of the time, firstly, I
feel perpetually tired, as if I had just walked about 25 miles. They tell me
that this is the effect that the spring air has on people here. Secondly, I am
suffering more than ever from the society of *strangers*, and all the more
because I have to speak in German and sometimes even in English! But
there are some unexpectedly pleasant times. For instance, I spent the whole
day yesterday at the house of the local Jurgenson, i.e. the principal music
publisher, Schirmer. At first I found it hard and was suffering, but towards
evening, when there was a circle of unusually kind and affectionate people,
I suddenly felt at ease and happy. But, truly, these people are very kind.
And in general I cannot praise enough the people here and their friendliness towards me. They are even too kind, and it is too difficult for me to
arrange an hour to myself. I like New York more and more. Incidentally,
Central Park is magnificent. It is remarkable that people of my generation
can remember very well when it was nothing but cows grazing in fields. I
have rehearsals almost every day. The new hall in which the *festival* will
take place is magnificent and its dimensions exceed all our halls.

10 May/28 April. I am going to visit the Niagara Falls, and on the 3rd I
will be conducting in Philadelphia; the 6th in Baltimore and on the 9th I
leave. The weather is marvellous, but too hot. All the trees have long since
come out. How far away from you all I am.[11]

6/24 May. 'Tchaikovsky is a tall, gray well built interesting man, *well on
to sixty* (?!!) He seems a trifle embarrassed, and responds to the applause by
a succession of brusque and jerky bows. But as soon as he grasps the baton
his self-confidence returns.' That's what I read this morning in the *New
York Herald* [6 May 1891]. It annoys me when they write about me personally and not just about the music. I cannot bear it when they remark on my
embarrassment and are surprised at my 'short, sharp' bows.[12]

The article in the *New York Herald* of 6 May 1891, p. 7, continued 'There is no sign
of nervousness about him as he taps for silence. He conducts with the authoritative
strength of a master and the band obeys his lead as one man.'

25 April/7 May. I am fifty-one. I am terribly agitated this morning.
There's a concert at two o'clock with the [Third] Suite. This peculiar fear
is an astonishing thing. How many times have I conducted this selfsame
suite? It goes perfectly well; what is there to be frightened of? And yet I
suffer intolerably. I don't think I have ever been in such a panic. Is this
because they pay attention to my appearance here and my shyness makes
itself apparent? However that may be I was once again given a superb reception and created, as they say in today's papers, 'a sensation'.[13]

I am having great difficulty in finding time to write letters. Whenever I
have a spare minute in the morning I write my diary. Today my activities in

[11] xvia. 104–5 (Kolya).   [12] *Diaries*, 273–4.   [13] Ibid. 274.

New York come to an end. Meanwhile I have had a magnificent success and the Suite in particular was very well received. The press have sung my praises to an extent that I never would have contemplated in Russia. In the intervals and after the concert the ladies would gather together in a great crowd to look at me and some of them would come up and give expression to their enthusiasm. They have all been terribly kind to me. The time is beginning to pass quickly and in ten days I am hoping to depart. Today and tomorrow will be difficult days, i.e. not one minute of freedom: but on the other hand on Monday I go *alone* to Niagara. After that I have to go to so many towns, one after the other, that I hope my day of departure will creep up unnoticed. I had a good birthday, or at least the second half of the day. The first half I suffered from anxiety and fear before conducting the Suite at an afternoon concert; but after its great success I refused all invitations and spent the whole of the rest of the day alone.[14]

26 April/8 May. I am besieged by visitors: reporters, composers, librettists, and, above all, absolute mountains of letters from all corners of America asking for *autographs*, to which I reply very conscientiously. Went to the rehearsal of the Piano Concerto. Went to Knabe's to thank them for the superb presentation which they made to me yesterday (a Statue of Liberty). But will they let me take such an object into Russia? There's no end to my visitors, including two Russian ladies. Since this was my first chance to have a heart-to-heart talk with a Russian lady there was a scene: tears suddenly came to my eyes, my voice quavered, and I could not restrain my sobbing. I rushed into another room and did not emerge for some time. I burn with shame when I think about this surprising episode.[15]

Carnegie, an amazing eccentric, who from being a telegraph boy, was transformed with the passing of the years into one of America's richest men, but who has remained a simple, modest man who does not at all turn his nose up at anyone, inspires an unusual warmth of feeling in me, perhaps because he is overflowing with goodwill towards me. Throughout the whole evening he displayed his liking for me in a remarkably individual way. He grasped me by the hand, crying out that I was uncrowned, but the most genuine king of music, embraced me (without kissing: here men never kiss each other), and in describing my greatness, stood on tiptoe and raised his arms above his head, and finally delighted the whole company by imitating me conducting. He did this so seriously and so well, so like me that I myself was delighted. His wife, a remarkably simple and sweet young woman, also expressed her kindly feelings towards me in a hundred different ways. All this was very gratifying for me but at the same time made me feel slightly ashamed.[16]

I will not describe the beauty of the Niagara Falls, for these things are difficult to express in words. The beauty and the grandeur of this sight are

---

[14] xvia. 108 (Modest).   [15] *Diaries*, 275.   [16] Ibid. 279.

truly amazing. After we had visited and had a good look at the part of the Falls which is more or less divided into several separate falls, of which two are enormous (the second one especially), we set off to skirt round the island towards the Three Sisters Islands. This whole walk is charming, especially at this time of year. The greenery is absolutely fresh and my favourite *dandelions* are blooming amongst the grass. I had a terrible desire to pick some of these yellow beauties smelling of freshness and of spring; but at every step you see a noticeboard with the reminder that you are not even allowed to pick *wild flowers*. Then I looked at the main waterfall, the *Horse Schoe Fall* [*sic*]. It is an awe-inspiring sight.[17]

27, 29, 30 April and 1 May [9, 10, 11 and 12 May]—conducted my own works with great success at the New York Festival. Then made a trip to Niagara, Washington, Philadelphia, and Baltimore. Conducted in the last two towns. Sailed from America on 9 May. The voyage was good again and so was the gale.

Arrived in Petersburg on 20 May, and here this morning [Maydanovo, 29 May].[18] I am home at last, and tremendously glad to be at the end of my travels.[19]

I have been *driven out* of Frolovskoye and will live at Maydanovo again for the time being.[20] Maydanovo is very gloomy. Apart from the results of the fire, everything else is going to rack and ruin, and even my own house doesn't look up to much at all.[21]

I have settled down to work. I am now writing the second act of the ballet, and when I have finished it I will start on my opera *King René's Daughter*. As well as that I have had a symphonic poem finished since last spring: *The Voyevoda* (on Pushkin's ballad). I will also score that in the summer. About orchestrating this piece: I have discovered a new orchestral instrument in Paris, something half-way between a small piano and a Glockenspiel, with a marvellous, heavenly sound. I want to use this instrument in my symphonic poem *The Voyevoda* and in the ballet. It is called the 'Celesta Mustel'. Since the instrument will be needed in Petersburg before Moscow it is preferable they they should send it from Paris to Jurgenson. But I would rather that it was not shown to anybody because I fear that Rimsky-Korsakov and Glazunov might get wind of it and make use of its unusual effect before I do.[22]

As his work progressed, and influenced by Taneyev's letters, Tchaikovsky gave some thought to Taneyev and to himself.

I know few people whose letters are such a pleasure to read as yours. Your future biographer will be most agreeably impressed by your constant air of cheerful, healthy optimism about life's problems. Albeit gradually, you

---

[17] *Diaries*, 281.   [18] xvia. 121 (Shpazhinskaya).
[19] xvia. 129 (Jurgenson).   [20] xvia. 80 (Panya).
[21] xvia. 130 (Jurgenson).   [22] xvia. 129–30 (Jurgenson).

move with a firm and even stride towards your goal, seeking no encouragement or urging on, sure of your success. I envy you. Your work is a
pleasure to you, because you do not have that feverish urge to finish things
as soon as possible, cost what it may; nor does it in any way stop you from
engaging in incidental activities, from devoting part of your time not only
to compiling a guide to counterpoint but even to practising that dismal
craft yourself, and, most astounding of all, enjoying it!!! You are, in short, a
wise man as well as an artist and from such a combination of qualities I
foresee a rich harvest. I think that your opera will be altogether special: it is
a work which will be truly outstanding in the originality of its conception
and the mature assurance of its execution. I have not the slightest intention
of reproaching you because you do not write much. The point is not to
write a lot, but to write well. Your quartet [in B♭ minor] is excellent. And I
am sure the opera will be the same. I, of course, do not conduct myself in
the manner of *wise men* and have finished sketching out the ballet, working
with feverish haste and in constant doubt about the adequacy of my abilities as a composer; nor must I miss this opportunity to bemoan the fate
which has constructed me in such a way that I always have to rush and put
myself under pressure. During next year I must write an opera and a ballet
which I have promised the management, finish and score the symphonic
ballad *The Voyevoda*, completely revise the *Sextet*, which has turned out a
disgraceful failure, and I must do all this as quickly as possible because in
addition I have to cope with productions of *The Queen of Spades* in Moscow, Hamburg, and Prague (and I regard my presence as essential), as well
as innumerable trips which I have promised to make all over the place. So I
must now at all costs first get rid of the burden of the opera and the ballet.
Writing the ballet has cost me an effort because I could feel a decline in my
powers of invention. We'll see how *the opera* goes. Despite the excellence of
the subject, which tempts me very much, if I find that it's going badly I
might abandon it. I am going through some sort of a crisis. Either I will
emerge the victor and will spill forth notes for a few more years yet or I will
lay aside my weapons.[23]

On the advice of Vsevolozhsky in June 1891 Karl Fyodorovich Waltz, the chief
stage manager and designer of the Bolshoy Theatre in Moscow, suggested to Tchaikovsky an outline for an opera-ballet *Watanabe*. Waltz wrote to Tchaikovsky:
'Vsevolozhsky promises to put this opera-ballet on simultaneously in Petersburg
and Moscow and to give it a magnificent production.'

I have read through *Watanabe* with the keenest pleasure. The subject is
charming, poetic in the extreme, yet effective. I couldn't be more willing to
write the music for it, but on this condition: *Watanabe* will be a *fairytale-
ballet* and not an *opera-ballet*. I do not understand, in fact I deny the
existence of that ill-defined and disagreeable artistic genre known as

---

[23] xvia. 164–5 (Taneyev).

opera-ballet. One thing or the other: either my characters will *sing* or they will *mime*. I find the two together quite inconceivable. An an opera *Watanabe* is not for me a suitable subject, because I allow the fantastic element in opera only in so far as it does not impede the actions of real, simple people, with their simple human passions and emotions. But I certainly cannot make the Prince of the Sun sing. Only people can sing, or possibly angels and demons when they intervene in human affairs on an equal footing with human beings. And then Watanabe, and Ga-tani, and Nao-Shik are for me creatures who lie beyond the real world, which means that I would have considerable difficulty in faithfully portraying them other than *orchestrally*. For that reason I regard *Watanabe* as an excellent subject for a ballet. As an opera it also has the disadvantage that a large part is played in the story by the *absence of light, of the sun*, and this is precisely the main theme of the story in the opera which I am writing now.[24]

I have started a serious study of Spinoza. I have bought masses of books about him as well as his own works. The more I get into him, the more do I admire him.[25]

Tchaikovsky made an enthusiastic study of Spinoza's works in the years 1891–3. He read with particular attention the *Ethics* and the *Correspondence*. These works, with Tchaikovsky's annotations, are in his library in the editions Moscow, 1892 and Petersburg 1891 respectively.

Living at Maydanovo is utterly hateful. Everything is dilapidated and in decline, the woods have gone, there's nowhere to go for a walk, and on top of everything these detestable holiday visitors!! The only tolerable thing here is the actual house I live in.[26]

Something very sad has happened. My watch has been stolen. This splendid watch was precious to me and it was a particularly daring thief who took it as his haul because it always lay on my night table (even during the day, because I did not wear it with my country clothes), and it was stolen either while I was working in the next room or when I was out walking. I have reported the matter but I don't suppose anything will come of it.[27]

This was the watch which Mme von Meck had given Tchaikovsky as a memento of his work on the opera *The Maid of Orleans*. The watch was not in fact found.

I have received your [Alferaki] letter and the romances, which I have played through. I have not got anything particularly new to add to what I have already said to you about your very significant capabilities as a composer. Nor do I wish pointlessly to repeat my regret that circumstances in life have not allowed you to go through strict training in counterpoint (which, there are good grounds for thinking, your talent needed). This is

---

[24] xvia. 150–1 (Waltz).   [25] xvia. 178 (Bob).
[26] xvia. 123 (Anna Merkling).   [27] xvia. 183 (Kolya).

obvious. I am sorry about your decision to restrict yourself to the sphere of romances. A real artist, even if he is truly only gifted with limited creative ability, which prevents him from composing outstanding works in the various branches of his art, must nevertheless be fired with enthusiasm for the broadest and greatest goals. Neither the years, nor any other obstacles should hold back his ambition. And why do you think that for the composition of a *chef-d'œuvre* in the category of romances, you don't need to possess an all-round technique in your chosen art? However much your technical deficiency may lead you to restrain yourself and limit the sphere of your creativity, you will never achieve anything greater than elegant amateurism. There is a lot which is very attractive and talented in your romances. As far as technique is concerned they are very neat. However, both in the harmony and in the form, in spite of all these qualities, there is evident throughout a certain clumsiness, an awkwardness, *raideur*. Moreover, 'in serving the muse there is no room for fussiness'; to this I would add 'bureaucratic fussiness', and this I am very, very sorry about. I shall be very upset if my assessment does not correspond with your own perfectly understandable self-respect as a composer. Please forgive me, but in such cases I have made it my rule to be sincere.[28]

I have nothing interesting to report about myself. I am working regularly and hard; I am living as usual a steady and sensible life. I have given up drinking vodka altogether and am very pleased about this; I now never feel sleepy and my digestion has much improved and I never get heartburn. I have heard from Modest that he is very happy at Grankino in spite of the presence there of Alina, whom he detests. In the evenings I sometimes play vint at Novikova's and also with some new acquaintances called Gurko. I do not avoid Novikova now and am not against getting to know the other inhabitants of the dachas because it is a hundred times better for my health and for a good night's rest to play vint than to tire my eyes and brain by a whole evening of reading.[29]

Yesterday evening I finished the rough sketches for my new ballet. This work has tired me out (I think the old man is beginning to be played out) and since I have besides a small matter of business in P'burg, I have decided instead of Moscow, where I was going, in order to avoid celebrating my name-day, to go for a few days to the Palmyra of the north. On my return I will get straight down to the opera.[30]

The draft of the ballet is finished and I went to Petersburg to revive myself after work, which had rather tired me. My life there was one of complete idleness. Went to the Zoo every day. Went to Peterhof. The weather was marvellous and I enjoyed being in an utterly *deserted* Petersburg. It is such a pleasure to be in a town where one does not have to visit anybody, positively *nobody*, nor does one have to receive visitors; it's like being a

[28] xvia. 187 (Alferaki).   [29] xvia. 154 (Anatoly).
[30] xvia. 155 (Alexandra Hubert).

foreign tourist, idly strolling along the pavements of this Palmyra of the north, which is, incidentally, astonishingly beautiful in summer.[31]

[Now] that I have been to P'burg I will get down to composing *King René's Daughter*. I find the subject really fascinating so I think that if my capacity for musical invention is not yet starting to expire I might write something very decent, the best I have ever done. I am certainly in no position to say at the moment how long it will take me to compose the draft sketches. Until they are properly finished I am incapable of coping with people and have to be on my own, at home.[32]

The more I immerse myself in writing the music for *Yolanta*, the more I admire the quality of the libretto. It has been excellently done and the verse is very, very fine in places.[33] I didn't start at the beginning but with the scene between Yolanta and Vaudémont. The music could be magnificent at that point but I don't think it has come out too well. The most sickening thing is that I am starting to repeat myself and much of this scene has come out like *The Sorceress*!!! But we shall see. I am more and more afflicted with doubts about myself. But perhaps it's not a general decline and I should just stop writing for the theatre for a time and concentrate on symphonies, piano pieces, quartets, and so on. I am tired of writing operas and ballets, but I'm not yet played out altogether. I hope not. It's strange that while I was writing the ballet I kept thinking it wasn't up to much but that when I started the opera I would show what I could do. Now I think that the ballet is good and the opera nothing special.[34] My work has suddenly taken a good turn. I know now that *Yolanta* will not disgrace itself.[35]

The time is drawing near when I will have to leave for Ukolovo [to see my brother Nikolay] and Kamenka, but *Yolanta* is far from finished. I'll probably have to delay finishing it until I come back; that would in fact be better because if I set myself to finish it now at all costs I'll just do it any old how. In any case, there's very little left to do. I'm quite content in general just now.[36]

I am back from my trip. I had a very pleasant few days with my brother Kolya. Then I spent about a week at Kamenka. When I was there I was very conscious of the loss we have all suffered.[37] I am very pleased with my trip. Ukolovo and life at Kolya's were very nice. I enjoyed the four days I spent with them. I went to Korennaya Pustyn and we spent a day at Fet's. It was the first time in my life that I had seen him and I found him very interesting.[38] I was touched by the friendly welcome he gave me. Judging by his memoirs, which were published in *Russky vestnik* [*The Russian Herald*], I had thought that he would not be particularly interesting to talk to. On the contrary, he turned out to be extraordinarily pleasant, full of

[31] xvia. 175 (Anna Merkling).   [32] xvia. 162 (Kolya).   [33] xvia. 180 (Bob).
[34] xvia. 186 (Modest).   [35] xvia. 189 (Bob).   [36] xvia. 190 (Modest).
[37] xvia. 198 (Anna Merkling).   [38] xvia. 199–200 (Anatoly).

individuality and humour. He read me a lot of his new poems which astonished me with the youthful vigour of their inspiration.[39]

I have finished my Symphonic Ballad *The Voyevoda*. Very pleased with it. Now I will get down to scoring the opera.[40] I am really persevering with my work. Time is terribly precious because I must at all costs finish scoring the opera and the ballet this winter.[41]

Feverish activity is starting up again. I have constantly to be in Moscow in connection with *The Queen of Spades*. I am going there for three weeks from 15 [October]. After that there will be concerts which I have promised to conduct in Moscow and Petersburg. Then I will have to go to Hamburg for the production of *Onegin*, and to Prague for *The Queen of Spades*. Then more work, more trips, more rushing around.[42]

Tchaikovsky conducted his Symphonic Ballad *The Voyevoda* at one of Ziloti's concerts in Moscow on 6 November 1891. He was not satisfied with the work, which was also coolly received by the audience, and destroyed the score.

Don't worry about *The Voyevoda*—it got what it deserved. I have no regrets because I am firmly convinced that it is a work which would have discredited me. It would be a different matter if I were young and inexperienced, but a hoary old ancient ought either to move onwards (and even that is possible, because Verdi, for instance, is still developing, and he is getting on for eighty), or he ought to maintain that level which he has already achieved. If this sort of thing happens any more I'll tear it up into little pieces again or I'll abandon composing altogether. Nothing on earth would induce me to keep on scribbling like Anton Grigoryevich [Rubinstein] when I have long since had nothing to say. I am finishing scoring *Yolanta*. I don't think I'll have to tear it up, but who knows?[43]

Ziloti hid the orchestral parts of The Voyevoda; after Tchaikovsky's death they were used to reconstruct the score which was published by Belyayev.

The Queen of Spades went off wonderfully [in Moscow]; the ensemble was beyond praise; Altani surpassed himself. The production is sumptuous, scarcely less so than in Petersburg. I liked Sionitskaya [Lisa] best. Medvedev was good but my memories of Figner are going to spoil any performance of Herman's part. It was a great success.[44]

I am terribly reluctant to leave. I have been orchestrating the introduction to *Yolanta* here [at Maydanovo] and have made a *draft* revision of the Sextet.[45]

On 14 December Tchaikovsky left for a major concert tour. He first went to Kiev, where he conducted two concerts.

[39] xvi*a*. 257–8 (K.R.).   [40] xvi*a*. 214 (Anatoly).
[41] xvi*a*. 220 (Anatoly).   [42] xvi*a*. 222 (Shpazhinskaya).
[43] xvi*a*. 276–7 (Jurgenson).   [44] xvi*a*. 262 (Anatoly).
[45] xvi*a*. 292 (Modest).

In Kiev I have been dealing with a large and very sound orchestra; people are very kind and are making a great fuss of me here and both of my concerts have in fact been a tremendous success. But I am increasingly convinced that I must not spend the rest of my life on tours like this; they take so much of my most precious possession—time; they tire me, and they cause so much worry, anxiety, and suffering. The suffering arises from the fact that there is never a minute in the day when I can be alone, and this is essential for me. Now it's all over and I am going to Kamenka; I'll spend two days there and then go on to Warsaw.[46]

I am in Warsaw now. Rehearsals have started and the orchestra is not even second-rate; I am far more tired than when I am in Moscow or Petersburg. I am spending my time with my former pupil Barcewicz, the famous violinist, and with the family of Mme Friede, the singer. It is a family remarkable for its cordial hospitality and for the fact that everybody is so pleasant. I will see the New Year in with them today. I go to the theatre in the evenings. The opera is not bad here. Yesterday (30 December) I saw [Mascagni's] famed *Cavalleria rusticana* for the first time. This really is a very remarkable opera, particularly in its astonishingly successful choice of subject. I wish Modya would sort out something like that for me.[47] The concert was outstanding. I am going to Hamburg [on 5/17 January, from Berlin] and the day after tomorrow i.e. 7/19th I am conducting *Eugene Onegin* in the theatre in Hamburg.[48]

[6/18 January]. There was *only one* rehearsal (of *Eugene Onegin* in Hamburg) which I conducted before the performance today. They have learnt the work extremely well and the production is not bad, but there are changes in the *recitatives* because of the German text and I couldn't help getting lost and muddling it. Despite all their attempts to persuade me I have withdrawn from conducting it because I am frightened of ruining the whole thing. By the way, the conductor here isn't just some middling character: he's a positive *genius*, and dying to conduct the first performance. I heard him conduct *the most astounding* performance of *Tannhäuser*. The singers, the orchestra, the producers, the conductor (they call him Mahler) are all in love with *Eugene Onegin*.[49]

The performance took place [on 7/19 January]. From the musical point of view it was superb. The best you can say of the production is that it was tolerable. Naturally we didn't get away without some comical details in the costumes and the scenery. Tatyana was excellent, graceful, and extraordinarily attractive. Onegin was very good so far as his voice was concerned. Lensky too was not bad at all. The orchestra and chorus were superb. It was a notable success. There were curtain calls after every scene, but no great enthusiasm, more a touch of coolness and mistrust.[50]

[46] xvia. 297 (Kolya).   [47] xvia. 303–4 (Kolya).   [48] xvib. 13 (Modest).
[49] xvib. 16 (Bob).   [50] xvib. 18 (Anatoly).

I am in Petersburg. I have postponed Holland till next year. My main concern is to get a few numbers of the new ballet scored; I have promised to play them at a concert of the Musical Society here. I am going to Maydanovo.[51] I will get down to scoring those numbers of the ballet which will go into the suite and then I'll see to the rest. I think I should finish it by the summer.[52]

The trip to Holland did not in fact take place.

I am relishing life at Maydanovo and enjoying the best winter month in the year [February]. I adore these bright days with a touch of frost, when the sun already has a hint of warmth and a suggestion of spring. My work has gone so well that the score of the ballet [suite] is already finished and Modest is taking it to Petersburg. Volodya Nápravník* is staying with me at the moment; he makes a most agreeable guest. He is working hard for an examination and spends even more hours a day at it than I do. His interest in music is a great source of pleasure to me because we enjoy playing duets together in the evenings; and on occasion I just get him to play me some of my favourite pieces.[53]

I am going to live in a house that I have taken at Klin. It's Sakharov's house, large and comfortable, on the road to Moscow, but outside town.† I have decided to carry on living in the wilds so that I can spend three months or so of the year in a furnished flat in Petersburg. My feeling is that it is essential for me to have a house in the country or, which is the same thing, in Klin so that I will know that if I suddenly feel like it there will always be available a peaceful quiet place where I can work. Moreover, the fact that I have got used to Klin plays a big part. There is a wonderful view from the house, and the garden is more than adequate.[54]

I am not long back from Petersburg. I played the ballet suite there [*The Nutcracker*]. It seemed to go off all right, not like the famed *Voyevoda*. The Russian spring thrills me! I am past myself with joy not to be abroad at this marvellous time of year![55]

I am going flat out scoring the ballet so as to have the work done by Easter. In April I am going to conduct for Pryanishnikov's private opera, and whilst I am in Moscow Alexey will move my possessions into the new place at Klin. It's a fine, big house, and convenient. I will have splendid rooms there, my own small garden, and no neighbours at all. I am very pleased with the move because Maydanovo is getting more and more objectionable.[56] The opera and ballet have already been delivered to the

---

* V. Nápravník—the conductor's son.
† Now the Tchaikovsky museum.

[51] xvi*b*. 27 (Jurgenson).   [52] xvi*b*. 29 (Jurgenson).   [53] xvi*b*. 37 (Anatoly).
[54] Ibid.   [55] xvi*b*. 57 (Ziloti).   [56] xvi*b*. 64 (Anatoly).

appropriate quarters and I am already thinking about a large new work: a symphony with a *secret* programme.[57]

I am in Moscow because of my promise to Pryanishnikov. I find myself much in sympathy with him and his partnership* and would like to help them in their new enterprise to the best of my ability. It will be difficult, unpleasant, even stupid (because what sort of an opera conductor will I make?), but it can't be helped.[58] So far I have conducted *Faust* and *The Demon*, and *Onegin* lies ahead.[59]

My Moscow torments came to an end when I conducted *Onegin*, which, of course, produced ovations.[60] More recently I have been living here at Klin, in my new abode. I personally am immensely pleased with my two huge, marvellous rooms, but it's dreadfully cold and damp for poor Alexey down below. So far we have had to light the stoves every day. Even so, despite all that, I am still very glad I have left rotten old Maydanovo. I feel much more *at home* here; there are lots of walks and living on the main road is very convenient because I can go for walks even in the rain without drowning in mud. I have been busy reading the proofs of some of my works and have also started composing a symphony.[61]

Bob and I left Petersburg on 3 June, spent a day in Berlin, a week in Paris (which we much enjoyed), and are now spending the third week in miserable, odious, insufferable Vichy. It would be wrong not to give Vichy its due in that the place is well-appointed, cheap, and well run. Nor, indeed, can one question the fact this it is doing us both good. But my God! how mournful and miserable! Thousands of people rushing around all over, never a moment to yourself, it's unbearable! When I have *work* to do I value and appreciate a certain monotony of life. But for a start you are forbidden to work here, and then there is no chance of even reading, never mind working. It may be a healthy life but it's a very boring one. Fortunately, the Vichy cure does not last long.[62] I think that the tap, which is closed at the moment, will open again only when I get back to my dear Russia, which, for all that it is so foul, I adore. I don't see how it can be otherwise. A performing artist can spend even decades away from his homeland, but a creative artist can work successfully only in his homeland.[63]

Authors never have anything sensible to say about their own works. I am at present reading Flaubert's letters with the greatest interest and they are peculiar in this respect. I think that the arts in general can scarcely have

* The Private Opera Partnership, of which Ippolit Petrovich Pryanishnikov was the impresario.

[57] xvi*b*. 70 (Ziloti).
[58] xvi*b*. 72 (Ippolitov-Ivanov).
[59] xvi*b*. 81 (Anatoly).
[60] xvi*b*. 85 (Modest).
[61] xvi*b*. 95–6 (Kolya).
[62] xvi*b*. 121–2 (Anna Merkling).
[63] xvi*b*. 120 (Ziloti).
[64] xvi*b*. 137 (Modest).
[65] xvi*b*. 127 (Kolya).

known a more agreeable person. He was something of a hero, a martyr to his art, and astonishingly intelligent as well![64]

There is an edition of Flaubert's letters (in French) in Tchaikovsky's library at Klin with many annotations and underlinings. Tchaikovsky was particularly taken by a letter from Flaubert to Feydeau, who had asked Flaubert to tell him about his work on the novel *Salammbô*. Flaubert replied: 'No, my dear fellow, it would embarrass me. You would start criticizing, and the more just your criticisms were, the more they would annoy me.' (p. 139)

Bob and I have arrived in P'burg; we went to the Zoo and the Aquarium Theatre, then had supper with Vasily Bertenson at Leiner's. I was surprised to be given an ovation at the Aquarium.[65]

The suite from *The Nutcracker* was performed at the Aquarium Theatre.
From Petersburg Tchaikovsky went back home to Klin.

In May, before I went abroad, I sketched the first movement and the Finale of the symphony. It made no progress at all when I was abroad, and now I have other things to do.[66] When I got back from Vichy I settled down to proofs and have been at it for *two solid months*. I have, admittedly, read all the proofs of both scores and of all the arrangements [*Yolanta* and *The Nutcracker*], and in addition I have also made easier arrangement of the ballet myself.[67] Then it might suddenly turn out that *Yolanta* and *The Nutcracker*, which are causing me so much trouble just now, are trash![68]

But at last tomorrow I will finish everything that I had to do. I think I have to thank my extremely sensible way of life, moderation in all things, exercise, and in general good healthy conditions for work, for the fact that I have not gone out of my mind from this hard labour. However, I am almost insane, don't understand anything, cannot use my reason, and am numb. Even my dreams consist of proofs lying about and sharps and flats not doing what they should, and all this merges in something tormenting, fateful, and terrible.[69]

I have to go to Vienna. Back in the spring they invited me to conduct a concert of my own works at the Vienna Exhibition; and they have now invited me in such kind and flattering terms that I thought it was my duty to accept the invitation. I put it this way because I see it as my duty to support the prestige of Russian music abroad in every way I can.[70]

Shortly before going abroad Tchaikovsky received a letter from Daniil Rathaus, a student at Kiev University, enclosing some poems.

I am not sufficiently competent in literary matters decisively to dispose one way or the other of the doubts which trouble you [Rathaus]. But as a *musician*, considering your poems from the point of view of their greater or lesser suitability for being set to music, I have to respond most positively

[64] xvib. 128 (Taneyev).   [67] xvib. 181 (Ziloti).   [68] xvib. 154 (Bob).
[69] xvib. 160 (Bob).   [70] xvib. 152 (Anna Merkling).

and tell you that I like your work. I cannot give you any precise indication of when I will manage to set all or any of your poems to music, but I can *firmly promise* that it will be done. There is one of them in particular which asks to be set to music: 'We sat together'. I must say frankly that I very frequently receive a lot of letters enclosing poems to be set to music and this is practically the first time that I have been able to reply with true gratitude and expressions of sincere enthusiasm. I *think* that you have a genuine talent and I flatter myself with the hope that persons of greater authority in the field of literary criticism will confirm my sincere opinion.[71]

It was not without pleasure that I set off at the end of August for Vienna because in the first place I needed a rest, and in the second I had thought I was going to conduct a splendid orchestra in a splendid hall. Nothing of the sort. The hall turned out to be a beer-cellar, and, though the orchestra did its best, in terms of numbers it was pitiful (eight first violins). I got annoyed and after the second rehearsal I went off with Sapelnikov and Sophie Menter to her place at Itter. We had a marvellous fortnight there. Then there was a very successful production of *The Queen of Spades* in Prague. When I got back home I settled down to the symphony. I have finished the draft and have now started scoring it. What it will be like I really don't know. Vile, I fear. That's all about the past and so far as plans for the future are concerned I am going to P'burg for a production of *Yolanta* and *The Nutcracker*. I will attend the hundredth performance of *Onegin*. I hope to finish scoring the symphony in December, and in January I am conducting two concerts in Odessa.[72]

[In Petersburg] there are rehearsals every day either for the opera or for the ballet, but progress is on the slow side. I am staying at the Grand Hotel in a very nice room, comfortable and convenient. Time passes unnoticed, neither sadly nor cheerfully, but quite fruitlessly because there can be no thought of doing any work.[73]

The premiere of *Yolanta* and *The Nutcracker* eventually took place on 6 December 1892 in the Mariinsky Theatre.

The opera and the ballet were a great success. The opera in particular was much liked. Both productions were magnificent, the ballet was even too magnificent—the eyes tire of so much opulence.[74]

The whole of the Petersburg press is busy cursing my latest offspring in a variety of styles. But it's a matter of utter indifference to me because it's not the first time it has happened and I know that in the end I will get my due. This abuse, I repeat, does not distress me, but none the less I have been in a foul state of mind all the time, which, of course, always happens in such cases. You spend a long time rapt in anticipation of something important,

[71] xvi*b*. 161–2 (Rathaus).   [72] xvi*b*. 181–2 (Ziloti).   [73] xvi*b*. 191 (Anatoly).
[74] xvi*b*. 201 (Anatoly).

then when it happens you feel an apathy, a revulsion from work, a sense of the emptiness and vanity of all our aspirations.[75]

While Tchaikovsky was in Petersburg in November 1892 the periodical *Petersburgskaya zhizn* [*Petersburg Life*] published an interview 'A Conversation with Tchaikovsky'. One of the questions concerned his attitude to the Mighty Handful.

The word 'handful' referred at the end of the sixties and in the seventies to a circle of musicians who were united by personal friendship and the identity of their musical tastes and opinions. One would imagine that such a grouping of talented men would be incapable of evoking anything but the warmest sympathy. What happened in the event, however, was that the 'handful' gradually acquired for itself an enormous number of enemies. The cause of this curious phenomenon is to be sought in the fact that some of those who represented the 'handful' in print attempted, laudably, if you wish, to extol their passionately admired friends and not infrequently went too far: they took to exaggerating and devoted their energies to excessively harsh mockery of everybody and everything which was either alien or unsympathetic to the group. The hostility which inevitably arose between [Balakirev's circle] and the rest of the Russian musical world gave rise to the idea that there was a conflict between two parties, one consisting of the 'handful', or the 'New Russian School' and the other consisting of everybody else. For some reason the latter party was called 'conservative'. This division into parties betrays a strange confusion of concepts, a colossal misunderstanding, and it is high time it was consigned to the past. As an example of the utter absurdity of this division into parties I would refer to the following fact, which is a source of regret to me personally. According to the accepted view of the Russian musical public, I belong to that party which is hostile to the Russian composer whom I love and admire more than any other alive: Rimsky-Korsakov. He is the finest ornament of the 'New Russian School'; but I belong to the old, retrograde school. Why? Rimsky-Korsakov has been subject to the influences of his time to a greater or lesser extent, and so have I. He has written programme symphonies, and so have I. This has not stopped him writing traditional symphonies, gladly writing fugues, and in general composing in a polyphonic vein; the same is true of me. In his operas he has accepted the influence of Wagner or some other, at all events modern, approach to operatic style; and so have I, though perhaps to a lesser extent. This has not stopped him from inserting the traditional cavatinas, arias, and ensembles into his operas; even less has it stopped me. For many years I was a professor at the Conservatoire, which is supposed to be hostile to the 'New Russian School' and to Rimsky-Korsakov as well! In short, despite all the differences of our musical natures, we are, it would seem, travelling along the same road; and, for my part, I am proud to have such a companion on the journey. And yet

[75] xvi*b*. 202 (Anatoly).

I am supposed to belong to the party which is opposed to Rimsky-Korsakov. There is a strange misunderstanding here which has had, and still has, regrettable consequences. It obscures a proper understanding by the public of what is going on in Russian music and gives rise to quite pointless hostility in a sphere where one would think the purest harmony ought to reign; it accentuates the extremes at both ends and ultimately it compromises us, the musicians, in the eyes of future generations. Lyadov and Glazunov, for instance, are also counted amongst my musical opponents, yet I am very fond of them and esteem their gifts.[76]

[76] *MC* 371–3.

25

1893

How short life is! How much one wants to do, to think about, to say ... but death is already lying in wait around the corner

After the St Petersburg production of *Yolanta* and *The Nutcracker* on 6 December, Tchaikovsky set off in mid-December 1892 on his usual concert tour abroad.

In Berlin I fell to meditating on important matters, fraught with consequences. I had looked very carefully through my new symphony, taking, so to speak, an objective attitude towards it; fortunately, I had not managed to orchestrate it and get it moving. My impression was most unflattering: this symphony was written simply for the sake of writing something—there is nothing remotely interesting or attractive about it. I decided to throw it away and forget about it. That decision is irrevocable and it is an excellent thing that I have taken it. But does it not follow that I am played out and that I have dried up? That is what I have been thinking about for three days. Perhaps *a story* could still summon up some inspiration in me, but I must no longer write pure music, i.e. symphonic or chamber. But then it would be very tedious to live without something to do, without work to absorb one's time, one's thoughts, one's abilities. So what am I to do? Snap my fingers and forget about composing? It's very difficult to decide. So I think and think and don't know what conclusion to come to. In any event, I have spent three unhappy days.[1]

It is truly astounding that I do not fall ill and go out of my mind from this phenomenal, monstrous homesickness. It is quite insane and gets worse every time I go abroad; because of this I will, of course, never go again *on my own*. From tomorrow this feeling will go and will be replaced by another, though a much less painful one. I am going to Montbéliard tomorrow with, I admit, a morbid *fear*, almost a *dread*, as though I were entering the realms of death and of those people who have long since vanished from the face of the earth.[2]

Tchaikovsky went to Montbéliard to see his old nanny Fanny Dürbach.

I will say something about my meeting with Mlle Fanny. I let her know from Basle when I would be arriving so that the old dear would not get into too much of a flap if I turned up unexpectedly. I arrived at Montbéliard at

---

[1] xvi*b*. 208 (Bob). [2] xvi*b*. 211–12 (Modest).

three o'clock on 1 January according to their system, and 20 December according to ours, and set off for Fanny's straight away. Although she is seventy now, she looks much younger, and in fact, strange though it may seem, *she has changed little*. I very much feared that there would be tears and scenes, but nothing of the sort. She welcomed me as though we had not met for perhaps a year—joyfully, affectionately, and with great simplicity. It was not long before we started on endless reminiscences about the past, and she produced a positive torrent of all manner of extraordinarily interesting details about our childhood, about mother, and about all of us. Then she showed me *our exercise books*, things I had written, letters, but most interesting of all were some extremely nice letters from mother. It's hard to put into words just how entrancing and magical it was to hear these stories and to read all these letters and exercise books. The past came alive in such detail in my memory that I seemed to be breathing the air of the house in Votkinsk, to be hearing the voices of mother, of Venichka, Khalit, Arisha, Akulina.* At times I got so carried away into that remote past that it was uncanny, but in the nicest way, and we were both holding back tears all the time. I was with her from three to eight and did not notice at all how the time passed. I spent the whole of the next day with her all the time. She gave me as a present a marvellous letter of mother's. In the evening I gave Fanny a parting embrace and left, promising to come again some time.[3] I was deeply affected in a strange, magical way: it was as though for two days I had travelled back to the forties, and [the past] had come alive for me with astonishing reality.[4] I was pleased, but it was uncanny as well.[5] After a gap of forty-four years to see someone once held in close affection, to recall the past as though it had happened just yesterday—it's a unique experience.[6]

The fuss connected with rehearsals, concerts, meeting people and so on didn't give me a minute's peace [in Brussels]. The concert was a brilliant success. The orchestra was big and very good, but they had got used to playing with a common-place, bad conductor who was not in the habit of observing nuances, so that it was incredibly difficult to get p or pp from them. Before I went to Brussels I spent a whole week in Paris, avoiding people I knew and trying by every means I could to stifle the homesickness which was consuming me. By the way, I saw a lot of Ziloti and his wife.[7]

In Brussels Tchaikovsky conducted the Suite No. 3, the First Piano Concerto (with Franz Rummel as soloist), the suite from *The Nutcracker*, the *Overture 1812*, and the Elegy and Waltz from the *Serenade* for string orchestra; some of his songs and piano pieces were also performed.

On his return to Russia Tchaikovsky went to Odessa.

* Members of the Votkinsk household (people of Tchaikovsky's own age, and servants).

[3] xvi*b*. 212–14 (Nikolay Tchaikovsky).   [4] xvi*b*. 215 (Modest).
[5] xvi*b*. 213 (Nikolay).   [6] xvii. 17 (Anatoly).
[7] xvii. 16 (Vladimir Nápravník).

My *homesickness* has gone, but all the same I cannot wait for this tour to come to an end.[8] I have never experienced the like of what is happening just now. They are honouring me here as though I were some great man, almost the saviour of the fatherland, and I am so pulled about in all directions that I can scarcely breathe. I have been here nearly two weeks now and in that time I have managed to conduct at five concerts, take innumerable rehearsals, and consume dozens of dinners and suppers given in my honour. It's all very tiring but it would be ridiculous to complain because eventually I will be glad to look back on all the enthusiasm and incredible ovations. I have also supervised the rehearsals of *The Queen of Spades* and I attended the three performances. I must thank God for the health which I command and which enables me to survive this sort of life for a full two weeks.[9] I have never received such praise anywhere. If only I might at some stage be given in Moscow or Petersburg even a fraction of what I was accorded in Odessa! But that is impossible, and in any case it is not necessary. What is necessary is that I should recover my faith in myself because it has been badly undermined; I think that I have played out my role. The painter Kuznetsov did an *astounding* portrait of me in Odessa.[10]

I was absolutely prostrate with tiredness from the endless celebrations. But I slept all day in the train and arrived at Kamenka fully recovered. However much I suffer from these tours I think that ultimately they are of use to me. All the same I am terribly in need of a period of solitude at the moment so I will go straight from here to Klin. I came to Kamenka mainly to see the old ladies.[11]

When he got back home Tchaikovsky settled down to work.

I am full of my new composition (the symphony) at the moment and I find it very difficult to tear myself away from working on it. I think it will be the best thing I have written.[12]

I want to say something about my present happy frame of mind concerning my work. I have destroyed the symphony which I composed and only partly scored in the autumn. And a jolly good thing too, because there was little of value in it, just an empty play of notes, no real inspiration. Whilst I was on my travels I had an idea for another symphony, a programme symphony this time; but the programme will be left as an enigma—let people guess it for themselves—and the symphony will actually be called 'Programme Symphony' (No. 6). This programme is so intensely personal that as I was mentally composing it on my travels I frequently wept copiously. When I got back I settled to the sketches and I worked with such fervour and speed that in less than four days I had completely finished the first movement and I already had a clear idea of the other movements in my

---

[8] xvii. 20 (Vladimir Nápravník).   [9] xvii. 24–5 (Anna Merkling).
[10] xvii. 27 (Modest).   [11] xvii. 28 (Anatoly).
[12] xvii. 42 (Anatoly).

head. Half of the third movement is already finished. From the point of view of form there will be much that is new in this symphony, and the Finale, incidentally, will not be a noisy Allegro but, on the contrary, a very unhurried Adagio. How glorious it is to realize that my time is not yet over and that I can still work. Of course, I could be mistaken, but I think not.[13]

The composing which he did in the course of his travels amounted to devising the main themes and considering the general plan of the work. But the real beginning of work on composing the Sixth Symphony was 4 February 1893, as Tchaikovsky himself noted on the sketches.

Work on the Sixth had been preceded by the composition of the Symphony in E♭ major, the material of which Tchaikovsky used for the Third Piano Concerto, the *Scherzo-fantaisie* for piano (Op. 72 No. 10), and for the unfinished Andante and Finale for piano and orchestra. But even before the E♭ major symphony Tchaikovsky had considered a programme symphony to be called 'Life'; he sketched the themes and indicated their programmatic significance. There is a theme entitled 'Why? Why? For what?'; there is a draft of the sections 'Youth', 'Obstacles! Nonsense', and a coda 'Onwards! Onwards!'.

I am the unhappiest of men: I roam between Moscow, Klin, Petersburg, Kharkov etc. and am quite unable to get settled anywhere to have even a short rest. Since leaving Odessa I have managed to go to Moscow four times, to Petersburg twice, and once to Nizhny and I have even developed a chronic headache. I am back from Moscow where I went specially to hear the suite *From Childhood* by Konius. It's a long time since I have felt so enthusiastic about anything! It's a delightful piece in every way.[14] There were endless celebrations in Kharkov which made me very tired. Incidentally, things went very well and were almost as great a success as in Odessa. I am [now] going to finish off the sketches for the Finale and Scherzo of the new symphony.[15]

At this time Anatoly was Vice-Governor of Nizhny Novgorod.

I have been travelling about an awful lot this winter and since last October I have really been a nomad, with no settled life. But I have had spells at home. During these spells I have written a new [symphony] and *I will certainly not tear this one up*. I also have some sketches for a piano concerto and I plan to do some work in the near future on some piano pieces.[16]

When he had finished the sketches for the symphony Tchaikovsky started writing the piano pieces, Op. 72, commissioned by Jurgenson.

I am dreadfully annoyed that the letter [to Modest] has got lost in which I praised him for his *Nal and Damayanti*. His libretto is very skilfully done, but the subject is not particularly to my taste. It's too far removed from life. I need a subject like [Mascagni's] *Cavalleria rusticana*.[17]

[13] xvii. 42–3 (Bob).   [14] xvii. 50 (Ziloti).   [15] xvii. 67 (Modest).
[16] xvii. 70 (Ippolitov-Ivanov).   [17] xvii. 79 (Bob).

Modest had written the libretto for Arensky.

I carry on cooking my musical pancakes. It's remarkable that I enjoy it more and find it easier the more I do. It was slow work at first and the first two pieces are the product of an effort of the will, but now I can't cope with the ideas which keep occurring to me one after the other throughout the day. So if *both* I and my publisher were able, I—not to stir from the country for a whole year, and he—to publish this great mass of stuff and pay me the fees, I could earn 36,500 roubles in a single year.[18] Alas! I am not likely to write thirty pieces. I have written eighteen in fifteen days. But I must stay [in Moscow] now, then I want to go to Nizhny, and on 29 [April] they are doing the first performance of Rakhmaninov's *Aleko* here. Then on 10 May I absolutely must go abroad. Perhaps I'll manage somehow to write a few more songs.[19]

I want to go to London direct. I want to get this trip done with as quickly as I can: I am so anxious to get down to scoring the new symphony which I finished in draft a long time ago. It is a long time since I have been so fond of one of my works as I am of this symphony. I feel that everybody who is sympathetic towards my music will like it more than anything I have ever written. I have spent all April at Klin but have not been able to work on it because my financial affairs are in a disgusting condition and I have written eighteen little piano pieces to improve them.[20]

Tchaikovsky went to England to receive an honorary doctorate at Cambridge.

I deliberately stayed at home an extra day so as to get one more opus copied out: the six songs.[21]

This was Op. 73 (Six songs to poems by Daniil Rathaus) composed between 23 April and 5 May 1893.

I spent a pleasant few days in Petersburg. I left in a good frame of mind but not an hour had passed before that insane homesickness started; it is not amenable to any form of description, and it always persecutes me now when I go abroad.[22] Is it not indeed strange that I voluntarily submit myself to these torments? Not only do I suffer from a misery which cannot be put into words (there is a passage in my new symphony which does, I think, express it well), but I also suffer from a hatred of other people, an ill-defined fear, and God alone knows what else.[23]

My Fourth Symphony was a huge success [in London].[24] The concert went off brilliantly: the unanimous view was that I had a real triumph, which meant that Saint-Saëns, who came on after me, suffered somewhat as a consequence of my remarkable success.[25] No less successful was the

[18] xvii. 81–2 (Bob).   [19] xvii. 86 (Modest).   [20] xvii. 89 (Ziloti).
[21] xvii. 89 (Jurgenson).   [22] xvii. 99 (Anatoly).   [23] xvii. 97 (Bob).
[24] xvii. 101 (Ziloti).   [25] xvii. 102 (Modest).

Cambridge concert, where we all (i.e. each of the *Doctors*) conducted our own works. *Francesca* went off well and provoked a great deal of applause.[26] The ceremony itself lasted for two whole days and consisted of the concert on the first day, a formal dinner, and a formal reception; on the second day there was the ceremony of conferring the doctorate, a formal lunch, and a reception given by the wife of the Chancellor, which brought things to a close. I have now left for London and tomorrow morning I go to Paris. I haven't quite come round yet.[27] But Cambridge as a whole—with its *colleges* like monasteries, its distinctive ways and customs preserving much of the medieval about them, with its buildings reminiscent of a very remote past—makes a very attractive impression.[28] Now that it is all over I am pleased to reflect on my success in England and the remarkable cordiality with which I was received everywhere.[29]

Tchaikovsky's visit to England coincided with the last days and the death of his close colleague Karl Albrecht.

I read about Karlusha's death in the papers while I was travelling. Although I had had no hope of him recovering I was still very sad and shed not a few tears.[30]

Tchaikovsky stayed with Sophie Menter at Itter then returned to Russia, to Grankino, to see Modest and Kolya Konradi.

There is no doubt about it: the Russian countryside is infinitely more to my taste than all the vaunted glories of Europe.[31] From here I will go to see my brother Nikolay for a short time. At the end of the summer and for the whole of the autumn I intend not to stir from Klin.[32]

Ukolovo, like the whole of southern Russia this summer, is glorious. Then I am going to Klin. I admit I am dying to spend some time at home. Moreover, I must get down as soon as I can to scoring my two big new works: the symphony and the piano concerto. I wrote both of them in dribs and drabs this last winter and spring. I finished the sketches at Grankino and I must hurry now to get it all done by 1 September.[33]

At last I am back home. Things are excellent here and I am tremendously pleased that I am going to be able to get on with my work. But I will have to spend a couple of days writing letters because there were thirty waiting for me here.[34] It is only at home that I can work properly. I am now up to the eyes in the symphony. The further I get with the scoring the more difficult do I find it. Twenty years ago I used to just charge on at full speed, never stopping to think, and it worked out all right.[35]

---

[26] xvii. 112 (Anatoly).   [27] xvii. 109–10 (Vladimir Nápravník).
[28] xvii. 114 (Jurgenson).   [29] xvii. 108 (Kolya).
[30] xvii. 123 (Jurgenson).   [31] xvii. 119 (Anatoly).
[32] xii. 123 (Jurgenson).   [33] xii. 127 (Anatoly).
[34] xvii. 136 (Anatoly).   [35] xvii. 142 (Modest).

Kostya and Volodya Shilovsky died one after the other this summer.[36]

The symphony is progressing. I am well satisfied with its content, but I am not satisfied, or, to put it more accurately, not absolutely satisfied with the orchestration. It's all coming out not quite as I imagined it. It will be quite normal and unsurprising if this symphony is torn to pieces or not properly appreciated—it wouldn't be the first time. But I definitely think it is by far the best and in particular *by far the most sincere* of all my pieces. I love it as I have never loved any other of my musical children.[37] I certainly can't go now because I am fit for nothing until I finish the symphony.[38] The work is going very well but I can no longer write so quickly as before, not because of a decline of my powers in old age but because I have become far more severe on myself and I lack my former self-confidence.[39]

I have finished scoring my new symphony. I have honestly never in my life felt so pleased with myself, so proud, so happy in the knowledge that I really have written something good.[40]

As I write this [20 August], they are burying my old friend and colleague Apukhtin in Petersburg. So many of my old friends are dying: Karlusha [Albrecht], both the Shilovskys, Apukhtin!!![41]

I am leaving for Hamburg via Petersburg, then I will come straight back to Petersburg to deal with my own affairs as well as with those of Modest and Bob. Kolya [Konradi] has found living with Modest unsatisfactory and has very unceremoniously, though observing the decencies, thrown him out. (That sounds harsh, but it is in fact what he has done.) Now Modest wants to move in with Bob and it's essential that I should go to help them because they would find it difficult to organize themselves on their own. I have finished the symphony and have been working under terrible strain recently. I am so utterly exhausted that I think it would be a good idea to go away for a little trip.[42]

It was at this time that the Grand Duke Konstantin suggested to Tchaikovsky that he should write a Requiem to verses by Apukhtin.

I am in some difficulty because of the fact that my last symphony, the one which I have just written and which is down for performance on 16 October, is imbued with a spirit very close to that which also infuses the *Requiem*. I think that I have made a success of the symphony and I am frightened of repeating myself if I immediately set about a work which in spirit and character is akin to its predecessor. It is no exaggeration to say that I have put my whole soul into this symphony.[43] I have read Apukhtin's *Requiem* several times, I have given the most careful thought to the extent to which it is suitable for being set to music, and I have ultimately come to a

[36] xvii. 136 (Anatoly).   [37] xvii. 155 (Bob).
[38] xvii. 159 (Bob).   [39] xvii. 164–5 (Anatoly).
[40] xvii. 165 (Jurgenson).   [41] xvii. 174 (Jurgenson).
[42] xvii. 171 (Anatoly).   [43] xvii. 186 (K.R.).

negative decision on the matter. If the music is to be worthy of it, the poem should have the power to fire my enthusiasm as a composer, to move me, to stir my heart, to excite my imagination. The overall spirit of this piece is, of course, amenable to a musical treatment and it is a spirit which to a considerable extent permeates my last symphony (especially the Finale). But if we can go into detail, there is much in Apukhtin's poem which, although it is expressed in fine verse, does not require music and is even in fundamental opposition to it. Such lines for instance as: '*They did not at this moment say to him: the choice is yours—to live or die*', '*From childhood on they told him day by day*' etc., etc. This whole tirade, imbued with a pessimistic attitude to life, these questions: '*Why was he born and why did he live?*' and so on—all this excellently expresses the impotence of the human mind faced with the insoluble questions of existence; but because it is not a direct reflection of feeling, and is rather a purely intellectual formulation, it is difficult to put to music. If one is to set a requiem to music it would be better to set the proper, medieval Latin text: this conveys superbly the weakness and fear which we experience when we see a loved one snatched from us by death.[44] There is another reason why I am not much inclined to set any sort of requiem to music. The requiem has a lot to say about *the judgement, the punishment, the vengeance of God* (!!!) But I do not believe in that sort of God, or at any rate that sort of *God* does not evoke in me those tears, that rapture, that worship of the Creator, the source of all that is good which would inspire me. If it were possible I would take the greatest delight in trying to set to music some texts from the Gospels. How many times, for instance, have I dreamt of writing a musical illustration of Christ's words: '*Come unto me all ye that labour and are heavy laden*'; or: '*For my yoke is easy, and my burden is light.*' How much infinite love and pity there is for man in these wonderful words! What infinite poetry in what might be called the *passionate* aspiration to dry the tears of sorrow and relieve the torments of suffering humanity . . .

On 7 October Tchaikovsky left Klin for Moscow, together with the cellists Brandukov and Poplavsky who had been staying with him. He was going to attend the requiem for his old colleague Nikolay Zverev, who had been a professor at the Conservatoire and had died recently.

Tchaikovsky left Klin and never returned. He arrived in St Petersburg on 10 October. He stayed with his brother and nephew on Malaya Morskaya (now 13/8 Gogol Street).

Tchaikovsky conducted the first performance of his Sixth Symphony in the Hall of the Nobility on 16 October 1893. Apart from the symphony, Tchaikovsky conducted the overture to Laroche's opera *Carmosina*, the First Piano Concerto (with Adele aus der Ohe as soloist), and the dances from Mozart's *Idomeneo*; Adele aus der Ohe played piano solos and Liszt's Spanish Rhapsody.

---

[44] xvii. 193–4 (K.R.).

Two days later, on 18 October, he sent Jurgenson the score of the symphony for publication.

Put this on the title-page: To Vladimir Lvovich Davydov. *Simphonie pathétique* (No. 6) Op. ??? *by P. Tchaikovsky*. Something odd is happening with this symphony: it's not that people don't like it but they are somewhat puzzled by it. So far as I am concerned personally, I am more proud of it than of any other of my works. But we'll soon have a talk about that because I will be in Moscow on Saturday.[45]

[45] xvii. 205 (Jurgenson).

26

18–28 October 1893

How sudden and simple, how natural and unnatural.
(Lev Tolstoy, from a letter to his wife)

The première of the Sixth Symphony (*Pathétique*) by Tchaikovsky took place on 16 October 1893 in the Assembly Hall of the Nobility in St Petersburg, conducted by the composer. A few days later alarming news spread throughout the town: Tchaikovsky was seriously ill. But on 24 October *Novosti i birzhevaya gazeta* [*The News and Stock Exchange Gazette*] No. 293 announced: 'The whole music world is alarmed by the news of *P. I. Tchaikovsky's serious illness*. Fortunately, according to the latest communiqué, P. I. Tchaikovsky's illness (presumed to be typhoid) is expected to have a favourable outcome.'

On the day of the composer's death, 25 October, the same newspaper (No. 294) included the following item: 'The virulent epidemic has also not spared our famous composer P. I. Tchaikovsky. He was taken ill on Thursday during the day and his illness immediately assumed a dangerous character.' Two medical bulletins follow and it is stated that 'at 2.30 a.m. the doctors left, having decided that the case was hopeless. At 3.0 a.m. P. I. Tchaikovsky was no more.'

Subsequently, the accounts by first-hand witnesses of Tchaikovsky's illness and death are remarkable for their mass of contradictions. But there is already a contradiction in the items quoted above: the first states that Tchaikovsky evidently has typhoid and that on 23 October he seemed to be improving. But in the account announcing his death, it states that the illness *immediately* assumed a dangerous character. It is true that the illness is not named, but in so far as an epidemic is mentioned, it is clear that cholera is involved. (In the summer of 1892 there was the most virulent epidemic of cholera in Russia. The following year it returned, although to a lesser degree. As a rule the outbreaks would die out towards autumn. This was the case in October 1893. Up to the end of the year there were only isolated cases mentioned in the newspaper reports about the movement of the cholera epidemic.)

All the new contradictions in interviews with witnesses evidently attracted the attention of the general public. A rumour began to spread through the town (possibly even before Tchaikovsky died) that the composer had committed suicide.

On the day after his death the *St Petersburg Gazette* wrote (26 October, No. 294): 'How could Tchaikovsky have contracted cholera when he lived in the most excellent conditions of hygiene and only arrived in St Petersburg a few days ago?'

The same edition included an interview with Doctor Bertenson, 'the first doctor to be summoned by Pyotr Ilich'. The doctor's initials are not given but it is known, from the memoirs of Vasily Bertenson as well as from Lev Bertenson and Modest

Tchaikovsky, that the first to be summoned was his friend Vasily Bertenson who regularly attended Tchaikovsky. In the interview the doctor said that Tchaikovsky began to feel ill on Thursday (21 October), but for the whole of that day and also part of the following day (Friday 22 October), he treated himself and 'did not seek medical help'. But on Friday evening (i.e. the evening of the 22nd) 'Doctor Bertenson was summoned' when 'it was already necessary for the combined strength of six men' to alleviate the suffering of the patient. Further on it states that the next day (Saturday 23 October) a significant improvement occurred and that Tchaikovsky was 'saved from cholera'. But on the other hand the same morning the doctors began to be concerned about another danger, 'the continuing sapping of his strength'. And they began to suspect an infection.

At the same time as the interview with Vasily Bertenson, the *News and Stock Exchange Gazette* printed an interview with Doctor Nikolay Mamonov, the assistant to Lev Bertenson who was a prominent clinical physician and physician to the tsar. He was called in by his brother Vasily. Mamonov was at Tchaikovsky's bedside until the end (he took it in turns with Lev Bertenson's other assistant, Doctor Alexander Zander). Mamonov recounted that Tchaikovsky felt unwell even on Wednesday, the day before he fell ill. (Whereas, according to Modest Tchaikovsky, on the day before his illness, the composer was completely well and even felt in excellent health late in the evening—from a letter to the editor, *Novoye vremya* [*New Times*], 1 Nov. 1893, No. 6350.)

On 27 October the *New Times* (No. 6345) printed an article by Lev Bertenson. The following appeared as a preamble to the article: 'The variety of eye-witness accounts appearing in print, concerning the illness of the late P. I. Tchaikovsky has caused us to turn to Doctor L. B. Bertenson, who was in charge of the treatment of the deceased composer.'

However, the picture painted by Lev Bertenson only made the discrepancies worse. Unlike his brother Vasily, Lev Bertenson emphasizes that there was a danger of uraemia from the very onset of the disease, but on Saturday 23 October, when according to Vasily Bertenson this danger had only just appeared, and when the general condition of the patient had improved, the composer was not only no better, but was already dying, and he died during Sunday night (24 October).

How can one explain such discrepancies? There can be only one solution: the doctors were trying to hide the truth. Since there were still a few isolated cases of cholera in St Petersburg that October, the original version mentioning typhoid was changed to cholera, a pitiless and inexorable disease which usually has a fatal outcome.

There is yet another surprising circumstance: Doctor Lev Bertenson's report does not stand up to scrutiny from a medical point of view. He said that on his first visit to Tchaikovsky, when he first became ill, he found 'the deceased in the so-called algid stage'. But the algid stage is the second stage of cholera. The third is the stage of reaction, i.e. when the patient either recovers or dies. Why was this? Why did the doctor mix up the stages of the disease? The answer can be found in Vasily Bertenson's memoirs: 'I must admit that I had never had occasion to witness a true case of cholera before this.'[1] This is quite understandable: the Bertenson brothers'

---

[1] Vasily Bertenson, 'Listki iz vospominaniy' ['Notes from my Memoirs'] in *P. I. Tchaikovsky v vospominaniyakh sovremennikov* [*P. I. Tchaikovsky remembered by his Contemporaries*], 4th edn. (Moscow, 1980), p. 342.

medical practice dealt exclusively with the circles of the St Petersburg élite and cholera did not touch these circles. This is why both doctors knew of cholera only from the literature. Lev Bertenson, too, was reduced to describing Tchaikovsky's illness not from his observation of the patient but from what he had once read. Deeply shocked and forced by circumstances to lie, the doctor used the terminology which he could remember, but in the wrong sequence.

This is also the only explanation of how a professional doctor could state that Tchaikovsky uttered words consciously and was able to give answers to questions when he was supposedly in a coma, although it is well known that a patient in a coma is not able to produce any conscious reaction, since he is 'decerebrate'. (It is interesting to note that it was precisely this part of Bertenson's account that Modest repeated almost word for word in his article—see below.)

Obviously the doctors were respectable and honest people who were incompetent when it came to such dubious matters as lying. Moreover they lost their heads under the strain of the unfolding catastrophe and became so confused that they could not agree on a unified story in their statements. They probably noticed this themselves, for a news item of the *New Times* for 28 October (No. 6346) states: 'L. B. Bertenson, who attended the late P. I. Tchaikovsky, has asked us to print the following: concerning P. I. Tchaikovsky's illness, some newspapers have reported my opinions and statements in such distorted form that I am forced to deny them, and my denial rests on the fact that I did not see any of the reporters except the reporter from *New Times* (see No. 6345). For this reason I could not have talked to any of them. Of the three bulletins which appeared in print, only two, appearing in abbreviated form (. . .) were written by me.' This concerns the bulletins which were pinned up on the door to Modest Tchaikovsky's apartment on the last day of the composer's life and which gave hourly information about the patient's condition. But even these bulletins did not coincide with Lev Bertenson's account!

Naturally all this confusion only strengthened the rumours. And then the composer's brother Modest took up his pen.

When Modest Tchaikovsky's archives were sorted through in 1938, two letters were discovered from Doctor Lev Bertenson, written after the composer's death. One is a short emotional note with expressions of sorrow at the terrible loss—the death of dear Pyotr Ilich. The other is extensive, in the form of an open letter, or rather guidelines. It is much less emotional, more businesslike, and the main content is devoted to a detailed description of Tchaikovsky's illness. (The note was discovered even earlier by the American musicologist, Nicolas Slonimsky, and printed in the book, *Tchaikovsky*, by Herbert Weinstock (New York, 1943), p. 364.) The second letter was in the Museum at Klin before the Second World War. It is not known whether it still exists or whether it was destroyed together with a number of other documents. At any rate, when I asked permission to see it in the 1950s in the course of my research, I was told that I could not because the letter had been lost. There is reason to believe that the second letter must have formed the basis for Modest Tchaikovsky's article. Otherwise how can one explain Modest's compulsion to recount the course of the composer's illness when he was at the patient's bedside all the time?

However, Modest was in such a state that he was incapable of taking in all of the doctor's detailed indications. A different picture altogether faced this man stricken with grief, and, despite his awareness of what he wanted to do, it was this picture which pushed Bertenson's document into the background for a time.

Modest Tchaikovsky's letter to the editor appeared on 1 November in a number of St Petersburg newspapers (I have used *New Times*, No. 6350). The article is called 'Tchaikovsky's illness' and begins as follows: 'To supplement the short but entirely accurate account of the last days of my brother's life by L. B. Bertenson, I consider it necessary, in order to put an end to various contradictory rumours, to hand over to you for publication as full an account as possible of everything to which I was a witness.'

Modest Tchaikovsky was probably simply not in a fit state to take in Lev Bertenson's indications. When you put together the accounts of the doctor and Tchaikovsky's brother the following points are glaringly obvious. In each document the symptoms of cholera are described, and its course is followed literally hour by hour, but each of the authors gives a different description. If one states that the patient suffered terrible convulsions, the other, describing the same hour, emphasizes that the convulsions had ceased. If, according to one, Tchaikovsky was fully conscious, the other affirms that at this time he was unconscious. And most surprising of all: according to the doctor the composer died not on the 25th but on 24 October, i.e. twenty-four hours previously. Besides this the descriptions of Modest Tchaikovsky and Lev Bertenson diverge from the published medical bulletins.

One essential detail stands out: Modest states that on the first day the patient had severe chest pains, and on the following day unquenchable thirst. In the doctor's account there is no mention of this, because these are not symptoms of cholera. But this is evidently what had particularly seared itself into the memory of Modest Tchaikovsky when he relived in torment his brother's suffering. (According to medical literature and to specialists—epidemiologists and toxicologists—such symptoms as sharp pain and thirst are not characteristic of cholera but on the other hand are typical of arsenic poisoning.)

As far as Modest's condition is concerned we have the following evidence: 'M. I. Tchaikovsky was crushed with grief to such an extent that he had to miss the requiem; he is in a private room in the company of a few devoted friends' (*News and Stock Exchange Gazette*, 25 Oct. 1893, No. 294). So it is not surprising that Lev Bertenson's instructions were unable to help Modest Tchaikovsky to describe what in reality never happened.

It is worth pointing out two more facts which play a part in the accounts of the witnesses mentioned above, and of others, and which subsequently appeared also in several memoirs. In some of the newspaper interviews there is mention of a glass of unboiled water, which Tchaikovsky drank, and which allegedly played a fateful role. However, some of the witnesses say that he drank the unboiled water on the day before, on the Wednesday evening (20 October) in a restaurant, but Modest states that the fateful glass was drunk on Thursday during the day (21st) at home, when the composer was already beginning to feel ill.

However, in all instructions for combating cholera it is forbidden not only to drink unboiled water but even to wash in it and boiled water is also recommended for washing dishes. We will leave aside the version about the restaurant since this figures mainly in memoirs, often at second hand. But it would be unthinkable for unboiled water to be served at table in any educated family (and it would be particularly unthinkable in the Tchaikovsky family, on whom cholera had once struck such a terrible blow!). But even if the composer had drunk unboiled water on that very day when he was already ill, nothing in his condition would have changed, since cholera does not usually strike instantly.

Various reports exist also about the bath which was essential for a cholera patient (in order to stimulate the working of the kidneys), but is not necessary in a case of poisoning. Lev Bertenson states that Tchaikovsky was given a bath on Saturday, but Modest indicates that it was on Sunday. But it is evident that they did not use the bath at all, which moreover is stated in Alexey Suvorin's diary: 'Tchaikovsky was buried yesterday. I am desperately sorry for him. The Bertenson brothers treated him and they did not give him a bath.'[2]

One must say that the very fact that the most detailed description of the illness of a great man and the method of treatment appeared widely in the Russian press, when it would have been more appropriate in a medical journal, is without precedent. Why was it necessary *after the composer's death* to describe in detail what his stools were like, how his kidneys were functioning and what treatment he was given? And why did both his brother and his doctor consider it necessary to give this kind of account? It is clear that it was in response to the rumours, a desire to establish (or to hide!) the truth. If there had not been important discrepancies in the accounts of eye-witnesses one could have assumed the former. But any lawyer will confirm that conflicting evidence from witnesses who are trying to convince the court of the truth of one or another version only demonstrates the unreliability of that version.

Apart from the contradictory evidence of the eye-witnesses, there is one more strange detail which cannot have failed to astonish Tchaikovsky's contemporaries, and undoubtedly caused perplexity: the failure to observe the most elementary precautions both at the patient's bedside and after his death. The government's orders concerning those who had died from cholera were very specific and everyone knew about them: 'In the event of a death from cholera the body should be removed from the house as soon as possible in a hermetically sealed coffin; it is also recommended that the arrangement of a widely attended funeral service or funeral banquet should be avoided.'[3]

In Tchaikovsky's house all these rules were violated. Fifteen people gathered round the bedside of the dying man, not counting the priest who had come with the Holy Sacrament to administer the Last Rites. The corpse was laid out for two days, first on the bed where he had died and then in an open coffin (the coffin was sealed only in the evening of the second day, i.e. the 26th). 'The deceased lies on a couch, as if he were alive and looks as if he is asleep. A photograph of the deceased was taken by the photographer of the Imperial Theatres', wrote *New Times* in its report for 25 October (26 October, No. 6344). The correspondent of the *Moskovskiye vedomosti* [*Moscow Gazette*] in his article on 26 October described how on the day before, the 25th, he could not get to the requiem service, but that on the 26th he attended two requiems, and moreover observed: 'Pyotr Ilich lies as if he were alive, his face calm, but it is as if the terrible pallor expresses the suffering which the dear departed underwent during the last three days of his life' (*Moscow Gazette*, 27 Oct.

[2] *Dnevniki A. S. Suvorina* [*The Diaries of A. S. Suvorin*] (Moscow–Petrograd, 1923), entry for 29 Oct. 1893.

[3] *Pravitelstvenny vestnik* [*Government Herald*], 2 July 1892, No. 142.

1893, No. 296). Only on the third day, 27 October, did the public file past a sealed coffin.

On the first two days requiem Masses took place in the presence of a constant stream of people. On 25 October at 2.0 p.m. (the body was still lying on the couch) and at 7.0 in the evening the chorus of the Russian opera sang and 'a mass of personalities were present from St Petersburg society and the musical world, men of letters, etc.' (*New Times*, 26 Oct. 1893, No. 6344). The next day (the 26th) the professors and students of the School of Jurisprudence attended the requiem.

Nikolay Rimsky-Korsakov remembered: 'It was strange that although the death was the result of cholera, there was free access to the requiem. I remember seeing Verzhbilovich (. . .) kiss the corpse's head and face.'[4]

On the evening of 25 October the sculptor Tselinsky made a death mask. This mask is yet another piece of evidence against the cholera version. Tchaikovsky's death mask is in the exhibition at the Museum at Klin. The face of the deceased is very sunken but peaceful, whereas the faces of those who have died of cholera are unrecognizably distorted by convulsions.

Time passed. By the 1920s Vasily Bertenson no longer concealed the truth about the cause of Tchaikovsky's death. And so he told the musicologist, Georgy Orlov, a friend of the now aged doctor's son, the pianist Nikolay Bertenson, that Tchaikovsky committed suicide. At about the same time the doctor Alexander Zander told the same story to his son Yury (Yury Zander was also a friend of Georgy Orlov and told him what his father had said to him). All this became known to me too since in the 1930s Georgy Orlov married me and we talked a lot about Tchaikovsky's death. Professor Alexander Ossovsky, the Director of the Research Institute for Music and Drama, where I worked after the war, also talked of Tchaikovsky's suicide. In other words the fact of the composer's suicide had long ceased to be a secret.

And so it was not cholera but suicide! It was a premeditated means of departing from life, made to look as if death was caused by a fatal illness. (Remember the attempt at suicide after his unsuccessful marriage when one autumn night in 1877 Tchaikovsky 'bathed' in the freezing waters of the Moscow River!)

The question naturally arises: when and why did the composer come to this desperate decision when he had reached the pinnacle of world fame? What event took place in St Petersburg during Tchaikovsky's last visit to the capital which could have forced him to commit this terrible deed?

I was given the answer to this question in the spring of 1966 by the late Alexander Voytov, formerly Curator of the Department of Numismatics at the Russian Museum in Leningrad.

This is what he told me:

In the list of students who graduated from the School of Jurisprudence at the same time as Tchaikovsky there appears the surname Jacobi. When I was a student at the School of Jurisprudence I spent all my holidays with the family of Nikolay Borisovich Jacobi, who died in 1902. His wife was a friend and

---

[4] N. A. Rimsky-Korsakov, *Letopis moyey muzykalnoy zhizni*, [*Chronicle of my Musical Life*] (Moscow, 1955), p. 194.

distant relative of my parents, was very fond of me and always welcomed me. In 1913, when I was in my last year at the School of Jurisprudence, the twentieth anniversary of Tchaikovsky's death was widely marked. And then, evidently under the influence of memories which came flooding back, Elizaveta Jacobi told me, under oath of secrecy, the story which, as she admitted, had long tormented her. She told me that she had decided that this was the moment to reveal it to me, because she was getting old and she felt that she did not have the right to carry this important and terrible secret with her to the grave. She said, 'You are interested in the history of School and the fate of its students. This is why you must know the whole truth, all the more so because it is so sad.' [Voytov devoted his life to collecting material on the history of the School of Jurisprudence and possessed a large library of books on this subject. He called himself 'the last jurisprudence student of the peace' since he graduated on the eve of the First World War in 1914.]

. . . The story begins in the autumn of 1893. Tchaikovsky was threatened with a serious catastrophe. Count Stenbock-Fermor had become concerned by the attentions which the composer was paying to his young nephew, and had written an indignant letter addressed to the Tsar and had handed this official letter for presentation to Alexander III to Jacobi, who was at that time Deputy Chief Procurator for the Department of Criminal Appeal in the Senate. Exposure would inevitably have threatened Tchaikovsky with unavoidable disgrace.

Exposure would also have threatened with disgrace the School of Jurisprudence and all graduates who had been fellow students of Tchaikovsky. But the honour of the uniform of the School was held sacred by all its graduates.

In order to prevent the matter from becoming public knowledge, Jacobi decided to act: he invited all the former fellow students of Tchaikovsky to his house, including the composer himself, and arranged a court of honour. In all there were eight men (the number cited by Elizaveta Jacobi exactly corresponds with the number of surviving fellow students who were living in St Petersburg at the time). Elizaveta Jacobi herself sat with her needlework in her usual place in the drawing room, which adjoined her husband's study. Voices could be heard coming from it from time to time, sometimes loud and emotional and sometimes dropping to a whisper. This went on for a very long time, almost five hours. Then Tchaikovsky came bursting out of the study. He was very pale and upset, almost ran straight past but made a sort of sideways bow and left without saying a word. All the others remained for a long time after that in the study and talked in low voices. But when the visitors had left, after swearing his wife to secrecy, Jacobi told her that they had discussed Stenbock-Fermor's letter to the Tsar. Jacobi had no right to impede the progress of the letter. And so the fellow students had taken a decision which Tchaikovsky had promised to observe. The letter could be suppressed only in the event of his death . . . A day or two later the news of his fatal illness was spreading throughout St Petersburg.

The version told by Voytov is confirmed by the witness account of Vera Kuznetsova, née Denisova, told to her granddaughter, Natalya Vladimirova-Kuznetsova.[5] Vera Kuznetsova (who died in 1955), the youngest sister of Olga Tchaikovskaya, Nikolay Tchaikovsky's wife, told the selfsame story about the verdict on Tchaikovsky at Jacobi's house. She found out about this from her sister, i.e. in fact from first hand: the elder brother of the composer and his wife knew how to keep secrets and there is no doubt that they were in on the affair from the beginning (remember that it was this couple who adopted Tatyana Davydova's son, Georges, and as a consequence had earned the complete confidence both of Pyotr and of Modest Tchaikovsky).

And this is what Galina von Meck, who died recently, recounted (the daughter of Tchaikovsky's niece Anna and Nadezhda von Meck's son Nikolay). In 1981 Galina von Meck, who had been living in England since the late 1930s, published her translation *Letters to his Family* [Pisma k blizkim] (not to be confused with the volume *Letters to his Relatives* [Pisma k rodnym] which was withdrawn immediately after its publication in 1940; *Letters to his Family*, even more shortened, is a selection from Tchaikovsky's enormous correspondence with the members of his family, published in 1955). In the Epilogue to the translation, Galina von Meck wrote: three days after Tchaikovsky had written to Jurgenson about the publication of the score of his Sixth Symphony (letter of 18 October) the composer returned home very upset about something: 'we shall never really know what—and not feeling very well. He asked his brother for a glass of water. When told that he would have to wait for the water to be boiled' Tchaikovsky 'ignored his brother's protests, went into the kitchen, filled a glass of water from the tap and drank it, saying something like, "Who cares anyway!" That same evening he felt quite ill.' (P. I. Tchaikovsky, *Letters to his Family*, an autobiography, trans. Galina von Meck with additional annotations by Percy M. Young (London, 1981), p. 555).

Three days after the 18th was the 21st. This is probably what happened: in the morning Tchaikovsky writes to Nápravník's wife to say that 'he is not going [to Moscow] today', then sets off for Jacobi's house, returns home 'very upset' and 'not feeling very well', drinks a glass of unboiled water (possibly taking poison with it), muttering something like 'Who cares anyway!' And then all the rest coincides exactly with the interview with Vasily Bertenson (see above), who said that Tchaikovsky felt ill on the evening of 21 October, the whole of the next day treated himself, and decided to call a doctor only on the evening of the 22nd. So in fact everything happened differently from what Lev Bertenson and Modest Tchaikovsky described, although the latter talked of pain in the region of the chest and of extreme thirst.

What happened in reality? Nobody will ever know. The version that Galina von Meck recounted was told her by the first cousin once removed of the composer, Alexander Litke, whom she became friendly with. Galina herself was two years old in 1893 and so she cannot be counted as a witness. However, Sanya Litke was one of the relatives who was present at Tchaikovsky's death and was an eyewitness to the tragedy.

But is it possible that this terrible sacrifice was made in vain? According to rumour, the court turned a blind eye to homosexuality—many of the tsar's own

5 Natalya Kuznetsova, 'Pismo k redaktoru' ['Letter to the Editor'] *Kontinent* (1988) No. 58, pp. 371–3.

relatives and his highest officials were homosexual. And it was only in cases of the scandalous exposure of highly placed officials that they were exiled to distant provinces, but they were not brought to trial, nor sent to Siberia. (There is mention of punishing homosexuality by the deprivation of all civil rights and banishment to Siberia in Article 995 of the Criminal Code of the Russian Empire, St Petersburg, 1868 and 1885.)

Of course, it was not repression that Tchaikovsky feared but the disgrace to his name. He was terrified not by punishment but by the loss of his honour . . . and the terrible deed was done.

It seemed that the secret of Tchaikovsky's 'court of honour' and his enforced suicide had been buried with him (those who knew about it—his brothers Modest and Nikolay, hid the truth for many years from all their relatives). But evidently documents existed in the archives. At all events, in 1960 at a lecture on forensic medicine in the First Leningrad Medical Institute, the case of Tchaikovsky was cited as an example of enforced suicide. (I was told about this by a doctor in Leningrad who was a student at that time and had been present at the lecture in question. As he lives in the Soviet Union, I cannot give his name, for obvious reasons.)

. . . In order to emphasize his recognition of the great composer's genius, Alexander III arranged the most grandiose funeral, to be conducted at the Ministry of the Imperial Court's expense. The funeral service was performed in the Kazan Cathedral, the first time such an honour had been granted to an ordinary citizen. Deputations from various societies and academic establishments, from various towns, and a crowd of several thousand accompanied the composer on his final journey. Traffic in the Nevsky Prospect was held up for several hours.

Tchaikovsky was buried in the Tikhvin Cemetery next to the Alexander Nevsky Monastery (now a 'necropolis' for outstanding personalities in the arts), near Glinka's tomb. Among the speakers was Tchaikovsky's fellow student, Vladimir Gerard, a man whom in his youth Tchaikovsky had loved whole-heartedly and unrequitedly. He could have been one of those who condemned Tchaikovsky to suicide in Jacobi's house. Gerard's speech at the grave side creates a painful impression with its leaden, official, and callous tone.

The untimely death of their beloved composer was a severe blow to his contemporaries. Chekhov was a great admirer of Tchaikovsky's talent and when he learnt of his death he sent a telegram to Modest: 'The news has shocked me. Terribly sad . . .'. It was at this time also that Tolstoy wrote to his wife from Yasnaya Polyana: 'I am very sorry about Tchaikovsky . . . More than as a musician I feel sorry for him as a man about whom there was something not altogether clear. How sudden and simple, how natural and unnatural, and how close to my heart.'

What Tolstoy does not quite say is highly significant: it serves as a sufficiently eloquent and definitive refutation of the false version of Tchaikovsky's death.

It is my passionate desire that my music should be widely known and that the number of those who like it, who find comfort and support in it should grow.

BIOGRAPHICAL GLOSSARY

Albrecht, Karl (Konstantin) Karlovich (1836–93) Teacher, cellist, Dean of Moscow Conservatoire.

Alexey, *see* Sofronov

Alyosha, *see* Sofronov

Anatoly, *see* Tchaikovsky, Anatoly Ilich

Apukhtin, Alexey Nikolayevich (1841–93) Friend of Tchaikovsky from their days at School of Jurisprudence. His nostalgic salon verses were frequently set by the composer.

Artôt, Désirée (1835–1907) Soprano with Italian opera company travelling in Russia. Tchaikovsky contemplated marrying her. Trained under Pauline Viardot.

Balakirev, Mily Alexeyevich (1837–1910) Russian nationalist composer. Central figure of the Mighty Handful. Forthright critic of Tchaikovsky's works but admired and encouraged him. Suggested Romeo and Juliet as a theme. Tchaikovsky trusted his judgement.

Blumenfeld, Stanislav Mikhaylovich (1850–97) Music teacher to the Davydov children. *See under* 'Georges' for his child by Tanya Davydova.

Bob, *see* Davydov, Vladimir Lvovich

Borodin, Alexander Porfiryevich (1833–87) Russian nationalist composer. Member of the Mighty Handful. Noted for his Second Symphony and opera *Prince Igor*.

Bortnyansky, Dmitry Stepanovich (1751–1825) Russian composer. Protégé of Catherine the Great. Studied in Italy. Wrote some operas and much unaccompanied choral music for religious use.

Bourgault-Ducoudray, Louis Albert (1840–1910) French composer and critic. Authority on folk music.

Brodsky, Adolph Davydovich (1851–1929) Violinist. Gave first performance of Violin Concerto.

Bülow, Hans Guido von (1830–94) German conductor and pianist. Gave prèmiere of First Piano Concerto. Wrote articles about Tchaikovsky and performed his works throughout Europe, doing much to establish his reputation outside of Russia.

Colonne, Edouard (1838–1910) French violinist, conductor and concert promoter.

Cui, César Antonovich (1835–1918) Russian nationalist composer. Member of the Mighty Handful. Military engineer and authority on fortifications. Severe critic of Tchaikovsky but discriminating and perceptive: aproved of *Romeo and Juliet* and Second String Quartet.

Dargomyzhsky, Alexander Sergeyevich (1813–69) Russian nationalist composer and pianist. Mainly operas and songs.

Davydov (Davidoff), Karl Yulevich (1838–89) Russian cellist and composer. Director of St Petersburg Conservatoire 1876–86.

Davydov, Lev Vasilyevich (Lyova) (1837–96) His father exiled to Siberia for his part in Decembrist uprising of 1825. Married Tchaikovsky's sister Alexander (Sasha) in 1860. His family estate of Kamenka became a home to the composer.

Davydov, Vladimir Lvovich (Bob) (1871–1906) Tchaikovsky's nephew, friend and correspondent.

Davydova, Alexandra Ilinichna née Tchaikovskaya (Sasha, Sanya) (1842–91) Tchaikovsky's sister. Married Lev Davydov. The whole family was much loved by the composer.

Davydova, Alexandra Ivanovna (1802–95) Widow of the Decembrist and mother of Lev Davydov.

Davydova, Anna Lvovna (1864–1942) Tchaikovsky's niece. Married Nikolay von Meck, son of the composer's benefactress.

Davydova, Natalya Lvovna (Tasya) (1868–1956) Tchaikovsky's niece. Married Nikolay Alexandrovich Rimsky-Korsakov, the widower of her sister Vera.

Davydova, Tatyana Lvovna (Tanya) (1862–87) Tchaikovsky's niece.

Davydova, Vera Lvovna (1863–89) Tchaikovsky's niece. Married Nikolay Alexandrovich Rimsky-Korsakov, who after her death married her sister Natalya.

Georges. Georges-Léon (1883–1940) Son of Tanya Davydova and Stanislav Blumenfeld. Adopted by Nikolay Tchaikovsky.

Glazunov, Alexander Konstantinovich (1865–1936) Russian composer. Symphonies and ballet music. More cosmopolitan than nationalist.

Glinka, Mikhail Ivanovich (1804–57) Leading Russian composer. Founded national school and was first to gain international reputation. Two operas: *A life for the Tsar* and *Ruslan and Lyudmila*.

Grand Duke Konstantin, *see* K.R.

Hubert, Nikolay Albertovich (1840–88) Student friend of Tchaikovsky. Subsequently critic and Professor of Theory, Moscow Conservatoire; Director 1881–83.

Ippolit, *see* Tchaikovsky, Ippolit Ilich

Ippolitov-Ivanov, Mikhail Mikhaylovich (1859–1935) Composer (*Caucasian Sketches*), conductor and head of Tiflis Conservatoire 1883–93; Director of Moscow Conservatoire 1906–22.

Jurgenson, Pyotr Ivanovich (1836–1903) Friend of Tchaikovsky and Russian publisher of many of his major works.

Kashkin, Nikolay Dmitriyevich (1839–1920) Friend of Tchaikovsky. Music critic. On staff of Moscow Conservatoire 1863–94.

Khomyakov, Alexey Stepanovich (1804–1860) Historian, religious thinker and poet.

Kolya (1.) In footnotes always: Konradi, Nikolay Hermanovich; (2.) Von Meck, Nikolay Karlovich; (3.) Tchaikovsky, Nikolay Ilich

Kondratyev, Nikolay Dmitriyevich (1837–87) Wealthy friend of the composer.

Konradi, Nikolay Hermanovich (Kolya) (1868–1922) Deaf-mute pupil of Modest Tchaikovsky.

Konshina, *see* Tchaikovskaya, Praskovya Vladimirovna

Kostya, *see* Shilovsky, Konstantin Stepanovich

Kotek, Iosif Iosifovich (1855–85) Pupil of Tchaikovsky. Violinist. House musician of Mme von Meck, which led to her relationship with Tchaikovsky.

K.R. Grand Duke Konstantin Konstantinovich Romanov (1858–1915) Member of ruling dynasty who published conventional lyric verse under pseudonym K.R.

Laroche, Herman Avgustovich (1845–1904) Friend and fellow student of Tchaikovsky at Conservatoire. One of the first critics to support the composer.

Lyova, *see* Davydov, Lev Vasilyevich

Mackar, Félix (1837–1903) Tchaikovsky's publisher in Paris.

Meck, Nadezhda Filaretovna von née Frolovskaya (1831–94) Wealthy music lover who at one stage employed Debussy as her house musician. Supported Tchaikovsky financially for many years. Extensive and musically informative correspondence with the composer, but they never met. Fourth Symphony dedicated to her. Her son, Nikolay, married Tchaikovsky's niece, Anna.

Meck, Nikolay Karlovich von (Kolya) (1863–1929) Son of Mme von Meck, Tchaikovsky's benefactress. Married the composer's niece, Anna Davydova.

Merkling, Anna Petrovna née Tchaikovskaya (1830–1911) Tchaikovsky's cousin.

Mighty Handful: '*Moguchaya kuchka*': term coined by the critic Stasov to cover the group of Balakirev, Borodin, Cui, Musorgsky, Rimsky-Korsakov. Sometimes known as 'the Five'. Russian nationalist composers based in St Petersburg. Tchaikovsky was a member of the more cosmopolitan group centred on Nikolay Rubinstein in Moscow. There were differences between the groups but these did not by any means amount to head-on opposition.

Milyukova, Antonina Ivanovna (1849–1917) Student at Moscow Conservatoire when Tchaikovsky was on the staff, although he did not know her at that stage. Married the composer in 1877 but they separated after only a few weeks. In mental hospital 1896–1917 but of questionable sanity long before.

Modest, Modya, *see* Tchaikovsky, Modest Ilich

Musorgsky, Modest Petrovich (1839–81) Most original and adventurous member of the Mighty Handful. His individual style not fully appreciated until the twentieth century. Tchaikovsky had reservations about his lack of polish. Opera *Boris Godunov* produced 1874.

Nápravník, Eduard Frantsevich (1839–1916) Bohemian conductor. Conductor of Imperial Russian Opera 1869–1916. Conducted many Tchaikovsky premières, including five of the operas.

Olkhovskaya, Zinaida Ilinichna née Tchaikovskaya (1829–78) Tchaikovsky's half-sister by his father's first marriage.

Olya, *see* Tchaikovskaya, Olga Sergeyevna

Panya, Parasha, *see* Tchaikovskaya, Praskovya Vladimirovna

Pryanishnikov, Ippolit Petrovich (1847–1921) Baritone; sang Onegin in Petersburg première. Impresario of Private Opera Partnership.

Rimsky-Korsakov, Nikolay Alexandrovich (1852–after 1906) Married Tchaikovsky's niece Vera Davydova and, on her death, her sister Natalya.

Rimsky-Korsakov, Nikolay Andreyevich (1844–1908) Member of the Mighty Handful. Influenced by nationalist works of Glinka and Balakirev. Colourful and masterly orchestrator as seen in *Sheherazade* and *Spanish Caprice*. Taught Glazunov and Stravinsky.

Rubinstein, Anton Grigoryevich (1829–94) Brother of Nikolay. Pianist and composer. Taught Tchaikovsky, who greatly admired his piano playing. Founder and first Director of St Petersburg Conservatoire 1862–67 and 1887–90.

Rubinstein, Nikolay Grigoryevich (1835–81) Brother of Anton. Founder and first Director of Moscow Conservatoire, 1866–81. Appointed Tchaikovsky to Conservatoire staff and conducted many premières of his works, including the first four symphonies. Taught Taneyev and Ziloti.

Sanya, Sasha, *see* Davydova, Alexandra Ilinichna

Shilovsky, Konstantin Stepanovich (Kostya) (1849–93) Brother of Vladimir. Actor at Maly theatre under name Loshivsky. Collaborated with Tchaikovsky on libretto for *Eugene Onegin*.

Shilovsky, Vladimir Stepanovich (Volodya) (1852–93) Brother of Konstantin. Pupil and friend of Tchaikovsky.

Shpazhinsky, Ippolit Vasilyevich (1844–1917) Dramatist. Wrote *The Sorceress* and adapted it as libretto for Tchaikovsky. The composer corresponded with his wife, Yuliya, after their marriage broke up.

Sofronov, Alexey Ivanovich (Alyosha) Tchaikovsky's manservant and companion.

Stasov, Vladimir Vasilyevich (1824–1906) First Russian music and art critic of note. Supported Mighty Handful, whose name he coined. Suggested programme for *The Tempest*.

Taneyev, Sergey Ivanovich (1856–1915) Composer and pianist. Opponent of nationalist school. Esteemed by Tchaikovsky who arranged his appointment as Director of Moscow Conservatoire (1885–89). Gave premières of Second and Third Piano Concertos.

Tanya, *see* Davydova, Tatyana Lvovna

Tasya, *see* Davydova, Natalya Lvovna

Tchaikovskaya, Alexandra Andreyevna née Assier (1813–54) Tchaikovsky's mother by his father's second marriage in 1833.

Tchaikovskaya, Elizaveta Mikhaylovna, formerly Alexandrova née Lipport Tchaikovsky's father's third wife by marriage of 1865.

Tchaikovskaya, Olga Sergeyevna née Denisova (Olya) Wife of Tchaikovsky's brother Nikolay.

Tchaikovskaya, Praskovya Vladimirovna née Konshina (Panya, Parasha) (1864–1956) Wife of Tchaikovsky's brother Anatoly.

Tchaikovsky, Anatoly Ilich (Tolya) (1850–1915) Tchaikovsky's brother, twin of Modest. Close to the composer. Successful career as lawyer and civil servant.

Tchaikovsky, Ilya Petrovich (1795–1880) Father of the composer.

Tchaikovsky, Ippolit Ilich (1843–1927) Brother of the composer. Career in the navy.

Tchaikovsky, Modest Ilich (Modya) (1850–1916) Tchaikovsky's brother and closest confidant. Twin of Anatoly. Produced librettos for *Queen of Spades* and *Yolanta* in collaboration with the composer.

Tchaikovsky, Nikolay Ilich (Kolya) (1838–1911) Tchaikovsky's brother.

Tolstoy, Alexey Konstantinovich (1817–75) Poet. Tchaikovsky set some of his lyrical verses.

Tolya, *see* Tchaikovsky, Anatoly Ilich

Viardot-Garcia, Pauline (1821–1910) Outstanding mezzo soprano. Wide repertoire performed throughout Europe, including Russia. Pupils included Désirée Artôt. Friend of Schumann and constant companion of Turgenev.

Volodya, *see* Shilovsky, Vladimir

Vsevolozhsky, Ivan Alexandrovich (1835–1909) Director of Imperial Theatres in St Petersburg 1881–99. Energetic in raising standard of ballet music. Suggested scenario for *Sleeping Beauty*.

Zaremba, Nikolay Ivanovich (1821–79) Tchaikovsky attended his theory and composition classes where he was given a firm traditional grounding in harmony and counterpoint.

Ziloti (Siloti), Alexander Ilich (1863–1945) Pianist. Studied with Nikolay Rubinstein and Tchaikovsky; also with Liszt.

Zinaida, *see* Olkhovskaya, Zinaida Ilinichna

INDEX OF TCHAIKOVSKY'S WORKS

GENERAL INDEX